A Guide to the World's Languages

VOLUME 1: CLASSIFICATION

A Guide to the World's Languages

Volume 1: Classification

Merritt Ruhlen

With a Postscript on recent developments

Stanford University Press
Stanford, California

Stanford University Press
Stanford, California

Printed in the United States of America
Original printing 1987
Printing with Postscript 1991
Last figure below indicates year of this printing:

97 96 95 94 93 92 91

Library of Congress Cataloging-in-Publication Data

Ruhlen, Merritt, 1944–
A guide to the world's languages / Merritt Ruhlen.
p. cm.
Includes bibliographical references and indexes.
Contents: v. 1. Classification, with a postscript.
ISBN 0-8047-1894-6 (pbk. : v. 1 : alk. paper)
1. Language and languages—Classification. I. Title.
P203.R8 1991
401′.2—dc20 90-21705
CIP

To Joseph H. Greenberg

Preface

This volume is the first in a projected series of three, which when complete will constitute a general guide to the world's languages:

Volume 1: *Classification*
Volume 2: *Language Data*
Volume 3: *Language Universals*

This first volume discusses the history and present status of the genetic classification of the world's languages and offers a complete classification. Volume 2 will provide certain kinds of linguistic and nonlinguistic information (e.g. location, number of speakers, genetic classification, consonants, vowels, pronouns, syntax) for a broad sample of the world's languages, and Volume 3 will survey the basic linguistic patterns that characterize human language around the world.

This first volume provides both a historical perspective on the development of (linguistic) genetic classification and a current assessment of the state of our knowledge. (Throughout this book I shall use the terms "genetic classification" and "linguistic classification" in place of the semantically more accurate, but stylistically awkward, "linguistic genetic classification.") Typological classification, based on structural similarities between languages, is not considered in this volume, though it will be treated in detail in Volume 3. Similarly, the historical implications of the present classification will also be explored in Volume 3.

Since human language impinges on so many related academic fields, and holds as well a general fascination for an even greater number of interested laymen, these volumes do not presume any special training on the part of the reader. In particular, this first volume does not assume any background in linguistics, genetics, or taxonomy. All that is required is a curiosity about how the world's languages are related, and about how this information has been discovered during the past two centuries. A few technical terms are introduced as needed, but the basic ideas are simple enough that the reader should encounter little difficulty.

Again with the aim of making this volume as accessible as possible to the interested layman, I have provided section-by-section topical bibliographies instead of a single comprehensive bibliography at the back of the book. By this system, the reader interested in, say, Nilo-Saharan, can easily find all the listed books and articles on that one family. Care must be taken, however, in tracing a particular citation in the text to the proper bibliography (and indeed to the proper section of that bibliography, since several bibliographies are broken into subsections).

All the linguistic maps in this volume are my own work, prepared from base maps published by the U.S. Geological Survey.

A brief sketch of the origin of this volume is perhaps in order. I first became aware of the need for a general guide to the world's languages while I was a graduate student at Stanford University from 1967 to 1973, and especially while I was working on Stanford's Language Universals Project from 1971 to 1977. During this period I compiled a *Guide to the Languages of the World* (Stanford, Calif., 1975), a self-published work containing information on roughly 700 languages. That book eventually sold some 2,500 copies, was used as a textbook at a number of universities in this country and abroad, and came to the attention of Stanford University Press, which expressed an interest in publishing a revised version.

From 1977 to 1980 I devoted my full time to collecting information on as many languages as possible, and the 7,000 data sheets I accumulated during that period contain information on about 2,000 different languages. These 2,000 languages are identified by an asterisk in the complete classification given in section 8.6, and the information itself will be found in the forthcoming Volume 2.

Since I had decided to arrange the information genetically (so that languages and groups would appear nearest the languages and groups to which they were most closely related) rather than alphabetically, as in the 1975 version (which made it easy to find individual languages, but difficult to perceive what traits characterized Romance, Germanic, Bantu, Polynesian, or any other language family), I had by late 1979 put together an overall classification of the world's languages that was based largely on C. F. Voegelin and F. M. Voegelin, *Classification and Index of the World's Languages* (New York, 1977). It was my intention to arrange the information I had collected in terms of this classification.

In November 1979 conversations with Donald Laycock and Darrell Tryon at the Australian National University in Canberra made me aware that both the Papuan and the Austronesian classifications given in the Voegelins' book had already been largely superseded by more recent work, and they proposed that I revise my classification. They also suggested pertinent literature to consult and other scholars I might contact for advice on specific groups.

In 1980 I decided that if I was going to revise the Papuan and Austronesian sections of the classification, I should also attempt to consult experts in other language families and solicit their criticism of the classification I was then using. Correspondence with more than 100 scholars as well as a careful review of the taxonomic literature during the early 1980's led to continual refinements and revisions of the classification. Furthermore, the addition of a historical sketch and current appraisal of each family eventually metamorphosed what began as a single chapter into the present volume. The linguistic information that formed the original focus of this *Guide* will now appear in Volume 2, and Volume 3 will explore the implications of the data presented in the first two volumes.

In addition to providing a complete classification of the world's languages and a historical discussion of how, when, and by whom this knowledge was discovered, this volume has a third goal, namely, to examine the spectacular taxonomic career of the American linguist Joseph Greenberg, who has undoubtedly clarified the relationships of the world's languages more than any other scholar ever has—or ever will. Greenberg fills the same niche in linguistic classification that Linnaeus does in biological taxonomy. While other linguists were content to pursue their careers working out minute details of small, closely related language families, apparently believing that this patchwork approach would one day knit itself into an overall classification of the world's languages, Greenberg had the audacity to classify, by himself, all the languages of Africa, the languages of New Guinea, and the languages of North and South America. His rejection of established dogma in African and Amerindian classification has been met with hostility and misguided attacks by a number of traditional scholars. Nevertheless, on questions of taxonomy he has seldom been found to be wrong. It has been my rare good fortune to have known Joseph Greenberg as a teacher, colleague, and friend over a period of almost 20 years, and it is with both admiration and affection that I dedicate this book to him.

Many people have helped me in quite varied ways in writing this volume, and I wish to express my appreciation to them all. First and foremost I must thank my parents, who made everything possible, and my wife Anca, who supported my writing of this volume in ways too numerous to mention.

I must also acknowledge the extraordinary support that Stanford University Press has provided me during the lengthy gestation period of this volume. William Carver, in particular, has guided and encouraged my work in a multitude of ways, and his contributions have truly been substantive, organizational, and stylistic. His constant support and ability to solve any apparent problem are greatly appreciated. J. G. Bell also provided able counsel from time to time, and his advice was always taken most seriously. I would also like to thank my two fine copy editors, Kathleen Much and Barbara Mnookin, who eliminated numerous infelicities and errors from the original manuscript and rendered the final product both clearer and more readable.

A third group of people whose contributions to this volume have been enormous, and are deeply appreciated, are the more than 100 scholars (most of whom I have never met) who generously offered me advice in trying to assemble the best classification possible on the basis of current knowledge. Their suggestions have had a profound impact on the final shape of the classification, and I wish to express my sincere gratitude to them all. Their names, together with their areas of expertise, are listed on pp. xix–xx, below. I must emphasize, however, that none of these specialists necessarily agrees with the views expressed in this volume or with the final classification, for which I assume sole responsibility. Those scholars who have supplied me with their own unpublished classifications and have allowed me to use them in this book deserve special thanks: Gabriel Manessy (Gur), M. Lionel Bender (Nilo-Saharan), Robin Thelwall (Nubian and Daju), Alexander Militarev (Berber), Robert Jones (Karen), Gérard Diffloth (Austroasiatic), Lawrence Reid (Philippine languages), Paul Black (Australian), Joseph H. Greenberg (Amerind), and Eugene Loos (Panoan). I would also like to thank Sydney Lamb for reading the entire manuscript and making a number of useful suggestions, and L. L. Cavalli-Sforza, for his illuminating conversations on biological taxonomy, genetics, and related areas.

Finally I would like to thank a number of personal friends who have helped me out in various and sundry ways: Moises Moreno, Russell Ruhlen, Victor Sapojnikoff, Michael Saunders, Michael Sullivan, Andrew Wilson, and John Wilson.

M.R.

Contents

Language Lists

Tables, Figures, and Maps

TABLES

FIGURES

MAPS

Specialists Consulted

Robert Austerlitz (Uralic, Chukchi-Kamchatkan)
Yvonne Bastin (Bantu)
M. Lionel Bender (Nilo-Saharan, Afro-Asiatic)
Paul K. Benedict (Sino-Tibetan, Austric)
Richard Bergman (Ubangian)
D. N. S. Bhat (Dravidian)
Robert Binnick (Mongolian)
Henrik Birnbaum (Slavic)
Paul Black (Cushitic, Australian)
Robert Blust (Austronesian)
Nicholas Bodman (Tibeto-Burman)
Lee E. Bohnhoff (Duru)
Luc Bouquiaux (Adamawa, Ubangian)
William Bright (Hokan)
Breandán Ó Buachalla (Celtic)
Robbins Burling (Burmese-Lolo)
Wallace L. Chafe (Siouan, Caddoan, Iroquoian)
Matthew Chen (Chinese)
Christos Clairis (Southern Andean)
Frans van Coetsem (Germanic)
James T. Collins (Maluku)
Bernard Comrie (Chukchi-Kamchatkan)
†Warren Cowgill (Indo-Hittite)
Irvine Davis (Ge)
Gyula Décsy (Uralic)
Desmond Derbyshire (Carib)
Gérard Diffloth (Austroasiatic)
Søren Egerod (Sino-Tibetan)
Christopher Ehret (Cushitic)
Murray Emeneau (Dravidian)
Ronald E. Emmerick (Iranian)
Harold C. Fleming (Omotic)
Thomas Gamkrelidze (Caucasian)
Ives Goddard (Algonquian)
Morris Goodman (Nilo-Saharan)
George Grace (Oceanic)
Joseph H. Greenberg (world)
Austin Hale (Sino-Tibetan)
Kenneth Hale (Australian, Uto-Aztecan)
Robert A. Hall, Jr. (Romance)
Robert Harms (Uralic)
André Haudricourt (New Caledonia)

Richard Hayward (Cushitic)
Robert Hetzron (Afro-Asiatic)
Carleton T. Hodge (Afro-Asiatic)
Larry Hyman (Grassfields Bantu)
V. V. Ivanov (Balto-Slavic)
Philip N. Jenner (Mon-Khmer)
Robert B. Jones (Karen)
Terrence Kaufman (Mayan)
Mary Key (South America)
M. Dale Kinkade (Salish)
Michael Krauss (Eskimo-Aleut, Na-Dene)
John R. Krueger (Altaic)
Ronald Langacker (Uto-Aztecan)
Margaret Langdon (Hokan)
†Donald Laycock (Indo-Pacific)
F. K. Lehman (Tibeto-Burman)
Winfred Lehmann (Indo-European)
†Fang-kuei Li (Tai)
W. B. Lockwood (Indo-European)
Eugene Loos (Panoan)
Horace G. Lunt (Slavic)
D. N. MacKenzie (Iranian)
Yakov Malkiel (Romance)
Gabriel Manessy (Gur)
Colin Masica (Indic)
James Matisoff (Tibeto-Burman)
David McAlpin (Dravidian)
Curtis McFarland (Philippines)
Alexander J. Militarev (Berber)
Marianne Mithun (Iroquoian)
David Moody (Borneo)
William Moulton (Germanic)
Paul Newman (Chadic)
Brian Newton (Greek)
Kemp Pallesen (Sama-Bajaw)
F. R. Palmer (Cushitic)
Andrew Pawley (Austronesian)
Rebecca Posner (Romance)
Ernst Pulgram (Italic)
Lawrence Reid (Philippines)
Calvin Rensch (Oto-Manguean)
David S. Rood (Siouan)
William J. Samarin (Adamawa, Ubangian)
J. David Sapir (West Atlantic)
Thilo C. Schadeberg (Kordofanian)
William R. Schmalstieg (Baltic)
Gary Simons (Santa Isabel, Southeast Solomons)
William A. Smalley (Miao-Yao)
Kenneth D. Smith (Borneo)
David Stampe (Munda)
Stanley Starosta (Austroasiatic)
Susan Steele (Uto-Aztecan)
Robin Thelwall (Nubian, Daju)
Laurence Thompson (Salish)
Darrell T. Tryon (Austronesian)
Robert Underhill (Turkic)
William S.-Y. Wang (Chinese)
E. O. J. Westphal (Khoisan)
Kay Williamson (Benue-Congo)
Alfred Willms (Berber)
Dean Worth (Chukchi-Kamchatkan)
Norman Zide (Austroasiatic)
David Zorc (Philippines, Australian)

Abbreviations

AA	*American Anthropologist.* Washington, D.C.
AAS	*Austroasiatic Studies,* 2 vols., ed. Philip N. Jenner, Laurence C. Thompson, and Stanley Starosta. Honolulu, 1976.
AL	*Anthropological Linguistics.* Bloomington, Ind.
AS	*Afroasiatic: A Survey,* ed. Carleton T. Hodge. The Hague, 1971.
ASEMI	*Asie du Sud-Est et Monde Insulindien.* Paris.
BAEB	*Bureau of American Ethnology Bulletin.* Washington, D.C.
CAAL	*Computational Analyses of Asian and African Languages.* Tokyo.
CSAL	*Comparative Studies in Amerindian Languages,* ed. Esther Matteson. The Hague, 1972.
CTIL	*Current Trends in Linguistics,* 14 vols., ed. Thomas A. Sebeok. The Hague, 1963–76.
EB	*Encyclopaedia Britannica,* 15th ed., 1974.
EXB	*L'expansion bantoue,* 3 vols., ed. Larry M. Hyman, Jan Voorhoeve, and Luc Bouquiaux. Paris, 1980.
GR	*Genetic Relationship, Diffusion and Typological Similarities of East & Southeast Asian Languages,* ed. Mantaro J. Hashimoto. Tokyo, 1976.
HNAI	*Handbook of North American Indians,* 20 vols., ed. William C. Sturtevant. Washington, D.C., 1978– .
IEL	*Inventaire des études linguistiques sur les pays d'Afrique noire d'expression française et sur Madagascar,* ed. Daniel Barreteau. Paris, 1978.
IJAL	*International Journal of American Linguistics.* Chicago.
LNA	*The Languages of Native America,* ed. Lyle Campbell and Marianne Mithun. Austin, Tex., 1979.

LSNA	*Linguistic Structures of Native America*, ed. C. Osgood. New York, 1946.
MKS	*Mon-Khmer Studies*. Honolulu.
NLA	*Native Languages of the Americas*, 2 vols., ed. Thomas A. Sebeok. New York, 1976–77.
NS	*Nilo-Saharan*, ed. Thilo C. Schadeberg and M. Lionel Bender. Dordrecht, 1981.
NSLE	*The Non-Semitic Languages of Ethiopia*, ed. M. Lionel Bender. East Lansing, Mich., 1976.
OL	*Oceanic Linguistics* Honolulu.
PL	*Pacific Linguistics*. Canberra.
PLNGLS	*Papuan Languages and the New Guinea Linguistic Scene*, ed. S. A. Wurm. 1975. *PL* C38.
UCPAAE	*University of California Publications in American Archaeology and Ethnology*. Berkeley.
UCPL	*University of California Publications in Linguistics*. Berkeley.

A Note on Notation

Although this volume does not employ a great deal of esoteric notation, some of its conventions and symbols may be unfamiliar to the general reader and so require a few words of explanation.

1. A dagger (†) identifies those languages, or language families, that are now extinct.

2. An asterisk (*) is used in two ways. Usually it identifies reconstructed (but historically unattested) words, e.g. Indo-European **akva-s* 'horse.' The second use of the asterisk is restricted to Chapter 8, where it identifies those languages whose sound system will in due course be found in Volume 2, e.g. *Iatmul.

3. A right arrow (→) is used to indicate that one language (or family) name has been replaced by another. For example, Barea → Nera means that the language frequently referred to as Barea is called Nera in this volume.

4. An equals sign (=) is used to point out alternate language (or family) names that for reasons discussed in section 8.1 are sometimes better known than the name adopted here, e.g. Nama (= Hottentot).

5. Brackets ([. . .]) enclose phonetic transcriptions, e.g. [dori] 'to wish for, desire.' In Chapter 8 the number of languages in any group is indicated in brackets, following the name of the group; e.g. CELTIC [4] means there are four extant Celtic languages.

6. Single quotes ('. . .') enclose English glosses of foreign words, e.g. French *chien* 'dog.'

7. Double quotes (". . .") are used to indicate direct quotation from a source or to call attention to a word or phrase, e.g. there are no "primitive" languages.

8. Italics are used for non-English words (e.g. French *chien* 'dog'), for individual letters in running text (treated as phonetic elements, whether in English or not), and for simple emphasis (e.g. *typological* traits like gender).

9. Names of language groups are given in capital letters (e.g. SLAVIC, ROMANCE) in the lists and in the classification itself; names of single languages are in capital-and-lower-case letters (e.g. Russian, English, Ohlone). In the case of single languages that are themselves independent branches of a family, either notation may be used, e.g. ALBANIAN or Albanian.

10. The less-than sign (<) indicates that a word, sound, or meaning derives historically from another, e.g. French *chien* < Latin *cane(m)*; French *š* < Latin *k*.

11. The greater-than sign (>) indicates that a word, sound, or meaning has changed into another over the course of time, e.g. Latin *cane(m)* > French *chien*; Latin *k* > French *š*.

12. The similar-to sign (~) indicates either (a) that certain forms alternate morphologically in a language, e.g. English *sing* ~ *sang* ~ *sung*, Indo-European **ped-* ~ **pod-* 'foot,' or (b) that variant forms of a root are found in different languages of a language family, e.g. Nilo-Saharan *tok* ~ *tek* ~ *dik* 'one.'

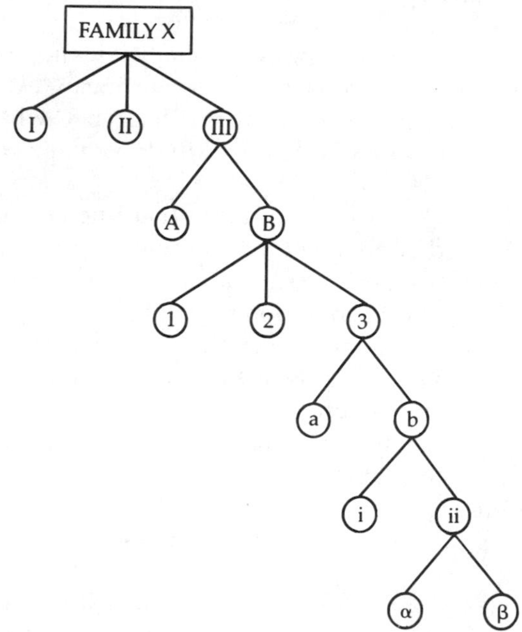

FAMILY X:
- I PRIMARY BRANCH
- II PRIMARY BRANCH
- III PRIMARY BRANCH:
  - A GROUP
  - B GROUP:
    - 1 SUBGROUP
    - 2 SUBGROUP
    - 3 SUBGROUP:
      - a BRANCH
      - b BRANCH:
        - i SUBBRANCH
        - ii SUBBRANCH:
          - α GROUP
          - β GROUP

13. A hyphen (-) is sometimes used to separate a root from its affixes, either prefixes (e.g. English *pre-fix*) or suffixes (e.g. Greek *dídō-mi* 'I give'). It is also used with prefixes and suffixes by themselves (e.g. the English prefix *pre-*, the Greek suffix *-mi* 'I') or following a root (e.g. Indo-European **ped-* ~ **pod-* 'foot').

14. The system of representing genetic tree structure is explained in section 8.2, but because such trees occur in lists throughout the book, a brief outline of the notation is given here. Genetic classifications are often represented in terms of branching diagrams, as in the figure on the facing page.

In this book such structures are represented by a system of indentation, where each successive level of branching is indicated by indentation to the right and each node is preceded by a letter or number to identify the taxonomic level of the group. Accordingly, the branching-tree diagram in the figure will have the representation shown in the list above.

A Guide to the World's Languages

VOLUME 1: CLASSIFICATION

Introduction

Classification, or taxonomy, is a fundamental pursuit of science, an indispensable first step in the search for understanding. Yet it is an area that tends to provoke fascination and deep interest in only a minority of scholars, and general boredom or lack of interest in the rest, be they biologists or linguists. In the development of comparative linguistics in nineteenth-century Europe, taxonomy was paramount, and substantial results were achieved, not only for Europe, but for the rest of the world as well. In the twentieth century a static "ahistorical" perspective has dominated linguistics, and taxonomy has been relegated to "historical linguistics" in the minds of many scholars. But despite its general neglect, discoveries since 1950 have been even more spectacular, and more far-reaching in their consequences, than the truly important results of the nineteenth-century pioneers. It is the aim of this volume to trace the history of language classification from its earliest beginnings to the present day, and to offer (in Chapter 8) a complete classification of the world's roughly 5,000 languages.

It is possible to classify languages in many ways, depending on the criteria chosen. One might, for example, divide the world's languages into two groups: those whose names begin with the letter P (e.g. Polish, Portuguese) and those that do not (e.g. English, Chinese). Such classifications are of course of no intellectual significance. Two kinds of classification *have* proved to be of great importance in the study of human language. *Typological* classification categorizes languages in terms of structural properties. For example, languages may be classified according to the number and kinds of vowels they use, or according to the order of the subject, verb, and object in a simple declarative sentence. Typological classification is important in many regards. Not only does it reveal that there are certain favored patterns in linguistic structure (e.g. the *i, e, a, o, u* vowel system), but it also allows us to perceive how such favored patterns influence, and are influenced by, other patterns over time. A typological classification thus offers us a window on the evolution and nature of language that transcends individual languages. Typological classification will figure prominently in the third volume of this *Guide*, but it is not the subject of this one.

Genetic classification, according to which languages are classified on the basis of common origin, is the second important kind. The idea is quite simple and is illustrated in the following example. Two thousand years ago Latin was spoken across a broad expanse of Europe by citizens of the Roman empire. With the destruction of the empire, Latin speakers were isolated from one another by invading Germanic, Slavic, Arabic, and Hungarian tribes. Gradually, over the centuries, the Latin spoken in what is today Rumania diverged from that spoken in present-day Italy, which in turn was increasingly different from the Latin spoken in present-day France or Spain. Each dialect continued to evolve along its own independent path, and the result is the contemporary Romance languages: Rumanian, Italian, French, Catalan, Spanish, and Portuguese, among others. Such genetic classifications, which trace the genealogy of a language family (Romance) from the parent language (Latin) to the daughter languages (Rumanian, Italian, etc.), are usually represented as "tree diagrams" (which are really inverted trees, with the branches pointing down), as here:

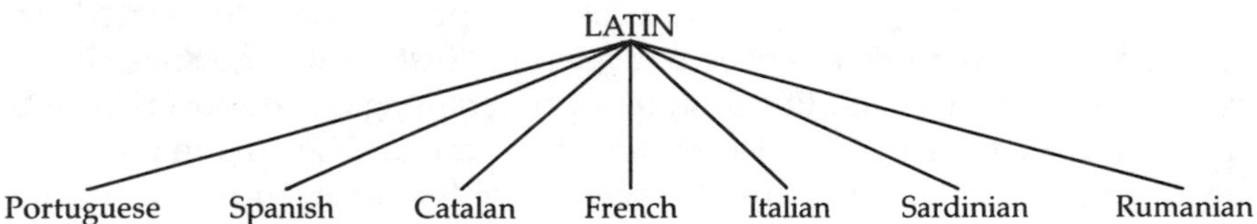

Such tree diagrams are an attempt to represent the historical development of a family of languages. The evidence offered to establish such a family is usually a set of etymologies in which each etymology contains forms from different languages that are both semantically and phonetically similar, and whose similarities are explained by the hypothesis of common origin. Continuing with our Romance example, one might cite Rumanian *mînă*, Sardinian *manu*, Italian *mano*, French *main*, Catalan *mà*, Spanish *mano*, and Portuguese *mão*, all of which mean 'hand.' In this case the hypothesis of common origin is confirmed by Latin *manus* 'hand,' but we are seldom so fortunate as to have historically attested forms of the parent language.

For the vast majority of the world's languages, nothing is directly known of the ancestor languages from which they derive, simply because these ancestor languages, unlike Latin, were never written down. In such cases we can often infer what the original form of a word must have looked like from the evidence of the surviving daughter languages, but such reconstructions are only approximate, because of the incompleteness and ambiguities of the available evidence. Fortunately, the recognition of valid genetic groupings does not depend on the reconstruction of earlier forms.

The membership of much larger language stocks—families of families—can also be deduced. It can be shown, for example, that the Romance family is but one branch of a larger and more ancient family that includes Armenian and Albanian, as well as Slavic, Germanic, Greek, Celtic, and Indic languages, among others. This larger group is known as the Indo-European (or Indo-Hittite) family. Although Indo-European reconstructions continue to undergo revision (and sometimes wholesale reevaluation) from time to time, the validity of the family itself is no longer questioned.

How many such larger groups are there? Disagreements persist, but during this century it has proved possible to reduce the number of distinct families to which the world's 5,000-odd languages belong to between 10 and 20. It has not yet been possible to demonstrate that all languages derive from a common source, though such a possibility cannot be ruled out. Nor is it possible to say where, when, or how human language developed. The problems posed by the origin of language are discussed, inconclusively, in section 7.4.

The general plan of this volume is as follows. The first chapter offers a brief introduction to the principles of genetic classification. After first placing the problem of genetic classification in its proper historical context, Chapter 2 traces the development of linguistic classification in Europe. Chapters 3–6 treat Africa, Asia, Oceania, and North and South America in a similar fashion. Chapter 7 assesses the prospects for future research, after first summarizing the methodological errors that must be avoided if progress is to be made in either large-scale groupings or low-level refinement. The problem of the origin and evolution of human language is also considered. Finally, Chapter 8 presents a complete classification of the world's languages, in three levels of detail: a brief index (section 8.4), a list of major genetic groups (8.5), and the complete classification (8.6).

But again, before turning to the history of genetic classification in Chapter 2, it is important that we develop a few basic notions concerning genetic classification, so that the reader may better understand the various controversies to be discussed in later chapters. Thus the reader who approaches this volume with an interest in some particular part of the world is advised to read Chapter 1 before proceeding to his or her area of interest. Chapters 2–6, by contrast, may to a large extent be read independently of one another. It is also advisable to read Chapter 1 before examining the classification in Chapter 8.

1

Genetic Classification: Principles and Methods

The idea that groups of languages that share certain systematic resemblances have inherited those similarities from a common origin is the basis for genetic classification. It is a simple, yet profound, idea, and seems today so obvious it is hard to imagine that it was not generally recognized until the late eighteenth century. As we shall see in Chapter 2, however, when the idea did finally penetrate the intellectual ethos, it triggered an explosion of research on the relationships of European languages that may be said to have inaugurated the modern scientific study of human language. In fact, in broadest terms, it would not be incorrect to view the entire development of linguistic science in nineteenth-century Europe as revolving around the gradual elucidation of this fundamental precept.

1.1 DEFINITIONS AND METHODS

Arguments over genetic classification usually concern either (1) the definition of genetic classification or (2) the method of "arriving at" a genetic classification. Let us consider first the question of definition.

Definition 1: A *genetic classification* is a subgrouping of all relevant languages into genetic nodes.

As illustrated in Fig. 1.1, a *subgrouping* is simply a branching diagram that subdivides the maximal domain A (i.e. all of the relevant languages) of the classification into smaller subgroups, or *nodes*: B, C, D, E, . . .

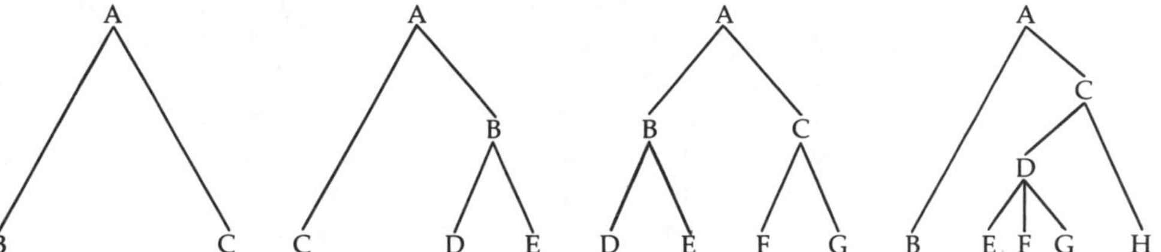

Fig. 1.1. Examples of subgroupings

Definition 2: A *genetic node* is a group of languages each of which is more closely related to the others in that group than to any language outside the group.

For the sake of lexical variety I shall use the equivalent terms (genetic) node, unit, and group interchangeably.

A genetic classification thus makes two statements. First, it affirms that certain languages are in fact related to each other (i.e. share a common ancestor). Second, it specifies how the languages are interrelated in the form of a branching diagram. Consider the classification described by Fig. 1.2. This subgrouping indicates not only that a, b, c, d, and e are related languages, but also that a and b are most closely related to each other, as are c, d, and e. In fact, a and b constitute the genetic node B, and c, d, and e constitute the genetic node C. Finally, B and C together compose a "higher" node A, which is the maximal domain of this genetic classification. Another genetic classification might also claim that the same languages a, b, c, d, and e are related, but might propose a very different subgrouping, like that in Fig. 1.3. And of course many other subgroupings are both reasonable and possible.

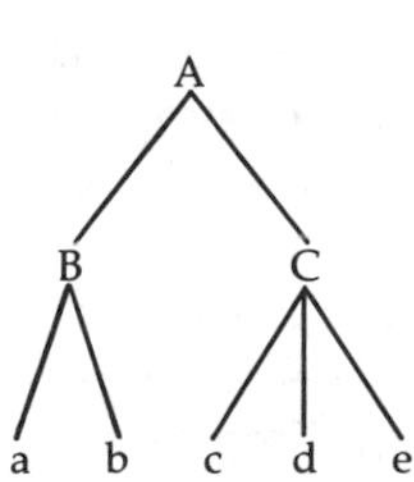

Fig. 1.2. A typical subgrouping

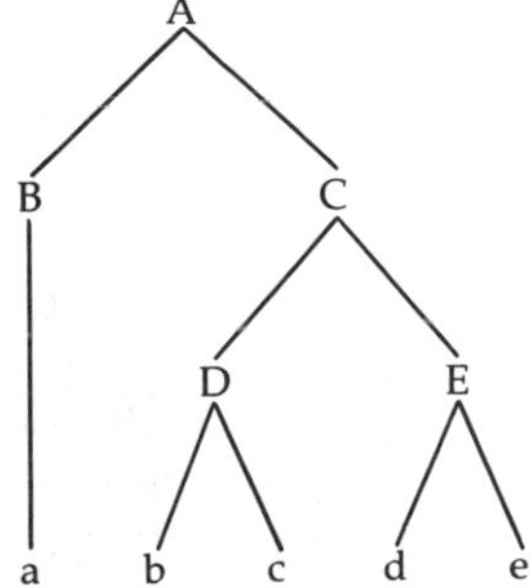

Fig. 1.3. A possible alternative subgrouping

Discovering the correct subgrouping is usually more difficult than simply determining when a group of languages is related, and for this reason more often leads to controversy. As we shall see below (see Table 1.1), even a modest amount of lexical evidence allows one to distinguish Indo-European (I-E) from non-Indo-European languages, and this distinction is so sharp that there are in fact no extant languages whose membership in (or exclusion from) I-E is in doubt. There is thus strong consensus on which languages make up the I-E family, and the same is true of the Romance, Slavic, and Germanic subfamilies. But the subgrouping of the languages within the I-E family (or within the Romance, Slavic, or Germanic subfamilies) is far from settled and remains even today a subject of scholarly debate.

1.2 CONTINUOUS AND DISCRETE VARIATION

One consequence of the fact that all languages are continually changing is that forms of speech that are mutually intelligible (i.e. dialects of one language) will gradually drift apart, provided only that they are isolated from each other for a sufficient period of time. Although languages are known to change at different rates during their histories (for reasons that are not completely clear), under most circumstances 500 years is probably sufficient to seriously impair mutual intelligibility, and 1,000 years will usually obliterate it entirely. Drift of this sort is of course gradual, and except where geographic or political barriers separate related neighboring tongues, there is likely to be a continuum of intermediate dialects in the borderlands. In fact, one of the principal problems in the subgrouping of languages involves this distinction between continuous and discrete variation. Within the Indo-European language family, the Romance, Slavic, and Germanic subfamilies are *discrete* groups. There are no languages that are ambiguous as to classification at this level; that is, there are no languages that appear to be half-Romance and half-Slavic. Rumanian, because it contains a sizable number of Slavic loanwords, is sometimes cited as such a hybrid, but in fact even a cursory examination reveals it to be overwhelmingly Romance in basic vocabulary, morphology, and syntax. The Slavic overlay is no more pronounced than the French overlay in English, which is also the result of large-scale borrowing.

Within closely related groups of languages (e.g. Romance, Slavic, Indic, Polynesian, or Bantu), however, one often encounters *continuous* variation. For example, historically at least, both Italian and French comprised numerous regional dialects that changed gradually as one traveled from village to village, from a form of speech that was clearly Italian to one that was unmistakably French. Although all villages could communicate with ease with neighboring villages, the end points (i.e. French and Italian) of this dialect chain were not mutually intelligible. Let us represent this situation as follows:

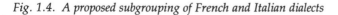

(1) French a b c d e f g Italian

Here a–g represent transitional forms of speech between Italian and French. Furthermore, let us assume for the sake of this example that only contiguous dialects are mutually intelligible; thus people in village c can communicate only with people in villages b and d. The problem that this extremely common phenomenon poses for the taxonomist is the following: although we would like to put "French dialects" in one group and "Italian dialects" in another, there is no non-arbitrary way of doing so in every case. In formal terms, what this means is that no subset of the dialects shown in (1) constitutes a genetic node as defined in definition 2 above.

To see why this is so, let us assume someone claims that French and dialects a–c constitute one genetic node and Italian and dialects d–g constitute another, as shown in Fig. 1.4. But dialect c is as close to dialect d as it is to dialect b, and it is in fact closer to dialect d (with which it is mutually intelligible) than it is to dialect a, even though dialect a is a member of the same genetic node. Obviously, our definition of genetic node is violated for this subgrouping, since French and dialects a, b, and c do not constitute "a group of languages each of which is more closely related to the others in that group than to any language outside the group."

Two points should be kept in mind. First, the problem of classifying dialects is formally the same as classifying languages; and the problem of classifying languages is the same as classifying groups of languages. Second, continuous and discrete variation are merely two facets of the same phenomenon. The transformation of dialects into distinct languages, and of continuous variation into discrete variation, are both the result of communicative isolation and the passage of time. These two factors alone are sufficient to transform continuous dialects into discrete languages, and discrete languages into discrete groups of languages. Nevertheless, since continuous variation is more apparent at the lower levels of classification, the problem of subgrouping becomes progressively more difficult as the languages

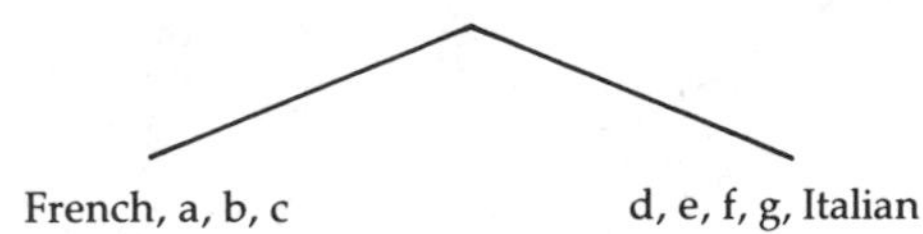

Fig. 1.4. A proposed subgrouping of French and Italian dialects

to be compared become more and more alike, until, as in the example just discussed, it becomes impossible to establish a non-arbitrary subgrouping.

In the case of the Romance languages, more than 1,500 years of communicative isolation have given the Eastern forms of Romance (i.e. the Rumanian dialects) a specific character that sets them apart from the rest of Romance. Most of the Western Romance idioms, however, show no such sharp cleavage into distinct groups, a consequence of there having been continuous contact, at least between neighboring languages, during the time of total isolation from Eastern Romance. The impression given by Western Romance, then, is that of one language gradually shading into the next, with few clear-cut boundaries. Subgrouping within Western Romance thus becomes arbitrary, and the lines of division often assume a geographic or political basis rather than a strictly linguistic one. The traditional subgroups of Western Romance (i.e. Italo-Romance, Rhaeto-Romance, Gallo-Romance, and Ibero-Romance) are to be understood in this sense.

Identical problems are often encountered in grouping dialects into languages. For example, let us assume there are five dialects related as in Fig. 1.5, where a line connecting two dialects indicates mutual intelligibility. Since all of these dialects are mutually intelligible with dialect A, this dialect is taken to be the "norm" of the language, and dialects B–E are said to be dialects of this language even though they themselves are not mutually intelligible. The choice of A as the norm here is likely (but not certain) to accord with the realities of the linguistic origins of these dialects, but in another case (see Fig. 1.6) no such convenient choice is available. Here there is

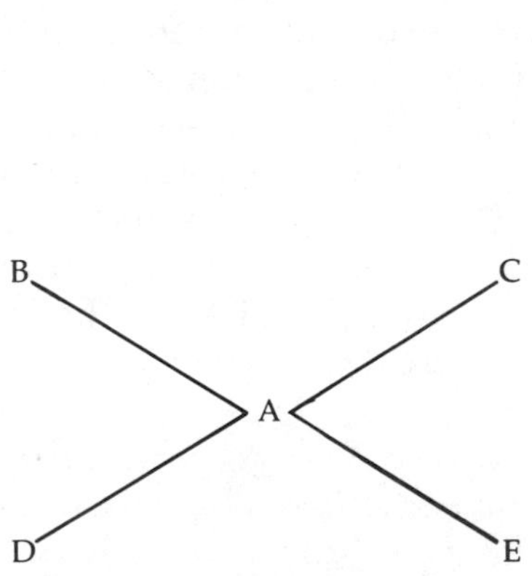

Fig. 1.5. Dialects that may be represented as a single language

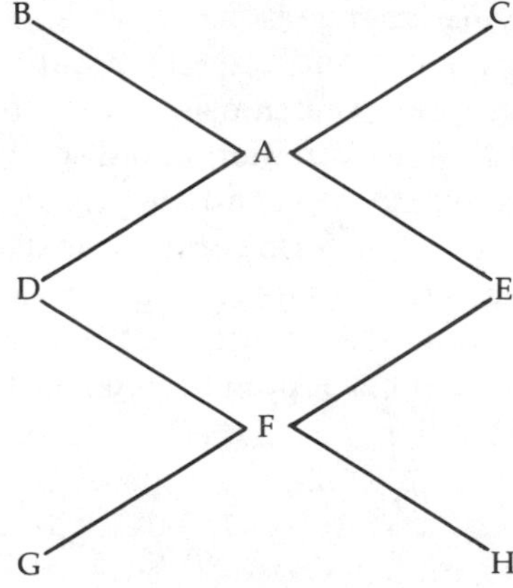

Fig. 1.6. Dialects that may be represented as multiple languages

no single dialect mutually intelligible with all other dialects. In cases like this linguists often can do no better than to divide the dialects into groups such that within each group there is at least one dialect intelligible with all other dialects in that group. In Fig. 1.6 language A might be defined as dialects A, B, C, and E and language F as D, F, G, and H. The arbitrary nature of such a subgrouping—several others would be as reasonable—should be evident. Moreover, in the real world the choice of a dialect to represent the norm of a language (a serious problem in countries trying to develop a standard national language) is often influenced by nonlinguistic factors. For instance, a dialect with numerous speakers or one enjoying high prestige—whatever its actual linguistic affinities for the other dialects—is much more likely to be chosen as the norm for a language than one with few speakers or low prestige.

1.3 GENETIC AFFINITY

Having defined the notion of genetic classification, and having discussed a few characteristic problems in identifying genetic nodes, let us now examine how one actually goes about discovering a genetic classification. The process involves two stages. During stage one the investigator seeks to establish "evidence" that certain languages are in fact related; during stage two "other evidence" is adduced for a particular subgrouping of the languages found to be related in stage one. The nature of the evidence required (or, as some might say, permitted) for proof of genetic affinity (stage one) or for proof of a subgrouping (stage two) is often at the center of classificatory controversies.

In attempting to ascertain genetic relationships, where does one start? According to Greenberg (1957: 42–43), the oldest and still "the swiftest and surest method" is the comparison of basic vocabulary for a large number of languages from some broad geographic area. Inevitably the languages compared will be found to group themselves into subgroups on the basis of systematic resemblances. Consider, for example, Table 1.1 (adapted from Greenberg 1957: 43), which shows the phonetic form of just nine basic words in 14 European languages. Yet even this meager evidence is sufficient to demonstrate that these 14 languages are to be divided into five groups (A, B, C, D, E), and furthermore that A, B, and C exhibit resemblances among themselves in which neither D nor E participate. The languages in group A are Germanic languages; those in group B, Romance languages; and those in C, Slavic languages. All three are branches of the Indo-European family. Group D includes two Finnic languages, and group E is the well-known language isolate Basque.

Table 1.1. Comparative Vocabulary of European Languages

Language	Word								
	one	two	three	head	eye	ear	nose	mouth	tooth
A Swedish	en	tvo	tre	hyvud	øga	øra	næsa	mun	tand
Dutch	ēn	tvē	drī	hȫft	ōx	ōr	nø̄s	mont	tant
English	wən	tuw	θrij	hɛd	aj	ijr	nowz	mawθ	tuwθ
German	ajns	tsvaj	draj	kopf	augə	ōr	nāze	munt	tsān
B French	œ̃/æ̃	dø	tRwa	tɛt	œj	ɔRɛj	ne	buš	dɑ̃
Italian	uno	due	tre	tɛsta	ok̄jo	orek̄jo	naso	bok̄a	dɛnte
Spanish	uno	dos	tres	kabesa	oxo	orexa	naso	boka	djente
Rumanian	un	doj	trej	kap	okj	ureke	nas	gurə	dinte
C Polish	jeden	dva	tši	glova	oko	uxo	nos	usta	zõp
Russian	adin	dva	tri	galava	oko	uxo	nos	rot	zup
Bulgarian	edin	dva	tri	glava	oko	uxo	nos	usta	zəb
D Finnish	yksi	kaksi	kolme	pǣ	silmæ	korva	nenæ	sū	ham̄as
Estonian	yks	kaks	kolm	pea	silm	korv	nina	sū	ham̄as
E Basque	bat	bi	hiryr	byry	begi	belari	sydyr	aho	orts

Within each of these groups the resemblances are so overwhelming that they require little comment even for the linguistically naive reader. Moreover, to a linguist familiar both with the precise phonetic meaning of each symbol and with the common evolutionary paths that transform one sound into another, the resemblances in Table 1.1 are even stronger and more apparent. The reader may observe how clearly and unambiguously the supposed "hybrid" Rumanian groups itself with the Romance languages. Note also the homogeneity of both the Slavic and Finnic groups.

The evidence for joining A, B, and C in an Indo-European family is admittedly less transparent, yet even here the reader should be able to perceive significant similarities among all three groups for the words 'one,' 'two,' 'three,' 'eye,' and 'nose'; and between A and B in their words for 'ear' and 'tooth.'

Genetic relationship is not, however, the sole source of sound/meaning resemblances such as those illustrated in Table 1.1. Three other possible causes must be entertained, and eliminated, before one may assert that the similarities in question derive from a common origin: chance, sound symbolism, and borrowing.

Since the number of distinct sounds used in human languages is relatively small, and furthermore, since certain sounds are common to (practically) all languages (e.g. *t, k, m, n, s, i, a, u*), inevitably chance resemblances between languages will arise from time to time. Usually such historical accidents are restricted to one-syllable words; Hockett (1958: 486) points out the similarity of German *nass* 'wet' and Zuni (an American Indian language of New Mexico) *nas* 'wet.' Occasionally one may encounter a two-syllable word with a chance resemblance, such as Rumanian *dori* 'to wish for, desire' and Lau (an Austronesian language spoken in the Solomon Islands) *dori* 'to wish for, desire.' How, one may justifiably ask, do we know that this similarity between Rumanian and Lau is nothing more than a chance resemblance? The answer is that all other causes may be ruled out in this case, leaving chance as the only possibility. First, borrowing is implausible because there has been no known historical contact between these peoples, and the immense geographic distance separating them more or less precludes such contact. Second, sound symbolism is eliminated as a possible cause because there is no intrinsic relationship between the sounds [dori] and the meaning 'desire' that is attested in the world's languages (more on this below). Third, genetic relationship may be ruled out by bringing into consideration other languages. As soon as this is done it becomes obvious, from abundant similarities, that Rumanian is a Romance language within the Indo-European family, whereas Lau is an Oceanic language within the Austronesian family. The cumulative weight of all the relevant evidence reveals the isolated, and therefore insignificant, nature of this particular resemblance.

The whole process of classifying languages into genetic groups on the basis of sound/meaning similarities is predicated on the fundamental assumption that *the relationship between sound and meaning is arbitrary in all human languages*. In general, this assumption holds true, as English 'dog,' French *chien*, Spanish *perro*, and Russian *sobaka* illustrate. Nevertheless, it has long been recognized that for a small group of words the assumption is invalid; in these few instances there is, in fact, an intrinsic connection between sound and meaning. The most obvious examples are onomatopoeic words, such as 'tinkle' and 'buzz' in English. But there are also a few non-onomatopoeic words that are known to display sound/meaning similarities in languages around the world. The two most famous examples are *mama* for 'mother' and *papa* (or *tata* ~ *dada*) for 'father.' It is also possible that there is sound symbolism between the front vowel [i] and the meaning 'here, this,' and between a non-front vowel [a] or [u] and the meaning 'there, that.' Such a pattern appears to have a global distribution.

Since sound symbolism affects such a small percentage of the words in any language's lexicon, the elimination of these few items from consideration in establishing genetic classifications represents more of a theoretical nuisance than a practical impediment. In point of fact, neither of the two nonhistorical causes of sound/meaning resemblances (i.e. chance and sound symbolism) greatly affects genetic classification. If a linguist cannot array more evidence (in the form of cross-language lexical similarities) than a few (possibly accidental) resemblances and several items known to be affected by sound symbolism, he is most unlikely to hazard any kind of guess at all about genetic classification.

The final nongenetic source of lexical resemblances is borrowing. It is probably true that whenever two languages come in contact for an extended period there will be borrowing of lexical items from one to the other, sometimes in both directions. Since relatively few languages have existed in such geographic isolation that they could avoid contact with other languages, it is understandable that the failure to recognize borrowed words has at times led to confusion in attempts at genetic classification. It is certainly true that the impact of lexical borrowing on genetic classification has attracted a good deal of scholarly attention. Probably too much, since, according to Greenberg (1957: 39), "while in particular and infrequent instances the question of borrowing may be doubtful, it is always possible to tell whether a mass of resemblances between two languages is the result of borrowing."

There are two principal techniques for detecting borrowed words. The first involves the recognized propensity for lexical borrowing to affect certain semantic domains (such as previously unknown cultural items, e.g. kangaroo, tobacco, television) and certain grammatical categories (nouns rather than verbs, rarely inflectional or derivational affixes). Although almost any word may be borrowed on occasion, there is no question that under most circumstances basic vocabulary (e.g. eye, nose, head, leg, and pronouns) is fairly resistant to borrowing. Because of the small, and specific, portion of the lexicon that borrowing tends to affect, it is normally not difficult to identify both the borrowed words and the donor language or languages.

A second technique for distinguishing borrowed words from genetic cognates is the extension of the range of comparison to other languages. For instance, let us assume that someone claims language X is genetically related to language A on the basis of certain lexical similarities. Let us assume further that language A is known to be a member of a language family that includes languages B, C, D, E, and F. Since X is claimed to be related to A, it must also be related to languages B–F. Therefore, one may anticipate finding similarities between X and B, X and C, etc., just as one has apparently discovered cognates between X and A. If, on the other hand, the lexical similarities turn out to be restricted to X and A, we may be fairly confident that we are dealing with borrowing. English displays numerous lexical similarities with French (e.g. face, poison, poor, ease, change, use, village), but very few with the other Romance languages. As a consequence, even in the absence of historical evidence, it would be clear that such words must have been borrowed from French.

The case of the Tai languages, of which Laotian and Standard Thai are the best known, offers an instructive example of how borrowed words may temporarily confound genetic classification. It was formerly thought, on the basis of phonological similarities (e.g. the presence of tone and monosyllabism) and a limited number of apparent cognates, that the Tai languages exhibited a distant genetic relationship with the Chinese languages, and hence with the Sino-Tibetan family as a whole. As we shall see, however, phonological similarities alone (such as the presence or absence of tone) are not reliable indicators of genetic affiliation. Furthermore, a closer examination of the supposed cognates revealed that the perceived similarities were almost uniquely with Chinese, and not with the other Sino-Tibetan languages. Today the Tai languages are generally considered to be most closely related to the widespread Austronesian family. The apparent cognates with Sino-Tibetan have turned out, on closer inspection, to be merely early borrowings between Chinese and Tai.

In establishing genetic affinity between languages, linguists have emphasized lexical similarities. This does not mean, however, that other evidence is without interest; in principle at least, everything should be taken into account, and in fact such factors as similarities in morphological irregularities may be of extremely high probative value. Nevertheless, lexical information is of paramount importance, especially in the initial stages of classification, because (1) it provides a large number of independent, and potentially differing, items; (2) it offers a point of comparison among all languages in the sense that certain fundamental vocabulary items may be expected to occur in all languages; and (3) often, especially in areas of the world lacking detailed linguistic documentation, lexical information is all that is available for comparison.

1.4 SUBGROUPING

Let us turn now to the second stage of language classification, the establishment of a subgrouping for the languages found to be related during stage one. It should be emphasized from the outset that the accuracy of the subgrouping obtained during stage two depends on having recognized, during stage one, all the relevant languages in a particular genetic unit. Where the true breadth of a language family has not been correctly delineated in stage one, the subgrouping implied by this (partial) information is likely to be incomplete, erroneous, or both. Success at stage two is thus crucially dependent on prior success at stage one. In subsequent chapters we shall encounter several examples where a failure to delimit correctly the extent of a genetic group of languages has undermined the proposed subgrouping. Identifying all the relevant languages is particularly troublesome for groups of languages with broad geographic distribution, such as Austronesian or Amerind.

If *lexical cognates* are the primary criterion for proof of genetic affinity, then *exclusively shared innovations* occupy a similar position with regard to subgrouping. Why are innovations so important? Let us not forget that in investigating genetic classification, we are attempting to understand the history and prehistory of linguistic groups. During stage one we adduce evidence that certain languages derive from a common ancestor. During stage two we form a hypothesis about how this common ancestor evolved into its currently extant (or historically attested) offspring. Genetic classification, if it is successful, is thus a reflection of history. Exclusively shared innovations are important in determining subgrouping because they attest to a period of common independent development. As a language evolves independently of related languages, it goes its own way, so to speak, innovating in its own individual way. Each such innovation, whether lexical, phonological, semantic, or syntactic, is an indication of the independent development of the language or group in question.

Not all putatively shared innovations carry the same weight, however. Some changes (e.g. the voicing of intervocalic *p, t, k*) occur so frequently in the world's languages that it is often difficult to be certain that such apparent innovations are not in reality separate but convergent developments. Accordingly, such innovations (representing known evolutionary paths of development) must be given less weight than truly idiosyncratic developments, such as most lexical innovations. It is highly unlikely, for example, that two languages would independently come to associate the sounds *tik* with the meaning 'finger.' Since lexical innovations do not represent evolutionary paths (and thus the possibility of convergence is all but eliminated), they carry more weight.

In theory, at least, the division of a group of languages into two parts may be established by the presence of a single exclusively shared innovation in one part but not in the other. In the real world, however, a single innovation is seldom convincing by itself, and in most instances a scholar will propose a set of shared innovations to justify a particular subgrouping. The greater the number of shared innovations, the more confident we may be that our division into two groups represents a true historical split.

Obviously the longer that two languages (or groups of languages) have been separated, the more innovations will be found in each. Thus the difficulty of discovering the historically correct subgrouping is to a large extent a function of the length of time between various proposed splits. The situation may be understood most easily by looking at a few simple diagrams. Consider the genetic subgrouping in Fig. 1.7. We define x as the length of time between Time A and Time B, and y as the length of time between Time B and Time C. The determining factor in whether one can discover (either easily or with difficulty) a subgrouping such as that in Fig. 1.7 is the ratio x/y. As this ratio increases, the subgrouping problem becomes progres-

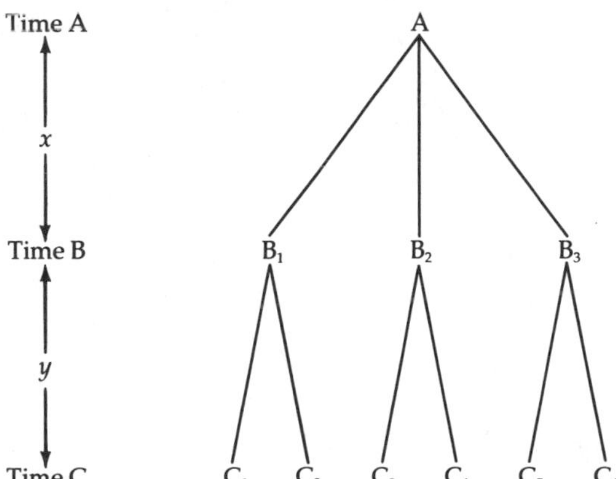

Fig. 1.7. A possible subgrouping of family A

sively simpler; as the ratio decreases, the subgrouping problem becomes more and more difficult, and eventually impossible. A case where x is large and y is small is illustrated in Fig. 1.8. The ratio x/y = 3,500/1,500 = 2 ⅓ is relatively large, and as we saw in Table 1.1, the correct subgrouping is evident even on inspection of only a few fundamental vocabulary items.

Consider next a case at the opposite end of the scale, where x is small with respect to y, as in Fig. 1.9. In this (somewhat simplified) example, spoken Latin divided into three distinct groups following the collapse of the Roman Empire around A.D. 500. In this instance the x/y ratio is comparatively small (500/1,000 = ½), and as Malkiel's (1978) historical survey clearly indicates, there has been no small number of classificatory disputes, and still no general consensus, on the internal relationships of the Romance languages.

Table 1.2 gives the equivalents of 14 words (the same nine words in Table 1.1 plus five pronouns) in 19 Romance languages or dialects. As we can see, whereas there is abundant evidence for the genetic unity of the group as a whole (stage one evidence), there is a relative paucity of evidence for sub-

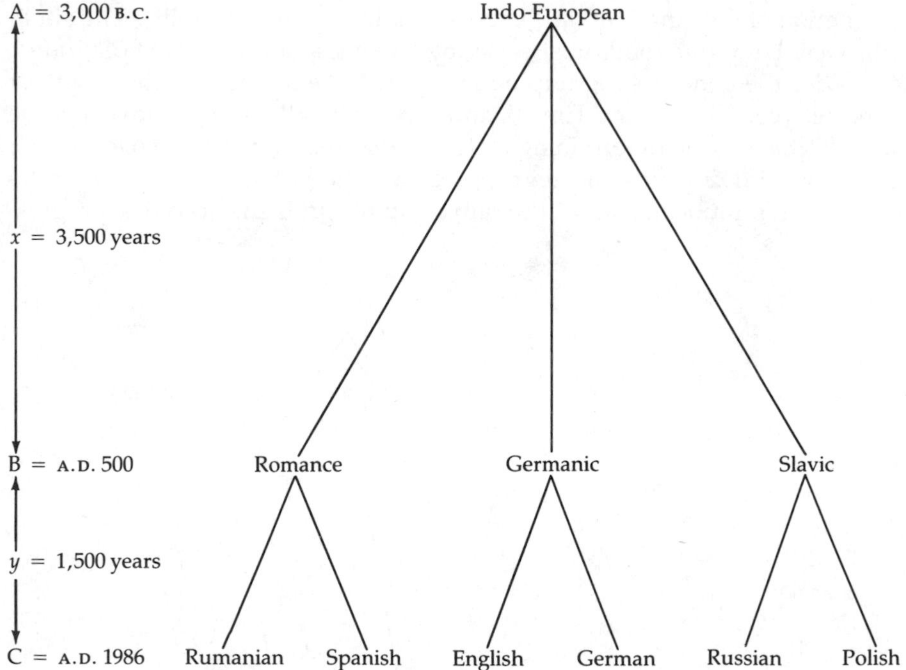

Fig. 1.8. Differentiation of the Indo-European family (partial)

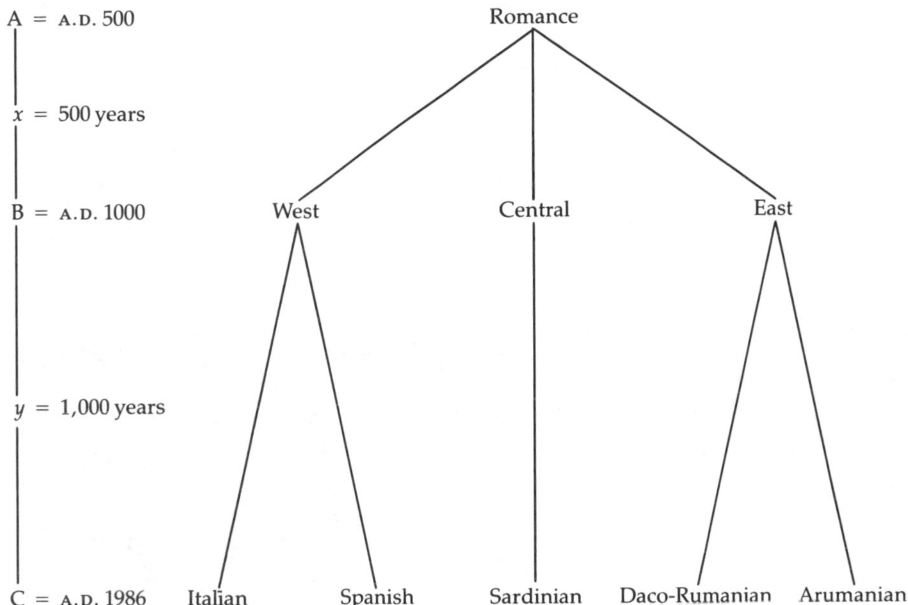

Fig. 1.9. Differentiation of the Romance family (partial)

grouping these languages (stage two evidence). There is in fact no obvious subgrouping suggested by the lexical evidence in Table 1.2.

A careful examination of Table 1.2 does, however, reveal a number of hints that the Rumanian dialects form a group of languages distinct from the rest of Romance:

1. The use of [gurə] 'mouth' (< Latin *gula* 'throat') in all the Rumanian dialects, as opposed to [buka] 'mouth' (or related cognates) in the other Romance languages is indicative, as is the discovery that Rumanian [gurə] has cognates in other Romance languages, cognates that have retained both the Latin meaning and the word-medial [l]. Furthermore, the Latin word *bucca* 'mouth' has not disappeared from the Rumanian dialects, but rather has undergone a semantic shift: 'mouth' > 'cheek' > 'buttock,' and this unusual semantic innovation is found in both Daco-Rumanian and Arumanian.

2. In the pronoun 'she,' the Rumanian dialects share the phonological innovation l > j. The Romance languages generally preserve a lateral (either [l] or [ʎ]) in this word. Only Sardinian, which has transformed the lateral into a retroflex stop [ḍ], and New World Spanish, in which [ʎ] has been reduced to [j] (the sound of 'y' in 'yet'), violate this distribution.

3. The Rumanian dialects have all raised the first vowel in *dinte* 'tooth,'

Table 1.2. Comparative Vocabulary of the Romance Languages

Language	Word						
	one	two	three	head	eye	ear	nose
Arumanian	un	doj	trej	kap	okʎju	ure̯akʎe	nare
Megleno-Rumanian	un	doj	trej	kap	wokʎu	ure̯akʎi	nas
Daco-Rumanian	un	doj	trej	kap	okj	ureke	nas
Istro-Rumanian	ur	doj	trej	kap	okʎu	urekʎe	nɑs
Dalmatian	join	doi	tra	kup	vakl(o)	orakla	nuos
Sardinian (Log)	unu	duos	tres	kabu/testa	oju/ogru	orija	nare
Sardinian (Camp)	unu	duus	tresi	kabu/testa	ogu	origa	nazu
Italian	uno	due	tre	kapo/tɛsta	ɔk̄jo	orek̄jo	naso
Friulian	un	doi	tre	čaf	voli	oreʎe	nas
Romansch	yn	duos	trais	čo	œʎ	uraʎa	nas
French	œ̃/æ̃	dø	tRwa	šɛf/tɛt	œj/jø	ɔRɛj	ne
Franco-Provençal	jõ	du/dɥe	tra	teta	žy	oreʎe	nɑs
Provençal	yn	dus	tres	kap/testa	ɛl	awreʎɔ	nas
Gascon	yn	dys	tres	kap	oeʎ/oej	awreʎe	nas
Catalan	un	dos	trɛs	kap	uʎ	urɛʎə	nas
Spanish (Spain)	uno	dos	tres	kabeθa	oxo	orexa	nariθ
Spanish (Mexico)	uno	dos	tres	kabesa	oxo	orexa	naris
Galician	un	dows	tres	kabeθa/testa	oʎo	oreʎa	nariθ
Portuguese	ũ	dɔjš	treš	kabesa	oʎu	urɛʎa	nariš

Language	Word						
	mouth	tooth	I	you	he	she	we
Arumanian	gurə	dintə	jo	tine	jelu	ja	noj
Megleno-Rumanian	gurə	dintɨ	jo	tu	jel^{ɯ}	ja	noj
Daco-Rumanian	gurə	dɨnte	jo	tu	jel	ja	noj
Istro-Rumanian	gurə	dɨnt	jo	tu	jel	jɑ	noj
Dalmatian	buka	diant	ju	toi	jal	jala	noi
Sardinian (Log)	buk̄a	dentə	dego/ego/eo	tue	iḏ̣u	iḏ̣a	nos
Sardinian (Camp)	buk̄a	dentə	deu	tui	iḏ̣u	iḏ̣a	nos
Italian	bok̄a	dɛntə	io	tu	eʎi	ela	noi
Friulian	buče	dɨnt	jo	tu	el	ele	nus
Romansch	buoča	dəint	eu	ty	el	ela	nus
French	buš/gœl	dɑ̃	žə	ty	il	ɛl	nu
Franco-Provençal	bɔθə	dɛ	ðo	ty	i(l)/e(l)	iʎi	no
Provençal	bokɔ	dent	jew	ty	el	ela	nusawtres
Gascon	buko	den(t)	žu	ty	et	elo	nuzaw
Catalan	bokə	den	žo	tu	eʎ	eʎə	nuzaltras
Spanish (Spain)	boka	djentə	jo	tu	el	eʎa	nosotros
Spanish (Mexico)	boka	djentə	jo	tu	el	eja	nosotros
Galician	boka	dente	eu	ti	el	ela	nɔs
Portuguese	boka	dẽti	ew	tu	eli	ela	nɔs

not an unusual type of change, but one that Table 1.2 indicates only for Friulian among the other Romance languages. (The phonological innovation of raising vowels before nasal consonants probably developed independently in Friulian and the Rumanian dialects.)

4. The retention of the *-kl-* cluster in the words for 'eye' and 'ear' in most Rumanian dialects (Standard Rumanian = Daco-Rumanian is an exception here) is a trait shared only by Dalmatian in Table 1.2. Whether the *retention* (as opposed to innovation) of a trait has any evidentiary value for subgrouping is a matter of scholarly disagreement.

The few words examined in Table 1.2 can only hint at the distinctness of Eastern Romance (= the Rumanian dialects). An examination of *all* the evidence, however, reveals an overwhelming number of innovations separating Eastern Romance from the rest of the Romance family.

Problems of subgrouping will reappear in later chapters, and the ideas outlined here will be further refined. For the moment Greenberg's (1957: 53) summary of the problems inherent in subgrouping, and the methodology appropriate to it, will serve to close our preliminary discussion of genetic classification:

> There is hardly a feature shared by certain related languages and not others for which convergence or borrowing is absolutely excluded as an explanation. Nevertheless, when in even more difficult cases the evidence is examined closely and in the light of general comparative reconstruction of the linguistic history of the entire family, certain groupings will normally emerge. Although . . . no single resemblance is ever completely decisive, it will be found that certain languages share with one another a far larger number of features, which may be innovations, than they do with related languages outside the subgroup, and that among these are some of those which are least likely to be the result of convergence, including shared sound shifts en masse, sporadic sound changes, new morphological formations, shared analogical shifts, including some of the rarer ones, and true lexical innovations. It is the sheer number of such resemblances, together with the inclusion of some of the types most likely to be innovations, that excludes convergence or borrowing as an over-all explanation.

1.5 TAXON NAMES

Just as biologists classify plants and animals in terms of *taxa* such as species, genus, family, order, class, and phylum, linguists use a similar terminology in classifying languages and groups of languages: dialect, language, family, stock, phylum. In the linguistic literature and in this volume, a *taxon* is any genetic node, as defined in definition 2 of section 1.1. It may be a "low-level" group such as Romance, Slavic, or Bantu, or a "high-level" unit such as Nilo-Saharan, Indo-Pacific, or Amerind. The common ancestor from which a low-level group of languages derives existed at a relatively recent date, whereas the common ancestor of a high-level group is considerably more ancient. In order to give a more precise indication of the level, or rank, of a taxon in a hierarchic classification, linguists, like biologists, assign the various taxa to different categories. Running from low-level (recent) to high-level (ancient), the linguistic terms commonly used are *dialect, language, family, stock,* and *phylum.* If finer gradations are needed, one may use the prefixes sub- and macro-: a subfamily is a branch of a family; a macrophylum is a group of phyla.

Linguists are, however, less consistent in their use of categorical names than are biologists; certain terms, especially family and phylum, are frequently used ambiguously. Thus, in addition to its proper categorical meaning (a group of related languages), family is often used synonymously with the generic terms "group," " node," and "unit"; that is, a family can be any genetic group at any level. Phylum, on the other hand, is often used to designate any genetic group, whether high-level or low-level, that is not known to be related to any other group. Thus the Chukchi-Kamchatkan and Eskimo-Aleut families are sometimes called phyla because they do not exhibit any evident relationship to any other group, even though they are clearly not ancient groupings of the Australian or Amerind sort.

The language/dialect distinction in linguistics parallels the species/variety distinction in biology. Whereas a species is usually thought of as a group of plants or animals that can interbreed and produce viable progeny, a language is a group of dialects among which there is mutual intelligibility.* As Cavalli-Sforza (1984) points out, in both instances we are dealing with communication, genetic in regard to species, linguistic in regard to language. But the analogy is not perfect, since the criterion of mutual intelligibility is less well defined than that of interbreeding. Mutual intelligibility ranges from close to 0 percent to close to 100 percent; interbreeding is usually an all-or-nothing proposition. As was noted in section 1.2, there are many gray areas in deciding what to call a language and what to call a dialect. Biological speciation is much more clear-cut. Yet the similarities, to which Darwin called attention in 1871, are indeed striking.

Pidgins and *creoles* are special kinds of languages. Pidgins are simplified languages that sometimes arise when people speaking distinct languages need to communicate. The simplified language is an amalgam of two (or more) languages, but generally one language is dominant. Another defining characteristic of pidgin languages is that no one speaks them as a native

*In linguistics "dialect" does not have the pejorative connotation that it often does in everyday parlance. It is simply a variety of speech that is similar to, but different from, other varieties of speech. The origin of the differences is usually the geographic or social separation of different groups.

(i.e. first) language; that is, they are spoken only by people who usually speak another language. Under certain circumstances a pidgin may become "creolized." Creoles differ from pidgins, initially at least, in only one respect: they are the first language (and sometimes the only language) of a group of people. Creole languages gradually lose the simplicity resulting from their unique origin as they evolve according to principles governing all human languages.

In this volume the various taxon names are used as they are throughout the linguistic literature. In particular, *family* and *phylum* are used with both of the meanings described above. *Group, node,* and *unit* are used interchangeably for genetic units at any level. *Stock* is used only for groups that are intermediate between families and phyla.

Benveniste, Émile. 1953. "La classification des langues," *Conférences de l'Institut de Linguistique de Paris* 11. Reprinted in Émile Benveniste, *Problèmes de linguistique générale*. Paris, 1966.

Birnbaum, Henrik. 1975. "Typological, Genetic, and Areal Linguistics—An Assessment of the State of the Art in the 1970s," *Foundations of Language* 13: 267–91.

Black, Paul. 1976. "Multidimensional Scaling Applied to Linguistic Relationships," *Cahiers de l'Institut de Linguistique de Louvain* 3, 5–6: 43–92.

Cavalli-Sforza, Luigi Luca. 1984. "Evolution of Language: Comments of a Biologist," paper presented at a conference on language change and language transmission, Stanford University, March 1984.

Chretien, C. D. 1963. "Shared Innovations and Subgrouping," *IJAL* 29: 66–68.

Dyen, Isidore, ed. 1973. *Lexicostatistics in Genetic Linguistics*. The Hague.

———. 1975. *Linguistic Subgrouping and Lexicostatistics*. The Hague.

Greenberg, Joseph H. 1953. "Historical Linguistics and Unwritten Languages," in A. L. Kroeber, ed., *Anthropology Today*. Chicago.

———. 1957. *Essays in Linguistics*. Chicago.

Grimes, Barbara F., ed. 1978. *Ethnologue 1978*. Huntington Beach, Calif.

Haas, Mary R. 1966. "Historical Linguistics and the Genetic Relationship of Languages," in *CTIL* 3.

Hetzron, Robert. 1976. "Two Principles of Genetic Reconstruction," *Lingua* 38: 89–108.

Hockett, Charles F. 1958. *A Course in Modern Linguistics*. New York.

Hoenigswald, Henry M. 1966. "Criteria for the Subgrouping of Languages," in Henrik Birnbaum and Jaan Puhvel, eds., *Ancient Indo-European Dialects*. Berkeley, Calif.

Kroeber, A. L. 1913. "The Determination of Linguistic Relationship," *Anthropos* 8: 389–401.

Malkiel, Yakov. 1978. "The Classification of Romance Languages," *Romance Philology* 31: 467–500.

Manessy-Guitton, Jacqueline. 1968. "La parenté généalogique," in André Martinet, ed., *Le langage*. Paris.

Mayr, Ernst. 1982. *The Growth of Biological Thought*. Cambridge, Mass.

Meillet, A. 1914. "Le problème de la parenté des langues," *Scientia* 15,35: 3.

Meillet, A., and M. Cohen, eds. 1952. *Les langues du monde*. Paris.
Schmidt, Wilhelm. 1926. *Die Sprachfamilien und Sprachenkreise der Erde*. Heidelberg.
Swadesh, Morris. 1967. "Lexicostatistic Classification," in Norman McQuown, ed., *Handbook of Middle American Indians* 5: *Linguistics*. Austin, Tex.
———. 1971. *The Origin and Diversification of Language*. Chicago.
Verguin, Joseph. 1968. "La situation linguistique du monde contemporain," in André Martinet, ed., *Le langage*. Paris.
Voegelin, C. F., and F. M. Voegelin. 1974. "Languages of the World," in *EB* 10: 662–72.
———. 1977. *Classification and Index of the World's Languages*. New York.
Washburn, Sherwood L., ed. 1963. *Classification and Human Evolution*. New York.
Zorc, R. David. 1982. "Micro- and Macro-Subgrouping: Criteria, Problems, and Procedures," in Rainer Carle et al., eds., *Studies in Austronesian Languages and Cultures*. Berlin.

2

Europe

All the languages currently spoken on the European continent, save Basque, belong to one of three language families: Indo-European, Uralic, and Caucasian. *Basque*, spoken in northern Spain by close to a million people, and elsewhere in the world by perhaps another million Basque emigrants, is a language isolate; that is, it has no obvious relationship with any other language. Some scholars believe it is distantly related to the Caucasian family, but this conjecture is hotly disputed by others.

The *Indo-European* family is the most widespread, covering most of Europe and extending through Asia Minor (Iran, Afghanistan, and Pakistan) into India. Emigrants, since 1500, have also carried Indo-European languages to the other continents, where they have often become the dominant languages (e.g. English in Australia and North America, Spanish and Portuguese in South America, Russian in northern Asia). The *Uralic* family, which includes Finnish and Hungarian, is found chiefly in northern Europe, but extends beyond the Urals into northwest Asia. Hungarian, however, is a Uralic island in central Europe, surrounded on all sides by Indo-European tongues. The *Caucasian* languages belong to two very divergent subfamilies, which possibly do not together constitute a valid genetic node. They are spoken in the mountains of the Caucasus, straddling southeast Europe and Asia Minor. Georgian is the only well-known Caucasian language.

This chapter traces the discovery and elaboration of the idea that languages may exhibit similarities because they are descendants of a common ancestor. After placing the question of language classification in the broader historical context of evolutionary studies (section 2.1), the chapter then surveys the period up to 1800 (section 2.2). Section 2.3 discusses the birth and development of comparative linguistics as it was first elaborated with respect to the Indo-European language family in the nineteenth century, and sections 2.4 and 2.5 treat the Uralic and Caucasian families, respectively. Subsequent chapters trace the development of genetic classification in other language families.

2.1 THE HISTORICAL CONTEXT

Today it does not seem startling that a single language, through the migration of a group of its speakers and their subsequent isolation, should in the course of time develop into two distinct languages, as the speech of the emigrants and that of the original group gradually drift apart. But this idea did not become current, and enjoy consensus, until the first half of the nineteenth century, though it had numerous precursors.

The "genetic hypothesis," considered by Hockett (1965: 185) to be the first major breakthrough in the field of linguistics, must be viewed in a broader historical context to be fully appreciated. For the nineteenth century witnessed a fundamental transformation of man's perception of himself, and his place in nature, that was perhaps as significant as the Copernican Revolution some 300 years earlier. In a number of disparate fields, including linguistics, geology, paleontology, and biology, a static, theologically inspired view of nature was replaced by a dynamic scientific approach. The most celebrated breakthrough was of course Charles Darwin's discovery (independently arrived at by Alfred Russel Wallace) that species may evolve gradually into other species through the operation of forces such as natural selection. Furthermore, Darwin, and linguists of the day like August Schleicher, did not fail to note the similarities between their respective disciplines. As Darwin remarked in one of his later works (1871: 40), "The formation of different languages and of distinct species, and the proofs that both have been developed through a gradual process, are curiously parallel."

To appreciate the extent of this intellectual transformation, let us for a moment try to view the natural world as an educated person might have in the first decade of the nineteenth century. In general, our outlook would have been constrained, if not dominated, by religious dogma in the form of "Creationism," the idea that the world and all its component parts (e.g. plants, animals, minerals) came into being by a single act of divine creation. Seventeenth-century theologians had even determined the precise date of the earth's creation: 9:00 A.M., Sunday, October 23, 4004 B.C. Similarities between certain animals (e.g. dog-wolf, cat-tiger, man-ape), and between certain plants, had of course been noticed, and even systematically classified by people such as Linnaeus. But they had not really been explained, except perhaps in terms of "divine order."

The absence of fossils in certain strata of the earth's crust was explained at the start of the nineteenth century by a theory called Catastrophism, according to which all life had periodically been wiped out by calamities such as floods and earthquakes. Following each of these disasters, new species of animals and plants were created by new acts of creation. The fact that plants and animals in later strata often appeared more advanced than similar forms in earlier strata was explained by the theory of Progressionism, which held that the Creator had made progressively more advanced forms after each disaster.

One of the dominant linguistic themes in the year 1800, as it had been for the preceding century, concerned the original language of mankind. The Old Testament reveals that all mankind originally shared a single uniform language, which God had felt obligated to confound at the Tower of Babel, lest the human race become too powerful. But the Bible does not specifically identify the original language, and the eighteenth century had witnessed unbridled speculation on this topic. The most popular candidate had for centuries been Hebrew, no doubt because most of the Old Testament was written in this language. From time to time other languages were also advocated; the Dutchman Goropius Becanus, for example, in 1569 argued patriotically for Dutch as mankind's original tongue.

To some extent this traditional world view had already begun to be undermined during the eighteenth century, and precursors of nineteenth-century developments may be cited in all the fields mentioned above. In biology, in particular, people such as Montesquieu, Pierre-Louis de Maupertuis, Denis Diderot, Georges Buffon, and Carolus Linnaeus had already, in the eighteenth century, questioned the idea of the immutability of species. Darwin's grandfather, Erasmus Darwin, was an outspoken advocate of evolution (or transmutation, as it was then known), and Lamarck explicitly proposed a theory of evolution in the first decade of the nineteenth century and even drew up a genealogical tree of the animal kingdom in 1809. Lamarck's explanations of the mechanisms that cause evolution, the most notorious of which was the heritability of acquired characteristics, are now generally considered incorrect, but his recognition of the existence of evolution has been amply confirmed. Although the idea of evolution was intuitively grasped by men like Lamarck, today we find the various explanations offered to account for it fanciful and erroneous. The key to evolution, natural selection, was to be Charles Darwin's contribution, but in 1800 that event lay 60 years in the future.

In the field of geology, James Hutton had proposed, toward the end of the eighteenth century, that the earth was in fact much older than most contemporaries conceded, and furthermore that the earth's surface had not been formed abruptly by a series of catastrophes, but slowly, by the gradual erosion that results from natural forces such as wind, rain, water, and ice. Hutton's theory, which came to be known as Uniformitarianism, was thought by many to be irreligious, and did not at first make appreciable inroads on the Biblically inspired doctrine of Catastrophism.

Hutton himself died in obscurity in 1797. By coincidence Charles Lyell was born that same year, and it was Lyell who would in the 1830's resurrect and prove the theory of Uniformitarianism. Lyell's *Principles of Geology* (1830), in addition to vindicating Hutton's earlier ideas, also had a significant influence on Darwin's thought. Lyell himself, though a close friend of Darwin's, was not initially a supporter of evolution. He withheld his assent until the publication of the *Origin of Species* (1859), at which time, however, he threw his considerable intellectual weight squarely behind Darwin's theory.

In the realm of human language, the eighteenth century had already seen opposition to the idea that Hebrew was mankind's original tongue. One of the most vocal opponents was the German mathematician G. W. Leibniz, who related Hebrew to Arabic, in the group where it rightly belongs. Toward the end of the century, attention began to shift from the identification of man's original language (on which no real progress had been made in spite of an enormous amount of effort) to the study of the Sanskrit language in far-off India. News of Sanskrit had for some time been filtering back to Europe, and it had already been noticed to exhibit striking similarities with European languages. In 1786 the orientalist William Jones, at a gathering of the Royal Asiatic Society in Calcutta, expressed the opinion that Sanskrit, Greek, and Latin, and probably also Gothic, Celtic, and Persian, "have sprung from some common source, which, perhaps, no longer exists" (quoted in Robins 1967: 134). This idea was to dominate linguistic research in the nineteenth century, and in the process the question of an original human language gradually faded from view—and in some quarters was even proscribed from scientific discussion.

By the end of the nineteenth century, an evolutionary approach involving gradual change over long periods of time had become dominant in geology, biology, paleontology, and linguistics. In geology the forces that had shaped the earth's surface were seen to be operating just as they had in the past. Moreover, the proposed age of the earth had grown considerably from the original church estimate of some 6,000 years. Uniformitarianism had replaced Catastrophism.

In biology the theory of evolution by natural selection won its battle with the Creationists after the appearance of the *Origin of Species* in 1859, though skirmishes between Creationists and Evolutionists still recur from time to time in the twentieth century, particularly in the United States. After Darwin it was understood that species are not immutable; rather, the species that now exist are simply the descendants of other species that once inhabited the earth. The recognition of a historical connection between all forms of life, and of the gradual evolution through time of more and more complex organisms, culminating in the relatively recent appearance on the earth of humans, contrasts sharply with the static picture of discrete and unchanging categories, all present on the earth from the beginning of time, that had been advocated by Creationists at the start of the century. In linguistics scholars had by the end of the nineteenth century developed methods for studying the genetic relationships of languages and even for reconstructing portions of languages (such as Indo-European) that had existed thousands of years earlier but that had left no written trace, their daughter languages (some extinct) being the only available evidence.

By 1900 educated persons, won over by the nineteenth-century successes in biology, geology, linguistics, and other fields, turned in progressively larger numbers to science for an understanding of the natural world. The role of the church as the ultimate arbiter in scientific disputes, long on the decline, more or less evaporated in the nineteenth century, and twentieth-century inquirers have looked increasingly to science for their final answers.

de Beer, Gavin. 1974. "Evolution," in *EB* 7: 7–23.
Bowler, Peter J. 1984. *Evolution: The History of an Idea*. Berkeley, Calif.
Campbell, Bernard. 1966. *Human Evolution*. Chicago.
Darwin, Charles. 1859. *The Origin of Species*. London.
———. 1871. *The Descent of Man*. London.
Greenberg, Joseph H. 1959. "Language and Evolution," in Betty J. Megger, ed., *Evolution and Anthropology: A Centennial Appraisal*. Washington, D.C.
Hockett, Charles F. 1965. "Sound Change," *Language* 41: 185–204.
Lyell, Charles. 1830. *Principles of Geology*. London.
Robins, R. H. 1967. *A Short History of Linguistics*. Bloomington, Ind.

2.2 THE LINGUISTIC BACKGROUND

It is difficult to determine who, and in what year, first realized that similarities between languages may (sometimes) be explained as traits inherited from a common ancestor. What is clear is that this notion took hold at the start of the nineteenth century and provoked a period of intense research on the Indo-European family and general comparative linguistics. The event traditionally identified as the starting point for this linguistic revolution is William Jones's address to the Royal Asiatic Society in 1786, but all the standard handbooks hasten to add that Jones was in fact neither the first to recognize similarities between Sanskrit and European languages nor the first to propose a genetic explanation for such resemblances. What he did was to state clearly, in a prominent forum, an idea whose time had come.

In delving into the historical background of the genetic hypothesis, there are two distinct questions we should not confuse. The first is when similarities between certain languages were first *noticed*; the second is when those resemblances were first *explained* as being due to historical descent from a common ancestor. With regard to the first question, we may safely assume that people have recognized similarities between their own speech and that of other fairly similar languages ever since human language developed on the earth, and probably recognized similarities even during the developmental stages leading up to human language. It is today impossible for, say, any Rumanian speaker to have modest contact with Italian, or even Spanish, without recognizing immediately that these two geographically distant languages resemble Rumanian in a way that neighboring Hungarian and Bulgarian do not. Wherever in the world languages are fairly similar, it seems likely that from time to time such similarities are, and always have been, duly noted.

Explaining similarities between languages is more difficult than simply noticing them, and consequently scholars did not generally reach the genetic hypothesis until the nineteenth century. Exactly when, and with regard to what group of languages, was the genetic hypothesis first formulated? It is difficult to find a precise answer in the literature. However, the historical record from Classical times to 1800, which is examined in the remainder of this section, does reveal a number of significant events.

Already in the first century B.C. the Romans were well aware of numerous resemblances between Greek, a language for which they had great respect, and their own language, Latin. These similarities were attributed to the Greek origin of the Latin-speaking people, one version of which is found in Book I of the *Aeneid*. Thus the Romans, in pre-Christian times, both recognized similarities between their language and another and gave a genetic (i.e. historical) explanation for them. This particular genetic explanation was, however, incorrect, because Latin and Greek both derive from Indo-European, rather than one from the other.

In early Christian times the monogenesis of all languages was widely accepted, on the strength of the Biblical account in *Genesis* of the origin of language diversity at the Tower of Babel (see p. 26). The assumption of Hebrew as mankind's original language was probably unfortunate for the development of genetic linguistics, for it meant that medieval and Renaissance scholars were facing an impossibility in trying to derive their own European languages from an unrelated Semitic language. To perform this Herculean feat scholars were forced, in relating Hebrew words to supposed European cognates, to take such phonetic and semantic liberties that the entire field of etymology sank into disrepute, from which it did not fully recover until the nineteenth century. Voltaire's observation that "etymology is a science in which the vowels count for nothing and the consonants for very little" is indicative of the low level of credibility that etymology had come to enjoy.

Around the twelfth century the recognition of similarities between languages, followed by a genetic hypothesis to explain them, began to appear in the written record. In Iceland an unknown scholar, in what has become known as the *First Grammatical Treatise*, concluded that Icelandic and English were related because they shared many similar words. Toward the end of the twelfth century, Giraldus Cambrensis asserted that Welsh, Cornish, and Breton were descendants of a single earlier language, which he called the "antiquum linguae Britannicae idioma." Today these languages are classified as the Brythonic branch of the Celtic family. Cambrensis went on to suggest a relationship between this "ancient Brittanic tongue" and Latin and Greek, pointing out lexical resemblances such as Latin *sal*, Greek *hals*, and Welsh *halen*, all of which mean 'salt.'

Probably no group of languages offered better prospects for the discovery of genetic linguistics than the Romance family. Here was a group of languages whose resemblances were obvious at a glance (see Table 1.2 above), and whose parent language, Latin, not only was abundantly attested in written records, but was even, throughout the Middle Ages, the spoken language of the church and the academic world. Yet despite these propitious circumstances (or perhaps even because of them), the Romance family did not play as large a role in unlocking the secrets of genetic classification as it might have. In light of the close-knit nature of the Romance group, it seems inescapable that resemblances between Italian, Provençal, French, and Spanish must have been noticed regularly throughout the Middle Ages, even if such observations were not written down. In the early fourteenth century the Italian poet Dante was fully aware of the lexical resemblances between Romance languages. He also knew that languages change and may break up into dialects. But he nonetheless never realized that the Romance languages were simply the historical continuation of the Latin spoken by the Romans more than 1,000 years earlier.

Apparently the genetic hypothesis was initially proposed for the Romance languages in the first half of the fifteenth century, although most of the standard Romance handbooks do not discuss the history of the genetic hypothesis with regard to Romance. A notable exception is Hall (1974: 231), who gives the following account: "A few fifteenth-century scholars, e.g. Flavio Biondo (1388–1463), had considered the modern idiom [i.e. Italian] to be the direct continuation, unchanged, of popular Latin; but others, beginning with Poggio Bracciolini (1380–1459) and Leonardo Bruni (1370–1444), saw that the modern Romance tongues, including Roumanian, were the result of linguistic change as it had affected Latin." Yet this early recognition of the genetic hypothesis did not instigate research on other language groups, but remained rather an isolated event, a dormant seed that would not begin to sprout for several more centuries.

In retrospect we can perhaps understand why the Romance example did not kindle success elsewhere, for the Romance group is, or at least was, almost unique in preserving the common ancestor (Latin) side by side with its daughter languages (Italian, French, Spanish, etc.). In the Middle Ages the anomalous, and artificial, nature of the preservation of Classical Latin was not clearly recognized. Nor was it realized that the ancestor of a group of languages may itself no longer exist, except in the form of its descendant languages. In fact the Romance case, which is probably the first widely recognized example of the genetic hypothesis, actually encouraged the search for linguistic ancestors among the world's *living* languages. If the special circumstances surrounding Latin contributed to the early recognition of the genetic hypothesis with respect to Romance, they probably obscured its implications for other language families.

Grammars of languages other than Latin and Classical Greek first began to appear at the end of the fifteenth century. During the following centuries grammars of languages from the most distant parts of the earth were published with greater and greater frequency. These grammars were written for a variety of purposes by a disparate group of authors that included missionaries, diplomats, explorers, and even an occasional layman inspired by nothing more than personal curiosity. They frequently suffer from a somewhat slavish adherence to Latin grammar, but since this was the only descriptive model widely available to Europeans at the time, a certain forced imitation was perhaps unavoidable in the beginning. Furthermore, a preoccupation with "universal grammatical categories," a legacy of the Greeks, made it seem natural to seek to identify those grammatical categories *assumed* to be universal, in particular grammars of individual languages. Despite their obvious flaws, these early grammars were of great importance for two reasons. First, they revealed beyond question that European languages possessed grammatical categories that were more often than not absent in other languages (e.g. gender), while at the same time grammatical categories widespread outside Europe were sometimes totally lacking in European languages (e.g. the distinction between inclusive and exclusive 'we,' first described in a Spanish grammar of Aymara in 1603).

The second important impact of the gradually accumulating linguistic documentation was that it led inevitably to a comparison of one language with another. As more and more languages became known, attempts were made to survey the world's languages. The first such general survey, the *Mithridates* of the Swiss scholar Conrad Gesner, appeared in 1555. That work (named after a king in Asia Minor in the first century B.C. who was reputed to know 25 languages) gave comparative wordlists for a number of languages. It derived Italian, Spanish, and French from Latin, and all languages from Hebrew.

Other general surveys followed at irregular intervals, often with a specimen translation of the Lord's Prayer in each language. In 1592 the German Hieronymous Megiser published *Specimen XL linguarum et dialectorum* (Specimens of Forty Languages and Dialects); a second edition in 1603 increased the number to 50.

One of the more ambitious early attempts at collecting wordlists, and thereby classifying languages into groups, was carried out by Catherine the Great of Russia toward the end of the eighteenth century. Catherine commissioned P. S. Pallas to collect and organize wordlists from a broad sample of the world's languages, and it is usually Pallas's name that is associated with the result of this project, which was published from 1786 to 1789 and contained information on 200 languages. However, according to Key (1977), it was really Catherine herself who decided the ordering of the languages in this work, and that order was to a very large extent genetic. Slavic languages came first, followed by Celtic, Greek, Romance, Germanic, Baltic, Caucasian, Finno-Ugric, Iranian, Semitic, Turkic, and so on. There were of course a few errors (e.g. Basque was included in Celtic, and Yiddish was placed in Semitic), and in the second half of the list the ordering becomes more geographic than genetic, with Hawaiian the last language listed. A second edition of this work (1791) added 80 more languages, including for the first time African and Amerindian tongues. Catherine's success in sorting out so many valid genetic groups is less surprising than one might think. In addition to having collected the requisite data for genetic classification (wordlists of 285 words each), Catherine was herself trilingual in German, Russian, and French, each of which is a member of a different branch of Indo-European. Ironically, although Catherine's classification of the world's languages began to appear the same year that William Jones delivered his famous pronouncement on Indo-European (1786), Catherine's contributions to genetic linguistics have today been all but forgotten, while Jones's discourse has assumed a quasi-mythical status.

During the first decade of the nineteenth century, a Spanish Jesuit, Lorenzo Hervás y Panduro, published a six-volume compendium containing material on 300 languages. The last *Mithridates* was published by J. C.

Adelung from 1806 to 1817 in four volumes, and contained, among other things, the Lord's Prayer in 500 languages. In that work Adelung recognized the affinity of Sanskrit with European languages, a topic then on the verge of replacing interest in comparative wordlists with attention to the recently established Indo-European (I-E) family.

With this gradual accumulation of linguistic documentation, it was inevitable that from time to time people would attempt to classify the known languages into groups, usually on the basis of lexical similarities. One of the more successful early attempts, by J. J. Scaliger, appeared in 1610. In that work Scaliger divided European languages into 11 groups on the basis of the word for 'God' in each (see List 2.1). Significantly, all 11 of these groups are correct genetic units, though some of the groups are now known to contain additional languages of which Scaliger was unaware. Scaliger did not recognize, and in fact explicitly denied, any relationship between these 11 groups, thus failing to recognize that groups 1, 2, 3, 4, 5, 9, and 10 belong to the I-E family (within which 9 and 10 constitute the Celtic subfamily), and 7 and 8 are members of what is today called the Finno-Ugric family.

List 2.1. European Language Families (Scaliger 1610)

1. SLAVIC 2. GERMANIC 3. ROMANCE 4. Greek 5. Albanian	6. TARTAR 7. Hungarian 8. Finnish (and Saami = Lapp)	9. Irish and Scottish Gaelic 10. Welsh and Breton 11. Basque

Scaliger's classification is unusual in the broad range of languages taken into consideration. More frequently the recognition of similarities between languages was more restricted, often being limited to just two languages. For example, in 1615 the Lithuanian Michalon claimed a relationship between Lithuanian and Latin, though he rejected one between the even more closely related Lithuanian and Russian. In 1671 the Swedish scholar G. Stiernhielm compared the inflectional endings of Latin *habere* 'to have' and Gothic *haban* 'to have' (the stems of which, *hab-*, are not cognate despite appearances), and concluded that both languages must be descendants of a common ancestor. In 1686 the Swedish scholar A. Jager, in a public lecture, pictured an ancient language spreading over Europe, breaking up into daughter languages, which in turn led to Persian, Greek, Romance, Slavic, Celtic, Gothic, and Germanic languages. Also recognized during the seventeenth century was the Baltic group (Lithuanian, Latvian, and Old Prussian), as well as the close affinity between this group and Slavic.

The eighteenth century witnessed additional discoveries of genetic links between various languages, including for the first time groups outside Europe. In 1702 Hiob Ludolf compared all known Semitic languages, and in 1707 E. Lhuyd founded comparative Celtic grammar by joining Scaliger's groups 9 and 10 to form the Celtic family. In 1730 the Swede Phillip Johann von Strahlenberg published a work in which he employed the mass comparison of basic vocabulary to classify the languages of Russia. According to Jakobson (1942: 603), Strahlenberg "established with an impressive exactitude nearly all the families of the non-Indo-European languages of Russia." In 1767 P. Coeurdoux asked the French Academy for an explanation of similarities between Sanskrit and Greek and Latin, similarities that he believed to be relics of mankind's original language. In 1786 William Jones gave his famous address and attributed the similarities to common origin, though he did not imply they went all the way back to the Tower of Babel.

In 1770 J. Sajnovics connected Hungarian with Lapp, and in 1799 Sámuel Gyarmathi established the affinity of Hungarian and Finnish. The genetic group to which Finnish, Lapp, and Hungarian belong is today called Finno-Ugric.

In 1778 William Marsden recognized striking similarities between languages on the east and west coasts of Africa; today these languages are considered members of the Bantu group. Three years later Marsden pointed out resemblances between the language of Madagascar (i.e. Malagasy) and the Polynesian languages, all of which belong to the Austronesian family. On this point, however, Marsden had already been foreshadowed by Hadrian Reland, who apparently had made a similar observation in 1706, and Frederick de Houtman, who had perceived the affinity between Malay and Malagasy as early as 1603. In the New World the Iroquoian, Algonquian, Carib, and Arawakan families were all identified before 1800.

We see then that by 1800 a not insignificant number of genetic groups had already been identified, but in most cases the true geographic extent of these groups was not yet known. For certain groups (e.g. Romance, Semitic, Finno-Ugric) the genetic hypothesis was already the accepted explanation for similarities, though for other groups, including I-E, the genetic hypothesis had been advanced without necessarily gaining wide acceptance. In the nineteenth century genetic classification left the realm of sporadic observations by isolated scholars and became for the first time the center of focus of intensive academic research. Although there was in fact great progress in classifying languages from all parts of the world in the nineteenth century, it was the I-E family that dominated attention and established the base for the development of general comparative linguistics. We shall explore that development in the following section.

Adelung, J. C. 1806–17. *Mithridates*, 4 vols. Berlin.
Bonfante, Giuliano. 1953. "Ideas on the Kinship of the European Languages from 1200 to 1800," *Cahiers d'Histoire Mondiale* 1: 679–99.
Davies, A. Morpurgo. 1975. "Language Classification in the Nineteenth Century," in *CTIL* 13.
Décsy, Gyula. 1973. *Die linguistische Struktur Europas*. Wiesbaden.
Gesner, C. 1555. *Mithridates*. Zurich.
Greenberg, Joseph H. 1957. *Essays in Linguistics*. Chicago.
Gyarmathi, Sámuel. 1799. *Affinitas linguae Hungaricae cum linguis Fennicae originis grammatice demonstrata*. Göttingen. Reprinted 1968, Bloomington, Ind.
Hall, Robert A., Jr. 1974. *External History of the Romance Languages*. New York.
Hervás y Panduro, Lorenzo. 1800–1805. *Catálogo de las lenguas de las naciones conocidas*, 6 vols. Madrid.
Jakobson, Roman. 1942. "The Paleosiberian Languages," *AA* 44: 602–20.
Key, Mary Ritchie. 1977. "The Linguistic Discoveries of Catherine the Great," in Robert J. Di Pietro and Edward L. Blansitt, Jr., eds., *The Third LACUS Forum, 1976*. Columbia, S.C.
Lhuyd, Edward. 1707. *Archaeologia Britannica*. London.
Lockwood, W. B. 1972. *A Panorama of Indo-European Languages*. London.
Ludolf, Hiob. 1702. "Dissertatio de harmonia linguae aethiopicae cum ceteris orientalibus," in *Grammatica Aethiopica*. Frankfurt.
Megiser, Hieronymous. 1592. *Specimen XL linguarum et dialectorum*. Frankfurt.
Mounin, Georges. 1970. *Histoire de la linguistique*. Paris.
Pallas, P. S., ed. 1786–89. *Linguarum totius orbis vocabularia comparativa*. St. Petersburg.
Pedersen, Holger. 1931. *Linguistic Science in the Nineteenth Century*. Cambridge, Mass. Reprinted 1962 as *The Discovery of Language*, Bloomington, Ind.
Robins, R. H. 1967. *A Short History of Linguistics*. Bloomington, Ind.
———. 1973. "The History of Language Classification," in *CTIL* 11.
Sajnovics, J. 1770. *Demonstratio idioma Ungarorum et Lapponum idem esse*. Copenhagen.
Scaliger, J. J. 1610. *Diatriba de Europaeorum linguis*. Paris.
von Strahlenberg, Phillip Johann. 1730. *Das nord- und östliche Theil von Europa und Asia*. Stockholm.

2.3 INDO-HITTITE

Although the Indo-Hittite (or Indo-European) family contains only about 140 of the world's 5,000 languages, its two billion speakers constitute almost half of the world's population. Since about 1500 A.D. Indo-European languages have been spread around the world by the European colonial movement to an extent that obscures their original provenance. Map 2.1 shows the geographic distribution of the Indo-Hittite family around 1500, though both the Anatolian and Tocharian branches (already extinct) are also shown.

The 10 branches that make up this family vary greatly in number of languages and number of speakers. Two of the branches, Anatolian and

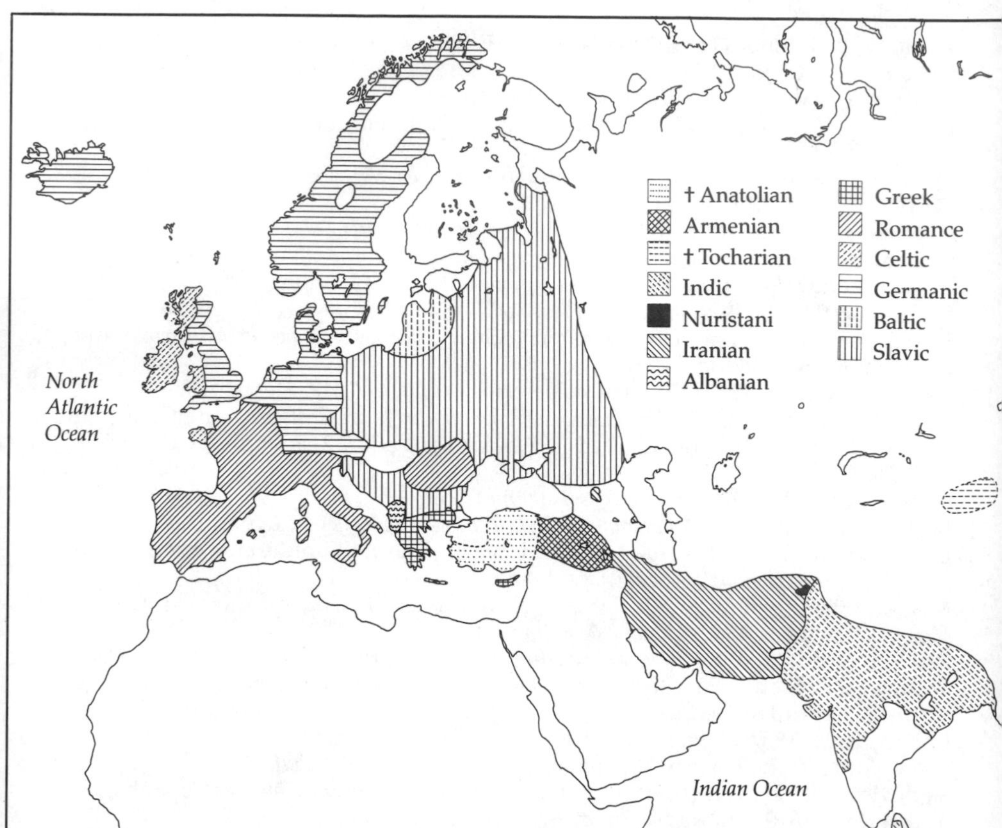

Map 2.1. The Indo-Hittite family. Turkish is now spoken where the Anatolian languages were spoken; several Turkic languages have supplanted Tocharian.

Tocharian, are extinct. Several *Anatolian* languages were formerly spoken in present-day Turkey; *Tocharian* languages were found in western China. Armenian and Albanian, though single languages, are independent branches of Indo-Hittite. *Armenian* has today about five million speakers, mostly in the U.S.S.R., though there are substantial numbers of Armenian speakers in many countries around the world. The original homeland of the Armenians was in what is today eastern Turkey. But a massacre by the Turks at the beginning of this century decimated the Armenian population in that region and scattered the survivors throughout the world. *Albanian* is spoken in Albania and surrounding parts of Yugoslavia and Greece by roughly four million people; it consists of two very divergent dialects (Gheg and Tosk), which are not mutually intelligible. Standard Albanian is based on the Tosk dialect. *Greek* is spoken in Greece by 10 million people. In addition to standard Greek, Tsakonian, with perhaps 10,000 speakers on the east coast of the Peloponnesus, continues the dialect of ancient Sparta.

Four *Celtic* languages in Ireland, in Great Britain, and on the north coast of France are all that is left of a family that once extended through Europe into Asia Minor. Breton, spoken in northern France by more than a million people, is numerically the strongest, but its use is discouraged by the French government. The use of Irish (= Gaelic) is encouraged by the Irish government, but the estimate of a half-million speakers is probably overoptimistic. Welsh, spoken in Wales, has an estimated 750,000 speakers. There are very few monolingual speakers of any Celtic language; those who speak Breton are mostly bilingual in French, those who speak the others are bilingual in English.

Originally a number of *Italic* languages were spoken in what is today Italy; all but Latin eventually became extinct. The descendants of Latin, known collectively as the *Romance* family, consist of some 16 languages with around 500 million speakers. The numerically strongest Romance languages (with millions of speakers in parentheses) are Spanish (200), Portuguese (130), French (66), Italian (60), Rumanian (22), Provençal (9), Catalan (6), and Sardinian (1). Spanish is spoken not only in Spain, but also in most of Central and South America. Portuguese is spoken in Brazil as well as Portugal. Various Provençal dialects are spoken in the south of France, but they have been steadily eroded by French, and the estimate of nine million speakers is probably exaggerated; almost all Provençal speakers are by now bilingual in French. Catalan is spoken primarily in eastern Spain, where it remains strong despite the efforts of the Franco regime to restrict its use.

About a dozen *Germanic* languages are spoken by some 450 million people. English, with about 300 million first-language speakers (and millions more who speak it as a second language) is numerically the strongest. Though English was originally restricted to Great Britain, the colonial movement has resulted in its being dominant today in Ireland, the United States, Canada, Australia, and New Zealand; it is also widely used in other parts of the world (e.g. India, South Africa). Other important Germanic languages (with millions of speakers in parentheses) are German (100), Dutch-Flemish (20), Swedish (9), Danish (5), Norwegian (5), Yiddish (4), Afrikaans (4), and Icelandic (.25). Yiddish has developed from German, and Afrikaans from Dutch. Despite their separate national status, Swedish, Danish, and Norwegian are mutually intelligible.

The *Balto-Slavic* family consists of 15 languages, with a total of some 290 million speakers, and has two clearly defined branches, Baltic and Slavic. Two *Baltic* languages survive today; Lithuanian has three million speakers, and Latvian, two million. Both are spoken along the western coast of the U.S.S.R., just north of Poland. The *Slavic* family contains roughly a dozen languages and 285 million speakers. Russian dominates, with 150 million first-language speakers and millions more who use it as a second language. Other Slavic languages, with millions of speakers in parentheses, are Ukrainian (40), Polish (35), Serbo-Croatian (17), Czech-Slovak (14), Byelorussian (10), Bulgarian (8), Slovene (2), and Macedonian (1). Ukrainian and Byelorussian (= White Russian) are spoken to the south and west, respectively, of Russian in the U.S.S.R. Serbo-Croatian is the national language of Yugoslavia, but Slovene is spoken in the north of that country, and Macedonian in the south.

The largest subfamily of the Indo-Hittite family is *Indo-Iranian*, with about 90 languages and 680 million speakers. Indo-Iranian languages are spoken in Iran, Afghanistan, Pakistan, India, Nepal, Bangladesh, and Sri Lanka. In addition, Romany, the language of the gypsies, is spoken in a number of mutually unintelligible dialects throughout western Europe and to a lesser degree in countries around the world. No fewer than 25 Indo-Iranian languages have a million speakers or more (the figures in parentheses below indicate number of speakers, in millions). In Iran there is Farsi (= Persian, 20), which extends into Afghanistan; Mazanderani (2); and Kurdish (5), also found in Iraq and Turkey. About 13 million Pashto speakers are found in Afghanistan and Pakistan. The most widespread Indic language is Hindi-Urdu, with 200 million first-language speakers and millions more second-language speakers; it is spoken in northern India and Pakistan. Sindhi (7) is also divided between India and Pakistan; Lahnda (15) and Baluchi (2) are found primarily in Pakistan. Nepali (10) is spoken in Nepal, and Sinhalese (10) on the island of Sri Lanka. Bengali (140) is spoken in Bangladesh and northeastern India. In addition to Hindi-Urdu, Bengali, and Sindhi, which are also spoken in neighboring countries, the following languages are located primarily in India: Awadhi (55), Marathi (45), Punjabi (40), Bihari (30), Gujarati (30), Oriya (20), Marwari (13), Kashmiri (3), Bhili (3), Pahari (2), Banjari (2), Garhwali (1), and Kumauni (1).

We begin our discussion of genetic classification with the Indo-Hittite family not because it is the most widespread in the world, but because it is in terms of this family that the principles of genetic classification were, in the nineteenth century, first established.

2.3.1 *History of Indo-Hittite Classification*

When William Jones delivered his famous address in 1786, several language families (e.g. Romance, Germanic, Slavic, Baltic, Celtic) had already been recognized for some time, and occasionally, as we saw in the preceding section, similarities *between* these families had been noticed. More often than not such comparisons were *binary* (i.e. only two families were taken into consideration), and the potential relevance of other languages or language groups was disregarded. This binary approach was characteristic of many prescientific classificatory attempts. A person speaking one language would by historical accident find himself in a locality where the people spoke a language with similarities to his own. Or a scholar interested in one group of languages might casually notice resemblances with another family. But there was seldom any attempt to collect, organize, and evaluate *all* of the evidence; research was directed more by happenstance than by design. It is to Jones's credit that he included six distinct groups in his putative family: Sanskrit, Greek, Latin, Germanic, Celtic, and Persian.

As soon as the I-E family was firmly established, during the second decade of the nineteenth century, the binary approach to language classification was superseded by what may be called the *global* approach. The binary approach examined only two pieces of a puzzle at a time; the global approach dictated that all pieces of the puzzle must be considered simultaneously. Any arbitrary restriction of the field of investigation to, say, two branches came to be considered methodologically inappropriate (unless of course those two branches were thought to share a special relationship, e.g. Indic and Iranian, Baltic and Slavic, Italic and Celtic). But the binary approach has remained in fashion in the classification of languages from other parts of the world up to the present day, often with lamentable consequences, which will be examined in section 6.3.

It would be hard to overestimate the importance of Sanskrit in the discovery and subsequent elaboration of the I-E family. That Sanskrit displayed similarities with European languages had been known, at the time of Jones's address, for some 200 years, ever since the Italian Filippo Sassetti, who lived on the west coast of India from 1581 to 1588, had reported striking resemblances between Sanskrit and Italian. Around 1800 the Romantic spirit of the times brought Sanskrit into great prominence in Europe; here was a language clearly affiliated with European tongues, yet found in far-off India. The idea that this exotic tongue was related to their own languages excited the imagination of European society. In 1808 F. von Schlegel claimed that Sanskrit was in fact the parent language of Greek, Latin, Persian, and Germanic, and was probably related to Armenian, Slavic, and Celtic. This claim has since been found to be incorrect, for Sanskrit represents merely one branch coordinate with each of the other branches. Yet Schlegel's book was enormously popular, and its success served both to attract the general attention of the public and to stimulate research on Sanskrit by the scholarly community.

Though it is peripheral to our concerns, we should nonetheless mention that the discovery of Sanskrit was important for the development of linguistic science in Europe in other ways. It turned out that besides being a cousin of the European languages, Sanskrit also possessed a long and distinguished tradition in descriptive (as opposed to historical) linguistics. Grammars of Sanskrit were far more sophisticated than any of the grammars hitherto prepared by European scholars following the Latin model. The most famous Sanskrit grammar, that of Panini, has been called by the American linguist Leonard Bloomfield (1933: 11) "one of the greatest monuments of human intelligence. . . . No other language, to this day, has been so perfectly described." Despite this illustrious descriptive tradition, however, the Indian grammarians, like the Greeks and Romans before them, had been obsessed with their own language and had paid scant attention to other tongues. They were primarily concerned with describing and preserving their sacred language, Sanskrit, and problems of language classification appear to have interested them not at all.

In spite of many valuable early observations connecting one I-E language (or language group) with another, a concentrated, sustained attack on the problem did not really get under way until the second decade of the nineteenth century. The first significant scholarly work was a prize-winning essay by a Dane, Rasmus Rask, completed in 1814 while the author was in Iceland, but not published until 1818. Through a careful examination and comparison of inflectional endings and basic vocabulary, and with an awareness of sound correspondences between languages that foreshadowed I-E research a half-century later, Rask proved beyond doubt that the Germanic, Latin, Greek, Slavic, and Baltic languages are all genetically related. Rask's monograph suffered, however, from two practical defects that undoubtedly diminished its impact. First, it was written in Danish, sharply curtailing its potential audience; and second, it ignored Sanskrit, a language that was at the time a fashionable topic in both popular society and learned circles.

The second influential book on the I-E family, by the German Franz Bopp, appeared in 1816 and suffered from neither of the defects of Rask's monograph. Like Rask, Bopp concentrated on inflectional endings and uncovered such an abundance of similarities that the genetic relationship of Latin, Greek, Germanic, Persian, and Sanskrit would never again be seriously questioned. Furthermore, Bopp demonstrated that Sanskrit was not the source of the I-E languages, but simply another branch of I-E, on the same taxonomic level as other branches such as Latin, Greek, Germanic, and Slavic.

It was not by chance that Rask and Bopp both chose inflectional endings as the focus of their research. As we have already seen, the science of etymology enjoyed a very poor reputation at this time, due primarily to its inability to distinguish probable (or even possible) phonetic and semantic shifts from improbable ones. Such lack of constraints had for centuries allowed scholars to derive words in any language from Biblical Hebrew through a series of totally improbable semantic and phonetic shifts. The search for cognates was further confounded by an inability to distinguish words that had been borrowed from another language from words that had been inherited from earlier stages of the same language. In choosing to investigate the inflectional apparatus of the I-E languages, Rask and Bopp avoided the problem of semantic similarity by examining inflectional endings whose semantic equivalency was taken for granted. Because inflectional endings are seldom borrowed, the confusing factor of loans was also eliminated. The only major variable was phonetic similarity, and this proved to be transparent enough to readily convince those who examined the evidence of the genetic unity of I-E.

It is nevertheless largely a historical accident that the I-E family was established by this line of proof. In the first place the I-E inflections are themselves accidents of history; many languages are structurally quite different from I-E and lack such inflections altogether. But even had the I-E languages been of a structurally different type, it seems unlikely that the absence of inflections would have retarded the recognition of I-E as a genetic unit for any significant length of time. Rather, the proof would have been made along different lines, most probably using fundamental vocabulary. The early reliance on inflections for proof of genetic affiliation served the same purpose as training wheels on a bicycle: one doesn't really need them to ride a bike (or even to *learn* to ride a bike), but the novice often feels comforted by their assistance. The early focus on inflectional resemblances was a similar crutch, as Holger Pedersen (1931: 245) has ably argued:

> That agreement in the inflectional system is an especially clear and striking proof of kinship, no one denies. But it is only an anachronism in theory, which has no significance in actual practice, when such an argument is still designated as the only valid proof. No one doubted, after the first communication about Tokharian, . . . that the language was Indo-European, although at that time virtually no similarities in inflection had been pointed out. Such similarities have since been shown, but even where they are almost obliterated, proof of kinship could be adduced from the vocabulary and from sound-laws.

I will suggest in section 3.6 that Pedersen is even here overcautious, and that proof of genetic kinship may in most cases be adduced from the fundamental vocabulary alone. Sound-laws, inflectional similarities, and other arbitrary classificatory criteria are no more decisive in determining genetic relationship than are lexical resemblances.

Although inflectional similarities served admirably to put the European scholarly community on the right track in the quest for the origin of their languages, exclusive reliance on this criterion at times impeded, rather than aided, language classification. Rask, for example, was fully aware of lexical resemblances between Celtic languages and the other languages for which he proposed genetic affiliation. But the Celtic languages do not display (or at least display less clearly) the inflectional similarities that linked the other groups so readily. Rask chose therefore to ignore the lexical resemblances as untrustworthy and excluded Celtic from his 1814 essay. Three years later Rask changed his mind on this point, and as soon as he became familiar with Sanskrit and Persian, he also added them to the family. Bopp apparently remained unconvinced of the I-E affinity of Celtic until his 1839 monograph.

By 1820 it had been established, primarily through the work of Rask and Bopp, that the Indo-European family covered most of Europe and extended through Asia Minor into northern India (see List 2.2).

List 2.2. The Indo-European Family (c. 1820)

INDO-EUROPEAN:
- I GREEK: Greek
- II ITALIC: Latin, . . .
- III CELTIC: Irish, Breton, . . .
- IV GERMANIC: German, English, . . .
- V SLAVIC: Russian, Polish, . . .
- VI BALTIC: Lithuanian, Latvian
- VII IRANIAN: Farsi (= Persian), . . .
- VIII INDIC: Sanskrit, Hindi, Bengali, . . .

Besides Rask and Bopp, there was a third major figure in the founding and initial development of comparative I-E grammar. This was the German scholar Jacob Grimm, who is better known for compiling and publishing, with his brother Wilhelm, a collection of children's stories, *Grimms' Fairy Tales*. Within the scholarly field Grimm produced a *Deutsche Grammatik* (Germanic Grammar), of which the second edition of Volume 1 (1822) is more often cited than the 1819 first edition. Grimm's work was influential in three respects. First, it uncovered the presence of ablaut (e.g. vowel alternation between morphologically related forms, as in 'sing, sang, sung') not only in Germanic, but in the I-E parent language as well. Second, it stressed the importance of systematic phonetic correspondences between related languages. Third, it served as a model for the comparative study of a branch of I-E, taking into account and weighing carefully the lower-level, more concrete evidence of the Germanic languages with the higher-level, more abstract evidence of the other branches of I-E.

Grimm was not the first to recognize systematic sound correspondences between related languages. Indeed it is clear that he owed much of his awareness on this point to Rask's monograph. But Grimm nonetheless popularized the notion of sound correspondence to such an extent that the most famous of all sound correspondences, though first stated explicitly by Rask, is today called Grimm's Law. Though Grimm may have discovered this correspondence in Rask's work, he neither named it after himself nor called it a law. The term Grimm's Law was invented by Max Müller in the 1860's. Since sound correspondences will play a central role in the subsequent history of the I-E family (and other genetic groupings as well), it is appropriate at this point to examine this most famous of all sound correspondences.

In simplest terms, Grimm's Law specifies the precise manner in which Germanic consonants are related to different consonants in the other branches of I-E. Using Gothic as the earliest attested Germanic language, the correspondences subsumed under Grimm's Law may be pictured in slightly simplified form as shown in Table 2.1 (adapted from Lyons 1968: 27). What the law represents, then, are the sound changes (or sound shifts, as Grimm would have called them) that transformed the I-E vocabulary into various Germanic cognates (the asterisks identify reconstructed sounds). Corresponding to a presumed I-E _*ped_ ~ _*pod_ 'foot,' we have Latin _pedis_, Greek _podos_, Sanskrit _padas_, Gothic _fotus_ (and English 'foot'), thus illustrating the first column of Table 2.1. Similar examples for the other columns may be found in the basic handbooks. It should be noted that the changes implied in Table 2.1 were not necessarily accomplished in a single step. If, for example, I-E _*g̤_ became Latin _h_, it is unlikely to have done so directly, as the sound correspondence implies:

(1) I-E *g̤ > Latin h

Far more likely, there were intermediate stages, now telescoped, separating the initial and final stages shown in (1). One might hypothesize a development such as:

(2) I-E *g̤ > k^h (as in Greek) > x > Latin h

If one understands the phonetics of the sounds listed in Table 2.1, it is apparent that Grimm's Law consists of three separate subrules, which account for the correspondences designated A, B, and C in Table 2.1:

Subrule A: I-E voiceless stops become voiceless fricatives in Germanic (p > f, t > θ, k > h).

Subrule B: I-E voiced stops become voiceless stops in Germanic (b > p, d > t, g > k).

Subrule C: I-E voiced aspirates become voiced stops in Germanic (b̤ > b, d̤ > d, g̤ > g).

Table 2.1. Grimm's Law

	Consonant group								
Language		A			B			C	
I-E	*p	*t	*k	*b	*d	*g	*b̤	*d̤	*g̤
Latin	p	t	k	b	d	g	f	f	h
Greek	p	t	k	b	d	g	p^h	t^h	k^h
Sanskrit	p	t	ś	b	d	ɟ	b̤	d̤	h
Gothic	f	θ	h	p	t	k	b	d	g

The extent to which these three subrules are interrelated, or causally connected, is still a matter of dispute.

The 1830's saw further significant developments in I-E research. In 1833, the year after Rask's death, Bopp began publishing the first comparative grammar of I-E. Publication of this work was not completed until 1852, and Old Slavic was included only starting with the second volume. Armenian was added to the second edition (1857–61), and the third and final edition appeared in 1868, the year after Bopp's death. Little attuned to the sound shifts that so fascinated both Rask and Grimm, Bopp remained all his life a devotee of morphology, especially inflectional morphology.

From 1833 to 1836 A. F. Pott published a work that both revitalized the long-moribund science of etymology and established comparative I-E phonetics. In 1839 Bopp demonstrated conclusively the I-E affinity of the Celtic languages, and in 1854 he recognized that Albanian constitutes a separate branch of I-E. Work on collateral branches of I-E was also progressing during this period, paralleling Grimm's work on Germanic. Among various important contributions, one may cite Diez (1836–44), von Miklosich (1852–75), Zeuss (1853), and Curtius (1858–62). The first linguistics journal devoted to the I-E family began to appear in 1851.

Of the second-generation Indo-Europeanists, no one was more colorful, or controversial, than the German August Schleicher. Originally trained as a botanist, Schleicher considered language a living organism, and linguistics a branch of the natural sciences. He thus rejected the traditional view of language as a set of social conventions passed on from generation to generation and properly studied within the humanities or social sciences. In a discipline that revered the quiet contemplation of ancient texts in libraries and private studies, Schleicher undertook what can only be described as anthropological fieldwork in the inhospitable Baltic region. The result was a splendid *Handbuch der litauischen Sprache* (Lithuanian Handbook). The first volume of this work (1856) was a grammar of Lithuanian, which was followed a year later by a second volume containing a collection of stories, songs, riddles, and proverbs upon which the grammar had been based.

Schleicher's investigation of Lithuanian paid off more handsomely than even he could have anticipated, for it turned out that modern Lithuanian is in certain respects as archaic as extinct languages known from documents several thousand years old (e.g. Sanskrit, Latin, Classical Greek). Indo-Europeanists had up to this time undervalued modern languages such as Lithuanian, which possessed no ancient texts, feeling that since languages are constantly changing, the modern stages could not possibly preserve any traits that would not be better preserved in the early texts. This belief was bolstered by the high esteem in which Sanskrit was held. Schleicher's work on Lithuanian showed very clearly that different areas of linguistic structure may age at different rates, and thus a language that is conservative with respect to inflectional morphology may be innovative with regard to phonology.

Whereas earlier scholars such as Rask, Bopp, Grimm, and Pott had been content with pointing out resemblances (such as cognate words) between different branches of I-E, Schleicher went one step further and attempted to use that information to reconstruct the I-E words from which the known cognates must have diverged. It was thus the I-E parent language itself, rather than its reflection in the daughter languages, that was the focus of Schleicher's *Compendium* (1861–62). In this work Schleicher introduced the practice of identifying reconstructed forms with an asterisk. The custom has been maintained ever since as a convenient way of distinguishing actually attested earlier stages from unattested reconstructions. For example, Schleicher reconstructed I-E **akva-s* on the basis of the following forms for 'horse':

(3)	Sanskrit	aśva-s	Avestan	aspa-
	Greek	híppo-s	Old English	eoh
	Latin	equu-s	Old Irish	ech

The attempt to reconstruct actual words led Schleicher to attempt a reconstruction of an entire fable in I-E, much to the chagrin of his more staid colleagues. Of course the reconstructed fable was incorrect in many respects; today an awareness of the overwhelming difficulties involved in such an enterprise discourages even the attempt. Yet for all its flaws, Schleicher's reconstructed fable served a useful purpose in focusing attention on the existence of the parent language itself, rather than merely dwelling on perceived similarities between daughter languages, as his predecessors were wont to do.

It was also Schleicher who first drew a branching tree diagram for the I-E family. Given his background as a botanist and his interest in evolutionary studies, this is not surprising. In his 1861 *Compendium* Schleicher proposed for the I-E family the subgrouping in List 2.3. I have substituted modern equivalents for names that have fallen into disuse; groups that are in fact single languages (e.g. Albanian) are not capitalized in the lists in this volume. One should note that all splits are binary, and that Armenian is still considered a member of the Iranian family. It was not until 1877 that the German scholar Heinrich Hübschmann finally sorted out the massive body of Iranian loanwords and demonstrated that Armenian, though a single language, constitutes a separate and distinct branch of I-E.

List 2.3. The Indo-European Family (Schleicher 1861)

INDO-EUROPEAN:
- I SLAVO-GERMANIC:
  - A GERMANIC
  - B BALTO-SLAVIC:
    - 1 BALTIC
    - 2 SLAVIC
- II INDO-CELTIC:
  - A INDO-IRANIAN:
    - 1 IRANIAN (including Armenian)
    - 2 INDIC
- [II INDO-CELTIC]
  - B GREEK-CELTIC:
    - 1 GREEK-ALBANIAN:
      - a GREEK
      - b Albanian
    - 2 ITALO-CELTIC:
      - a ITALIC
      - b CELTIC

It is also not surprising that the ex-botanist Schleicher should have been one of the first to embrace Darwinian principles, as he did in an 1863 monograph. It must have seemed to Schleicher in the 1860's that he was riding the wave of the future; yet subsequent history reveals that in many respects it was the wave of the past. Research on I-E in the nineteenth century is often divided into two periods. The first period began with the pioneering work of Rask, Bopp, and Grimm and lasted roughly through the 1860's. The second phase commenced in the 1870's and extended into the twentieth century. When Schleicher died in 1868, at the age of 47, the first phase of I-E research was drawing to a close. During the second period certain themes that had played a prominent role in the early work would either fade in importance (e.g. inflectional endings, Sanskrit) or disappear altogether (e.g. Schleicher's treatment of language as a living organism). Other issues, some of them foreshadowed in the first period, arose to take their place (e.g. phonetics, sound laws, the regularity of sound change, syntax).

It is customary in appraising the work of the early scholars to emphasize their genuine insights and to pass over in silence their sometimes obvious (from a modern vantage point) errors. I have done this consciously up to this point. But before turning to the second phase of I-E research, I should at least mention some of the inadequacies of the early work:

1. The early scholars were notoriously poor phoneticians, often displaying a total confusion between the sounds of a language and the letters of an alphabet used to represent them. Grimm, for example, considered the German word *Schrift* 'writing' to contain eight sounds, with the letter *f* representing the two sounds *ph*! In fact, the word contains but five sounds: [šrift].

2. Despite repeated warnings, Sanskrit was from the start accorded too much importance in determining the structure of I-E. Its archaic inflectional morphology, considered the key area in early work on genetic classification, had led many scholars to assume (incorrectly) that Sanskrit was comparably old in other areas of linguistic structure as well. Schleicher's work on Lithuanian only tarnished the image of Sanskrit as being most faithful to I-E structure. Not until the second period of research did it become clear just how distant Sanskrit was, in some respects, from the original I-E language.

3. Schleicher's work, in particular, suffered from a rather slavish adherence to *a priori* notions of symmetry, beauty, and elegance, which he presumed were attributes of the "perfect" proto-language. We have already seen that his I-E subgrouping (List 2.3) involved only binary branchings. Schleicher's proto-language was itself based on threes: three vowels (*i, a, u*), three places of articulation (*p, t, k*), and three manners of articulation (*t, d, dh*(= d)). Later scholars were more willing to let the evidence speak for itself, without imposing upon it some preconceived ideal pattern.

4. From the modern vantage point the most embarrassing of the defects of the early period were the related beliefs that (a) languages, like plants and animals, pass through periods of growth, maturity and decay; and (b) the relative "stage" of a language could be determined by its structural type. Schleicher was a major advocate of both views, as was the German diplomat Wilhelm von Humboldt. Schleicher believed that throughout prehistory (that is, roughly up to the time when I-E was spoken) human languages, like species, had been gradually progressing in complexity and sophistication. I-E supposedly represented the "mature" stage of language development, followed in the last several thousand years by various degrees of decay and decline in different branches. Languages other than I-E were presumed to have advanced at different rates, some having remained in a primitive state (e.g. Chinese), while others had progressed to a stage intermediate between primitive Chinese and advanced I-E (e.g. Turkish, Hungarian). Whether a language was advanced or primitive depended on its structural type, according to which *isolating* languages like Chinese were taken to be the primitive stage of language development, *agglutinating* lan-

guages like Turkish and Hungarian were seen as an intermediate stage, and *inflectional* languages such as I-E represented the highest stage.

Both of these theories are today discounted. Without exception, linguists agree that there are no "primitive" languages extant. Nor are there any linguistic "missing links" connecting full-fledged human speech with a more primitive communication system. In some ill-defined sense linguists consider all human languages currently spoken to be "equal." Of course it is possible to say that French and English have complex vowel systems, that Caucasian languages have complex consonant systems, and that Oceanic languages often have intricate pronominal systems. It is *not* possible at present to assign a weight to each aspect of linguistic structure in such a way that the total complexity of a language could be measured. Nor is it clear exactly what such a measure would mean even if it were in fact possible to arrive at one. Certainly English, and European languages in general, do not appear to function less effectively than Oceanic languages, despite having, by Oceanic standards, a very rudimentary pronominal system. Nor do languages that have many consonants (e.g. Georgian, Nama) appear superior in any recognizable way to languages with relatively few consonants (e.g. Hawaiian, Sentani). In fact, it is not even clear whether having a large consonant inventory is advantageous, detrimental, or irrelevant to the efficient functioning of language.

To a large extent the preoccupation with the organic growth of language was a residue of the earlier concern with the origin of human language. During the second period of I-E research, it was realized that human languages spoken, say, 5,000 years ago (e.g. I-E) did not differ in any fundamental way from contemporary languages. Meillet (1922b: 469) described this fundamental change in outlook after 1875 as follows: "Indo-European comparative grammar was no longer concerned with a would-be organic period, a period of development about which nothing was known; rather it simply continued into a slightly more remote past the research of Romance, Germanic, Celtic, Slavic, and Iranian scholars, obtaining the same kind of results by means of the same methods."

The supposed hierarchy from primitive isolating languages through agglutinating to advanced inflectional languages was entirely the product of a pervasive ethnocentrism that colored much of nineteenth-century thought. It was then fervently believed by many (as it still is by a few) that European languages, customs, religions, and "races" were superior to their counterparts in other regions of the world. Inflectional languages were taken to be the highest form of language by definition rather than by demonstration. In fact, it turned out that the modern Chinese languages, which were usually cited as the chief example of the pure isolating type, derive from an Old

Chinese that was apparently inflectional. The contemporary view is that this taxonomy is of limited value because many languages do not fall neatly into just one category. Moreover, there is no evidence that languages of any structural type are more "advanced" than languages of some other structural type.

It is, however, not the poor phonetics, overvaluation of Sanskrit, belief in the organic growth of language, or alleged superiority of some languages over others that primarily distinguishes linguists of the first period from those of the second. Rather, the chief difference lies in their attitude toward sound correspondences or, to be more precise, in their attitude toward the *regularity* of such sound shifts. The early scholars never envisaged sound correspondences as being in any sense absolute; there were simply too many exceptions to even the most famous sound shifts for them to be swept under the rug and ignored. For Grimm (as quoted in Robins 1967: 172), "the sound shift is a general tendency; it is not followed in every case." However, a series of revolutionary discoveries, made primarily during the 1870's, led many linguists to the conclusion that sound correspondences exhibit far greater regularity than had previously been recognized. A group of young scholars based in Leipzig went so far as to proclaim that "sound laws admit of no exceptions" (August Leskien, quoted in Hockett 1965: 187). Karl Verner's more moderate version of the "regularity hypothesis" is perhaps a better description of the new spirit: "There must be a rule for exceptions to a rule; the only question is to discover it" (quoted in Robins 1967: 184).

This new doctrine of regular sound change triggered an acrimonious debate between the so-called Young Grammarians (including Karl Brugmann, Hermann Osthoff, August Leskien, Vilhelm Thomsen), who championed the regularity of sound change, and the Old Guard (especially G. Curtius, but also such able younger scholars as Johannes Schmidt, Hermann Collitz, and Hugo Schuchardt), who refused to accept the doctrine of absolute regularity. This bitter dispute was not resolved by the conversion of one side by the other; the hostility involved probably precluded that. In fact, a division between proponents and opponents of regular sound change has persisted to the present day in attenuated form. Ordinarily a fundamental division of any science into two camps must eventually work itself out, for otherwise there will develop two versions of the same science, an intolerable (or at least undesirable) state of affairs. There was, however, a curious aspect of this particular dispute that made its resolution unnecessary: both sides *worked as if* sound change were regular, and both groups produced significant research; both sides recognized that scholars of the early period had overlooked a great deal of subtle regularity in the I-E evidence. The discovery of explanations for seemingly recalcitrant exceptions led the Young Grammarians to the belief that all such exceptions were potentially explainable, whereas their opponents were willing to grant only that regularity in the I-E family existed on a level hitherto unnoticed. The acceptance of the "regularity hypothesis" in the 1870's (either as an article of faith by the Young Grammarians or simply as a working hypothesis by their opponents) is considered by Hockett (1965: 188) to be the second great breakthrough in the field of linguistics.

As an illustration of the work done by the Young Grammarians, let us examine one of the most celebrated discoveries of the 1870's. We have already seen earlier in this chapter (Table 2.1) how Grimm's Law describes the relationship of Germanic consonants to those of other branches of I-E. According to Grimm's Law, we should expect Latin *t* and Sanskrit *t* to correspond to Germanic θ, as it does in the word 'brother':

(4)

Sanskrit	bhrā́tar-
Latin	frāter
Gothic	brōθar

It was recognized from the outset, however, that there are a host of exceptions to Grimm's Law in which *b*, *d*, and *g* are found in place of "expected" *f*, θ, and *h*, respectively. (The precise phonetic character of *b*, *d*, and *g* in early Germanic is in dispute; voiced fricatives (β,ð,γ) are a likely possibility.) One such example is the word 'father':

(5)

Sanskrit	pitár-
Latin	pater
Gothic	fadar

The rather numerous exceptions of this nature did not trouble the early linguists like Rask and Grimm, who did not expect sound change to be regular. But they did trouble the Young Grammarians, who demanded explanations for apparent exceptions. In this case the explanation was supplied by Karl Verner (1877), in the same article in which he had boldly proclaimed that "there must be a rule for exceptions to a rule; the only question is to discover it." The explanation Verner offered had to do with the position of the accent in Sanskrit and Greek (and hence also presumably in the I-E parent language). Verner noticed that if the Sanskrit and Greek accents *precede* the *t*, then development was according to Grimm's Law (see (4) above), but if the accents *did not precede* the *t*, the result was *d* (see (5) above). Verner's Law, as it came to be known, accounted for the exceptional appearance of certain *b*'s and *g*'s as well; it may be thought of as an amendment to Grimm's Law stipulating that *p,t,k* have the exceptional outcome *b,d,g* in just those cases where the I-E accent (as revealed by Sanskrit and Greek) did not precede the consonant in question. Pedersen (1931: 282–83) stressed the importance of Verner's discovery:

> The effect of Verner's article . . . was immeasurable. Now there were no more exceptions to the Germanic sound-shift, and this absence of exceptions necessarily had quite as strong an effect upon the whole conception of linguistics as the chief laws applying to the sound-shifts had exerted in their time. Then, scholars were beginning to understand that there were laws of phonology; now, they were awaking to the fact that such laws operate regularly. . . . Verner's discovery suggested how exhaustively one must study the phenomena and how accurately one must discriminate, to understand the development of sounds. It was, in fact an emphatic warning not to regard any such development as a mere whim of language.

Notwithstanding the instantly recognized brilliance of Verner's insight, it would not have had the impact it did, had it been an isolated instance. But it was not. Rather, Verner's Law was embedded in a mosaic of other discoveries that pushed linguists to the conclusion that sound change is regular. Limitations of space do not permit an exhaustive treatment of the many discoveries of this fascinating era, but a few more examples seem mandatory in dealing with an era so rich in discovery.

In 1878, the year after the appearance of Verner's article, the Law of Palatals was published. Originally perceived by Vilhelm Thomsen (but apparently independently discovered by Verner, Esaias Tegnér, Ferdinand de Saussure, Hermann Collitz, and Johannes Schmidt), this law cleared up a number of outstanding problems and also laid to rest the notion that Sanskrit was archaic in all respects. Consider the following words for 'and':

(6)

Sanskrit	ča
Latin	que
Greek	te

Schleicher (1861–62) posited a three-vowel system for I-E, parallel to Sanskrit's three short vowels:

(7)

i　　u

a

But if I-E had these three vowels and passed them down intact to Sanskrit, two problems arise. First, why were some Sanskrit *k*'s palatalized to *č* (the sound in '*ch*ur*ch*'), while other *k*'s were unaffected, before the vowel *a* (cf. Sanskrit *ča* 'and' with Sanskrit *kas* 'who')? Second, why did I-E **a* change into *e* in certain words (the same words) belonging to the European I-E languages? These anomalies were eliminated by the Law of Palatals, which showed once again how I-E scholarship had been led astray by the overvaluation of Sanskrit. As part of the Law of Palatals it was recognized that, with respect to the vowel system, it was the European languages that preserved the original I-E system:

(8)

i		u
e		o
	a	

Sanskrit had undergone two sound changes (*e* > *a* and *o* > *a*), thus arriving at the (short) vowel system shown in (7), but these mergers took place only *after* the vowel *e* had palatalized preceding *k*'s. Thus Sanskrit *ča* may be traced back to I-E as follows:

(9) I-E *ke > *če > Sanskrit ča

The Law of Palatals demonstrated clearly the danger of overvaluing one language at the expense of others, and it also showed how the motivating factor in a sound change may itself subsequently disappear through the action of other sound changes.

One final work, by the Swiss scholar Ferdinand de Saussure, should be mentioned. In 1878, at the age of 21, Saussure published a brilliant analysis of the I-E vowel system using the methods of the Young Grammarians. In this monograph Saussure suggested (among other things) that the I-E parent language must have had certain vowels that subsequently disappeared from all attested I-E languages. Using what is today called the method of internal reconstruction, Saussure argued that the I-E parent language must have had two "sonorant coefficients," which disappeared after either lengthening or changing the timbre of a preceding vowel. Reviewers of Saussure's *Mémoire* suggested that these "sonorant coefficients" were most probably consonants rather than vowels. Saussure's bold conjecture was never verified during his lifetime, but the discovery of Hittite in the early twentieth century revealed an I-E language that had maintained "sonorant coefficients" (or "laryngeal consonants," as they came to be called) in at least some of the positions that Saussure had predicted. The Polish scholar Jerzy Kuryłowicz first pointed this out in 1927, 14 years after Saussure's death.

The discovery of the regularity of sound change had several salutary effects on the field of linguistics. On the one hand, it both encouraged, and was encouraged by, the rapidly developing field of phonetics. At the same time, by focusing attention on the residue of exceptions to established sound laws, linguists became more aware of other factors affecting the evolution of language. Among those factors responsible for exceptions to sound laws, the following were quickly recognized:

1. *Loanwords*, long the bugaboo of I-E research, were often found to be exceptions to general sound laws. Heinrich Hübschmann, beginning in 1875, used this new awareness to distinguish the innumerable Iranian loans from the true Armenian lexical heritage and to establish the basic sound laws of Armenian. Only when the Iranian loans were filtered out of the vocabulary was Hübschmann able to demonstrate that Armenian is not a member of the Iranian branch of I–E, as previously believed, but rather a separate and independent branch.

2. The disturbing influence of *writing* or *script* on regular phonetic development also became apparent.

3. A whole host of *sporadic phonetic processes* (e.g. assimilation/dissimilation at a distance, metathesis, haplology, contamination) were seen typically to affect single words rather than the entire vocabulary.

4. Of all the forces counteracting regular sound change, *analogy* turned out to be one of the most pervasive. Although the influence of analogy on language had long been recognized, it is arguable that analogy can only be truly appreciated against a background of regular sound change. As long as arbitrary sporadic sound changes were tolerated, as they were in the early period of linguistic research, the true nature of analogy remained obscure. To illustrate the role of analogy in linguistic evolution consider the following forms:

(10)	Greek	phérō	'I bear'	eî-mi	'I go'	dídō–mi	'I give'
	Sanskrit	bhárā–mi	'I bear'	ḗ-mi	'I go'	dádā–mi	'I give'

In Sanskrit the first-person marker *-mi* (cognate with English 'me') is affixed regularly to all verbs; in Greek, however, there is a group of verbs to which the suffix *-mi* is not added (e.g. *phérō*). In the early period, when Sanskrit was considered the most faithful descendant of I-E and I-E was itself considered the paragon of human language, the completely regular Sanskrit pattern shown in (10) was assumed to have been inherited directly from I-E. The problem of when and why Greek had lost this ending in certain verbs was unresolved. In 1868 Wilhelm Scherer, a precursor of the Young Grammarians, argued that it was in fact Greek that preserved the I-E state and Sanskrit that had innovated. He pointed out that *all* of the European branches of I-E, as well as the older Iranian documents, preserved verbs that did not take the *-mi* suffix, at least in part. In Germanic and Slavic the class of *-mi* verbs had also grown at the expense of the suffixless verbs, though not so completely as in Sanskrit. From the 1870's onward analogy assumed greater importance as its role in leveling out the idiosyncrasies of regular sound change was perceived more clearly.

The demise of the organic theory of linguistic growth and decay, the devaluation of Sanskrit, the growing awareness that linguistic change was far more tightly constrained than had been thought, and a better understanding of phonetics all necessitated a thorough reevaluation of the results of the early period. The older handbooks of Bopp and Schleicher were rendered obsolete and had to be replaced, rather than revised, by a work written from the new perspective. To fill this void Karl Brugmann published, between 1897 and 1916, a two-volume comparative grammar of I-E that remains today "the latest full-scale treatment of the family" (Cowgill 1974: 434).

During the second period of research, Schleicher's subgrouping of I-E (List 2.3 above) underwent several substantial modifications: (1) Armenian was demonstrated to be an independent branch of I-E, not a member of the Iranian branch; (2) higher-level groupings between branches were eliminated, with the exception of Indo-Iranian, Balto-Slavic, and Italo-Celtic; and (3) in 1880 F. von Bradke divided the I-E languages into two groups, a Western group characterized by the retention of initial *k-* in the word for 'hundred' (e.g. Latin *centum*) and an Eastern group in which this *k-* has been assibilated to *s-*, *š-*, or *s^j-* (e.g. Avestan *satem*). At the close of the nineteenth century, the subgrouping of the I-E family was conceived to be something like that in List 2.4. In this scheme the geographic position of Albanian seemed anomalous, since it is an Eastern (i.e. *satem*) language found in what is basically Western territory (if one discounts the recent Slavic expansion). Prehistorical migration from a more Eastern position was the usual explanation, though no supporting evidence was adduced.

List 2.4. The Indo-European Family (c. 1900)

INDO-EUROPEAN:	
I EASTERN (= satem):	II WESTERN: (= centum)
A INDO-IRANIAN:	A GERMANIC
1 INDIC	B ITALO-CELTIC:
2 IRANIAN	1 ITALIC
B Armenian	2 CELTIC
C Albanian	C GREEK
D BALTO-SLAVIC:	
1 BALTIC	
2 SLAVIC	

During the first decade of the twentieth century, unexpected archaeological discoveries in Asia revealed two additional branches of I-E, Hittite and Tocharian, which are both *centum* languages in an area (Asia) that was supposed to know only *satem* languages. The Eastern-Western (= *centum-satem*) dichotomy of I-E languages dissolved with the discovery of these two extinct *centum* languages, illustrating the danger of basing genetic classification on a single phonological trait.

Around the turn of the century, archaeologists discovered documents in Chinese Turkestan in a hitherto unknown language. Written in a North Indian script (some were even bilingual), and dating from around the seventh century A.D., these texts revealed two similar languages, now called Tocharian A and B, whose I-E affinity was obvious. The proof of affiliation was published in 1908 by the Germans Emil Sieg and Wilhelm Siegling. Also obvious was the fact that Tocharian constitutes a separate branch of I-E. It was probably extinct by the beginning of the second millennium A.D.

In 1887 a cache of clay tablets, ancient correspondence between Egyptian kings and Middle East potentates, was unearthed in Egypt. All were written in cuneiform, and all but three of the several hundred tablets were in Akkadian, a Semitic language used at that time as an international diplomatic language in the region. One letter was in Hurrian, an extinct language of unknown affiliation spoken around 1400 B.C. in what is today southern Turkey. The final two letters were in an unknown language. In 1902 the Norwegian scholar Jørgen Knudtzon published these two letters with a translation and critical commentary. He argued that the letters, addressed to the king of Arzawa (thought by scholars to have been located somewhere in southeast Asia Minor), were in an I-E tongue, possibly the language of the Hittites mentioned in the Bible. This proposal was greeted with skepticism; unlike Tocharian, the language was not transparently I-E, and the evidence was admittedly slim.

Confirmation of Knudtzon's conjecture was not long in coming, though it arrived by a rather circuitous route. In 1893 a French archaeological expedition to what is today central Turkey had discovered 14 tablets in an unknown language. The contents of these tablets had been published in Paris in 1898. An English scholar, A. H. Sayce, pointed out that the language of these tablets was the same as that of the Arzawa letters. Sayce's observation led the German Hugo Winckler to undertake an expedition to the site (Boğazköy, 95 miles [150 km] east of Ankara, Turkey); from 1905 to 1907 thousands of additional tablets were discovered in what turned out to be Hattusa, the capital of the ancient Hittite empire. Dating from roughly 1550–1200 B.C., these tablets were older than any previously known I-E inscriptions. Decipherment progressed rapidly, and in 1915 the Czech scholar Friedrich Hrozný proposed the I-E affinity of Hittite; two years later he published the first Hittite grammar. Despite an abundance of tablets (whose number would eventually grow to 25,000) skepticism about the I-E nature of Hittite continued into the early 1920's. Hittite largely lacked the complex inflectional apparatus scholars had come to expect of an I-E language (especially an early one), and its vocabulary contained a sizable non-I-E element.

Nevertheless, as more and more texts became available in the 1920's, the I-E affinity of Hittite gained general acceptance.

In 1926 the American linguist Edgar Sturtevant proposed that the archaic character of Hittite and its remoteness from other branches of I-E were due to the fact that Hittite is a *sister* language of I–E, rather than a *daughter* language, as had been previously assumed. Thus for Sturtevant and his supporters, I-E and Hittite (more precisely, the Anatolian group, of which Hittite is one member) are co-equal branches of Indo-Hittite. Bloomfield (1933: 64, 312) presents the subgrouping for Indo-Hittite given in List 2.5. Notice that in addition to the exclusion of Anatolian from I-E proper, the Italo-Celtic group has been discounted. Italic and Celtic had been joined together largely (but not exclusively) on the basis of an *r-* passive. With the discovery of the same *r-* passive in Tocharian and Hittite, it was realized that this particular trait did not indicate any special relationship between Italic and Celtic (because it was not shared by them exclusively).

Sturtevant's Indo-Hittite proposal has met with a decidedly mixed reaction. Although most linguists today reject it outright (e.g. Jerzy Kuryłowicz; Jaan Puhvel 1966), a few accept it (Bloomfield 1933: 64; Hockett 1958: 591; Cowgill 1975, 1979; Greenberg 1987). The Balto-Slavic unity also remains in dispute, but is probably accepted by the majority of scholars. Voegelin and Voegelin (1977) present a subgrouping that discounts both the Balto-Slavic group and Sturtevant's Indo-Hittite hypothesis (see List 2.6).

List 2.5. The Indo-Hittite Family (Bloomfield 1933)

INDO-HITTITE:
- I †ANATOLIAN: Hittite, Luwian, Palaic, Lydian
- II INDO-EUROPEAN:
  - A Armenian
  - B †TOCHARIAN
  - C INDO-IRANIAN:
    - 1 INDIC
    - 2 IRANIAN
  - D Albanian
  - E GREEK
  - F ITALIC
  - G CELTIC
  - H GERMANIC
  - I BALTO-SLAVIC:
    - 1 BALTIC
    - 2 SLAVIC

List 2.6. The Indo-European Family (Voegelin & Voegelin 1977)

INDO-EUROPEAN:
- I †ANATOLIAN
- II Armenian
- III †TOCHARIAN
- IV INDO-IRANIAN:
  - A INDIC
  - B NURISTANI
  - C IRANIAN
- V Albanian
- VI GREEK
- VII ITALIC
- VIII CELTIC
- IX GERMANIC
- X BALTIC
- XI SLAVIC

2.3.2 *Present Status of Indo-Hittite Classification*

Within the Indo-Hittite family there is scholarly consensus that the following subfamilies constitute genetic nodes, as defined in section 1.1:

(11)	ANATOLIAN	ITALIC
	Armenian	ROMANCE
	TOCHARIAN	CELTIC
	INDO-IRANIAN	GERMANIC
	Albanian	BALTIC
	GREEK	SLAVIC

Indo-Hittite (or Indo-European) is itself, of course, a valid genetic group. With regard to Indo-Hittite subgrouping, one continuing dispute involves the proper position of Anatolian, which is for most scholars simply a coordinate branch of I-E on a par with Italic, Celtic, Germanic, Albanian, etc. Other scholars, as we have seen, regard Anatolian as coordinate with a group containing *all* other Indo-Hittite languages (i.e. the traditional I-E family, including Tocharian).

The scholarly community remains quite divided on the validity of Sturtevant's Indo-Hittite hypothesis, with supporters a decided minority. Three factors have apparently inhibited an objective appraisal of Sturtevant's thesis. (1) Some scholars have undoubtedly been reluctant to replace the traditional (and venerated) label Indo-European with the newfangled term Indo-Hittite. (2) The fact that Anatolian is attested solely by inscriptions from a few languages that have been extinct for millennia has not helped its case for being taken as a genetic group coordinate with the far-flung I-E family. Whether or not a language (or group of languages) is extinct, or has relatively few speakers, has no bearing on its proper position in a genetic classification. Notwithstanding, languages with many speakers have always received special treatment in the linguistic literature, and sometimes unwarranted prominence in genetic classifications. (3) The acceptance of Anatolian as a sister language of I-E, rather than simply one of many daughters, reduces the traditional I-E family to a taxonomically less significant position. Although it may seem surprising that sober scholars could let their judgments be swayed by the mere position of a group of languages in a genetic classification, such has in fact been the case on several occasions. Some Bantuists, for example, were less than enthusiastic about Greenberg's "demotion" of the huge Bantu family to a modest taxonomic position within the Niger-Congo family.

As we saw in section 2.3.1, there were in the nineteenth century several proposals for combining various of the groups listed in (11) into higher-level groupings. Today, however, none enjoys much favor, with the exception of Balto-Slavic, which, though still controversial, is quite probably a valid genetic unit. The once popular Italo-Celtic, on the other hand, has lost support, though Cowgill (1970) suggests that Italic and Celtic were neighboring dialects of late Proto-I-E that shared perhaps as few as five common innovations before going their separate ways. Indo-Hittite is thus currently considered to consist of two groups, Anatolian and I-E, with I-E itself comprising nine coordinate branches (see List 2.7). For those who reject the Indo-Hittite hypothesis, I-E would consist of 10 or 11 first-order groups, depending on whether or not Baltic and Slavic are joined in a Balto-Slavic family.

List 2.7. The Indo-Hittite Family (1986)

INDO-HITTITE:	
I †ANATOLIAN	E GREEK
II INDO-EUROPEAN:	F ITALIC
A Armenian	G CELTIC
B †TOCHARIAN	H GERMANIC
C INDO-IRANIAN	I BALTO-SLAVIC
D Albanian	

Let us turn now to the internal subgrouping of the families listed in (11) above. For the small *Anatolian* group the internal structure is not well understood. Although it is clear that Luwian (both hieroglyphic and cuneiform) and Lycian form one unit, the relationship of this group to Hittite, Palaic, and Lydian is unclear. Questions of subgrouping do not arise for *Armenian* and *Albanian* (single languages) or *Tocharian* (two languages).

Indo-Iranian consists of three well-defined subfamilies: Indic, Nuristani, and Iranian. Within *Indic* the Sinhalese-Maldivian group and Romany (the language of the gypsies) stand apart from the rest of the Indic languages, between many of which there are transitional dialects making further subgrouping difficult, if not impossible. (*Dardic*, however, seems to be a valid genetic group at some level.) *Nuristani* represents a small group of languages intermediate between Indic and Iranian. Within *Iranian* there is a fairly clear-cut division between Eastern and Western branches, but little consensus on further subgrouping.

In antiquity *Greek* constituted a single fairly homogeneous language, with a few aberrant dialects. Modern Greek is a continuation of a *koine* based on the Attic dialect of classical times, which succeeded in obliterating all other dialects (e.g. Arcadian, Aeolic, Locrian, Ionic, Mycenaean) except for Tsakonian, which continues the Laconian dialect of ancient Sparta.

Tsakonian is apparently moribund, retaining no more than 10,000 speakers on the east coast of the Peloponnesus.

The internal subgrouping of the *Italic* group is not well understood; some of the languages are not even clearly Italic. It is clear that of the original Italic group (whatever its constituents may have been) only a single language, Latin, survived. Latin has survived, of course, in the form of the modern Romance languages. Within *Romance* there is a clear distinction between Eastern (Rumanian) and Western (Italian, French, Catalan, Spanish, Portuguese) groups. The chief classificatory problems involve the position of the heterogeneous Sardinian dialects and the extinct (since 1898) Dalmatian language, formerly spoken on the northwest coast of Yugoslavia. Dalmatian has been classified as both Eastern and Western by various scholars (and sometimes even by the same scholar at different stages of his career). It shares similarities with both Rumanian and Italian, and linguists do not yet agree on which of the two it is most closely related to. The position of Sardinian is even more problematical, since it does not obviously belong to either Eastern or Western Romance; Hall (1974) considers it coordinate with the rest of Romance. Leaving aside Dalmatian, Eastern Romance is itself clearly divided into Northern and Southern groups, with Daco-Rumanian (= Standard Rumanian) and Istro-Rumanian constituting the Northern group and Arumanian and Megleno-Rumanian the Southern group. Within most of Western Romance there are (or at least were until fairly recently) transitional dialects between contiguous languages (e.g. Italian-French-Provençal-Gascon-Catalan-Spanish-Galician-Portuguese) that make further subgrouping somewhat arbitrary. Catalan, for instance, has been included in both the Ibero-Romance and Gallo-Romance groups by different scholars.

Celtic languages were once spoken throughout Europe (including present-day Spain, France, and Italy) and into Asia Minor (Turkey), but all of these Continental and Asian languages became extinct early on, with little known about them save their existence. These extinct Celtic languages are usually placed in a Continental subgroup to distinguish them from the four surviving Celtic languages, which belong to an Insular group originally restricted to the British Isles. The Insular group itself has two clear subgroups: the Goidelic group, consisting of Irish (= Gaelic), Scottish Gaelic, and the extinct Manx (spoken on the Isle of Man into this century), and the Brythonic group, consisting of Breton, Welsh, and the extinct Cornish. Though currently spoken on the northwest coast of France (in Brittany), Breton is not the survivor of an earlier Continental Celtic tongue, but rather represents a reintroduction of Celtic speech from the British Isles, believed to have taken place around A.D. 500. Cornish was formerly spoken in Cornwall, England, but was gradually eroded by English, becoming extinct during the eighteenth century.

Germanic consists of three subgroups: East, North, and West. All the languages of the East group (e.g. Gothic, Vandalic, Burgundian) are now extinct. The North group is made up of the Scandinavian languages (Danish, Swedish, and Norwegian; each is to a large extent mutually intelligible with the other two), Icelandic, and Faeroese, the latter spoken on the Faeroe Islands north of Great Britain. West Germanic languages include German, Luxembourgeois, Dutch, English, and Frisian. Luxembourgeois is one of three official languages in Luxembourg; it is reported to be as distinct from Standard German as Dutch. Spoken in Holland and Germany, Frisian consists of three sharply divergent dialects (East, West, and North), no doubt distinct languages if the criterion of mutual intelligibility were rigorously applied. Afrikaans and Yiddish are offshoots of Dutch and German, respectively, and Flemish is a dialect of Dutch. Certain scholars (E. Schwarz and W. Lehmann) believe that the North and East groups form a higher-level grouping, so that the original schism in Germanic was into Western and Eastern groups, with the latter subsequently dividing into Northern and Eastern subgroups.

The *Baltic* group consists of two subgroups. Old Prussian, extinct since the seventeenth century, made up the West Baltic subgroup. East Baltic consists of the two extant Baltic languages, Latvian and Lithuanian, and several extinct tongues.

Like Germanic, the *Slavic* family has three distinct branches. Russian, Byelorussian, and Ukrainian belong to East Slavic. West Slavic comprises Polish, Czech, Slovak, and several minor tongues. Czech and Slovak are mutually intelligible. South Slavic comprises four languages: Slovene, Serbo-Croatian, Macedonian, and Bulgarian. Slovene consists of a number of sharply differentiated dialects scattered amid the mountains of northern Yugoslavia. The other three are fairly homogeneous. Some scholars believe the primary division was into East and West Slavic, with South Slavic being a subsequent offshoot of West Slavic.

INDO-HITTITE

Baldi, Philip. 1983. *An Introduction to the Indo-European Languages*. Carbondale, Ill.

Birnbaum, Henrik, and Jaan Puhvel, eds. 1966. *Ancient Indo-European Dialects*. Berkeley, Calif.

Bloomfield, Leonard. 1933. *Language*. New York.

Bomhard, Allan R. 1976. "The Placing of the Anatolian Languages," *Orbis* 25: 199–239.

Bopp, Franz. 1816. *Über das Conjugationssystem der Sanskritsprache in Vergleichung mit jenem der griechischen, lateinischen, persischen und germanischen Sprache*. Frankfurt.

———. 1833–52. *Vergleichende Grammatik des Sanskrit, Zend, Griechischen, Lateinischen, Litthauischen, Altslawischen, Gotischen, und Deutschen*. Berlin.

———. 1839. *Über die celtischen Sprachen vom Gesichtspunkte der vergleichenden Sprachforschung*. Berlin.
Brugmann, Karl. 1897–1916. *Grundriss der vergleichenden Grammatik der indogermanische Sprachen*, 2 vols. Strassburg.
Buck, Carl Darling. 1949. *A Dictionary of Selected Synonyms in the Principal Indo-European Languages*. Chicago.
Cardona, George, H. M. Hoenigswald, and A. Senn, eds. 1970. *Indo-European and Indo-Europeans*. Philadelphia.
Collinge, Neville E. 1985. *The Laws of Indo-European*. Amsterdam.
Cowgill, Warren. 1970. "Italic and Celtic Superlatives and the Dialects of Indo-European," in Cardona et al., cited above.
———. 1974. "Indo-European Languages," in *EB* 9: 431–38.
———. 1975. "More Evidence for Indo-Hittite: The Tense-Aspect Systems," *Proc. Eleventh International Congress of Linguists* 2: 557–70.
———. 1979. "Anatolian *hi*-Conjugation and Indo-European Perfect: Instalment II," in Erich Neu and Wolfgang Meid, eds., *Hethitisch und Indogermanisch*. Innsbruck.
Diderichsen, Paul. 1974. "The Foundation of Comparative Linguistics: Revolution or Continuation?" in Dell Hymes, ed., *Studies in the History of Linguistics*. Bloomington, Ind.
Djakonov, I. M. 1976. "Mesto frigijskogo sredi indoevropejskix jazykov," *Drevnij Vostok* 2: 158–64.
Hamp, Eric P. 1966. "The Position of Albanian," in Birnbaum and Puhvel, cited above.
———. 1972. "Albanian," in *CTIL* 9.
Hockett, Charles F. 1958. *A Course in Modern Linguistics*. New York.
———. 1965. "Sound Change," *Language* 41: 185–204.
Jullian, Camille. 1916. "L'époque italo-celtique. De son existence," *Revue des Études Anciennes* 18: 263–76.
Knudtzon, Jørgen. 1902. *Die zwei Arzawa-briefe*. Leipzig.
Lane, George S. 1966. "On the Interrelationship of the Tocharian Dialects," in Birnbaum and Puhvel, cited above.
Lyons, John. 1968. *Introduction to Theoretical Linguistics*. Cambridge, Eng.
Manessy-Guitton, Jacqueline. 1968. "L'indo-européen," in André Martinet, ed., *Le langage*. Paris.
Meillet, A. 1922a. *Introduction à l'étude comparative des langues indo-européennes*. Paris.
———. 1922b. "Aperçu du developpement de la grammaire comparée," in Meillet, cited above.
———. 1950. *Les dialectes indo-européens*. Paris.
Metcalf, George J. 1974. "The Indo-European Hypothesis in the Sixteenth and Seventeenth Centuries," in Dell Hymes, ed., *Studies in the History of Linguistics*. Bloomington, Ind.
Pedersen, Holger. 1931. *Linguistic Science in the Nineteenth Century*. Cambridge, Mass.
Pott, A. F. 1833–36. *Etymologische Forschungen auf dem Gebiete der indogermanischen Sprachen*. Lemgo, Germany.
Puhvel, Jaan. 1966. "Dialectal Aspects of the Anatolian Branch of Indo-European," in Birnbaum and Puhvel, cited above.
Rask, Rasmus. 1818. *Undersøgelse om det gamle Nordiske eller Islandske Sprogs Oprindelse*. Copenhagen.
Robins, R. H. 1967. *A Short History of Linguistics*. Bloomington, Ind.

de Saussure, Ferdinand. 1878. *Mémoire sur le système primitif des voyelles dans les langues indo-européennes*. Leipzig.
Scherer, Wilhelm. 1868. *Zur Geschichte der deutschen Sprache*. Berlin.
von Schlegel, F. 1808. *Über die Sprache und Weisheit der Indier*. Heidelberg.
Schleicher, August. 1861–62. *Compendium der vergleichenden Grammatik der indogermanischen Sprachen*. Weimar.
———. 1863. *Die darwinische Theorie und die Sprachwissenschaft*. Weimar.
Sieg, Emil, and Wilhelm Siegling. 1908. *Tocharisch, die Sprache der Indoskythen*. Berlin.
Sturtevant, Edgar H. 1942. *The Indo-Hittite Laryngeals*. Baltimore.
———. 1962. "The Indo-Hittite Hypothesis," *Language* 38: 105–10.
Verner, Karl. 1877. "Eine Ausnahme der ersten Lautverschiebung," *Zeitschrift für vergleichende Sprachforschung* 23: 97–130.
Voegelin, C. F., and F. M. Voegelin. 1977. *Classification and Index of the World's Languages*. New York.
Watkins, Calvert. 1966. "Italo-Celtic Revisited," in Birnbaum and Puhvel, cited above.
Wilbur, Terence H., ed. 1977. *The Lautgesetz-Controversy: A Documentation (1885–86)*. Amsterdam.

INDO-IRANIAN

Emeneau, Murray B. 1966. "The Dialects of Old Indo-Aryan," in Birnbaum and Puhvel, cited above under Indo-Hittite.
Morgenstierne, Georg. 1961. "Dardic and Kafir Languages," in *The Encyclopaedia of Islam* 2: 25.
Strand, Richard F. 1973. "Notes on the Nuristani and Dardic Languages," *Journal of the American Oriental Society* 93: 297–305.

IRANIAN

Comrie, Bernard. 1981. "Iranian Languages," in Bernard Comrie, *The Languages of the Soviet Union*. Cambridge, Eng. [This section is the work of J. R. Payne.]
Emmerick, R. E. 1974. "The Iranian Languages," in *EB* 9: 450–57.
MacKenzie, D. N. 1961. *Kurdish Dialect Studies*, 2 vols. London.
———. 1969. "Iranian Languages," in *CTIL* 5.
Oranskij, I. M. 1963. *Iranskie jazyki*. Moscow.

GREEK

Buck, Carl Darling. 1933. *Comparative Grammar of Greek and Latin*. Chicago.
Cowgill, Warren C. 1966. "Ancient Greek Dialectology in the Light of Mycenaean," in Birnbaum and Puhvel, cited above under Indo-Hittite.
Curtius, Georg. 1858–62. *Grundzüge der griechischen Etymologie*. Leipzig.

ITALIC

Beeler, Madison S. 1966. "The Interrelations within Italic," in Birnbaum and Puhvel, cited above under Indo-Hittite.
Buck, Carl Darling. 1933. *Comparative Grammar of Greek and Latin*. Chicago.
Polomé, Edgar G. 1966. "The Position of Illyrian and Venetic," in Birnbaum and Puhvel, cited above under Indo-Hittite.
Pulgram, E. 1958. *The Tongues of Italy*. Cambridge, Mass.

ROMANCE

Bec, Pierre. 1970–71. *Manuel pratique de philologie romane*, 2 vols. Paris.
Diez, Friedrich. 1836–44. *Grammatik der romanischen Sprachen*, 2 vols. Bonn.
Elcock, W. D. 1960. *The Romance Languages*. London.
Hall, Robert A., Jr. 1950. "The Reconstruction of Proto-Romance," *Language* 26: 6–27.
———. 1974. *External History of the Romance Languages*. New York.
Malkiel, Yakov. 1978. "The Classification of Romance Languages," *Romance Philology* 31: 467–500.

CELTIC

Pedersen, Holger. 1909–13. *Vergleichende Grammatik der keltischen Sprachen*, 2 vols. Göttingen. Translated 1937 as *A Concise Comparative Celtic Grammar*, by Henry Lewis and Holger Pedersen. Göttingen.
Zeuss, Johann Kaspar. 1853. *Grammatica celtica*. Paris.

GERMANIC

van Coetsem, Frans, and Herbert L. Kufner, eds. 1972. *Toward a Grammar of Proto-Germanic*. Tübingen.
Grimm, Jacob. 1822. *Deutsche Grammatik*. Göttingen.
Haugen, Einar. 1976. *The Scandinavian Languages*. London.
Hirt, H. 1931–34. *Handbuch des Urgermanischen*, 3 vols. Heidelberg.
Keller, R. E. 1961. *German Dialects*. Manchester, Eng.
Lehmann, Winfred P. 1966. "The Grouping of the Germanic Languages," in Birnbaum and Puhvel, cited above under Indo-Hittite.
Moulton, William G., Einar Haugen, and Marvin I. Herceg. 1974. "Germanic Languages," in *EB* 8: 15–31.
Prokosch, E. 1939. *A Comparative Germanic Grammar*. Philadelphia.
Voyles, J. B. 1972. "The Problem of West Germanic," *Folia Linguistica* 5: 117–50.

BALTO-SLAVIC

Leumann, Manu. 1955. "Baltisch und Slavisch," in Hans Krahe, ed., *Corolla Linguistica. Festschrift Ferdinand Sommer*. Wiesbaden.
Schmalstieg, William R. 1974. "A Question Without a Clear Answer: One Aspect of the Relations Between Baltic and Slavic," *Suvaziavimo Darbu* 8: 181–88.
Senn, A. 1966. "The Relationships of Baltic and Slavic," in Birnbaum and Puhvel, cited above under Indo-Hittite.
Szemerényi, Oswald. 1957. "The Problem of Balto-Slav Unity—A Critical Survey," *Kratylos* 2: 97–123.

BALTIC

Endzelins, Janis. 1971. *Comparative Phonology and Morphology of the Baltic Languages*. The Hague.
Schleicher, August. 1856–57. *Handbuch der litauischen Sprache*, 2 vols. Prague.
Stang, Christian S. 1966. *Vergleichende Grammatik der baltischen Sprachen*. Oslo.
Toporov, V. N., ed. 1966. "Baltijskie jazyki," in *Jazyki narodov SSSR* 1. Moscow.

SLAVIC

Birnbaum, Henrik. 1966. "The Dialects of Common Slavic," in Birnbaum and Puhvel, cited above under Indo-Hittite.
de Bray, R. G. A. 1969. *Guide to the Slavonic Languages*. London.
Ivanov, V. V. 1974. "Slavic Languages," in *EB* 16: 866–74.
Jakobson, Roman. 1955. *Slavic Languages*. Oxford.
Lunt, Horace. 1968. "Slavic Languages," in *EB* 20: 644–46.
von Miklosich, Franz. 1852–75. *Vergleichende Grammatik der slavischen Sprachen*. Vienna.
Shevelov, G. 1965. *Prehistory of Slavic*. New York.
Vaillant, A. 1950–66. *Grammaire comparée des langues slaves*. Paris.

2.4 URALIC-YUKAGHIR

The Uralic-Yukaghir family, comprising two dozen languages and spoken by some 22 million people, is located for the most part in northern Eurasia, extending from Scandinavia across the Ural mountains into northern Asia, as shown in Map 2.2. The most divergent language of the group is *Yukaghir*, which has several hundred speakers in Northeast Asia. The

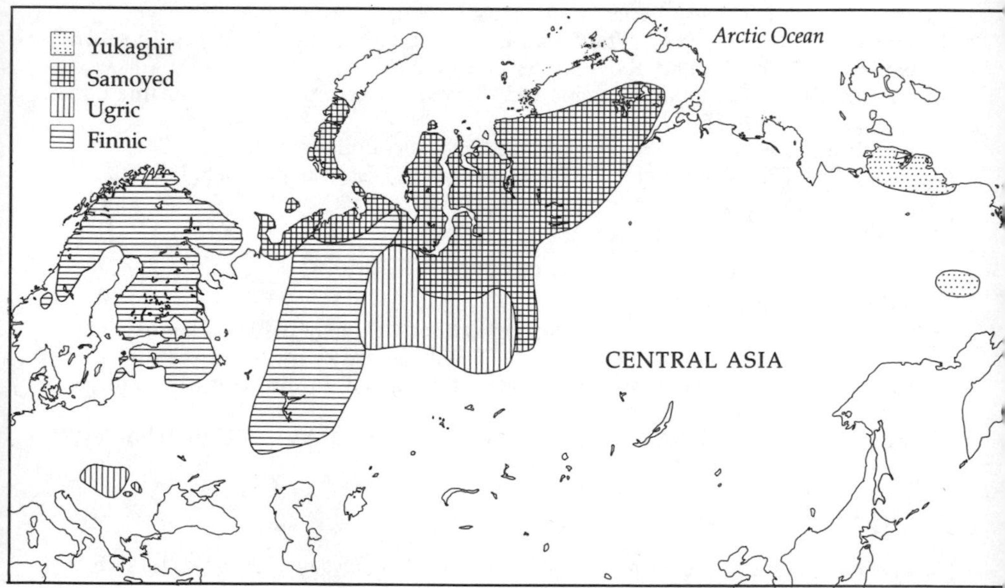

Map 2.2. The Uralic-Yukaghir family

Uralic family itself has two well-defined branches. The *Samoyed* group, situated on both sides of the Ural mountains in northern Eurasia, has four extant languages and perhaps 30,000 speakers. The second branch, the *Finno-Ugric* family, with 19 languages and about 22 million speakers, also contains two branches. The *Ugric* family is composed of two languages spoken just east of the Ural mountains in western Asia (Xanty, Mansi) and Hungarian, a Uralic island in central Europe surrounded on all sides by Indo-European languages. Hungarian's 14 million speakers account for more than half of all Uralic speakers. The second branch of Finno-Ugric is the *Finnic* family, most of whose languages are found in the Baltic region (Finland, Estonia, northern Scandinavia), though some Finnic languages are found on the western side of the Ural mountains. The best known Finnic languages are Finnish (with five million speakers), Estonian (with a million), and various Saami (= Lapp) languages (with around 30,000 speakers) spoken in northern Scandinavia and on the Kola Peninsula of the U.S.S.R.

2.4.1 *History of Uralic-Yukaghir Classification*

The first mention of a Uralic people in the historical record occurs in Tacitus's *Germania* (A.D. 98), where the Finns are described as inhabiting a region northeast of the Germanic territory. The earliest recorded observation of similarities between two Uralic languages is usually attributed to the Norwegian landowner Othere, who noted resemblances between Lapp and Karelian around A.D. 890. The Samoyed peoples are first mentioned in *Nestor's Chronicle* (c. 1113). The western, or European, Samoyeds came under Russian rule during the twelfth century; the Asian, or trans-Uralic, Samoyeds remained outside the Russian sphere until the fourteenth century. Recognition that the Samoyed languages are related to the Finnic languages did not come until the early eighteenth century.

At the end of the fifteenth century, European scholars noticed the resemblance between *Hungaria* and *Yugria* (a group of settlements just east of the Ural Mountains). A Ugric connection was assumed at this time, but no linguistic evidence was adduced.

In 1671 a Swedish scholar, Georg Stiernhielm, remarked that Estonian and Lapp resemble Finnish in numerous ways and that Finnish, in turn, shares many words with Hungarian. At about the same time a German scholar, Martin Vogel, compared Finnish, Lapp, and Hungarian in an attempt to prove a relationship among them, but his work was never published. These two scholars were apparently the first to perceive the outlines of what has since come to be known as the Finno-Ugric family.

The year 1717 saw two publications of importance for Uralic classification. First, a Swedish professor, Olaf Rudbeck, proposed about 100 etymologies linking Hungarian with Finnish. According to Collinder (1965: 34), some 40 of these etymologies are still considered valid. The second important publication was G. W. Leibniz's *Collectanea Etymologica*, in which the German scholar J. G. von Eckhart proposed a relationship among Finnish, Estonian, Livonian, Hungarian, Xanty, and Samoyed, thus for the first time linking the Samoyed languages with the Finno-Ugric group previously recognized by Stiernhielm. This larger grouping is today known as the Uralic family.

In 1730 the Swedish army officer Phillip Johann von Strahlenberg published a work in which he correctly delineated, for the first time, all the branches of the Finno-Ugric family except Lapp. In 1770 a German historian, August Ludwig von Schlözer, added Lapp to Strahlenberg's classification. At this point all the constituent branches of Finno-Ugric were known, as was the connection between the Finno-Ugric and Samoyed languages. The basic structure of the Uralic family had thus been roughly worked out at least six years before William Jones's celebrated address, which *opened* the era of I-E studies.

The fact that a few scholars had discovered the linguistic relationships of the Uralic languages by the close of the eighteenth century does not mean that this knowledge was either widespread or widely believed. Hungarian intellectuals of the time, for instance, fancied that the Turkic tribes in the east were their nearest relatives and had little use for rumors of similarities with Baltic or Siberian languages. In Hungary, at least, the wild unfettered Romanticism of the epoch chose to ignore the sober linguistic facts.

Despite the hostile climate, however, in 1770 the Hungarian Jesuit J. Sajnovics attempted to show, by comparing inflectional endings and lexical similarities, that Hungarian and Lapp are related. Since the Saami are racially distinct from the Hungarians (and from the Baltic peoples as well), and since they occupy what would today be called a modest position on the socioeconomic scale, many Hungarians were outraged at Sajnovics's proposal, which was condemned "as an impious act of sacrilege and regarded by a so-called 'patriotic public' as a slight on the nation's honour. Preference was given to authors less inclined to dissipate illusions." (Zsirai 1951: vi).

In 1799 another Hungarian, Sámuel Gyarmathi, who had been both influenced and encouraged by the German Schlözer, published the most significant work on Uralic languages up to that time. Gyarmathi's work represents an advance over Sajnovics's, in that he took into consideration all of the Uralic languages about which he had information (including Samoyed) and did not artificially restrict his investigation to only two languages. Gyarmathi established that (1) Hungarian's closest relatives are Xanty and Mansi, the three of which form a Ugric subfamily; (2) this Ugric group shows numerous affinities with the Finnic family; and (3) both display similarities with the Samoyed languages. Although many of Gyarmathi's proposed etymologies were later discredited, it nevertheless remains true that "a substantial proportion of the accepted . . . Finno-Ugrian etymologies was established for the first time by Gyarmathi" (Zsirai 1951: xiv).

At the beginning of the nineteenth century, the classification of Uralic languages was much better understood than that of the I-E family. Furthermore, Uralic relationships had been established by the *same* methods later employed by the early Indo-Europeanists, namely, the discovery of *lexical* similarities (Strahlenberg) and *inflectional* similarities (Sajnovics, Gyarmathi). Why, then, was comparative linguistics in the nineteenth century developed almost entirely in terms of the I-E family, with the Uralic heritage being largely ignored? Pedersen (1931: 241) suggests two principal reasons: "The Finno-Ugric languages were too far beyond the horizon and interest of most European scholars, and, besides, the problems to be solved were too difficult because the languages are very distantly related, and lack old documents." I believe Pedersen's first cause, a lack of interest on the part of the European community, was the crucial factor. The Uralic languages are in fact not as distantly related as Pedersen implies, and as we saw above, they had already been fairly accurately classified by the end of the eighteenth century. Their major handicap was that practically without exception the Uralic languages are "marginal," both geographically and politically. The sole exception was Hungarian, but in Hungary the intellectual climate was hostile to the development of Finno-Ugric comparative linguistics.

During the nineteenth century there were no major revisions in Uralic classification, though some details were clarified and a growing body of evidence supported the classifications of earlier scholars. In 1800 the Samoyed languages were the least well known, and their precise position within the Uralic family had not yet been firmly established. Although the first Samoyed grammar appeared in 1811, the Samoyed languages remained poorly documented until the work of the Finnish linguist M. A. Castrén. Castrén visited all the Samoyed-speaking areas during a series of field trips in the 1840's and classified the various Samoyed dialects into five languages, divided into Northern and Southern subgroups. In addition to clarifying the internal relationships of the Samoyed family, Castrén was the first scholar to show that the fundamental division in Uralic is between the Samoyed languages and all the rest of the family, i.e. Finno-Ugric. Because of this discovery Castrén is sometimes referred to as the founder of Uralic linguistics. His most important work, a comparative grammar of the Samoyed languages, appeared in 1854, two years after his death.

In the final decades of the nineteenth century, two additional scholars consolidated and expanded the knowledge of the Uralic family. The first of these was a German, József Budenz, who spent the last 20 years of his life as the leading Finno-Ugric specialist in Hungary. In his major work, a comparative dictionary of the Finno-Ugric elements in Hungarian, Budenz proposed close to 1,000 correspondences between Hungarian and various Finnic languages and laid to rest forever the erroneous notions concerning Hungarian's closest relatives. Though Budenz concentrated primarily on Finno-Ugric languages, he did avail himself of the opportunity to elicit five stories and some sentences from a Samoyed family of five that was being exhibited at the Budapest zoo in 1882.

A final scholar of importance was the Hungarian linguist Ignác Halász. In a work published in 1893–94 Halász proposed 245 Uralic cognates and noted numerous grammatical agreements between the Samoyed and Finno-Ugric families. His work has been called "the first thorough proof of the Samoyed-Finno-Ugric relationship" (Hajdú 1963: 87).

2.4.2 *Present Status of Uralic-Yukaghir Classification*

Within the Uralic family the following groups of languages are believed to constitute valid genetic nodes:

(12)	SAMOYED	FINNIC
	FINNO-UGRIC	PERMIC
	UGRIC	SAAMIC (= LAPPIC)
	OB-UGRIC	BALTIC FINNIC

Some linguists would add an additional group, Volgaic, made up of the two languages Mari and Mordvin (Austerlitz 1968, Sauvageot & Menges 1973, Haarmann 1974, Voegelin & Voegelin 1977). Other scholars, however, deny any special relationship between these two languages (Collinder 1965, Harms 1974).

List 2.8. The Uralic Family (1986)

URALIC:
I SAMOYED:
  A NORTH
  B SOUTH
II FINNO-UGRIC:
  A UGRIC:
    1 Hungarian
    2 OB-UGRIC
  B FINNIC

List 2.9. Proposed Subgroupings of the Finnic Family

Collinder 1965	*Austerlitz 1968*	*Sauvageot & Menges 1973*
FINNIC:	**FINNIC:**	**FINNIC:**
I Mordvin	I PERMIC	I BALTIC FINNIC
II Mari	II VOLGAIC	II SAAMIC
III BALTIC FINNIC	III NORTH FINNIC:	III VOLGAIC
IV SAAMIC	A SAAMIC	IV PERMIC
V PERMIC	B BALTIC FINNIC	

Harms 1974	*Voegelin & Voegelin 1977*
FINNIC:	**FINNIC:**
I PERMIC	I PERMIC
II Mari	II FINNO-VOLGAIC:
III WEST FINNIC:	A VOLGAIC
A Mordvin	B FINNO-LAPPIC:
B NORTH FINNIC:	1 SAAMIC
1 SAAMIC	2 BALTIC FINNIC
2 BALTIC FINNIC	

The subgrouping of the units in (12) is at the highest levels quite uncontroversial, with practically all scholars supporting the subgrouping for Uralic in List 2.8. Divergence of opinion is presently restricted to the Finnic subfamily of Uralic. Here there is, first, disagreement over the validity of the Volgaic group, and second, different proposals for subgrouping the constituent branches of Finnic (Baltic Finnic, Saamic, Permic, and either Volgaic or Mari and Mordvin). List 2.9 shows five proposed subgroupings for the Finnic languages. The classification of Finnic adopted in this book follows Austerlitz (1968).

The Yukaghir language is spoken in northeastern Siberia by several hundred people. Though it is not a Uralic language *stricto sensu,* it "is obviously related to the Uralic languages" (Collinder 1955: xii). Yukaghir is often considered a language isolate, that is, a language not known to be related to any other language (see Voegelin & Voegelin 1977: 355). Yet the evidence offered in Collinder (1940, 1965) and Harms (1977) demonstrates beyond doubt the affinity of Yukaghir with the Uralic family. Collinder (1965: 30) summarizes the evidence as follows:

> The features common to Yukaghir and Uralic are so numerous and so characteristic that they must be remainders of a primordial unity. The case system of Yukaghir is almost identical with that of Northern Samoyed. The imperative of the verbs is formed with the same suffixes as in Southern Samoyed and the most conservative of

> the Fenno-Ugric languages. . . . There are striking common traits in verb derivation. Most of the pronominal stems are more or less identical. Yukaghir has half a hundred words in common with Uralic, in addition to those that may fairly be suspected of being loanwords. . . . It is worth noting that all the Fenno-Ugric languages deviate more from Samoyed in their case inflection than Yukaghir does.

It thus appears that Yukaghir, and the closely related, but extinct, Chuvantsy and Omok, are taxonomically coordinate with the entire Uralic family (see List 2.10).

List 2.10. The Uralic-Yukaghir Family (Collinder 1965)

URALIC-YUKAGHIR:
- I YUKAGHIR
- II URALIC:
  - A SAMOYEDIC
  - B FINNO-UGRIC:
    - 1 UGRIC
    - 2 FINNIC

Austerlitz, Robert. 1968. "L'ouralien," in André Martinet, ed., *Le langage*. Paris.

Budenz, József. 1873–81. *Magyar-ugor összehasonlító szótár*. Budapest. Reprinted as *A Comparative Dictionary of the Finno-Ugric Elements in the Hungarian Vocabulary*, n.d., Bloomington, Ind. [Despite its title this reprint is in Hungarian.]

Castrén, M. A. 1854. *Grammatik der samojedischen Sprachen*. St. Petersburg.

Collinder, Björn. 1940. *Jukagirisch und Uralisch*. *Uppsala Universitets Årsskrift* 8.

———. 1955. *Fenno-Ugric Vocabulary*. Stockholm.

———. 1957. *Survey of the Uralic Languages*. Stockholm.

———. 1965. *An Introduction to the Uralic Languages*. Berkeley, Calif.

Comrie, Bernard. 1981. "Uralic Languages," in Bernard Comrie, *The Languages of the Soviet Union*. Cambridge, Eng.

Décsy, Gyula. 1965. *Einführung in die finnisch-ugrische Sprachwissenschaft*. Wiesbaden.

Gulya, János. 1974. "Some Eighteenth Century Antecedents of Nineteenth Century Linguistics: The Discovery of Finno-Ugrian," in Dell Hymes, ed., *Studies in the History of Linguistics*. Bloomington, Ind.

Gyarmathi, Sámuel. 1799. *Affinitas linguae Hungaricae cum linguis fennicae originis grammatice demonstrata*. Göttingen. Reprinted 1968, Bloomington, Ind.

Haarmann, Harold. 1974. *Die finnisch-ugrischen Sprachen*. Hamburg.

Hajdú, Peter. 1963. *The Samoyed Peoples and Languages*. Bloomington, Ind.

Harms, Robert T. 1974. "Uralic Languages," in *EB* 18: 1022–32.

———. 1977. "The Uralo-Yukaghir Focus System: A Problem in Remote Genetic Relationship," in Paul J. Hopper, ed., *Studies in Descriptive and Historical Linguistics*. Amsterdam.

Leibniz, G. W., ed. 1717. *Collectanea etymologica*. Hanover.

Pedersen, Holger. 1931. *Linguistic Science in the Nineteenth Century*. Cambridge, Mass.

Sajnovics, J. 1770. *Demonstratio idioma Ungarorum et Lapponum idem esse*. Copenhagen.
Sauvageot, A., and K. H. Menges. 1973. "Ural-Altaic Languages," in *EB* 22: 775–77.
von Strahlenberg, Phillip Johann. 1730. *Das nord- und östliche Theil von Europa und Asia*. Stockholm.
Voegelin, C. F., and F. M. Voegelin. 1977. *Classification and Index of the World's Languages*. New York.
Zsirai, Miklós. 1951. "Sámuel Gyarmathi, Hungarian Pioneer of Comparative Linguistics," *Acta Linguistica Academiae Scientiarum Hungaricae* 1: 5–17.

2.5 CAUCASIAN

Approximately three dozen Caucasian languages are spoken in the Caucasus of the U.S.S.R. by some five million people. The geographic distribution of the Caucasian family is shown in Map 2.3. The Caucasian family is composed of two very different subfamilies, and it is possible that these two subfamilies, North and South Caucasian, do not constitute a valid genetic node. Georgian, with 3.3 million speakers, is the only well-known

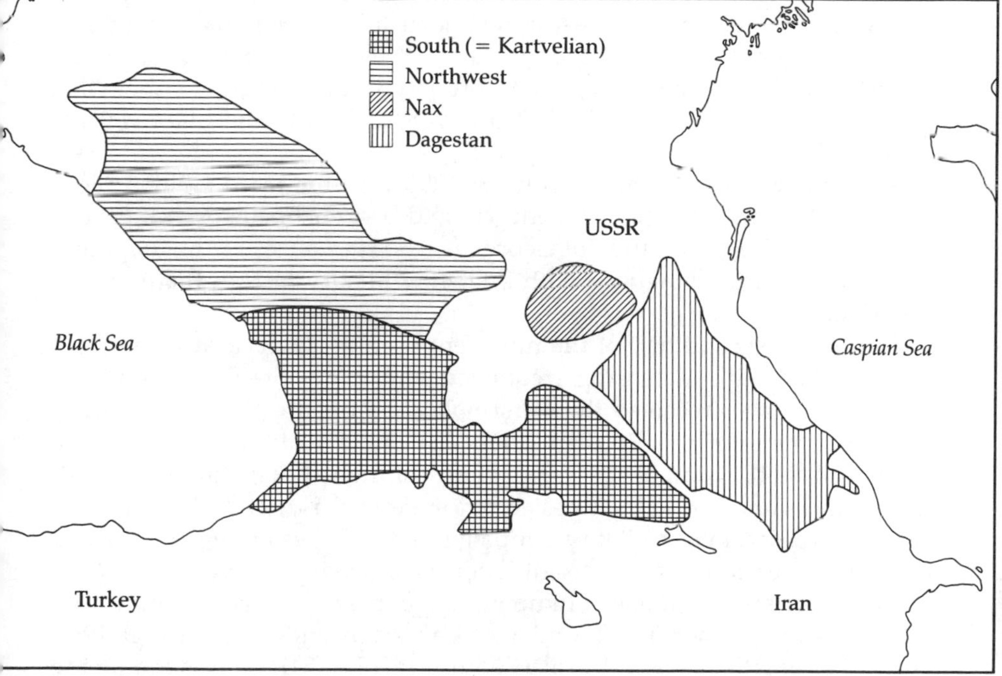

Map 2.3. The Caucasian family

Caucasian language. One North Caucasian language, Kabardian, has attained a certain linguistic notoriety as a language with few vowels and numerous consonants.

2.5.1 *History of Caucasian Classification*

I have been unable to determine precisely who it was that first recognized, and offered evidence for, the various genetic groups constituting the Caucasian family. As a consequence, the following brief historical perspective will be a good deal less satisfying than I would like. It will consist mainly of an enumeration of scholars who have studied, and made some contribution to, Caucasian linguistics, but the contribution of each with regard to genetic classification will remain regrettably vague.

The earliest mention of the multiplicity of languages spoken in the Caucasus Mountains was made by the Greek geographer Strabo around the beginning of the Christian era. But these languages attracted very little scholarly attention until the late eighteenth century, at which time the region was coming increasingly under Russian control.

The first person to study the Caucasian languages in a systematic way was a German doctor, Johann Anton Güldenstädt. During the second half of the eighteenth century, Güldenstädt published information on the diverse North Caucasian languages and proposed a classification of them that was not, according to Vogt (1942: 245), "very different from that currently accepted."

The German linguist Heinrich Julius Klaproth continued Güldenstädt's work in the early nineteenth century, and a Frenchman, Marie-Félicité Brosset, undertook the study of Georgian, a South Caucasian language and the only Caucasian language with a lengthy literary history (dating from the fifth century A.D.).

During the second half of the nineteenth century, Caucasian languages were studied with increasing frequency, and many previously undocumented languages received their first published treatments. In this regard one must mention the Russian orientalist Franz Anton Schiefner, who from 1854 to 1873 published descriptions of eight Caucasian languages. During this same period the Russian officer Peter Karlovich Uslar, who had earlier taken part in the military campaigns in the Dagestan region, devoted himself to the study of Caucasian languages, producing grammatical descriptions of six previously unknown languages. Uslar is sometimes regarded as the "father and founder of Caucasian linguistics" (Vogt 1942: 246); according to Sala and Vintilă-Rădulescu (1981: 54), he was the first to propose that all Caucasian languages share a common origin.

The final work of the nineteenth century on Caucasian languages was published in 1895 by another former officer in the Russian army, R. von Eckhart. This general survey of Caucasian languages contained information on a greater number of Caucasian languages than earlier works and was quite successful in Europe even though it was not highly regarded by scholars.

The most important scholar of the early twentieth century was the German Adolf Dirr, who from 1904 to 1913 published monographs on nine North Caucasian languages, mostly of the Dagestan region. In 1924 Dirr founded the first linguistics journal devoted to Caucasian languages, *Caucasia*, and in 1928 he published an introduction to Caucasian linguistics containing sketches of 35 languages.

2.5.2 *Present Status of Caucasian Classification*

Whether or not all Caucasian languages derive from a single source has never been resolved to the satisfaction of most linguists. There is no question that the South Caucasian, or Kartvelian, languages form a valid genetic group. Furthermore, most linguists accept that the North Caucasian languages constitute a valid family with two branches, a compact Northwestern group and a distantly related, and more heterogeneous, Northeastern group. The principal taxonomic dispute in the twentieth century has been whether the North Caucasian and South Caucasian families share a common ancestor. Although certain scholars have supported a single Caucasian family (e.g. Friedrich Müller, A. Trombetti, Hans Vogt, and most Soviet linguists), others remain unconvinced. The Russian linguist N. S. Trubetzkoj (1922: 185) considered the attempt to connect North and South Caucasian to be "fantasy" so long as regular sound correspondences had not been established between the two families.

A second area of disagreement has to do with the relationship of the Nax group to other Northern subgroups. There have been three proposals: (1) the Nax group is intermediate between Northeast and Northwest Caucasian and thus constitutes one of three primary branches of North Caucasian (Catford 1977, B.G. Hewitt in Comrie 1981); (2) the Nax group forms one of two primary branches of Northeast Caucasian (Eckhart 1895, Dirr 1928, Dumézil 1952, Klimov 1965, Gamkrelidze & Gudava 1974), the other branch containing the remainder of the Northeastern languages; and (3) the Nax group is simply one of several Northeastern subgroups (Trubetzkoj 1922, Deeters 1963, Voegelin & Voegelin 1977). These three subgroupings are illustrated in List 2.11. The classification adopted in this book follows subgrouping 2.

List 2.11. Proposed Subgroupings of the North Caucasian Languages

I	II	III
NORTH CAUCASIAN:	**NORTH CAUCASIAN:**	**NORTH CAUCASIAN:**
I NORTHWEST	I NORTHWEST	I NORTHWEST
II NAX	II NORTHEAST:	II NORTHEAST:
III NORTHEAST	A NAX	A NAX
	B DAGESTAN:	B AVARO-ANDI-DIDO
	1 AVARO-ANDI-DIDO	C LAK-DARGWA
	2 LAK-DARGWA	D LEZGIAN
	3 LEZGIAN	

Ignoring low level genetic units whose members are sometimes treated as dialects of one language, other times as distinct languages (e.g. Mingrelian-Laz, Abxaz-Abaza, Chechen-Ingush, Bezhta-Hunzib), the following Caucasian groups are fairly well established as valid genetic units:

(13)	SOUTH CAUCASIAN	AVARO-ANDI-DIDO
	NORTH CAUCASIAN	ANDI
	NORTHWEST CAUCASIAN	DIDO
	NORTHEAST CAUCASIAN	LAK-DARGWA
	NAX	LEZGIAN

Dagestan may be added to this list only if subgrouping 2 in List 2.11 above is correct. The Caucasian classification used in this book has the structure given in List 2.12.

Several scholars have attempted to relate the language isolate Basque, spoken in northern Spain, with Caucasian languages. The putative rela-

List 2.12. The Caucasian Family (Gamkrelidze & Gudava 1974)

CAUCASIAN:
- I SOUTH
- II NORTH:
  - A NORTHWEST
  - B NORTHEAST:
    - 1 NAX
    - 2 DAGESTAN:
      - a AVARO-ANDI-DIDO
      - b LAK-DARGWA
      - c LEZGIAN

tionship would be a very distant one, and the majority of scholars remain skeptical. For evidence supporting the connection, the reader should consult Bouda (1948, 1949), Lafon (1933, 1952b), and Michelena (1968).

Bouda, Karl. 1948. "Baskisch-kaukasisch," *Zeitschrift für Phonetik* 2: 182–202.

———. 1949. *Baskisch-kaukasische Etymologien*. Heidelberg.

Catford, J. C. 1977. "Mountain of Tongues: The Languages of the Caucasus," *Annual Review of Anthropology* 6: 283–314.

Comrie, Bernard. 1981. "Caucasian Languages," in Bernard Comrie, *The Languages of the Soviet Union*. Cambridge, Eng. [This chapter is the work of B. G. Hewitt.]

Deeters, Gerhard. 1963. "Die kaukasischen Sprachen," in *Armenisch und kaukasische Sprachen*. Leiden.

Dirr, Adolf. 1928. *Einführung in das Studium der kaukasischen Sprachen*. Leipzig.

Dumézil, Georges. 1952. "Langues caucasiennes," in A. Meillet and M. Cohen, eds., *Les langues du monde* 1. Paris.

von Eckhart, R. 1895. *Die Sprachen des kaukasischen Stämmes*. Wiesbaden.

Gamkrelidze, Thomas V., and T. E. Gudava. 1974. "Caucasian Languages," in *EB* 3: 1011–15.

Geiger, B., et al. 1959. *Peoples and Languages of the Caucasus*. The Hague.

Klimov, G. A. 1965. *Kavkazskie jazyki*. Moscow.

Kuipers, Aert H. 1963. "Caucasian," in *CTIL* 1.

Lafon, R. 1933. "Basque et les langues kartvèles," *Revue Internationale des Études Basques* 24,2.

———. 1951–52. "Concordances morphologiques entre le basque et les langues caucasiques," *Word*, 2 parts, 7: 227–44, 8: 80–94.

———. 1952. "Quelques rapprochements entre les langues caucasiques du nord et les langues kartvèles," *Études Basques et Caucasiques* (Salamanca).

Michelena, Luis. 1968. "L'euskaro-caucasien," in André Martinet, ed., *Le langage*. Paris.

Sala, Marius, and Ioana Vintilă-Rădulescu. 1981. *Limbile lumii*. Bucharest.

Trubetzkoj, N. S. 1922. "Les consonnes laterales des langues caucasiques-septentrionales," *Bulletin de la Société Linguistique de Paris* 23: 184–204.

Voegelin, C. F., and F. M. Voegelin. 1977. *Classification and Index of the World's Languages*. New York.

Vogt, Hans. 1942. "La parenté des langues caucasiques," *Norsk Tidsskrift for Sprogvidenskap* 12: 242–57.

3

Africa

There are many more languages in Africa than in Europe, and their classification has been comprehensively worked out only in this century. The three European phyla discussed in the previous chapter contain some 200 languages, almost half of which are really spoken in Asia (primarily the Indo-Iranian branch of Indo-European). The four phyla into which African languages are currently classified comprise close to 1,500 languages. Languages of the *Afro-Asiatic* family are spoken across a wide belt covering most of the northern third of Africa and extending into western Asia. More than 1,000 *Niger-Kordofanian* languages are spoken throughout most of the southern two-thirds of Africa, with the large Bantu subfamily occupying most of the southern half of the continent. Although one *Nilo-Saharan* language (Songhai) is spoken in western Africa (i.e. Mali, Burkina Fasso, Niger), most Nilo-Saharan languages are found in central and east-central Africa. *Khoisan* languages were probably originally spoken over most of the southern third of Africa. However, the Bantu expansion from the northwest and the European occupation of the South have overwhelmed and extinguished most of these languages. Several dozen Khoisan languages are still spoken by small groups in South Africa, Namibia, Botswana, and Angola, where the dominant languages are either Bantu (e.g. Zulu, Xhosa) or Indo-European (e.g. Afrikaans, English). The two most divergent Khoisan languages are in fact found in northern Tanzania.

3.1 THE HISTORY OF AFRICAN CLASSIFICATION

Our earliest records of Sub-Saharan languages are Arabic documents dating from the tenth to twelfth centuries. Although a few wordlists of African languages were collected during the Middle Ages, it was not until the fifteenth and sixteenth centuries that Europeans began to gather such information in any quantity. The seventeenth century witnessed a flowering of scholarship on African languages, including dictionaries of Coptic (1636), Nubian (1638), and Kongo (1652) and grammars of Nama (1643),* Kongo (1659), Geez (1661), and Amharic (1698), among others.

During most of the eighteenth century African scholarship ebbed, but in the last quarter of the century, two African language families were clearly discerned. In 1776 a French abbé, Lievin Bonaventure Proyart, recognized that three Bantu languages must derive from a common source, which, however, he incorrectly assumed still existed. It is likely that the Englishman William Marsden perceived the Bantu group as early as 1778, though the first written record to this effect dates from 1816. In the early nineteenth century several more scholars independently discovered the Bantu group. The early recognition of Bantu is not surprising, since Bantu is a large group of closely related languages that covers most of the southern third of Africa. Because the Bantu family is about as closely related as the Romance group (cf. Table 1.2), it can hardly be missed by anyone who examines even a few Bantu languages. (The term Bantu, however, was not coined until 1858.)

The other linguistic group to be recognized in the eighteenth century was the Semitic family. The German scholar Ludwig von Schlözer is often credited with having recognized, and named, the Semitic family in 1781. But the affinity of Hebrew, Arabic, and Aramaic had been recognized for centuries by Jewish and Islamic scholars, and this knowledge was published in Western Europe as early as 1538 (see Postel 1538). Around 1700 Hiob Ludolf, who had written grammars of Geez and Amharic (both Ethiopic Semitic languages) in the seventeenth century, recognized the extension of the Semitic family into East Africa. Thus when von Schlözer named the family in 1781, he was merely recognizing genetic relationships that had been known for centuries. Three Semitic languages (Aramaic, Arabic, and Hebrew) were long familiar to Europeans both because of their geographic proximity and because the Bible was written in Hebrew and Aramaic.

During the first half of the nineteenth century, two additional families were postulated. In 1808 Heinrich Lichtenstein divided the languages of Southern Africa into two groups, Bantu and Nama. The first attempt at an overall classification of African languages was published in 1826 by Adrien Balbi. Balbi connected Nama with the Bushman languages, as did James C. Prichard (1826). The principal distinction between the Nama and the Bushmen is cultural, not linguistic. The Nama are cattle-herders; the Bushmen are hunters and gatherers. Both groups, however, share a distinct racial

*The name Hottentot is felt to be pejorative and has therefore been replaced by Nama throughout this work.

type, sometimes called Bushmanoid, which distinguishes them rather clearly from the surrounding Negroid Bantu speakers. Furthermore, the languages of the Nama and Bushmen both use clicks. It is likely that such genetically (in the linguistic sense) irrelevant traits as racial type and clicks were at first the major criteria for connecting Nama and the Bushman languages. The connection turned out to be correct, but the supporting linguistic evidence did not come until later.

Also widely recognized by 1850 was a group of languages known as Hamitic, which was usually taken to include Ancient Egyptian (now extinct) and the Berber and Cushitic families. Furthermore, most scholars admitted by then that the Hamitic languages showed such striking affinities with the Semitic family that a common origin could hardly be doubted. The overall family became known in the 1860's as Hamito-Semitic.

Thus at midcentury there were three recognized language families in Africa: Bantu, Nama-Bushman, and Hamito-Semitic. Unfortunately there were still hundreds of languages that did not appear to fit into any of these families. This rather substantial residue was more often than not lumped into a single ill-defined group with a name like "Negroland" or "Mid-African." Speakers of these languages were for the most part Negroid and were situated geographically in the middle of Africa, in a belt running from coast to coast, with Hamito-Semitic speakers to the north and Bantu and Nama-Bushman speakers to the south. Relationships among these numerous and heterogeneous languages were not at all clear. Some scholars candidly admitted that the Negro group was based primarily on physical traits rather than linguistic similarities. In revising Prichard's *Natural History of Man* (1843), the Englishman Edwin Norris wrote in 1855 that "hitherto the Negroes have been deemed to be one race from physiological rather than philological evidence" (quoted in Cole 1971: 21).

During the second half of the nineteenth century, two influential classifications of African languages appeared, both first published in the 1860's and revised periodically by their authors over the next several decades. The German Egyptologist Karl Richard Lepsius published various versions of his classification between 1863 and 1880. His final classification, from his *Nubische Grammatik* (Nubian Grammar), is given in List 3.1.

The other important classification was the work of an Austrian linguist, Friedrich Müller, who offered a complete classification of the world's languages in his *Grundriss der Sprachwissenschaft* (Outline of Linguistics). Müller's classification appeared first in 1867, with revised versions as late as 1888. The African portion of his classification had six subdivisions (see List 3.2). Of these six groups, Müller believed that only Semitic and Bantu were valid genetic units, with the status of the others in doubt. Müller acknowledged that Semitic and Hamitic were related at some level, but the precise relationship remained unclear.

List 3.1. African Language Families (Lepsius 1880)

SEMITIC

HAMITIC:
I †Ancient Egyptian
II CUSHITIC
III BERBER-HAUSA
IV NAMA-BUSHMAN

NEGRO:
I BANTU
II MIXED NEGRO (all the rest)

List 3.2. African Language Families (Müller 1877)

SEMITIC

HAMITIC:
I †Ancient Egyptian
II CUSHITIC
III BERBER

NUBA-FULA

NEGRO

BANTU

NAMA-BUSHMAN

The chief differences between Lepsius and Müller were the following. (1) To the traditional Hamitic group (see List 3.2) Lepsius added other languages not usually considered Hamitic: Hausa (which he linked with Berber) and Nama. (2) Lepsius lumped the Negro and Bantu groups into one family, whereas Müller kept them separate. (3) From the Negro family Müller extracted a heterogeneous Nuba-Fula group, which subsequent scholarship proved to be totally unjustified. Both Lepsius and Müller used nonlinguistic criteria, such as skin color, hair type, and mode of subsistence, in establishing their classifications. Lepsius, in addition, used typological traits, such as the presence or absence of gender, which do not lead to valid genetic groups.

During the first half of the twentieth century, two Germans dominated work on African linguistics, particularly in matters of classification. The first was the Bantuist Carl Meinhof; the second was his student Diedrich Westermann. Unlike their nineteenth-century predecessors, neither ever proposed a complete classification of African languages, but their views on most of the vital issues in language grouping can be inferred from their published works.

Meinhof made his reputation in Bantu linguistics and then used that authority to dominate the entire African field for close to half a century. In 1910 he proposed that the ill-defined Mid-African, or Negro, group be renamed Sudanic, and he expressed the belief that all these languages would one day be shown to be related. He did not claim to have demonstrated the relationships himself. The following year Westermann attempted to prove the genetic unity of Meinhof's Sudanic group, which at this point was defined mostly in negative terms: it included all those languages that were neither Semitic, Hamitic, Bantu, nor Nama-Bushman. In *Die Sudansprachen* (The Sudanic Languages; 1911), Westermann compared five West African languages with three East African languages. Although he felt he had accomplished the task assigned him by Meinhof, he was aware that the evidence linking the Eastern and Western languages was not altogether satisfactory.

In 1912 Meinhof published *Die Sprachen der Hamiten* (The Languages of the Hamites) in which he extended Lepsius's expansion of the Hamitic group. We may recall that to the traditional Hamitic group (Ancient Egyptian, Berber, Cushitic), Lepsius had added Nama and Hausa. Meinhof now proposed Hamitic affiliation for Fula, Maasai, Bari, Nandi, Sandawe, and Hadza. Thus for Meinhof African languages fell into one of three groups, Bantu, Sudanic, or Hamito-Semitic (see List 3.3). Despite objections from various critics with regard to both the Hamitic and the Sudanic group, Meinhof's classification remained in fashion through the 1940's.

Westermann, however, had increasing doubts about certain aspects of Meinhof's classification. The Sudanic group, in particular, seemed less and less secure. In 1927, when he published his best work, "Die westlichen Sudansprachen und ihre Beziehungen zum Bantu" (The West Sudanic Languages and Their Relationship to Bantu), Westermann left aside the disparate East Sudanic languages altogether and concentrated instead on the relatively more clear-cut West Sudanic family. In this work Westermann established the genetic unity of the West Sudanic family and offered the most accurate subgrouping yet proposed for West Sudanic. In addition, he cited sufficient similarities between West Sudanic and Bantu that some kind of genetic relationship was apparent, though he declined to be specific about its exact nature.

Neither of these ideas was original with Westermann; numerous scholars had noticed scattered resemblances among West African languages, and between West African languages and Bantu, from the mid-nineteenth century on. Westermann, however, marshaled the evidence in such detail that both conclusions became inescapable (though Westermann himself was noncommittal on both, perhaps out of deference to his mentor Meinhof). In 1940 Westermann suggested the classification of African languages given in List 3.4, but he made it clear that not all the groups were necessarily valid genetic units.

In 1950 African linguistic classification was, in its broadest outline, not significantly different from views prevailing a century earlier. To be sure, there had been progress in delineating low-level genetic groups (e.g. Chadic, Nubian), but there had been remarkably little success in establishing how the numerous small families fit together in larger groupings. At this point the American linguist Joseph H. Greenberg proposed, in a series of articles (Greenberg 1949–50, 1954; published together as Greenberg 1955), a complete classification of African languages that differed in certain dramatic ways from prevailing opinion. In a classification that Greenberg

List 3.3. African Language Families (Meinhof c. 1912)

BANTU

SUDANIC:
I EAST
II WEST

HAMITO-SEMITIC:
I SEMITIC
II HAMITIC:
A †Ancient Egyptian
B CUSHITIC
C BERBER
D Hausa
E Maasai
F Fula
G Nama

List 3.4. African Language Families (Westermann 1940)

KHOISAN:
I NAMA
II BUSHMAN

NEGRO:
I NILOTIC
II BANTU
III SUDANIC:
A NIGRITIC
B MANDE
C SEMI-BANTU
D INNER SUDAN

HAMITO-SEMITIC:
I SEMITIC
II HAMITIC

termed "conservative," the languages of Africa were divided into 16 groups, the genetic unity of each being, according to Greenberg, "in the class of the obvious." That classification is shown in List 3.5. Greenberg's classification, which was hailed by Welmers (1956: 558) as "a significant mid-century milestone . . . almost sensational in its scope and originality" and characterized by Cole (1960: 223) as "the first attempt at a pan-African classification on genetic principles," was revolutionary in several important respects.

As Cole emphasized, Greenberg's classification was based solely on *genetic* principles. Hitherto all attempts at pan-African classifications had followed genetic principles only in identifying such obvious groups as Bantu and Semitic. When confronted with a bewildering diversity in the remaining hundreds of African languages, all earlier classifiers had abandoned ge-

List 3.5. African Language Families (Greenberg 1949–50)

1. KHOISAN	8. MABAN
2. AFRO-ASIATIC (formerly Hamito-Semitic)	9. TEMEIN
3. NIGER-CONGO (formerly West Sudanic)	10. KOMAN
4. KORDOFANIAN	11. Songhai
5. CENTRAL SAHARAN	12. Mimi
6. CENTRAL SUDANIC	13. Fur
7. EASTERN SUDANIC	14. Berta
	15. Kunama
	16. Teuso

netic principles, as articulated by Indo-Europeanists in the nineteenth century (see section 2.3), and had resorted either to *nonlinguistic* factors such as skin color, hair type, and mode of existence or to *typological* traits like gender. By the end of the nineteenth century, it was well known that the use of such criteria does not produce valid genetic groups. Why, then, were they used for African languages? I have already suggested one reason: the traditional linguistic criteria did not seem to work for most African languages. But there was a second factor, which was equally important. This was the widespread belief among European scholars that European languages were "special," and that, though the principles of Indo-European comparative grammar might be valid in theory for the rest of the world's languages, in the real world the lack of ancient documents for almost all African languages, the (supposed) primitive nature of the African peoples, and so forth, all conspired to make genetic classification intractable, except for many low-level groups.

First and foremost, Greenberg reaffirmed the irrelevance of nonlinguistic and typological traits for the genetic classification of languages. All 16 of his groups were based on the *same* linguistic principles, and they were all claimed to be valid *genetic* groups. Physical and cultural attributes of speakers were for the first time ignored. Second, he demonstrated that traditional comparative linguistics may be used successfully in any part of the world, regardless of the technological level of the people or the literary history of their languages. Greenberg's reclassification of African languages had three important results:

1. The Hamitic group was eliminated. Greenberg showed that each of the three original members of Hamitic (Ancient Egyptian, Berber, Cushitic) constitutes an independent branch of Hamito-Semitic, and that the Chadic family (including Hausa) constitutes a fifth branch. Since there was no valid Hamitic group, and since the term Hamitic had racial (and racist) connotations, Greenberg proposed that the family name Hamito-Semitic be replaced by Afro-Asiatic, the only language family spoken in both Africa and Asia (see List 3.6).

2. The other languages that had been added to Hamitic by Lepsius and Meinhof were shown to belong to various groups: (a) Fulani was included in the West Atlantic family of Niger-Congo, as several French scholars had already suggested; (b) Nama was placed in the Khoisan group; (c) the so-called Nilo-Hamitic languages (e.g. Maasai, Nandi, Bari) formed one branch of the Nilotic family, which itself was one of seven branches of Greenberg's Eastern Sudanic group.

3. Greenberg added the Adamawa and Ubangian families to Westermann's West Sudanic phylum and renamed it Niger-Congo. Bantu was shown to be a subgroup of a subgroup of Niger-Congo, as in List 3.7.

List 3.6. The Afro-Asiatic Family (Greenberg 1950)

AFRO-ASIATIC (formerly Hamito-Semitic):
I †Ancient Egyptian
II SEMITIC
III BERBER
IV CHADIC
V CUSHITIC

List 3.7. The Niger-Congo Family (Greenberg 1954)

NIGER-CONGO (formerly West Sudanic):
I WEST ATLANTIC
II MANDE
III GUR (= VOLTAIC)
IV KWA
V IJO
VI ADAMAWA-UBANGIAN
VII BENUE-CONGO:
  A BANTU
  . . .

Greenberg did not deny the possibility of further consolidation of the 16 groups in List 3.5 as more and better information became available, and in fact suggested that similarities between Niger-Congo and Kordofanian, and between Mimi and Maban, might ultimately lead to such larger groupings. In 1954 he published an update to his classification in which the 16 original groups were reduced to 12 by the addition of Mimi to the Maban group and the grouping of Berta, Kunama, Eastern Sudanic, and Central Sudanic in a higher-level node, which he called Macro-Sudanic (see List 3.8).

In 1963 Greenberg published the definitive version of his classification, in which all African languages were shown to belong to one of four phyla. The major differences between this work and his previous classification were (1) the grouping of Kordofanian with Niger-Congo to form a family called Niger-Kordofanian, and (2) the grouping of all non-Khoisan, non-Afro-Asiatic, non-Niger-Kordofanian languages (i.e. branches 5–16 in List 3.5) in a fourth phylum, for which he proposed the name Nilo-Saharan. This highly diversified family corresponds very roughly with what had been known as the East Sudanic languages in the earlier literature. The

List 3.8. The Macro-Sudanic Family (Greenberg 1954)

MACRO-SUDANIC:
I Berta
II CENTRAL SUDANIC
III EASTERN SUDANIC-KUNAMA:
  A Kunama
  B EASTERN SUDANIC

Macro-Sudanic family, which Greenberg renamed Chari-Nile, was considered to be one of six primary branches of Nilo-Saharan.

Greenberg's 1963 classification has formed the basis of all subsequent work on African classification. By eliminating the irrelevant nongenetic criteria that had vitiated all previous classifications, Greenberg demonstrated that the principles of genetic classification established in the nineteenth century for European languages were equally valid for African languages. It was, one might say, a demonstration of linguistic uniformitarianism that put African linguistic classification back on track after a century of relative stagnation, and in some instances even regression (e.g. the ill-conceived Hamitic group). Greenberg's 1963 classification is shown in List 3.9.

List 3.9. African Language Phyla (Greenberg 1963)

AFRO-ASIATIC:
- I †Ancient Egyptian
- II SEMITIC
- III BERBER
- IV CHADIC
- V CUSHITIC:
  - A NORTHERN
  - B CENTRAL
  - C EASTERN
  - D WESTERN
  - E SOUTHERN

NIGER-KORDOFANIAN:
- I KORDOFANIAN
- II NIGER-CONGO:
  - A WEST ATLANTIC
  - B MANDE
  - C GUR (= VOLTAIC)
  - D KWA
  - E BENUE-CONGO
  - F ADAMAWA-UBANGIAN

NILO-SAHARAN:
- I Songhai
- II SAHARAN
- III MABAN
- IV Fur
- V CHARI-NILE:
  - A EASTERN SUDANIC
  - B CENTRAL SUDANIC
  - C Berta
  - D Kunama
- VI KOMAN

KHOISAN:
- I Hadza
- II Sandawe
- III SOUTHERN AFRICA:
  - A NORTHERN
  - B CENTRAL
  - C SOUTHERN

Balbi, Adrien. 1826. *Atlas ethnographique du globe ou classification des peuples anciens et modernes d'après leurs langues*, 2 vols. Paris.

Barreteau, Daniel, ed. 1978. *Inventaire des études linguistiques sur pays d'Afrique noire d'expression française et sur Madagascar*. Paris.

Cole, Desmond T. 1960. "African Linguistic Studies, 1943–60," *African Studies* 19: 219–29.

———. 1971. "The History of African Linguistics to 1945," in *CTIL* 7.

Dalby, David. 1970. "Reflections on the Classification of African Languages," *African Language Studies* (London) 11: 147–71.

Goodman, Morris F., David W. Crabb, and Oswin Köhler. 1974. "African Languages," in *EB* 1: 218–32.
Greenberg, Joseph H. 1949–50, 1954. "Studies in African Linguistic Classification," *Southwestern Journal of Anthropology*, 8 parts, 5 (1949), 6 (1950), 10 (1954).
———. 1955. *Studies in African Linguistic Classification*. Branford, Conn.
———. 1963. *The Languages of Africa*. Bloomington, Ind.
———. 1964. "The History and Present Status of African Linguistic Studies," in *Proceedings of the First International Congress of Africanists*. Evanston, Ill.
———. 1969. "African Languages," in *Collier's Encyclopedia* 1: 243–47.
Gregersen, Edgar A. 1977. *Language in Africa: An Introductory Survey*. New York.
Heine, Bernd. 1972. "Historical Linguistics and Lexicostatistics in Africa," *Journal of African Languages* 11: 7–20.
Heine, Bernd, Thilo C. Schadeberg, and Ekkehard Wolff, eds. 1981. *Die Sprachen Afrikas*. Hamburg.
Hoffman, Carl. 1974. "The Languages of Nigeria by Language Families," unpublished paper, Department of Linguistics, University of Ibadan.
Köhler, Oswin. 1975. "Geschichte und Probleme der Gliederung der Sprachen Afrikas," in H. Baumann, ed., *Die Völker Afrikas und ihre traditionellen Kulturen*. Wiesbaden.
Lepsius, Karl Richard. 1880. *Nubische Grammatik*. Berlin.
Lichtenstein, Heinrich. 1808. "Bemerkungen über die Sprachen der Sudafrikanischen wilden Volkerstämme," *Allgemeines Archiv für Ethnographie und Linguistik* 1: 259–331.
Meinhof, Carl. 1910. *Die moderne Sprachforschung in Afrika*. Berlin.
———. 1912. *Die Sprachen der Hamiten*. Hamburg.
Müller, Friedrich. 1867. *Grundriss der Sprachwissenschaft*. Vienna.
Postel, Guillaume. 1538. *De originibus seu de Hebraicae linguae et gentis antiquitate deque variarum linguarum affinitate liber*. Paris.
Prichard, James C. 1826. *Researches into the Physical History of Man*. London.
———. 1843. *The Natural History of Man*. London.
Welmers, William E. 1956. Review of *Studies in African Linguistic Classification*, by Joseph H. Greenberg, *Language* 32: 556–63.
———. 1973. *African Language Structures*. Berkeley, Calif.
Westermann, Diedrich. 1911. *Die Sudansprachen*. Hamburg.
———. 1927. "Die westlichen Sudansprachen und ihre Beziehungen zum Bantu," *Mitteilungen des Seminars für orientalische Sprachen* (Berlin) 29,3.
———. 1940. "Sprache und Erziehung," in H. Baumann, R. Thurnwald, and D. Westermann, eds., *Volkerkunde von Afrika*. Essen.

3.2 AFRO-ASIATIC

Roughly 240 Afro-Asiatic languages are spoken across the northern third of Africa, from Morocco and Mauritania on the Atlantic seaboard to Egypt, the Sudan, Ethiopia, and Somalia on the east coast. In addition, languages of the Semitic branch are spoken in many countries of the Near East (e.g. Saudi Arabia, Jordan, Israel, Lebanon, Syria, Iraq). This geographic distribution is shown in Map 3.1.

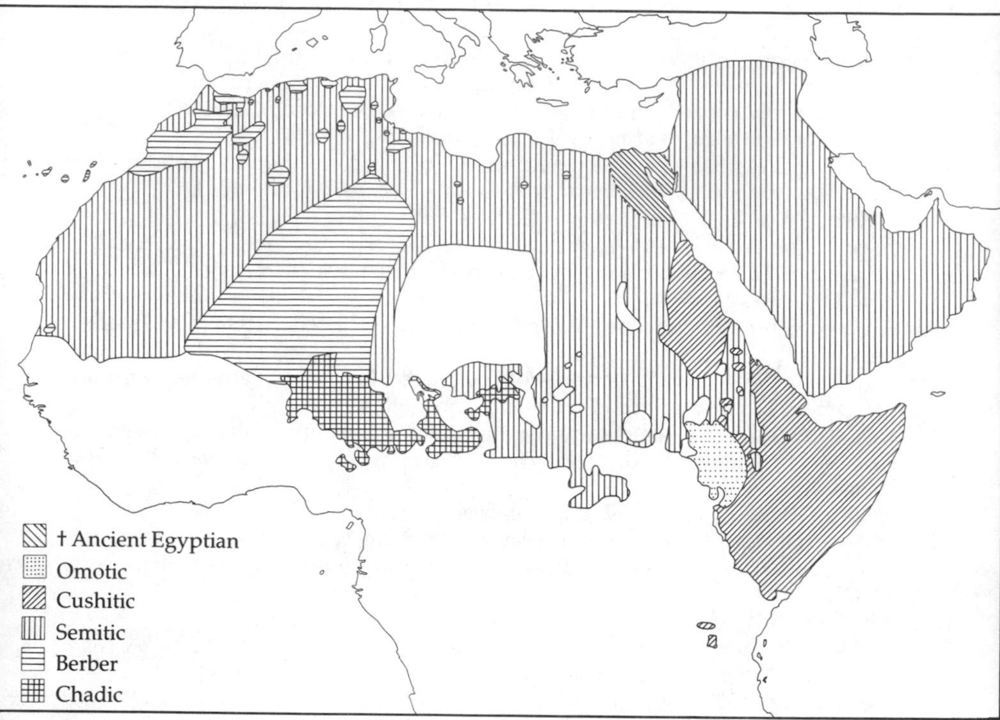

Map 3.1. The Afro-Asiatic family. Arabic is now spoken in the area where Old Egyptian once prevailed.

Afro-Asiatic languages are spoken by an estimated 175 million people, but only a few languages, with numerous speakers, account for most of the total. Arabic alone has some 100 million speakers. The next most important, in sheer numbers, are Hausa (with 12 million native speakers and an additional 13 million who speak it as a second language), Amharic (8 million), Oromo (7 million), Tigrinya (4 million), Shilha (3 million), Hebrew (3 million), Tamazight (2 million), Somali (2 million), Kabyle (1 million), and Riff (1 million).

The Afro-Asiatic phylum has six distinct branches. *Ancient Egyptian,* which was known in its last years as Coptic, became extinct in the seventeenth century. It was spoken in the region that is today Egypt. Most of the 11 million *Berber* speakers are found in Morocco and Algeria, with roughly five million each. Berber languages are also found in small numbers in Tunisia, Libya, Mauritania, and Senegal. The widely dispersed Tuareg are found in Niger, Mali, and Nigeria. Originally, Berber languages were spoken over most of northern Africa, but the Arab expansion from the Arabian

Peninsula, beginning in the seventh century, has largely submerged the original Berber tongues; most Berber speakers (especially men) are today bilingual in Arabic. The *Chadic* family, with about 125 languages and some 30 million speakers, is located primarily in Chad, Niger, Nigeria, Cameroon, and the Central African Republic. A single language, Hausa, accounts for about 80 percent of Chadic speakers. There are a little more than a million *Omotic* speakers, mostly in western Ethiopia and northern Kenya, speaking some three dozen languages. About 35 *Cushitic* languages, with 12 million speakers, are found in the Sudan, Ethiopia, Kenya, Somalia, and Tanzania. *Semitic* languages are spoken in much of northern Africa and the Near East. Altogether there are some 20 languages and 120 million speakers, though Arabic, with 100 million speakers, accounts for most of this total. Most Semitic languages are found in Ethiopia.

3.2.1 *History of Afro-Asiatic Classification*

For cultural and geographic reasons the Semitic family was the first branch of Afro-Asiatic (indeed the first African family) to be recognized as a genetic group of languages by European scholars. A Frenchman, Guillaume Postel, reported the affinity of Hebrew, Arabic, and Aramaic in 1538, a connection long known to Jewish and Islamic scholars. In 1702 Hiob Ludolf extended this Semitic nucleus to include the Ethiopic Semitic languages of East Africa, and finally in 1781 von Schlözer proposed the name Semitic.

During the first half of the nineteenth century, Ancient Egyptian and the Berber and Cushitic families became associated in a group called Hamitic, the defining characteristic of which was that the Hamitic languages all showed resemblances to the Semitic family. The Berber scholar Francis W. Newman sought to establish the relationship of Hausa to the Hamito-Semitic group in 1844, an affinity accepted by Max Müller in the 1850's and Karl Lepsius in the 1860's. Furthermore, it soon became apparent that Hausa was related to other languages in a family now known as Chadic. H. Barth established the affinity of Hausa and Logone in 1862, and in 1884 G. A. Krause added Musgu, Bade, Margi, and others to the group. Thus by the late nineteenth century a fairly coherent picture of the Hamito-Semitic family had emerged, as shown in List 3.10. Lepsius, as we saw in the preceding section, incorrectly included Nama in the Hamitic group, but most scholars did not follow him on this point.

Despite the fairly clear evidence of the Hamito-Semitic affinity of Hausa (and hence the whole Chadic family), many scholars continued to express reservations, or even outright denial, until the mid-twentieth century. Greenberg's 1950 classification effectively ended the century-old debate.

List 3.10. The Hamito-Semitic Family (late 19th century)

HAMITO-SEMITIC:
I SEMITIC
II HAMITIC:
  A †Ancient Egyptian
  B BERBER
  C CUSHITIC
  D CHADIC

Why should scholars have persisted for so long in excluding Chadic languages from Hamito-Semitic when the linguistic evidence makes it obvious that this is where they belong? The answer is that although Semitic, Cushitic, Berber, and Ancient Egyptian are (or were) spoken by people of a predominantly Caucasoid racial type, speakers of Chadic languages are Negroid, and for this reason alone they were segregated from Hamito-Semitic and incorrectly lumped with the other "Negro" languages.

Most nineteenth-century scholars (and a good many in the twentieth century as well) suffered from an ethnocentrism that often included outright racism. For scholars who fervently believed in the superiority of the "white race," white languages, and the like, the idea of a black branch (Chadic) in a white family (Hamito-Semitic) was disconcerting, if not repugnant. Despite the fact that a portion of the scholarly community had been continuously aware of the Hamito-Semitic affinity of Hausa and other Chadic languages from the mid-nineteenth century on, many scholars continued either to reject or to ignore this clear linguistic fact until the mid-twentieth century. Two events finally brought about the acceptance of Chadic as a member of Hamito-Semitic. The first was the work of Johannes Lukas in the 1930's, which established quite clearly the Chadic family (Lukas called it Chado-Hamitic); the second was Greenberg's 1950 classification, which summarized previous arguments and adduced additional evidence for the inclusion of Chadic in Hamito-Semitic.

In rejecting Hamitic as a valid genetic group, Greenberg was in effect rejecting what had become the favored subgrouping for the Hamito-Semitic family (see List 3.10 above). As with Chadic, so too with Hamitic were Greenberg's proposals decisive, though not original. As early as 1860 C. Lottner had proposed four primary branches for Hamito-Semitic (see List 3.11). Such a subgrouping was also advocated by several French linguists in the early twentieth century (Pierre Lacau, Maurice Delafosse, and Marcel Cohen), but it was Greenberg's rejection of Hamitic that finally tipped the scales in its favor (with the inclusion of Chadic as a fifth branch).

List 3.11. The Hamito-Semitic Family (Lottner 1860)

HAMITO-SEMITIC:
I †Ancient Egyptian
II SEMITIC
III BERBER
IV CUSHITIC

List 3.12. The Afro-Asiatic Family (Greenberg 1950)

AFRO-ASIATIC (formerly Hamito-Semitic):
I †Ancient Egyptian
II SEMITIC
III CUSHITIC
IV BERBER
V CHADIC

What was original in Greenberg's treatment of Hamito-Semitic, which he renamed Afro-Asiatic (a term first used by Delafosse in 1914), was the combination of including Chadic and breaking up the fallacious Hamitic group into three independent branches, thus producing the subgrouping in List 3.12. In proposing this subgrouping, Greenberg was not claiming that all five branches of Afro-Asiatic are in fact equidistant from each other, but rather was rectifying the error of grouping Ancient Egyptian, Cushitic, and Berber together in a family (Hamitic) for which there was no linguistic evidence. More recent proposals for Afro-Asiatic subgrouping will be discussed below.

3.2.2 *Present Status of Afro-Asiatic Classification*

Although Afro-Asiatic has proved to be the least controversial of Greenberg's four African phyla, a number of disputes and revisions have developed in the 30 years since it was first proposed. The most significant revision involves the Cushitic family. In contrast to Berber and Semitic, which are very close-knit families whose internal unity cannot be questioned, the constituent branches of Cushitic are quite disparate, and doubt has arisen that they constitute a valid genetic unit. In his 1950 classification Greenberg followed the Italian M. M. Moreno, who in the late 1930's had divided the Cushitic languages into four subgroups: Northern, Central, Eastern, and Western. In 1963 Greenberg added a fifth branch, Southern, which consists of several languages spoken to the south of the main body of Cushitic languages (see List 3.13).

In 1969 an American linguist, Harold C. Fleming, proposed that Western Cushitic is not a part of Cushitic at all, but rather constitutes a sixth primary branch of Afro-Asiatic, for which he suggested the name Omotic. His proposal gained fairly wide support in the 1970's. Recently the inclusion of the Northern branch (which is in fact a single language, Beja) in Cushitic has also been questioned by a number of scholars, including Fleming,

List 3.13. The Cushitic Family (Greenberg 1963)

CUSHITIC:
I NORTHERN
II CENTRAL
III EASTERN
IV WESTERN
V SOUTHERN

M. Lionel Bender, and Robert Hetzron. Hetzron (1980) has proposed a revised subgrouping for Cushitic (which for him excludes both Omotic and Beja) in which the Eastern group is divided into two distinct primary groups (Highland and Lowland), with Southern Cushitic being a subbranch of the latter. The Cushitic classification adopted in this volume follows suggestions from Christopher Ehret; Omotic is excluded, and Beja is treated as coordinate with the rest (i.e. Central, Eastern, Southern).

Within Afro-Asiatic there is near unanimity that Ancient Egyptian, Semitic, Chadic, and Berber are valid genetic nodes, although there is disagreement over whether Cushitic constitutes one, two, or three nodes (depending on the status one grants Omotic and Beja). No clear subgrouping has yet emerged for the five to seven groups that make up Afro-Asiatic, though several tentative suggestions have recently been made. List 3.14 illustrates a sample of current views, ranging from the essentially agnostic position of Hetzron to the more highly structured proposals of Ehret, Newman, Fleming, and Bender. It is apparent that there is as yet little consensus on the internal relationships of Afro-Asiatic.

Finally, let us turn briefly to the internal subgrouping of the various Afro-Asiatic subfamilies. Cushitic (discussed above) and Ancient Egyptian (a single language) require no further comment. Hetzron (1974) summarizes the history of Semitic classification, which was to a large extent established by German scholars in the late nineteenth and early twentieth centuries. The classification adopted in this volume follows Hetzron (1972, 1974) in dividing the Semitic family into two primary subgroups: (1) an extinct Eastern branch, which consisted of a single language, Akkadian, and (2) a Western branch with two subbranches, (a) Central and (b) South. The Central group has three components (Aramaic, Canaanite, Arabic), and the Southern group has two (South Arabian, Ethiopic) (see List 3.15).

Because the Chadic family contains a large number of poorly documented languages, its internal relationships have only recently begun to be clarified. Early classifications were organized along geographic, rather than *st 3.14. Proposed Subgroupings of the Afro-Asiatic Family*

Voegelin & Voegelin 1977

AFRO-ASIATIC:
- I †Ancient Egyptian
- II SEMITIC
- II BERBER
- V CHADIC
- V CUSHITIC
- VI OMOTIC

Ehret 1979

AFRO-ASIATIC:
- I OMOTIC
- II ERYTHRAIC:
  - A CHADIC
  - B CUSHITIC
  - C NORTH AFRO-ASIATIC:
    - 1 †Ancient Egyptian
    - 2 BERBER-SEMITIC:
      - a BERBER
      - b SEMITIC

Newman 1980[a]

AFRO-ASIATIC:
- I BERBER-CHADIC:
  - A BERBER
  - B CHADIC
- II EGYPTIAN-SEMITIC:
  - A †Ancient Egyptian
  - B SEMITIC
- III CUSHITIC:
  - A Beja
  - B CUSHITIC PROPER

Fleming 1981

AFRO-ASIATIC:
- I OMOTIC:
- II AFRO-ASIATIC PROPER:
  - A CUSHITIC
  - B BEJA-CHADIC-BERBER-ANCIENT EGYPTIAN:
    - 1 Beja
    - 2 CHADIC-BERBER:
      - a CHADIC
      - b BERBER
    - 3 †Ancient Egyptian
  - C SEMITIC

Greenberg 1981

AFRO-ASIATIC:
- I OMOTIC:
- II AFRO-ASIATIC PROPER:
  - A †Ancient Egyptian
  - B SEMITIC
  - C BERBER
  - D CHADIC
  - E CUSHITIC

Bender 1981

AFRO-ASIATIC:
- I NORTH:
  - A †Ancient Egyptian
  - B SEMITIC
  - C BERBER
- II WEST (= CHADIC)
- III Beja
- IV SOUTH:
  - A CUSHITIC
  - B OMOTIC

Hetzron 1982

AFRO-ASIATIC:
- I †Ancient Egyptian
- II SEMITIC
- III BERBER
- IV CHADIC
- V Beja
- VI CUSHITIC
- VII OMOTIC

---

[a]Newman excludes Omotic from Afro-Asiatic.

List 3.15. The Semitic Family (Hetzron 1972, 1974)

SEMITIC: I †EAST (Akkadian) II WEST: A CENTRAL: 1 Aramaic 2 ARABO-CANAANITE: a CANAANITE b ARABIC	[II WEST] B SOUTH: 1 South Arabian 2 ETHIOPIC: a NORTH b SOUTH

linguistic, lines. Greenberg (1963) divided the family into nine subgroups, without further specification of relationships. Newman and Ma (1966) distinguished two first-order groups, Biu-Mandara and Plateau-Sahel. Further research, however, led Newman (1977) to divide Plateau-Sahel into two first-order groups (i.e. East Chadic and West Chadic) coordinate with Biu-Mandara. In addition, Newman considers the small Masa group a provisional fourth branch, since it does not appear to share the defining characteristics of any of the other three groups. The Chadic classification presented in this volume, as shown in List 3.16, is based on Newman (1977).

No firm picture of the internal relationships of the Berber family has yet emerged. I have adopted the classification shown in List 3.17, which follows in the main Militarev (1984). Some scholars doubt that Guanche (formerly spoken in the Canary Islands) is in fact Berber; others (Hetzron 1982, Militarev 1984) consider it a primary subgroup of Berber opposed to all the rest of the family.

In the Omotic family there is a clear-cut cleavage between a small Southern branch and a larger Northern group. The Northern branch, in turn, consists of three subgroups: Dizoid, Mao, and Gonga-Gimojan. The classification shown in List 3.18 follows Fleming's work. The Mao group represents the most problematical area—some scholars are skeptical that the Mao group is really Omotic.

List 3.16. The Chadic Family (Newman 1977)

CHADIC:
I MASA
II EAST
III BIU-MANDARA
IV WEST

List 3.17. The Berber Family (Militarev 1984)

BERBER:	[III BERBER PROPER]
I †Guanche	C WESTERN: Zenaga
II †East Numidian (= Old Libyan)	D NORTHERN:
III BERBER PROPER:	1 ATLAS: Shilha, Tamazight
A EASTERN: Siwa, Awjila, Sokna	2 KABYLE: Kabyle
B TUAREG	3 ZENATI

List 3.18. The Omotic Family (Fleming 1976a,b, 1981)

OMOTIC:	
I SOUTH	[II NORTH]
II NORTH:	C GONGA-GIMOJAN:
A DIZOID	1 GONGA
B MAO	2 GIMOJAN

AFRO-ASIATIC

Bender, M. Lionel. 1981. Personal letter.

Cohen, David. 1968. "Les langues chamito-sémitiques," in André Martinet, ed., *Le langage*. Paris.

Cohen, Marcel. 1947. *Essai comparatif sur le vocabulaire et la phonétique du chamito-sémitique*. Paris.

Diakonoff, Igor M. 1965. *Semito-Hamitic Languages*. Moscow.

———. 1974. "Hamito-Semitic Languages," in *EB* 8: 589–98.

Ehret, Christopher. 1979. "Omotic and the Subgrouping of the Afroasiatic Language Family," in Robert L. Hess, ed., *Proceedings of the Fifth International Congress on Ethiopian Studies*. Chicago.

Fleming, Harold C. 1981. Personal letter.

Greenberg, Joseph H. 1949–50, 1954. "Studies in African Linguistic Classification," *Southwestern Journal of Anthropology* 8 parts, 5 (1949), 6 (1950), 10 (1954).

———. 1955. *Studies in African Linguistic Classification*. Branford, Conn.

———. 1963. *The Languages of Africa*. Bloomington, Ind.

———. 1981. Personal communication.

Hetzron, Robert. 1982. Personal letter.

Hodge, Carleton T. 1968. "Afroasiatic '67," *Language Sciences* 1: 13–21.

———. 1970. "Afroasiatic: An Overview," in *CTIL* 6.

———. 1976. "Lisramic (Afroasiatic): An Overview," in *NSLE*.

———, ed. 1971. *Afroasiatic: A Survey*. The Hague.

Lottner, C. 1860–61. "On Sister Families of Languages, Specially Those Connected with the Semitic Family," *Transactions of the Philological Society*, 2 parts, 1860, 20–27; 1861, 112–32.

Newman, Paul. 1980. *The Classification of Chadic Within Afroasiatic*. Leiden.

Postel, Guillaume. 1538. *De originibus seu de Hebraicae linguae et gentis antiquitate deque variarum linguarum affinitate liber*. Paris.
Voegelin, C. F., and F. M. Voegelin. 1977. *Classification and Index of the World's Languages*. New York.

BERBER

Applegate, Joseph R. 1971. "The Berber Languages," in *AS*.
Militarev, Alexander. 1984. Personal letter.
Newman, Francis W. 1844. *On the Structure of the Berber Language*. London.
Willms, Alfred. 1980. *Die dialektale Differenzierung des Berberischen*. Berlin.

CHADIC

Barreteau, Daniel. 1978. "Les langues tchadiques," in *IEL*.
Lukas, Johannes. 1936. "The Linguistic Situation in the Lake Chad Area of Central Africa," *Africa* 9: 332–49.
———. 1937. *Zentralsudanische Studien*. Hamburg.
Newman, Paul. 1977. *Chadic Classification and Reconstructions*. *Afroasiatic Linguistics* (Malibu, Calif.) 5,*1*.
Newman, Paul, and Roxana Ma. 1966. "Comparative Chadic: Phonology and Lexicon," *Journal of African Languages* (London) 5: 218–51.
Terry, Robert R. 1971. "Chadic," in *AS* and *CTIL* 7.

OMOTIC

Bender, M. Lionel. 1975. *Omotic: A New Afroasiatic Language Family*. Carbondale, Ill.
Fleming, Harold C. 1969. "The Classification of West Cushitic within Hamito-Semitic," in D. F. McCall, ed., *Eastern African History*. New York.
———. 1976a. "Cushitic and Omotic," in M. L. Bender et al., *Language in Ethiopia*. London.
———. 1976b. "Omotic Overview," in *NSLE*.

CUSHITIC

Black, Paul. 1974. "Lowland East Cushitic: Subgrouping and Reconstruction," Ph.D. dissertation, Yale University.
Ehret, Christopher. 1976. "Cushitic Prehistory," in *NSLE*.
———. 1980. *The Historical Reconstruction of Southern Cushitic Phonology and Vocabulary*. Berlin.
———. 1982. Personal letter.
Heine, Bernd, Franz Rottland, and Rainer Vossen. 1979. "Proto-Baz: Some Aspects of Early Nilotic-Cushitic Contacts," *Sprache und Geschichte in Afrika* 1: 75–91.
Hetzron, Robert. 1980. "The Limits of Cushitic," *Sprache und Geschichte in Afrika* 2: 7–126.
Moreno, M. M. 1940. *Manuale di Sidamo*. Rome.
Palmer, F. R. 1971. "Cushitic," in *AS*.
Sasse, Hans-Jürgen. 1979. "The Consonant Phonemes of Proto-East-Cushitic (PEC): A First Approximation," *Afroasiatic Linguistics* (Malibu, Calif.) 7: 1–67.
Tucker, A. N. 1967. "Fringe Cushitic," *Bulletin of the School of Oriental and African Studies* 30: 656–80.
Zaborski, Andrzej. 1976. "Cushitic Overview," in *NSLE*.

SEMITIC

Fleisch, Henri. 1947. *Introduction à l'étude des langues sémitiques*. Paris.
Goldenberg, Gideon. 1977. "The Semitic Languages of Ethiopia and their Classification," *Bulletin of the School of Oriental and African Studies* 40: 461–507.
Gray, Louis H. 1934. *Introduction to Semitic Comparative Linguistics*. New York.
Hetzron, Robert. 1972. *Ethiopian Semitic: Studies in Classification*. Manchester, Eng.
———. 1974. "La division des langues sémitiques," in André Caquot and David Cohen, eds., *Actes du premier congrès international de linguistique sémitique et chamito-sémitique*. The Hague.
Ludolf, Hiob. 1702. "Dissertatio de harmonia linguae aethiopicae cum ceteris orientalibus," in *Grammatica Aethiopica*. Frankfurt.
Moscati, Sabatino, et al. 1964. *An Introduction to the Comparative Grammar of the Semitic Languages*. Wiesbaden.
von Schlözer, Ludwig. 1781. *Repertoire für Biblische und Morgenländische Literatur* 8.
Ullendorff, Edward. 1971. "Comparative Semitic," in *AS*.
Wechter, Pinchos. 1941. "Ibn Barun's Contribution to Comparative Hebrew Philology," *Journal of the American Oriental Society* 61: 172–87.

3.3 NIGER-KORDOFANIAN

The vast Niger-Kordofanian phylum covers most of the southern two-thirds of Africa, as seen in Map 3.2. The small *Kordofanian* group, with some 30 languages and 200,000 speakers, is one of two primary branches. Kordofanian languages are spoken in the Sudan, where they are isolated from the rest of the Niger-Kordofanian phylum by Afro-Asiatic and Nilo-Saharan languages. The other primary branch, *Niger Congo*, contains more than 1,000 languages and has some 180 million speakers.

The *Bantu* subgroup of Niger-Congo covers most of the southern half of Africa and itself accounts for close to 500 languages and probably more than 100 million speakers. Bantu languages are found in all African countries that lie south of a line running from southeastern Nigeria to southern Kenya. Other important Niger-Congo subfamilies (e.g. *West Atlantic, Mande, Gur* [= Voltaic]) are located in West Africa in a belt running from Senegal to Cameroon. The *Adamawa-Ubangian* subfamily, however, lies north of the Bantu family in a belt running from eastern Nigeria into the Sudan. The numerically strongest Niger-Congo languages (with millions of speakers in parentheses) are Mandinka (3), Bambara (1.5), Mende (1), Dyula (1), Fula (= Fulani, 8), Wolof (2), More (= Mossi, 2), Ijo (1), Akan (2), Ewe (1), Yoruba (8), Igbo (6), Efik (2), Tiv (1), and the Bantu languages Losengo, Kikuyu, Kamba, Sukuma, Swahili, Sango, Kongo, Luganda, Luyia, Rwanda, Rundi, Luba, Bemba, Nyanja, Makua, South Mbundu, Shona, Tswana, Sotho, Xhosa, Zulu, Tsonga, and Ronga, each of which has more than a million speakers. Swahili is used as a *lingua franca* along the east coast of Africa by upwards of 20 million people.

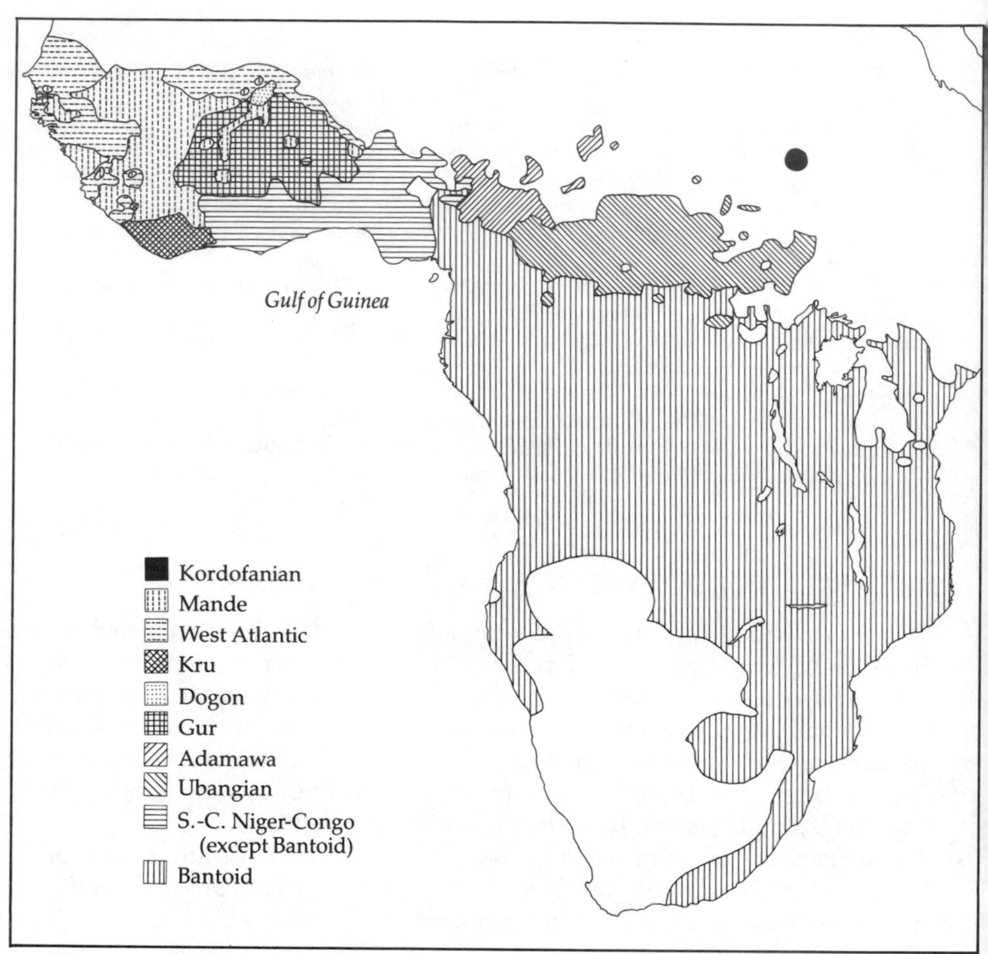

Map 3.2. The Niger-Kordofanian family

3.3.1 *History of Niger-Kordofanian Classification*

As we saw in section 3.1, the first part of the Niger-Kordofanian phylum to be recognized was the widespread and closely related Bantu family, whose unity was already apparent in the eighteenth century. During the second half of the nineteenth century, a number of different language families were established in West Africa. In 1854 a German missionary, Sigismund W. Koelle, published what is now recognized as a landmark in African linguistics: the *Polyglotta Africana*. This work contained comparative wordlists from 156 African languages, with all entries written in a standard phonetic alphabet developed by Lepsius. Koelle grouped the languages, on the basis of perceived similarities, into 11 groups, with 40 languages left unclassified. Of the six branches making up Greenberg's (1963a) Niger-Congo family (see List 3.19), all but Adamawa-Ubangian were foreshadowed in the *Polyglotta*.

List 3.19. The Niger-Congo Family (Greenberg 1963a)

NIGER-CONGO:

I WEST ATLANTIC
II MANDE
III GUR (= VOLTAIC)
IV KWA
V BENUE-CONGO
VI ADAMAWA-UBANGIAN

Koelle's first group was West Atlantic (named by him). His second group contained Mande languages, though the name Mande was first applied to the group in 1867 by H. Steinthal. Koelle's third, fifth, and sixth groups contained languages belonging to the Kwa family (Kru, Ewe, Yoruba, Igbo, Edo, Nupe); the name Kwa was coined by G. A. Krause in 1885. The fourth group contained Gur (also known as Voltaic) languages. The term Gur was proposed for the group in 1885 by G. A. Krause; Voltaic was suggested by Delafosse in 1911. Both names are still widely used. Koelle's groups 8–11, which he distinguished from the other groups as "South African" languages, contained various components of Benue-Congo, including Bantu. The name Benue-Congo was proposed by Greenberg in 1963 as an extension of Westermann's Benue-Cross group, from which the Bantu family had been excluded. The only Niger-Congo branch that was not distinguished in Koelle's work is the Adamawa-Ubangian family. Delafosse recognized and named the Ubangian family in 1924, but the Adamawa group went unnoticed until Greenberg (1950) joined it with the Ubangian family.

Striking similarities among the various West African families, and between these families and Bantu, were also noticed by numerous scholars during the last half of the nineteenth century. Bishop O. E. Vidal had recognized the affinity of certain languages of Sierra Leone with the Bantu family in 1852. A decade later Wilhelm Bleek asserted that a single family covered most of Southern and West Africa. Other scholars arrived independently at the same conclusion. It is thus clear that a rough outline of the Niger-Congo family had already emerged in the nineteenth century.

Unfortunately, the first half of the twentieth century witnessed regression, rather than progress, in untangling Niger-Congo relationships. In the work of Meinhof, Malcolm Guthrie, and others, the affinity of Bantu and West African languages is discounted, with similarities being attributed to loans from one language to another. Bantu is regarded as a separate and distinct family. Although Westermann was reluctant to commit himself to any precise declaration about the relationship between Bantu and West African languages, it seems likely that he conceived the relationship as one of coordinate branches. When, in 1950, Greenberg proposed that Bantu was genetically a branch of a branch (i.e. Benue-Congo) of Niger-Congo, he was in fact recommending a return to views that had been prevalent a century earlier. Greenberg's proposals were met with hostility from some Bantuists, who resented having their formerly independent family accorded a taxonomically less significant position in the Niger-Congo family. The evidence in favor of Greenberg's classification of Bantu was so overwhelming, however, that it quickly gained general acceptance.

List 3.20. The West Sudanic Family (Westermann 1927)

WEST SUDANIC:
I KWA
II BENUE-CROSS
III TOGO-REMNANT
IV GUR (= VOLTAIC) (including Songhai)
V WEST ATLANTIC (excluding Fula)
VI MANDE

Although Westermann had failed to grasp the nature of the relationship between Bantu and the West African languages he called West Sudanic, he nonetheless had made considerable progress in delineating the subgroups within West Sudanic, as his 1927 classification, shown in List 3.20, demonstrates. Greenberg's (1963a) revision of this classification entailed relatively few changes: (1) Bantu was included in Benue-Cross, which was accordingly renamed Benue-Congo; (2) the Togo-Remnant group was added to Kwa; (3) Songhai was removed from Gur (and Niger-Kordofanian); (4) Fula was added to West Atlantic; and (5) Adamawa-Ubangian was proposed as an additional primary branch.

In 1963 Greenberg joined the large Niger-Congo family with the small Kordofanian group to form Niger-Kordofanian, the possibility of which he had already foreseen in 1954.

3.3.2 *Present Status of Niger-Kordofanian Classification*

During the past two decades classificatory work on Niger-Kordofanian has concentrated almost entirely on the subgrouping of the family. The only group of languages whose membership in Niger-Kordofanian has been questioned is the Kadugli branch of Kordofanian. Thilo C. Schadeberg, who has worked extensively on Kordofanian languages, concludes "that it is presently not possible to assume a genetic relationship between Kadugli and (Niger-)Kordofanian" (Schadeberg 1981a: 304) and goes on to suggest that membership in Nilo-Saharan is a distinct possibility. (In personal correspondence both Morris Goodman and Lionel Bender have pointed out similarities between Kadugli and languages belonging to Nilo-Saharan.) Greenberg (1963a: 149) already recognized that the Kadugli group "shows considerable divergence from the remainder" of the Kordofanian languages.

List 3.21. The Kordofanian Family (Greenberg 1963a)

KORDOFANIAN:
I KADUGLI
II KORDOFANIAN PROPER:
A KATLA
B HEIBAN
C TALODI
D RASHAD

The classification adopted in this volume, shown in List 3.21, retains Kadugli as a branch of Kordofanian, but considers it coordinate with the other four branches. The five subfamilies that make up Kordofanian are all valid genetic nodes; so too is Kordofanian Proper. Whether the higher-level node Kordofanian is itself correct depends on whether or not Kadugli is directly related to the other four groups. It is now widely accepted that the Kordofanian languages are distantly related to the Niger-Congo family.

The subgrouping of Niger-Congo, which contains roughly 1,000 languages, is exceedingly difficult. Greenberg (1963a) laid the foundation for future research by dividing Niger-Congo into six primary groups (see List 3.19, above). Furthermore, he recognized that these six branches are not equidistant: "Kwa and Benue-Congo are particularly close to each other and in fact legitimate doubts arise concerning the validity of the division between them. On the other hand West Atlantic seems more remotely related to the other group and Mande the most distant of all" (Greenberg 1963a: 39).

William Welmers had suggested as early as 1956 that the Mande family was the most divergent group; work by Welmers, Kay Williamson, and others has confirmed Greenberg's suspicion that Kwa and Benue-Congo are in fact not distinct subgroups. Greenberg (1963a: 39) also considered the inclusion of Kru and Ijo in Kwa to be "tentative," and several French scholars (e.g. Calame-Griaule 1978: 66) have questioned the Gur affiliation of the Dogon language as posited by Greenberg and others. In an attempt to refine the subgrouping of Niger-Congo, Patrick R. Bennett and Jan P. Sterk (1977) have proposed a reclassification of Niger-Congo that reflects the modifications suggested above (see List 3.22). The languages traditionally assigned to Kwa and Benue-Congo now constitute the node South Central Niger-Congo, with a single exception: the Kru group, tentatively included by Greenberg in Kwa, is placed in North Central Niger-Congo.

List 3.22. The Niger-Kordofanian Family (Bennett & Sterk 1977)

NIGER-KORDOFANIAN:
- I KORDOFANIAN
- II MANDE
- III NIGER-CONGO:
  - A WEST ATLANTIC
  - B CENTRAL NIGER-CONGO:
    - 1 NORTH:
      - a KRU
      - b GUR (= VOLTAIC)
      - c ADAMAWA-UBANGIAN
    - 2 SOUTH:
      - a WESTERN
      - b IJO
      - c EASTERN:
        - i CENTRAL NIGER
        - ii YORUBOID
        - iii EDO
        - iv LOWER NIGER
        - v JUKUNOID
        - vi DELTA-CROSS
        - vii EFIKOID
        - viii EASTERN CROSS
        - ix BENUE-ZAMBESI

The Niger-Kordofanian classification adopted in this volume follows Bennett and Sterk's proposed subgrouping with a few exceptions: (1) Mande is considered closer to Niger-Congo than Kordofanian; (2) Dogon is treated as a fourth branch of North Central Niger-Congo; and (3) within South Central Niger-Congo, (a) the Western branch is divided into four subbranches rather than two, and (b) their Bantoid subgrouping has been replaced by one following Greenberg's (1974) Bane-Bantu dichotomy.

The internal subgrouping of the various families that constitute the

Niger-Congo phylum presents a host of problems, only the most important of which can be touched upon here. Despite its genetic distance from the rest of Niger-Congo, the Mande group is internally quite homogeneous and forms a well-defined genetic node. Work by Welmers has established two primary branches, each consisting of two subbranches. There is, in addition, a single language, Bobo-Fing, that appears to lie outside either primary branch (see List 3.23).

List 3.23. The Mande Family (Welmers 1971)

MANDE:
- I Bobo-Fing
- II NORTHERN-WESTERN:
  - A NORTHERN
  - B SOUTHWESTERN
- III SOUTHERN-EASTERN:
  - A SOUTHERN
  - B EASTERN

List 3.24. The West Atlantic Family (D. Sapir 1971)

WEST ATLANTIC:
- I Bijago
- II NORTHERN:
  - A SENEGAL
  - B CANGIN
  - C BAK
  - D EASTERN SENEGAL–GUINEA BISSAU
  - E MBULUNGISH-NALU
- III SOUTHERN:
  - A Sua
  - B Limba
  - C MEL

Like Mande, the West Atlantic family is subdivided into two groups and an isolated language, Bijago, which appears to form an independent primary branch. Unlike Mande, however, the West Atlantic group is extremely heterogeneous, and in fact the validity of a West Atlantic node has been questioned by Dalby (1965). Bennett and Sterk (1977: 248) summarize the internal diversity of West Atlantic as follows:

> West Atlantic . . . is a very diverse group, containing at least three major subdivisions. It is possible that some language groups traditionally assigned to West Atlantic are in fact coordinate branches of Niger-Congo. There is no apparent common innovation linking West Atlantic, and evaluation of its status as a well-defined subgroup of Niger-Congo must await further detailed investigation. At present, all that can be said is that the lexicostatistical distance between branches of West Atlantic is nearly as great as that between West Atlantic and the remainder of Niger-Congo.

The classification used in this volume follows the work of J. David Sapir (1971), as shown in List 3.24.

The Kru family is a close-knit group. Lafage (1978) subdivides it into two groups and three languages isolated from the main body of Kru speakers, as in List 3.25.

List 3.25. The Kru Family (Lafage 1978)

KRU:
I Aizi
II Kuwaa
III Seme
IV EASTERN
V WESTERN

List 3.26. The Gur Family (Manessy 1978)

GUR:
I Bariba
II KULANGO-LORHON
III SENUFO-TUSYA
IV CENTRAL:
  A KURUMFE-OTI-VOLTA
  B DOGHOSE-GURUNSI

With Gur (= Voltaic) we are again dealing with a diverse family. As I noted above, the assignment of Dogon to Gur by Westermann, Greenberg, and others is still a subject of dispute. Within Gur there are two fairly well-defined groups (Central and Senufo), as well as a few smaller groups or isolated languages. I have in the main followed the subgrouping worked out by Gabriel Manessy (see List 3.26), especially with regard to the Central branch.

The Adamawa-Ubangian branch of Niger-Congo is both diverse and poorly documented; the internal subgrouping is consequently less firmly established than for other groups. The fundamental dichotomy into two branches, Adamawa and Ubangian, is beyond doubt, since the gulf between the two is deep. Within each branch the relationships are less clear; Adamawa shows greater internal diversity than Ubangian. For Adamawa I have followed Boyd (1978), for Ubangian Barreteau and Moñino (1978) and Bouquiaux and Thomas (1980), as shown in List 3.27.

List 3.27. The Adamawa-Ubangian Family (Boyd 1978, Barreteau & Moñino 1978, Bouquiaux & Thomas 1980)

ADAMAWA-UBANGIAN:
I ADAMAWA:
  A Kam
  B Longuda
  C Fali
  D Nimbari
  E Kim
  F WAJA
  G CHAMBA
  H DAKA
  I DURU
  J MUMUYE-YENDANG
[I ADAMAWA]
  K MBUM-MUNDANG
  L YUNGUR
  M BAMBUKA
  N BUA
II UBANGIAN:
  A GBAYA-GBANZILI
  B BANDA
  C ZANDE
  D AMADI
  E MONDUNGA

List 3.28. The South Central Niger-Congo Family (Bennett & Sterk 1977, Greenberg 1974, and others)

SOUTH CENTRAL NIGER-CONGO:

- I IJO-DEFAKA
- II WESTERN:
  - A VOLTA-COMOE
  - B CENTRAL TOGO
  - C GÃ-ADANGME
  - D TOGO
- III EASTERN:
  - A CENTRAL NIGER
  - B YORUBA–NORTHERN AKOKO
  - C EDO
  - D LOWER NIGER
  - E JUKUNOID
  - F DELTA CROSS
  - G LOWER CROSS
  - H UPPER CROSS
  - I BENUE-ZAMBESI:
    - 1 CARA
    - 2 NYIMA:
      - a PLATEAU
      - b WEL:
        - i BENDI
        - ii BANTOID:
          - α NON-BANTU:
            - I MAMBILA-VUTE
            - II TIV-BATU
          - β BROAD BANTU:
            - I BANE:
              - A JARAWAN-EKOID
              - B MAMFE
              - C GRASSFIELDS
              - D MENCHUM
              - E BEBOID
              - F TIKAR
            - II NARROW BANTU:
              - A NORTHWEST
              - B CENTRAL

The remainder of the Niger-Congo family consists of those languages that have traditionally been assigned to either the Kwa or the Benue-Congo families. The difficulties inherent in subgrouping a large number (c. 750) of similar languages have already been underscored by the untenability of even the Kwa-Benue-Congo distinction. Bennett and Sterk (1977) have proposed the name South Central Niger-Congo for the group containing Kwa and Benue-Congo languages. Within this group it is possible to identify numerous low-level genetic groups (e.g. Volta-Comoe, Edo, Jukunoid, Plateau, Grassfields, Bantu), but establishing the correct subgrouping for these many groups is by its very nature an extremely delicate problem, especially within the very closely related Bantoid group.

For the overall structure of South Central Niger-Congo (see List 3.28), I have generally followed Bennett and Sterk (1977), with the exception that the Bantoid subgrouping is organized according to Greenberg (1974). Most of the subgroups within South Central Niger-Congo are based on Hoffman (1974), with modifications suggested by Kay Williamson. Subgroups within Bantoid follow a variety of sources (including Hyman 1980a, Stallcup 1980a,b, Hombert 1980, Leroy 1980); the Bantu family is based on Bastin (1978). In general the South Central Niger-Congo languages become more and more similar as one progresses down the tree until, with the Narrow Bantu family, we have a group of languages so closely related that they are sometimes described (a bit facetiously) as 500 dialects of a single language.

NIGER-KORDOFANIAN

Bennett, Patrick R., and Jan P. Sterk. 1977. "South Central Niger-Congo: A Reclassification," *Studies in African Linguistics* (UCLA) 8: 241–73.
Greenberg, Joseph H. 1963a. *The Languages of Africa*. Bloomington, Ind.

KORDOFANIAN

Schadeberg, Thilo C. 1981a. "The Classification of the Kadugli Language Group," in *NS*.
———. 1981b. *A Survey of Kordofanian*, 4 vols. Hamburg. In progress. Vols. 1 (The Heiban Group) and 2 (The Talodi Group) have appeared.

NIGER-CONGO

Crabb, David W. 1974. "Niger-Congo Languages," in *EB* 1: 221–25.
Greenberg, Joseph H. 1949–50, 1954. "Studies in African Linguistic Classification," *Southwestern Journal of Anthropology*, 8 parts, 5 (1949), 6 (1950), 10 (1954).
———. 1955. *Studies in African Linguistic Classification*. Branford, Conn.
Hoffman, Carl. 1974. "The Languages of Nigeria by Language Families," unpublished paper, Department of Linguistics, University of Ibadan.
Koelle, Sigismund W. 1854. *Polyglotta Africana*. London.
Westermann, Diedrich. 1911. *Die Sudansprachen*. Hamburg.

———. 1927. "Die westlichen Sudansprachen und ihre Beziehungen zum Bantu," *Mitteilungen des Seminars für orientalische Sprachen* (Berlin) 29,3.

———. 1935. "Nominalklassen in westafrikanischen Klassensprachen und in Bantusprachen," *Mitteilungen des Seminars für orientalische Sprachen* (Berlin) 38,*3*: 1–55.

MANDE

Houis, Maurice. 1963. "Rapport sur les langues du groupe mandé," in *Actes du second colloque international de linguistique négro-africaine*. Dakar.

Kastenholz, Raimund. 1979. "Essai de classification des dialectes mandé-kan," *Sprache und Geschichte in Afrika* 1: 205–23.

Platiel, Suzanne. 1978. "Les langues mandé," in *IEL*.

Welmers, William E. 1958. "The Mande Languages," *Georgetown University Monograph Series* 11: 9–24.

———. 1971. "Niger-Congo, Mande," in *CTIL* 7.

WEST ATLANTIC

Dalby, David. 1965. "The Mel Languages: A Reclassification of Southern 'West Atlantic,'" *African Language Studies* 6: 1–17.

Sapir, J. David. 1971. "West Atlantic: An Inventory of the Languages, Their Noun Class Systems, and Consonant Alternation," in *CTIL* 7.

Sauvageot, Serge. 1978. "Les langues ouest-atlantiques," in *IEL*.

Westermann, Diedrich. 1928. "Die westatlantische Gruppe der Sudansprachen," *Mitteilungen des Seminars für orientalische Sprachen* (Berlin) 31,*1*: 63–86.

GUR (VOLTAIC)

Bendor Samuel, John T. 1971. "Niger-Congo, Gur," in *CTIL* 7.

Calame Griaule, Geneviève. 1978. "Le dogon," in *IEL*.

Manessy, Gabriel. 1963. "Rapport sur les langues voltaïques," in *Actes du second colloque international de linguistique négro-africaine*. Dakar.

———. 1969. *Les langues gurunsi*. Paris.

———. 1978. "Les langues voltaïques," in *IEL*.

———. 1980. *Contribution à la classification généalogique des langues voltaïques: le proto-central*. Paris.

Prost, André. 1964. *Contribution à l'étude des langues voltaïques*. Dakar.

Swadesh, Mauricio, et al. 1966. "A Preliminary Glottochronology of Gur Languages," *The Journal of West African Languages* (Cambridge, Eng.) 3,*2*: 27–65.

KRU

Lafage, Philippe. 1978. "Les langues kru," in *IEL*.

Marchese, Lynell. 1979. *Atlas linguistique kru*. Abidjan.

Vogler, P. 1974. "Le problème linguistique kru: éléments de comparaison," *Journal de la Société des Africanistes* 44,2.

KWA

Greenberg, Joseph H. 1963b. "History and Status of the Kwa-Problem," in *Actes du second colloque international de linguistique négro-africaine*. Dakar.

Hérault, Georges. 1978. "Les langues kwa," in *IEL*.
Stewart, John M. 1971. "Niger-Congo, Kwa," in *CTIL* 7.

ADAMAWA

Boyd, Raymond. 1974. *Étude comparative dans le groupe adamawa*. Paris.
———. 1978. "Les langues adamawa," in *IEL*.
Samarin, William J. 1971. "Adamawa-Eastern," in *CTIL* 7.

UBANGIAN (= EASTERN)

Barreteau, Daniel, and Yves Moñino. 1978. "Les langues oubanguiennes," in *IEL*.
Bouquiaux, Luc, and Jacqueline M. C. Thomas. 1980. "Le peuplement oubanguien," in *EXB* 3.
Samarin, William J. 1971. "Adamawa-Eastern," in *CTIL* 7.

BENUE-CONGO

Guarisma, Gladys. 1978. "Les langues bantoïdes non bantoues," in *IEL*.
Shimizu, Kiyoshi. 1971. "Comparative Jukunoid: An Introductory Survey," Ph.D. dissertation, University of Ibadan.
Williamson, Kay. 1971. "The Benue-Congo Languages and Ijo," in *CTIL* 7.
———. 1973. *Benue-Congo Comparative Wordlist* 2. Ibadan.
Williamson, Kay, and Shimizu Kiyoshi. 1968. *Benue-Congo Comparative Wordlist* [1]. Ibadan.
Wolff, Hans. 1959. "Niger Delta Languages I: Classification," *AL* 1,*8*: 32–53.

BANTOID AND BANTU

Alexandre, Pierre. 1968. "Le bantu et ses limites," in André Martinet, ed., *Le langage*. Paris.
Bastin, Yvonne. 1978. "Les langues bantoues," in *IEL*.
Bouquiaux, Luc, ed. 1980. *L'expansion bantoue*, vols. 2 and 3. Paris.
Bryan, M. A. 1959. *The Bantu Languages of Africa*. London.
Coupez, A., E. Evrard, and J. Vansina. 1975. "Classification d'un échantillon de langues bantoues d'après la lexicostatistique," *Africana Linguistica* 6: 131–58.
Gerhardt, Ludwig. 1980. "An Attempt at a Lexicostatistic Classification of Some Bantu and Some Not-So-Bantu Languages," in *EXB* 2.
Greenberg, Joseph H. 1974. "Bantu and Its Closest Relatives," *Studies in African Linguistics* (UCLA), Supplement 5: 115–19.
Guthrie, Malcolm. 1948. "Classification of the Bantu Languages," in *Handbook of African Languages*. London.
———. 1953. "The Bantu Languages of Western Equatorial Africa," in *Handbook of African Languages*. London.
———. 1967–71. *Comparative Bantu*, 4 vols. Farnborough, Eng.
———. 1971. "The Western Bantu Languages," in *CTIL* 7.
Heine, Bernd. 1973. "Zur genetischen Gliederung der Bantu-Sprachen," *Afrika und Übersee* 56: 164–85.
———. 1980a. "Methods in Comparative Bantu Linguistics (The Problem of Bantu Linguistic Classification)," in *EXB* 2.
———. 1980b. "Some Recent Developments in the Classification of Bantoid," in *EXB* 2.

Henrici, A. 1973. "Numerical Classification of Bantu Languages," *African Language Studies* 16: 82–104.
Hombert, Jean-Marie. 1980. "Le groupe noun," in *EXB* 1.
Hyman, Larry M. 1980a. "Reflections on the Nasal Classes in Bantu," in Hyman, *Noun Classes*, cited below.
———., ed. 1980b. *Noun Classes in the Grassfields Bantu Borderland*. Southern California Occasional Papers in Linguistics 8.
Hyman, Larry M., and Jan Voorhoeve, eds. 1980. *L'expansion bantoue* vol. 1. Paris.
Johnston, Harry H. 1919–22. *A Comparative Study of the Bantu and Semi-Bantu Languages*, 2 vols. Oxford.
Kähler-Meyer, Emmi. 1971. "Niger-Congo, Eastern Bantu," in *CTIL* 7.
Leroy, Jacqueline. 1980. "The Ngemba Group," in *EXB* 1.
Leroy, Jacqueline, and Jan Voorhoeve. 1978. "Les langues bantoues des grassfields au Caméroun," in *IEL*.
Maddieson, Ian, and Kay Williamson. 1975. "Jarawan Bantu," *African Languages* 1: 125–63.
Meinhof, Carl. 1948. *Grundzüge einer vergleichenden Grammatik der Bantusprachen*. Hamburg.
Schadeberg, Thilo C. 1980. "Situation actuelle de la classification des langues bantoues (au sens étroit) du Caméroun," in *EXB* 2.
Stallcup, Kenneth. 1980a. "La géographie linguistique des Grassfields," in *EXB* 1.
———. 1980b. "The Momo Languages," in *EXB* 1.
———. 1980c. "The Guthrie Criteria and Batibo Moghamo: The Mistaken Identity of the Bantus Who Stayed Home," in *EXB* 2.

3.4 NILO-SAHARAN

Nilo-Saharan languages are spoken in the interior of Africa, from Mali in the west to Egypt, the Sudan, Ethiopia, Kenya, and Tanzania on the east coast. Their geographic distribution is shown in Map 3.3. They are often found in "islands," surrounded by either Afro-Asiatic or Niger-Congo languages. Altogether there are about 140 languages, with a total of perhaps 11 million speakers. Few of the languages have attracted much attention. Kanuri, Luo, and Nubian each have a million speakers, and Maasai and Songhai are somewhat well known from the ethnographic literature.

3.4.1 *History of Nilo-Saharan Classification*

The untangling of the relationships among the numerous and disparate languages of Central and East Africa, culminating in Greenberg's (1963) Nilo-Saharan hypothesis (see List 3.9, above), proceeded at a considerably slower pace than was the case with the other three African language phyla. There are several reasons why Nilo-Saharan was the last phylum to be recognized and why it remains the most controversial of Greenberg's four phyla. (1) European contact with speakers of Nilo-Saharan languages gen-

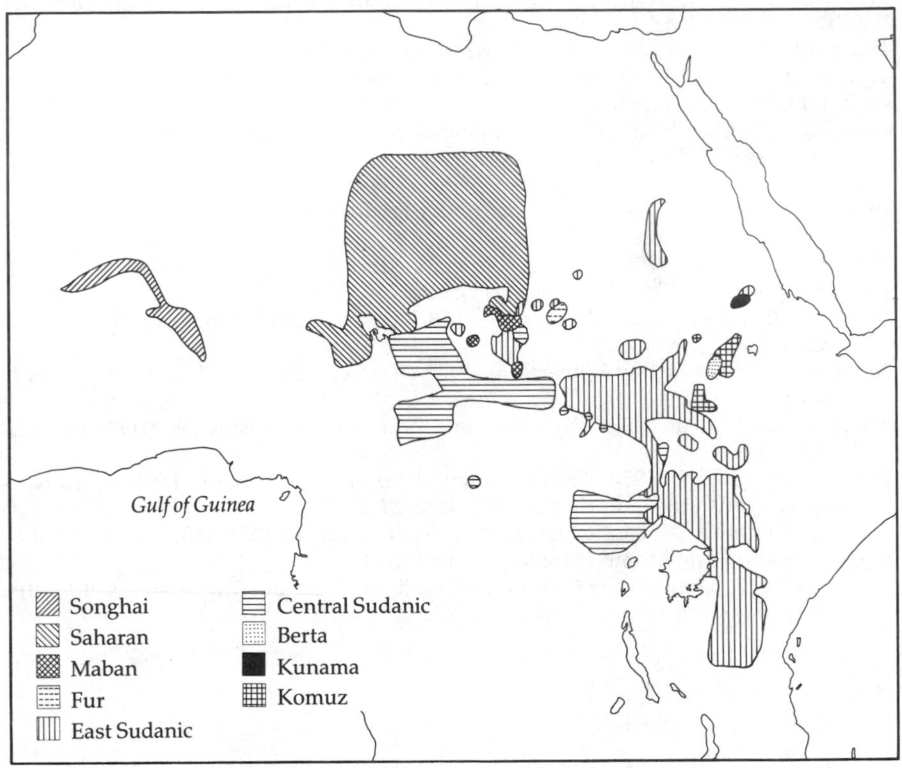

Map 3.3. The Nilo-Saharan family

erally took place at a later date than with speakers of Niger-Kordofanian, Afro-Asiatic, and Khoisan languages primarily because these three phyla are (or were) spoken along the African coast; Nilo-Saharan is restricted to more inaccessible areas of Central Africa. (2) A consequence of this relative inaccessibility is that Nilo-Saharan has always been a "literature-poor" phylum (i.e. there are fewer and poorer sources of information), like Khoisan, in stark contrast with the "literature-rich" Afro-Asiatic and Niger-Kordofanian phyla. (3) Nilo-Saharan contains fewer languages (c. 140) than either Afro-Asiatic (c. 200) or Niger-Kordofanian (c. 1,000). (4) Probably the most critical factor, however, is that the affinity of the various constituents of Nilo-Saharan is simply less obvious than in the case of the other three phyla. This internal heterogeneity was quite apparent in Greenberg's first classification, in 1950, which posited 12 independent families rather than a single phylum. (5) Of these 12 independent groups, four are single languages (Songhai, Fur, Kunama, Berta), and several others (Saharan, Maban,

Koman) contain only a few languages. Isolated languages, and small groups, are intrinsically more difficult to classify than large groups, for the simple reason that they contain fewer witnesses to their historical past.

During the nineteenth and early-twentieth centuries a number of low-level groups were recognized in Central and East Africa. Heinrich Barth noted the affinity of two Saharan languages in 1853; Lepsius identified Nilotic in 1880; Friedrich Müller perceived the Bongo-Bagirmi, Moru-Madi, and Mangbetu-Asua groups in 1889; Maurice Gaudefroy-Demombynes discovered the Maban group in 1907; and so forth. The isolated languages (Songhai, Fur, Berta, and Kunama) came to European attention during roughly the same period.

One often finds in the history of classification that a larger family is built around a smaller group of languages that serves as a kind of reference point, or nucleus, for the expanded family. The Semitic family served this purpose within Afro-Asiatic (see section 3.2) and the same was also true to some extent for Bantu within Niger-Kordofanian (see section 3.3). The subgrouping that results from combining families in this way is usually of dubious value, having more to do with the historical accretion of knowledge than with the genetic relationships of the languages. The demise of the Hamitic family, discussed in section 3.2, illustrates the point. For Nilo-Saharan, the Nilotic languages played this pivotal role.

In the early twentieth century two of the principal unresolved questions were the precise definition of the Nilotic group and the identification of possible relatives of the group, however defined. In 1902 Harry Johnston divided the Nilotic languages into two branches. Ten years later Meinhof asserted that these two groups, which he called Nilotic (e.g. Dinka, Nuer, Luo, Shilluk) and Nilo-Hamitic (e.g. Maasai, Bari, Nandi) were in fact *not* related, thus contradicting the opinion of such earlier scholars as Lepsius and Johnston. Pointing to the presence of gender in certain Nilo-Hamitic languages (e.g. Maasai), and its absence in Nilotic, Meinhof proposed that languages in the Nilo-Hamitic group were "mixed languages," the products of a Nilotic mother and a Hamitic father. Meinhof chose to overlook the numerous similarities in vocabulary between the two groups, preferring to rely on the typological feature of gender.

The fortunes of Nilo-Hamitic fared as poorly as those of Hamitic itself, and for much the same reason. Both groups were based on typological traits and a fallacious theory of language mixture. When Greenberg rejoined the two groups in 1950, he was in fact returning to a view widely held a half-century earlier. Subsequently, in 1955, Oswin Köhler showed that the group previously called Nilo-Hamitic comprised instead two distinct groups, both of which appear equally distant from the "Nilotic" group. He proposed calling these two branches Eastern and Southern Nilotic; the traditional "Nilotic" group was renamed Western Nilotic.

List 3.29. The Nilotic Family (Köhler 1955)

NILOTIC: I WESTERN: A LUO B DINKA-NUER II EASTERN: A BARI B LOTUXO-TESO	III SOUTHERN: A KALENJIN B TATO

Greenberg (1963: 128) accepted this tripartite division, with the qualification that "if anything, Eastern Nilotic . . . is closer to Western Nilotic . . . than it is to Southern Nilotic . . . and may once have formed a unity with it." The structure of the Nilotic family is shown in List 3.29.

Long before the Nilo-Hamitic controversy was resolved, similarities between Nilotic (in the broad sense) and certain other languages were recognized. In 1912 Westermann proposed a Niloto-Sudanic family linking three groups of what later became known as Central Sudanic with Nilotic. This Niloto-Sudanic family was in turn taken to be one component of a larger Eastern Sudanic phylum that also included Nubian, Kunama, and probably Berta. In 1920 G. W. Murray proposed affiliation between Nilotic and Nubian, Nera, Gaam, and Kunama. Carlo Conti Rossini (1926) also connected Kunama with various East Sudanic languages (in Greenberg's sense), and Westermann (1935) connected Murle with Nilotic. In 1940 A. N. Tucker presented evidence connecting five branches of Greenberg's Central Sudanic family, though Tucker himself refrained from drawing this obvious conclusion. The Central Sudanic and Eastern Sudanic families that Greenberg postulated in 1950 were thus groupings that had been foreshadowed, albeit sometimes ambiguously, in the work of earlier scholars.

At that time Greenberg did not attempt to link the various languages and language groups that would eventually constitute Nilo-Saharan, cautioning that "a hypothesis . . . of affiliation between Central Sudanic and Eastern Sudanic is as venturesome as the suggestion of a connection between Indo-European and Ural-Altaic." Four years later, however, he took the first step by proposing a Macro-Sudanic family made up of Central Sudanic, Eastern Sudanic, Kunama, and Berta (see List 3.8, above); in 1956 Greenberg changed the name Macro-Sudanic to Chari-Nile, which had been suggested by Welmers. Finally, in 1963, Greenberg offered evidence for an even more comprehensive family, which he named Nilo-Saharan, and of which Chari-Nile was one of six branches, the other five being two isolates (Songhai, Fur) and three small groups (Saharan, Maban, Koman) (see List 3.30).

List 3.30. The Nilo-Saharan Family (Greenberg 1963)

NILO-SAHARAN:	
I Songhai	V CHARI-NILE:
II SAHARAN	A EASTERN SUDANIC
III MABAN	B CENTRAL SUDANIC
IV Fur	C Berta
	D Kunama
	VI KOMAN

3.4.2 *Present Status of Nilo-Saharan Classification*

There have been several developments in Nilo-Saharan classification since Greenberg's (1963, 1971) pioneering work, the most important of which is the demise of the Chari-Nile node. Shafer (1959), Goodman (1970), and Bender (1976) all disputed Greenberg's claim that Central Sudanic, East Sudanic, Kunama, and Berta form a higher-level group (i.e. Chari-Nile). Greenberg accepts their arguments to the extent that he now considers Central Sudanic and East Sudanic independent branches of Nilo-Saharan, but he continues to believe that Kunama and Berta are genetically closest to the East Sudanic family.

Another recent development, mentioned in section 3.3, has been the suggestion by several scholars that the Kadugli group, which Greenberg (1963) considered distantly related to the Kordofanian languages, may in fact turn out to be a member of Nilo-Saharan.

Of all the languages Greenberg included in Nilo-Saharan, only the affinity of Songhai has elicited serious reservations. As a language clearly distant genetically from any other language (or group of languages), Songhai has had a controversial taxonomic history. Delafosse (1914) considered it closest to the Mande group, though most linguists of the early twentieth century treated it as an isolate with no known relatives. This was Greenberg's position in 1950, though three years later he suggested a possibility of affiliation with Niger-Congo. In 1963, however, he included it in the newly formed Nilo-Saharan phylum. Several scholars have recently revived Delafosse's Mande affiliation of Songhai (e.g. Mukarovsky 1966, Creissels 1981), thus calling into question its inclusion in Nilo-Saharan. Welmers (1973: 15) also stresses the relative isolation of Songhai from the rest of Nilo-Saharan: "Within Nilo-Saharan, the most basic subdivision appears to be between Songhai and all the other languages." Despite these misgivings, Greenberg continues to regard Songhai as firmly Nilo-Saharan.

The classification adopted in this volume follows Greenberg (1963, 1971),

List 3.31. The Nilo-Saharan Family (Greenberg 1971, Bender 1982)

NILO-SAHARAN:

- I Songhai
- II SAHARAN
- III MABAN
- IV FUR
- V EAST SUDANIC
  - A EASTERN:
    - 1 NUBIAN
    - 2 SURMA
    - 3 Nera
    - 4 EASTERN JEBEL
  - B WESTERN:
    - 1 NYIMANG
    - 2 TEMEIN
    - 3 TAMA
    - 4 DAJU
  - C NILOTIC:
    - 1 WESTERN
    - 2 EASTERN
    - 3 SOUTHERN
  - D KULIAK
- VI CENTRAL SUDANIC:
  - A WEST CENTRAL:
    - 1 BONGO-BAGIRMI
    - 2 Kresh
  - B EAST CENTRAL:
    - 1 MORU-MADI
    - 2 MANGBETU-ASUA
    - 3 MANGBUTU-EFE
    - 4 Balendru
- VII Berta
- VIII Kunama
- IX KOMUZ:
  - A Gumuz
  - B KOMAN

as modified by Bender (1976, 1982); see List 3.31. Bender's modifications include (1) the elimination of the Chari-Nile node in favor of four independent primary branches (i.e. Central Sudanic, East Sudanic, Kunama, and Berta); (2) a revision in the subgrouping of East Sudanic that unites Nubian, Surma, Nera, and Eastern Jebel in an Eastern branch, and Nyimang, Temein, Tama, and Daju in a Western branch; (3) moving Kibet from the Tama group to the Maban group; (4) grouping Biltine (one of several languages that have been called Mimi in earlier literature) with Fur; (5) calling the Koman group Komuz to reflect its bipartite nature (= Gumuz + Koman); and (6) renaming several branches of East Sudanic (i.e. Didinga-Murle → Surma, Barea → Nera, Tabi → Eastern Jebel, Teuso → Kuliak). The classification within the constituent groups of Nilo-Saharan follows the sources cited in the bibliography with a few exceptions. The Nubian and Daju groups are based on unpublished work by Robin Thelwall. It has been suggested that Central Sudanic has two primary branches, one uniting Bongo-Bagirmi and Kresh, the other containing the rest. This was the position of Delafosse (1924), followed by Tucker and Bryan (1956); Greenberg (1971: 434) mentions such a subgrouping as a possibility, but does not commit himself to it.

On the basis of a recent analysis of Nilo-Saharan pronoun systems, Bender (1983a) suggests that the nine primary branches of Nilo-Saharan in List 3.31 should be reduced to six by joining (1) Kunama and Berta and (2) Maban, Fur, East Sudanic, and Central Sudanic as higher-level units within Nilo-Saharan. Furthermore, Bender considers East Sudanic and Central Sudanic the nucleus of the last mentioned group.

Barth, Heinrich. 1854. "Letter to K. R. Lepsius," *Zeitschrift der Gesellschaft für Erkunde zu Berlin* 2: 372–74, 384–87.
Bender, M. Lionel. 1976. "Nilo-Saharan Overview," in *NSLE*.
———. 1981. "Some Nilo-Saharan Isoglosses," in *NS*.
———. 1982. Personal letter.
———. 1983a. "Pronoun Patterns in Nilo-Saharan," paper presented at the Second Nilo-Saharan Linguistics Colloquium.
———. 1983b. "The Eastern Jebel Languages," in Jonathan Kaye, ed., *Current Approaches to African Linguistics*. Dordrecht.
Bryan, M. A. 1948. *Distribution of the Nilotic and Nilo-Hamitic Languages of Africa*. London.
Caprile, Jean-Pierre. 1978a. "La famille nilo-saharienne," in *IEL*.
———. 1978b. "Les langues maba," in *IEL*.
———. 1978c. "Le groupe des langues du Soudan central," in *IEL*.
———. 1978d. "Les langues du Soudan oriental," in *IEL*.
Conti Rossini, Carlo. 1926. *Lingue nilotiche*. Rome.
Creissels, Denis. 1981. "De la possibilité de rapprochements entre le songhay et les langues niger-congo (en particulier mandé)," in *NS*.
Delafosse, Maurice. 1914. *Esquisse générale des langues de l'Afrique et plus particulièrement de l'Afrique française*. Paris.
———. 1924. "Les langues du Soudan et de la Guinée," in A. Meillet and M. Cohen, eds., *Les langues du monde*. Paris.
Ehret, Christopher. 1983. "Nilotic and the Limits of Eastern Sudanic: Classificatory and Historical Conclusions," in Rainer Vossen and Marianne Bechhaus-Gerst, eds., *Nilotic Studies*. Berlin.
Gaudefroy-Demombynes, Maurice. 1907. *Documents sur les langues de l'Oubangui-Chari*. Paris.
Goodman, Morris F. 1970. "Some Questions on the Classification of African Languages," *IJAL* 36: 117–22.
———. 1974. "Chari-Nile and Nilo-Saharan Languages," in *EB* 1: 225–28.
Greenberg, Joseph H. 1949–50, 1954. "Studies in African Linguistic Classification," *Southwestern Journal of Anthropology*, 8 parts, 5 (1949), 6 (1950), 10 (1954).
———. 1953. "Historical Linguistics and Unwritten Languages," in A. L. Kroeber, ed., *Anthropology Today*. Chicago.
———. 1955. *Studies in African Linguistic Classification*. Branford, Conn.
———. 1957. "Nilotic, 'Nilo-Hamitic,' and Hamito-Semitic: A Reply," *Africa* 27: 364–77.
———. 1963. *The Languages of Africa*. Bloomington, Ind.
———. 1971. "Nilo-Saharan and Meroitic," in *CTIL* 7.
Hohenberger, J. 1958. "Some Notes on Nilotic, 'Nilo-Hamitic,' and Hamito-Semitic by Joseph H. Greenberg," *Africa* 28: 37–41.

Huntingford, G. W. B. 1956. "The 'Nilo-Hamitic' Languages," *Southwestern Journal of Anthropology* 12: 200–222.
Johnston, Harry. 1902. *The Uganda Protectorate*. London.
Jouannet, Francis. 1978. "Les langues sahariennes," in *IEL*.
Köhler, Oswin. 1955. *Geschichte der Erforschung der nilotischen Sprachen, Afrika und Übersee* 28.
Lepsius, Karl Richard. 1880. *Nubische Grammatik*. Berlin.
Meinhof, Carl. 1912. *Die Sprachen der Hamiten*. Hamburg.
Mukarovsky, H. G. 1966. "Über die Stellung der Mandesprachen," *Anthropos* 61: 679–88.
Müller, Friedrich. 1889. "Die aequatoriale Sprachfamilie in Zentral-Afrika," *Sitzungsberichte der Kais. Akademie der Wissenschaften in Wien, Philosophisch-Historische Classe* 119.
Murray, G. W. 1920. "The Nilotic Languages, a Comparative Essay," *Journal of the Royal Anthropological Institute* 50: 327–68.
Schadeberg, Thilo C., and M. L. Bender, eds. 1981. *Nilo-Saharan: Proceedings of the First Nilo-Saharan Linguistics Colloquium*. Dordrecht.
Shafer, Robert. 1959. "Phonétique comparée du nigéro-sénégalien (Mandé)," *Bulletin d'Institut Français d'Afrique Noire* 21: 179–200.
Tersis, Nicole. 1978. "Le groupe songhay-zarma," in *IEL*.
Thelwall, Robin. 1981. "Lexicostatistical Subgrouping and Lexical Reconstruction of the Daju Group," in *NS*.
Tucker, A. N. 1940. *The Eastern Sudanic Languages*. London.
Tucker, A. N., and M. A. Bryan. 1956. *The Non-Bantu Languages of North-Eastern Africa*. London.
Vossen, Rainer. 1981. "The Classification of Eastern Nilotic and its Significance for Ethnohistory," in *NS*.
Welmers, William E. 1973. *African Language Structures*. Berkeley, Calif.
Westermann, Diedrich. 1912. *The Shilluk People*. Berlin.
———. 1935. "Charakter und Einteilung der Sudansprachen," *Afrika* 8: 129–48.

3.5 KHOISAN

There are today about 30 Khoisan languages, with a total of 120,000 speakers. It is believed that Khoisan languages were originally spoken throughout most of southern Africa. But the Bantu expansion from the north and the Dutch invasion from the south (both by agricultural societies that could support large populations, and with advanced weapons to boot) overwhelmed the Khoisan peoples, who today eke out their living surrounded by Bantu and/or Germanic languages. As seen in Map 3.4, most Khoisan languages are found in South Africa, Namibia, Botswana, and Angola. Two distantly related languages, however, are spoken in northern Tanzania. Within the Khoisan family only Nama (= Hottentot) is at all well known. Khoisan languages are renowned for their use of "clicks" as ordinary consonants.

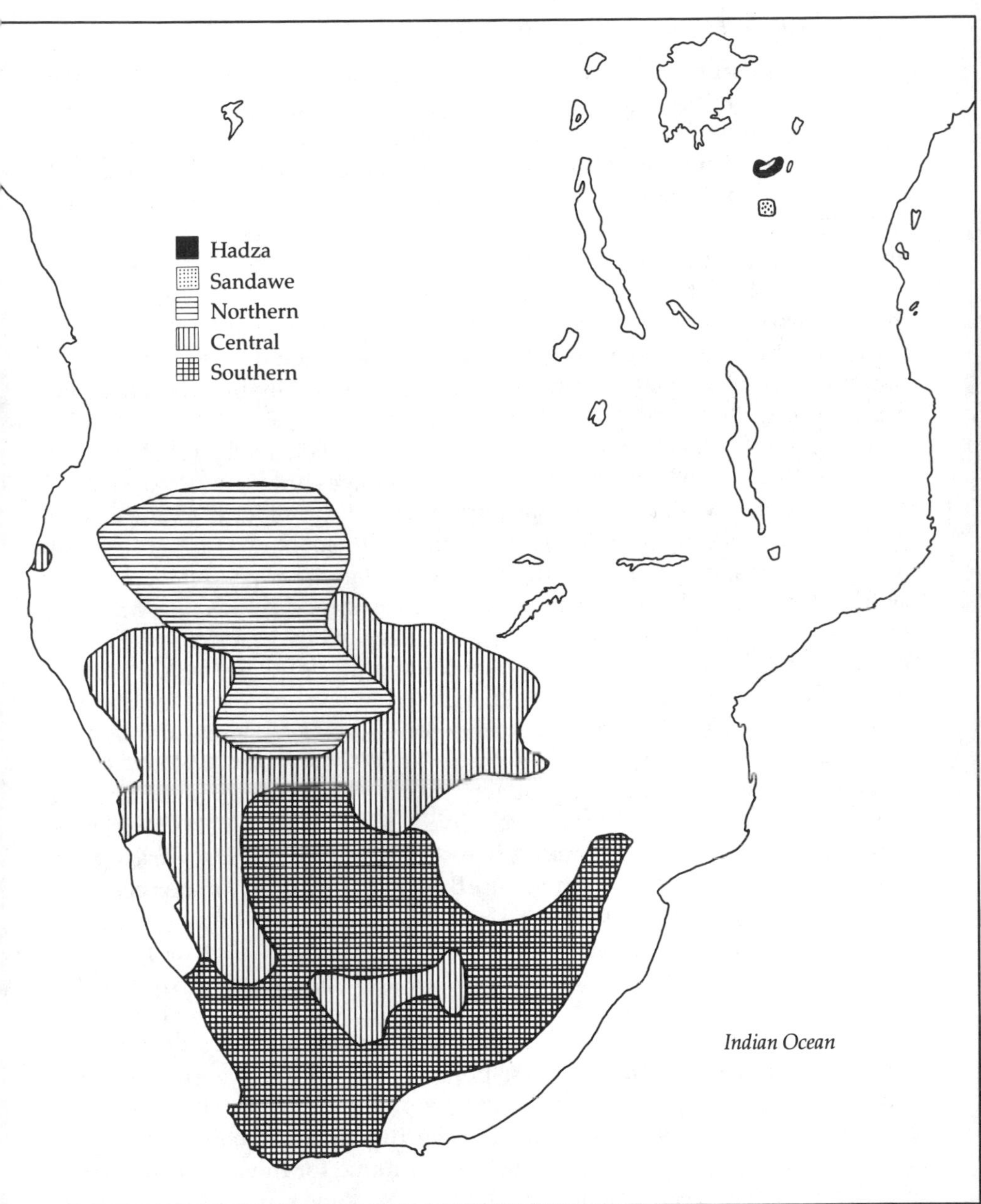

Map 3.4. The Khoisan family

3.5.1 *History of Khoisan Classification*

As we saw in section 3.1, the distinctness of the Nama and Bushman languages from the surrounding Bantu group was recognized early in the nineteenth century by Lichtenstein and others, no doubt in large measure because of the distinctive clicks and the physical appearance (Bushmanoid) of the speakers. In 1847 John W. Appleyard, in a series of articles on the languages of Southern Africa, asserted that "the dialects of the Bushmen are very numerous, though all furnish sufficient evidence of a common origin with those of the Hottentot family" (quoted in Cole 1971: 15). The fact that the two groups practice a different mode of existence (cattle herding for the Nama, hunting and gathering for the Bushmen) led to their initial separation into two groups, a distinction that was eventually incorporated into linguistic classifications, where it had no relevance.

The first classification of Khoisan languages is usually attributed to Wilhelm Bleek (1858), who divided the languages into gender and genderless groups, a dichotomy that happened to correspond to the Nama (gender)-Bushman (genderless) distinction. Or so Bleek thought, for it turns out that some Bushman languages do in fact have gender.

Bleek's work on Khoisan languages was continued by his sister-in-law, Lucy Lloyd, and his daughter, Dorothea Bleek. Four years after Wilhelm Bleek's death in 1875, Lucy Lloyd began the study of Qxû (= !Kung), the first such investigation of a language from what has become known as the Northern group. The first grammatical description (H. Vedder's grammar of Qxû) of a Bushman language did not appear, however, until 1910.

The 1920's witnessed a flurry of activity on Khoisan languages that laid the foundation for all further research. In the early 1920's Albert Drexel proposed a classification incorporating two click languages of East Africa (Sandawe and Hadza) with the Nama and Bushman groups. A major advance occurred in 1927, when Dorothea Bleek divided the Bushman languages into three groups: Northern, Central, and Southern; two years later she showed that Nama, rather than constituting an independent branch of the family, belongs instead to the Central group. It was also in the late 1920's that the term Khoisan was coined to designate the family as a whole. This name combines the Nama word for person (*Khoi* or *Kxoe*) with the Nama word for the Bushmen (*San*); it was first proposed in 1928 by the anthropologist L. Schultze as a designation for the Bushmanoid racial type. Two years later I. Schapera adopted Khoisan as a name for the linguistic family.

Alongside the developments sketched above, some scholars took a different taxonomic direction, attempting to link Nama with the Hamitic family (see section 3.1). Lepsius first proposed this affiliation in 1863, and it was incorporated in Meinhof's expanded Hamitic family in the early twentieth century. With the demise of the original Hamitic family (and its extension to Nilo-Hamitic as well as Nama), occasioned by Greenberg's midcentury classification, the supposed Nama-Hamitic link fell into disfavor and is not, to my knowledge, presently adhered to by anyone, unlike Nilo-Hamitic, which continues to have a few diehard supporters.

Greenberg's 1950 classification followed the work of Dorothea Bleek in dividing the Khoisan languages into three groups, with Nama included in the Central branch. The two East African click languages, Sandawe and Hadza, were treated as distantly related to the other Khoisan languages. Thus for Greenberg the Khoisan phylum consists of three primary branches, two of which are single languages. The third branch contains three subgroups (see List 3.32).

List 3.32. The Khoisan Family
(Greenberg 1949–50/1954, 1963)

KHOISAN:
I Hadza
II Sandawe
III SOUTHERN AFRICA:
  A NORTHERN
  B CENTRAL
  C SOUTHERN

3.5.2 *Present Status of Khoisan Classification*

The most controversial aspect of Khoisan classification has been the affiliation of the two isolates, Hadza and Sandawe, with the rest of the phylum. Although both languages are spoken in relative proximity in Tanzania, some 3,000 miles (4,800 km) from the Southern Africa group, they exhibit no more similarity to each other than they do to the Khoisan languages spoken in the south. The evidence (see Greenberg 1963) that links these geographically isolated languages with the bulk of Khoisan tongues farther south is not of the overwhelming variety that makes the Bantu, Semitic, or Mande families apparent from even a cursory examination of the evidence. It is, rather, of a subtle variety that can be discovered only by the patient accumulation of a substantial body of data, from which a small but significant number of similarities may be culled. It is the kind of evidence that characterizes much of Greenberg's work, in Africa as well as in Oceania (see section 5.2) and the New World (see Chapter 6).

The South African scholar E. O. J. Westphal, a specialist in Khoisan languages, disputes the affiliation of Hadza and Sandawe with the other

Khoisan languages on essentially two grounds: (1) these two isolates do not exhibit *regular sound correspondences* with the rest of the Khoisan group; and (2) if the two isolates (which are found almost side by side some 3,000 miles from the other languages) cannot be shown to be related to each other within their own specific East African context, then it is impossible to prove their genetic affiliation by comparing them with a family of languages spoken thousands of miles away.

Westphal's first objection is a general criticism of Greenberg's work that will be dealt with in detail in the following section (3.6). The second objection also merits examination, since it involves a fundamental principle of genetic classification that is often not fully appreciated.

Westphal (1971: 382) states categorically that "if Hatsa and Sandawe belong to the same family then this should be apparent from a direct comparison of these two languages." One of the great merits of Greenberg's methodology of "mass comparison" is that it is able to overcome obstacles that appear insurmountable to the "binarist" (i.e. a linguist who tackles genetic classification by asking the question, Is language X related to language Y?). Greenberg's method is in fact so powerful that it is possible, under certain circumstances, to prove that languages are genetically related even if they share *not a single cognate*.

Let us assume for the moment that Hadza and Sandawe each share 20 plausible cognates with the Southern Africa Khoisan group, but that they share *none* with each other. Since the links between Hadza and the southern languages, and between Sandawe and the southern languages, are fairly strong, it follows from the principle of transitivity that Hadza and Sandawe must themselves be related, since they are demonstrably related to the same family, i.e. Southern African Khoisan. But this is obviously a conclusion that cannot be obtained if one arbitrarily limits one's perspective to the two isolates, between which we have assumed there are no similarities at all. It is only in the richer context of mass comparison that the lines of genetic affiliation can emerge. In fact, the evidence Greenberg offered to connect Hadza and Sandawe is considerably stronger than our hypothetical figures. Of the 116 etymologies he adduced in support of the Khoisan phylum as a whole, Hadza participates in 75, and Sandawe figures in 52. Hadza and Sandawe occur together, however, in only 11 of the etymologies.

The inadequacy of the binary approach to language classification has been recognized since the nineteenth century. Furthermore, during the development of Indo-European comparative linguistics itself, scholars did not attempt to prove the affinity of, say, Albanian and Armenian by a direct confrontation of these two languages alone. Rather the proof was invariably made in terms of the *higher-level unit* (Indo-European) to which both belonged. The same is true of biological classification, in which, as Greenberg (1979: 20) observes: "It has occurred to no biologist . . . to write a special treatise to prove that sparrows are genetically related to whales by a direct and exclusive comparison between the two. Yet no biologist doubts the relationship, since they are both vertebrates." While such ad hoc binary comparisons would be considered a joke in biological taxonomy, they are still widely practiced by certain segments of the linguistic community, to the dismay and chagrin of more seasoned taxonomists (see section 6.3).

The Southern African subgroup of Khoisan consists of three distinct branches: Northern, Central, and Southern. The first two are internally fairly homogeneous; the Southern branch is composed of two distinct families (Ta'a and !Wi). Köhler (1974: 230) suggests that the Central and Northern groups are genetically closer to each other than either is to the Southern group. Köhler regards Sandawe as significantly closer to South African Khoisan than is Hadza, an opinion shared by Elderkin (1982), who also points out resemblances between Hadza and Omotic, Chadic, and Kuliak. Westphal (1971), on the other hand, considers the three South African groups to be independent families not relatable either to each other or to Hadza and Sandawe, on the basis of present evidence.

Bleek, Dorothea F. 1927. "The Distribution of the Bushman Languages in South Africa," in *Festschrift Meinhof*. Hamburg.

———. 1929. *Comparative Vocabularies of Bushman Languages*. Cambridge, Eng.

———. 1956. *A Bushman Dictionary*. New Haven, Conn.

Bleek, Wilhelm. 1858. *The Library of Sir George Grey*, 2 vols. London.

Cole, Desmond T. 1971. "The History of African Linguistics to 1945," in *CTIL* 7.

Drexel, Albert. 1921–25. "Gliederung der afrikanischen Sprachen," *Anthropos*, 4 parts, 16–17 (1921–22): 73–108; 18–19 (1923–24): 12-39; 20 (1925): 210–43, 444–60.

Elderkin, E. D. 1982. "On the Classification of Hadza," *Sprache und Geschichte in Afrika* 4: 67–82.

Greenberg, Joseph H. 1949–50, 1954. "Studies in African Linguistic Classification," *Southwestern Journal of Anthropology*, 8 parts, 5 (1949), 6 (1950), 10 (1954).

———. 1955. *Studies in African Linguistic Classification*. Branford, Conn.

———. 1963. *The Languages of Africa*. Bloomington, Ind.

———. 1979. "The Classification of American Indian Languages," in Ralph E. Cooley et al., eds., *Papers of the 1978 Mid-America Linguistics Conference at Oklahoma*. Norman, Okla.

———. 1986. *Language in the Americas*. Stanford, Calif.

Köhler, Oswin. 1974. "Khoisan Languages," in *EB* 1: 228–32.

———. 1981. "Les langues khoisan," in Jean Perrot, ed., *Les langues dans le monde ancien et moderne*. Paris.

Lepsius, Richard. 1863. *Standard Alphabet*. London.

Schapera, I. 1930. *The Khoisan Peoples of South Africa*. London.

Schultze, L. 1928. *Zur Kenntnis des Korpers der Hottentotten und Buschmänner*. Jena.

Westphal, E. O. J. 1962a. "A Reclassification of Southern African Non-Bantu Languages," *Journal of African Languages* 1: 1–8.
———. 1962b. "On Classifying Bushman and Hottentot Languages," *African Language Studies* 3: 30–48.
———. 1963. "The Linguistic Prehistory of Southern Africa: Bush, Kwadi, Hottentot, and Bantu Linguistic Relationships," *Africa* 33: 237–65.
———. 1971. "The Click Languages of Southern and Eastern Africa," in *CTIL* 7.

3.6 CRITICISM OF GREENBERG'S METHODOLOGY

In the 20 years that have passed since the appearance of Greenberg's pivotal 1963 classification of African languages, there has developed in the scholarly community a curious ambivalence toward his work. Greenberg's *results* are now generally accepted by the vast majority of African specialists and have constituted the basic framework for research on African classification over the past two decades. Furthermore, it is widely acknowledged that serious work on African classification had been severely impeded by a number of "pseudo-issues," of which Meinhof's extended Hamitic family is probably the most notorious. In addition to providing a complete classification of African languages, Greenberg's work was instrumental in identifying and eliminating these spurious issues from the scholarly debate.

But if Greenberg's results have won general acceptance, his *methods*, curiously enough, have not. Indeed, his methodology of "mass comparison," which he now prefers to call "multilateral comparison," remains almost as controversial today as it was in the 1950's. It is of interest to examine how and why this unusual situation has developed, for it illuminates the single chief impediment to continued progress in genetic classification, not only in Africa, but in the rest of the world as well.

As Greenberg has stressed since his earliest work, the technique of multilateral comparison is the oldest, quickest, and most effective method of untangling genetic relationships over a wide area. It consists essentially of collecting wordlists, usually restricted to several hundred basic vocabulary items, from as wide a range of languages as possible. The vocabulary items may be either *lexical* (e.g. 'hand,' 'sky,' 'red,' 'go') or *grammatical* (e.g. PLURAL, PAST TENSE, MASCULINE). Once a substantial number of wordlists has been assembled, their comparison inevitably leads to the grouping of languages into a certain number of obviously valid genetic units (e.g. Romance, Germanic, Semitic, Austronesian, Athabaskan, Algonquian), with perhaps a residue of languages not readily classifiable either because they are remote from any of the established groups or because there is insufficient material available to determine their affiliation.

Once the low-level groups have been identified on the basis of numerous shared cognates, the next step is the comparison of these groups among themselves. Although the similarities will not be as startling as they are at the lowest level of classification (see Table 1.2 in section 1.4), significant resemblances among certain of the groups will usually be apparent (see Table 1.1 in section 1.3). Genetic classification can be continued as long as there are groups to compare, but historically there has been a bias against carrying it beyond fairly obvious groups (e.g. Indo-European, Uralic, Bantu, Austronesian, Salish) for reasons that will be discussed both in this section and in section 7.3.

The principal objection to Greenberg's methodology is that, although he has discovered substantial numbers of apparent cognates for the groups he postulates, these sets of cognates do not exhibit the *regular sound correspondences* (see section 2.3) that many linguists have come to regard as "the only real proof of genetic relationship" (Welmers 1973: 5). For István Fodor (1969), Greenberg's "entire method is vitiated, in fact, annihilated," by the failure to demonstrate "the existence of phonetic laws, which is the standard of all comparisons of genetic purpose" (p. 24). According to Fodor, "the proof of the affinity of languages is regular correspondence of their sounds" (p. 86) and "without sound laws the genetic relations of the African languages cannot be proved" (p. 135). Furthermore, this point of view is by no means restricted to Africanists, as the following citations indicate:

> Without sound correspondences among the languages being considered, etymology is nothing more than a game and does not constitute proof (Meillet 1937: 462).

> Sauvageot . . . has pointed out as the main weakness of most of the previous works in [Ural-Altaic comparative studies] the indiscriminate comparison of words which somehow resembled each other. Sauvageot states that only such comparisons count which permit of establishing regular sound correspondences (Poppe 1965: 128).

> The interrelationships of North and South Caucasian are as yet uncertain because of the absence of any regular sound correspondences between them (Gamkrelidze 1974: 1011).

> In order to prove that a group of languages is genetically related, it is necessary . . . to detail the regular changes by which each modern language has developed from the proto-system. Simply remarking on recurrent similarities and counting possible cognates may suggest a genetic relationship, but it does not constitute proof (Dixon 1980: 221).

> The fundamental criterion for cognation is systematic sound correspondences in basic vocabulary (McAlpin 1981: 128).

More characteristic of prevailing views, at least with respect to African classification, is the following measured opinion of Welmers (1973: 5–6):

> Greenberg has not, to be sure, demonstrated the existence of regular phonetic correspondences among all the languages in any of the four language families he posits for Africa, though it has already been implied that such correspondences are the only real proof of genetic relationship. However, . . . evidence that falls short of clear demonstration of regular phonetic correspondences may nevertheless be overwhelming. . . . The nature of the similar forms with similar meanings which Greenberg cites, and the number of them, is such that the fact of genetic relationship can be considered established.

While accepting Greenberg's results in full, Gregersen (1977: 122) too is troubled by the absence of sound correspondences in Greenberg's proposed etymologies, a defect that he believes "raises the important issue of eventually *rigorizing* the evidence for Greenberg's conclusions" (emphasis added).

The notion that the ultimate proof of genetic affinity is the presence of regular sound correspondences represents a peculiar twentieth-century distortion of nineteenth-century comparative linguistics, as well as a misunderstanding of the nature of scientific proof. In the first place, many linguists presently have the mistaken impression that the Indo-European family was somehow "proved" by the discovery of regular sound correspondences: "In the methodology worked out by Indo-Europeanists, only the establishment of sound correspondences was taken as proof of genetic relationship" (Gregersen 1977: 103).

Nothing could be further from the truth, for the Indo-European family was well established, even with regard to its constituent branches, long before sound laws and sound correspondences came into vogue (see section 2.3). The emphasis that the Neo-Grammarians placed on regular sound laws had nothing whatever to do with validating the Indo-European family, the existence of which had not been in doubt since the early nineteenth century. In fact, as Greenberg, Paul Newman, Ives Goddard, and others have stressed, it is the prior recognition of valid genetic groups that leads to the discovery of sound correspondences, rather than the other way around: "The proof of genetic relationship does not depend on the demonstration of historical sound laws. Rather, the discovery of sound laws and the reconstruction of linguistic history normally emerge from the careful comparison of languages already presumed to be related" (Newman 1970: 39).

Furthermore, many linguists today are laboring under the delusion that regular sound correspondences, which stand out so sharply when one examines low-level genetic groups like Bantu, Romance, and Semitic, will one day be discovered *to the same degree* in more ancient groupings such as Niger-Congo and Nilo-Saharan. This is essentially what Welmers (1963: 416) means when he writes that "for all of Greenberg's four families, genetic relationship has not yet been demonstrated *in the same way* as it has for the homogeneous Bantu group itself, or for Indo-European." However, as

Greenberg (1969: 429) makes clear, there is a whole host of perturbative influences on regular sound change (and hence on regular sound correspondences), accepted by even the strictest Neo-Grammarian, "which must produce greater and greater variety of correspondences as time goes on." Like any part of linguistic structure, correspondences are subject to the same kinds of change that continually affect all languages everywhere. As time goes by, these correspondences are gradually, but continually, obscured until eventually they become indiscernible. What Greenberg's work on genetic classification demonstrates quite clearly is that even after correspondences have been eroded to the point of invisibility, it is still often possible to identify sufficient cognates so that the genetic unity of a group is not in doubt.

Three final points must be touched upon briefly. First, sound correspondences even at the lowest levels of classification (e.g. Bantu, Romance) are not exceptionless laws, as Fodor (1969) somewhat naïvely believes; and in traditional comparative linguistics etymologies are not usually dismissed for failing to obey a phonetic law, provided they appear otherwise sound. Second, sound correspondences do not discriminate between loanwords and true cognates, as is sometimes alleged, with only true cognates obeying sound laws. In this regard one should not forget the numerous sound laws established by Wulff (1934) to link the Tai languages with Sino-Tibetan, a relationship now almost universally abandoned, since the Tai "cognates" are currently considered to be early loanwords from (and into) Chinese. Finally, it is worth remarking that there is no analog to sound correspondences in biological classification, which is nonetheless recognized as being in a more advanced state than linguistic classification.

If, as has been argued above, regular sound correspondences are neither necessary nor sufficient for demonstrating genetic relationship, how are we to explain the almost blind faith many linguists place in them as the "ultimate proof" of genetic affinity? The answer lies in a widespread misunderstanding of the nature of scientific proof. Consider what the biologist Ernst Mayr (1982: 25–26) has to say about this notion:

> Descartes endeavored to present only such conclusions and theories as had the certainty of a mathematical proof. Although there have always been some dissenters, the belief that a scientist had to supply absolute proof for all his findings and theories prevailed until modern times. It dominated not only the physical sciences, where proof of the nature of a mathematical proof is often possible, but also the biological sciences. Even here, inferences are often so conclusive that they can be accepted as proof. . . . In many cases, however, and perhaps in the majority of the conclusions of the biologists, it is impossible to supply proof of such certainty. . . . Eventually the physicists also realized that they could not always give absolute proof, . . . and the new theory of science no longer demands it. Instead, scientists are satisfied to consider as true either that which appears most probable on the

basis of available evidence, or that which is consistent with more, or more compelling, facts than competing hypotheses.

In this context it becomes clear that the use of sound correspondences to "prove" genetic affiliation represents a misguided attempt to provide a mathematical proof for a question that is not susceptible to such a proof. There is no litmus test for the detection of genetic relationships, as the unsuccessful attempts to use inflectional similarities (in the nineteenth century) and sound correspondences (in the twentieth century) for this purpose attest. Rather we must be satisfied with "inferences . . . so conclusive that they can be accepted as proof." The etymologies that Greenberg offers for his African families are of precisely this nature.

Dixon, R. M. W. 1980. *The Languages of Australia*. Cambridge, Eng.

Fodor, István. 1969. *The Problems in the Classification of the African Languages*. Budapest.

Gamkrelidze, Thomas V. 1974. "Caucasian Languages," in *EB* 3: 1011–15.

Greenberg, Joseph H. 1969. Review of *The Problems in the Classification of the African Languages*, by István Fodor, *Language* 45: 427–32.

———. 1987. *Language in the Americas*. Stanford, Calif.

Gregersen, Edgar A. 1977. *Language in Africa*. New York.

Mayr, Ernst. 1982. *The Growth of Biological Thought*. Cambridge, Mass.

McAlpin, David W. 1981. *Proto-Elamo-Dravidian: The Evidence and Its Implications*. Philadelphia.

Meillet, Antoine. 1937. *Introduction à l'étude comparative des langues indo-européennes*. Paris.

Newman, Paul. 1970. "Historical Sound Laws in Hausa and in Dera (Kanakuru)," *The Journal of West African Languages* 7: 39–51.

Poppe, Nicholas. 1965. *Introduction to Altaic Linguistics*. Wiesbaden.

Welmers, William E. 1963. Review of *The Languages of Africa*, by Joseph H. Greenberg, *Word* 19: 407–17.

———. 1973. *African Language Structures*. Berkeley, Calif.

Wulff, Kurt. 1934. *Chinesisch und Tai: Sprachvergleichende Untersuchungen*. *Det Kgl. Danske Videnskabernes Selskab., Historisk-filologiske Meddelelser* 20,3.

4

Asia

Asia differs dramatically from Africa in the number, diversity, and distribution of the languages. Whereas in Africa we find many families, each containing numerous languages, intertwined in such a way that the genetic picture remained muddled into the twentieth century, in Asia the families are considerably fewer in number. They usually contain relatively few languages, and, practically without exception, they are sharply delineated from neighboring families. For all of these reasons most Asian families were recognized fairly early in the development of genetic linguistics. For northern Asia Strahlenberg had already outlined the major families by 1730, and in South Asia the picture was clarified during the nineteenth century, at least with regard to the major genetic groups.

Before we examine these various groups in greater detail, a brief survey of Asian families will help to orient the reader. Beginning with the northwest corner of Asia, and proceeding roughly counterclockwise, the linguistic picture presents itself as follows. In the northwest we find the *Samoyed* family, a branch of Uralic (see section 2.4). Several branches of the *Indo-Hittite* family (see section 2.3) are (or were) found in Southwest Asia (Iranian, Armenian, Anatolian) or South Asia (Indic, Tocharian). The *Altaic* family, which extends from Turkey across Central Asia into Siberia, is usually taken to include the Turkic, Mongolian, and Tungus families, and sometimes Korean, Japanese, and Ainu as well. The *Dravidian* family is found in southern India, with a few scattered outliers farther north. The *Austroasiatic* family comprises two branches, the small Munda family in northeast India and the larger, and more diverse, Mon-Khmer family, found in Southeast Asia and on the Nicobar Islands in the Bay of Bengal.

Languages belonging to the *Sino-Tibetan* family are found over a wide area of East Asia from Tibet and Nepal throughout China and extending southward into India, Burma, and Laos.

Three additional small families are found in Southeast Asia. Several dozen *Daic* languages cover a broad belt from southern China through Laos and Thailand as far south as the Malay Peninsula. The *Miao-Yao* family contains only a handful of languages, spoken in numerous scattered enclaves in southern China, Vietnam, Laos, and Thailand. The small *Chamic* group, found in southern Vietnam, in Kampuchea, and on the Chinese island of Hainan, belongs to the large Austronesian family, which covers most of Oceania and will be discussed in section 5.1.

In North and Northeast Asia we find only a few small families and several language isolates. The *Chukchi-Kamchatkan* family is spoken on the Chukchi and Kamchatkan peninsulas. West of the Chukchi-Kamchatkan family, the Yukaghir language is the sole survivor of a previously more numerous group whose closest relative appears to be the Uralic family (see section 2.4). Farther west still, in North Asia, Ket is the sole surviving member of the *Yeniseian* family. Its genetic affiliation is unknown, with the most common proposal (Sino-Tibetan) enjoying little support. Several varieties of Eskimo are spoken in northeastern Siberia, but most Eskimo dialects are found along the northern perimeter of North America, and they will be discussed in that context (see section 6.1).

Finally, there are three language isolates in Asia. *Gilyak* is spoken on the island of Sakhalin, just off the east coast of Asia. It is most often linked with the Chukchi-Kamchatkan and Eskimo-Aleut families farther to the north. In this regard Roman Jakobson (1942: 604) suggested a number of plausible cognates between Gilyak and Aleut. The other two isolates are found in India. Spoken by several hundred people in Northeast India, *Nehali* is sometimes grouped with Austroasiatic. *Burushaski* is spoken by some 50,000 people in a mountainous region of northern India; its genetic affiliation remains a complete mystery.

Though there have been many attempts to link one Asian family with another, few have garnered much support. Two such proposals are the *Austric* phylum (originally conceived as including Austronesian and Austroasiatic) and the *Austro-Tai* stock (which originally linked Austronesian with the Daic family). Both proposals are discussed in section 4.5.

Benedict, Paul K. 1942. "Thai, Kadai, and Indonesian: A New Alignment in Southeastern Asia," *AA* 44: 576–601.
Jakobson, Roman. 1942. "The Paleosiberian Languages," *AA* 44: 602–20.
Klaproth, H. J. 1823. *Asia Polyglotta*. Paris.

Shorto, H. L. 1979. "The Linguistic Protohistory of Mainland South East Asia," in R. B. Smith and W. Watson, eds., *Early South East Asia*. New York.
von Strahlenberg, Phillip Johann. 1730. *Das nord- und östliche Theil von Europa und Asia*. Stockholm.

4.1 ALTAIC

The Altaic family is composed of three subfamilies (Turkic, Mongolian, Tungus) and three isolated languages (Korean, Japanese, Ainu), as seen in Map 4.1. Altogether there are approximately 60 languages and 250 million speakers. Some 30 *Turkic* languages are spoken by 80 million people across a wide belt extending from Turkey eastward through the U.S.S.R. into northwestern China. With 40 million speakers, Turkish is the best known Turkic language, but Uzbek, Azerbaijani, Tatar, Uighur, Kazakh, Turkmen, Chuvash, Kirghiz, and Bashkir all have more than a million speakers (and in some cases considerably more). A dozen *Mongolian* languages, with three million speakers, are found in Mongolia and surrounding portions of the U.S.S.R. and China. One Mongolian language (Moghol) is spoken in Afghanistan. Some 16 *Tungus* languages, with 80,000 speakers, are found in scattered "islands" throughout much of Asiatic U.S.S.R. and parts of northern China. The best-known Tungus language is Manchu, spoken in

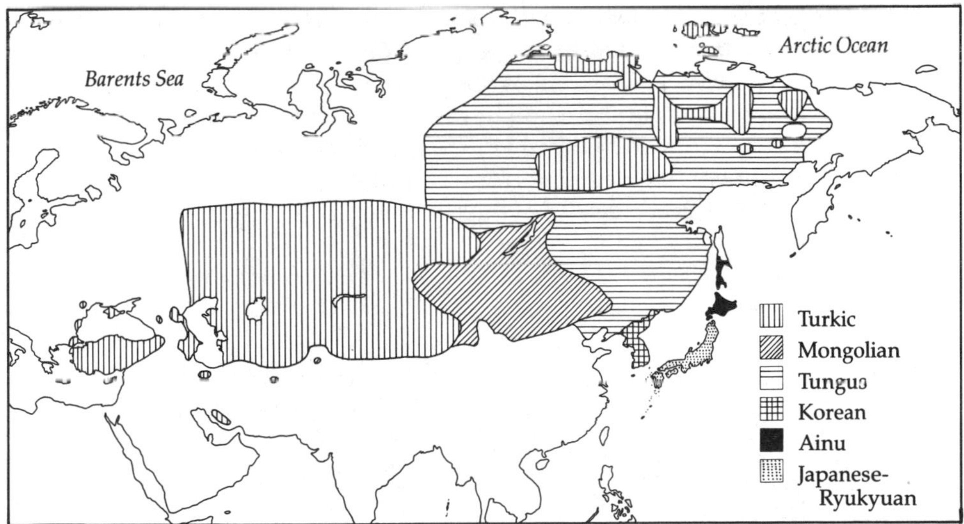

Map 4.1. The Altaic family

northeastern China. Estimates at the number of Manchu speakers range from almost three million to zero (the explanation for this discrepancy is that, although there are several million ethnic Manchu in China, the Manchu language is either extinct or on the verge of extinction). *Korean* (55 million speakers) is spoken primarily in Korea, and *Japanese* (115 million) primarily in Japan. *Ainu* is spoken in northern Japan and on the southern portion of Sakhalin Island (U.S.S.R.) to the north. Estimates of 15,000 Ainu in Japan and 1,500 in the U.S.S.R. apparently refer to ethnic Ainu; the Ainu language is close to extinction.

4.1.1 *History of Altaic Classification*

The study of the Altaic family has had a long and stormy history, and even today there is considerable disagreement among specialists over exactly which languages belong to the family. As I mentioned in section 3.4, one often finds in the history of genetic classification that some close-knit family serves as a nucleus around which increasingly larger families are built. With Altaic we find an unusual development in the opposite direction: the original conception of Altaic in the nineteenth century was considerably broader than it is today.

The first grammars of individual Altaic languages appeared during the seventeenth century; the first classification of languages now considered Altaic is found in Strahlenberg (1730), where a Tatar family is posited, as shown in List 4.1. Nineteenth-century scholars proposed revisions of this family that either expanded its scope (e.g. Rasmus Rask, Max Müller) or narrowed it (e.g. M. A. Castrén, W. Schott). In 1834 Rask added Eskimo, Chukchi-Kamchatkan, and Basque to the family and renamed it Scythian; he also correctly grouped Manchu with Tungus, not Mongolian, a point on which Strahlenberg had been in error (see List 4.2).

Max Müller enlarged Rask's Scythian family in 1855 by including Thai,

List 4.1. The Tatar Family (Strahlenberg 1730)

TATAR:
I FINNO-UGRIC
II TURKIC
III SAMOYED
IV MONGOL-MANCHU
V TUNGUS
VI CAUCASIAN

List 4.2. The Scythian Family (Rask 1834)

SCYTHIAN:
I MONGOLIAN
II MANCHU-TUNGUS
III TURKIC
IV URALIC
V ESKIMO
VI CHUKCHI-KAMCHATKAN
VII CAUCASIAN
VIII Basque

List 4.3. The Altaic Family (Schott 1849)

ALTAIC:
- I CHUDIC:
  - A FINNO-UGRIC
  - B SAMOYED
- II TATAR:
  - A TURKIC
  - B MONGOLIAN
  - C TUNGUS

List 4.4. The Ural-Altaic Family (20th century)

URAL-ALTAIC:
- I URALIC:
  - A FINNO-UGRIC
  - B SAMOYED
- II ALTAIC:
  - A TURKIC
  - B MONGOLIAN
  - C TUNGUS

Tibetan, Dravidian, and Malay; he renamed the family Turanian. Rask's and Müller's proposals turned out to be deadends; it was the work of Castrén and Schott, both of whom pruned Caucasian from Strahlenberg's Tatar family, that led to contemporary views. Both Castrén and Schott rejected the facile typological approach and insisted on lexical and morphological similarities; that is, they insisted on the same standard of proof that had been required of Indo-European. Both men reached their conclusions around the middle of the nineteenth century. In 1849 Schott proposed an Altaic (or Chudic-Tatar) family composed of a Chudic (or Finnic) branch and a Tatar branch, as in List 4.3.

Castrén's views, which were not published until 1862, 10 years after his death, were very similar to Schott's, with the exception that he believed Turkic to be closer to Chudic than to Mongolian or Tungus. On this point modern scholarship has sided with Schott. Schott's classification is in fact quite modern in conception, though his terminology is no longer used. What he called Altaic is now known as Ural-Altaic; Chudic has been replaced by Uralic (see section 2.4); and Tatar corresponds to the modern definition of Altaic (see List 4.4).

During the century following Schott's and Castrén's work, the Ural-Altaic family (to use the modern terminology) developed in two directions. First, the validity of the genetic link between Uralic and Altaic was increasingly questioned, and the most widespread opinion today rejects such a link. Nevertheless, there has always been a small group of scholars who have not only steadfastly defended the Ural-Altaic family, but even expanded it to include Chukchi-Kamchatkan, Eskimo-Aleut, Indo-European (and, for some, Dravidian, South Caucasian, and Semitic). In addition, Korean, Japanese, Ainu, and Gilyak are frequently included in the expanded family, which is known most commonly as Nostratic or Eurasiatic. The question of possible genetic links between well-established families (of which the Ural-Altaic hypothesis is one example) is discussed in section 7.3.

The second line of development has been the expansion of Altaic Proper (= Turkic, Mongolian, and Tungus) to include Korean, Japanese, and Ainu. Korean was first connected with Altaic in 1823 by H. J. Klaproth. The Austrian scholar Anton Boller sought to show in 1857 that both Korean and Japanese were related to the Ural-Altaic family. In the late 1920's the Russian linguist E. D. Polivanov and the Finnish linguist G. J. Ramstedt (usually regarded as the founder of comparative Altaic linguistics) both offered evidence linking Korean to Altaic Proper. In 1966 the American linguist Samuel E. Martin proposed more than 300 etymologies connecting Korean with Japanese (an idea first suggested in 1717), and in 1971 another American linguist, Roy A. Miller, sought to demonstrate the affinity of Japanese with both Korean and Altaic Proper.

Ainu has been associated with Altaic less often than Korean or Japanese, though Street (1962) suggested such a relationship in the context of a larger North Asiatic family. Recently Patrie (1982) has adduced considerable evidence linking Ainu with the rest of Altaic, including both Japanese and Korean.

4.1.2 Present Status of Altaic Classification

There is no consensus today on either the membership or the subgrouping of the Altaic family. At one extreme are those linguists who reject even Altaic Proper as a valid genetic group (e.g. Clauson 1956, Doerfer 1963, Comrie 1981); at the other extreme are those who believe Altaic Proper is genetically related both to languages farther west (Uralic, Indo-European) and farther east (Korean, Japanese, Ainu, Gilyak, Chukchi-Kamchatkan, Eskimo-Aleut) in a family called Eurasiatic (e.g. Greenberg 1979, 1986). Between these two extremes lie a number of intermediate proposals, some of which are illustrated in List 4.5.

In weighing the scholarly support for these various configurations, I conclude that Altaic Proper (= Turkic, Mongolian, Tungus) is now widely accepted as a valid genetic group. The affiliation of Korean with this complex has also gained considerable support, and Japanese appears to be gaining in popularity as a member of Altaic, though still in a minority position. Ainu has been mentioned less often in connection with Altaic, but Patrie (1982) changes this state of affairs significantly. Looking westward, the defenders of the Uralic connection are in a decreasing minority. Those who include even more distant groups such as Indo-European, Chukchi-Kamchatkan, or Eskimo-Aleut are seldom accorded much attention by Altaicists.

The present unresolved state of Altaic classification has several causes. First of all, except in the case of Altaic Proper, the genetic affinity of the

List 4.5. Proposed Subgroupings of the Altaic Family

Schott 1849

ALTAIC:
- I TURKIC
- II MONGOLIAN
- III TUNGUS

Ramstedt 1952–57

ALTAIC:
- I TURKIC
- II MONGOLIAN
- III TUNGUS
- IV Korean

Street 1962

NORTH ASIATIC:
- I KOREAN-JAPANESE-AINU:
  - A Ainu
  - B KOREAN-JAPANESE:
    - 1 Korean
    - 2 Japanese
- II ALTAIC:
  - A EAST:
    - 1 TUNGUS
    - 2 MONGOLIAN
  - B WEST:
    - 1 Chuvash
    - 2 TURKIC

Poppe 1965

ALTAIC:
- I Korean
- II ALTAIC PROPER:
  - A TURKIC:
    - 1 Chuvash
    - 2 TURKIC PROPER
  - B MONGOLIAN-TUNGUS:
    - 1 MONGOLIAN
    - 2 TUNGUS

Miller 1971

ALTAIC:
- I WESTERN:
  - A Chuvash
  - B TURKIC
- II EASTERN:
  - A MONGOLIAN
  - B TUNGUS-KOREAN-JAPANESE:
    - 1 TUNGUS
    - 2 KOREAN-JAPANESE:
      - a Korean
      - b Japanese

various groups and languages is not obvious. Second, because of the distant relationships involved, as well as the broad geographic distribution of the languages in question, Altaic classification has all too often been investigated with a "binary approach" (see section 3.5), where the focus of the investigation has been artificially restricted to those languages in which a particular scholar happens to have expertise. Although binary comparisons may suggest a genetic connection between two languages (or groups of languages), they do not tell us the nature of that link, thus producing a muddled picture with respect to subgrouping. What Altaicists frequently overlook is that even if Korean (or Japanese) *is* related to Altaic Proper, this does not necessarily mean that Korean and Altaic Proper constitute a valid genetic group. English, French, and Spanish are all related, but they form no valid group. As will be made clear in section 7.3, the failure to study the Altaic problem in a sufficiently broad context is primarily responsible for the present unsettled state of affairs. Third, Altaic comparative linguistics has been plagued by the fallacy of negative evidence. Some critics of Altaic Proper, for example, point out that whereas Turkic and Mongolian have very similar color words, the corresponding terms in Tungus are totally different. Therefore, they claim, the Altaic affinity of Tungus is called into question. Though arguments of this nature are surprisingly common (and not just in Altaic studies), they are of no importance, because no one either pretends or demands that related languages be similar in every detail. Lexical innovation, through either borrowing or invention, is a fact of life that in no way undermines genetic classification. Finally, the fact that most members, or putative members, of Altaic are either language isolates (e.g. Korean, Ainu) or small homogeneous groups (e.g. Turkic, Mongolian, Japanese) renders the classificatory problems more difficult than with large diverse groups.

The Altaic classification adopted in this volume is similar in conception to Street (1962) and Patrie (1982), though with a slightly different terminology (see List 4.6). The validity of defining Altaic in this manner will be examined again in section 7.3 in the context of an even broader Eurasiatic family.

List 4.6. The Altaic Family (Street 1962, Patrie 1982)

ALTAIC:
- I ALTAIC PROPER:
  - A TURKIC
  - B MONGOLIAN-TUNGUS:
    - 1 MONGOLIAN
    - 2 TUNGUS
- II KOREAN-JAPANESE:
  - A Korean
  - B Ainu
  - C JAPANESE-RYUKYUAN:
    - 1 Japanese
    - 2 Ryukyuan

List 4.7. The Turkic Family (Voegelin & Voegelin 1977)

TURKIC:
- I BOLGAR: Chuvash
- II COMMON TURKIC:
  - A SOUTHERN
  - B EASTERN
  - C WESTERN
  - D CENTRAL
  - E NORTHERN

Let us turn now to subgrouping within the various constituents of Altaic. With respect to Altaic Proper there have been two principal views, turning on whether Mongolian is closer to Turkic (e.g. Vladimirtsov 1929) or to Tungus (e.g. Street 1962, Poppe 1965, Miller 1971).

Of the three families constituting Altaic Proper, Turkic and Mongolian are both extremely homogeneous, and Tungus is apparently only slightly less so. According to Poppe (1965: 107), contemporary views on Turkic derive from the classification of Alexandr Samojlovich (1922), "which, with some minor changes, is the basis for present-day classification." Within Turkic a single language, Chuvash (the sole surviving member of the Bolgar group), stands at some distance from the rest of the family. Of the five geographic groups making up Common Turkic, the Northern is the most divergent. The classification followed here (List 4.7) is based on Voegelin and Voegelin (1977), with certain modifications suggested by Robert Underhill (personal communication).

Within the Mongolian family Moghol is isolated from the rest, and Dagur and the Monguor languages are somewhat less distant from the very homogeneous Oirat-Khalkha nucleus. The classification adopted in this volume (List 4.8) follows Binnick (1981).

List 4.8. The Mongolian Family (Binnick 1981)

MONGOLIAN:
I WESTERN: Moghol
II EASTERN:
  A Dagur
  B MONGUOR
  C OIRAT-KHALKHA:
    1 OIRAT-KALMYK
    2 KHALKHA-BURIAT

List 4.9. The Tungus Family (Voegelin & Voegelin 1977)

TUNGUS:
I NORTHERN
II SOUTHERN:
  A SOUTHWESTERN
  B SOUTHEASTERN:
    1 NANAJ
    2 UDIHE

The Tungus family is divided into distinct Northern and Southern branches. Although speakers of Northern languages are found over an enormous area covering most of Siberia, the relatively compact Southern group displays far greater diversity, being itself bifurcated into Southwestern and Southeastern groups. The classification followed, shown in List 4.9, comes from Voegelin and Voegelin (1977).

ALTAIC

Boller, Anton. 1857. *Nachweis, dass das Japanische zum ural-altaischen Stämme gehort.* Vienna.

Castrén, M. A. 1862. "Über die Personalaffixe in den altaischen Sprachen," in *Kleinere Schriften*. St. Petersburg.

Clauson, Gerard. 1956. "The Case Against the Altaic Theory," *Central Asiatic Journal* 2: 181–87.

Comrie, Bernard. 1981. "Altaic Languages," in Bernard Comrie, *The Languages of the Soviet Union*. Cambridge, Eng.

Doerfer, Gerhard. 1963. *Turkische und mongolische Elemente im Neupersischen*. Wiesbaden.

Greenberg, Joseph H. 1979. "The Classification of American Indian Languages," in Ralph E. Cooley et al., eds., *Papers of the 1978 Mid-America Linguistics Conference at Oklahoma*. Norman, Okla.

———. 1987. *Language in the Americas*. Stanford, Calif.

Hazai, Georg. 1974. "Altaic Languages," in *EB* 1: 635–39.

Klaproth, H. J. 1823. *Asia Polyglotta*. Paris.

Martin, Samuel E. 1966. "Lexical Evidence Relating Korean to Japanese," *Language* 42: 185–251.

Menges, Karl H. 1975. *Altajische Studien* 2: *Japanisch und Altajisch*. Wiesbaden.

Miller, Roy Andrew. 1971. *Japanese and the Other Altaic Languages*. Chicago.

Müller, Max. 1855. *The Languages of the Seat of War in the East*. London.

Patrie, James. 1982. *The Genetic Relationship of the Ainu Language*. Honolulu.

Polivanov, E. D. 1927. "K voprosu o rodstvennyx otnoshenijax korejskogo i altajskix jazykov," *Izvestija Akademii Naux* (Leningrad).

Poppe, Nicholas. 1960. *Vergleichende Grammatik der altaischen Sprachen*. Wiesbaden.

———. 1965. *Introduction to Altaic Linguistics*. Wiesbaden.

Ramstedt, G. J. 1928. "Remarks on the Korean Language," *Mémoires de la Société Finno-Ougrienne* 58: 441–53.

———. 1952–57. *Einführung in die altaische Sprachwissenschaft*, 2 vols. Helsinki.

Rask, Rasmus K. 1834. "Den skytiske Sproget," *Sammlede tilldels forhen utrykte Afhandlingen* (Copenhagen) 1.

Samojlovich, Alexandr N. 1922. *Nekotorye dopolnenija k klassifikatsii turetskix jazykov*. Petrograd.

Schott, W. 1849. *Über das altaische oder finnisch-tatarische Sprachengeschlecht*. Berlin.

von Strahlenberg, Phillip Johann. 1730. *Das nord- und östliche Theil von Europa und Asia*. Stockholm.

Street, John C. 1962. Review of *Vergleichende Grammatik der altaischen Sprachen*, by Nicholas Poppe, *Language* 38: 92–98.

Vladimirtsov, B. J. 1929. *Sravnitel'naja grammatika mongol'skogo pis'mennogo jazyka i xalxaskogo narechija*. Leningrad.

Voegelin, C. F., and F. M. Voegelin. 1977. *Classification and Index of the World's Languages*. New York.

TURKIC

Menges, Karl H. 1968. *The Turkic Languages and Peoples*. Wiesbaden.

Underhill, Robert. 1982. Personal letter.

MONGOLIAN

Binnick, Robert I. 1981. *On the Classification of the Mongolian Languages*. Project on Mongolian Historico-Comparative Syntax, Scarborough College, University of Toronto.

Doerfer, Gerhard. 1964. "Klassifikation und Verbreitung der mongolischen Sprachen," in *Mongolistik*. Leiden.

Poppe, Nicholas. 1955. *Introduction to Mongolian Comparative Studies*. Helsinki.
———. 1970. *Mongolian Language Handbook*. Washington, D.C.

TUNGUS

Benzing, J. 1956. *Die tungusischen Sprachen*. Wiesbaden.

4.2 CHUKCHI-KAMCHATKAN

Five Chukchi-Kamchatkan languages, with a total of 23,000 speakers, are found in northeastern Siberia, primarily on the Chukchi and Kamchatkan peninsulas (see Map 4.2). According to Jakobson (1942: 602), the Chukchi-Kamchatkan (= Luorawetlan) family was first perceived by S. Krasheninnikov, who connected Chukchi and Koryak in 1775. In 1798 N. Cherepanov added Kamchadal to the group. The first serious treatise on these languages was published by L. Radloff in 1861, and the first comparative study of the family was made by W. Bogoras in 1922.

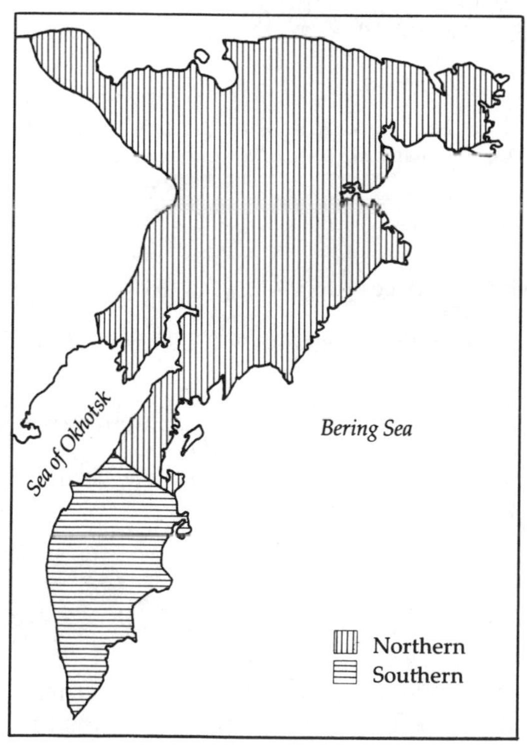

Map 4.2. The Chukchi-Kamchatkan family

In the twentieth century two additional members of the group have been recognized, both of which were previously treated as dialects of Koryak. Kerek became isolated from the other Koryak dialects and has undergone substantial Chukchi influence. Alyutor has only recently been recognized by the Soviet authorities as a language distinct from Koryak. The subgrouping of the family is fairly straightforward. There is a basic, and deep, division between a Southern branch, with Kamchadal as the sole member, and a Northern branch comprising the other four languages. Within the Northern group Chukchi apparently stands somewhat apart from the other three (see List 4.10).

List 4.10. The Chukchi-Kamchatkan Family

CHUKCHI-KAMCHATKAN:
I NORTHERN:
  A Chukchi
  B KORYAK:
    1 Kerek
    2 Koryak
    3 Alyutor
II SOUTHERN: Kamchadal

The most promising external links for the Chukchi-Kamchatkan family appear to lie with the Eskimo-Aleut family and the Gilyak isolate. These possibilities are discussed in section 7.3.

Austerlitz, Robert. 1974. "Paleosiberian Languages," in *EB* 13: 914–16.
Bogoras, W. 1922. *Chukchee*. Washington, D.C.
Comrie, Bernard. 1981. "Paleosiberian and Other Languages," in Bernard Comrie, *The Languages of the Soviet Union*. Cambridge, Eng.
Jakobson, Roman. 1942. "The Paleosiberian Languages," *AA* 44: 602–20.
Radloff, L. 1861. *Über die Sprache der Tschuktschen und ihr Verhältniss zum Korjakischen*. St. Petersburg.
Skorik, P. J. 1968. "Chukotsko-kamchatskie jazyki," in *Jazyki narodov SSSR* 5. Moscow.
Worth, Dean S. 1963. "Paleosiberian," in *CTIL* 1.

4.3 DRAVIDIAN

There are about two dozen Dravidian languages, with a total of perhaps 145 million speakers. As shown in Map 4.3, they are found predominantly in southern India, but there are a few outliers, separated from the main

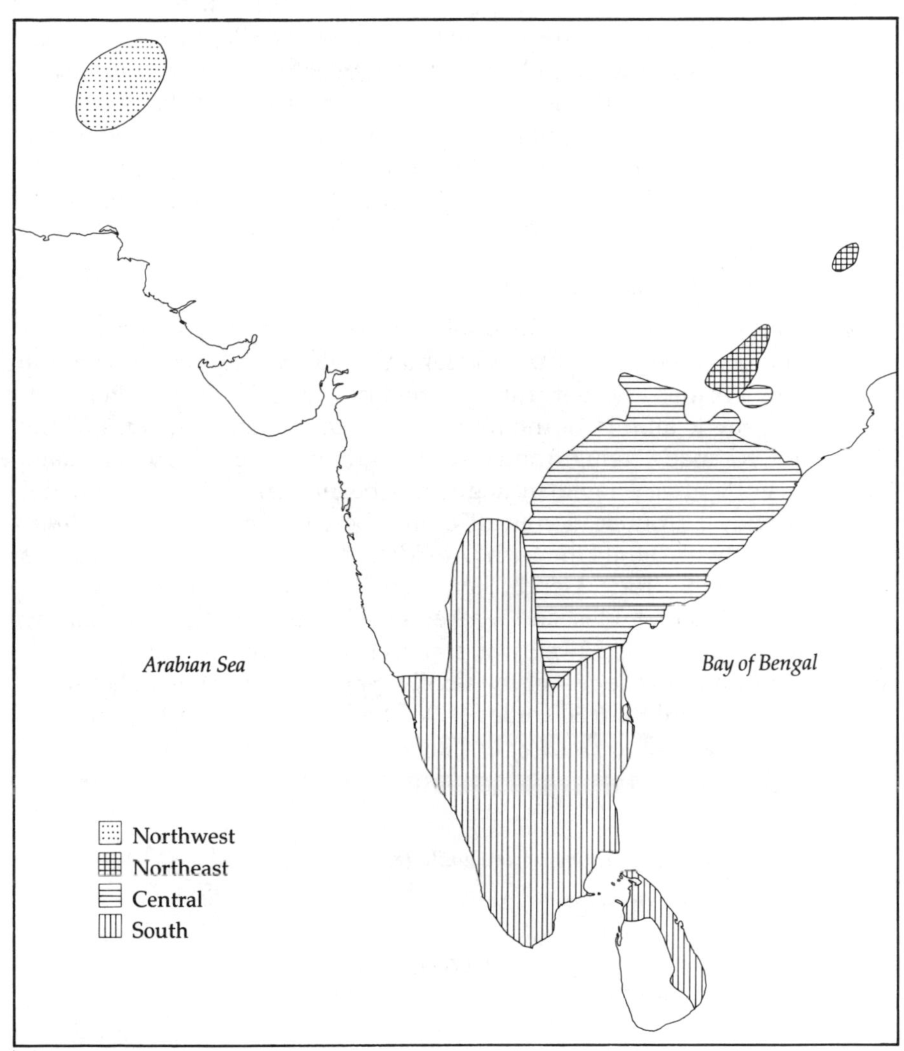

Map 4.3. The Dravidian family

body of Dravidian speakers, in eastern India (Malto, Kurux, Kui) and southern Pakistan (Brahui). The extinct language Elamite, formerly spoken in what is today southwestern Iran, has also been considered distantly related to the Dravidian family. The best-known Dravidian languages are Telugu, Tamil, Malayalam, and Kannada. They are the only Dravidian languages with literary traditions dating from pre-Christian times, and together they account for over 95 percent of the Dravidian population.

4.3.1 History of Dravidian Classification

Although grammars of individual Dravidian languages appeared as early as the seventeenth century, the family itself was not recognized until 1816, when a British civil servant stationed in India, Francis W. Ellis, proposed the genetic affinity of the four literary Dravidian languages (Tamil, Malayalam, Kannada, Telugu) and three nonliterary tongues (Tulu, Kodagu, Malto). Comparative Dravidian linguistics began, auspiciously, four decades later with the publication in 1856 of Robert A. Caldwell's *Comparative Grammar*. Caldwell coined the term Dravidian (based on a Sanskrit word for Tamil); added Kota, Toda, Gondi, Kui, Kurux, and Brahui to the seven languages enumerated by Ellis; and worked out the rudiments of comparative Dravidian linguistics. Caldwell was somewhat unclear regarding the relationship of Brahui to the rest of the family. Spoken in what is today southwest Pakistan, more than 800 miles (1,280 km) from the nearest Dravidian language, Brahui had, according to Caldwell, "a Dravidian element" in its vocabulary, but he stopped short of granting it full-fledged membership in

List 4.11. The Dravidian Family (Konow 1906)

DRAVIDIAN:
- I NORTH: Brahui
- II CENTRAL AND SOUTH:
  - A CENTRAL:
    - 1 GONDI-TELUGU: Gondi, Kui, Kolami, Naiki, Telugu
    - 2 KURUX-MALTO: Kurux, Malto
  - B SOUTH:
    - 1 TODA-KANNADA:
      - a KANNADA
      - b TODA-KOTA: Toda, Kota
    - 2 Kodagu
    - 3 Tulu
    - 4 TAMIL-MALAYALAM: Tamil, Malayalam

List 4.12. The Dravidian Family (Zvelebil 1974)

DRAVIDIAN:
- I NORTH:
  - A Brahui
  - B KURUX-MALTO
- II CENTRAL:
  - A KOLAMI-PARJI
  - B TELUGU-KUI:
    - 1 Telugu
    - 2 GONDI-KUI
- III SOUTH:
  - A Tulu
  - B TAMIL-KANNADA:
    - 1 KANNADA
    - 2 TAMIL-TODA:
      - a KOTA-TODA
      - b TAMIL-KODAGU:
        - i Kodagu
        - ii TAMIL-MALAYALAM

the Dravidian family. Nevertheless, by the end of the nineteenth century, it had become apparent that Brahui was in fact Dravidian, though perhaps the family's most divergent member. This was the position taken in Konow (1906: 285), where the Dravidian subgrouping in List 4.11 was proposed.

The first half of the twentieth century saw little progress in Dravidian classification, but during the 1960's contributions by several linguists (including M. B. Emeneau, B. Krishnamurti, and P. S. Subrahmanyam) led to a new view of Dravidian subgrouping containing three primary branches, as given in List 4.12.

4.3.2 *Present Status of Dravidian Classification*

In the past decade the initial enthusiasm for the tripartite subgrouping of List 4.12 was tempered by a growing disenchantment with certain aspects of the classification. McAlpin (1981: 21), summarizing these developments, cites two major defects. First, Brahui and Kurux-Malto do not constitute a valid genetic group. The evidence supporting this grouping (i.e. Emeneau 1962) was scant from the start, and the principal shared innovation linking the two was shown during the 1970's to be independent, but convergent developments. Second, Kolami-Parji and Telugu-Kui do not form a valid genetic node; Krishnamurti (1969) suggests that Telugu-Kui

List 4.13. The Dravidian Family (Andronov 1978, McAlpin 1981)

Andronov 1978

DRAVIDIAN:
- I Brahui
- II DRAVIDIAN PROPER:
  - A KURUX-MALTO
  - B CENTRAL AND SOUTH:
    - 1 GONDI-KUI
    - 2 KOLAMI-TAMIL:
      - a KOLAMI-PARJI
      - b TELUGU-TAMIL:
        - i Telugu
        - ii TULU-TAMIL:
          - α Tulu
          - β KANNADA-TAMIL

McAlpin 1981

DRAVIDIAN:
- I Brahui
- II DRAVIDIAN PROPER:
  - A KURUX-MALTO
  - B CENTRAL AND SOUTH:
    - 1 KOLAMI-PARJI
    - 2 TELUGU-KUI
    - 3 TAMIL-TULU (= SOUTH DRAVIDIAN)

may be closer to South Dravidian than to Kolami-Parji. Thus, for both North and Central Dravidian the requisite shared innovations are lacking. There are, according to McAlpin, five secure nodes within the Dravidian family: Brahui, Kurux-Malto, Kolami-Parji, Telugu-Kui, and South Dravidian. Precisely how these five nodes fit together is unresolved; two recent proposals are shown in List 4.13. Languages whose precise position in the family continues to be controversial are Telugu (formerly believed to be most closely related to South Dravidian, but now subgrouped with Gondi-Kui), Tulu (apparently standing at some distance from the rest of South Dravidian), and a few preliterate languages only recently discovered (e.g. Koraga, Kurumba, Bellari).

A final development in the 1970's saw the revival of the theory that the Dravidian family is related to the extinct Elamite language, spoken from roughly 2,000 B.C. to 500 B.C. in what is today southwest Iran. This hypothesis was first put forth in the mid-nineteenth century by several different scholars, including Caldwell. During the 1970's the hypothesis was rediscovered and elaborated by McAlpin; for a detailed summary of these developments, consult McAlpin (1981).

The Dravidian classification adopted in this volume (List 4.14) is a slightly modified version of McAlpin's subgrouping, in which Central Dravidian has been retained as a genetic unit, but North Dravidian has not.

For a discussion of proposed genetic links between Dravidian and other language families, see section 7.3 below.

List 4.14. The Elamo-Dravidian Family (McAlpin 1981 and others)

ELAMO-DRAVIDIAN:
I †Elamite
II DRAVIDIAN:
  A NORTHWEST: Brahui
  B DRAVIDIAN PROPER:
    1 NORTHEAST (= KURUX-MALTO)
    2 CENTRAL:
      a KOLAMI-PARJI
      b TELUGU-KUI
    3 SOUTH:
      a Tulu
      b TAMIL-KANNADA

Andronov, M. S. 1965a. *Dravidijskie jazyki*. Moscow.
———. 1965b. "Lexicostatistic Analysis of the Chronology of Disintegration of Proto-Dravidian," *Indo-Iranian Journal* 7: 170–86.
———. 1978. *Sravnitel'naja grammatika dravidijskix jazykov*. Moscow.
Caldwell, Robert A. 1856. *A Comparative Grammar of the Dravidian or South-Indian Family of Languages*. London.
Emeneau, Murray B. 1962. *Brahui and Dravidian Comparative Grammar*. UCPL 27.
———. 1969. "The Non-Literary Dravidian Languages," in *CTIL* 5.
Konow, Sten. 1906. *Munda and Dravidian Languages*, vol. 4 of George A. Grierson, ed., *Linguistic Survey of India*. Delhi.
Krishnamurti, B. 1969. "Comparative Dravidian Studies," in *CTIL* 5.
McAlpin, David W. 1974. "Toward Proto-Elamo-Dravidian," *Language* 50: 89–101.
———. 1975. "Elamite and Dravidian: Further Evidence of Relationship," *Current Anthropology* 16: 105–15.
———. 1980. "Is Brahui Really Dravidian?" *Proceedings of the Berkeley Linguistic Society* 6: 66–72.
———. 1981. *Proto-Elamo-Dravidian: The Evidence and Its Implications*. Philadelphia.
Subrahmanyam, P. S. 1969. "The Central Dravidian Languages," in S. Agesthialingom and N. Kumaraswami Raja, eds., *Dravidian Linguistics*. Annamalainagar.
Zvelebil, Kamil V. 1970. *Comparative Dravidian Phonology*. The Hague.
———. 1974. "Dravidian Languages," in *EB* 5.
———. 1977. *A Sketch of Comparative Dravidian Morphology* 1. The Hague.

4.4 SINO-TIBETAN

After Indo-Hittite, the Sino-Tibetan family is the most populous language family in the world, with close to a billion speakers. Sino-Tibetan

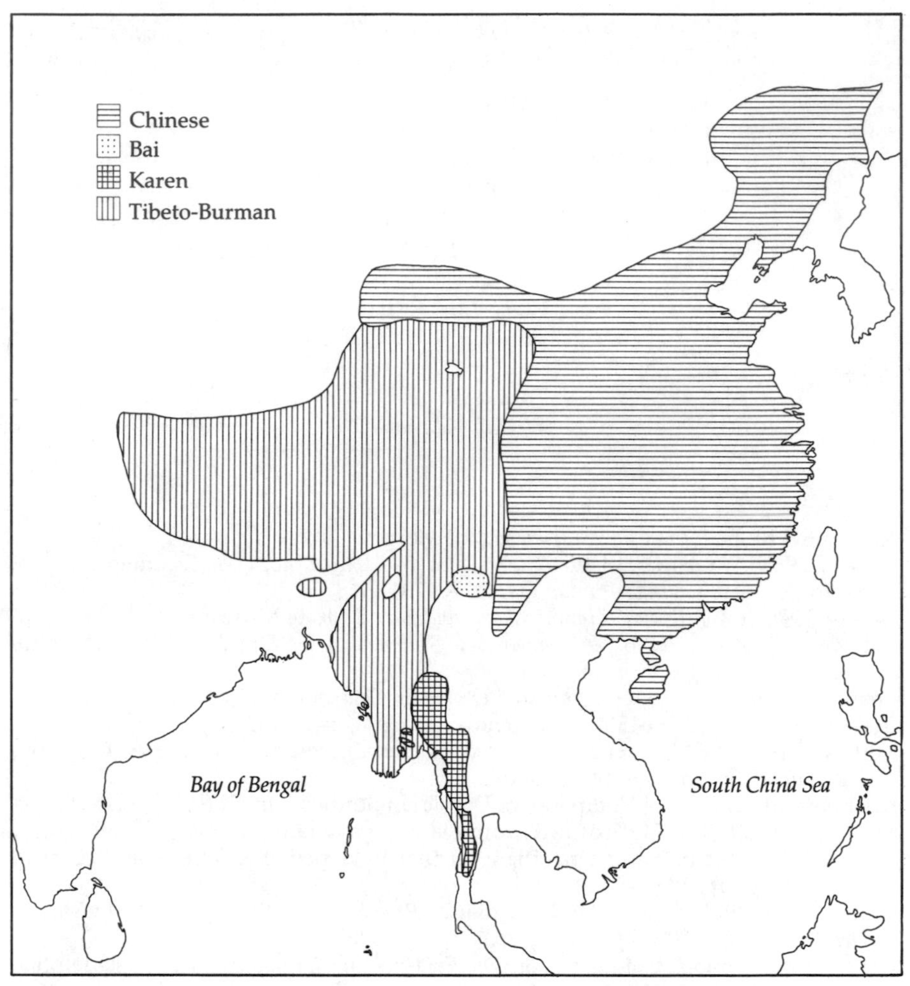

Map 4.4. The Sino-Tibetan family

languages are found primarily in China, India, Nepal, and Burma. To a lesser degree they are also found in the northern parts of Thailand, Laos, and Vietnam. Their geographic distribution is shown in Map 4.4. Except for Chinese, however, few of the languages have many speakers. Estimates for the number of speakers of each of the Chinese "dialects" (really separate languages) are difficult to come by. By my estimate there are currently some

927 million total Chinese speakers for the eight languages into which the Chinese continuum has been (somewhat arbitrarily) divided, with a distribution roughly as follows: Mandarin (680), Wu (69), Yue (= Cantonese, 53), Southern Min (36), Xiang (29), Kejia (28), Gan (21), Northern Min (11). These figures may be too low. Except for Chinese, however, few Sino-Tibetan languages have many speakers or are well known. Burmese, with some 22 million speakers, and Tibetan, with four million, are the only exceptions. The Hani language, spoken in southern China by more than one million people, is the only other Sino-Tibetan language with a million speakers, but it is hardly well known. Most Sino-Tibetan languages are spoken by small numbers of people, and their names are known only to specialists.

4.4.1 *History of Sino-Tibetan Classification*

In the sources I have been able to consult, the early history of the Sino-Tibetan family remains regrettably vague. What is clear is that during the nineteenth century there first appears in the linguistic literature an Indo-Chinese family, defined for the most part typologically by traits like tone and monosyllabism. Its membership varied somewhat from scholar to scholar but followed the general pattern shown in List 4.15. Most scholars excluded Mon-Khmer from this family, and the affinity of the small Miao-Yao group was also problematical. The Tai languages appeared to have a special relationship with Chinese. According to Konow (1909: 12), the large and diverse Tibeto-Burman family was first recognized in 1828 by B. H. Hodgson, and the first Tibeto-Burman classification was attempted by Max Müller in 1854. At the end of the century, August Conrady proposed a family uniting Chinese, Tai, and Tibeto-Burman (List 4.16).

In the early twentieth century Konow (1909: 1), among others, noted that the subfamilies lumped together under the rubric Indo-Chinese belonged to two distinct families: (1) Mon-Khmer and (2) Chinese, Tai, and Tibeto-

List 4.15. The Indo-Chinese Family (19th century)

INDO-CHINESE:
I CHINESE
II TAI
III KAREN
IV TIBETO-BURMAN
V MIAO-YAO
?VI MON-KHMER

List 4.16. The Indo-Chinese Family (Conrady 1896)

INDO-CHINESE:
I SINITIC (= CHINESE)
II TAI
III TIBETO-BURMAN

List 4.17. Proposed Subgroupings of the Sino-Tibetan Family

Konow 1909	*Li 1937*
SINO-TIBETAN:	**SINO-TIBETAN:**
I SINO-TAI:	I SINO-TAI:
A SINITIC	A SINITIC
B TAI	B TAI
II TIBETO-BURMAN	C MIAO-YAO
	II TIBETO-BURMAN

Benedict 1942	*Shafer 1955*
SINO-TIBETAN:	**SINO-TIBETAN:**
I SINITIC	I SINITIC
II TIBETO-KAREN:	?II TAI
A KAREN	III BODIC
B TIBETO-BURMAN	IV BURMIC
	V BARIC
	VI KAREN

Burman. For the latter family Konow proposed the subgrouping shown in List 4.17. Fang-kuei Li presented a similar classification in 1937, though he included Miao-Yao (List 4.17).

Although a few scholars were skeptical of the Chinese-Tai connection, it was largely accepted until 1942, when a young American linguist, Paul K. Benedict, proposed that the nearest affiliation of the Tai group was with the Austronesian family and not with Sino-Tibetan. In fact a similar opinion had been offered by Gustav Schlegel as early as 1902. Whether the roots shared by Chinese and Tai are merely early loans, as Benedict maintains, or represent the residue of a common origin, as suggested by Manomaivibool (1976) and others, continues to divide the linguistic community. Furthermore, even if these roots are loans, the direction of borrowing is often in dispute. Nevertheless, whether or not Chinese and Tai are genetically related at some level, it would appear that Tai's *closest* relatives are the Austronesian languages.

For Benedict (1942: 600) the Sino-Tibetan family was constituted as shown in List 4.17. He explicitly excluded Miao-Yao from Sino-Tibetan, linking it tentatively with Tai, Austronesian, and (until 1966) Austroasiatic in an Austric phylum (see section 4.5).

In 1955 Robert Shafer presented a classification of Sino-Tibetan in which both the Sino-Tai and Tibeto-Burman nodes were discounted. In addition, Shafer expressed reservations about the inclusion of Tai (see List 4.17).

4.4.2 *Present Status of Sino-Tibetan Classification*

Renewed interest in classificatory problems during the late 1960's and the 1970's has led to a growing consensus that Sino-Tibetan is made up of just three subfamilies: Sinitic, Karen, and Tibeto-Burman. Those who would also include Tai or Miao-Yao appear to be in a decreasing minority; Benedict (1976: 172) excludes both categorically: "The real problem . . . has always been why anyone . . . has ever seriously taken the Kam-Tai and/or M[iao]-Y[ao] languages to be true 'blood cousins' of S[ino]-T[ibetan], given the almost total lack of any basic ties in the respective lexicons."

There is agreement that Karen is closer to Tibeto-Burman than to Sinitic within Sino-Tibetan, but whether it is taxonomically coordinate with Tibeto-Burman, as in Benedict's proposal (see List 4.17), or simply a subgroup thereof is unresolved. Of the three constituents that make up Sino-Tibetan, both Sinitic and Karen are small, very close-knit families whose genetic unity is clear. Traditionally Sinitic and Chinese have been considered synonyms. However, Greenberg (1953) remarks, concerning the Bai (= Minchia) language(s), that "when the obvious Chinese borrowings are accounted for, the language still appears to show a special affinity to Chinese in fundamentals, so that it should probably be included in the Sinitic subbranch." His suggestion was generally ignored, and Voegelin and Voegelin (1977: 90) classified Bai as a member of Burmese-Lolo within Tibeto-Burman. According to Benedict (1983), new material on the Bai language(s) indicates that Greenberg was correct, and that Sinitic consists of two branches, Chinese and Bai. The third constituent, Tibeto-Burman, is large and more diverse, but still well defined, though the precise relationship of Karen to the Tibeto-Burman nucleus remains a problem. The internal structure of Tibeto-Burman is not at all clear, as the various subgrouping proposals in List 4.18 suggest.

The Sino-Tibetan classification adopted in this volume (List 4.19) follows Benedict (1942, 1972, 1983) for the overall subgrouping, but the Tibeto-Burman family is based primarily on Shafer (1955, 1974). The classification is thus similar to Egerod's (1974). In addition, certain modifications have been made on the basis of Matisoff (1980) and Bradley (1976). The Tibeto-Burman subgrouping should be considered provisional, for it is certain that future research will necessitate substantial revision. For a comprehensive review of different Tibeto-Burman subgroupings, consult Hale (1982).

Let us close this section by examining a curious development in the scholarly appraisal of Sino-Tibetan during the twentieth century. For Konow (1909: 2), Tibeto-Burman was "very closely related" to Sinitic. Three decades later Benedict (in a work not published until 1972) termed this same relationship "a distant one" (p. 2). Recently Lehman (1975: 218) implied

List 4.18. Proposed Subgroupings of the Tibeto-Burman Family

Konow 1909

TIBETO-BURMAN:
- I TIBETAN
- II HIMALAYAN
- III NORTH ASSAM
- IV BODO
- V NAGA
- VI Kachin
- VII KUKI-CHIN
- VIII BURMESE

Shafer 1955

TIBETO-BURMAN:[a]
- I TIBETIC
- II BARIC
- III BURMIC

Benedict 1972

TIBETO-BURMAN:
- I TIBETAN-KANAURI
- II BAHING-VAYU
- III ABOR-MIRI-DAFLA
- IV BURMESE-LOLO
- V Kachin
- VI KUKI-NAGA
- VII BARIC

Voegelin & Voegelin 1977

TIBETO-BURMAN:
- I TIBETAN
- II GYARUNG-MISHMI
- III BURMESE-LOLO
- IV NAGA-KUKI-CHIN
- V BODO-NAGA-KACHIN
- VI KAREN

[a]Shafer did not posit a TIBETO-BURMAN node, but these three groups are what remains after one excludes SINITIC, TAI, and KAREN from his Sino-Tibetan family.

List 4.19. The Sino-Tibetan Family (Benedict 1942, Shafer 1955, and others)

SINO-TIBETAN:
- I SINITIC:
    - A BAI
    - B CHINESE
- II TIBETO-KAREN:
    - A KAREN
    - B TIBETO-BURMAN:
        - 1 TIBETIC
        - 2 BARIC
        - 3 BURMIC:
            - a KUKI-NAGA
            - b KACHIN-LUIC
            - c BURMESE-MOSO:
                - i MOSO
                - ii BURMESE-LOLO:
                    - α BURMIC
                    - β LOLO

that the Sino-Tibetan family is as yet unproved: "While I fully subscribe to the view that actual proof of genetic relationship is founded upon explicit *Lautlehren* [sound laws], I believe that B[enedict] has *all but* proved the S[ino]-T[ibetan] hypothesis. He has listed so many fairly obvious cognate sets . . . that their cumulative effect alone precludes serious doubt."

How can it be that the dramatic increase in both the quantity and quality of Sino-Tibetan sources during this century seems to have had the effect of eroding confidence in the Sino-Tibetan family? Have these new materials really called into question the validity of Sino-Tibetan? Of course not. What has happened in the study of Sino-Tibetan parallels what happened in African classification: the standard of proof of genetic affinity has been modified to such an extent by the requirement of regular sound correspondences that even such obvious groupings as Sino-Tibetan fail to meet the new requirements. The striking similarity between the quotation from Lehman above and the one from Welmers on African languages (page 121) illustrates the pervasiveness of the current malaise caused by the insistence on sound correspondences as proof of genetic affinity. Further discussion of this issue may be found in section 3.6.

SINO-TIBETAN

Benedict, Paul K. 1942. "Thai, Kadai, and Indonesian: A New Alignment in Southeastern Asia," *AA* 44: 576–601.

———. 1972. *Sino-Tibetan: A Conspectus*. Cambridge, Eng.

———. 1976. "Sino-Tibetan: Another Look," *Journal of the American Oriental Society* 96: 167–97.

———. 1983. Personal letter.

Bodman, Nicholas C. 1980. "Proto-Chinese and Sino-Tibetan: Data Towards Establishing the Nature of the Relationship," in Frans van Coetsem and Linda R. Waugh, eds., *Contributions to Historical Linguistics: Issues and Materials*. Leiden.

Bradley, David. 1976. "Akha and Southern Loloish," in Mantaro J. Hashimoto, ed., *Genetic Relationship, Diffusion, and Typological Similarities of East and Southeast Asian Languages*. Tokyo.

Chao, Yuen Ren. 1943. "Languages and Dialects in China," *Geographical Journal* 102: 63–66.

Chen, Matthew. 1976. "From Middle Chinese to Modern Peking," *Journal of Chinese Linguistics* 4: 113–277.

Conrady, August. 1896. *Eine indochinesische causativ-denominativ Bildung und ihr Zusammenhang mit den Tonaccenten*. Leipzig.

Egerod, Søren C. 1974. "Sino-Tibetan Languages," in *EB* 16: 796–806.

Greenberg, Joseph H. 1953. "Historical Linguistics and Unwritten Languages," in A. L. Kroeber, ed., *Anthropology Today*. Chicago.

Lehman, F. K. 1975. Review of *Sino-Tibetan: A Conspectus*, by Paul K. Benedict, *Language* 51: 215–19.

Li, Fang-kuei. 1937. "Languages and Dialects of China," in *Chinese Yearbook*. Shanghai. Reprinted in *Journal of Chinese Linguistics* 1 (1972): 1–13.

Manomaivibool, Prapin. 1976. "Thai and Chinese—Are They Genetically Related?" *CAAL* 6: 11–31.
Shafer, Robert. 1955. "Classification of the Sino-Tibetan Languages," *Word* 11: 94–111.
———. 1974. *Introduction to Sino-Tibetan*. Wiesbaden.
Voegelin, C. F., and F. M. Voegelin. 1977. *Classification and Index of the World's Languages*. New York.

TIBETO-BURMAN

Benedict, Paul K. 1972. *Sino-Tibetan: A Conspectus*. Cambridge, Eng.
Bradley, David. 1979. *Proto-Loloish*. London.
Burling, Robbins. 1959. "Proto-Bodo," *Language* 35: 433–53.
———. 1967. *Proto Lolo-Burmese*. Bloomington, Ind.
Hale, Austin. 1982. *Research on Tibeto-Burman Languages*. Berlin.
Jones, Robert B., Jr. 1961. *Karen Linguistic Studies*. *UCPL* 25.
Konow, Sten. 1909. *Tibeto-Burman Family*, vol. 3, part 1 of George A. Grierson, ed., *Linguistic Survey of India*. Delhi.
Luce, G. H. 1959. "Introduction to the Comparative Study of Karen Languages," *Journal of the Burma Research Society* 42,*1*: 1–18.
Matisoff, James A. 1978. *Variational Semantics in Tibeto-Burman*. Philadelphia.
———. 1980. "The Languages and Dialects of Tibeto-Burman," unpublished manuscript.
Miller, Roy Andrew. 1969. "The Tibeto-Burman Languages of South Asia," in *CTIL* 5.

4.5 AUSTRIC: MIAO-YAO, AUSTROASIATIC, DAIC

The Austric phylum is a controversial grouping that consolidates four families: Miao-Yao, Austroasiatic, Daic (= Kadai), and Austronesian. Altogether the Austric phylum contains close to 1,200 languages, with a total of around 293 million speakers. In this section we will discuss the Austric hypothesis and its three Asiatic subfamilies, Miao-Yao, Austroasiatic, and Daic (see Map 4.5). The Austronesian family is dealt with in section 5.1.

Four *Miao-Yao* languages are spoken in scattered "islands" throughout southern China (mainly Guizhou Province) and the northern regions of Vietnam, Laos, and Thailand. The Miao language is composed of several divergent dialects with perhaps a total of five million speakers. Mien (= Yao) has about one million.

The *Austroasiatic* family has approximately 150 languages and 56 million speakers, unequally divided into two important subfamilies, Munda and Mon-Khmer. Ten *Munda* languages are spoken in northeastern India by six million people; Santali (4 million) and Mundari (2 million) account for most of the speakers. *Mon-Khmer* languages are spoken throughout much of Southeast Asia, primarily in Laos, Vietnam, and Kampuchea, but also in Thailand, Burma, the Malay Peninsula, and the Nicobar Islands in the An-

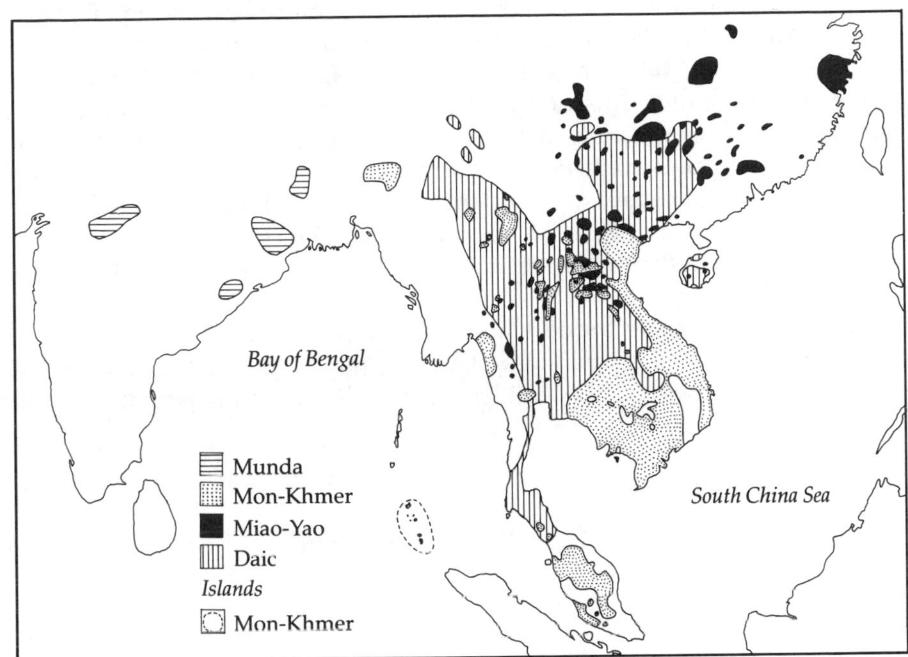

Map 4.5. The Miao-Yao, Austroasiatic, and Daic families

daman Sea. One Mon-Khmer language (Khasi) is found in northeast India. There are about 140 Mon-Khmer languages, with a total of 50 million speakers, but only Vietnamese (47 million) and Khmer (= Cambodian, 7 million) are well known.

The *Daic* family has around 60 languages, which are spoken by an estimated 50 million people in Thailand, Laos, northern Vietnam, Burma, and southern China, and also on Hainan Island in the Gulf of Tonkin. The best-known languages are Thai (= Siamese, 30 million speakers) and Lao (= Laotian, 17 million). Other Daic languages with more than a million speakers are Zhuang (13 million), Northern Tai (6 million), Southern Tai (4 million), Bouyei (2 million), Shan (2 million), Zhongjia (2 million), Kam (1.5 million), and Li (1 million).

4.5.1 *History of Austric Classification*

The linguistic relationships within Southeast Asia remained obscure until the second half of the nineteenth century, when the genetic picture slowly began to be delineated. The process was gradual; only after roughly a century of work (c. 1850–1950) were the basic outlines clear, and indeed even today there are questions that have not been fully resolved. The history of Austric is intertwined with that of Sino-Tibetan in respect to two families, Tai and Miao-Yao, which have been assigned to Sino-Tibetan by some linguists and to Austric by others. The borderline between the well-defined Sino-Tibetan family and the controversial Austric phylum has consequently fluctuated over the years, with a growing consensus that both Tai and Miao-Yao either are independent families or belong to Austric rather than to Sino-Tibetan. Fig. 4.1 compares the differing subgroups of the major Southeast Asian language families as conceived today and at the start of this century.

Until the 1850's the Munda languages were thought to belong to the Dravidian family, since speakers of both groups were of the same racial type. In 1854, however, Max Müller separated the Munda languages from

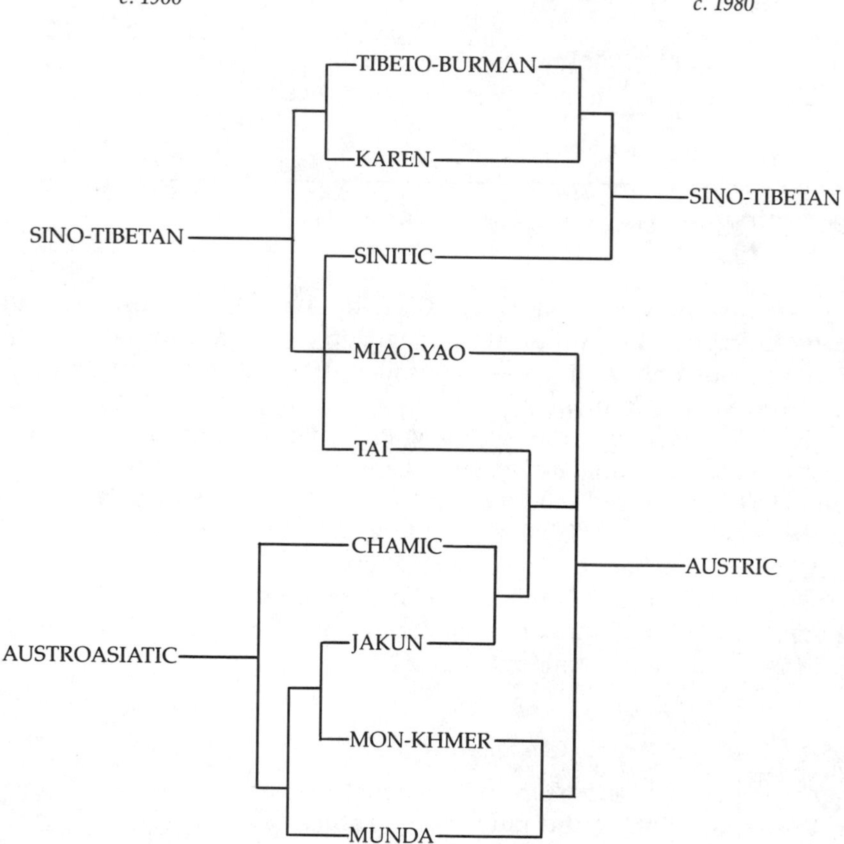

Fig. 4.1. Subgrouping of Southeast Asian families, 1900 and 1980

Dravidian and coined the term Munda for the family. At about the same time J. R. Logan and F. Mason pointed out similarities between Munda languages and languages farther east belonging to what is now called the Mon-Khmer family; Logan also called attention to resemblances between Khasi, spoken in India, and Mon-Khmer. The larger grouping, comprising Mon-Khmer and Munda, was dismissed by scholars such as James M. Hasswell and C. J. F. S. Forbes during the latter part of the nineteenth century. On the other hand, Ernst Kuhn presented evidence in 1889 substantiating the link between the Munda family and Mon, Khmer, the languages of Malacca, and those of the Nicobar Islands, though he hesitated to call it a genetic connection. He referred instead to a "common substratum." During the twentieth century the grouping that comprises Munda and Mon-Khmer has become known as Austroasiatic and its validity as a genetic node is now well established.

In 1906 the Austrian anthropologist Wilhelm Schmidt proposed that the Austroasiatic family (= Munda + Mon-Khmer) and the Austronesian family (formerly known as Malayo-Polynesian and covering the greater part of Oceania; see section 5.1) together constitute an even larger family, which he named Austric (see List 4.20). Schmidt cited striking correspondences in prefixes and infixes (the latter being a fairly rare phenomenon in human language), as well as certain lexical agreements, to substantiate his argument.

The Austric hypothesis has been controversial from the start and is no less so today. Indeed, given the fragmentary nature of the evidence and the generally hostile attitude toward proposals of this type, it could hardly have been otherwise. From today's perspective it is clear that Schmidt's classification contained several errors: (1) Chamic and Jakun are misclassified as Austroasiatic; both are members of Austronesian; (2) the Viet-Muong

List 4.20. The Austric Family (Schmidt 1926)

AUSTRIC:[a]
I AUSTROASIATIC:
  A ASLIAN
  B CENTRAL:
    1 Khasi
    2 NICOBAR ISLANDS
    3 PALAUNGIC
  C SOUTHEAST AND NORTHWEST:
    1 MON-KHMER:
      a MONIC
    [1 MON-KHMER]
      b Khmer
      c BAHNARIC
      d JAKUN
    2 MUNDA
  D CHAMIC
II AUSTRONESIAN:
  A INDONESIAN
  B OCEANIC

[a]In this list, as throughout this volume, modern names have been substituted for some of the original terminology, e.g. Malaccan → Aslian, Southeast Mixed → Chamic.

group was incorrectly classified as Sino-Tibetan; it is now known to be a member of Mon-Khmer; and (3) the Tai and Miao-Yao groups were also incorrectly placed in Sino-Tibetan. As we shall see directly, the Tai languages are closest genetically to the Austronesian family, and the Miao-Yao languages appear to belong to the Austric complex, or at the very least to Austro-Tai.

In the early 1940's a young American linguist, Paul K. Benedict, recognized a small family of languages in southern China that had obvious affinities with the Tai family. He named this group the Kadai family. Furthermore, he noticed that both this Kadai group and the Tai family appeared to share more cognates with the Austronesian family than with the Sinitic branch of Sino-Tibetan, with which they were usually associated. An examination of the supposed Sinitic-Tai cognates revealed that the words in question (e.g. numbers, cultural items) were almost certainly loans, and that the basic vocabulary (e.g. body parts, pronouns) indicated an unmistakable Austronesian affiliation. Benedict published his findings in 1942 and simultaneously clarified both Sino-Tibetan and Austric classification. Benedict only tentatively included Miao-Yao in Austric at this point (see List 4.21).

As Benedict himself noted, the Austro-Tai hypothesis had been foreshadowed in studies published a half century or so earlier. In 1887 Terrien de Lacouperie had suggested a relationship between Li (a Kadai language) and Formosan languages (which belong to Austronesian). Two years later E. H. Parker had recognized similarities between Li and Tai languages, and in 1902 Gustav Schlegel called attention to similarities between Tai and Malay (an Austronesian language). No one, however, had systematically surveyed the available evidence, and drawn the obvious conclusions, until Benedict (1942). Even though his Austro-Tai proposal flew in the face of established dogma, it gained support in the 1950's (e.g. Greenberg 1953).

List 4.21. The Austric Family (Benedict 1942)

AUSTRIC:
?I MIAO-YAO:
  A MIAO
  B YAO
II AUSTROASIATIC:
  A MON-KHMER
  B VIET-MUONG
  C MUNDA
III AUSTRO-TAI:
  A TAI
  B KADAI
  C AUSTRONESIAN

Nonetheless, some linguists still cling to the traditional view (i.e. that Tai is closest to Chinese).

Schmidt's Austric hypothesis, however, has been less successful. Sebeok (1942) reviewed it negatively, and Greenberg (1953) concluded that "the Austric hypothesis cannot be accepted on present evidence." As for Miao-Yao, Greenberg (1953) found it to be "a separate branch of Sino-Tibetan, no more divergent than, say, the Karen languages of Burma."

After leaving the linguistic scene for some two decades to pursue a career in psychiatry, Benedict returned to the problem of Austro-Tai in the mid-1960's and increased the number of putative Austro-Tai roots from 30 to around 400. The Austro-Tai hypothesis was strengthened by material from the Kam-Sui group, first recognized by Fang-kuei Li in the early 1940's. Like the Kadai family, Kam-Sui is a small "Tai-like" group of languages displaying affinities with both Tai and Austronesian languages. Benedict considerably bolstered the case for Austro-Tai, but he retreated in his support of Austric, reinterpreting the connection between Austroasiatic and Austronesian as a "substratum relationship" rather than a true genetic bond. Miao-Yao was treated as a separate entity "with Austroasiatic . . . the most likely affiliation" (Benedict 1966–67: 327).

In 1975 Benedict published his collected writings on Austro-Tai, including a comprehensive glossary of Austro-Tai roots. In this work he included the Miao-Yao group in an expanded version of the Austro-Tai family, as shown in List 4.22. A connection between this expanded Austro-Tai stock and the Austroasiatic family (i.e. the Austric hypothesis) was still denied, though in rather equivocal terms: "There are indications of a very early linkage (less than a full genetic relationship) between A[ustro]-T[ai] and the Austroasiatic . . . languages. Our present analysis confirms this linkage. [However,] we must still think in terms of a 'linkage' or 'substratum' rather than of a fully reconstructable language stock" (Benedict 1975: 135).

Like Benedict, Greenberg revised his classification of these language families, coming to feel that both his earlier inclusion of Miao-Yao in Sino-Tibetan and his dismissal of Austric were incorrect. By 1980 he viewed the Austric phylum roughly as we see it in List 4.23.

List 4.22. The Austro-Tai Family (Benedict 1975)

AUSTRO-TAI:
I MIAO-YAO
II TAI-AUSTRONESIAN:
  A DAIC
  B AUSTRONESIAN

List 4.23. The Austric Family (Greenberg 1980)

AUSTRIC:
I MIAO-YAO
II AUSTROASIATIC
III AUSTRO-TAI:
  A DAIC
  B AUSTRONESIAN

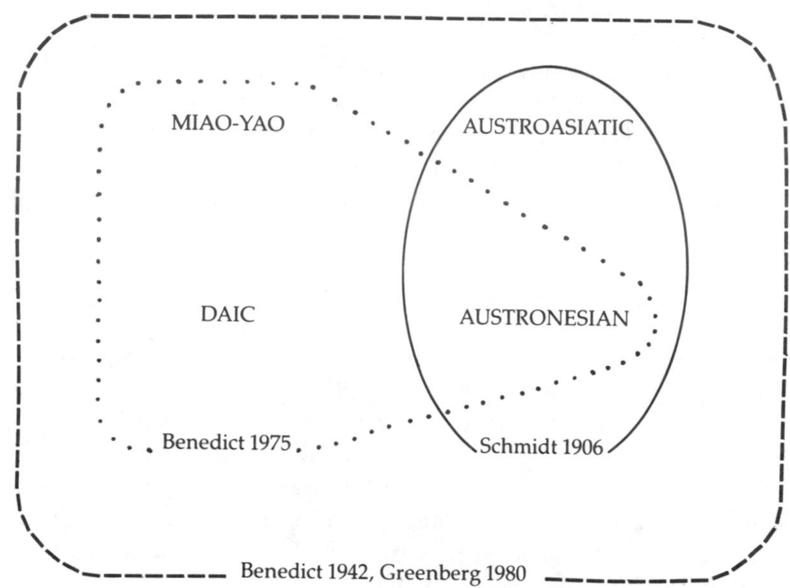

Fig. 4.2. Different definitions of Austric

4.5.2 Present Status of Austric Classification

There is, as yet, no consensus on the validity of the Austric phylum, with strong opinions on both sides of the issue. Furthermore, even among those who support an Austric grouping there are differences on which families are to be included, as Fig. 4.2 illustrates. For the overall subgrouping of Austric, I have adopted Benedict's (1942) position (List 4.21, above).

The internal subgrouping of the four constituents of Austric differs in the degree of clarity attained. The relationships are fairly straightforward for Miao-Yao, less so for Austroasiatic and Daic, and quite complex and unsettled for Austronesian (see section 5.1). The Miao-Yao family is bifurcated into the Miao language as one group and the small Yao (= Mien) family as the other. According to Benedict (1983), Daic apparently has two branches, Lati-Gelao and Li-Kam-Tai, with the latter group containing the Kam-Sui and Tai families.*

The Austroasiatic family is larger and more diverse than either Miao-Yao or Daic, and no definitive subgrouping for the family has so far been established. List 4.24 illustrates five proposals, by Schmidt (1926), Sebeok (1942),

*It is customary to use the spelling Tai for the group of languages to which Thai (=Siamese= Standard Thai) belongs

List 4.24. Proposed Subgroupings of the Austroasiatic Family

Schmidt 1926

AUSTROASIATIC:
- I ASLIAN
- II CENTRAL:
  - A Khasi
  - B PALAUNGIC
  - C NICOBAR ISLANDS
- III MON-KHMER-MUNDA:
  - A MON-KHMER:
    - 1 MONIC
    - 2 Khmer
    - 3 BAHNARIC
    - 4 JAKUN
  - B MUNDA
- IV CHAMIC

Sebeok 1942

AUSTROASIATIC:
- I MUNDA
- II MON-KHMER:
  - A MON-KHMER PROPER:
    - 1 MONIC
    - 2 Khmer
    - 3 BAHNARIC
    - 4 PEARIC
  - B CHAMIC
  - C ASLIAN
  - D NICOBAR ISLANDS
  - E PALAUNGIC-KHMUIC
  - F Khasi

Pinnow 1959, 1963

AUSTROASIATIC:
- I WESTERN:
  - A Nahali
  - B MUNDA
- II EASTERN:
  - A NICOBAR ISLANDS
  - B PALAUNG-KHMER:
    - 1 Khasi
    - 2 PALAUNGIC
    - 3 MON-KHMER:
      - a MONIC
      - b Khmer
      - c BAHNARIC
    - 4 ASLIAN

Voegelin & Voegelin 1977

AUSTROASIATIC:
- I ASLIAN (including JAKUN)
- II MON-KHMER
- III MUNDA
- IV NICOBAR ISLANDS

Diffloth 1974

AUSTROASIATIC:
- I MUNDA
- II NICOBAR ISLANDS
- III MON-KHMER:
  - A Khasi
  - B PALAUNGIC
  - C MONIC
  - D KHMUIC
  - E VIET-MUONG
  - F KATUIC
  - G BAHNARIC
  - H PEARIC
  - I Khmer
  - J SEMANG
  - K SAKAI
  - L SEMELAIC

Pinnow (1959, 1963), Diffloth (1974), and Voegelin and Voegelin (1977). It now appears that a dozen different subfamilies constitute Austroasiatic:

(14)

MUNDA	BAHNARIC
Khasi	Khmer
PALAUNGIC	PEARIC
KHMUIC	MONIC
VIET-MUONG	ASLIAN
KATUIC	NICOBAR ISLANDS

The Austroasiatic subgrouping adopted in this volume represents Gérard Diffloth's current appraisal, which he has been kind enough to share with me. Diffloth divides Austroasiatic into two branches; the Munda family constitutes one branch, and the remaining 11 families constitute the second branch, commonly known as Mon-Khmer. The Munda family consists of Northern and Southern branches. The Munda classification followed in this volume is based on suggestions from David Stampe and Norman Zide. Mon-Khmer, according to Diffloth, has three branches, North, East, and South, as shown in List 4.25. This Mon-Khmer subgrouping should be regarded as tentative and will likely undergo further modification as research on Austroasiatic classification proceeds.

List 4.25. The Austroasiatic Family (Diffloth 1982)

AUSTROASIATIC:
I MUNDA
II MON-KHMER:
A NORTH:
1 Khasi
2 PALAUNGIC-KHMUIC
3 VIET-MUONG
B EAST:
1 KATUIC
2 BAHNARIC
3 Khmer
4 PEARIC
C SOUTH:
1 MONIC
2 ASLIAN
3 NICOBAR ISLANDS

AUSTRIC

Benedict, Paul K. 1942. "Thai, Kadai, and Indonesian: A New Alignment in Southeastern Asia," *AA* 44: 576–601.
———. 1976a. "Austro-Thai and Austroasiatic," in *AAS* 1.
———. 1976b. "Shorto: In Defense of Austric—Comment," *CAAL* 6: 105–8.
Diffloth, Gérard. 1976. "An Appraisal of Benedict's Views on Austroasiatic and Austro-Thai Relations," in *South-East Asian Studies*, Discussion Paper No. 82, Kyoto University.

Greenberg, Joseph H. 1953. "Historical Linguistics and Unwritten Languages," in A. L. Kroeber, ed., *Anthropology Today*. Chicago.
———. 1980. Personal communication.
Hevesy, W. F. de. 1930. "On W. Schmidt's Munda-Mon-Khmer Comparisons (Does an 'Austric' Family of Languages Exist?)," *Bulletin of the School of Oriental and African Studies* 6: 187–200.
Schmidt, Wilhelm. 1906. *Die Mon-Khmer-Völker, ein Bindeglied zwischen Volkern Zentralasiens und Austronesiens*. Braunschweig.
———. 1926. *Die Sprachfamilien und Sprachenkreise der Erde*. Heidelberg.
Shorto, Harry L. 1976. "In Defense of Austric," *CAAL* 6: 95–104.

MIAO-YAO

Haudricourt, André G. 1971. "Les langues miao-yao," *ASEMI* 2, 4: 31–51.
Mao, Tsung-wu, and Chou Tsu-yao. 1962. "A Brief Description of the Languages of the Yao People," *Chung-kuo yu-wen* 113: 141–48.
Miao Language Team. 1962. "A Brief Description of the Miao Language," *Chung-kuo yu-wen* 111: 28–37. Reprinted in 1972 in Herbert C. Purnell, Jr., ed., *Miao and Yao Linguistic Studies*. Cornell University Data Paper 88.
Purnell, Herbert C., Jr. 1970. "Toward a Reconstruction of Proto-Miao-Yao," Ph.D. dissertation, Cornell University.

AUSTROASIATIC

Diffloth, Gérard. 1974. "Austro-Asiatic Languages," in *EB* 2: 480–84.
———. 1982. Personal letter.
Haudricourt, André G. 1966. "The Limits and Connections of Austroasiatic in the Northwest," in Zide, ed., *Studies*, listed below.
Kuhn, Ernst. 1889. *Beiträge zur Sprachenkunde Hinterindiens*. Munich.
Pinnow, Heinz-Jürgen. 1959. *Versuch einer historischen Lautlehre der Kharia-Sprache*. Wiesbaden.
———. 1963. "The Position of the Munda Languages Within the Austroasiatic Family," in H. L. Shorto, ed., *Linguistic Comparison in South East Asia and the Pacific*. London.
Sebeok, Thomas A. 1942. "An Examination of the Austroasiatic Language Family," *Language* 18: 206–17.
Thomas, David D. 1964. "A Survey of Austroasiatic and Mon-Khmer Comparative Studies," *MKS* 1: 149–63.
Voegelin, C. F., and F. M. Voegelin. 1977. *Classification and Index of the World's Languages*. New York.
Zide, Norman H. 1969. "Munda and Non-Munda Austroasiatic Languages," in *CTIL* 5.
———, ed. 1966. *Studies in Comparative Austroasiatic Linguistics*. The Hague.

MUNDA

Konow, Sten. 1906. *Munda and Dravidian Languages*, vol. 4 of George A. Grierson, ed., *Linguistic Survey of India*. Delhi.
Stampe, David. 1981. Personal letter.
Zide, Norman H. 1969. "Munda and Non-Munda Austroasiatic Languages," in *CTIL* 5.

MON-KHMER

Benjamin, Geoffrey. 1976. "Austroasiatic Subgroupings and Prehistory in the Malay Peninsula," in *AAS* 1.

Diffloth, Gérard. 1975. "Les langues mon-khmer de Malaisie, classification historique et innovations," *ASEMI* 6,4: 1–19.

Ferlus, Michel. 1974. "Le groupe viet-muong," *ASEMI* 5,*1*: 69–73.

Grierson, George A. 1904. *Mon-Khmer and Siamese-Chinese Families*, vol. 2 of Grierson, ed., *Linguistic Survey of India*. Delhi.

Headley, Robert K., Jr. 1976. "Some Considerations on the Classification of Khmer," in *AAS* 1.

———. 1978. "An English-Pearic Vocabulary," *MKS* 7: 61–94.

Huffman, Franklin E. 1976. "The Relevance of Lexicostatistics to Mon-Khmer Languages," in *AAS* 1.

Martin, Marie A. 1974. "Remarques générales sur les dialectes pear," *ASEMI* 5,*1*: 25–34.

Schmidt, Wilhelm. 1906. *Die Mon-Khmer-Völker, ein Bindeglied zwischen Völkern Zentralasiens und Austronesiens*. Braunschweig.

Thomas, David D. 1973. "A Note on the Branches of Mon-Khmer," *MKS* 4: 139–41.

———. 1979. "The Place of Alak, Tampuan, and West Bahnaric," *MKS* 8: 171–86.

Thomas, David D., and Robert K. Headley, Jr. 1970. "More on Mon-Khmer Subgrouping," *Lingua* 25: 398–418.

AUSTRO-TAI

Benedict, Paul K. 1942. "Thai, Kadai, and Indonesian: A New Alignment in Southeastern Asia," *AA* 44: 576–601.

———. 1966–67. "Austro-Thai Studies," *Behavior Science Notes*, 3 parts, 1 (1966), 2 (1967).

———. 1975. *Austro-Thai: Language and Culture*. New Haven, Conn.

Egerod, Søren C. 1976. "Benedict's Austro-Thai Hypothesis and the Traditional Views on Sino-Thai Relationship," *CAAL* 6: 51–59.

Gedney, William J. 1976. "On the Thai Evidence for Austro-Thai," *CAAL* 6: 65–81.

Wulff, Kurt. 1942. *Über das Verhältnis des Malayo-Polynesischen zum indochinesischen*. Copenhagen.

DAIC

Benedict, Paul K. 1983. Personal letter.

Brown, J. M. 1965. *From Ancient Thai to Modern Dialects*. Bangkok.

Li, Fang-kuei. 1960. "A Tentative Classification of Tai Dialects," in S. Diamond, ed., *Culture in History*. New York.

———. 1965. "The Tai and Kam-Sui Languages," *Lingua* 14: 148–79.

———. 1974. "Tai Languages," in *EB* 17: 989–92.

———. 1977. *A Handbook of Comparative Tai*. Honolulu.

5

Oceania

Close to 40 percent of the world's languages are spoken on the islands of the Pacific and Indian oceans. With perhaps a few exceptions, they belong to one of three families: Austronesian (formerly Malayo-Polynesian), Indo-Pacific (or Papuan), or Australian. The *Austronesian* family is the most widespread and the most numerous, but also the most close-knit of the three. Austronesian languages are spoken on practically every island from Madagascar to Easter Island, and from Formosa to New Zealand. Yet despite this enormous geographic distribution, their genetic unity is transparent. Languages belonging to the *Indo-Pacific* phylum are concentrated on New Guinea and surrounding islands, often in propinquity to Austronesian tongues. The languages belonging to Indo-Pacific display a bewildering diversity, and their genetic unity is still not accepted by many scholars. One of the few "islands" of the South Pacific that Austronesian speakers never inhabited, so far as we know, is the largest, Australia. The *Australian* family is coterminous with Australia itself. All Australian languages are spoken in Australia and, before the English invasion at least, only Australian languages were found there. The validity of the Australian family is by now both well established and widely accepted. It represents nonetheless an ancient grouping whose genetic unity is by no means obvious.

Capell, A. 1962. *A Linguistic Survey of the South-Western Pacific*. Noumea, New Caledonia.

Grace, George W. 1968. "Classification of the Languages of the Pacific," in Andrew P. Vayda, ed., *Peoples and Cultures of the Pacific*. Garden City, N.Y.

Salzner, Richard. 1960. *Sprachenatlas des Indopazifischen Raumes*, 2 vols. Wiesbaden.

Wurm, Stephen A., and Shirô Hattori, eds. 1981–83. *Language Atlas of the Pacific Area*, 2 vols. Stuttgart.

5.1 AUSTRIC: AUSTRONESIAN

The alleged genetic connections between the Austronesian family and the Miao-Yao, Austroasiatic, and Daic families of Southeast Asia were discussed in section 4.5. In this section we will examine the Austronesian family, which extends from Madagascar, off the east coast of Africa, through Indonesia and the Philippines and across the Pacific Ocean to Hawaii and Easter Island. The geographic distribution of the Austronesian family is shown in Map 5.1.

Austronesian comprises close to 1,000 languages with an estimated 180 million speakers. If we draw a line separating New Guinea and islands to the east of it from those to the west (most of Indonesia, the Philippines, Formosa, Madagascar), there are roughly equal numbers of languages on either side of the line, but almost all the speakers are in the western half. Even though close to 500 Austronesian languages are spoken on New Guinea and islands farther east, they probably claim fewer than two million speakers, compared with an estimated 179 million Austronesian speakers in the western half (primarily in Indonesia and the Philippines).

Only two Austronesian languages outside the Philippines and Indonesia have more than a million speakers. Malagasy, on the island of Madagascar, has 8 million, and Malay has 10 million in Malaysia, with perhaps 15 million speakers of various dialects (some extremely divergent) elsewhere.

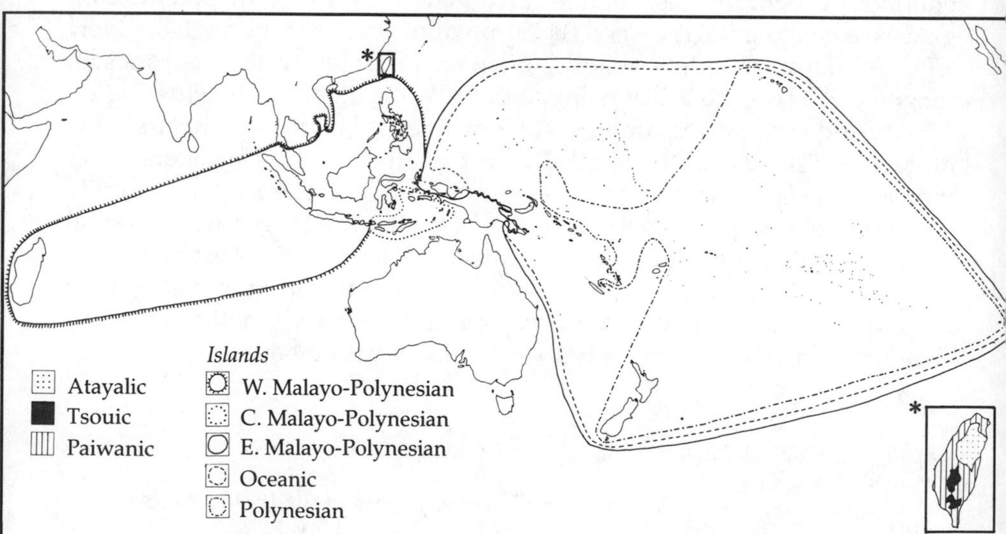

Map 5.1. The Austronesian family

A form of Malay, known as Bahasa Indonesia (= Indonesian), has been adopted as the national language of Indonesia, where it is spoken by perhaps 10 million people as their first language, and by tens of millions more as a second language. Indonesia has no fewer than 12 Austronesian languages with a million or more speakers: Javanese (50, plus 25 million who speak it as a second language), Sundanese (25), Madurese (8), Minangkabau (7), Bali (3), Bugis (= Buginese, 2.5), Makassarese (2), Achinese (2), Toba Batak (2), Sasak (1.5), Lampung (1.5), and Rejang (1). In the Philippines there are eight languages with a million or more speakers: Cebuano (10), Tagalog (10), Ilocano (5), Hiligaynon (4), Bikol (3), Samar-Leyte (2), Kapampangan (1.5), and Pangasinan (1). The Philippine national language (Pilipino) is based on Tagalog. Several Austronesian languages are spoken on the island of Formosa, where they have been largely submerged by the influence of Chinese immigration during the last several centuries. The numerically strongest language, Ami, has around 100,000 speakers, and most others have only a few thousand or less. Several are already extinct. Some Austronesian languages of Polynesia are fairly well known despite having relatively few speakers (e.g. Samoan, Tahitian, Hawaiian).

5.1.1 *History of Austronesian Classification*

As early as 1603 a Dutchman, Frederick de Houtman, perceived the relationship between Malay and Malagasy. A little over a century later another Dutchman, Hadrian Reland (1706), recognized similarities among the languages of Polynesia, the East Indies, and Madagascar. In 1778 the Polynesian family was correctly identified by a member of Cook's second voyage around the world (1772–75), John Reinold Forster. Given the very close-knit nature of the Polynesian family, this early discovery is not surprising. Like Bantu, the Polynesian languages are sometimes described as dialects of a single language. In 1782 William Marsden noted similarities between the languages of Madagascar and Easter Island. Despite these early precursors, both Dyen (1971a) and Collins (1980) credit Lorenzo Hervás y Panduro with having "definitely established" the Austronesian family in 1784, two years before William Jones's famous pronouncement on Indo-European.

The Austronesian affinity of the aboriginal languages of Formosa was first noticed by J. H. Klaproth in 1822. Because of the present domination of Formosa by the Chinese, it is often forgotten that until the initial Chinese invasion of 1626, Formosa was inhabited solely by Austronesian speakers. In a work published from 1836 to 1839, Wilhelm von Humboldt provided sketches of several Polynesian and Indonesian languages and proposed the name Malayo-Polynesian for the family.

Lying between the Indonesian languages and the Polynesian languages was a large group that came to be known as Melanesian. They were at first not regarded as members of Malayo-Polynesian; their membership in the family came to be accepted only gradually during the second half of the nineteenth century. Hans Conon von der Gabelentz published grammatical sketches of various Melanesian languages in 1861, expressing the view that the Melanesian languages constitute a valid linguistic family and that, in addition, the Melanesian and Polynesian languages share numerous similarities that cannot be attributed to borrowing. In linking the Melanesian and Polynesian groups in this manner, Gabelentz foreshadowed what has become known as the Oceanic subgroup of Austronesian.

In 1885 R. H. Codrington published a book on the Melanesian languages and emphatically underlined their unmistakable Malayo-Polynesian affinity. He attributed the reluctance of some scholars to include the Melanesian languages in Malayo-Polynesian to their speakers' "misfortune to be black" (quoted in Grace 1959: 5). Just as in Africa, where the Chadic family was long excluded from Afro-Asiatic because Chadic speakers are black and the rest of the family is not (see section 3.2), so too in Oceania were the Melanesian speakers at first denied their proper place in the Malayo-Polynesian family solely because of their race. Nineteenth-century scholars expected congruity between race and linguistic group, and those cases that did not meet their expectations were often handled poorly.

Although the Oceanic subgroup of Austronesian had been adumbrated in the work of Gabelentz, it was explicitly recognized by Hendrik A. Kern in 1886. Furthermore, Kern demonstrated that Fijian, which had previously been considered a Melanesian language because its speakers are dark-skinned, is in fact most closely related to the languages of the light-skinned Polynesians.

Not until the final decade of the nineteenth century was it discovered that not all of the Melanesian languages were Malayo-Polynesian. Sidney Ray reported non-Malayo-Polynesian languages in Southeast New Guinea in 1892, and a decade later Wilhelm Schmidt demonstrated their presence in Northeast New Guinea as well. Ray proposed the term Papuan for these non-Malayo-Polynesian languages, restricting "Melanesian" to Malayo-Polynesian tongues. The classification of the Papuan languages of New Guinea and surrounding islands is discussed in section 5.2 below.

Schmidt (1899a) proposed the name Austronesian in place of Malayo-Polynesian. During the twentieth century Austronesian has become the most widely used term for the family as a whole, and Malayo-Polynesian has been given a more restricted definition, or eliminated altogether. In another study published the same year, Schmidt (1899b) concluded that (1) the Melanesian languages were definitely Austronesian; (2) the Melanesian group is older than the Polynesian group, in the sense that the original

Melanesian language was spoken much earlier than the original Polynesian language; and (3) the languages most closely related to the Polynesian family are Fijian, Rotuman, the languages of the southern Solomons, and, to a lesser degree, those of the central New Hebrides.

By the beginning of the twentieth century, practically all of the Austronesian-speaking areas of the world had been identified. For taxonomists the problem of delimiting the Austronesian domain was replaced by the more difficult problem of unraveling the internal relationships of the myriad Austronesian languages. (A second—and during the first half of the twentieth century more important—focus of Austronesian research was the reconstruction of Proto-Austronesian, often attempted with remarkable success.) At the turn of the century, the subgrouping of the Austronesian family was viewed as follows. First, the Polynesian family constituted one clear-cut group, and together with the Melanesian languages formed a higher-level node called Oceanic. Second, the remainder of the Austronesian family, that is, the non-Oceanic languages, were lumped together under the rubric Indonesian. And third, it was realized that some of the Melanesian languages were in fact genetically closer to the Polynesian family than to the other Melanesian languages. Schmidt (1926) called such languages "transitional" Melanesian, implying that they were transitional between Melanesian languages proper and the Polynesian family (see List 5.1). Such a bipartite division of Austronesian has remained popular to this day, sometimes under the guise of a Western (= Indonesian)/Eastern (= Oceanic) terminology (see Pawley 1974).

The most influential Austronesianist of the first half of the twentieth century was the German Otto Dempwolff, who, in a three-volume work published from 1934 to 1938, proposed more than 2,000 lexical items for Austronesian. Dempwolff also carefully worked out many of the major sound correspondences exhibited by the Austronesian family and for the

List 5.1. The Austronesian Family (Schmidt 1926)

AUSTRONESIAN:
- I INDONESIAN:
  - A WEST
  - B EAST
- II OCEANIC:
  - A MELANESIAN:
    - 1 MELANESIAN PROPER
    - 2 MICRONESIAN (excluding Chamorro and Palauan)
  - B "TRANSITIONAL" MELANESIAN
  - C POLYNESIAN

first time stated precisely the criteria defining the Oceanic subgroup. But Dempwolff was not primarily interested in questions of classification and never suggested a complete subgrouping for the whole family. His views were probably not significantly different from Schmidt's.

The precise position of the border between Oceanic and Indonesian was clarified only in the 1950's through the work of Wilhelm Milke and George Grace, and is presently drawn at roughly 136 degrees east longitude.

One of the weaknesses of this early classificatory work on Austronesian was that, although the evidence that had been developed in support of the Oceanic branch was substantial, evidence demonstrating the validity of Indonesian was all but nonexistent. During the past two decades the unitary nature of Indonesian has been increasingly called into question by a number of scholars, as we see in List 5.2.

Dyen (1965) published a lexicostatistical classification indicating that the Austronesian family is composed of some 40 different primary branches. At the same time he questioned the validity of the Oceanic subgroup on the grounds that his data located the area of greatest internal diversity in Oceanic territory. In this confrontation between Dyen's quantitative approach and the traditional qualitative methods of comparative linguistics, the latter have carried the day, and Dyen's proposals currently have few adherents.

5.1.2 *Present Status of Austronesian Classification*

Despite the renewed interest in Austronesian classification over the last decade or so, and the many significant contributions that have appeared during that time, no widely accepted subgrouping of the family as a whole has yet emerged. The reasons are not hard to pinpoint. The Austronesian family presents three of the chief ingredients for taxonomic difficulties. First, it consists of a *large* number of very *similar* languages. Second, with a few exceptions (e.g. Malay-Indonesian, Tagalog, Cebuano), Austronesian tongues are spoken by small groups in remote areas of the world and are therefore usually considered of no interest to anyone but the dedicated scholar or missionary. The literature dealing with them has been both incomplete and uneven in quality, but happily this situation has been ameliorated somewhat in recent years by a wealth of new publications. Third, most Austronesianists have chosen to investigate only a small portion of the vast Austronesian domain. Relatively few scholars have been so audacious as to attempt to handle the entire family, yet without such a global perspective the chances of discovering a defensible subgrouping for Austronesian are slim. Recent work by Blust is encouraging in this regard.

What, one might ask, is presently known of the internal relationships of the Austronesian family? First, Austronesian is itself a well-defined genetic

List 5.2. Proposed Subgroupings of the Austronesian Family

Haudricourt 1962

AUSTRONESIAN:
- I NORTHERN (= FORMOSAN)
- II WESTERN (= INDONESIAN)
- III EASTERN (= OCEANIC):
  - A MICRONESIAN
  - B MELANESIAN
  - C POLYNESIAN

Blust 1978

AUSTRONESIAN:
- I ATAYALIC (= FORMOSAN)
- II TSOUIC (= FORMOSAN)
- III PAIWANIC (= FORMOSAN)
- IV MALAYO-POLYNESIAN:
  - A WESTERN
  - B CENTRAL-EASTERN:
    - 1 CENTRAL
    - 2 EASTERN:
      - a SOUTH HALMAHERA–NORTHWEST NEW GUINEA
      - b OCEANIC

Benedict 1983

AUSTRONESIAN:
- I ATAYALIC (= FORMOSAN)
- II TSOUIC-MALAYO-POLYNESIAN:
  - A TSOUIC (= FORMOSAN)
  - B PAIWANIC-MALAYO-POLYNESIAN:
    - 1 PAIWANIC (= FORMOSAN)
    - 2 MALAYO-POLYNESIAN

Dahl 1973

AUSTRONESIAN:
- I FORMOSAN
- II NON-FORMOSAN:
  - A WESTERN (= INDONESIAN)
  - B EASTERN (= OCEANIC):
    - 1 MELANESIAN
    - 2 POLYNESIAN

Reid 1982

AUSTRONESIAN:
- I ATAYALIC (= FORMOSAN)
- II TSOUIC (= FORMOSAN)
- III PAIWANIC (= FORMOSAN)
- IV SOUTH MINDANAO (= PHILIPPINE)
- V AMI-EXTRA-FORMOSAN:
  - A Ami
  - B EXTRA-FORMOSAN:
    - 1 OUTER PHILIPPINES:
      - a NORTHERN PHILIPPINES
      - b SOUTHERN PHILIPPINES
    - 2 MALAYO-POLYNESIAN:
      - a WESTERN:
        - i MESO-PHILIPPINE
        - ii CELEBES
        - iii BORNEO
        - iv SAMA-BAJAW
        - v SUNDIC
      - b CENTRAL-EASTERN

unit. With the exception of Maisin (spoken on the southeast coast of mainland Papua New Guinea) and the languages of the Reef Islands and Santa Cruz, there are no disputes on which languages belong to the family. The exceptional languages just mentioned have been variously classified as Papuan-influenced Austronesian languages or Austronesian-influenced Papuan languages. The position followed here is that Maisin is basically an Austronesian tongue, probably belonging to the Oceanic subgroup. The Reef Islands–Santa Cruz languages are considered Papuan languages, forming part of the East Papuan branch of Indo-Pacific.

Second, within Austronesian there appears to be a growing consensus that the Formosan languages occupy a special position, as all the subgroupings in List 5.2 indicate. It now seems likely that these languages constitute either one or several primary branches of Austronesian. Furthermore, work by Blust indicates that all extra-Formosan Austronesian languages constitute a single primary branch, which he calls Malayo-Polynesian (M-P). Within M-P the Oceanic subgroup appears to be a valid genetic node, as do innumerable small families (e.g. Polynesian, Micronesian, Loyalty Islands, Bashiic, South Mindanao, Piru Bay). How these numerous subfamilies fit together within M-P is a primary subject of current research, and continued refinement (or even revision) of the picture is to be expected in the coming years.

The Austronesian classification presented here is based on the sources cited in the bibliography at the end of this section, as well as on the valuable advice of the dozen or so scholars who were kind enough to share their expertise with me and whose assistance I have already acknowledged at the beginning of this volume. The overall framework for Austronesian follows Blust (1978)—see List 5.2—in positing four primary branches, three Formosan groups (Atayalic, Tsouic, Paiwanic), and the remainder of the family (M-P). Within M-P Blust groups the well-defined Oceanic node with a group of languages spoken on the northwest coast of New Guinea and the southern portion of Halmahera to form a subgroup called Eastern M-P. This in turn he subgroups with languages spoken in the Maluku region of Indonesia to form the node Central-Eastern M-P, which constitutes one of two primary branches of M-P. The other, Western M-P, contains the remainder of the Austronesian languages. These embrace most Indonesian languages; all Philippine languages; and a few scattered outliers on the Malay Peninsula (Malay, Jakun), in Vietnam and Kampuchea and on Hainan Island (the Chamic family), on Madagascar (Malagasy), and in Micronesia (Chamorro, Palauan, and possibly Yapese).

The subgrouping within Western M-P is perhaps the least studied and least understood area of Austronesian classification. Although it has been

List 5.3. The Austronesian Family (Blust 1978, Pawley 1972, and others)

AUSTRONESIAN:
- I ATAYALIC
- II TSOUIC
- III PAIWANIC
- IV MALAYO-POLYNESIAN:
  - A WESTERN:
    - 1 Chamorro
    - 2 Palauan
    - 3 Yapese
    - 4 NORTHERN PHILIPPINES
    - 5 SOUTHERN PHILIPPINES
    - 6 MESO-PHILIPPINE
    - 7 SOUTH MINDANAO
    - 8 CELEBES
    - 9 BORNEO
    - 10 SAMA-BAJAW
    - 11 SUNDIC
  - B CENTRAL-EASTERN:
    - 1 CENTRAL:
      - a CENTRAL MALUKU
      - b SOUTH-EAST MALUKU
    - 2 EASTERN:
      - a SOUTH HALMAHERA–NORTHWEST NEW GUINEA
      - b OCEANIC:
        - i Maisin
        - ii SARMI-YOTAFA
        - iii SIASSI
        - iv MARKHAM
        - v MILNE BAY–CENTRAL PROVINCE
        - vi KIMBE
        - vii NEW BRITAIN
        - viii NEW IRELAND–TOLAI
        - ix ADMIRALTY ISLANDS
        - x BOUGAINVILLE
        - xi CHOISEUL
        - xii NEW GEORGIA
        - xiii SANTA ISABEL
        - xiv SANTA CRUZ
        - xv SOUTHERN NEW HEBRIDES
        - xvi NEW CALEDONIA
        - xvii LOYALTY ISLANDS
        - xviii REMOTE OCEANIC:
          - α MICRONESIAN
          - β SOUTHEAST SOLOMONS
          - γ CENTRAL AND NORTHERN NEW HEBRIDES
          - δ CENTRAL PACIFIC:
            - I ROTUMAN-FIJIAN
            - II POLYNESIAN

customary to include a Philippine group as one component of Western M-P, Reid (1981) questions the validity of such a node. Moreover, it has long been realized that there are "Philippine-like" languages in northern Borneo and Celebes, so the southern border of a Philippine node is far from clear. In List 5.3 groups 4–7 of Western M-P (i.e. Northern Philippines, Southern Philippines, Meso-Philippine, South Mindanao) constitute the traditional Philippine group. Of the four non-Philippine groups within Western M-P, only Sama-Bajaw seems secure as a valid genetic group (at some level). The geographic nature of the other three groups (Celebes, Borneo, Sundic) is apparent in their names; their validity as well-defined nodes is dubious. It will surely turn out that the 11 subgroups of Western M-P shown in List 5.3 are not all equidistant from one another. However, until someone proposes an overall subgrouping for Western M-P, this provisional classification will have to suffice.

The internal subgroupings of the four Philippine groups and Sama-Bajaw follow, in the main, a classification compiled by Lawrence Reid on the basis of a wide range of published and unpublished materials. I have modified his classification slightly by condensing somewhat the number of distinct languages in South-Central Cordilleran, Central Philippine, and Sama-Bajaw. A few other modifications reflect McFarland (1980) and Zorc (1982). For the classification of the other Western M-P groups I have relied heavily, but not exclusively, on Wurm and Hattori (1983).

The Oceanic subgrouping is based broadly on the work of Andrew Pawley, with a few modifications introduced on the basis of Wurm and Hattori (1981). The individual Oceanic subgroups reflect a variety of sources, which are listed in the bibliography to this section. Finally, Yapese, which has been classified here as an ungrouped language within Western M-P (like Chamorro and Palauan), may in fact turn out to be a member of Oceanic; its position is at present unclear.

The general structure of the Austronesian family adopted in this volume is shown in List 5.3.

AUSTRONESIAN

Benedict, Paul K. 1983. Personal letter.

Blust, Robert. 1978. "Eastern Malayo-Polynesian: A Subgrouping Argument," in *PL* C61.

———. 1981. "The Reconstruction of Proto-Malayo-Javanic: An Appreciation," *Bijdragen tot de Taal-, Land- en Volkenkunde* 137: 456–69.

———. Forthcoming. *Austronesian Languages*. Cambridge, Eng.

Cense, A. A., and E. M. Uhlenbeck. 1958. *Critical Survey of Studies on the Languages of Borneo*. The Hague.

Collins, James T. 1980. "The Historical Relationships of the Languages of Central Maluku, Indonesia," Ph.D. dissertation, University of Chicago.
Dahl, Otto Christian. 1973. *Proto-Austronesian*. Lund.
Dempwolff, Otto. 1934–38. *Vergleichende Lautlehre des austronesischen Wortschätzes*, 3 vols. Berlin.
Dyen, Isidore. 1965. *A Lexicostatistical Classification of the Austronesian Languages*. *IJAL Memoir* 19.
———. 1971a. "The Austronesian Languages and Proto-Austronesian," in *CTIL* 8.
———. 1971b. "The Chamic Languages," in *CTIL* 8.
Grace, George W. 1955. "Subgrouping of Malayo-Polynesian: A Report of Tentative Findings," *AA* 57: 337–39.
———. 1966. "Austronesian Lexicostatistical Classification: A Review Article," *OL* 5: 13–31.
———. 1976. "History of Research in Austronesian Languages of the New Guinea Area: General," in S. A. Wurm, ed., cited below.
Hervás y Panduro, Lorenzo. 1784. *Catalogo delle lingue*. Cesena.
Houtman, Frederick de. 1603. *Spraeck ende woord-boeck, inde Maleysche ende Madagaskarsche Talen met vele Arabische ende Turcsce woorden*. Amsterdam.
Hudson, Alfred B. 1967. *The Barito Isolects of Borneo*. *Cornell University Data Paper* 68.
———. 1970. "A Note on Selako: Malayic Dayak and Land Dayak Languages in Western Borneo," *Sarawak Museum Journal* 18: 301–18.
Humboldt, Wilhelm von. 1836–39. *Über die Kawi-Sprache auf der Insel Java*, 3 vols. Berlin.
Lincoln, Pete. 1977. "Listing Austronesian Languages," 2 parts, 1: "Oceanic Languages," 2: "Languages West of Oceanic." Unpublished manuscripts.
Moody, David C. 1984. "Conclusion," in Julie K. King and John Wayne King, eds., *Languages of Sabah: A Survey Report*, *PL* C78.
Pawley, Andrew. 1974. "Austronesian Languages," in *EB* 2: 484–94.
Reid, Lawrence A. 1982. Personal letter.
Schmidt, Wilhelm. 1899a. "Die sprachliche Verhältnisse Oceaniens (Melanesiens, Polynesiens, Mikronesiens und Indonesiens) in ihrer Bedeutung für die Ethnologie," *Mitteilungen der anthropologischen Gesellschaft* (Vienna) 29: 245–58.
———. 1899b. *Über das Verhältniss der melanesischen Sprachen zu den polynesischen und untereinander*. Vienna.
———. 1900–1901. "Die sprachlichen Verhältnisse von Deutsch Neu-Guinea," *Zeitschrift für Afrikanische und Ozeanische Sprachen*, 2 parts, 5: 345–84, 6: 1–99.
———. 1926. *Die Sprachfamilien und Sprachenkreise der Erde*. Heidelberg.
Wurm, S. A., ed. 1976. *New Guinea Area Languages and Language Study: Austronesian Languages*. *PL* C39.
Wurm, S. A., and Shirô Hattori, eds. 1983. *Language Atlas of the Pacific Area* 2. Stuttgart.

FORMOSA

Dyen, Isidore. 1963. "The Position of the Malayo-Polynesian Languages of Formosa," *Asian Perspectives* 7: 261–71.
———. 1971. "The Austronesian Languages of Formosa," in *CTIL* 8.
Ferrell, Raleigh. 1969. *Taiwan Aboriginal Groups: Problems in Cultural and Linguistic Classification*. Taipei.

———. 1980. "Phonological Subgrouping of Formosan Languages," in Paz Buenaventura Naylor, ed., *Austronesian Studies*. Ann Arbor, Mich.
Klaproth, J. H. 1822. *Asia Polyglotta*. Paris.
Loukotka, Čestmír, and Peter A. Lanyon-Orgill. 1958. "A Revised Classification of the Formosan Languages," *Journal of Austronesian Studies* 1,*3*: 56–63.
Nikigawa, A. 1953. "A Classification of the Formosan Languages," *Journal of Austronesian Studies* 1,*1*: 145–51.
Tsuchida, Shigeru. 1976. *Reconstruction of Proto-Tsouic Phonology*. Tokyo.

PHILIPPINE

Allison, E. Joe. 1974. "Proto-Danao: A Comparative Study of Maranao, Maguindanao and Iranon," M.A. thesis, University of Texas, Arlington.
Charles, Mathew. 1974. "Problems in the Reconstruction of Proto-Philippine Phonology and the Subgrouping of Philippine Languages," *OL* 13: 457–510.
Chretien, C. Douglas. 1962. "A Classification of Twenty-One Philippine Languages," *Philippine Journal of Science* 91: 485–506.
Elkins, Richard E. 1974. "A Proto-Manobo Word List," *OL* 13: 601–42.
Gallman, Andrew F. 1974. "A Reconstruction of Proto-Mansakan," M.A. thesis, University of Texas, Arlington.
Harmon, Carol W. 1974. "Reconstructions of Proto-Manobo Pronouns and Case-Marking Particles," *University of Hawaii Working Papers in Linguistics* 6,*6*: 13–46.
Headland, Thomas N. 1975. "Report of Eastern Luzon Language Survey," unpublished manuscript. Manila.
Llamzon, Teodoro A., and Maria Teresita Martin. 1976. "A Subgrouping of 100 Philippine Languages," in *PL* C42.
McFarland, Curtis D. 1974. "The Dialects of the Bikol Area," Ph.D. dissertation, Yale University.
———. 1980. *A Linguistic Atlas of the Philippines*. Tokyo.
McKaughan, Howard. 1971. "Minor Languages of the Philippines," in *CTIL* 8.
Palleson, Alfred K. 1977. "Culture Contact and Language Divergence," Ph.D. dissertation, University of California, Berkeley.
Reid, Lawrence A. 1974. "The Central Cordilleran Subgroup of Philippine Languages," *OL* 13: 511–60.
———. 1978. "Problems in the Reconstruction of Proto-Philippine Construction Markers," in *PL* C61.
———. 1981. "The Demise of Proto-Philippines," paper presented at the Third International Conference on Austronesian Linguistics, Bali, Indonesia, Jan. 1981.
Tharp, James A. 1974. "The Northern Cordilleran Subgroup of Philippine Languages," *University of Hawaii Working Papers in Linguistics* 6,*6*: 53–114.
Thomas, David, and Alan Healey. 1962. "Some Philippine Language Subgroupings," *AL* 4,*9*: 22–33.
Walton, Charles. 1979. "A Philippine Language Tree," *AL* 21: 70–98.
Zorc, R. David. 1974. "Internal and External Relationships of the Mangyan Languages," *OL* 13: 561–600.
———. 1977. *The Bisayan Dialects of the Philippines: Subgrouping and Reconstruction*. *PL* C44.
———. 1982. Personal letter.

OCEANIC

Beaumont, C. H. 1972. "New Ireland Languages: A Review," in *PL* A35.
Bender, Byron W. 1971. "Micronesian Languages," in *CTIL* 8.
Codrington, R. H. 1885. *The Melanesian Languages*. Oxford.
Dutton, T. E. 1976a. "Austronesian Languages: Eastern Part of South-Eastern Mainland Papua," in *PL* C39.
———. 1976b. "Magori and Similar Languages of South-East Papua," in *PL* C39.
Gabelentz, Hans Conon von der. 1861. *Die melanesischen Sprachen*. Leipzig.
Haudricourt, André G. 1971. "New Caledonia and the Loyalty Islands," in *CTIL* 8.
Izui, Hisanosuke. 1965. "The Languages of Micronesia: Their Unity and Diversity," *Lingua* 14: 349–59.
Kern, Hendrik A. 1886. *Die Fidji-taal vergeleken met hare verwanten in Indonesie en Polynesie*. Amsterdam.
Levy, Richard. 1980. "Languages of the Southeast Solomon Islands and the Reconstruction of Proto-Eastern-Oceanic," in Paz Buenaventura Naylor, ed., *Austronesian Studies*. Ann Arbor, Mich.
Lithgow, David R. 1976. "Austronesian Languages: Milne Bay and Adjacent Islands (Milne Bay Province)," in *PL* C39.
McElhanon, K. A. 1978. *A Classification of the Languages of the Morobe Province, Papua New Guinea*. Canberra.
Milke, Wilhelm. 1958. "Zur inneren Gliederung und geschichtlichen Stellung der ozeanisch-austronesischen Sprachen," *Zeitschrift für Ethnologie* 83: 58–62.
———. 1965. "Comparative Notes on the Austronesian Languages of New Guinea," *Lingua* 14: 330–48.
Pawley, Andrew. 1972. "On the Internal Relationships of Eastern Oceanic Languages," in R. C. Green and M. Kelly, eds., *Studies in Oceanic Culture History* 3. Honolulu.
———. 1976. "Austronesian Languages: Western Part of South-Eastern Mainland Papua," in *PL* C39.
———. 1978. "The New Guinea Oceanic Hypothesis," *Kivung* 11: 99–151.
Ray, Sidney. 1893. "The Languages of British New Guinea," in *Transactions of the Ninth International Congress of Orientalists, London, 1892*.
Tryon, D. T. 1976. *New Hebrides Languages: An Internal Classification*. *PL* C50.
———. 1982. "The Languages of the Solomon Islands: The Present Position," in Rainer Carle et al., eds., *Gava': Studies in Austronesian Languages and Cultures*. Berlin.
Wurm, Stephen A., and Shirô Hattori, eds. 1981. *Language Atlas of the Pacific Area* 1. Stuttgart.

POLYNESIAN

Biggs, Bruce. 1971. "The Languages of Polynesia," in *CTIL* 8.
Clark, Ross. 1979. "Language," in Jesse D. Jennings, ed., *The Prehistory of Polynesia*. Cambridge, Mass.
Elbert, Samuel H. 1953. "Internal Relationships of Polynesian Languages and Dialects," *Southwestern Journal of Anthropology* 9: 147–73.
Grace, George W. 1959. *The Position of the Polynesian Languages Within the Austronesian Language Family*. Bloomington, Ind.

Green, Roger. 1966. "Linguistic Subgrouping Within Polynesia: The Implications for Prehistoric Settlement," *Journal of the Polynesian Society* 75: 6–38.
Green, Roger, and Andrew Pawley. n.d. *The Linguistic Subgroups of Polynesia*. Wellington, N.Z.
Kirk, Jerome, and P. J. Epling. 1973. "Taxonomy of the Polynesian Languages," *AL* 15: 42–70.
Pawley, Andrew. 1966. "Polynesian Languages: A Subgrouping Based on Shared Innovations in Morphology," *Journal of the Polynesian Society* 75: 39–64.
———. 1967. "The Relationships of Polynesian Outlier Languages," *Journal of the Polynesian Society* 76: 259–96.
Walsh, D. S., and Bruce Biggs. 1966. *Proto-Polynesian Word List 1*. Auckland.

5.2 INDO-PACIFIC

Although there are more than 700 distinct Indo-Pacific (or Papuan) languages spoken on New Guinea and neighboring islands, they count as speakers fewer than three million people. The Papuan language with the most speakers is Enga, which is spoken in the Western Highlands of Papua New Guinea by about 165,000 people. To the west of New Guinea, Papuan languages are found on Halmahera, Timor, Alor, and Pantar; east of New Guinea they are spoken on New Britain, New Ireland, Bougainville, the Solomons, the Reef Islands, and Santa Cruz. In addition to the Papuan languages spoken on islands surrounding New Guinea, it has been suggested that the indigenous languages of the Andaman Islands (in the Andaman Sea just west of lower Thailand) and the extinct languages of Tasmania (off the southeast coast of Australia) are distantly related to this family. The geographic distribution of the Indo-Pacific family is illustrated in Map 5.2. None of the Indo-Pacific languages can truly be called "famous." At best a few have attracted some attention in the anthropological literature.

5.2.1 *History of Indo-Pacific Classification*

The languages of New Guinea remained until quite recently among the least studied of any in the world. Despite the fact that approximately 1,000 distinct languages (roughly 20 percent of the world total) are spoken in New Guinea, making it the area of the world with the greatest concentration of languages (and greatest diversity as well), these languages were virtually ignored by the scholarly community until the 1950's. In 1950 only a handful of small language families had been recognized in various parts of the island, and for most of New Guinea little was known at all. The two decades from 1955 to 1975 witnessed a veritable explosion of research, and today our knowledge of the classification of these languages has reached a point that seemed unattainable only 30 years ago. With minor exceptions,

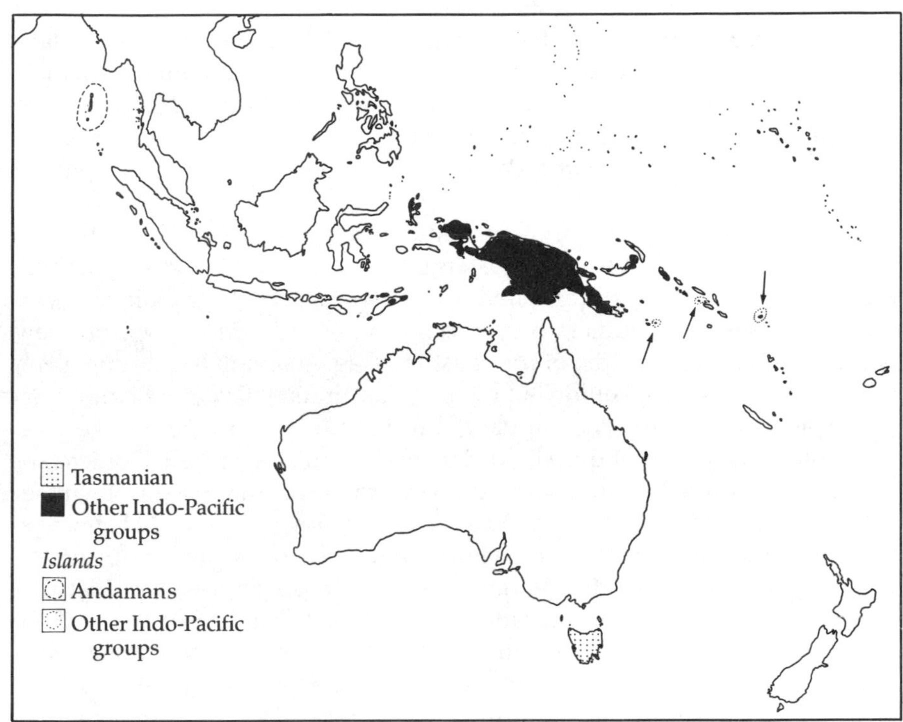

Map 5.2. The Indo-Pacific family

all of New Guinea is now known linguistically, and a general understanding of the genetic relationships of these languages has been reached, though, as we shall see, many problems remain.

As I noted in the preceding section (5.1), although the Malayo-Polynesian (M-P) family was identified during the eighteenth century, the affinity of the so-called Melanesian languages (which fall geographically between the Malayan and Polynesian families) with M-P came to be accepted only during the second half of the nineteenth century. The chief impediment to including the Melanesian languages in the M-P family appears to have been the fact that speakers of Melanesian languages have dark skins, whereas the M-P family, as originally conceived, contained only light-skinned Indonesians and Polynesians. The eventual inclusion of the Melanesian languages in M-P (which, thus expanded, came to be called Austronesian [AN]) raised the question of whether *all* Melanesian languages were in fact AN, or whether there might not be some non-AN Melanesian languages as well. Several early claims to have discovered such languages turned out to be false, the languages in question having proved to be AN, and it was not until 1892 that Sidney Ray demonstrated the existence of non-AN languages in southeastern New Guinea. Ray proposed the name Papuan (a term already in use) for these non-AN languages, restricting Melanesian to the AN languages of Melanesia. At the start of the twentieth century, Wilhelm Schmidt documented Papuan languages on the northern part of the island as well.

There are several reasons why Papuan languages were identified so much later than the AN family. Most important, no doubt, was the fact that Papuan languages are concentrated on a single island (New Guinea), with only a few scattered outliers on surrounding islands. Moreover, on New Guinea itself a large portion of the coastline was inhabited by AN speakers, who, with their boats, could visit the first explorers without the latter even having to touch shore. The Papuans, on the other hand, were largely restricted to the interior of the island. The first wordlist of a New Guinea language was collected in 1616, almost a century after the first European set foot on New Guinea (1526). This language was, however, an AN language, as were all the languages on which information became available during the following two centuries. It was not until 1822 that a Papuan wordlist was finally collected, some four decades after the M-P family had been firmly established. During the nineteenth century information on Papuan languages began to trickle in, but was still completely overshadowed by AN research. Finally, it is likely that the great diversity of Papuan languages, in the face of AN homogeneity, contributed to their neglect. In any event, the distinction between AN and Papuan languages did not become clear until Ray (1893).

During the first half of the twentieth century, Papuan languages were discovered elsewhere on New Guinea and surrounding islands. In Western New Guinea they were documented primarily by Dutch missionaries. Table 5.1 lists those Papuan families that had been identified by the mid-1950's; references may be found in Wurm (1975, 1982).

With the exception of the Australian scholar Arthur Capell, who was a pioneer in all three areas of Oceanic research (Austronesian, Australian, and Papuan), the academic world showed scant interest in the myriad diverse Papuan languages during the first half of this century, and by 1950 the common belief was that the New Guinea area contained innumerable small families (only a few of which had been identified), that displayed no relationship either among themselves or to languages outside New Guinea. Four separate research projects radically altered this picture during the 1950's and 1960's: (1) the work of H. K. J. Cowan (1957a,b,c, 1959, 1963); (2) the studies of Joseph H. Greenberg (1958, 1960, 1971); (3) numerous publications of the New Guinea branch of the Summer Institute of Linguistics;

Table 5.1. Early Identification of Papuan Groups

Year	Recognized by	Group (current name)
1872	P. J. B. C. Robidé van der Aa	North Halmahera
1900	W. Schmidt	West Papuan (= West New Guinea + North Halmahera)
1905	W. Schmidt	Torricelli (Schmidt connected two languages: Valman and Monumbo)
1907	S. Ray	Eleman
1908	W. Schmidt	Central Solomons
1912	G. Frederici	Sko
1914	A. R. Radcliffe-Brown	Andaman Islands
1915	H. van der Veen	North Halmahera
1918	J. H. P. Murray, S. Ray	Marind (partial)
1919	S. Ray	Rai Coast
1922	F. Kirschbaum	Ndu
1941	K. H. Thomas	Sko
1944	A. Capell	Timor
1949	P. Drabbe	Kolopom
1950	J. H. M. C. Boelaars	Marind (expanded)
1950's	P. Drabbe	Awyu, Awyu-Dumut, Bulaka River
1951	K. Laumann	Nor-Pondo
1951	S. Wurm	Kiwaian
1951	A. Capell	Madang
1956	D. Laycock	Upper Sepik
1957	H. K. J. Cowan	West Papuan, North Papuan

and (4) the research of Stephen A. Wurm and his colleagues at the Australian National University, summarized in Wurm (1975, 1982).

H. K. J. Cowan was a Dutch civil servant and self-taught linguist who devoted considerable time and energy to the languages of Netherlands New Guinea, where he served. He was especially interested in their classification and was among the first to propose the existence of widespread genetic relationships in the New Guinea area. In 1957 Cowan postulated both a West Papuan family (uniting certain languages of Northwest New Guinea with a group of languages spoken in North Halmahera) and a North Papuan family (comprising various languages from Northern New Guinea). Cowan expanded the West Papuan family in the late 1950's to include additional New Guinea languages, and in the early 1960's he proposed the inclusion of the languages of Timor Island as well.

After finishing his work on the classification of African languages in the mid-1950's (see Chap. 3), the American linguist Joseph Greenberg turned his attention to the two areas of the world where genetic classification was least advanced, South America and the New Guinea area. His conclusions regarding South America are discussed in section 6.3; we shall now examine those concerning New Guinea.

Employing essentially the same methods that had proved successful in classifying African languages (i.e. the compilation of lists of basic vocabulary for a wide range of languages, with whatever grammatical information was available), Greenberg concluded that the non-AN languages of New Guinea and surrounding islands were all (or almost all) genetically related. He reported his findings in a paper delivered to the Association for Asian Studies in 1960. During the 1960's Greenberg continued to expand his data base, and in 1971 he finally published the evidence he had accumulated that

> the bulk of non-Austronesian languages of Oceania, from the Andaman Islands on the west in the Bay of Bengal to Tasmania in the southeast, forms a single group of genetically related languages for which the name Indo-Pacific is proposed. The major exception to this generalization is constituted by the indigenous languages of Australia, nearly all of which are generally accepted as related to each other. This Australian stock does not seem to align genetically with Indo-Pacific and is excluded from it, at least tentatively. With regard to the remaining languages, membership in the overall family can be asserted with varying degrees of confidence (Greenberg 1971: 807).

Greenberg proposed 14 subgroups for the Indo-Pacific phylum; the seven on New Guinea were given geographic designations (Central, North, South, Southwest, West, East, Northeast), and the seven outside New Guinea were named after the island(s) on which they were spoken (Andaman Islands, Tasmanian, Halmahera, Timor-Alor, Bougainville, New Britain, Central Melanesian [= Central Solomons + Santa Cruz]). As a first approximation to the internal relationships, Greenberg suggested the subgrouping shown in List 5.4. Greenberg's West Papuan group corresponded closely with Cowan's, though he included a few additional languages. Greenberg extended Cowan's North Papuan family eastward to include languages from Australian New Guinea (now Papua New Guinea).

List 5.4. The Indo-Pacific Phylum (Greenberg 1971)

INDO-PACIFIC:
- I ANDAMAN ISLANDS
- II †TASMANIAN
- III NUCLEAR NEW GUINEA:
  - A CENTRAL NEW GUINEA:
    - 1 KAPAUKU-BALIEM
    - 2 HIGHLANDS
    - 3 HUON
  - B NORTH NEW GUINEA
  - C SOUTH NEW GUINEA
  - D SOUTHWEST NEW GUINEA
- IV WEST PAPUAN:
  - A WEST NEW GUINEA
  - B NORTH HALMAHERA
  - C TIMOR-ALOR
- V EAST NEW GUINEA
- VI NORTHEAST NEW GUINEA
- VII PACIFIC:
  - A BOUGAINVILLE
  - B NEW BRITAIN
  - C CENTRAL MELANESIAN:
    - 1 CENTRAL SOLOMONS
    - 2 SANTA CRUZ

As evidence for the Indo-Pacific hypothesis, Greenberg proposed 84 etymologies linking the 14 subgroups. In addition, he offered sets of etymologies for those subgroups whose existence was not already established (e.g. North New Guinea). A limited amount of grammatical information, primarily concerning the distribution of pronominal etyma, was adduced as corroboration of the lexical evidence.

In addition to the individual efforts of Cowan and Greenberg, two organizations have helped clarify the classification of Papuan languages. Founded in the mid-1950's, the New Guinea branch of the Summer Institute of Linguistics (SIL, a missionary organization that produces literacy materials and Bible translations) has published numerous grammars, dictionaries, and other specialized studies on the languages of New Guinea. Some SIL members (notably Alan and Phyllis Healey, Kenneth McElhanon, Karl Franklin, Bruce Hooley, Oren Claassen, Richard Lloyd) have also made significant contributions to the classification of Papuan languages.

The other organization actively involved in investigating New Guinea languages is the Australian National University, which has sponsored a research program under the direction of Stephen Wurm since the mid-1950's. The result has been extensive new field research in previously unknown regions by numerous scholars, of whom Wurm, Donald Laycock, Clemens Voorhoeve, Thomas Dutton, and John Z'graggen have been most prominent. The classification of Papuan languages has been a prime concern of Wurm and his colleagues from the beginning, and one may discern in their work two phases. During the initial phase emphasis was placed on documenting all of the existing families; it became increasingly clear during the 1950's and early 1960's that there were in fact a number of genetic groups in New Guinea that were much larger than previously suspected. Furthermore, the earlier notion that Papuan languages were spoken only by small numbers of people had to be revised with the discovery in the Highlands of languages with more than 100,000 speakers.

Eventually, as small families grew into increasingly larger stocks, these stocks began to "bump into" each other, or rather, it was seen that a case could be made for classifying some languages as members of more than one stock. The implication was clearly that these stocks must be components of an even broader genetic unit. The second phase of classificatory work began with this recognition. Wurm took the first steps toward such a consolidation in the early 1960's, and in 1965 Carl and Florence Voegelin followed him in setting up a large-scale grouping that became known as the Central New Guinea Macro-Phylum. This broad grouping continued to expand until, in 1970, it had grown to such an extent that a new name was felt appropriate; in that year McElhanon and Voorhoeve rechristened it the Trans–New Guinea (TNG) phylum.

List 5.5. The Trans–New Guinea Phylum (Wurm 1982)

TRANS–NEW GUINEA:	[B EASTERN]
I MAIN SECTION:	5 MANUBARAN
A CENTRAL AND WESTERN:	6 YAREBAN
1 FINISTERRE-HUON	7 MAILUAN
2 EAST NEW GUINEA HIGHLANDS	8 DAGAN
3 CENTRAL AND SOUTH NEW GUINEA–KUTUBUAN	II MADANG-ADELBERT RANGE
4 ANGAN	III TEBERAN–PAWAIAN
5 GOGODALA-SUKI	IV TURAMA-KIKORIAN
6 MARIND	V INLAND GULF
7 KAYAGAR	VI ELEMAN
8 SENTANI	VII TRANS-FLY–BULAKA RIVER
9 DANI-KWERBA	VIII MEK
10 WISSEL LAKES–KEMANDOGA	IX SENAGI
11 MAIRASI–TANAH MERAH	X PAUWASI
12 WEST BOMBERAI	XI NORTHERN
B EASTERN:	XII NIMBORAN
1 BINANDEREAN	XIII KAURE
2 GOILALAN	XIV SOUTH BIRD'S HEAD
3 KOIARIAN	XV KOLOPOM
4 KWALEAN	XVI TIMOR-ALOR-PANTAR

List 5.6. Papuan Language Phyla Other Than the Trans–New Guinea Phylum (Wurm 1982)

WEST PAPUAN:	**[TORRICELLI]**
I Amberbaken	IV MAIMAI
II BIRD'S HEAD	V KOMBIO-ARAPESH
III BORAI-HATTAM	VI MARIENBERG
IV NORTH HALMAHERA	VII MONUMBO
EAST BIRD'S HEAD	**SEPIK-RAMU:**
GEELVINK BAY	I Gapun
	II SEPIK
SKO	III LEONARD SCHULTZE
KWOMTARI-BAIBAI	IV NOR-PONDO
	V RAMU
ARAI	**EAST PAPUAN:**
AMTO-MUSIAN	I YELE-SOLOMONS-NEW BRITAIN
TORRICELLI:	II BOUGAINVILLE
I Urim	III REEF ISLANDS–SANTA CRUZ
II WEST WAPEI	
III WAPEI-PALEI	

The TNG phylum itself gradually increased in size until around 1975, when it reached its present proportions. Although it is still substantially less inclusive than Greenberg's Indo-Pacific phylum, it nonetheless contains two-thirds of all Papuan languages spoken in New Guinea and over 80 percent of all speakers. List 5.5 shows the TNG phylum as currently conceived. In addition to the TNG phylum, Wurm and colleagues recognize 10 other phyla and eight isolated languages, all of which are considered independent on the basis of present evidence. The eight isolates are Warenbori, Taurap, Yuri, Busa, Nagatman, Porome, Pauwi, and Massep; the 10 phyla are shown in List 5.6. Sepik-Ramu contains about 100 languages, Torricelli about 50, and West Papuan and East Papuan roughly 25 each. The other families contain fewer than 10 languages each.

Although attention has been focused increasingly on higher-level groupings since around 1960, considerable progress on lower levels of classification has also been achieved, and many new families have been identified during the past two decades. Table 5.2 lists some of the more important discoveries; references may be found in Wurm (1975, 1982).

Table 5.2. Recent Identification of Papuan Groups

Year	Recognized by	Group
1960	S. Wurm	East New Guinea Highlands
1962	A. Capell	Dani-Kwerba, Binanderean, Turama-Kikorian and others
1962	W. Davenport	Reef Islands–Santa Cruz
1962	A. Healey	Ok, Awin-Pa
1964	W. Steinkrauss, A. Pence	Goilalan
1964	R. Loving, J. Bass	Senagi, Kwomtari-Baibai, Amto-Musian
1965	G. Allen, C. Hurd	Bougainville
1965	D. Laycock	Sepik
1967	M. Bromley	Mek (formerly Goliath)
1968	J. Lloyd, A. Healey	Angan
1968	D. Laycock	Torricelli
1968	C. Voorhoeve	Central and South New Guinea
1968	K. McElhanon	Huon
1968	W. Dye, P. Townsend, W. Townsend	Sepik Hill
1969	T. Dutton	Eastern Trans–New Guinea (formerly Southeast New Guinea)
1969	K. Franklin	Inland Gulf
1970	O. Claassen, K. McElhanon	Rai Coast
1970	K. McElhanon	Finisterre
1970	S. Wurm	Trans-Fly
1970	K. McElhanon, C. Voorhoeve	Trans–New Guinea
1971	J. Z'graggen	Ramu
1971	J. Greenberg	East Papuan (= Pacific)
1973	D. Laycock	Sepik-Ramu
1973	F. S. Watuseke, J. C. Anceaux	Timor-Alor-Pantar
1973	K. Franklin, C. Voorhoeve	Kutubuan

5.2.2 *Present Status of Indo-Pacific Classification*

Reactions to Greenberg's Indo-Pacific hypothesis have been mixed. Blust (1978) found it "bold and brilliant" (p. 475), with the grammatical evidence offered in support of Indo-Pacific showing Greenberg "at his best, displaying the patient, encyclopaedic scholarship, unifying insight, and methodological soundness that combine to assure his position as one of the great linguists of our time. . . . In sum, Greenberg's argument, right or wrong, seems destined profoundly to affect all future thinking about linguistic relationships in this part of the world" (pp. 476–77); and in reexamining Cowan's West Papuan phylum, Capell (1975: 685) found "the comparisons presented by Greenberg . . . to be valid and fully acceptable"; but others disagree. Probably the most controversial aspect of Greenberg's hypothesis has been the inclusion of the (extinct) Tasmanian languages in the Indo-Pacific phylum. Wurm (1975, 1982) found Greenberg's evidence unconvincing, and Crowley and Dixon (1981: 420) consider it "outrageous."

It should be borne in mind that much of the problem of classifying the Tasmanian languages derives from the fact that the Tasmanian people were exterminated before much of anything had been learned of their languages. The little material that was gathered is of very poor quality. Though one might anticipate, on geographic grounds, a connection between Tasmanian and Australian languages, evidence for it has been elusive at best. Recently Blake (1981: 63) has suggested 10 possible cognates connecting an Australian language of western Victoria and one Tasmanian dialect. Greenberg, by contrast, proposed 20 cognates linking the Tasmanian languages with other groups of Indo-Pacific.

Franklin (1973a) gives a negative appraisal of the Indo-Pacific hypothesis on the basis of Greenberg's treatment of the languages of the Gulf District of Papua New Guinea. However, since all the Papuan languages of the Gulf District are now accepted as genetically related (as members of either TNG or Indo-Pacific), Franklin's article deals in effect with questions of subgrouping and not with the ultimate validity of Indo-Pacific. The claim that errors in low-level subgrouping call into question the validity of higher-level nodes is obviously false; innumerable controversies over Austronesian subgrouping have never affected the validity of Austronesian itself.

There have been to date only two full-scale classifications of Papuan languages: Greenberg (1971), using multilateral comparison, and Wurm (1975, 1982), based in large measure on lexicostatistical analysis. The overall structure of both classifications has been illustrated in Lists 5.4–5.6 above. But since the two classifications employ completely different terminology, it is not readily apparent from these lists how they are alike and how they differ. In 1981 I compared these two classifications in order to determine their similarities and differences, and I will now briefly summarize my findings.

As has already been mentioned, one of the primary differences is that Greenberg's classification is considerably more inclusive than Wurm's. Wurm's TNG phylum *excludes* (1) the languages of the Andaman Islands, (2) Tasmanian, (3) the Papuan languages found on islands to the east of New Guinea (Greenberg's Pacific group, Wurm's East Papuan), (4) much of Greenberg's North New Guinea group, and (5) part of Greenberg's West Papuan family. Wurm does not simply dismiss the resemblances between these groups and the TNG phylum; in fact he (1982: 255) concedes that lexical agreements between the Andaman languages and the West Papuan phylum-Timor-Alor-Pantar stock "are quite striking and amount to virtual formal identity . . . in a number of instances." Nevertheless Wurm prefers to attribute the resemblances to "widespread old substrata" rather than to common origin. He also finds TNG "substratum influence" responsible for resemblances among the East Papuan languages, hypothesizing that "at least some East Papuan Phylum languages were driven out of the New Guinea mainland by speakers of Trans-New Guinea Phylum languages" (Wurm 1975: 798, 799).

Wurm admits only a portion of Cowan's (and Greenberg's) West Papuan group into the TNG phylum, namely the South Bird's Head, West Bomberai, and Timor-Alor families. The remainder of Cowan's West Papuan phylum is treated as three independent phyla: Geelvink Bay, East Bird's Head, and (a diminished) West Papuan that now includes only those languages on the extreme northwest tip of New Guinea and in Northern Halmahera. Similarities between the (reduced) West Papuan and TNG phyla are again attributed to substratum influence (see Wurm 1982: 204).

With the exception of the small Sko family, all of Cowan's North Papuan phylum has now been incorporated in the TNG phylum. "In spite of the quite sizable Trans–New Guinea Phylum lexical elements in [Sko], which includes verbs and pronouns," Wurm (1982: 72) excludes it from the TNG phylum because it fails to exhibit the "typological and structural" criteria characteristic of that phylum. Moving in a different direction, Greenberg expanded Cowan's North Papuan family to include the Sepik-Ramu and Torricelli families. He calls this expanded stock North New Guinea. We may note that Greenberg's North New Guinea group corresponds to four genetically independent families in the Wurm classification: Sepik-Ramu, Torricelli, Sko, and TNG.

Although the differences between the two classifications are by no means inconsequential, there are also important similarities:

1. Both classifications concur on the genetic unity of the Papuan languages spoken on Bougainville, New Britain, the Solomon Islands, and Santa Cruz. Greenberg calls this group Pacific; Wurm, East Papuan. Furthermore, the subgroupings proposed are practically identical, the sole difference being that Greenberg subgroups the Solomon group with the Santa

Cruz languages, whereas Wurm subgroups them with the New Britain languages.

2. Both classifications concur on a genetic unit that Greenberg calls Northeast New Guinea and Wurm calls Madang-Adelbert Range.

3. There is also very close agreement on the genetic unity of the languages in Greenberg's East New Guinea group, which corresponds almost exactly with the Eastern branch of the Main Section of the TNG phylum.

4. Of Greenberg's seven mainland groups, five (Central, Southwest, South, East, and Northeast New Guinea) correspond to constituents of Wurm's TNG phylum. In addition, portions of Greenberg's West New Guinea and North New Guinea groups are included in the TNG phylum.

List 5.7. The Indo-Pacific Phylum (Greenberg 1971, Wurm 1982)

INDO-PACIFIC:

- I †TASMANIAN
- II ANDAMAN ISLANDS
- III TRANS–NEW GUINEA:
  - A MAIN SECTION:
    - 1 CENTRAL AND WESTERN:
      - a FINISTERRE-HUON
      - b EAST NEW GUINEA HIGHLANDS
      - c CENTRAL AND SOUTH NEW GUINEA–KUTUBUAN
      - d ANGAN
      - e GOGODALA-SUKI
      - f MARIND
      - g KAYAGAR
      - h SENTANI
      - i DANI-KWERBA
      - j WISSEL LAKES–KEMANDOGA
      - k MAIRASI–TANAH MERAH
      - l WEST BOMBERAI
    - 2 EASTERN:
      - a BINANDEREAN
      - b GOILALAN
      - c KOIARIAN
      - d KWALEAN
      - e MANUBARAN
      - f YAREBAN
      - g MAILUAN
      - h DAGAN

[III TRANS–NEW GUINEA]

  - B MADANG–ADELBERT RANGE
  - C TEBERAN-PAWAIAN
  - D TURAMA-KIKORIAN
  - E INLAND GULF
  - F ELEMAN
  - G TRANS-FLY–BULAKA RIVER
  - H MEK
  - I SENAGI
  - J PAUWASI
  - K NORTHERN
  - L NIMBORAN
  - M KAURE
  - N SOUTH BIRD'S HEAD
  - O KOLOPOM
  - P TIMOR-ALOR
- IV WEST PAPUAN
- V EAST BIRD'S HEAD
- VI GEELVINK BAY
- VII SKO
- VIII KWOMTARI-BAIBAI
- IX ARAI
- X AMTO-MUSIAN
- XI TORRICELLI
- XII SEPIK-RAMU
- XIII EAST PAPUAN

5. The most important similarity between the two classifications is simply that the vast majority of Papuan languages are now recognized as forming a single genetic unit. Whether that unit encompasses two-thirds of the Papuan languages (TNG) or nearly all of them (Indo-Pacific), the long-lived myth of New Guinea as a land beyond the pale of genetic classification has finally been laid to rest.

Whether the widespread similarities among Papuan languages of Oceania will prove to be the residue of an ancient genetic unity, as Greenberg claims, or simply the result of borrowing (i.e. substratum influence), as Wurm suggests, it is too early to tell. So much important work has been done in recent years that it is easy to lose sight of the fact that we are still in the initial stages of the investigation of Papuan classification, and as more material accumulates, our understanding of the relationships among these diverse languages is likely to continue to undergo revision. The classification adopted in this volume, outlined in List 5.7, represents a compromise between the two classifications discussed above. At the highest level Indo-Pacific is used to designate a phylum consisting of all the Papuan languages, but the internal subgrouping within Indo-Pacific follows Wurm (1982). The classification of the languages of the Andaman Islands follows Bradley (1983).

Anceaux, J. C. 1958. "Languages of the Bomberai Peninsula," *Nieuw-Guinea Studien* 2: 109–21.

Blake, Barry J. 1981. *Australian Aboriginal Languages*. Sydney.

Blust, Robert. 1978. Review of *Current Trends in Linguistics*, VIII: *Linguistics in Oceania*, ed. Thomas A. Sebeok, *Language* 54: 467–80.

Bradley, David. 1983. "Map of Andaman and Nicobar Islands," in S. A. Wurm and Shirô Hattori, eds., *Language Atlas of the Pacific Area* 2, Map 37. Stuttgart.

Capell, Arthur. 1944. "Peoples and Languages of Timor," *Oceania* 14: 330–37.

———. 1975. "The 'West Papuan Phylum': General, and Timor and Areas Further West," in *PLNGLS*.

Cowan, H. K. J. 1957a. "A Large Papuan Language Phylum in West New Guinea," *Oceania* 28: 159–67.

———. 1957b. "Prospect of a 'Papuan' Comparative Linguistics," *Bijdragen tot de Taal-, Land- en Volkenkunde* 113: 70–91.

———. 1957c. "Een tweede grote Papoea-taalgroepering in Nederlands-Nieuw-Guinea," *Nieuw Guinea Studien* 1: 106–18.

———. 1959. "La classification des langues papoues," *Anthropos* 54: 973–81.

———. 1963. "Le buna' de Timor: une langue 'ouest-papoue,'" *Bijdragen tot de Taal-, Land- en Volkenkunde* 119: 387–400.

Crowley, Terry, and R. M. W. Dixon. 1981. "Tasmanian," in R. M. W. Dixon and Barry J. Blake, eds., *Handbook of Australian Languages* 2. Amsterdam.

DuBois, Cora Alice. 1944. *The People of Alor*. Minneapolis.

Franklin, K. J. 1973a. "The Gulf Area in the Light of Greenberg's Indo-Pacific Hypothesis," in Franklin, *PL* C26, cited below.

———, ed. 1973b. *The Linguistic Situation in the Gulf District and Adjacent Areas, Papua New Guinea*. *PL* C26.

Grace, George W. 1968. "Classification of the Languages of the Pacific," in Andrew P. Vayda, ed., *Peoples and Cultures of the Pacific*. Garden City, N.Y.

Greenberg, Joseph H. 1958. "Report on the Classification of the Non-Austronesian Languages of the Pacific," unpublished manuscript.

———. 1960. "Indo-Pacific Etymologies," unpublished manuscript.

———. 1971. "The Indo-Pacific Hypothesis," in *CTIL* 8.

Laycock, D. C., and C. L. Voorhoeve. 1975. "History of Research in Papuan Languages," in *PLNGLS*.

Laycock, D. C., and S. A. Wurm. 1975. "Possible Wider Connections of Papuan Languages," in *PLNGLS*.

McElhanon, K. A. 1971. "Classifying New Guinea Languages," *Anthropos* 66: 120–44.

———. 1978. *A Classification of the Languages of the Morobe Province, Papua New Guinea*. Canberra.

McElhanon, K. A., and C. L. Voorhoeve. 1970. *The Trans–New Guinea Phylum: Explorations in Deep-Level Genetic Relationships*. *PL* B16.

Plomley, N. J. B. 1976. *A Word-List of the Tasmanian Aboriginal Languages*. Hobart.

Ray, Sidney H. 1893. "The Languages of British New Guinea," *Transactions of the Ninth International Congress of Orientalists, London, 1892*.

Ruhlen, Merritt. 1981. "A Comparison of Two Classifications of Papuan Languages," unpublished manuscript.

Schmidt, Wilhelm. 1900–1901. "Die sprachlichen Verhältnisse von Deutsch Neu-Guinea," *Zeitschrift für Afrikanische und Ozeanische Sprachen*, 2 parts, 5: 345–84, 6: 1–99.

———. 1952. *Die tasmanischen Sprachen*. Utrecht.

Voegelin, C. F., and F. M. Voegelin. 1965. *Languages of the World: Indo-Pacific fascicle five*. *AL* 7.

Wurm, Stephen A. 1971. "The Papuan Linguistic Situation," in *CTIL* 8.

———. 1974. "Papuan Languages," in *EB* 13: 977–78.

———. 1982. *Papuan Languages of Oceania*. Tübingen.

———, ed. 1975. *Papuan Languages and the New Guinea Linguistic Scene*. *PL* C38.

Wurm, Stephen A., and K. McElhanon. 1975. "Papuan Language Classification Problems," in *PLNGLS*.

Zide, Norman H. 1985. "Robert Colebrooke and the First Linguistic Notice of the Andamanese Languages," unpublished manuscript.

5.3 AUSTRALIAN

About 170 Australian languages are still spoken by some 30,000 people. There are perhaps another 20,000 Aborigines who no longer speak their original language. All but about 50 of these languages appear to be rapidly heading for extinction in the next generation or two, and a good number of Australian tongues have already disappeared in this, and the previous, century. The numerically strongest language is the Western Desert Language, spoken over a wide area of Western Australia by perhaps 5,000

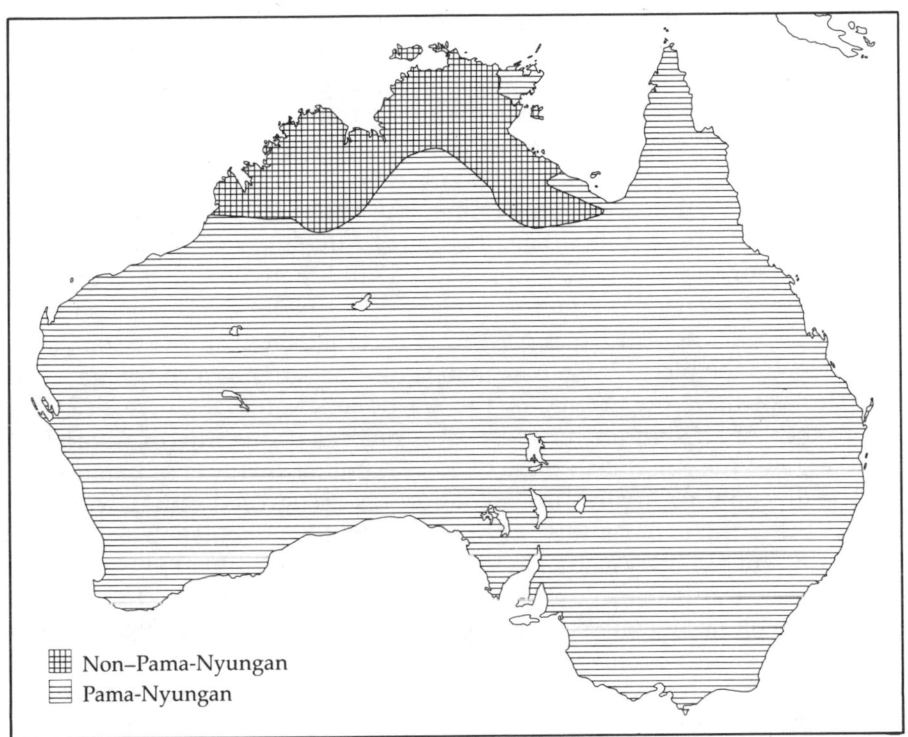

Map 5.3. The Australian family

people. Languages in the eastern third of Australia are for the most part either extinct or moribund. The Australian languages that have been best able to maintain themselves are found in the Northern Territory and Western Australia. Like the Papuan languages of New Guinea, there are no famous Australian languages. They are generally known only to anthropologists and linguists who specialize in their study. The geographic distribution of the Australian family is shown in Map 5.3.

5.3.1 *History of Australian Classification*

Although European explorers landed in Australia as early as 1616, the first recording of an Aboriginal language was made only in 1770, when a member of Captain Cook's expedition collected some information on Guugu Yimidhirr. The first English settlement, on the present site of Sydney, was begun in 1788, and the founding of Hobart in 1803 marked the invasion of Tasmania. The history of the study of Australian Aboriginal languages is neither long nor complex. Since the English invasion of Australia the Aborigines have, in the best of times, been the subject of "benign neglect," and in the worst of times, the object of periodic acts of genocide. Under such conditions the study of their languages could hardly thrive. During the nineteenth century investigation of Australian languages was almost exclusively the domain of missionaries and amateurs, who produced materials that from a modern vantage point leave much to be desired. During the first half of the twentieth century, the situation deteriorated during what Dixon (1980: 16) calls "the dark ages of Australian Aboriginal policy." Most amateur and missionary work ceased, and there was no government-sponsored research. Except for an occasional isolated scholar, such as Arthur Capell, linguistic work on Australian languages came to a standstill. In the 1960's the picture began to change for the better as a consequence of the work of three organizations: the Australian National University (and later other Australian universities), the Australian Institute of Aboriginal Studies, and the Australian branch of the Summer Institute of Linguistics.

The diversity of Australian languages was recognized only toward the end of the eighteenth century; previously it had been widely believed that there was but a single Australian language. The first book on an Australian language (Awabakal) was published in 1827 by the missionary L. E. Threlkeld, who followed it with a grammar of the same language in 1834. Awabakal became extinct around 1850.

Australian linguistics in the nineteenth century created few milestones. One, however, was the recognition by George Grey in 1841 that all Australian languages have a common origin. Grey had explored parts of Western Australia and had compiled wordlists from languages across the continent. He detected a number of cognates that spanned the entire continent and on this basis posited "a community of origin for the aborigines" (quoted in Dixon 1980: 12). The second, and final, milestone of the nineteenth century was the publication of Edward M. Curr's *The Australian Race* in 1886–87. Curr was a sheep farmer north of Melbourne, who collected wordlists for almost 500 languages and dialects and on the basis of their comparison continued the task begun by Grey of identifying pan-Australian cognates.

The first serious attempt at a genetic classification of Australian languages was published in 1919 by the Austrian cleric Wilhelm Schmidt. Schmidt's contribution to the classification of Asian and Oceanic languages has already been discussed in sections 4.5 and 5.2 above. But Schmidt had a particular and enduring fascination for Australian languages, as manifested in the two monographs he published in 1919 and in the compendium on the Tasmanian languages that appeared in 1952, two years before his death at the age of 86. Though he never visited Australia, Schmidt gathered together in Vienna all the published material he could find on Australian languages (relying heavily on Curr's wordlists). In 1919 he proposed a classification that recognized a relatively homogeneous group covering the southern two-thirds of Australia and a very diverse Northern group that appeared to consist of a number of families related neither to the Southern group nor to each other. The diversity of the Northern languages had been largely overlooked by nineteenth-century investigators such as Grey and Curr, who had really only perceived the uniformity of the large Southern group.

Although Schmidt may be credited with being the first to recognize the diversity of the Northern languages, his denial of the genetic unity of all Australian languages did not gain general acceptance. As early as 1923 the American anthropologist Alfred L. Kroeber (better known for his work on American Indian languages) examined the Curr vocabularies and concluded that Australian languages did in fact constitute a valid genetic family, though the Northern region was clearly the most diverse area. (Some 30 years later Greenberg [1953] examined the Curr vocabularies and arrived at conclusions identical to Kroeber's.) Capell (1937) also expressed a belief in the unity of Australian languages and investigated the neglected Northern languages in the early 1940's. In 1956, building on the earlier observations of Grey, Curr, Schmidt, and Kroeber, Capell proposed more than 50 lexical and grammatical cognates distributed throughout the Australian continent, north and south.

In the early 1960's the American linguist Kenneth Hale showed that the Eastern portion of Schmidt's diverse Northern group consisted in reality of phonologically aberrant Southern languages. In redrawing the boundary between Northern and Southern languages, Hale proposed the name Pama-Nyungan for the homogeneous Southern group, combining the words for 'man' from the Northeast and Southwest corners of Australia. Except for the exclusion of the Northeastern languages, Schmidt's proposed subgrouping of the Pama-Nyungan family was quite good; it forms the basis of our current understanding of Pama-Nyungan classification.

In 1966 two similar classifications of Australian languages, based on lexicostatistical analysis, were proposed by O'Grady, Voegelin, and Voegelin and by O'Grady, Wurm, and Hale. The Australian phylum was divided into 29 first-order subgroups, one of which was Pama-Nyungan. The other 28 groups (some consisting of a single language) were restricted to north central and northwest Australia. This lexicostatistic classification was admittedly tentative, and later research uncovered a number of errors. No one, however, has yet proposed any alternative hypothesis for the higher levels of classification.

5.3.2 *Present Status of Australian Classification*

It is generally accepted today that all the indigenous languages of the Australian continent, including the language of the western Torres Straits (Kala Lagaw Ya = Mabuiag), but excluding Meriam (a Papuan language spoken in the eastern Torres Straits) and the extinct Tasmanian languages, are genetically related. Dixon (1980: 225) expresses reservations about the affinity of Tiwi and Djingili with the rest of the languages, but concedes that they may yet prove to be Australian. The majority of scholars already accept them as such.

Within this ancient Australian phylum it is possible to discern many low-level genetic groups consisting of a handful of languages (e.g. Yiwaidjan, Gunwinyguan, West Barkly, Daly) as well as one low-level genetic group encompassing most Australian languages (i.e. Pama-Nyungan). Several peculiarities of the Australian situation, such as the extreme phonological homogeneity of all Australian languages and their lexical diversity, have so far prevented any clarification of the internal relationships of the Australian phylum. Dixon (1980: 226) even questions the validity of Pama-Nyungan as a genetic subgroup of the Australian phylum, but most scholars continue to regard it as a valid subgroup at some level.

The Australian classification followed here is based on Walsh and Wurm (1981), which is itself a revised version of the 1966 lexicostatistic classification discussed above. Following the advice of Paul Black (1982), I have modified the Walsh and Wurm classification by (1) condensing the number of distinct languages listed (here as elsewhere in this volume, one dialect has often been chosen to represent a language that may have several other dialects), (2) replacing the names (or their spelling) with others in a good number of instances (Australian language names have numerous variant spellings, sometimes a dozen or more, and there is no accepted standardization), and (3) altering certain details of the subgrouping. Echoing Dixon's sentiments, Black finds many aspects of the present classification woefully inadequate, but no better proposals are currently available. We may hope that the current revival of interest in the classification of Australian languages, manifested in the work of Dixon, Black, and others, will eventually lead to an even better understanding of the internal relationships of this unique family.

The Australian phylum consists of 15 isolated languages (Enindhilyagwa, Ndjébbana, Yanyuwa, Gagudju, Kungarakany, Mangarayi, Mingin, Nakkara, Nunggubuyu, Tiwi, Waray, Limilngan, Umbugarla, Gunbudj, Murrinh-Patha) and 15 groups. Leaving aside the 15 isolated languages, the structure of the rest of the Australian phylum is illustrated in List 5.8.

List 5.8. The Australian Family (Walsh & Wurm 1982, Black 1982)

AUSTRALIAN:
I YIWAIDJAN
II Mangerrian
III GUNWINYGUAN
IV BURARRAN
V MARAN
VI WEST BARKLY
VII GARAWAN
VIII LARAGIYAN
IX DALY
X DJAMINDJUNGAN
XI DJERAGAN
XII BUNABAN
XIII NYULNYULAN
XIV WORORAN
XV PAMA-NYUNGAN:
A YUULNGU
B TANGIC
C PAMAN
D YALANJIC
E YIDINYIC
F DYIRBALIC
G NYAWAYGIC
H MARIC
I WAKA-KABIC
J †DURUBALIC

[XV PAMA-NYUNGAN]
K GUMBAYNGGIRIC
L YUIN-KURIC
M WIRADHURIC
N Baagandji
O †YOTAYOTIC
P †KULINIC
Q †NGARINYERIC-YITHAYITHIC
R KARNIC
S WAGAYA-WARLUWARIC
T GALGADUNGIC
U ARANDIC
V SOUTH-WEST:
1 NGUMBIN
2 MARNGU
3 NGAYARDA
4 MANTHARDA
5 KANYARA
6 †KARDU
7 WADJARI
8 WATI
9 NGARGA
10 †Nyungar
11 Ngadjunmaya
12 YURA

Alpher, Barry. 1972. "On the Genetic Subgrouping of the Languages of Southwestern Cape York Peninsula, Australia," *OL* 11: 67–87.

Black, Paul. 1980. "Norman Pama Historical Phonology," in Bruce Rigsby and Peter Sutton, eds., *Papers in Australian Linguistics* 13. *PL* A59.

———. 1982. Personal letter.

Blake, Barry J. 1981. *Australian Aboriginal Languages*. Sydney.

Capell, Arthur. 1937. "The Structure of Australian Languages," *Oceania* 8: 27–61.

———. 1940. "The Classification of Languages in North-West Australia," *Oceania* 10: 241–72.

———. 1942. "Languages of Arnhem Land," *Oceania*, 2 parts, 12: 364–92, 13: 24–51.

———. 1956. *A New Approach to Australian Linguistics*. Sydney.

———. 1971. "History of Research in Australian and Tasmanian Languages," in *CTIL* 8.

———. 1979. "The History of Australian Languages: A First Approach," in Stephen A. Wurm, ed., *Australian Linguistic Studies*. *PL* A54.

Curr, E. M. 1886–87. *The Australian Race*, 4 vols. London.
Dixon, R. M. W. 1980. *The Languages of Australia*. Cambridge, Eng.
Greenberg, Joseph H. 1953. "Historical Linguistics and Unwritten Languages," in A. L. Kroeber, ed., *Anthropology Today*. Chicago.
Hale, Kenneth L. 1964. "Classification of the Northern Paman Languages, Cape York Peninsula, Australia: A Research Report," *OL* 3: 248–65.
Kroeber, Alfred L. 1923. "Relationship of the Australian Languages," *Journal and Proceedings of the Royal Society of New South Wales* 57: 101–17.
Oates, W. J., and Lynette F. Oates, eds. 1970. *A Revised Linguistic Survey of Australia*. Canberra.
O'Grady, G. N. 1966. "Proto-Ngayarda Phonology," *OL* 5: 71–130.
———. 1979. "Preliminaries to a Proto Nuclear Pama-Nyungan Stem List," in Stephen A. Wurm, ed., *Australian Linguistic Studies*. *PL* A54.
O'Grady, G. N., C. F. Voegelin, and F. M. Voegelin. 1966. *Languages of the World: Indo-Pacific fascicle six*. *AL* 8,2.
O'Grady, G. N., S. A. Wurm, and K. Hale. 1966. *Map of Aboriginal Languages of Australia*. Victoria, B.C.
Schmidt, Wilhelm. 1919a. *Die Gliederung der australischen Sprachen*. Vienna.
———. 1919b. *Die Personalpronomina in den australischen Sprachen*. Vienna.
———. 1952. *Die tasmanischen Sprachen*. Utrecht.
Walsh, M. J., and S. A. Wurm. 1981. "Language Maps of Australia and Tasmania," in S. A. Wurm and Shirô Hattori, eds., *Language Atlas of the Pacific Area* 1, Maps 20–23. Stuttgart.
Wurm, Stephen A. 1971. "Classification of Australian Languages, including Tasmanian," in *CTIL* 8.
———. 1972. *Languages of Australia and Tasmania*. The Hague.
———. 1974. "Australian Aboriginal Languages," in *EB* 2: 430-31.

6

North and South America

As Rowe (1974) points out, grammars of New World languages began to appear in the sixteenth century, no later than those of European, Asian, and African languages. During the sixteenth century at least six New World grammars appeared (Tarascan, Quechua, Nahuatl, Zapotec, Mixtec, Tupi), and the seventeenth century saw the appearance of 15 more. Only two of the New World grammars published before 1700, however, dealt with languages spoken north of Mexico (Timucua, Massachusett).

During the eighteenth century linguistic materials accumulated in ever-increasing numbers, and finally in the nineteenth century problems of classification were seriously investigated for the first time. Toward the end of the nineteenth century, John W. Powell (1891) classified the languages north of Mexico into 58 independent families, many of which contained but a single language. An even greater number of low-level genetic groups were identified in Central and South America. Brinton (1891) recognized 73 in South America alone. At the beginning of the twentieth century, more than 150 distinct New World families had been identified, though much of South America was still poorly known.

During the first half of the twentieth century, several scholars attempted to reduce the total number of families by combining certain groups into more comprehensive stocks. Chief among these scholars was Edward Sapir, who suggested in 1929 that the languages north of Mexico could be reduced to just six phyla, and those of Central America to 15.

In South America, however, the number of distinct families increased from 73 (Brinton 1891) to 77 (Rivet 1924) to 94 (Loukotka 1935) to 114 (Loukotka 1944) to 117 (Loukotka 1968). Furthermore, Sapir's (1929) article turned out to be a watershed in the classification of North American languages; most Amerindian scholars after Sapir (including his students) came to feel that he had gone too far in consolidation. In 1964 a conference on the classification of American Indian languages north of Mexico replaced Sapir's six phyla with 16 independent families; 12 years later another conference on a similar theme proposed 62 distinct genetic groups north of Mexico (see Campbell and Mithun 1979). Combining Loukotka's (1968) 117 South American families with Campbell and Mithun's (1979: 3–69) 62 North American families, and adding perhaps 20 families restricted to Central America, brings us to a total of roughly 200 distinct genetic groups, according to the current consensus of Amerindian scholars.

This is certainly a startling figure. If the rest of the world's languages can be subsumed in a dozen or so families, as I have indicated in this volume, or even in the several dozen families that more conservative linguists might postulate, the figure does not approach 100, much less 200. The mystery is compounded by the fact that man's presence in the New World is of recent date compared with the rest of the world. On these grounds alone one should expect less diversity in the New World than elsewhere.

One linguist has argued for a radically different view of New World languages since the mid-1950's. After completing his work on African classification (see Chap. 3), Joseph Greenberg turned his attention to the two areas of the world for which there was little understanding of the genetic relationships of languages, New Guinea and South America. (His conclusions regarding the New Guinea area are discussed in section 5.2.)

Soon after Greenberg began investigating South American Indian languages in the mid-1950's, he realized that they could not be fruitfully investigated by themselves, since lexical cognates characterizing these languages were also found in the languages of Central America and much of North America. After expanding his purview to the entire New World, Greenberg soon concluded that New World languages grouped themselves into but three genetic units: *Eskimo-Aleut*, *Na-Dene*, and *Amerind*. He reported his findings in a paper delivered in 1956, but not published until 1960. Greenberg continued to gather Amerindian data during the 1960's and especially the 1970's, and finally published the evidence supporting his tripartite classification in 1987. It is in terms of this classification that New World languages will be examined in this volume.

Brinton, Daniel G. 1891. *The American Race*. Philadelphia.

Campbell, Lyle, and Marianne Mithun, eds. 1979. *The Languages of Native America*. Austin, Tex.

Greenberg, Joseph H. 1960. "The General Classification of Central and South American Languages," in *Men and Cultures: Selected Papers of the Fifth International Congress of Anthropological and Ethnological Sciences, Philadelphia, 1956*. Philadelphia.

———. 1987. *Language in the Americas*. Stanford, Calif.

Loukotka, Čestmír. 1935. "Clasificación de las lenguas sudamericanas," *Lingüística Sudamericana* 1. Prague.
———. 1944. "Klassifikation der südamerikanischen Sprachen," *Zeitschrift für Ethnologie* 74: 1–69.
———. 1968. *Classification of South American Indian Languages*. Los Angeles.
Powell, John Wesley. 1891. "Indian Linguistic Families of America North of Mexico," *Seventh Annual Report, Bureau of American Ethnology*. Washington, D.C.
Rivet, Paul. 1924. "Langues de l'Amérique du Sud et des Antilles," in Antoine Meillet and Marcel Cohen, eds., *Les langues du monde*. Paris.
Rowe, John Howland. 1974. "Sixteenth and Seventeenth Century Grammars," in Dell Hymes, ed., *Studies in the History of Linguistics*. Bloomington, Ind.
Sapir, Edward. 1929. "Central and North American Indian Languages," in *Encyclopaedia Britannica*, 14th ed., 5: 138–41.

6.1 ESKIMO-ALEUT

There are about 10 Eskimo-Aleut languages, with a total of 85,000 speakers. Aleut is spoken in the Aleutian Islands (Alaska) by some 700 people; an additional 1,500 Aleuts no longer speak the language. It is also spoken in the Commander Islands (U.S.S.R.) by roughly 20 members of the total Aleut population of 400. Several varieties of Eskimo are spoken across the northern perimeter of North America, from Alaska in the west through Canada to Greenland in the east. There are, in addition, about 600 speakers of three Eskimo languages spoken in northeastern Siberia (U.S.S.R.). The geographic distribution of the Eskimo-Aleut family is shown in Map 6.1.

It is sometimes forgotten that the Eskimo were known in Europe centuries before Columbus first reached the New World. The Vikings landed in Greenland early in the ninth century A.D. and by the end of the century established permanent settlements that would last into the fifteenth century. Since Greenland was already inhabited by Eskimo before the arrival of the Vikings, knowledge of the Eskimo gradually filtered back to Europe via Norse travelers.

The study of the Eskimo language(s), however, dates only from the mid-eighteenth century, when Paul Egede published the first (Greenlandic) Eskimo dictionary (1750) and grammar (1760). These works were described by Hoijer (1976: 4) as "the foundations of Eskimo linguistic studies." The enormous geographic distribution of the Eskimo languages was not at first appreciated, but by 1836 Albert Gallatin was able to sketch the boundaries of the Eskimo family "with considerable precision" (Powell 1891). The second landmark in Eskimo linguistics was Samuel Petrus Kleinschmidt's Greenlandic grammar (1851) and dictionary (1871), which showed a notable advance in linguistic sophistication over Egede's works.

Apparently the first person to perceive the affinity of Eskimo and Aleut was the Dane Rasmus Rask, whose work on Indo-European was discussed

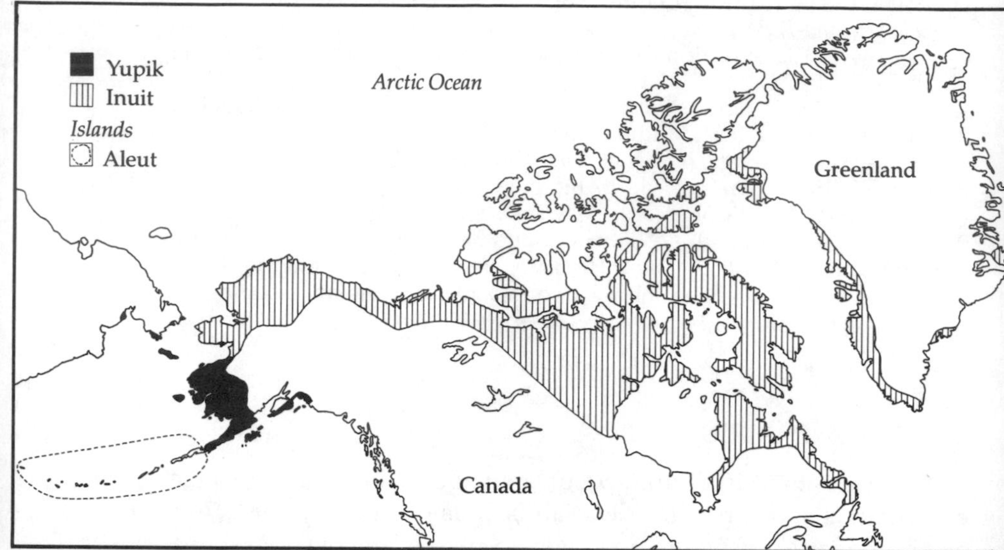

Map 6.1. The Eskimo-Aleut family

in section 2.3. According to Pedersen (1931: 136), Rask made his observation around 1818 in a manuscript that remained unpublished for almost a century. In any event, by the time of the Powell classification (1891), it was generally agreed that Eskimo and Aleut formed one genetic group.

Early in the twentieth century it was realized that there were basically two varieties of Eskimo, an Eastern type (Inuit or Inupiaq) and a Western type (Yupik). The border between these two varieties was at first placed between Alaska and Canada, but in the 1950's it became apparent that the true border was located at Norton Sound on the west coast of Alaska.

There have been numerous attempts to link the Eskimo-Aleut family with other families. The question of the external connections of Eskimo-Aleut is taken up in section 7.3.

List 6.1. The Eskimo-Aleut Family (Krauss 1976, 1979)

ESKIMO-ALEUT:
- I Aleut
- II ESKIMO:
  - A INUIT
  - B YUPIK:
    - 1 ALASKAN
    - 2 SIBERIAN

The internal relationships of the Eskimo-Aleut family are fairly clear and uncontroversial. There is a sharp cleavage between Aleut and Eskimo and a clear distinction between Inuit and Yupik Eskimo. The classification followed here, based on Krauss (1976, 1979), is shown in List 6.1.

Bergsland, Knut. 1974. "Eskimo-Aleut Languages," in *EB* 6: 962–64.
Egede, Paul. 1750. *Dictionarium Gronlandico-Danico-Latinum*. Hafniae [Copenhagen].
———. 1760. *Grammatica Gronlandica Danico-Latina*. Hafniae [Copenhagen].
Gallatin, Albert. 1836. "Synopsis of the Indians Within the United States East of the Rocky Mountains and in the British and Russian Possessions in North America," *Archaeologia Americana* 2: 1–422.
Hoijer, Harry. 1976. "History of American Indian Linguistics," in *NLA* 1.
Kleinschmidt, Samuel Petrus. 1851. *Grammatik der grönländischen Sprache*. Berlin.
———. 1871. *Den gronlandske Ordbog*. Copenhagen.
Krauss, Michael E. 1976. "Eskimo-Aleut," in *NLA* 1.
———. 1979. "Na-Dene and Eskimo-Aleut," in *LNA*.
Pedersen, Holger. 1931. *Linguistic Science in the Nineteenth Century*. Cambridge, Mass.
Powell, John Wesley. 1891. "Indian Linguistic Families of America North of Mexico," in *Seventh Annual Report, Bureau of American Ethnology*. Washington, D.C.
Thalbitzer, William. 1921. "The Aleutian Language Compared with Greenlandic," *IJAL* 2: 40–57.
Woodbury, Anthony C. 1984. "Eskimo and Aleut Languages," in William C. Sturtevant, ed., *Handbook of North American Indians* 5: *Arctic*. Washington, D.C.

6.2 NA-DENE

The Na-Dene phylum consists of three independent languages (i.e. Haida, Tlingit, Eyak) and the Athabaskan family. Their geographic distribution is shown in Map 6.2. There are approximately 300 speakers of *Haida* on the Queen Charlotte Islands (off the west coast of Canada) and in the Alaskan panhandle. There are an additional 1,700 Haida who no longer speak the language. Of the total *Tlingit* population of 10,000, only 2,000 still speak the language. Most speakers reside in southeastern Alaska, though there are perhaps 100 speakers in Canada. Originally spoken along the southeastern coast of Alaska, *Eyak* had only two surviving speakers, both old, in the late 1970's and may now be extinct.

About 30 *Athabaskan* languages, with an estimated 200,000 speakers, are spoken in most of the Alaskan interior, much of western Canada, and the American Southwest (i.e. Arizona and New Mexico). Formerly Athabaskan languages were also spoken on the northern California and Oregon coasts, but these languages are now either extinct or bordering on extinction. The numerically largest Athabaskan language is Navajo, spoken in New Mexico and Arizona by 130,000 people. An additional 20,000 Navajo no longer

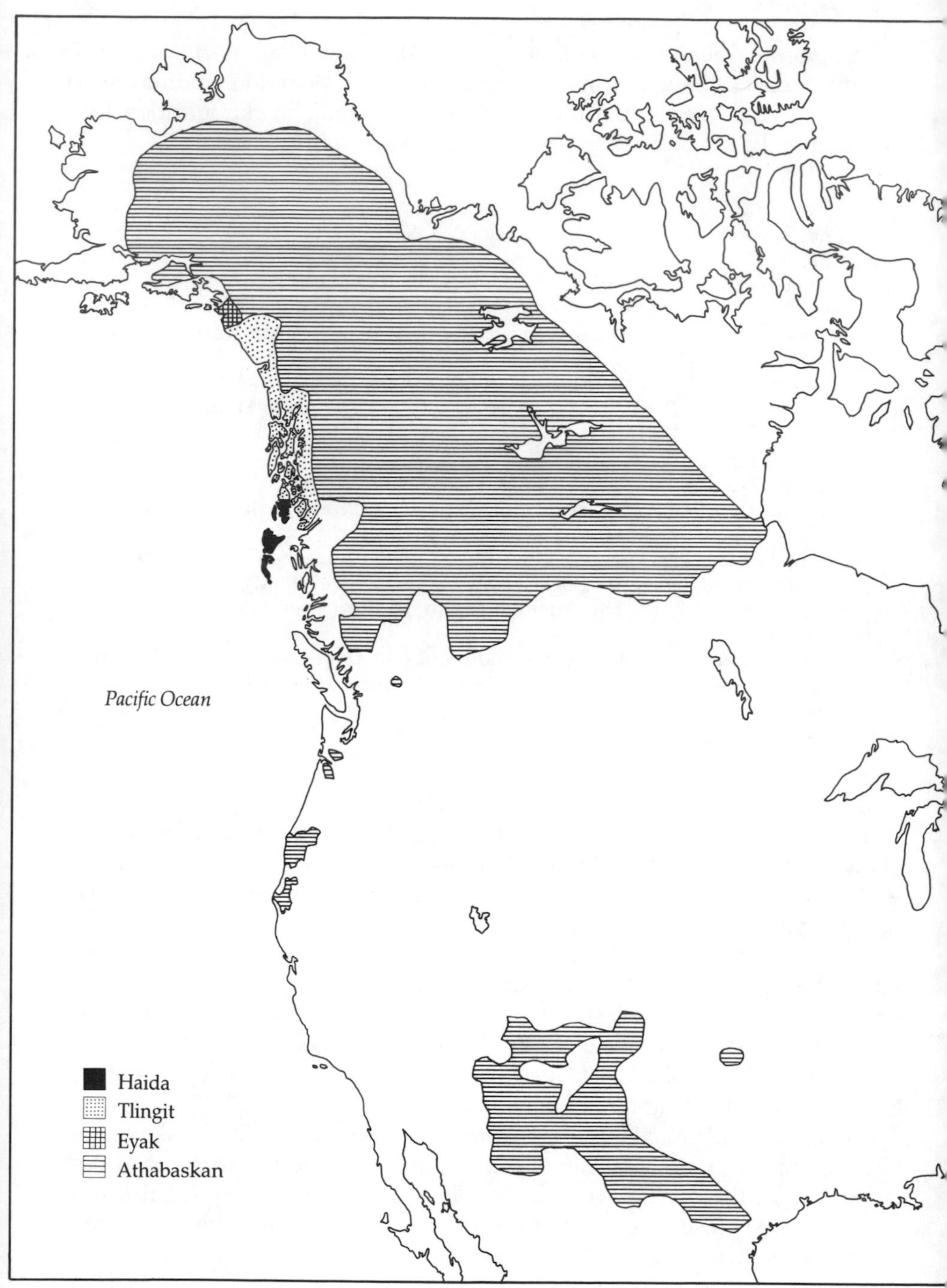

Map 6.2. The Na-Dene family

speak the language, which is the only American Indian language north of Mexico with more than 100,000 speakers.

6.2.1 *History of Na-Dene Classification*

According to Krauss (1964: 127), information on all three constituents of the Na-Dene phylum (Haida, Tlingit, Athabaskan) was first published in the eighteenth century. Edward Thompson's Chipewyan vocabulary (1742) was apparently the first linguistic work on an Athabaskan language; material on Tlingit (1786) and Haida (1791) was gathered toward the end of the century. The possibility that Tlingit and Haida are genetically related was first entertained at the close of the eighteenth century. A Russian linguist, Rezanov, collected the first Eyak data in 1805. Although he perceived similarities between Eyak, Tanaina (an Athabaskan language), and Tlingit, he attributed them to borrowing rather than to common origin. In 1816 Adelung and Vater discussed a possible relationship between Athabaskan, Eyak, and Tlingit, but reached no firm conclusions.

By the mid-nineteenth century Russian linguists had arrived at an understanding of the Na-Dene phylum that differed little from that reached by Americans a century later (see Krauss 1976: 334). With the sale of Alaska to the United States in 1867, however, the Na-Dene languages passed out of the Russian zone of inquiry into the American.

Gallatin, in his 1836 classification of North American Indian languages, recognized the Athabaskan family, though only its Northern varieties. In addition to the large Athabaskan-speaking territory in Alaska and Western Canada, there are two isolated Athabaskan enclaves far to the south. Pacific Coast Athabaskan was spoken on the Oregon-California coast; today these languages are all either extinct or moribund. Apachean, comprising Navajo and various dialects of Apache, is found in Arizona and New Mexico. Pacific Coast Athabaskan and Apachean were first connected with the Northern languages by William Turner and Horatio Hale in the 1850's.

In the Powell classification of 1891, Athabaskan, Tlingit, and Haida were listed as independent families, though Powell mentioned the possibility that Tlingit and Haida might be related. The Eyak language did not appear in Powell's classification or in any other American work of this period; both the Eyak themselves and the earlier Russian sources on their language were overlooked by American investigators until the 1930's.

In 1894 Franz Boas concluded on "structural" grounds that Tlingit and Haida were genetically related, though he admitted that lexical cognates were few. In the American literature the Na-Dene hypothesis was first formulated by Edward Sapir in 1915. Building on the earlier observations of Boas and John Swanton, Sapir proposed close to 100 cognates shared by

Athabaskan and Tlingit or Haida (or both), which accounted, according to Sapir, for only a third of those he had discovered. Sapir's proposals stirred up quite a controversy (see Goddard 1920), for the scholarly climate, then as now, was not receptive to such distant relationships. Boas, in fact, had become disenchanted with genetic classification in general, and with the Athabaskan-Tlingit-Haida connection in particular, coming to feel that it was impossible to distinguish borrowing and areal convergence from true genetic affinity. In this regard his views contrasted sharply with those of Sapir, for whom the Na-Dene family was but one of many proposals consolidating what had previously been considered independent languages or families. Other examples of Sapir's work in this vein are discussed in the following section (6.3).

The question of whether it is possible to distinguish genetic affiliation from borrowing continues to divide linguists to the present day. "Diffusionists," such as Boas, felt it was impossible to differentiate borrowed traits from inherited ones, particularly at deeper levels of relationship. "Geneticists," such as Alfred Kroeber and Sapir, did not deny that the diffusion of traits occurs. Rather, they contended that it was never of such a massive or ambiguous nature that it was impossible to distinguish the inherited core of a language from later superficial accretions. Some scholars did eventually turn this issue into an either/or proposition. The dichotomy was unfortunate since, as Haas (1966: 150) stresses, "The truth of the matter is that both cognates *and* borrowed words have a story to tell about earlier connections."

Eyak was rediscovered by Frederica de Laguna in 1930 and thus came to the attention of American scholars for the first time. Sapir immediately recognized that Eyak was related to, but not a member of, the Athabaskan family, and subsequently Fang-kuei Li and Michael Krauss reached the same conclusion.

Since 1950 the Na-Dene hypothesis has received further support from the work of Dell Hymes and especially Heinz-Jürgen Pinnow. Quite recently Krauss (1979) and Levine (1979) have questioned the inclusion of Haida in Na-Dene, but Greenberg (1987) criticizes their demurral.

6.2.2 *Present Status of Na-Dene Classification*

The nucleus of the Na-Dene phylum is the Athabaskan family, whose close-knit genetic unity has been recognized for over a century. Clearly related to the Athabaskan family, but not a member of it, is the Eyak language, which is now on the verge of extinction. It is also universally accepted that Tlingit is distantly related to the Athabaskan-Eyak nucleus, but opinion is divided on whether Haida too is to be included in the Na-Dene complex.

Sapir, Hymes, Pinnow, and Greenberg support its inclusion; Krauss and Levine remain unconvinced.

Perhaps the most difficult problem in Na-Dene taxonomy concerns the internal relationships of the close-knit Athabaskan family. Krauss (1976, 1979) doubts that any valid internal subgrouping can be established for Athabaskan. Nevertheless, based on the sources listed in the bibliography to this section, we can make certain observations about the internal structure of the family. (1) Of the three geographic groups that make up Athabaskan, only Pacific Coast Athabaskan and Apachean constitute valid genetic nodes. (2) The Northern group comprises several primary branches, though the precise number and their constituent languages are difficult to determine because of the homogeneity of Northern Athabaskan and the paucity of materials on some languages. (3) Apachean is both more homogeneous and more closely related to the Northern languages than is the Pacific Coast group. (4) Among the Northern groups the greatest diversity lies in the west (mainly Alaska), whereas in the east (Canada) the diversity is considerably less, with mutually intelligible dialects covering large areas. (5) Within the Pacific Coast group there is a clear division into Oregon and California branches. (6) Within Apachean a single language, Kiowa Apache, is opposed to the remainder of the languages. (7) The Apachean and Pacific Coast groups appear to have broken away from different sections of the Northern dialect complex. Specifically, Apachean shows greatest affinity with Sarcee, and Pacific Coast Athabaskan with Tahltan. The Athabaskan

List 6.2. The Na-Dene Family (Sapir 1929 and others)

NA-DENE:
- I Haida
- II ATHABASKAN-TLINGIT:
  - A Tlingit
  - B ATHABASKAN-EYAK:
    - 1 Eyak
    - 2 ATHABASKAN:
      - a TANAINA-AHTNA
      - b INGALIK-KOYUKON
      - c TANANA–UPPER KUSKOKWIM
      - d TUTCHONE
      - e TAHLTAN-KASKA
      - f †Tsetsaut
      - g PACIFIC COAST:
        - i OREGON
        - ii CALIFORNIA

[2 ATHABASKAN]
- h CANADIAN:
  - i HAN-KUTCHIN
  - ii HARE-CHIPEWYAN
  - iii BEAVER-SEKANI
  - iv CARRIER-CHILCOTIN
  - v †Kwalhioqua
  - vi Sarcee
- i APACHEAN:
  - i Kiowa Apache
  - ii NAVAJO-APACHE

classification adopted here attempts to represent these seven statements, as well as a host of low-level relationships described in Krauss (1976, 1979). The subgrouping for Na-Dene as a whole follows Sapir (1929), with the addition of Eyak in the appropriate position (List 6.2).

Adelung, J. C., and J. S. Vater. 1816. *Mithridates*. Berlin.

Boas, Franz. 1894. "Classification of the Languages of the North Pacific Coast," in *Memoirs of the International Congress of Anthropologists, 1893*.

Gallatin, Albert. 1836. "Synopsis of the Indians within the United States East of the Rocky Mountains and in the British and Russian Possessions in North America," *Archaeologia Americana* 2: 1–422.

Goddard, P. E. 1920. "Has Tlingit a Genetic Relation to Athapaskan?," *IJAL* 1: 266–79.

Greenberg, Joseph H. 1987. *Language in the Americas*. Stanford, Calif.

Haas, Mary R. 1966. "Historical Linguistics and Genetic Relationship," in *CTIL* 3.

Hoijer, Harry. 1938. "The Southern Athapascan Languages," *AA* 40: 75–87.

———. 1956. "The Chronology of the Athapaskan Languages," *IJAL* 22: 219–32.

———. 1960. "Athapascan Languages of the Pacific Coast," in Stanley Diamond, ed., *Culture in History*. New York.

Hymes, Dell. 1956. "Na-Dene and Positional Analysis of Categories," *AA* 58: 624–38.

Krauss, Michael E. 1964. "Proto-Athapaskan-Eyak and the Problem of Na-Dene: The Phonology," *IJAL* 30: 118–31.

———. 1976. "Na-Dene," in *NLA* 1.

———. 1979. "Na-Dene and Eskimo-Aleut," in *LNA*.

Levine, Robert D. 1979. "Haida and Na-Dene: A New Look at the Evidence," *IJAL* 45: 157–70.

Li, Fang-kuei. 1965. "Some Problems in Comparative Athabascan," *Canadian Journal of Linguistics* 10: 129–34.

Pinnow, Heinz-Jürgen. 1966. *Grundzüge einer historischen Lautlehre des Tlingit: Ein Versuch*. Wiesbaden.

———. 1968. "Genetic Relationship vs. Borrowing in Na-Dene," *IJAL* 34: 204–11.

———. 1976. *Geschichte der Na-Dene-Forschung*. Berlin.

Powell, John Wesley. 1891. "Indian Linguistic Families of America North of Mexico," *Seventh Annual Report, Bureau of American Ethnology*. Washington, D.C.

Sapir, Edward. 1915. "The Na-Dene Languages, A Preliminary Report," *AA* 17: 534–58.

———. 1929. "Central and North American Languages," in *EB* 5: 138–41.

Viitso, Tiit-Rein. 1976. "On Classifying the Athapaskan Languages," *Linguistica Acta et Commentationes Universitatis Tartuensis* 401.

6.3 AMERIND

Before the European invasion of the New World in the sixteenth century, languages belonging to the Amerind phylum were spoken from what is today northern Canada to the tip of South America (see Maps 6.3–6.5). Dur-

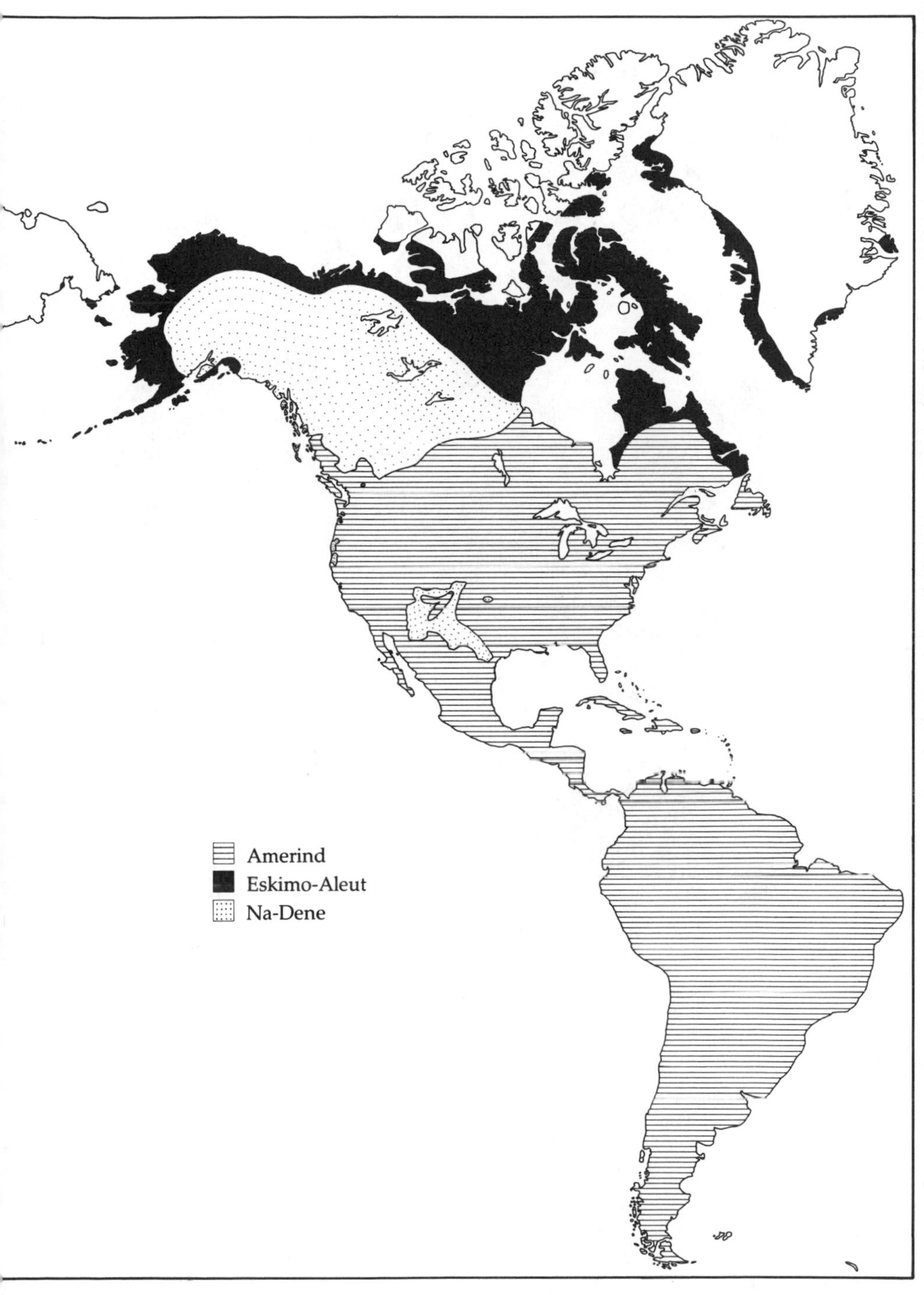

Map 6.3. The Amerind family

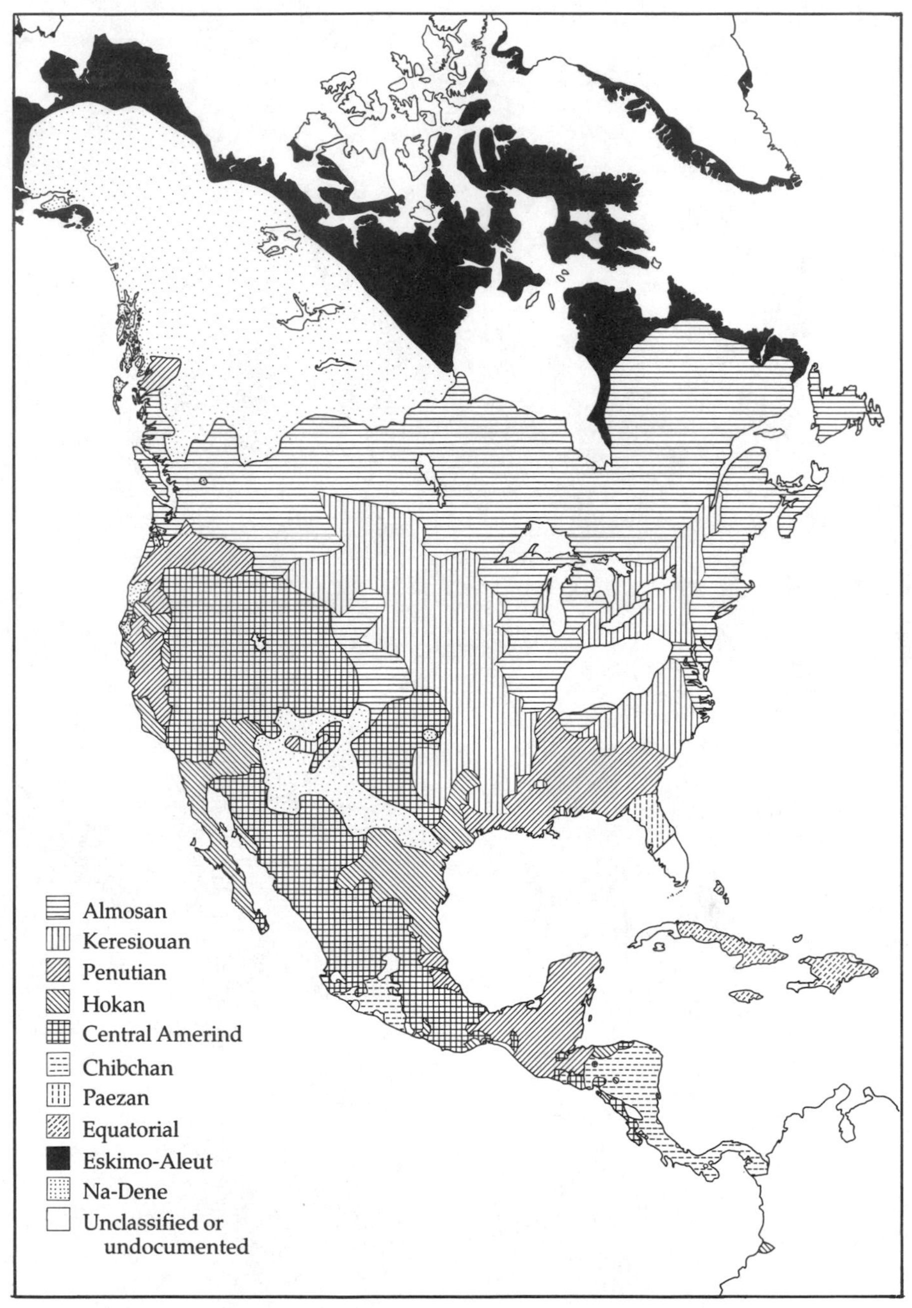

Map 6.4. The Amerind family, North and Central America

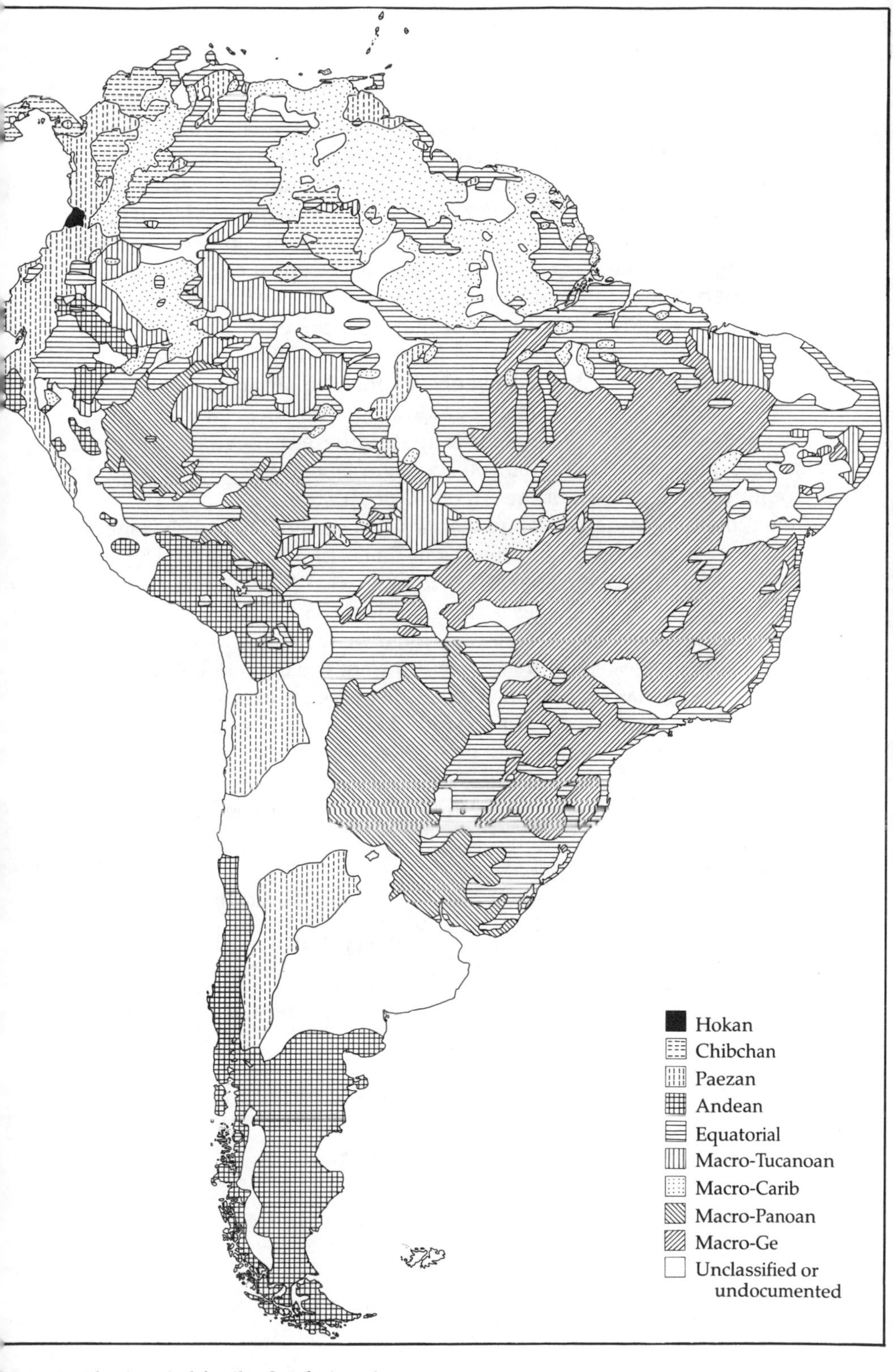

Map 6.5. The Amerind family, South America

ing the past 500 years many of the Native American tribes and languages have disappeared, often without a trace. Today an Indo-European language (English, Spanish, or Portuguese) is politically dominant in every country of North, Central, and South America, and the native Indian languages enjoy second-class status, or worse. We can only roughly estimate the number of surviving native languages and their number of speakers, particularly for South America, which is much more poorly documented than North and Central America. My estimate is that there are currently about 600 surviving Amerind languages, spoken by a total of roughly 18 million people. Were all the speakers divided evenly among the languages, the average would be almost 30,000 speakers per language. But the actual distribution of speakers among the languages is quite different. Seventeen Amerind languages have more than 100,000 speakers (see Table 6.1), and they account for over 90 percent of the Amerind population.

The remaining Amerind languages would average about 1,400 speakers each. But even this figure is deceiving in that, although roughly 20 percent of Amerind languages are spoken north of Mexico (United States and Canada), these 140 or so languages account for less than 2 percent of the Amerind population. This fact is well illustrated in Table 6.1, where we notice that all the languages listed are spoken south of the United States. (Navajo, as we have seen, has more than 100,000 speakers, but it belongs to the Na-Dene phylum.) Many North American Indian languages have only a handful of speakers left (usually old people, the younger generation having

Table 6.1. Amerind Languages with More Than 100,000 Speakers

Language[a]	Millions of speakers	Location
Quechua	7.00	Colombia, Ecuador, Peru, Bolivia
Guarani	3.00	Paraguay, Brazil, Argentina
Aymara	1.50	Peru, Bolivia
Nahuatl (=Aztec)	1.00	Southern Mexico
Quiche (Mayan)	.87	Guatemala
Yucatec (Mayan)	.53	Southern Mexico
Zapotec	.50	Southern Mexico
Mapudungu (=Araucanian)	.44	Chile
Cakchiquel (Mayan)	.41	Guatemala
Mazahua	.35	Southern Mexico
Totonac	.27	Southern Mexico
Kekchi (Mayan)	.27	Guatemala
Mam (Mayan)	.26	Guatemala
Mixtec	.25	Southern Mexico
Otomi	.22	Southern Mexico
Mazatec	.12	Southern Mexico
Tzotzil (Mayan)	.11	Southern Mexico
TOTAL	17.10	

[a]Some of these "languages" are in reality complexes of mutually unintelligible dialects, e.g. Quechua, Nahuatl, Otomi, Zapotec, Mixtec.

adopted English) and are clearly destined for extinction in the very near future.

Despite having limited numbers of speakers, a number of North American Indian languages are well known, having been borrowed into English as place names, e.g. Illinois, Massachusett, Cheyenne, Alabama, Omaha, Dakota, Biloxi, Wichita, Mohave, Kalispel. Others have become famous around the world via Western movies, e.g. Comanche, Muskogee (= Creek), Cherokee, Mohawk.

Information on the numerous families that make up the Amerind phylum (e.g. Algonquian, Iroquoian, Uto-Aztecan) may be found in Table 8.2.

6.3.1 *History of Amerind Classification*

As I mentioned above, the collection of linguistic information for New World languages did not lag behind that for the rest of the world. During the sixteenth century the first wordlists were gathered by European explorers, and a few grammars appeared. The seventeenth and eighteenth centuries saw a steady increase in the number of grammars, mostly the work of missionaries. Finally, in the nineteenth century, problems of genetic classification were systematically attacked for the first time.

The first New World language to be recorded was apparently Laurentian (a Northern Iroquoian language), a wordlist of which was collected during Jacques Cartier's first voyage to the Gulf of Saint Lawrence in 1534. (The wordlist may actually have been taken down some time later, since Cartier took two Indians back to France to meet the king.) There is some dispute whether Laurentian is an earlier stage of the modern Huron language or a language closely related to Huron that became extinct. Regardless, it was clearly a Northern Iroquoian language.

The Iroquoian family was also apparently the first genetic group in North America to be identified by European scholars. As early as 1635 Paul LeJeune recognized it, or at least its Northern branch. The Southern branch, consisting of a single language (Cherokee), was added to the family in 1797 by Benjamin S. Barton, though the relationship had perhaps been perceived by David Zeisberger in 1768. Barton also included the Tuscarora language in Iroquoian for the first time; though geographically Southern (originally spoken in eastern North Carolina), Tuscarora belongs with the Northern branch, not with neighboring Cherokee.

The other major linguistic family indigenous to the Atlantic seaboard, the Algonquian family, was no doubt recognized early, but I have not been able to determine either by whom or at what date it was first noticed. In northern Florida a language was spoken that was neither Iroquoian nor Algonquian; the genetic affinity of Timucua (now extinct) has been the subject of lively controversy over the years, and we shall return to this question below. A grammar of Timucua, published in 1614, is the earliest North American grammar listed in Rowe (1974).

At the beginning of the nineteenth century, in North America, only the languages of the Atlantic Coast were documented at all well. West of the Mississippi River there were known to be a number of tribes, but almost nothing was known of their languages. Work on California languages was begun only in the nineteenth century by a Spanish priest, Felipe Arroyo de la Cuesta.

Men such as Thomas Jefferson recognized the value of wordlists for the detection of genetic relationships (and hence of migratory paths of the Native American peoples). Jefferson explicitly instructed Lewis and Clark to collect such wordlists as they could during their expedition across the continent from 1803 to 1806. The materials they gathered were deposited in Washington, D.C., upon their return, but were quickly lost and have never been found.

During the early nineteenth century typological classification was more common than genetic classification, and indeed the two were often not carefully distinguished. Stephen Duponceau and John Pickering, both lawyers by profession and philologists by avocation, believed that all New World languages were characterized by polysynthesis (i.e., what would constitute an entire sentence in European languages was contained in a single word in so-called polysynthetic languages), a trait that was presumed to be absent from the languages of the rest of the world. It was not until the end of the century that this belief in structural uniformity was finally laid to rest, largely through the work of Franz Boas. Polysynthesis is by no means characteristic of all New World languages, nor is it entirely absent from the rest of the world.

The first serious attempt at a classification of North American languages was made by Albert Gallatin in 1836. Sometimes referred to as the Father of American Linguistics, Gallatin reduced the 81 tribes on which he had data to 28 families by comparing basic vocabulary. Twelve years later he increased the number to 32 for North America north of Mexico, but excluding California, for which no materials were yet available. Gallatin's classification is still recognized as a turning point in Amerindian classification; the American linguist Mary Haas (1969b: 244) has called it "a landmark in the history of the genealogical classification of North American languages [that] was not superseded until the work of Powell and his coworkers completed what Gallatin had begun." Gallatin, we might add, believed that all North American languages were ultimately related.

The last half of the nineteenth century saw the gradual accumulation of data on languages of the western United States, in particular the previously unknown area of California. Toward the end of the century, there developed a race between two men to compile the first comprehensive classification of North American languages. Daniel Brinton was a doctor who had been intensely interested in the American Indian all his life. He eventually quit his medical practice to devote his full time to the study of American Indian languages, after 1886 as a professor at the University of Pennsylvania. Brinton's competitor was an army major, geologist, and explorer who had founded the Bureau of American Ethnology in 1879 and served as its first director, John Wesley Powell. Brinton's classification was published in 1891; though Powell's classification bore the same date, it did not in fact appear until 1892. The two classifications were only roughly similar in scope, since Brinton's covered all of North and South America; Powell's was restricted to North America north of Mexico. Furthermore, Brinton produced his classification by himself, whereas Powell may be more accurately described as the supervisor, rather than the author, of the classification that bears his name, as we shall see presently.

When Brinton published *The American Race* in 1891, he intended it as "the first attempt at a systematic classification of the whole American race on the basis of language" (p. ix). Brinton estimated some 80 families for North America and an equal number for South America, but all of them, he believed, shared a fundamental unity: "The psychic identity of the Americans is well illustrated in their languages" (p. 55). Brinton divided all the New World languages into five geographic groups; List 6.3 shows his classification, with representative families from each of the groups.

Brinton's classification was the first for South America and formed a foundation for all future work in this area. For North America the classification was soon eclipsed by Powell's, which was based on more complete information to which Brinton had been denied access. More precisely, Brinton had asked to see the materials that had been gathered at the Bureau of American Ethnology. Powell responded that Brinton could see the materials on condition that he not use them in his work, "a proviso scarcely so liberal as I had expected," lamented Brinton (1891: xii).

Powell's classification was a group effort by the staff of the Bureau of American Ethnology, and in the actual determination of the classification Powell himself played an inconsequential role. According to Kroeber, the final classification "was made for Powell, who was a geologist and an army major, by Henshaw the ornithologist when Powell found that he would never get his philologist-linguists like Gatschet, Hewitt, and Pilling to come through with the commitment of a classification" (quoted in Campbell & Mithun 1979: 12). The Powell classification, as it became known, identified 58 families north of Mexico, over half of which were language isolates (i.e. single languages with no known relatives). Furthermore, fully two-thirds of the 58 families were found west of the Rocky Mountains. Thirty-two languages were classified as language isolates: Adaizan, Atakapa, Beothuk, Chimariko, Tsimshian, Chinook, Chitimacha, Chumash, Esselen, Kala-

List 6.3. New World Language Families (Brinton 1891; partial list)

I	II	III
NORTH ATLANTIC:	**NORTH PACIFIC:**	**CENTRAL:**
A ESKIMO-ALEUT	A Tlingit	A UTO-AZTECAN
B Beothuk	B Haida	B OTOMIAN
C ATHABASKAN	C SAHAPTIN–NEZ PERCE	C Tarascan
D ALGONQUIAN	D SALISH	D TOTONACAN
E IROQUOIAN	E CHIMAKUAN	E ZAPOTECAN-MIXTECAN
F MUSKOGEAN	F PALAIHNIHAN	F MIXE-ZOQUE
G COAHUILTECAN	G YANAN	G CHINANTECAN
H CADDOAN	H MAIDUAN	H MANGUEAN
I SIOUAN	I COSTANOAN	I TEQUISTLATECAN
J Kiowa	J Karok	J MAYAN
	K Yuki	K Huave
	L YUMAN	L Subtiaba
	M TANOAN	M Jicaque
	N Zuni	N Xinca
	O Keres	

IV	V
SOUTH PACIFIC:	**SOUTH ATLANTIC:**
A CHIBCHAN	A TUPI
B PAEZAN	B GE
C TIMOTE	C ARAWAKAN
D Cuna	D CARIB
E CHOCO	E PANOAN
F Quechua	F TACANAN
G Aymara	G ZAPAROAN
	H JIVAROAN
	I Mapudungu

puya, Karankawa, Keres, Kiowa, Kutenai, Tlingit, Coos, Klamath, Natchez, Karok, Salinan, Shasta, Sahaptin, Haida, Takelma, Timucua, Tunica, Tonkawa, Yuchi, Washo, Yurok, Wiyot, Zuni. In addition to these isolates, the Powell classification identified the 26 families in List 6.4.

The Powell classification has been widely praised over the years and is generally regarded as the second important classification of North American languages, completing what Gallatin had begun a half-century earlier. Edward Sapir called it a "monumental work, . . . the cornerstone of the linguistic edifice in aboriginal North America" (quoted in Hoijer 1976: 9). Recently both Lamb (1964) and Campbell and Mithun (1979) have suggested

List 6.4. Language Families North of Mexico (Powell 1891)

ESKIMO-ALEUT	PALAIHNIHAN	COSTANOAN
ATHABASKAN	POMO	WINTUN
ALGONQUIAN	YANAN	YOKUTS
CHIMAKUAN	YUMAN	YUKI-WAPPO
WAKASHAN	COAHUILTECAN	MUSKOGEAN
SALISH	CAYUSE-MOLALA	TANOAN
CADDOAN	YAKONAN	NUMIC
SIOUAN	MAIDUAN	PIMIC-TARACAHITIC-CORACHOL
IROQUOIAN	MIWOK	

that the Powell classification is not as praiseworthy as many believe. A genetic classification may err in two ways. The first is to group languages that do not belong together; the second is not to combine languages (or groups of languages) that do belong together. On the first count the Powell classification has often been praised for the fact that all 58 "Powell units," as they are sometimes called, are valid genetic nodes. Lamb (1964: 119) objects that this is hardly deserving of praise "since, with the exception of Salish and his Piman (Pimic plus Taracahitic plus Coric), every grouping made was of languages so closely related that there could be no doubt of a recent common origin."

The main defect of the Powell classification is that it failed to recognize higher-level groupings, some of which had already been demonstrated in the literature. In this regard Powell's classification is less satisfactory than that of Brinton, who not only identified the Uto-Aztecan family, but gave it its name, remarking that "the relationship of these numerous bands is unquestionable" (Brinton 1891: 118). According to Powell (1891: 175), the relationship of Aztec to the more northerly Uto-Aztecan languages had been claimed by Johann Buschmann (among others), "but this relationship has yet to be demonstrated." Lamb (1964: 115) points out that Powell was confused on this point: "Although Buschmann did not include Aztec in the group [Uto-Aztecan], he presented sufficient evidence to show that it belonged." Though Buschmann did join the Numic languages with the Pimic, Taracahitic, and Corachol groups of northern Mexico, it was not until 1879 that Gatschet explicitly added Aztec to the group, a position accepted by Brinton but not by Powell.

Furthermore, Powell did not combine Miwok and Costanoan, though their relationship had been demonstrated by Robert Latham in 1856. Finally, we may note that Brinton, but not Powell, recognized the affinity of Yuman, Seri, and Tequistlatecan, which are today considered members of the Hokan phylum.

In sum, the Powell classification is perhaps neither as perfect as supporters sometimes contend nor as flawed as some critics would suggest. It accomplished essentially what it set out to do, namely, to delineate all of the linguistic families of North America. As Powell made clear, it was not intended as a final classification, but rather as a beginning. In that capacity it served its purpose admirably.

The appearance of the Powell classification (and the less influential Brinton classification) in 1891 brought to a close the initial phase in the genetic classification of New World languages.* All of North America (north of Mexico) had been fairly well charted and the languages reduced to 58 genetic units. Central and South America were less well documented, but here too Brinton's work constituted a baseline for future research. The second phase in the study of Amerindian classification took place during the period 1900–1930, but it was the second decade of the century that witnessed the most remarkable and controversial discoveries. This phase was characterized by a gradual reduction in the number of North American families; by 1929 Edward Sapir had managed to reduce the 58 Powell units to just six stocks.

As I mentioned above, certain of the Powell units had already been consolidated before 1891; Miwok-Costanoan had been established in 1856 and Uto-Aztecan by 1879. So the period of consolidation really overlaps somewhat with the period of discovery. Nevertheless, relatively little consolidation took place until the twentieth century. Some of the earliest intimations of more comprehensive genetic groupings are due to the German-American anthropologist Franz Boas, who suggested in 1894 that "structural similarities" indicated a common origin for Athabaskan, Tlingit, and Haida. On similar grounds Boas saw a common origin for the Salish, Wakashan, and Chimakuan families. But by the time Sapir offered lexical support for grouping Athabaskan, Tlingit, and Haida in a family that he named Na-Dene (see section 6.2), Boas had become disillusioned with genetic classification, having come to feel that it was impossible to separate borrowings from true cognates. Although Boas remained a towering figure in American anthropology until his death in 1942, his main contribution was not in the area of linguistic classification. Indeed, in this field he appears to have had a negative impact.

One might well mark the beginning of the "reductionist phase" of Amerindian classification, as it is sometimes called, with the arrival of Alfred Kroeber at the University of California at Berkeley in 1901. With the zeal characteristic of a recent Ph.D. (from Columbia University), Kroeber quickly set to work gathering wordlists for all California Indian languages, with the hope that their comparison might lead to some consolidation in the 22 fami-

*See Voegelin & Voegelin 1967 for a discussion of the three phases of Amerindian classification.

lies that Powell had postulated for California. The reductionist phase began slowly, and the first consolidation (linking Shasta and Palaihnihan) was proposed in 1905 by Kroeber's colleague and future collaborator, Roland Dixon. The following year Boas assigned the extinct Adaizan language to the Caddoan family, and Natchez to Muskogean. In 1910 Dixon added Chimariko to the Shasta-Palaihnihan group, and Kroeber combined Miwok and Costanoan, returning to a position first advocated by Latham in 1856. In 1911 Kroeber noted certain "structural similarities" between Wiyot and Yurok, spoken side by side on the coast of northern California and, according to Powell, related neither to each other nor to any other language.

In 1913 the reductionist phase began in earnest; the year was also a turning point in Amerindian classification, and the issues raised then continue to reverberate to the present day. Two articles in particular startled the scholarly community; one was by Dixon and Kroeber, the other by Sapir. Dixon and Kroeber reported the results of their survey of California families, reducing Powell's 22 families to nine. The principal reductions resulted from the establishment of a Penutian family (combining Miwok-Costanoan, Maiduan, Yokuts, and Wintun) and a Hokan family, which was an expanded version of the Shasta-Palaihnihan-Chimariko group adumbrated by Dixon some years before. Karok, Pomo, Yanan, Esselen, and Yuman were now added to the earlier group. In addition to the newly discovered Penutian and Hokan stocks, Chumash and Salinan were joined in an Iskoman family; Wiyot and Yurok, whose similarities Kroeber had perceived in 1911, were set up as a Ritwan family. This substantial consolidation reduced the number of California families to Penutian, Hokan, Iskoman, Ritwan, Athabaskan, Klamath, Yuki, Washo, and Numic.

Like Boas, Edward Sapir was born in Germany, but he was brought to the United States at the age of five. After receiving an M.A. in Germanic languages, he became interested in American Indian languages through contact with Boas. His curiosity led to fieldwork with the Indians of Washington, Oregon, and California, and a doctorate in linguistics from Columbia in 1909. Sapir had spent the academic year 1907–8 in Berkeley, where, according to Campbell and Mithun (1979: 26), he had been "caught up in the reductionist zeal of Kroeber and Dixon which prevailed at the time." In 1913, the same year that Kroeber and Dixon announced their sweeping reorganization of California families, Sapir made the startling discovery that Wiyot and Yurok (joined by Dixon and Kroeber in a Ritwan group) are displaced Algonquian languages, or at the very least more closely related to Algonquian than to any other language. Since the Algonquian family is found predominantly east of the Mississippi River, and the nearest Algonquian language was 600 miles (1,000 km) away, an Algonquian affinity for Wiyot and Yurok was totally unexpected. Moreover, although Wiyot and Yurok were neighboring languages on the northern California coast, it is by no means clear that they are more closely related to each other than either is to Algonquian. Thus Dixon and Kroeber's Ritwan might not be a valid genetic node after all, though Sapir left the possibility open.

An irate Truman Michelson, the leading Algonquianist of the day, issued a stinging rebuttal to Sapir's claims the following year, offering five counterarguments: (1) Wiyot and Yurok have un-Algonquian traits, (2) Sapir's morphological resemblances were "purely fanciful," (3) Sapir's alleged pronominal similarities must be accidental, since they are found in other Indian languages as well, (4) Wiyot and Yurok possess certain non-Algonquian morphological elements, (5) the cumulative weight of arguments 1 through 4! Michelson (1914: 367) concluded triumphantly that "enough has been said to show the utter folly of haphazard comparisons."

A clearly exasperated Sapir responded to Michelson's criticism the following year. First, Sapir rebuked Michelson for concentrating on the un-Algonquian and non-Algonquian features of Wiyot and Yurok (what I have called the fallacy of negative evidence in section 4.1) and failing to pay attention to the numerous threads connecting Wiyot and Yurok with Algonquian: "the really convincing *positive* points raised in my paper are sedulously avoided" (Sapir 1915: 189). Second, Sapir pointed out that raising questions about a few etymologies that may well be invalid does not undermine the value of the rest of the etymologies that still massively support the connection. Regarding Michelson's failure to appreciate the evidential value of some 200 etymologies, including pronominal similarities of a most intimate nature, Sapir wrote: "There is no accounting for tastes, but it seems to me that such callousness deserves to be called linguistic cynicism almost as much as scientific sobriety" (pp. 189–90).

Michelson added yet another rejoinder, to which Sapir replied briefly, closing the debate. Needless to say, neither succeeded in convincing the other. Inevitably other scholars took sides, with Boas joining Michelson, and Dixon and Kroeber supporting Sapir. It is often claimed that this "controversy was not settled until 1958, when Haas presented irrefutable evidence of the Algonquian-Ritwan relationship" (Hoijer 1976: 15). In point of fact Sapir had himself offered irrefutable evidence in his original 1913 article. Although it is true that this proof was not universally accepted until the 1950's, the scholarly *acceptance* of proof is an altogether different question from that of *proof* itself, as the history of science has repeatedly shown.

With the Algonquian-Ritwan debate in full swing, Sapir announced yet another consolidation, joining Haida, Tlingit, and the Athabaskan family in a stock to which he gave the name Na-Dene. This too provoked a storm of controversy, with Pliny Goddard the principal critic (see section 6.2). Other consolidations were made with increasing rapidity, including the extension of both the Hokan and Penutian families to include languages outside California. Hokan was extended to Mexico by Kroeber in 1915 with the addition of Seri and Tequistlatecan, and by Walter Lehmann in 1920 with the inclusion of Tlapanecan. In 1917 Sapir added to Hokan both the South Texas Coahuiltecan family (established by John Swanton in 1915) and the Iskoman family of California that had been left ungrouped by Dixon and Kroeber (1913). During the 1920's Sapir extended Penutian northward to include languages from Oregon, Washington, and British Columbia, and in 1929 he added a Mexican branch to Penutian comprising Mixe-Zoque and Huave.

During this same period scholars were also at work consolidating Powell's groups outside California. In 1910 John Harrington presented evidence linking Kiowa with Tanoan and suggested that this expanded Tanoan family was related to Uto-Aztecan, a position subsequently adopted by Sapir (1929) and supported by Whorf and Trager (1937). In the Southeast Swanton joined Tunica, Chitimacha, and Atakapa in 1919, and Natchez and Muskogean in 1924. Leo Frachtenberg (1920) revived the Mosan group (= Salish, Wakashan, and Chimakuan), which had been suggested (but then abandoned) by Boas at the close of the nineteenth century. In 1921 Sapir suggested an affinity between Yuchi, a language isolate, and the Siouan family. A few residual problems in California were also cleared up, with Dixon and Kroeber assigning Washo to Hokan in 1919 and Sapir adding Klamath to Penutian in 1929.

In 1929 Sapir published a classification of North and Central American languages that, as it turned out, both summarized and climaxed the reductionist phase of Amerindian classification. This classification, which differed in only a few details from one he proposed in Sapir (1921a), divided the languages north of Mexico into six stocks and those of Central America into 15. Furthermore, Sapir asserted that "Middle America, in spite of its special cultural position, is distinctly a part of the whole North American linguistic complex and is connected with North America by innumerable threads" (1929: 141). The Sapir classification is shown in Lists 6.5 and 6.6. List 6.6 excludes certain groups that Sapir had classified as branches of more northerly families (e.g. Tlapanecan, Tequistlatecan, Aztecan), though Mixe-Zoque-Huave appears in both lists. Sapir considered his classification "suggestive but not demonstrable in all its features at the present time" (p. 139), and he foresaw the likelihood of at least some of the Central American families being linked to stocks farther north.

The 1930's and 1940's were, with a few exceptions, uneventful for Amerindian classification. Freeland and Sapir (1930) added support to the connection between Mixe-Zoque and (California) Penutian, and Whorf and Trager (1937) offered evidence for Aztec-Tanoan such that the connection became generally accepted. During the 1930's Whorf is reported to have proposed a Macro-Penutian stock consisting of Penutian, Aztec-Tanoan, Zuni, Mayan, Totonacan, Tunica, Xinca, and Lenca, but the evidence was

List 6.5. North American Families (Sapir 1929)

ESKIMO-ALEUT

ALGONQUIAN-MOSAN:

I ALGONQUIAN-RITWAN:
    A ALGONQUIAN
    ?B Beothuk
    C RITWAN:
        1 Wiyot
        2 Yurok
II Kutenai
III MOSAN:
    A WAKASHAN
    B CHIMAKUAN
    C SALISH

NA-DENE:

I Haida
II ATHABASKAN-TLINGIT:
    A Tlingit
    B ATHABASKAN

PENUTIAN:

I CALIFORNIA:
    A MIWOK-COSTANOAN
    B YOKUTS
    C MAIDUAN
    D WINTUN
II OREGON:
    A Takelma
    B COAST: Coos, Siuslaw, Yakonan
    C Kalapuya
III Chinook
IV Tsimshian
V PLATEAU:
    A Sahaptin
    B MOLALE-CAYUSE
    C Klamath
VI MEXICAN:
    A Huave
    B MIXE-ZOQUE

AZTEC-TANOAN:

I UTO-AZTECAN:
    A AZTECAN
    B PIMIC
    C NUMIC
II KIOWA-TANOAN:
    A Kiowa
    B TANOAN
?III Zuni

HOKAN-SIOUAN:

I HOKAN-COAHUILTECAN:
    A HOKAN:
        1 NORTHERN:
            a KAROK-PALAIHNIHAN:
                i Karok
                ii Chimariko
                iii SHASTA-PALAIHNIHAN
            b YANAN
            c POMO
        2 Washo
        3 ESSELEN-YUMAN:
            a Esselen
            b YUMAN
        4 SALINAN-SERI:
            a Salinan
            b Chumash
            c Seri
        5 TEQUISTLATECAN
    B TLAPANECAN
    C COAHUILTECAN:
        1 Tonkawa
        2 COAHUILTECAN PROPER:
            a Coahuilteco
            b Cotoname
            c Comecrudo
        3 Karankawa
II Yuki
III Keres
IV TUNICA-CHITIMACHA:
    A TUNICA-ATAKAPA
    B Chitimacha
V IROQUOIAN-CADDOAN:
    A IROQUOIAN
    B CADDOAN
VI EASTERN:
    A SIOUAN-YUCHI:
        1 Yuchi
        2 SIOUAN
    B NATCHEZ-MUSKOGEAN:
        1 Natchez
        2 MUSKOGEAN
        ?3 Timucua

List 6.6. Central American Families (Sapir 1929)

Chinantec	MISKITO-SUMO-MATAGALPA	Paya
†Janambre	MIXE-ZOQUE-HUAVE	Tarascan
Jicaque	MIXTEC-ZAPOTEC	TOTONACAN
Lenca	†Olive	†Waicuri
MAYAN	OTOMIAN-MANGUE	Xinca

never published. Less dramatic but still controversial was McQuown's (1942) proposal of a Mexican branch of Penutian combining Mayan and Totonacan with Mixe-Zoque.

These few contributions aside, interest in classificatory problems was dormant and did not reawaken until the 1950's. This dormant period is sometimes blamed on Sapir's "premature" 1929 classification, which supposedly stifled further interest. It seems more likely that this waning of interest in taxonomy reflects the changing *zeitgeist* of the 1930's, when methodological issues increasingly supplanted descriptive and classificatory problems as the focus of scholarly attention. Furthermore, the structure of language was increasingly investigated from a synchronic (ahistorical), rather than a diachronic (historical), perspective, and this new orientation also diminished interest in classification. Finally, as we have just seen, problems of classification had been thrashed out in minute detail over a period of 20 years (1910–30). Eventually such arguments become repetitive, and the quarrels tiresome even to the participants; their exhaustion seems to have been at least a contributing factor in the almost total cessation of taxonomic research.

In whatever field classification is carried out, scholars tend to divide themselves into two categories. At one pole there are the "lumpers," who manifest a predilection for combining entities into more comprehensive groups. At the other are the "splitters," who tend to divide groups into a greater number of distinct entities. The second phase of Amerindian classification was clearly dominated by the lumpers, with Dixon, Kroeber, and Sapir leading the way. During the third phase of Amerindian classification, running from roughly 1950 to the present, a reaction set in against what were perceived as Sapir's excesses, and splitters have dominated the scene now for three decades. Mary Haas, a student of Sapir's and probably the leading Amerindian scholar of the second half of the twentieth century, has been a leading advocate of a more conservative approach to genetic classification than Sapir's. In addition to doing fieldwork throughout much of North America, Haas directed the survey of California Indian languages at the University of California (Berkeley) that has produced a wealth of new linguistic material on California languages. She has also been responsible for the training of a good number of those scholars currently engaged in Amerindian research.

As Sapir himself candidly admitted, evidence had not been published for all the groupings in his 1929 classification. When scholars returned to classificatory problems in the 1950's, in part encouraged to do so by the new materials becoming available, they adopted a relatively conservative stance that accepted only those portions of Sapir's classification for which evidence had been adduced. Their view of the Sapir classification was, therefore, roughly as follows. Eskimo-Aleut and Na-Dene were accepted unchanged, though it was sometimes claimed, despite Sapir's work, that "the Nadene super-stock, which unites Athapaskan, Haida, and Tlingit, is still unsupported" (Hoijer 1976: 15). Aztec-Tanoan was accepted, except for the inclusion of Zuni, which was reinterpreted as a language isolate. Penutian continued to be considered a valid genetic group, though the inclusion of the Mexican branch remained in dispute. Algonquian-Mosan was broken up into four independent families (Algonquian-Ritwan, Salish, Wakashan, Chimakuan) and two language isolates (Beothuk and Kutenai).

The grouping that came in for the most criticism was Hokan-Siouan, which was reputedly Sapir's "wastepaper basket" stock, into which he lumped everything else once the relatively clear-cut families had been factored out. Hokan-Siouan was broken up into six families (Hokan, Tunica-Chitimacha, Iroquoian, Caddoan, Siouan, Natchez-Muskogean) and four isolates (Yuki, Keres, Yuchi, Timucua).

The opening salvo of the third phase of research on Amerindian classification was Haas's (1951) proposal of a Gulf group, combining Sapir's Tunica-Chitimacha and Boas's Natchez-Muskogean. In 1953 Morris Swadesh, like Haas a student of Sapir's, published evidence supporting the Mosan (Salish, Wakashan, Chimakuan) stock, the existence of which had been suggested by Boas in 1894 and Frachtenberg in 1920. That same year Swadesh published a paper with Joseph Greenberg claiming that the Jicaque language of Honduras belonged to the Hokan phylum. In 1958 Haas demonstrated the existence of sound correspondences between Algonquian and Gulf, thus for the first time directly linking elements of two of Sapir's six stocks. Furthermore, if Algonquian and Gulf form a valid genetic group, then Sapir's Algonquian-Mosan does not. That same year Haas also discovered sound correspondences connecting Wiyot and Yurok with Algonquian, effectively ending the Sapir-Michelson debate.

In the early 1960's a need was felt to reassess the status of Amerindian classification, and toward that end a conference, attended by 30 specialists, was held in 1964. That conference reached a "consensus" classification, summarizing "Phase III" work to that point. This consensus classification, discussed in Voegelin and Voegelin (1967), is illustrated in List 6.7.

Although there was little activity in Amerindian classification following

List 6.7. North American Families (Voegelin & Voegelin 1967)

CHUKCHI-ESKIMO:
I ESKIMO-ALEUT
II CHUKCHI-KAMCHATKAN

NA-DENE:
I Haida
II Tlingit
III ATHABASKAN (including Eyak)

MACRO-ALGONQUIAN:
I ALGONQUIAN-RITWAN:
A ALGONQUIAN
B Wiyot
C Yurok
II GULF:
A NATCHEZ-MUSKOGEAN
B TUNICA-CHITIMACHA
C Tonkawa

MACRO-SIOUAN:
I IROQUOIAN
II SIOUAN
III Catawba
IV CADDOAN
V Yuchi

HOKAN:
I Shasta
II PALAIHNIHAN
III POMO
IV YUMAN-SERI
V TEQUISTLATECAN
VI TLAPANECAN
VII †YANAN
VIII Salinan
IX †Chumash
X †Comecrudo
XI †Chimariko
XII Washo
XIII Karok
XIV COAHUILTECAN
XV †Esselen
XVI Jicaque

PENUTIAN:
I YOKUTS
II MAIDUAN
III WINTUN
IV MIWOK-COSTANOAN
V SAHAPTIN–NEZ PERCE
VI †Cayuse
VII †Molale
VIII Coos
IX YAKONAN
X KALAPUYA
XI Takelma
XII Chinook
XIII Tsimshian
XIV Zuni
XV MIXE-ZOQUE
XVI MAYAN
XVII CHIPAYA-URU
XVIII TOTONACAN
XIX Huave

AZTEC-TANOAN:
I TANOAN
II UTO-AZTECAN

OTO-MANGUEAN
Keres

YUKI-WAPPO
†Beothuk
Kutenai
†Karankawa

CHIMAKUAN

SALISH

WAKASHAN
†Timucua
Tarascan

List 6.8. North American Families (Campbell & Mithun 1979)

ESKIMO-ALEUT	Washo	†Molale
NA-DENE	†Salinan	Coos
Haida	Karok	†Alsea
ALGONQUIAN-RITWAN	†Chumash	Siuslaw
MUSKOGEAN	†Cotoname	†Takelma
†Natchez	†Comecrudo	Kalapuya
†Atakapa	†Coahuilteco	Chinook
Chitimacha	†Aranama	Tsimshian
†Tunica	†Solano	Zuni
Tonkawa	†Esselen	TANOAN
SIOUAN	Jicaque	UTO-AZTECAN
IROQUOIAN	TLAPANECAN	Keres
CADDOAN	TEQUISTLATECAN	YUKI-WAPPO
Yuchi	YOKUTS	†Beothuk
YUMAN	MAIDUAN	Kutenai
Seri	WINTUN	†Karankawa
POMO	MIWOK	CHIMAKUAN
PALAIHNIHAN	COSTANOAN	SALISH
Shasta	Klamath	WAKASHAN
†YANAN	Sahaptin	†Timucua
†Chimariko	†Cayuse	†Adai

the 1964 conference, and certainly no major discoveries, a second conference on the classification of New World languages was held in 1976, with the results published in Campbell and Mithun (1979). This second "consensus classification," shown in List 6.8, increased the number of independent genetic units in North America (including some, but not all, of the indigenous languages of Mexico) to a whopping 63, dismembering almost every genetic group that had previously been postulated, including not only the extended versions of Hokan and Penutian, but even their California nuclei, which had been the cornerstones of Phase II research. According to Campbell and Mithun (1979: 39), this "classification . . . is conservative and not very controversial, but rather represents something of an encapsulation of current received opinion."

It seems rather doubtful that all the participants in this conference would truly subscribe to every aspect of Campbell and Mithun's classification. In particular, it seems difficult to believe that Haas could accept Campbell and Mithun's (1979: 43) assertion that "as yet there has been no sufficient demonstration that any two of the variously proposed branches [of Hokan] are actually related genetically," when only a decade earlier she wrote that Sapir's (1917) Hokan cognates "stand up remarkably well in the light of more recent knowledge, and the paper therefore ought to have been adequate to establish the validity of the Hokan stock" (Haas 1964: 74).

For Central America Campbell (1979) contributes an equally conservative classification. Omitting groups already listed for North America (e.g. Uto-Aztecan, Tlapanecan, Tequistlatecan, Seri), he identifies the Central American groups shown in List 6.9.

In contrast to the substantial activity on North and Central American Indian languages during this century, South America has been largely ignored. Those few scholars who did conduct taxonomic research on South American languages generally contented themselves with a simple listing of numerous diverse groups, and no major consolidations of the kind that took place in North America were proposed until Greenberg's address in 1956 and subsequent work. The initial classification of South American Indian languages by Brinton (1891) was followed by similar attempts by Alexander F. Chamberlain (1903, 57 families; 1913, 83 families), Paul Rivet (1924, 77 families), and Čestmír Loukotka (1935, 94 families; 1944, 114 families; 1968, 117 families). Most of the linguistic research on Central American and especially South American Indian languages since 1950 has been the work of the Summer Institute of Linguistics (SIL), which began work in Central America in 1935 and in South America in 1946. Although SIL linguists have produced a wealth of new descriptive material and many low-level genetic classifications, they have not attempted an overall classification of American Indian languages.

Returning to North America, what are we to make of the apparent regression in Amerindian classification to a position little different from views prevailing at the start of this century? Can it be that Dixon, Kroeber, and Sapir, who were thought to have made seminal discoveries in Amerindian classification, had merely deluded themselves? Is it possible that Sapir, so often described as a genius in questions of taxonomy, had in fact overstepped the bounds of reasonable genetic classification to the extent implied in Lists 6.7 and 6.8? This apparently is what "current received opinion" would have us believe. Were Sapir alive today to witness the dismemberment of much of his life's work, I suspect he would feel that "such callousness deserves to be called linguistic cynicism almost as much as scien-

List 6.9. Central American Families (Campbell 1979)

OTO-MANGUEAN	Tarascan
Jicaque	Cuitlatec
Huave	Xinca
MIXE-ZOQUE	Lenca
MAYAN	Paya

tific sobriety." Sapir, however, died in 1939, so we cannot turn to him for a solution to our dilemma.

Fortunately for Amerindian classification there was one scholar working outside of the normal "Phase III" paradigm. This was the American linguist Joseph Greenberg, whose contributions to African classification (see Chap. 3) and Oceanic classification (see section 5.2) have already been examined. When Greenberg had completed his classification of African languages in the mid-1950's, he began to investigate the two remaining areas of the world, New Guinea and South America, where genetic classification had not progressed beyond the simple enumeration of numerous small groups. Using multilateral comparison (see section 3.6), Greenberg quickly realized that South American Indian languages were connected to those of Central and North America "by innumerable threads," as Sapir (1929) had described the cohesiveness of North and Central America. Greenberg reported his preliminary findings in 1956 at the Fifth International Congress

List 6.10. New World Families (Greenberg 1960)

ESKIMO-ALEUT

NA-DENE

AMERIND:

I NORTHERN BRANCHES (e.g. ALGONQUIAN, SALISH, SIOUAN, IROQUOIAN)
II HOKAN
III PENUTIAN (including MIXE-ZOQUE, Huave, MAYAN, and TOTONACAN)
IV AZTEC-TANOAN
V OTO-MANGUEAN
VI Tarascan
VII MACRO-CHIBCHAN:
  A CHIBCHAN
  B PAEZAN
VIII ANDEAN-EQUATORIAL:
  A ANDEAN
  B JIVAROAN
  C MACRO-TUCANOAN
  D EQUATORIAL (including ARAWAKAN and TUPI)
IX GE-PANO-CARIB:
  A MACRO-GE
  B MACRO-PANOAN
  C Nambikuara
  D Huarpe
  E MACRO-CARIB
  F Taruma

of Anthropological and Ethnological Sciences; a brief summary of the results (see List 6.10) was published in the Proceedings of the Congress in 1960, though without supporting evidence.

Greenberg's startling claim that all the languages of North, Central, and South America could be assigned to only three genetic families (Eskimo-Aleut, Na-Dene, Amerind) has been generally ignored by Amerindian specialists. It is not even mentioned in Campbell and Mithun's (1979) survey of Amerindian classification. Over the past quarter-century, with concentrated attention since 1970, Greenberg has compiled comparative wordlists of New World languages. An estimated quarter-million entries have been collected in 20-odd notebooks (copies of which may be found in Stanford University's Green Library), drawing together information on New World languages from roughly 3,000 different sources. This is the largest and most detailed compilation of New World vocabularies ever assembled.

Greenberg has previously revealed portions of the evidence for his tripartite classification (1979, 1981), but it is only in his most recent work (1987) that the extraordinary breadth and depth of the evidence becomes apparent. In support of the Amerind phylum Greenberg offers over 300 etymologies (involving basic vocabulary and pronouns, the elements of language least susceptible to borrowing) connecting different Amerind groups from Canada to the tip of South America. The nature and distribution of the evidence are such that the existence of the Amerind phylum may be considered established. Furthermore, evidence has recently been offered from dentition and gene distributions in the New World that corroborates Greenberg's tripartite classification of the peoples in the Western Hemisphere, although he of course based his division solely on linguistic evidence. The convergence of these three independent lines of inquiry is discussed in Greenberg, Turner, and Zegura (1985).

As revolutionary as Greenberg's proposals are, they were foreshadowed in the earlier literature in a number of interesting ways. As I have mentioned, some nineteenth-century linguists asserted that all New World languages were genetically related in a single family, the defining characteristics of which were essentially typological (i.e. the so-called polysynthetic structure of Amerindian languages). These early claims were not, however, supported by evidence and must be considered to reflect a certain *parti pris* of the early investigators. Furthermore, Boas finally put an end to the long-lived myth that all Amerindian languages are polysynthetic, thus undermining what had been taken to be their genetic basis. Finally, nowhere in the nineteenth-century literature is there any awareness of the individuality of the Na-Dene languages with respect to other Amerindian groups; Athabaskan (later Na-Dene) was simply regarded as one group among many. For all these reasons I do not believe there were any true precursors to the Greenberg classification in the nineteenth century.

The first intimation of the Amerind phylum may be traced to the Sapir-Michelson controversy (discussed above), though neither participant was aware at the time of the import of their dispute over Amerindian pronouns. Part of the evidence that Sapir had offered in support of Algonquian-Ritwan was the presence of a first-person pronoun ('I') with *n-* as the characteristic consonant and a second-person pronoun ('you') characterized by *m-*. Michelson responded that this same distribution of *n-* and *m-* was found in a fair number of North American languages in addition to Algonquian, Wiyot, and Yurok. To this assertion Sapir replied, lamely, that Michelson was confusing a few sporadic resemblances with a set of significant cognates. In reality, however, Michelson was citing evidence that the Algonquian-Ritwan family was merely one component of an even larger genetic group, and it is this larger grouping, not just Algonquian-Ritwan, that is characterized by *n-* and *m-*, respectively, in the first- and second-person pronouns. Interpreted in this manner, Michelson's critique in no way affects Sapir's claim of genetic affinity between Algonquian, Wiyot, and Yurok.

Several years later, when reviewing a grammar of a Bolivian Indian language, Sapir was struck by the presence of a second-person pronoun in *m-*, remarking (1917a: 184) that "the curiously widespread American second singular *m-* meets us here once more (*mi* 'thou')." A year later he discovered that not only was second-person *m-* found in South America, but so too was first-person *n-*. At this point Sapir realized that there must be an enormous family of languages stretching from North America through Central America and deep into South America, for he wrote in a letter dated August 1, 1918: "Getting down to brass tacks, how in the Hell are you going to explain general American *n-* 'I' except genetically? It's disturbing, I know, but (more) non-committal conservatism is only dodging, after all, isn't it? Great simplifications are in store for us. . . . It seems to me that only now is American linguistics becoming really interesting, at least in its ethnological bearings" (quoted in Darnell & Sherzer 1971: 27).

Although Sapir did not pursue this line of inquiry in his later work, I believe this early recognition of two distinguishing traits of the Amerind phylum clearly foreshadows Greenberg's conclusions some four decades later. Interestingly, one critic of Sapir's work in genetic classification, his former teacher Franz Boas, was also aware of the embarrassingly wide distribution of certain Amerindian pronouns, suggesting in 1917 that "the frequent occurrence of similar sounds for expressing related ideas (like the personal pronouns) may be due to obscure psychological causes rather than to genetic relationship" (quoted in Haas 1966a: 102).

Not only was Sapir aware of the apparent existence of an enormously widespread American stock by 1918, but even earlier he had remarked on the fact that Eskimo-Aleut and Na-Dene seemed to stand apart from other New World languages. In his 1916 study he suggested that "the peopling of

America was not a single historical process, but a series of movements of linguistically unrelated peoples, possibly from different directions and certainly at very different times. This view strikes me as intrinsically highly probable. As the latest linguistic arrivals in North America would probably have to be considered the Eskimo-Aleut and the Na-Dene (Haida, Tlingit, and Athabaskan)" (pp. 454–55).

Other scholars, over the years, have perceived at least part of the Amerind phylum. Benjamin Whorf (1935: 608) proposed a Macro-Penutian phylum incorporating Penutian, Aztec-Tanoan, Zuni, Mayan, Totonacan, and possibly Tunica. Since Whorf published no evidence for his assertion, we cannot be sure whether he had recognized a large portion of the Amerind family, but it is not unlikely. In the mid-1950's Morris Swadesh (1954, 1956) postulated a Penutoid stock containing languages of North, Central, and South America. In support of Penutoid, Swadesh (1954: 309–11) offered 13 Penutoid etymologies and two pronouns: *ni*/*na* 'I' and *mi*/*ma* 'you,' the first of which has as common variants *ña* and, especially in South America, *ja*. In 1960 he wrote that "recent research seems to show that the great bulk of American languages form a single genetic phylum going far back in time. . . . Eskimo-Aleutian and Nadenean seem to stand apart, and may therefore represent later waves of migration" (p. 896). In his later work Swadesh considerably revised his classification of New World languages, in line with his growing belief that all the world's languages were related in a vast network of connections. However, he provided little evidence for his sweeping revisions, which were based primarily on lexicostatistics. Although Swadesh's later taxonomic work diverged significantly from his earlier views, his 1954 and 1960 papers, at least, seem to foreshadow the Amerind phylum and its distinctness from both Na-Dene and Eskimo-Aleut. Recently both Matteson (1972) and Key (1981a,b,c, 1983) have presented evidence that is consonant with Greenberg's Amerind phylum.

In addition to these possible precursors of Greenberg's Amerind stock, one encounters not infrequently in the literature remarks that all but admit the existence of an enormous Amerindian family: "It must be kept in mind that most of the specialists who have immersed themselves in the study of large numbers of American Indian languages believe that almost all of them are genetically related to one another" (Kaufman 1974: 960).

Yet another factor should have led to the recognition of broad genetic connections in the New World, but in fact did not. Since the nineteenth century, and with increasing frequency in recent decades, numerous scholars have observed striking similarities between supposedly "independent" genetic groups. In the bibliography at the end of this section I have included (under Amerind) a representative sample of various proposals linking two or more Amerind groups. The groups they connect are indicated in brackets following each entry. Connections of this sort have been so numerous and widespread that it has seemed at times that the comparison of *any* two Amerind groups produced a list of tantalizing similarities. Phase III linguists reacted to these seemingly pervasive interconnecting genetic links by dismissing them all as random "noise," much in the spirit of Michelson (1914). For example, Goddard (1979: 376), in discounting Sapir's proposed Hokan affiliation for the Coahuiltecan group (which he also discounts), remarks "how easy it is to find lexical resemblances between groupings of large numbers of poorly recorded languages."

It is time we face the fundamental question: how can we reconcile Greenberg's reduction of New World phyla to just three (Eskimo-Aleut, Na-Dene, Amerind), and the compelling evidence behind it, with the prevailing "consensus" view (summarizing Phase III research) that the New World contains dozens, if not hundreds, of independent families? Why was a genetic unit that was sensed by Sapir (and perhaps others), and proved by Greenberg, invisible to scholars working within the Phase III paradigm? How are we to explain the failure of Phase III scholars to extend and consolidate the splendid foundation that had been bequeathed them by Dixon, Kroeber, and Sapir? And what was it that eventually led them to try to destroy the foundation itself?

In fact, a whole complex of factors has contributed to the failure of the Phase III paradigm. One of the primary factors was that Phase III scholars adopted different standards of proof of genetic affinity. In the classifications of Gallatin, Brinton, Powell, Kroeber, and Sapir, lexical and grammatical resemblances, if sufficient in number and plausible both phonologically and semantically, were the cornerstone of proof of genetic relationship. Their methods are often referred to disparagingly by Phase III scholars as the "inspection of crude word lists," the "'laundry-list' approach," or "simple lexical scanning" (Campbell & Mithun 1979: 10, 50, 53). In lieu of a set of shared cognates, Phase III scholars have relied on either the establishment of sound correspondences or the reconstruction of the parent stock as the ultimate proof of genetic affinity.

The changing standard of proof reflects, I believe, the changing academic climate from the 1930's on. As I have noted, during the 1930's methodological issues became paramount. When taxonomic questions were again broached in the 1950's, scholars felt it necessary to develop a more rigorous theoretical foundation than the impressionistic cognate sets of earlier scholars. For this reason sound laws (sometimes referred to as "phonetic equations" to emphasize their supposed mathematical precision) and reconstruction were substituted for the earlier criterion of cognation. The deleterious effects of this decision were discussed in section 3.6. The fact is, the new standard of proof not only was incapable of extending Phase II research, it was even unable to substantiate Phase II results and consequently led directly to the sense of disillusionment and frustration that is apparent in Campbell and Mithun (1979), Shipley (1980), and elsewhere.

Equally disastrous for Amerindian classification was the rise in popularity of the binary approach to taxonomy, which involves the comparison of two languages (or two groups), usually chosen for comparison quite by accident, in order to establish a genetic connection between the two. As Lamb (1964) pointed out, practitioners of the binary approach fail to distinguish language classification from the establishment of genetic relationship. Although the binary approach may suggest a genetic relationship, it tells us next to nothing about classification. According to Lamb (1964: 109), "The question that should be of greatest concern for language classification . . . is not whether or not a given pair of languages is related, but how close or distant the relationship is."

To illustrate the deficiencies of the binary approach, let us consider a specific example. In 1964–65 Roland Olson sought to show that the Chipaya language of Bolivia is related to the Mayan languages of Central America. Even if one grants that a genetic relationship between the two is indicated by his cognate sets, there is no evidence that Chipaya and Mayan are more closely related *to each other* than either is to other languages. In light of Greenberg's findings it is now clear that Chipaya and Mayan are related (as members of Amerind), but they have no special relationship to each other. Mayan remains a member of Penutian, and Chipaya belongs to the Arawakan branch of Equatorial. The only reason Mayan was even compared with Chipaya is that Olson happened to have first-hand experience with both groups. Comparing Mayan with Chipaya is like comparing Irish and Bengali to prove they are related. Although such a proof might be possible, it would be tortured and incomplete, for the simple reason that much of the evidence demonstrating the affinity of Irish and Bengali (or Chipaya and Mayan) is contained in neither language. For amplification of this point see section 3.5. The failure to understand this fundamental principle of genetic classification has unfortunately led to a great deal of wasted time and energy. We may hope that the day when arbitrary pairs of languages are compared under the guise of genetic classification is now over.

The binary approach and the insistence on regular sound correspondences and/or reconstruction are probably the most serious defects of Phase III research, but at least a half-dozen others warrant brief mention:

1. Silverstein (1979: 651) observes that "there has been for a long time a peculiar development of comparative-historical Amerindian linguistics. . . . This trend has sought doctrinally to work 'from the bottom up' and from present to past unidirectionally." Ignoring the lessons of comparative Indo-European linguistics, many Americanists have come to believe that to reach greater time depths and more comprehensive classifications one must first

reconstruct the proto-languages for all the low-level genetic groups. Only after these proto-languages (e.g. Proto-Penutian, Proto-Hokan, Proto-Algonquian) have been established is it legitimate to compare them, in turn, to see if greater consolidations are possible (i.e. Amerind). Except in Phase III Amerindian linguistics, it has been firmly established since the nineteenth century that it is more fruitful to attack genetic classification simultaneously from the bottom up and from the top down, since each approach informs the other. The attempt to turn genetic classification into a kind of linguistic Rubik's cube constitutes a deviation from established principles of historical linguistics.

2. As is often the case, political boundaries play a large role in determining who studies which languages. American linguists tend to study languages of the United States, perhaps keeping abreast of developments across the border in Mexico and Canada, but they are very unlikely to pay much attention to South America. Within the United States a similar compartmentalization occurs between states. Yet from the perspective of genetic linguistics, these arbitrary political boundaries are meaningless, and taxonomic research that pays them any attention at all cannot but suffer as a result. In addition, of course, there is great disparity in the relative wealth of various countries, as well as very different attitudes toward the Native American population. Both factors have no doubt contributed to South America's relative isolation from the rest of Amerindian linguistics.

3. Paralleling the arbitrary political boundaries are the equally arbitrary institutional and personal boundaries that have increasingly dictated that a scholar confine himself to one language, or at most one language family. As Langdon (1979: 597) candidly admits, "The number of scholars who have had direct contact with more than one branch of Hokan is extremely limited." Key (1979: 17) reports that "in South America it is rare that an investigator knows more than one language well." Obviously the extreme specialization characteristic of contemporary academic studies makes the discovery of deep genetic relationships unlikely.

4. The consensus classifications summarizing Phase III research fail to take into account that it is impossible for individual scholars of specific languages and families to distinguish general Amerind traits from language-specific or family-specific ones. A Hokan specialist, for example, cannot distinguish the roots that Hokan shares with other Amerind groups from those that define Hokan itself unless he is familiar with *all* the potentially related Amerind groups. In fact, the term consensus classification is something of a misnomer, implying as it does that a group of scholars have all examined a body of evidence and have reached similar conclusions based on it. In reality, each scholar has examined a *different* set of data (his particular language or family), and the consensus refers to each scholar's willing-

ness to accept other scholars' work if they will accept his. The pitfalls and dangers of such "classification by committee" are too obvious to dwell on and represent once again a basic misunderstanding of the nature of genetic classification on the part of Phase III scholars.

5. Phase III linguists tend to believe that combining groups that do not belong together constitutes a far more serious error than not combining groups that do. This bias is reflected most clearly in the second consensus classification, which is little more than an enumeration of obvious low-level genetic groups. In reality, as Lamb (1964: 107) observes, "It is just as bad to leave apart two related groups as it is to put together two unrelated ones."

6. Many scholars believe it is impossible to classify a language unless one possesses complete, linguistically sophisticated materials. A short wordlist collected by a person with no linguistic training is therefore considered of little or no value. In reality, as Kroeber, Sapir, and Greenberg realized full well, it is often possible to classify a language accurately on the basis of the most meager and poorly recorded materials if they happen to contain a few diagnostic cognates. As any historian knows, all information is imperfect in some respect, but "to throw out all evidence that does not attain to an arbitrary standard of fineness is sterile as well as unreasonable" (Dixon & Kroeber 1919: 113).

It should be abundantly clear from the preceding discussion that genetic classification carried out within the Phase III paradigm stood no chance of making any significant progress. Operating with a methodological mythology largely of its own creation, Phase III represents not a continuation of the pioneering work of Phase II, but a blind alley that led nowhere. Rather it is the work of Greenberg that picks up where Sapir left off. In both methodology and results, Greenberg's classification carries the work of Kroeber and Sapir to its logical conclusion, confirming Sapir's suspicion that "great simplifications are in store for us."

Table 6.2, overleaf, presents a chronological listing of the earliest identification of New World families. The list is neither complete (Algonquian and Siouan, among others, are lacking) nor in all probability totally accurate, and should be considered a first approximation. For a few groups two dates and names are given, indicating that the discovery was foreshadowed by an earlier scholar.

6.3.2 *Present Status of Amerind Classification*

In attempting to assess the present status of Amerindian classification, I find myself in something of a quandary, since I am confronted with two diametrically opposed views. Current received opinion posits dozens of genetically independent families in the New World; Greenberg (1987) pro-

Table 6.2. Initial Identification of New World Families

Year	Recognized by	Group (current name)
1635	P. LeJeune	Iroquoian (Northern branch only)
1645	A. Pérez Ribas	Uto-Aztecan (Corachol, Nahuatl)
1768	D. Zeisberger	Iroquoian (including Cherokee)
1782	S. F. Gilij	Arawakan, Carib
1797	B. Smith	Iroquoian (including Cherokee and Tuscarora)
1800	L. Hervás y Panduro	Mayan (Yucatec, Quichean)
1816	J. C. Adelung, J. S. Vater	Mayan (Yucatec, Quichean, Huastec)
1818	R. Rask	Eskimo-Aleut
1840's	A. Gallatin	Numic
1844	J. Gregg	Caddoan
1852	W. Turner	Athabaskan (Northern, Apachean)
1854	R. Latham	Ritwan (= Wiyot and Yurok)
1856	R. Latham	Miwok-Costanoan
1856	W. Turner	Athabaskan (Northern, Pacific Coast, Apachean)
1856	W. Turner	Uto-Aztecan (Numic, Takic), Yuman
1859	J. Buschmann	Uto-Aztecan (all branches except Aztecan)
1864	M. Orozco y Berra	Oto-Manguean
1867	Martius	Ge, Macro-Ge
1872	S. Powers	Yuki-Wappo
1874	F. Pimentel	Mixe-Zoque
1879	A. Gatschet	Uto-Aztecan (including Aztecan), Tanoan
1883	H. de Charencey	Mixe-Zoque
1884	O. Stoll	Mayan
1889	F. Boas	Wakashan
1890	M. Uhle	Chibchan
1891	D. Brinton	Hokan (Yuman, Seri, Tequistlatecan), Otomian
1894	F. Boas	Na-Dene (Athabaskan, Tlingit, Haida), Mosan (Salish, Chimakuan, Wakashan)
1902	S. A. Lafone y Queredo	Macro-Panoan (Tacana, Chimane)
1905	F. Belmar	Mangean
1910	J. Harrington	Tanoan (including Kiowa), Aztec-Tanoan
1910	W. Lehmann	Misumalpan
1911	P. Rivet	Macro-Carib
1912	W. H. Mechling	Chinantecan, Zapotecan
1913	E. Sapir	Algic (= Algonquian, Wiyot, and Yurok)
1913	R. Dixon, A. Kroeber	(California) Hokan, (California) Penutian, Ritwan (Wiyot, Yurok)
1915	E. Sapir	Na-Dene (Athabaskan, Tlingit, Haida)
1915	J. Swanton	Coahuiltecan
1920	W. Lehmann	Tlapanecan
1924	P. Radin	Mexican Penutian (Huave, Mixe-Zoque, Mayan)
1924	J. Swanton	Natchez-Muskogean
1926	P. González Casanova	Popolocan
1929	E. Sapir	Penutian (including Mixe-Zoque and Huave), Almosan
1942	N. McQuown	(Mexican) Penutian (Mayan, Mixe-Zoque, Totonacan)
1951	M. Haas	Gulf
1956	J. Greenberg	Amerind, Chibchan-Paezan, Macro-Ge, Macro-Panoan, Macro-Carib, Andean, Equatorial, Macro-Tucanoan
1978	J. Greenberg	Northern Amerind (Almosan-Keresiouan, Penutian, Hokan), Central Amerind (Uto-Aztecan, Tanoan, Oto-Manguean)
1984	J. Greenberg	Almosan-Keresiouan

vides compelling evidence that there are but three: Eskimo-Aleut, Na-Dene, and Amerind. More conservative linguists will no doubt feel that the traditional classification, listing dozens of families, should be retained until Greenberg's proposals have had a chance to be evaluated by other scholars. But since the inadequacies of more conservative classifications are so grievous, and since Greenberg's evidence is so overwhelming, I have had little difficulty in opting to follow Greenberg's minority opinion. I urge all who are interested in the classification of American Indian languages to review the evidence presented in Greenberg (1987) for themselves. In the remainder of this section I will take for granted the existence of the Amerind family.

Before turning to the internal subgrouping of Amerind and its various components, it will be useful to review those groups whose genetic unity is beyond question. I believe the following families fall into this category:

(15)	ALGIC (= ALGONQUIAN-RITWAN)	TANOAN
	ALGONQUIAN	UTO-AZTECAN
	CHIMAKUAN	OTO-MANGUEAN
	WAKASHAN	CHIBCHAN-PAEZAN
	SALISH	MACRO-GE
	CADDOAN	MACRO-PANOAN
	SIOUAN	MACRO-CARIB
	IROQUOIAN	ANDEAN
	HOKAN	EQUATORIAL
	PENUTIAN	MACRO-TUCANOAN

Within these families there are of course subfamilies whose genetic validity is equally secure (e.g. Yuman and Pomo within Hokan, Mayan and Miwok-Costanoan within Penutian); these will be mentioned below in the discussion of the subgrouping of the families listed in (15).

Once the true dimensions of the Amerind phylum are recognized, the entire classification problem becomes one of subgrouping, as Greenberg (1960: 791) pointed out. *All* the languages are related, but which ones are more closely related to which others? What well-defined subgroups are there, and how do they relate to each other? Given the inherent difficulties in discovering the subgrouping of a family (particularly a large and ancient one), as compared with the relatively easier task of identifying the family itself, it should be clear that whatever subgrouping is proposed for Amerind must be considered merely a first approximation, subject to modification and revision as research proceeds. Greenberg (1987) suggests the internal classification of Amerind shown in List 6.11.

This classification calls for a number of observations. (1) Contrary to prevailing opinion (and Greenberg's expectations), Sapir's Algonquian-Mosan

List 6.11. The Amerind Phylum (Greenberg 1987)

AMERIND:
- I NORTHERN AMERIND:
  - A ALMOSAN-KERESIOUAN:
    - 1 ALMOSAN:
      - a Kutenai
      - b MOSAN:
        - i CHIMAKUAN
        - ii WAKASHAN
        - iii SALISH
      - c ALGIC:
        - i RITWAN
        - ii ALGONQUIAN
    - 2 KERESIOUAN:
      - a KERESAN
      - b SIOUAN-YUCHI
      - c CADDOAN
      - d IROQUOIAN
  - B PENUTIAN (including Zuni, Gulf, Yuki-Wappo, Huave, Totonacan, Mixe-Zoque, and Mayan)
  - C HOKAN (including Yurimangui)
- II CENTRAL AMERIND:
  - A TANOAN
  - B UTO-AZTECAN
  - C OTO-MANGUEAN
- III CHIBCHAN-PAEZAN (including Timucua, Tarascan, and Cuitlatec)
- IV ANDEAN (including Mapudungu)
- V EQUATORIAL-TUCANOAN:
  - A MACRO-TUCANOAN (including Nambikuara)
  - B EQUATORIAL (including Jivaroan and Chipaya)
- VI GE-PANO-CARIB:
  - A MACRO-CARIB
  - B GE-PANO:
    - 1 MACRO-PANOAN
    - 2 MACRO-GE

grouping is supported. (2) Keres, previously regarded as an isolate, is a member of Keresiouan within Almosan-Keresiouan, perhaps closest to the Iroquoian family. (3) Yuki-Wappo is a displaced member of the Gulf group. (4) Gulf is a member of Penutian. (5) Oto-Manguean, Tanoan, and Uto-Aztecan form a stock Greenberg calls Central Amerind. (6) Tarascan, Timucua, and Cuitlatec, long considered isolates, are all assigned to Chibchan-Paezan. (7) Nambicuara, which Greenberg (1960) included in Ge-Pano-Carib, has been reassigned to Macro-Tucanoan. (8) The Ge-Pano-Carib stock posited in Greenberg (1960) has been retained, but the Andean-Equatorial stock posited there has been divided into two coordinate branches, Andean and Equatorial-Tucanoan. (9) In North America Penutian, Hokan, and Almosan-Keresiouan have been joined in a higher-level grouping called Northern Amerind.

The internal classification of the numerous Amerind families poses a whole host of problems, only the most salient of which can be touched on here. The internal subgroupings adopted in this volume reflect the sources listed in the bibliography to this section, relevant portions of Voegelin and Voegelin (1977), and the expert advice of some 20 Amerindian scholars, whose assistance I have acknowledged at the beginning of this volume. None of these scholars, of course, is responsible for the use I have made of their advice. Let us examine the various Amerind families in the order in which they are listed in (15) above.

Algic. The name Algic was suggested by Teeter (1965: 225) as a replacement for Algonquian-Ritwan. Of the three components of Algic, Algonquian is a close-knit family covering much of the eastern United States and Canada, and Wiyot and Yurok are (or were—Wiyot is recently extinct and Yurok is moribund) single languages spoken side by side on the coast of northern California, some 600 miles (1,000 km) from the nearest Algonquian language. Sapir's (1913) discovery of the relationship between Algonquian, Wiyot, and Yurok, and the controversy it provoked, have been examined above in some detail. Sapir's aim in this debate was to establish the validity of Algic (= Algonquian-Ritwan); he was noncommittal about the validity of Ritwan. Teeter (1965: 224) expresses doubt regarding Ritwan, whereas Haas (1966a: 103) considers it an open question. Goddard (1981) believes Ritwan is "probably a subgroup, though [this] has not yet been demonstrated." Recently Berman (1982) has suggested two possible innovations supporting a Ritwan group. To my knowledge, the possibility that either Wiyot or Yurok is closer to Algonquian than the other has never been raised. Given the dissimilarity between Wiyot and Yurok, however, this possibility cannot be ruled out *a priori*.

Algonquian. Despite its enormous geographic spread, the Algonquian family is a close-knit group whose internal homogeneity is now generally accepted. Eastern Algonquian, comprising those languages spoken along the Atlantic seaboard, is the only clearly distinguished subgroup. Goddard (1979: 105) suggests that Blackfoot "is the most divergent language of the family." The Algonquian subgrouping followed in this volume (see List 6.12) is based on Goddard (1978a,b, 1979, 1981).

List 6.12. The Algonquian Family (Goddard 1978a,b, 1979)

ALGONQUIAN:	[II ALGONQUIAN PROPER]
I Blackfoot	F Menominee
II ALGONQUIAN PROPER:	G Fox
A Cheyenne	H †Illinois
B Arapaho	I Shawnee
C Cree	J EASTERN: Micmac,
D Ojibwa	Passamaquoddy,
E Potawatomi	Eastern Abenaki, etc.

List 6.13. The Salish Family (Thompson 1979)

SALISH:
I Bella Coola
II SALISH PROPER:
  A COAST:
    1 CENTRAL
    2 †Tillamook
  B TSAMOSAN:
    1 INLAND
    2 MARITIME
  C INTERIOR:
    1 NORTHERN
    2 SOUTHERN

Chimakuan. Since the Chimakuan family consists of only two languages (one of which is extinct), the question of subgrouping does not arise.

Wakashan. The small Wakashan family is sharply differentiated into Northern (= Kwakiutlan) and Southern (= Nootkan) branches.

Salish. According to current opinion, a single language, Bella Coola, is coordinate with the remainder of the family, which itself is divided into three subgroups. The Salish classification adopted here (List 6.13) follows Thompson (1979).

Caddoan. The Caddoan family is structured like an onion, with Pawnee and its divergent dialect Arikara at the center, and with Kitsai, Wichita, and Caddo progressively farther away from the nucleus (List 6.14).

Siouan. There is a deep cleavage between Catawba and the rest of the Siouan family, so deep in fact that some scholars do not regard Catawba as a Siouan language. Such reservations are, however, terminological, not substantive, since it is generally accepted today that Catawba is more closely

List 6.14. The Caddoan Family (Chafe 1979)

CADDOAN:
I SOUTHERN: Caddo
II NORTHERN:
  A Wichita
  B PAWNEE-KITSAI:
    1 †Kitsai
    2 PAWNEE-ARIKARA

List 6.15. The Siouan Family (Rood 1979)

SIOUAN:
I Catawba
II SIOUAN PROPER:
  A Mandan
  B NORTHERN PLAINS: Crow, Hidatsa
  C MISSISSIPPI VALLEY:
    1 Dakota
    2 DHEGIHA
    3 CHIWERE-WINNEBAGO
  D †SOUTHEAST:
    1 †Tutelo
    2 †BILOXI-OFO

related to Siouan than to any other language or group. Siouan Proper is itself divided into three subgroups and the difficult-to-classify single language Mandan. Tutelo was apparently so divergent from Biloxi-Ofo that the validity of the Southeast group is in question. List 6.15 proposes a tentative subgrouping, subject to revision.

Iroquoian. Cherokee is distantly but clearly related to the rest of the Iroquoian family. The remaining languages, called Northern Iroquoian, are all closely related, with the languages of the Five Nations (plus the extinct Susquehannock) constituting one subgroup and Tuscarora-Nottoway another (List 6.16).

Hokan. Unlike such close-knit families as Algonquian, Salish, and Iroquoian, Hokan is an ancient grouping consisting of several subfamilies

List 6.16. The Iroquoian Family (Mithun 1979)

IROQUOIAN:
I NORTHERN:
  A †Laurentian
  B †Huron
  C FIVE NATIONS:
    1 †Susquehannock
    2 MOHAWK-ONEIDA
    3 SENECA-ONONDAGA:
      a Onondaga
      b SENECA-CAYUGA
  D TUSCARORA-NOTTOWAY
II SOUTHERN: Cherokee

(e.g. Pomo, Yuman), a number of isolated languages (e.g. Karok, Shasta, Washo, Seri), and a few outliers (e.g. Yurimangui, Jicaque, Tlapanec, Coahuiltecan), whose affinity with the rest of Hokan continues to be a matter of dispute. In the context of recent attempts to break up the Hokan stock into many independent families, questions of subgrouping have obviously fallen by the wayside. Furthermore, no Amerindian group has suffered so grievously from binary comparisons as Hokan. Since a binary approach to language classification is useless in determining subgrouping, it is not surprising that there has been no progress in unraveling the internal relationships of Hokan in the past half-century. The Hokan subgrouping adopted in this volume (List 6.17) is based on Sapir (1929), as modified by Rivet (1942), Greenberg and Swadesh (1953), and Greenberg (1987); the internal structure of Pomo follows Halpern (1964), and Yuman follows Langdon (1981).

List 6.17. The Hokan Stock (Sapir 1929 and others)

HOKAN:	IV SERI-YUMAN:
I NORTHERN:	A Seri
A Karok	B YUMAN
B Shasta	V †WAICURI-QUINIGUA
C †Chimariko	VI COAHUILTECAN
D PALAIHNIHAN	VII TEQUISTLATECAN
E †YANAN	VIII SOUTHERN:
F POMO	A TLAPANECAN
II Washo	B Jicaque
III SALINAN-CHUMASH	C †Yurimangui

Penutian. Penutian is, like Hokan, an ancient and controversial grouping that was first recognized in California and later found to extend southward into Mexico and, in the case of Penutian, northward into Canada. Yet the internal texture of Penutian, characterized by continuity, contrasts sharply with the discontinuous nature of Hokan. Whereas only two languages were added to Hokan after 1925 (Yurimangui, Jicaque), Penutian has shown a particular predilection for expansion, often in different directions in the work of different scholars. The Penutian classification adopted here (List 6.18) is based on Sapir (1929), as modified by McQuown (1942) and Greenberg (1987). The Muskogean classification follows Haas (1979), and the Mayan subgrouping is based on Kaufman (1982).

Greenberg's Penutian stock differs from earlier proposals in two important respects: (1) the Gulf group, first established in Haas (1951) and previously linked to Algonquian (Haas 1958a) and to Hokan (Swadesh 1954), is for the first time included in Penutian; and (2) the Yuki-Wappo family, considered by Shipley (1976: 447) "the most intriguing and problematical in California," is included in the Gulf group. Despite the fact that Yuki and the distantly related Wappo (*pace* Sawyer 1980) are (or were) spoken in northern California, over 2,000 miles (3,200 km) from the nearest Gulf language, the affinity of Yuki-Wappo with Gulf is, in Greenberg's opinion, so obvious that had they been spoken in Louisiana they would have been included in the Gulf group without fanfare.

List 6.18. The Penutian Stock (Sapir 1929, Greenberg 1987, and others)

PENUTIAN:
- I CANADIAN: Tsimshian
- II WASHINGTON: Chinook
- III OREGON
- IV PLATEAU
- V CALIFORNIA:
  - A WINTUN
  - B MAIDUAN
  - C YOKUTS
  - D MIWOK-COSTANOAN
- VI NEW MEXICO: Zuni
- VII GULF:
  - A TUNICA-CHITIMACHA
  - B YUKI-WAPPO
  - C NATCHEZ-MUSKOGEAN:
    - 1 †Natchez
    - 2 MUSKOGEAN
- VIII MEXICAN:
  - A Huave
  - B TOTONACAN
  - C MIXE-ZOQUE
  - D MAYAN

The inclusion of Yuki-Wappo in Penutian, and even in Gulf, had been foreshadowed in the literature, but since Yuki has been compared over the years with various groups and languages, the earlier proposals attracted little attention. In 1906 Kroeber compared Yuki and Yokuts (a Penutian language) and noted a structural similarity, though he did not claim they were related. Radin (1919) first connected Yuki with Penutian, and Shipley (1957) suggested 32 Yuki-Penutian cognates. Sapir (1929), on the other hand, included Yuki in his rather amorphous Hokan-Siouan phylum, and Swadesh (1954) placed Yuki in his "Hokogian" (= Hokan + Gulf) family. Gursky (1965a) also assigned Yuki to Hokan, and Elmendorf (1963, 1964) proposed links with Siouan and Yuchi. In spite of these diverse proposals (or perhaps because of them), both consensus classifications left Yuki-Wappo as an isolated family without known relatives. Greenberg's discovery that Yuki and Wappo are displaced Gulf languages confirms a suspicion expressed in Swadesh (1954). Swadesh (1954: 324), who grouped Yuki with Gulf and (Southern) Hokan (i.e. Coahuiltecan), quotes a letter from Robert Melton supporting his conclusions:

> Ethnological evidence [indicates] that the Yuki do not "belong" in California, and have had seemingly direct contact with the Pueblo and SW, most likely in passage

from near New Orleans. The chiefship pattern among the Yuki is very un-Californian and very possibly closer to the SE than elsewhere. They were the most warlike in California, except for the extreme South. They sound *re* . . . like . . . Chitimacha [a Gulf language of Southern Louisiana].

Tanoan. Tanoan is a small, close-knit family. All the Tanoan languages except Kiowa are (or were) spoken in Pueblo societies in what is today New Mexico. Since Kiowa was originally spoken throughout the Great Plains, from Montana to Mexico, it was at first assumed that Kiowa would prove to be the most divergent member of the family. Such expectations, however, proved false, and it is now generally agreed that the geographic and cultural distance between Kiowa and the remainder of the family is not matched by a similar linguistic divergence. Davis (1979) suggests that Tiwa (sometimes considered a single language, though there is a fairly sharp division between Northern and Southern subgroups) is closest to the extinct Piro. Furthermore, Tiwa(-Piro) is genetically closest to Tewa, and Kiowa and Towa may also constitute a subgroup of Tanoan, though the evidence for this is less clear than in the case of Tiwa-Tewa (see List 6.19).

Uto-Aztecan. A general consensus has developed that Uto-Aztecan is composed of eight genetic units: six families (Numic, Takic, Pimic, Taracahitic, Corachol, Aztecan) and two isolated languages (Tübatulabal, Hopi). (The Giamina language, now extinct, may have been a ninth branch.) Divergence of opinion arises solely with regard to their subgrouping. List 6.20 compares three proposals. The validity of Shoshonean and and the validity of Sonoran (with or without Aztecan) are of course independent questions; Lamb (1964: 122) reports that Kroeber accepted Shoshonean but rejected Sonoran. The Uto-Aztecan classification adopted in this volume (List 6.21) is based on Lamb (1964).

According to Steele (1979), some scholars believe that Tübatulabal is most closely related to Numic, Hopi is closest to Takic, and Southern Numic and Central Numic constitute a group coordinate with Western Numic.

List 6.19. The Tanoan Family
(Davis 1979)

TANOAN:
- I KIOWA-TOWA
- II TEWA-TIWA:
  - A Tewa
  - B TIWA-PIRO:
    - 1 †Piro
    - 2 TIWA:
      - a NORTHERN
      - b SOUTHERN

List 6.20. Proposed Subgroupings of the Uto-Aztecan Family

Whorf 1935, Lamb 1964	*Voegelin, Voegelin & Hale 1962*	*Heath 1975 (reported in Steele 1979)*
UTO-AZTECAN:	**UTO-AZTECAN:**	**UTO-AZTECAN:**
I NUMIC	I SHOSHONEAN:	I NORTHERN:
II Tübatulabal	A NUMIC	A NUMIC
III TAKIC	B Tübatulabal	B Tübatulabal
IV Hopi	C TAKIC	C TAKIC
V PIMIC	D Hopi	D Hopi
VI TARACAHITIC	II SONORAN:	II SOUTHERN:
VII CORACHOL	A PIMIC	A PIMIC
VIII AZTECAN	B TARACAHITIC	B TARACAHITIC
	C CORACHOL	C CORACHOL
	III AZTECAN	D AZTECAN

List 6.21. The Uto-Aztecan Family (Lamb 1964 and others)

UTO-AZTECAN:	IV Hopi
I NUMIC:	V PIMIC:
A WESTERN	A PIMAN
B CENTRAL	B TEPEHUAN
C SOUTHERN	VI TARACAHITIC:
II Tübatulabal	A †Tubar
III TAKIC:	B TARAHUMARA-GUARIJIO
A †Gabrielino	C CAHITA
B SERRAN	VII CORACHOL
C CUPAN:	VIII AZTECAN:
1 Luiseño	A †Pochutla
2 CAHUILLA-CUPEÑO	B AZTEC PROPER

Oto-Manguean. A half-dozen small families (Otomian, Mixtecan, Popolocan, Chinantecan, Zapotecan, Manguean) and the isolated language Amuzgo make up the Oto-Manguean family. The classification adopted here (List 6.22) is based on Rensch (1976), who has elaborated the basic structure postulated by Robert Longacre. Some linguists have proposed the inclusion of Huave and Tlapanecan in Oto-Manguean. Greenberg (1987), however, classifies them as (Mexican) Penutian and Hokan, respectively, and I have followed that position. Attempts at an internal subgrouping of the seven Oto-Manguean branches have not yet identified any higher-level groupings. In particular, the (extinct) Manguean branch, which was geographically separated from the remainder of the family by almost 700 miles (1,100 km), does not show a comparable linguistic divergence.

List 6.22. The Oto-Manguean Family (Rensch 1976)

OTO-MANGUEAN:	IV POPOLOCAN
I OTOMIAN	V CHINANTECAN
II MIXTECAN	VI ZAPOTECAN
III Amuzgo	VIII †MANGUEAN

Chibchan-Paezan. All seven South American stocks (i.e. Chibchan-Paezan, Andean, Macro-Tucanoan, Equatorial, Macro-Carib,Macro-Panoan, Macro-Ge) derive from the work of Greenberg (1960, 1986). The subgrouping within these seven stocks follows in the main Greenberg (1986), though Voegelin and Voegelin (1977) and Grimes (1984) have also been used.

Chibchan-Paezan, extending from Central America deep into South America, consists of two families, Chibchan and Paezan (see List 6.23). Several languages that had long been regarded as language isolates (Tarascan, Cuitlatec, Timucua) are included in Chibchan-Paezan in Greenberg (1987). Tarascan and Cuitlatec (both spoken in southern Mexico) have been added to the Chibchan branch, and Timucua is included in Paezan. The addition of Timucua (formerly spoken in northern Florida, but long extinct) is surprising, in that Chibchan-Paezan languages were thought to be restricted to Central and South America. Nevertheless, Greenberg's conclusions are similar to those of Granberry (1970, as reported in Crawford 1979), who

List 6.23. The Chibchan-Paezan Stock (Greenberg 1987)

CHIBCHAN-PAEZAN:	II PAEZAN:
I CHIBCHAN:	A †Timucua
A Tarascan	B Warao
B †Cuitlatec	C †Kunza
C Xinca	D †Betoi
D Lenca	E †Chimu
E Paya	F Itonama
F YANOMAM	G †HUARPE
G NUCLEAR CHIBCHAN:	H †JIRAJARAN
1 Motilon	I MURA
2 Cuna	J NUCLEAR PAEZAN:
3 MISUMALPAN	1 †Andaqui
4 RAMA	2 CHOCO
5 TALAMANCA	3 INTER-ANDINE
6 GUAYMI	4 BARBACOAN
7 †ANTIOQUIA	
8 ARUAK	
9 CHIBCHAN PROPER	

List 6.24. The Andean Stock (Greenberg 1987)

ANDEAN:	IV QUECHUAN
I †NORTHERN:	V AYMARAN
A †Culli	VI SOUTHERN:
B †Sec	A †Puelche
C †Leco	B MAPUDUNGU (= ARAUCANIAN)
D †CATACAO	C QAWASQAR-YAMANA
E †CHOLONA	D PATAGONIAN
II URARINA-WAORANI	
III CAHUAPANAN-ZAPAROAN	

concluded that Timucua was genetically closest to Warao (a Paezan language of Venezuela).

Andean. The Andean family extends down the western coast of South America from present-day Ecuador to Tierra del Fuego. Although Andean contains fewer languages (about 20) than any other South American branch of Amerind, its speakers account for approximately half of the *entire Amerind* population. The extremely large number of Quechua speakers and significant numbers of Aymara and Mapudungu (= Araucanian) speakers (see Table 6.1) accounts for about nine million people. Greenberg (1987) subdivides the Andean family into a half-dozen branches, as shown in List 6.24. On the subgrouping within Southern Andean, I have followed the advice of Christos Clairis (personal communication).

Macro-Tucanoan. About 50 languages make up the Macro-Tucanoan stock. Most of the languages are found in what is today western Brazil, but there are outliers in both southern and eastern Brazil. According to Greenberg (1987), the family is composed of seven subfamilies and a dozen isolated languages (see List 6.25). The Tucanoan subgrouping adopted in this volume follows Waltz and Wheeler (1972).

List 6.25. The Macro-Tucanoan Stock (Greenberg 1987)

MACRO-TUCANOAN:	X †Pankararu
I †Auishiri	XI Shukuru
II Canichana	XII Uman
III Capishana	XIII CATUQUINAN
IV †Gamella	XIV HUARI
V Iranshe	XV ARUTANI-SAPE
VI Koaia	XVI NAMBIKUARAN
VII Movima	XVII PUINAVE-MAKU
VIII Muniche	XVIII TICUNA-YURI
IX Natu	XIX TUCANOAN

List 6.26. The Equatorial Stock (Greenberg 1987)

EQUATORIAL:	XII MACRO-ARAWAKAN:
I Cayuvava	A Katembri
II Camsa	B †Otomaco
III †Taruma	C TINIGUAN
IV Trumai	D GUAHIBAN
V †Tusha	E ARAWAKAN:
VI Yuracare	1 †Guamo
VII PIAROA-SALIBA	2 †Taino
VIII †TIMOTE	3 Chamicuro
IX JIVAROAN	4 ARAWAN
X ZAMUCOAN	5 CHIPAYAN
XI KARIRI-TUPI	6 CHAPACURAN
	7 MAIPURAN

Equatorial. The Equatorial family contains more languages (about 150) and is more widespread than any of the other six branches of Amerind found in South America. Its geographic distribution is enormous, extending from the islands of the Caribbean as far south as Uruguay; on an east-west axis it literally spans the entire continent. Two subfamilies of Equatorial, Arawak (about 80 languages) and Tupi (about 50), account for most of the languages and much of its broad distribution. Greenberg (1987) subdivides the family into a half-dozen isolated languages and a half-dozen subfamilies, as illustrated in List 6.26.

Macro-Carib. Greenberg (1987) joins two single languages and two small families with the larger and more widespread Carib family to form the Macro-Carib stock (see List 6.27). For the most part these 50 languages are spoken in the northern regions of South America, from Colombia to French Guiana, though there is one group of Carib languages located far to the south in central Brazil. The Carib classification followed in this volume comes from Durbin (1977).

List 6.27. The Macro-Carib Stock (Greenberg 1987)

MACRO-CARIB:
I Andoke
II †Cucura
III PEBA-YAGUAN
IV BORA-WITOTO
V CARIB

List 6.28. The Macro-Panoan Stock (Greenberg 1987)

MACRO-PANOAN:
I †CHARRUAN
II LULE-VILELA
III MASCOIAN
IV Chimane (= Moseten)
V MATACO-GUAICURU:
  A GUAICURUAN
  B MATACO
VI PANO-TACANA:
  A PANOAN
  B TACANAN

Macro-Panoan. About 50 languages are all that survive today of a family that once extended from Peru to Uruguay. Macro-Panoan unites a few small families (some extinct), the language isolete Chimane (= Moseten), and the more numerous and widespread Panoan and Tacanan subfamilies. Panoan and Tacanan form one higher-level grouping, and Mataco and Guaicuruan another, as seen in List 6.28.

Macro-Ge. Languages belonging to the Macro-Ge stock were originally spoken over a broad expanse of eastern South America. Today there are only about two dozen surviving languages and the internal structure of the family is far from clear. About all that can be said with assurance is that the Ge and Kaingang families are most closely related to each other, as shown in List 6.29.

The following bibliography, like all the others in this volume, is arranged topically. Since this bibliography is the longest in the book, and is subdivided into almost two dozen subsections, the reader who wishes to look up a particular citation in the text must be careful to look under the appro-

List 6.29. The Macro-Ge Stock (Greenberg 1987)

MACRO-GE:
I Rikbaktsa
II Fulnio
III Guato
IV Opaye
V †Oti
VI Caraja
VII BORORO
VIII BOTOCUDO
IX †CHIQUITO
X †KAMAKAN
XI †PURI
XII YABUTI
XIII MASHAKALI
XIV GE-KAINGANG:
  A KAINGANG
  B GE

priate subsection. Books and articles are classified in this bibliography as *narrowly* as possible. This means that a book dealing exclusively with Algonquian languages will be listed under Algonquian, even if it has been referred to in a more general context in the text itself. This topical arrangement also means that some works published by a scholar in the same year are, according to convention, distinguished by *a* and *b* following the date, even though the titles may be in different subsections of the bibliography. The first subsection (Amerind) contains works of a general nature as well as a sampling of books and articles that have called attention to similarities between supposedly independent Amerind groups. In the latter case the groups (or languages) compared are given in brackets following the source.

AMERIND

Allen, Louis. 1931. "Siouan and Iroquoian," *IJAL* 6: 185–93. [Siouan, Iroquoian]

Boas, Franz. 1894. "Classification of the Languages of the North Pacific Coast," in *Memoirs of the International Congress of Anthropology, 1893*.

———. 1920. "The Classification of American Languages," *AA* 22: 367–76.

———. 1929. "Classification of American Indian Languages," *Language* 5: 1–7.

Bright, William O. 1974. "North American Indian Languages," in *EB* 13: 208–13.

Brinton, Daniel G. 1891. *The American Race: A Linguistic Classification and Ethnographic Description of the Native Tribes of North and South America*. Philadelphia.

———. 1897. "On the Affinities of the Otomi Language with Athabaskan Dialects," *Tenth International Congress of Americanists (1894)*, pp. 151–62. [Otomian, Athabaskan]

Campbell, Lyle. 1973. "Distant Genetic Relationship and the Maya-Chipaya Hypothesis," *AL* 15: 113–35. [Mayan, Chipaya]

———. 1978. "Distant Genetic Relationship and Diffusion: A Mesoamerican Perspective," *Actes du XLIIe Congrès International des Américanistes* 4: 595–605.

———. 1979. "Middle American Languages," in *LNA*.

Campbell, Lyle, and Marianne Mithun, eds. 1979. *The Languages of Native America*. Austin, Tex.

Chafe, Wallace. 1964. "Another Look at Siouan and Iroquoian," *AA* 66: 852–62. [Siouan, Iroquoian]

———. 1976. *The Caddoan, Iroquoian, and Siouan Languages*. The Hague. [Caddoan, Iroquoian, Siouan]

Chamberlain, A. F. 1913. "Linguistic Stocks of South American Indians," *AA* 15: 236–47.

Crawford, James M. 1979. "Timucua and Yuchi: Two Language Isolates of the Southeast," in *LNA*.

Darnell, Regna, and Joel Sherzer. 1971. "Areal Linguistic Studies in North America: A Historical Perspective," *IJAL* 37: 20–28.

Davis, Irvine E. 1974. "Keresan-Caddoan Comparisons," *IJAL* 40: 265–67. [Caddoan, Keres]

Dixon, Roland B., and Alfred L. Kroeber. 1913. "New Linguistic Families in California," *AA* 15: 647–55.

———. 1919. "Linguistic Families of California," in *UCPAAE* 16.

Elmendorf, W. W. 1963. "Yukian-Siouan Lexical Similarities," *IJAL* 29: 300–09. [Yukian, Siouan]
———. 1964. "Item and Set Comparison in Yuchi, Siouan, and Yukian," *IJAL* 30: 328–40. [Yuchi, Siouan, Yukian]
Gallatin, Albert. 1836. "A Synopsis of the Indian Tribes of North America," *Transactions and Collections of the American Antiquarian Society* 2,1: 1–422.
Goddard, Ives. 1979. "The Languages of South Texas and the Lower Rio Grande," in *LNA*.
Greenberg, Joseph H. 1960. "The General Classification of Central and South American Languages," in Anthony F. C. Wallace, ed., *Selected Papers of the Fifth International Congress of Anthropological and Ethnological Sciences*. Philadelphia.
———. 1979. "The Classification of American Indian Languages," in Ralph E. Cooley et al., eds., *Papers of the 1978 Mid-America Linguistics Conference at Oklahoma*. Norman, Okla. [Amerind]
———. 1981. "The External Relationships of the Uto-Aztecan Languages," paper delivered at Uto-Aztecan Conference, Tucson, Ariz. [Uto-Aztecan, Tanoan, Oto-Manguean]
———. 1987. *Language in the Americas*. Stanford, Calif. [Amerind]
Greenberg, Joseph H., Christy G. Turner, and Stephen L. Zegura. 1985. "Convergence of Evidence for the Peopling of the Americas," *Collegium Antropologicum* 9: 33–42.
Grimes, Barbara F., ed. 1984. *Ethnologue*. 10th ed. Dallas.
Gursky, Karl-Heinz. 1963. "Algonquian and the Languages of Southern Texas," *AL* 5,9: 17–21. [Algonquian, Hokan]
———. 1965a. "Ein lexikalischer Vergleich der Algonkin-Golf- und Hoka-Subtiaba-Sprachen," *Orbis* 14: 160–215. [Algonquian, Gulf, Hokan]
———. 1965b. "Lexical Similarities between Caddoan and Algonkian-Gulf," *AL* 7,4: 104–9. [Caddoan, Algonquian, Gulf]
———. 1965c. "Zur Frage der historischen Stellung der Yuki-Sprachfamilie," in *Abhandlung der Volkerkundlichen Arbeitsgemeinschaft* 8.
———. 1966. "Ein Vergleich der grammatikalischen Morpheme der Golf-Sprachen und der Hoka-Subtiaba-Sprachen," *Orbis* 15: 511–37. [Gulf, Hokan]
———. 1968. "Gulf and Hokan-Subtiaban: New Lexical Parallels," *IJAL* 34: 21–41. [Gulf, Hokan]
———. 1974. "Der Hoka-Sprachstamm. Eine Bestandsaufnahme des lexikalischen Beweis materials," *Orbis* 23: 170–215. [Hokan, Penutian]
Haas, Mary R. 1951. "The Proto-Gulf Word for 'water' (with Notes on Siouan-Yuchi)," *IJAL* 17: 71–79. [Gulf, Siouan, Yuchi]
———. 1958a. "A New Linguistic Relationship in North America: Algonkian and the Gulf Languages," *Southwestern Journal of Anthropology* 14: 231–64. [Algonquian, Gulf]
———. 1959. "Tonkawa and Algonquian," *AL* 1,2: 1–6. [Algonquian, Tonkawa]
———. 1960. "Some Genetic Affiliations of Algonkian," in Stanley Diamond, ed., *Culture in History*. New York. [Algonquian, Ritwan, Mosan, Gulf, Tonkawa]
———. 1963. "The Muskogean and Algonkian Words for 'skunk,'" *IJAL* 29: 65–66. [Algonquian, Muskogean]
———. 1964. "California Hokan," in *UCPL* 34. [Penutian, Yuki, Hokan]
———. 1965. "Is Kutenai Related to Algonkian?" *Canadian Journal of Linguistics* 10: 77–92. [Algonquian, Kutenai]

———. 1966b. "Historical Linguistics and Genetic Relationship," in *CTIL* 3.
———. 1969a. "American Indian Languages and Historical Linguistics," in Mary Haas, *The Prehistory of Languages*. The Hague.
———. 1969b. "Grammar or Lexicon? The American Indian Side of the Question from Duponceau to Powell," *IJAL* 35: 239–55.
———. 1976. "American Indian Linguistic Prehistory," in *NLA* 1.
———. 1978a. "The Study of American Indian Languages: A Brief Historical Sketch," in Mary R. Haas, *Language, Culture, and History*. Stanford, Calif.
———. 1978b. "The Problem of Classifying American Indian Languages: From Duponceau to Powell," in Mary R. Haas, *Language, Culture, and History*. Stanford, Calif.
———. 1979. "Southeastern Languages," in *LNA*.
Hamp, Eric P. 1967. "On Maya-Chipayan," *IJAL* 33: 74–76. [Mayan, Chipayan]
———. 1971. "On Mayan-Araucanian Comparative Phonology," *IJAL* 37: 156–59. [Mayan, Mapudungu]
Harrington, J. P. 1943. "Hokan Discovered in South America," *Journal of the Washington Academy of Science* 33: 334–44. [Hokan, Quechua]
Hewson, John. 1968. "Beothuk and Algonkian: Evidence Old and New," *IJAL* 34: 85–93. [Algonquian, Beothuk]
———. 1971. "Beothuk Consonant Correspondences," *IJAL* 37: 244–49. [Algonquian, Beothuk]
Hoijer, Harry. 1976. "History of American Indian Linguistics," in *NLA* 1.
Holt, Dennis G. 1977. "Evidence of Genetic Relationship Between Chibchan and Uto-Aztecan," *Proceedings of the Berkeley Linguistic Society* 3: 283–92. [Uto-Aztecan, Chibchan]
Ibarra Grasso, Dick Edgar. 1961. "La lingüística indigena de Bolivia y las lenguas andinas," in *A William Cameron Townsend*. Mexico City.
Kaufman, Terrence. 1974. "Meso-American Indian Languages," in *EB* 11: 956–63.
Key, Harold, and Mary Key. 1967. *Bolivian Indian Tribes*. Norman, Okla.
Key, Mary Ritchie. 1979. *The Grouping of South American Indian Languages*. Tübingen.
———. 1981a. "North and South American Linguistic Connections," *La Linguistique* 17,*1*: 3–18. [Amerind]
———. 1981b. "South American Relationships with North American Indian Languages," *Boletín de Filología* 31: 331–50. [Amerind]
———. 1981c. *Intercontinental Linguistic Connections*. Irvine, Calif. [Amerind]
———. 1983. "Comparative Methodology for Distant Relationships in North and South American Languages," *Language Sciences* 5: 133–54. [Amerind]
Klein, Harriet E. Manelis, and Louisa R. Stark, eds. 1985. *South American Indian Languages*. Austin, Tex. [Amerind]
Landar, Herbert. 1977. "South and Central American Indian Languages," in *NLA* 2.
Lehmann, Walter. 1920. *Zentral-Amerika*, 2 vols. Berlin.
Loukotka, Čestmír. 1935. *Clasificacíon de las lenguas sudamericanas*. Prague.
———. 1944. "Klassifikation der sudamerikanischen Sprachen," *Zeitschrift für Ethnologie* 74: 1–69.
———. 1968. *Classification of South American Indian Languages*. Los Angeles.
Mason, J. Alden. 1950. "The Languages of South American Indians," *Handbook of South American Indians* 6: 157–317.
Matteson, Esther. 1972. "Toward Proto Amerindian," in *CSAL*.
McClaran, Marlys. 1977. "Mexico," in *NLA* 2.

McQuown, Norman A. 1955. "The Indigenous Languages of Latin America," *AA* 57: 501–70.
———, ed. 1967. *Handbook of Middle American Indians, 5: Linguistics*. Austin, Tex.
Nimuendaju, Curt. 1931–32. "Idiomas indigenas del Brasil," *Revista del Instituto de Etnologia de la Universidad de Tucuman* 2: 543–618.
Noble, G. Kingsley. 1965. "On the Genetic Affiliations of Timucua, an Indigenous Language of Florida," *Journal de la Société des Américanistes* 54: 359–76.
Olson, Ronald D. 1964–65. "Mayan Affinities with Chipaya of Bolivia," *IJAL*, 2 parts, 30: 313–24, 31: 29–38. [Mayan, Chipaya]
Perez Gonzalez, Benjamin. 1975. "Clasificacíones lingüísticas," in Evangelina Arana de Swadesh, ed., *Las lenguas de Mexico* 1. Mexico City.
Powell, John Wesley. 1891. "Indian Linguistic Families of America North of Mexico," *Seventh Annual Report, Bureau of American Ethnology*. Washington, D.C.
Radin, Paul. 1919. "The Genetic Relationship of the North American Indian Languages," in *UCPAAE* 14.
———. 1944. "The Classification of the Languages of Mexico," *Tlalocan* 2: 259–65.
Ribeiro, Darcy, and Mary Ruth Wise. 1978. *Los grupos etnicos de la amazonia peruana*. Lima.
Rivet, Paul. 1924. "Langues de l'Amérique du Sud et des Antilles," in Antoine Meillet and Marcel Cohen, eds., *Les langues du monde*. Paris.
Rood, David S. 1973. "Swadesh's Keres-Caddo Comparisons," *IJAL* 39: 189–90. [Caddoan, Keres]
Rowe, John Howland. 1974. "Linguistic Classification Problems in South America," in Patricia J. Lyon, ed., *Native South Americans*. Boston.
Sapir, Edward. 1916. *Time Perspective in Aboriginal American Culture: A Study in Method*. Ottawa. Reprinted in 1949 in David G. Mandelbaum, ed., *Selected Writings of Edward Sapir in Language, Culture and Personality*. Berkeley, Calif.
———. 1917a. Review of Benigno Bibolotti, *Moseteno Vocabulary and Treatises*, *IJAL* 1: 183–84.
———. 1921a. "A Bird's-Eye View of American Languages North of Mexico," *Science* 54: 408.
———. 1929. "Central and North American Indian Languages," in *Encyclopaedia Britannica*, 14th ed., 5: 138–41.
Shipley, William. 1976. "California," in *NLA* 1.
Stark, Louisa R. 1970. "Mayan Affinities with Araucanian," *Papers from the Chicago Linguistic Society* 6: 57–69. [Mayan, Mapudungu]
———. 1972. "Maya-Yunga-Chipayan: A New Linguistic Alignment," *IJAL* 38: 119–35. [Mayan, Chimu, Chipayan]
Steward, J. H., ed. 1950. *Handbook of South American Indians*. *BAEB* 143.
Sturtevant, William C. 1959. "Authorship of the Powell Linguistic Classification," *IJAL* 25: 196–99.
Suárez, Jorge A. 1974. "South American Indian Languages," in *EB* 17: 105–12.
———. 1983. *The Mesoamerican Indian Languages*. Cambridge, Eng.
Swadesh, Morris. 1954. "Perspectives and Problems of Amerindian Comparative Linguistics," *Word* 10: 306–32. [Amerind]
———. 1960. "On Interhemisphere Linguistic Connections," in Stanley Diamond, ed., *Culture in History*. New York.
———. 1964a. "Linguistic Overview," in Edward Norbeck and Jesse D. Jennings, eds., *Prehistoric Man in the New World*. Chicago.

———. 1964b. "Afinidades de las lenguas amerindias," *Akten des 34.Internationalen Amerikanisten Kongress*, pp. 729–38. [Amerind]
———. 1967. "Linguistic Classification in the Southwest," in Dell Hymes and W. Bittle, eds., *Studies in Southwestern Ethnolinguistics*. The Hague.
Swanton, J. R. 1952. "The Indian Tribes of North America," in *BAEB* 145.
Thompson, Laurence C. 1976. "The Northwest," in *NLA* 1.
Tovar, Antonio. 1961. *Catálogo de las lenguas de América del Sur*. Buenos Aires.
Trager, George L. 1948. "The Indian Languages of Brazil," *IJAL* 14: 43–48.
Trager, George L., and Felicia E. Harben. 1958. "North American Indian Languages," *Studies in Linguistics, Occasional Papers* 5.
Voegelin, C. F. 1941. "North American Indian Languages Still Spoken and Their Genetic Relationships," in Leslie Spier, A. Irving Hallowell, and Stanley S. Newman, eds., *Language, Culture, and Personality*. Menosha, Wis.
Voegelin, C. F., and F. M. Voegelin. 1965. "Classification of American Indian Languages," *AL* 7,7: 121–50.
———. 1967. Review of *Die nordamerikanischen Indianersprachen*, by H. J. Pinnow, *Language* 43: 573–83.
———. 1973. "South Western and Great Basin Languages," in *CTIL* 10.
———. 1977. *Classification and Index of the World's Languages*. New York.
Whorf, Benjamin L., and George L. Trager. 1937. "The Relationship of Uto-Aztecan and Tanoan," *AA* 39: 609–24. [Uto-Aztecan, Tanoan]
Witkowski, Stanley R., and Cecil H. Brown. 1978. "Mesoamerican: A Proposed Language Phylum," *AA* 80: 942–44. [Mayan, Zoquean, Huave, Totonacan, Lenca, Jicaque, Oto-Manguean]

ALGIC

Berman, Howard. 1982. "Two Phonological Innovations in Ritwan," *IJAL* 48: 412–20.
Goddard, Ives. 1975. "Algonquian, Wiyot, and Yurak," in M. D. Kinkade et al., eds., *Linguistics and Anthropology*. Lisse, Neths.
———. 1981. Personal letter.
Haas, Mary R. 1958b. "Algonkian-Ritwan: The End of a Controversy," *IJAL* 24: 159–73.
———. 1966a. "Wiyot-Yurok-Algonkian and Problems of Comparative Algonkian," *IJAL* 32: 101–7.
Kroeber, Alfred L. 1911. "The Languages of the Coast of California North of San Francisco," in *UCPAAE* 9.
Michelson, Truman. 1914. "Two Alleged Algonquian Languages of California," *AA* 16: 361–67.
Sapir, Edward. 1913. "Wiyot and Yurok, Algonkin Languages of California," *AA* 15: 617–46.
———. 1915. "Algonkin Languages of California: A Reply," *AA* 17: 188–94.
Teeter, Karl V. 1965. "The Algonquian Verb: Notes Toward a Reconsideration," *IJAL* 31: 221–25.
———. 1974. "Some Algic Etymologies," *IJAL* 40: 197–201.

ALGONQUIAN

Bloomfield, Leonard. 1925. "On the Sound System of Central Algonquian," *Language* 1: 130–56.

———. 1946. "Algonquian," in *LSNA*.
Cowan, William, ed. 1980. *Papers of the 11th Algonquian Conference*. Ottawa.
Goddard, Ives. 1967. "Notes on the Genetic Classification of the Algonquian Languages," in *Contributions to Anthropology: Linguistics 1 (Algonquian). National Museum of Canada Bulletin* 214.
———. 1978a. "Eastern Algonquian Languages," in *HNAI* 15.
———. 1978b. "Central Algonquian Languages," in *HNAI* 15.
———. 1979. "Comparative Algonquian," in *LNA*.
Teeter, Karl. 1964. "Algonquian Languages and Genetic Relationship," in Horace G. Lunt, ed., *Proceedings of the 9th International Congress of Linguists*. The Hague.
———. 1967. "Genetic Classification in Algonquian," in *Contributions to Anthropology: Linguistics 1 (Algonquian). National Museum of Canada Bulletin* 214.
———. 1973. "Algonquian," in *CTIL* 10.

MOSAN

Andrade, Manuel J. 1953. "Notes on the Relations Between Chemakum and Quileute," *IJAL* 19: 212–15.
Frachtenberg, Leo J. 1920. "Abnormal Types of Speech in Quileute," *IJAL* 1: 295–99.
Klokeid, Terry J. 1969. "Notes on the Comparison of Wakashan and Salish," *University of Hawaii Working Papers in Linguistics* 1,7: 1–19.
Swadesh, Morris. 1953a. "Mosan," *IJAL*, 2 parts, 19: 26–44, 223–36.
———. 1953b. "Salish-Wakashan Comparisons Noted by Boas," *IJAL* 19: 290–91.

SALISH

Jorgensen, Joseph G. 1969. *Salish Language and Culture*. Bloomington, Ind.
Swadesh, Morris. 1950. "Salish Internal Relationships," *IJAL* 16: 157–67.
Thompson, Laurence C. 1973. "The Northwest," in *NLA* 1.
———. 1979. "Salishan and the Northwest," in *LNA*.

WAKASHAN

Jacobsen, William H., Jr. 1979. "Wakashan Comparative Studies," in *LNA*.

CHIMAKUAN

Jacobsen, William H., Jr. 1979. "Chimakuan Comparative Studies," in *LNA*.

SIOUAN

Chafe, Wallace L. 1973. "Siouan, Iroquoian, and Caddoan," in *CTIL* 10.
———. 1976. *The Caddoan, Iroquoian and Siouan Languages*. The Hague.
Matthews, G. Hubert. 1958. "Handbook of Siouan Languages," Ph.D. dissertation, University of Pennsylvania.
Rood, David S. 1979. "Siouan," in *LNA*.
Siebert, F. T., Jr. 1945. "Linguistic Classification of Catawba," *IJAL*, 2 parts, 11: 100–104, 221–28.
Voegelin, C. F. 1941. "Internal Relationships of Siouan Languages," *AA* 43: 246–49.
Wolff, Hans. 1950. "Comparative Siouan," *IJAL*, 4 parts, 16: 61–66, 113–21, 168–78; 17: 197–204.

CADDOAN

Boas, Franz. 1906. "Some Philological Aspects of Anthropological Research," *Science* 23: 641–45.

Chafe, Wallace L. 1973. "Siouan, Iroquoian, and Caddoan," in *CTIL* 10.

———. 1976. *The Caddoan, Iroquoian and Siouan Languages*. The Hague.

———. 1979. "Caddoan," in *LNA*.

Taylor, Allan R. 1963. "The Classification of the Caddoan Languages," *Proceedings of the American Philosophical Society* 107: 51–59.

IROQUOIAN

Chafe, Wallace L. 1973. "Siouan, Iroquoian, and Caddoan," in *CTIL* 10.

———. 1976. *The Caddoan, Iroquoian and Siouan Languages*. The Hague.

Hoffman, Bernard G. 1959. "Iroquois Linguistic Classification from Historical Materials," *Ethnohistory* 6: 160–85.

Lounsbury, Floyd G. 1978. "Iroquoian Languages," in *HNAI* 15.

Mithun, Marianne. 1979. "Iroquoian," in *LNA*.

HOKAN

Dixon, Roland B. 1905. "The Shasta-Achomawi: A New Linguistic Stock with Four New Dialects," *AA*: 213–17.

———. 1910. "The Chimariko Indians and Language," in *UCPAAE* 5.

Greenberg, Joseph H., and Morris Swadesh. 1953. "Jicaque as a Hokan Language," *IJAL* 19: 216–22.

Haas, Mary R. 1964. "California Hokan," in *UCPL* 34.

Halpern, A. L. 1964. "A Report on a Survey of Pomo Languages," in *UCPL* 34.

Jacobsen, William H., Jr. 1979. "Hokan Inter-Branch Comparisons," in *LNA*.

Joel, Judith. 1964. "Classification of the Yuman Languages," in *UCPL* 34.

Kroeber, Alfred L. 1915. "Serian, Tequistlatecan, and Hokan," in *UCPAAE* 11.

———. 1943. "Classification of the Yuman Languages," in *UCPL* 1.

Langdon, Margaret. 1974. *Comparative Hokan-Coahuiltecan Studies: A Survey and Appraisal*. The Hague.

———. 1979. "Some Thoughts on Hokan with Particular Reference to Pomoan and Yuman," in *LNA*.

———. 1981. Personal letter.

McLendon, Sally. 1973. *Proto Pomo*. *UCPL* 71.

Rivet, Paul. 1942. "Un dialecte hoka colombien: le yurumangí," *Journal de la Société des Américanistes* 34: 1–59.

Sapir, Edward. 1917b. "The Position of Yana in the Hokan Stock," in *UCPAAE* 13.

———. 1920. "The Hokan and Coahuiltecan Languages," *IJAL* 1: 280–90.

———. 1925. "The Hokan Affinity of Subtiaba in Nicaragua," *AA* 27: 402–35.

Swanton, John R. 1915. "Linguistic Position of the Tribes of Southern Texas and Northeastern Mexico," *AA* 17: 17–40.

PENUTIAN

Broadbent, S., and C. A. Callaghan. 1960. "Comparative Miwok: A Preliminary Study," *IJAL* 26: 301–16.

Callaghan, Catherine A. 1958. "California Penutian: History and Bibliography," *IJAL* 24: 189–94.
Freeland, L. S., and E. Sapir. 1930. "The Relationship of Mixe to the Penutian Family," *IJAL* 6: 28–33.
Haas, Mary R. 1941. "The Classification of the Muskogean Languages," in Leslie Speir, A. Irving Hallowell, and Stanley S. Newman, eds., *Language, Culture, and Personality*. Menasha, Wis.
Hamp, Eric P. 1975. "On Zuni-Penutian Consonants," *IJAL* 41: 310–12.
Jackson, Frances L. 1972. "Proto-Mayan," in *CSAL*.
Kaufman, Terrence. 1982. Personal letter.
Kroeber, Alfred L. 1906. "The Yokuts and Yuki Languages," in Berthold Laufer, ed., *Boas Anniversary Volume*. New York.
———. 1910. "The Chumash and Costanoan Languages," in *UCPAAE* 9.
McQuown, Norman A. 1942. "Una posible síntesis lingüística Macro-Mayance," *Mayas y Olmecas* 2: 37–38.
———. 1956. "The Classification of the Mayan Languages," *IJAL* 22: 191–95.
Newman, Stanley S. 1964. "Comparison of Zuni and California Penutian," *IJAL* 30: 1–13.
Pitkin, Harvey, and William Shipley. 1958. "Comparative Survey of California Penutian," *IJAL* 24: 174–88.
Robertson, John S. 1977. "A Proposed Revision in Mayan Subgrouping," *IJAL* 43: 105–20.
Sapir, Edward. 1921b. "A Characteristic Penutian Form of Stem," *IJAL* 2: 58–67.
———. 1922. "The Takelma Language of Southwestern Oregon," *BAEB* 40,2: 1–296.
———. 1926. "A Chinookan Phonetic Law," *IJAL* 4: 105–10.
Sawyer, Jesse O. 1980. "The Non-Genetic Relationship of Wappo and Yuki," in Kathryn Klar, Margaret Langdon, and Shirley Silver, eds., *American Indian and Indoeuropean Studies*. The Hague.
Shipley, William. 1957. "Some Yukian-Penutian Lexical Resemblances," *IJAL* 23: 269–74.
———. 1980. "Penutian Among the Ruins: A Personal Assessment," *Proceedings of the Berkeley Linguistic Society* 6: 437–41.
Silverstein, Michael. 1979. "Penutian: An Assessment," in *LNA*.
Swadesh, Morris. 1956. "Problems of Long-Range Comparison in Penutian," *Language* 32: 17–41.
Swanton, John R. 1919. *A Structural and Lexical Comparison of the Tunica, Chitimacha, and Atakapa Languages*. *BAEB* 68.
———. 1924. "The Muskhogean Connection of the Natchez Language," *IJAL* 3: 46–75.

UTO-AZTECAN

Hale, Kenneth. 1964. "The Subgrouping of Uto-Aztecan Languages: Lexical Evidence for Sonoran," *International Congress of Americanists, Proceedings* 25,2: 511–18.
Lamb, Sydney M. 1964. "The Classification of the Uto-Aztecan Languages: A Historical Survey," in *UCPL* 34.
Langacre, Ronald W., ed. 1977. *An Overview of Uto-Aztecan Grammar*. Dallas.
Mason, J. Alden. 1936. "The Classification of the Sonoran Languages," in Robert H. Lowie, ed., *Essays in Anthropology Presented to A. L. Kroeber*. Berkeley, Calif.

Miller, Wick R. 1964. "The Shoshonean Languages of Uto-Aztecan," in *UCPL* 34.
———. 1967. *Uto-Aztecan Cognate Sets*. *UCPL* 48.
Steele, Susan. 1979. "Uto-Aztecan: An Assessment for Historical and Comparative Linguistics," in *LNA*.
Voegelin, C. F., F. M. Voegelin, and Kenneth Hale. 1962. *Typological and Comparative Grammar of Uto-Aztecan*, 1: *Phonology*. *IJAL Memoir* 17.
Whorf, Benjamin L. 1935. "The Comparative Linguistics of Uto-Aztecan," *AA* 37: 600–608.

TANOAN

Davis, Irvine. 1979. "The Kiowa-Tanoan, Keresan, and Zuni Languages," in *LNA*.
Harrington, John P. 1910. "On Phonetic and Lexical Resemblances Between Kiowan and Tanoan," *AA* 12: 119–23.

OTO-MANGUEAN

de Angulo, Jaime, and L. S. Freeland. 1933. "Zapotekan Linguistic Group," *IJAL*, 2 parts, 8: 1–38, 111–30.
Longacre, Robert E. 1957. *Proto Mixtecan*. Bloomington, Ind.
———. 1961. "Swadesh's Macro-Mixtecan Hypothesis," *IJAL* 27: 9-29.
Rensch, Calvin. 1973. "Otomanguean Isoglosses," in *CTIL* 11.
———. 1976. *Comparative Oto-Manguean Phonology*. Bloomington, Ind.
———. 1977. "Classification of the Oto-Manguean Languages and the Position of Tlapanec," in David Oltrogge and Calvin Rensch, *Two Studies in Middle American Comparative Linguistics*. Arlington, Tex.
———. 1978. "Typological and Genetic Consideration in the Classification of the Otomanguean Languages," *Actes du XLIIe Congrès International des Américanistes* 4: 623–33.
Swadesh, Morris. 1960. "The Oto-Manguean Hypothesis and Macro-Mixtecan," *IJAL* 26: 79–111.

CHIBCHAN-PAEZAN

Wheeler, Alva. 1972. "Proto Chibchan," in *CSAL*.

MACRO-GE

Davis, Irvine. 1968. "Some Macro-Je Relationships," *IJAL* 34: 42–47.
Hamp, Eric P. 1969. "On Maxacali, Karaja, and Macro-Je," *IJAL* 35: 269–70.
Wilbert, Johannes. 1962. "A Preliminary Glottochronology of Ge," *AL* 4,2: 17–25.

MACRO-PANOAN

Girard, Victor. 1971. *Proto-Takanan Phonology*. *UCPL* 70.
Key, Mary Ritchie. 1968. *Comparative Tacanan Phonology*. The Hague.
Suárez, Jorge A. 1969. "Moseten and Pano-Tacanan," *AL* 11: 255–66.

MACRO-CARIB

Durbin, Marshall. 1977. "A Survey of the Carib Language Family," in Ellen B. Grasso, ed., *Carib Speaking Indians*. Tucson, Ariz.

ANDEAN

Clairis, Christos. 1985. Personal letter.
Parker, Gary J. 1963. "La clasificacíon genética de los dialectos quechuas," *Revista del Museo Nacional* (Lima) 32: 241–52.

EQUATORIAL

Rodrigues, Arion D. 1958. "Classification of Tupi-Guarani," *IJAL* 24: 231–34.

ARAWAKAN

Matteson, Esther. 1972. "Proto Arawakan," in *CSAL*.
Noble, G. Kingsley. 1965. *Proto-Arawakan and Its Descendants*. Bloomington, Ind.

MACRO-TUCANOAN

Waltz, Nathan E., and Alva Wheeler. 1972. "Proto Tucanoan," in *CSAL*.

7

Prospects for Future Research

After a period of relative quiescence, genetic classification has, since 1950, undergone a renaissance, with discoveries as remarkable as any made by the nineteenth-century pioneers. More scholars than ever before are currently interested in taxonomy, despite the pejorative connotation that the word taxonomic has acquired in recent years in certain linguistic circles. Moreover, there is every indication that this renewed interest will continue for the remainder of this century. In this chapter, after first summarizing various methodological errors that should be avoided in future research, I will indicate the directions that work should take, with respect both to low-level refinement and large-scale groupings.

7.1 METHODOLOGICAL ERRORS TO AVOID

Some of the errors discussed in this section have fortunately become rare in recent years; others continue to flourish. I will discuss here only the most fundamental and most common ones.

Among the most basic errors, especially in the early literature, was the belief that the principles of genetic linguistics, as developed for Indo-European languages, were not readily applicable to languages in other parts of the world that lacked early written records or were spoken by people with a low level of technology and/or non-Caucasian racial traits. It is now well established that the principles of genetic classification are valid for the entire human population. That genetic linguistics happened to be discovered largely in terms of the Indo-European languages merely by happenstance is still not fully appreciated.

A second major error has been the adoption of too narrow a purview. This may manifest itself in several ways. At its worst it involves the binary comparison of two languages (or groups), usually arbitrarily selected, in an attempt to prove that they are related. This approach confuses genetic relationship with classification, the latter being a far more powerful concept encompassing the former. In order to investigate genetic classification fruitfully, one must make every effort to work on a valid genetic node, though the node itself may represent a group of languages that has only recently diverged from a common origin (e.g. Slavic, Bantu, Polynesian, Mayan) or one of considerable antiquity (e.g. Nilo-Saharan, Australian, Amerind). It is incumbent on the investigator to study the *entire group* as fully as possible and to ignore arbitrary geographic and political boundaries. One can no more study Amerind by comparing, say, Penutian and Algonquian than one can study Indo-European in terms of Slavic and Celtic alone. In classificatory work it is far better to err by comparing too many languages than too few, so where there is legitimate doubt about the boundary of some genetic group, an investigator would be well advised to include in his study any possible member of the group.

A related error involves the comparison of one family with only *part* of another family. Thus, for example, Indo-European is still sometimes compared directly with Semitic. There is no longer any doubt, however, that Semitic is but one branch of Afro-Asiatic, so any meaningful comparison must be between Indo-European and *all* of Afro-Asiatic. Should it turn out that resemblances are restricted to Indo-European and Semitic, this would constitute a strong argument that the similarities are due to borrowing and not to common origin.

One of the more serious errors in contemporary classification involves the artificial standards of proof of genetic affinity that are still followed by many linguists. In the attempt to recognize valid cognates, criteria such as the presence of regular correspondences and the reconstruction of protoforms are still commonly invoked. On the semantic side, some scholars even go so far as to require an identity of meaning among cognates. Obviously, research limited by such artificial constraints as these will be unable to probe very deeply into the past.

The early error of confusing genetic classification, which is based on common origin, with classifications based either on typological (e.g. tone, word order) or nonlinguistic criteria (e.g. race, level of technology) is encountered less frequently today than in the past. Similarly, the problem of distinguishing borrowed words from the inherited stock is now handled with greater sophistication than in an earlier day. Borrowing has befuddled genetic classification in two ways. First, the failure to distinguish borrowed roots from inherited ones undermines the basis of genetic classification.

Equally pernicious, however, has been the belief that borrowing may operate almost without constraints; from this perspective, shared by Franz Boas, Malcolm Guthrie, and others, almost any potential cognate can be attributed to borrowing. Recent studies in bilingualism (see Grosjean 1982) have confirmed what astute scholars have always known: borrowing takes place under very special circumstances, usually involving bilingualism, and affects a fairly limited area of vocabulary (chiefly nouns). The idea that any root can "radiate out," contaminating languages at great distances, confuses the relative ease of cultural diffusion of artifacts with the much more restrictive nature of linguistic diffusion.

One still encounters today, though with decreasing frequency, arguments to the effect that family A and family B cannot be related because differences in some area of linguistic structure (e.g. morphology, color terminology, numerals) are simply too profound. This is what I have referred to as the fallacy of negative evidence; scholars who advance such arguments fail to appreciate that in detecting common origin it is similarities that count, not differences.

With regard to subgrouping, both methodology and characteristic errors are different from those associated with proving genetic affinity. One common error results from an unsophisticated handling of putative innovations, either by giving all innovations equal weight or by failing to recognize that some apparent innovations may in reality be retentions from the proto-language. If a root is found in just one of, say, eight branches of a family, many scholars assume the root to be an innovation of that branch and fail to realize that it may instead be a root of the proto-language that has survived only in that branch. Second, one frequently encounters a rivalry between different subgrouping criteria, usually in the form of a "shared innovations" vs. "lexicostatistics" debate. Such arguments are essentially futile, since *all* methods of discovering the underlying historical reality should be used, where possible. When different methods (based on different assumptions) all point in the same direction, we may have greater confidence that the indicated subgrouping is correct. And when they differ, we should recognize that these methods are imperfect, and that some work better than others in certain contexts. This failure to distinguish clearly methods and goals has led at times to proposed subgroupings that are inherently implausible. (A similar adherence to supposed methodological principles has also led to the postulation of totally improbable sound systems for reconstructed languages.)

Another common subgrouping error derives from the widespread belief that an error of commission is far more serious than an error of omission. In reality, both kinds of errors are equally serious, and the scholar who fails to work out the subgrouping in as much detail as possible cannot be said to have completely fulfilled the task of classification.

A final subgrouping error results from failing to recognize the *hierarchical* nature of a subgrouping. For a long time it was believed that the Bantu family was an independent family related to West Sudanic (= Niger-Congo). In fact, the autonomous status of the Bantu family is a historical artifact that does not correspond to linguistic reality. Bantu is rather merely one subfamily of the vast Niger-Congo stock. An analogous development took place with respect to Melanesian (= Oceanic) and Polynesian languages. The lesson to be learned from these examples is that subgrouping is more than simply stringing together related groups.

7.2 LOW-LEVEL REFINEMENT

Although the discovery of distant genetic relationships is intrinsically more exciting than working out the internal structure of low-level genetic nodes, the latter type of work has the advantage of being more readily approachable without an enormous period of preparation. Furthermore, there are innumerable areas where someone with the requisite background could make a substantial contribution to linguistic taxonomy in a reasonable period of time, depending of course on the size and difficulty of the problem tackled. Therefore, someone who wishes to engage in taxonomic research would be well advised to begin with a clearly delineated group whose internal subgrouping has never been worked out. Such modest projects are likely to be far more beneficial for linguistic taxonomy (and more instructive for the investigator) than the pursuit of some fanciful hunch that, say, Haida is really an Altaic language.

In approaching a problem of subgrouping, the principal criterion for determining valid subgroups is the establishment of shared innovations for each subgroup postulated. Not all innovations are of equal importance, since many phonological and semantic shifts may reflect the independent operation of universal tendencies rather than a shared innovation. For example, the voicing of voiceless stops between vowels or before nasal consonants is such a common shift that it may easily take place independently in different languages. An associated problem is that closely related languages often "drift" in similar directions, beyond what could be expected on the basis of universal tendencies alone. I do not wish to imply that phonological and semantic innovations are without value. On the contrary, they can at times, and particularly in sufficient number, be probative, but they must be handled with care.

Because they combine the arbitrariness of sound and meaning, lexical innovations are particularly important. Two languages are hardly likely to invent the same word (say, the sounds *plok* with the meaning 'sky') independently of one another. Therefore, lexical innovations are fairly impervious to phenomena such as convergence and drift, and relatively greater weight should be given them for this reason.

One final aspect of subgrouping merits attention. Consider the following comments from Welmers (1973: 15–16):

> Language division usually appears to take the form of bifurcation; it must normally be expected that the model for the origin of four branches would be one of the following:

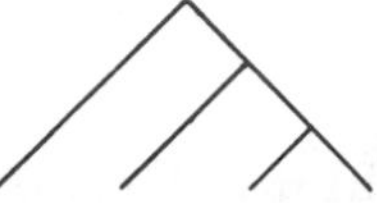

> A three-way division from a single node is historically possible, of course; but where there is adequate evidence for reconstructing language history, few such cases have been demonstrated. References to "coordinate branches" should not be taken as actual hypotheses of multiple divisions from single nodes; they are more likely to be, by implication, mere admissions that the order of bifurcations is not clear from the evidence to date.

I think Welmers is generally correct on this point. Many linguists confuse the indeterminacy of the data with historical reality. There is, however, another factor that leads away from strict bifurcations, namely, the heterogeneity of any living language, particularly one that has many speakers or is spread over a large area. Suppose that languages A, B, and C have developed from dialects a, b, and c of an original language L. Then a simple trichotomy more accurately describes the historical developments than a bifurcation. In most instances, however, it is unclear whether multiple branchings are due to the indeterminacy of the data, to dialect divisions already present in the original language, or to a combination of the two. The many examples of multiple branching in the classification presented in section 8.6 (e.g. Nilo-Saharan, 9; Indo-European, 9; Central and Western Trans–New Guinea, 12; Australian, 15; Oceanic, 17) are to be interpreted in this light. In some cases (e.g. Oceanic) we may be fairly certain that the seeming multiplicity of primary branches is due to a fairly rapid expansion over a large area rather than to dialect differences in Proto-Oceanic. In other cases (perhaps Indo-European) the different branches may well derive from different dialects of the proto-language, at least in part.

In closing this section, I would like to return to a topic that has appeared several times earlier in this volume, namely, the dispute between those who would represent linguistic relationships by a *tree* structure and those who prefer a *wave* model. Branching-tree diagrams are appropriate for representing sharp cleavages between languages (or groups of languages) where bundles of isoglosses clearly distinguish one entity from another. The wave model, on the other hand, seems better suited to describing cases where sharp divisions are absent and overlapping isoglosses make the establishment of a family tree impossible. Whereas the family tree model emphasizes the discrete nature of linguistic groups, the wave model underscores their clinal properties. These clinal properties are most apparent at the lower levels of classification, such as among the dialects of a highly diversified language (e.g. Ijo, German, Kurdish, Bikol, Zapotec) or among closely related languages spoken over a continuous geographic area (e.g. Bantu, Indic, Chinese, Athabaskan). Tree structure, however, is most obvious at higher levels of classification (e.g. between the various subfamilies that make up Afro-Asiatic, Indo-European, or Amerind).

Although the hierarchical (tree) and clinal (wave) properties of genetic classifications are sometimes portrayed as competing (or even conflicting) tendencies, they are in fact complementary properties that are simultaneously present at all levels. As early as 1872 Johannes Schmidt recognized that the seemingly distinct branches of Indo-European (e.g. Celtic, Italic, Germanic, Slavic) exhibit overlapping isoglosses, though they are few in number and hence overshadowed by the innumerable differences between these families. Furthermore, dialects of a single language frequently are separated by bundles of isoglosses just as languages are. Viewed in this light, the long-simmering feud between the "wave school" and the "tree school" can be seen to be misguided, for we are not dealing with an either/or situation. Both hierarchical and clinal properties are consequences of linguistic evolution that may be present at any level of a genetic classification. The classification offered in the following chapter should be interpreted in this way. At the highest levels the branching indicates primarily sharp divisions between distinct groups, though the possibility of overlapping isoglosses is never excluded. At the lowest levels the branching represents relative distance between languages (or groups of languages), but there is often no sharp boundary separating them into distinct groups.

7.3 LARGE-SCALE GROUPINGS

In Chapters 2–6, I reviewed the history of genetic classification and suggested that the taxonomic literature indicates the world's currently extant languages, except for a small number of language isolates (e.g. Basque, Burushaski, Nehali, Ket), belong to one of the 17 families shown in List 7.1.

As I have attempted to make explicit in the discussion of each of these families, they vary in what might be called genetic transparency, from the small, close-knit Eskimo-Aleut and Chukchi-Kamchatkan families to the large and very ancient Australian and Indo-Pacific. The other groups fall somewhere between these two extremes.

List 7.1. The World's Language Families (Ruhlen 1987)

KHOISAN	URALIC-YUKAGHIR	SINO-TIBETAN
NIGER-KORDOFANIAN	ALTAIC	AUSTRIC
NILO-SAHARAN	CHUKCHI-KAMCHATKAN	INDO-PACIFIC
AFRO-ASIATIC	ESKIMO-ALEUT	AUSTRALIAN
CAUCASIAN	ELAMO-DRAVIDIAN	NA-DENE
INDO-HITTITE		AMERIND

Although the reduction of the world's roughly 5,000 languages to a mere 17 families would be considered a radical step by a good number of contemporary linguists, there are indications that even further consolidation is not only possible, but necessary. The bibliography to this section includes (under the rubric Genetic Links Between Families) a list of articles and books that discuss, either favorably or unfavorably, the possibility of genetic links among these 17 families; this listing is intended to be representative of such proposals and is in no way exhaustive. In seeking a more comprehensive classification, one must avoid the trap of binary comparison, which at this level of research seems so tempting. Rather, one should adopt a global approach, taking into account *all* of the world's languages, as Dyen (1959: 546) suggested: "Greenberg's method of determining 'valid relationships' by 'mass comparison' without limitation as to number seems to imply that the optimum comparison is that of all the languages in the world at once. In fact, I think we must agree with this proposition; for, in effect, the discovery of genetic relationships is a way of partitioning the set of all languages in the world."

The problem with studies attempting to "prove," for example, the Ural-Altaic hypothesis is that they invariably limit themselves to citing evidence that the two families are genetically related and never face up to the even more important question of whether the two families (Uralic and Altaic in this instance) are more closely related *to each other* than to any other language or group—that is, they constitute a valid genetic node. It is the failure to address just this issue that makes all of the various Altaic proposals so inconclusive. Japanese may well be related to Altaic, but is it more closely related to Altaic than to Korean, Ainu, Gilyak, Chukchi-Kamchatkan, and other languages? This is the question that Altaicists should, but almost never do, tackle. They content themselves with a piece of the puzzle.

As one can see in the bibliography to this section, certain families (e.g. Ural-Altaic, Indo-European-Uralic) have been alleged to be related many times, by different scholars, whereas other families (e.g. Khoisan and Amerind) have not, to my knowledge, ever been linked directly. The mere fact that certain proposals are more common than others does not necessarily ensure that they are more valid. The numerous proposals linking Indo-European with various other families are as much a reflection of the Eurocentric bias of the linguistic literature as they are of the relationships themselves. Nevertheless, though there are disagreements on details (rather substantial details, it must be admitted), the literature cited in the bibliography to this section indicates fairly clearly that there are genetic relationships between European and Asian families. Precisely which families are to be included in this vast phylum is still in dispute. This complex of European and Asian families has been referred to as Nostratic, Eurasiatic, and Mitian, the last term being based on the characteristic first- and second-person pronouns of the stock (*mi* 'I,' *ti* 'you'). Recognition that certain Eurasiatic families were related came as early as 1576, when Martin Frobischer proposed a relationship between Uralic and Eskimo. In 1869 Vilhelm Thomsen linked Indo-European with Uralic, and we saw in section 4.1 that Uralic has been widely connected with Altaic since the nineteenth century. In the twentieth century a number of scholars have argued for Eurasiatic connections. List 7.2 illustrates several such proposals. Where precisely the bounds of Eurasiatic lie is a matter to be resolved by future research.

List 7.2. Proposed Subgroupings of the Eurasiatic (= Nostratic) Phylum

Pedersen 1931

EURASIATIC:
- I SEMITIC
- II INDO-EUROPEAN
- III URALIC
- IV Yukaghir
- V ALTAIC
- VI ESKIMO-ALEUT

Illich-Svitych 1971–84, Menges 1977, Birnbaum 1978

EURASIATIC:
- I WESTERN:
  - A AFRO-ASIATIC
  - B SOUTH CAUCASIAN
  - C INDO-EUROPEAN
- II EASTERN:
  - A URALIC
  - B DRAVIDIAN
  - C ALTAIC

Collinder 1965

EURASIATIC:
- I INDO-EUROPEAN
- II URALIC-YUKAGHIR
- III ALTAIC-KOREAN
- IV CHUKCHI-KAMCHATKAN
- V ESKIMO-ALEUT

Greenberg 1987

EURASIATIC:
- I INDO-HITTITE
- II URALIC-YUKAGHIR
- III ALTAIC
- IV KOREAN-JAPANESE:
  - A Korean
  - B Ainu
  - C JAPANESE-RYUKYUAN
- V CHUKCHI-ESKIMO:
  - A Gilyak
  - B CHUKCHI-KAMCHATKAN
  - C ESKIMO-ALEUT

List 7.3. The World's Language Families (Greenberg 1987)

KHOISAN	SOUTH CAUCASIAN	AUSTRO-TAI
NIGER-KORDOFANIAN	EURASIATIC	INDO-PACIFIC
NILO-SAHARAN	DRAVIDIAN	AUSTRALIAN
AFRO-ASIATIC	SINO-TIBETAN	NA-DENE
NORTH CAUCASIAN	AUSTROASIATIC	AMERIND

Greenberg (1987) classifies the world's languages into the 15 families shown in List 7.3. Proposals for joining North Caucasian and South Caucasian in a single Caucasian family were discussed in section 2.5 and those for uniting Austroasiatic and Austro-Tai in an Austric phylum, in section 4.5. Among other proposals for further consolidation, the most common are the following. (1) Niger-Kordofanian has been linked with Nilo-Saharan by Gregersen (1972), Boyd (1978), and Bender (1981), supporting a position advocated by L. Homburger (1941). (2) As List 7.2 indicates, both Afro-Asiatic (often just the Semitic branch) and South Caucasian (= Kartvelian) have been linked with Indo-European. (3) The external relationships of the Dravidian family have long been a subject of controversy, with proposals as varied as Uralic, Australian, and Nilo-Saharan. The Nilo-Saharan connection appears the most promising. (4) Sino-Tibetan and various members of Austric have been linked by scholars since the nineteenth century, chiefly on the basis of typological similarities and undiagnosed borrowings. (5) Wurm (1982) suggests that the Indo-Pacific and Australian phyla may some day be shown to be related, a possibility that Greenberg (1971) entertained but left in abeyance. (6) Na-Dene has been compared with Chinese by Sapir (1925), Shafer (1952, 1957), and Swadesh (1952), and with various Amerind groups.

The ultimate question is, of course, whether all human languages are genetically related, in which case the problem of classification would be reduced to one of subgrouping. This question is sometimes confused with that of monogenesis, though as Lamb (1964) points out, the questions are distinct. It is possible that all extant human languages are related, but that the theory of the monogenesis of language is not correct. This would be the case if human language had originated independently several times, and all but one strain had eventually become extinct. It is also possible that not all human languages are related. These are questions that, for some decades now, scholars have shied away from for essentially two reasons. First, the scholarly climate has not been receptive to such distant proposals, and the increasing specialization in academia has led in the other direction. Second, scholars supporting either monogenesis or the relatability of all lan-

Table 7.1. A Possible Global Etymology (Greenberg 1976)

Phylum	Form(s)	Meaning	Source[a]
Nilo-Saharan	tok~tek~dik	'one'	Greenberg (1963)
(South) Caucasian	tit-i	'finger'	Gamkrelidze (1984)
	tito	'single'	Gamkrelidze (1984)
Indo-European	*d(e)ik	'to point'	
Uralic	ik~odik~γtik	'one'	Collinder (1977)
Ainu	tek	'hand'	
Japanese	te	'hand'	
Eskimo-Aleut	tik(-eq) (Esk.)	'index finger'	
	tik(-laq) (Al.)	'middle finger'	
Sino-Tibetan	*tik	'one'	Benedict (1976)
Yeniseian	*tok	'finger'	Bengtson (1986)
Miao-Yao	*ntoʔ	'finger'	Benedict (1975)
Austroasiatic	*tiʔ	'hand, arm'	Benedict (1975)
Austro-Tai	*diaŋ	'finger, point'	Benedict (1975)
Indo-Pacific	tong~tang~teng	'finger, hand, arm'	Greenberg (1971)
Na-Dene	t'ek~tikhi~łaq, (ka-)tleek~	'one'	
	tłʔeq~(ka-)tliki	'finger'	
Amerind	tik	'finger'	Greenberg (1987)

[a]Where no source is cited I have found the forms myself in various standard dictionaries.

guages run the risk of being branded Creationists and of therefore having their work disregarded by colleagues. Although these questions have been considered by many to be beyond the pale of scientific investigation, there are indications that this stone wall of opposition is beginning to crumble, and future consolidation of some of the groups in List 7.3 is likely.

Most scholars have in recent years assumed, without bothering to examine the evidence, that the stocks in List 7.3 must be so ancient that any trace of relationship would have long since disappeared, even if some (or all) of the groups did in fact derive from a common source. Greenberg, however, reported in a public lecture in 1976 that he had noticed a number of roots common to several of these groups. One example he cited was the root *tik* with the meaning 'finger' or 'one.' Table 7.1 illustrates some possible members of this cognate set. Bengtson (1986) proposes 45 such global etymologies.

7.4 THE ORIGIN AND EVOLUTION OF LANGUAGE

Few questions in the study of human language have attracted as much attention, provoked as much controversy, or resisted so resolutely their answers as that of the origin of language. As we saw in sections 2.1 and 2.2, this question was much debated during the eighteenth century, when Hebrew was generally considered mankind's original tongue. The development of comparative linguistics in the nineteenth century (see section 2.3) shifted attention from the origin of language to the origin of the European languages, a more tractable problem. Speculation on the origin of language continued, of course, throughout the nineteenth century, but the topic fell out of fashion with scholars, and the Linguistic Society of Paris, weary of the idle speculation, banned its discussion in 1866. In general the question of the origin of language remained out of favor through the 1960's as scholars shifted their attention from language change to language structure, that is, from a basically historical perspective to a static one.

The past decade, however, has witnessed a resurgence in interest in this once-banned topic (see Hewes 1973, Lieberman 1975, 1984, Sagan 1977, Lyons 1977, Bickerton 1981, Leakey 1981, Itzkoff 1983). In 1975 the New York Academy of Sciences held a conference on the Origins and Evolution of Language and Speech (see Harnad, Steklis, & Lancaster 1976), at which some 70 papers were delivered on subjects as diverse as the linguistic competence of apes, language and the neurobiology of the human brain, the relationship between language and other cognitive systems, paleoneurological evidence for language origins, child language acquisition and language origins, and sign language and the gestural theory of language origins.*

Yet despite the remarkable advances in our understanding of biology, genetics, paleontology, linguistics, the human brain, and semiotic systems that have been made during the past century, there was a total lack of consensus among the 1975 conference's participants on almost every question related to the origin of language. This suggests that we are not perceptibly closer to a solution to the enigma than were scholars of the nineteenth century. On the basic questions of when, how, and why human language developed, there was much interesting speculation, with a number of "plausible scenarios" suggested, but there was virtually no convincing evidence produced to show that one particular scenario was the historically correct one. So that we may better understand the difficulty of the problem, let us briefly review some of the lines of research found in recent studies on the origin of language.

7.4.1 *Human Relatives*

As soon as it was realized that man is part of the animal kingdom, and in particular phylogenetically closest to the Old World apes, attempts were made to study the communicative systems and the physiology of apes and

*One topic that was curiously overlooked at the conference was any attempt to assess what had become known in the last century about both the diversity and the uniformity of the world's languages. Although ape language was discussed at length and in great detail, the world's extant human languages were accorded very little attention.

monkeys to determine, first, why it was that monkeys and apes do not talk, and, second, what kind of rudimentary communication system they might have from which human language could have gradually evolved. Though the early studies had revealed little more than a high degree of similarity in the vocal apparatus of man and ape, the topic was resurrected in the 1970's, when several psychologists attempted to teach apes human language. One attempt to teach normal spoken English to a chimpanzee was generally unsuccessful, but other attempts, using sign language and arbitrary tokens manipulated by computer, revealed that chimps could learn much more of language than had hitherto been believed. In this regard it is useful to make a distinction between language and speech. Language is a symbolic communicative system that represents meaning in terms of some arbitrary code. In all human languages (leaving aside sign language) the medium used to encode meaning is sound, and for this reason language and speech are often used synonymously. Chimps, for whatever reason, are not very adept at using the sounds of human language, but they are much more gifted in using sign language. Although no one claims that chimps can approach human competence in the use of sign language, they can apparently learn a good deal of it and even use it creatively, an attribute that many believe is restricted to man. (Interestingly, chimps also seem to have a concept of self, shown by their ability to recognize themselves in mirrors. Monkeys and lower primates lack this ability.)

There is still great controversy over the meaning of these recent studies. Some linguists, such as Noam Chomsky and his followers, generally maintain that human language is unrelated to the chimp's cognitive capabilities. Ronald Myers (1976: 755) expresses this viewpoint when he writes that "the speech of man has evolved not from the vocal responses of lower primates, but rather speech has developed *de novo* in man during his evolutionary development beyond the level of monkeys or, indeed, apparently, of the apes." Many others, however, believe it would be premature to dismiss this possibility, given our present rudimentary knowledge of the questions involved. According to Pribram (1976: 798), "The facts supporting biological evolution make it unlikely that human language has sprung *de novo* with no relationship to subhuman primate forms of communication."

7.4.2 *Human Ancestors*

If human relatives were poorly known in the nineteenth century, human ancestors were scarcely known at all. The discovery of man's closest ancestors in the fossil record has been largely a twentieth-century development. Though human paleontology is by its very nature incomplete, great advances have been made, particularly in recent decades. The sketch that I present below is based largely on Eldredge and Tattersall (1982) and Pilbeam (1984), whose views are widely if not universally accepted. The purpose of the following discussion of paleontology is to place the study of the origin and evolution of language in its proper biological context; it is not to defend any particular detail in the controversial area of human evolution.

The three great apes are thought to have branched off from the evolutionary line leading to *Homo sapiens* in the following order: (1) orangutan (16 million years before present [B.P.]), (2) gorilla (10 million B.P.), and (3) chimpanzee (7 million B.P.). The fossil record of man's ancestors from the period 8 million to 4 million B.P. remains a gap in our knowledge. When traces of mankind's ancestors reappear, in eastern Africa, around 4 million B.P., they are in the form of a creature who has been named *Australopithecus afarensis*. Small in stature (3′ to 4½′ in height and weighing 50–100 lbs.) and small in brain size (450 cc), this ancestor shared one important trait with modern humans. Unlike apes and monkeys, it walked erect on two feet. So far as we know, it had no tools and did not use fire.

This trait of bipedality defines a family containing man and "man-like" creatures, known collectively as hominids. The hominids in turn are usually divided into two genera, *Australopithecus* and *Homo*. The earliest known form of *Australopithecus* (*A. afarensis*) is attested from roughly 4–3 million B.P. About 3 million B.P. a different variety of *Australopithecus* (*A. africanus*) replaced *A. afarensis*. *A. africanus* is represented in the fossil record from roughly 3–2 million B.P. and then apparently split into *A. robustus* (which became extinct around 1½ million years ago) and *Homo habilis*, which leads to modern man. Like the various australopithecine fossils, remains of *H. habilis* are so far known only from Africa. Descendants of *H. habilis*, *H. erectus*, are the only known human ancestors from the period 1.5–0.5 million B.P., and they are the first hominids found outside Africa. They were also our first ancestors to use fire and, with *H. habilis*, the first to use tools that have left a trace in the archaeological record. *H. erectus* is attested in Asia and Africa from roughly 1.6 million B.P. to 300,000 B.P.

Between 400,000 and 300,000 years ago *H. erectus* disappeared and our own species, *H. sapiens*, appeared on the earth for the first time. An early type of *H. sapiens* is attested from 300,000 B.P. to 40,000 B.P. in Africa, Europe, and Asia, and is usually referred to as "archaic" *H. sapiens* to distinguish it from the type presently found on the earth (i.e. *H. sapiens sapiens*). One form of archaic *H. sapiens*, *H. sapiens neanderthalensis*, flourished in Europe and the Near East between 160,000 B.P. and 35,000 B.P., and then suddenly was replaced by *H. sapiens sapiens* everywhere, beginning around 40,000 years ago. After 40,000 B.P., migrations carried mankind's ancestors to northern Eurasia, Australia, the Pacific Islands, and the New World.

During the evolution from *Australopithecus* to *Homo sapiens sapiens*, there were a number of significant developments in both the biological and the cultural realm. Size in general, and brain size in relation to body weight in particular, steadily increased, with most modern humans standing between 4½ and 6½ feet tall and weighing between 100 and 200 lbs. From at least the time of *H. habilis*, our ancestors used stone tools, at first primitive and then, with *H. erectus* and *H. sapiens*, progressively more complex and more varied. Big-game hunting was practiced by *H. erectus*, and ritual burial is attested from more than 100,000 years ago. Some kind of cultural and/or biological transition appears to have taken place between 40,000 and 30,000 years ago. "Neanderthals" suddenly disappeared, and *H. sapiens sapiens* just as suddenly spread over the entire earth. More advanced kinds of tools, art, and other artifacts are attested for the first time. Less than 12,000 years ago agriculture was first practiced, in the Near East, and the transition from a nomadic hunterer-gatherer way of life to a sedentary agricultural society began. Finally, between 6,000 B.P. and 5,000 B.P., writing was invented and history proper begins.

Having thus briefly sketched the human ancestry, let us turn to the question of what, if anything, we can say about the linguistic capabilities of these various creatures. The linguistic ability of modern man (*H. sapiens sapiens*) is well known, if not well understood, but since language leaves no fossil evidence, it would seem at first blush impossible to say anything at all about the speech (or lack thereof) of our extinct ancestors. But several attempts have nevertheless been made in recent years. Lieberman (1975) proposed that Neanderthal man, though a member of our species, had linguistic abilities that differed significantly from our own. On the basis of a reconstruction, using fossil evidence, of the vocal tract, Lieberman has argued that Neanderthals would have been incapable of producing (1) vowels such as [i], [u], and [a], (2) velar consonants (e.g. *k*, *g*, *ŋ*), or (3) a nasal-nonnasal distinction (i.e. the difference between *m* and *b*, or *n* and *d*). All three of these traits are characteristic of virtually every human language, as a perusal of the data in Volume 2 clearly shows. If Neanderthals really had such limitations, their speech would have been nothing like any extant human language. The validity of Lieberman's reconstruction (made in collaboration with his co-worker Edmund S. Crelin) was called into question at the 1975 conference by E. Lloyd Du Brul (1976: 640), who claimed that such beings would not have been able to open their mouths, much less talk, and by Dean Falk (1976: 725), who argued that Lieberman's Neanderthals would not have been able to swallow either. Lieberman also claimed in 1975 that Neanderthal language possessed a syntax with a "transformational component," apparently reflecting his infatuation at that time with the transformational model. His most recent and most comprehensive treatment of the origin of language (Lieberman 1984) specifically rejects some of his earlier positions; and if it does not offer us any definitive answers, it provides an excellent summary of what is known and points squarely in the proper direction—toward biology.

Another putative method of investigating the linguistic capabilities of human ancestors has been the examination of fossil endocasts, that is, fossils representing the inside of a skull, where the brain once was. Some scholars have claimed to be able to discern "Broca's area" or "Wernicke's area" (see section 7.4.3) in endocasts from australopithecines, but most paleobiologists consider such claims nothing more than legerdemain. According to Ralph L. Holloway (1976: 330), "There is no good paleoneurological evidence as yet from the fossil hominid record that either proves or disproves when this or that hominid acquired the capacity for language."

The nature of the linguistic evolution that led to human language has several interpretations. On the one hand are those who maintain a strict Darwinian position of slow, gradual, progressive, and constant change over long periods of time. Others, however, believe that evolution, biological and linguistic, usually proceeds by swift and sharp transitions between stages, though any stage may persist with great stability over long periods of time. Contrary to Darwin's expectations, the fossil record simply does not support his conception of slow gradual change. A number of linguists have proposed that language also evolved by fits and starts, rather than by slow steady progression. The idea is often expressed that there were certain critical "thresholds" that led from one stage to another, though what those thresholds were, and when (and how often) they took place remain matters of conjecture.

One hypothesis is that when the computing power of the brain passed some critical level, it became a qualitatively different instrument. Another proposal is that the original symbiosis of sound and meaning, the definitional quality of a word, led to an explosive growth in vocabulary. Indirect support for such a view has been cited from child language acquisition, from language learning by apes, and from Helen Keller's experience in learning language, in all of which a rapid explosive growth in vocabulary has been observed. Though there is no direct evidence, it seems likely that a similar phenomenon occurred at some point in the development of human language. A third proposal, found in Bickerton (1981), is that the crucial step in the "hominization" of mankind was the transition from monopropositional sentences to multipropositional sentences. Although the idea of certain thresholds separating qualitatively different stages is appealing, there is really no direct evidence at present for any specific stage. As far as dates are concerned, the period 70,000–30,000 (or 40,000–30,000) years ago is frequently cited as a time of rapid development, but what those developments might have been we can only speculate.

This brings us to a final question. Do all of the world's roughly 5,000 languages represent the same stage of development, or have some reached a higher level than others? As we saw in section 2.3, nineteenth-century linguists considered the inflectional stage of European languages more advanced than the agglutinating stage (e.g. Turkish), which was in turn more advanced than the primitive isolating stage (e.g. Chinese). Modern linguists generally consider all languages to be equal, or at least at the same stage of development. Wang (1976) proposes that language evolved from an "emergent state," during which language as we know it developed, into a "steady state," where the basic linguistic structures are simply shifting around, rather than evolving further to a higher stage. Bickerton (1981: 299), however, claims that "the belief that all existing languages are at the same level of development [has] no empirical foundation," and I must agree with him on this point. Both the nineteenth-century racism that arranged languages in an order running from primitive to advanced and the contemporary egalitarian view represent the prevailing ideologies of the different centuries more than anything else. It is not at all clear how we would recognize a language that was a stage ahead of (or behind) others. There can be no question that language developed through an emergent state, but whether that emergent state is over and a steady state has been achieved has yet to be demonstrated. Possibly the generally perceived steady state is rather the reflection of a long stable period of linguistic development, perhaps from a single origin, rather than the cessation of the emergent stage.

7.4.3 *The Human Brain*

During the nineteenth century it was first noticed that people whose brains had been damaged in certain areas, as the result of accidents, exhibited a corresponding impairment in language. Lesions to Broca's area affected the production of sounds, whereas lesions to Wernicke's area tended to affect the perception of sounds. Different forms of aphasia are associated with each area. Unfortunately, many aspects of language (e.g. the lexicon) defy any neat localization in the brain, and even the location of Wernicke's area can be specified only probabilistically. Oscar Marin (1976: 902) concludes that "it would seem premature, at this stage, to try to plug linguistic theory into the brain."

It has long been known that the human brain is lateralized, that is, the left and right hemispheres serve different functions. In most normal adults language is controlled by the dominant (left) hemisphere, where both Broca's area and Wernicke's area are usually located. Furthermore, human language appears to be controlled primarily by the brain's neocortex, whereas the communicative abilities of lower animals seem to be controlled by the limbic system. The neocortex is a much later evolutionary development than the limbic system, though it is by no means restricted to man.

Several scholars have attempted to use our meager understanding of the brain to approach the problem of language origins. Claims that Broca's area can be discerned in australopithecine endocasts is one example, though in all likelihood a purely fanciful one. Others have attempted to correlate brain weight (especially in relationship to body weight) with the evolution of language, but it is now generally thought that brain structure is more important than brain size alone.

Brain lateralization has also been adduced as a potential clue to the origin of language. The fact that both "handedness" and human language are intimately tied up with lateralization has been interpreted by some as support for the "gestural" origin of language. The vast majority of people are right-handed, and it is the left hemisphere that controls the right hand, just as it is the left hemisphere that controls language (in most people). Furthermore, brain lateralization apparently also existed in *Homo erectus* over a half million years ago, as indicated by the stone tools associated with the Chinese variety of *H. erectus*, which display right-handed chipping. Since it now appears that chimpanzees (but not monkeys) also exhibit some degree of lateralization, this trait may be a necessary criterion for human speech, but not a sufficient one.

According to Marin, Saffran, and Schwartz (1976: 868–69), "The human brain is a vastly complex instrument; its operating principles with respect to language, and indeed, to behavior in general are practically unknown." As long as this remains the case it is unlikely that a study of the brain will be able to shed much light on the origin of language.

7.4.4 *Child Language Acquisition*

The German biologist Ernst Haeckel noted in the nineteenth century that "ontogeny recapitulates phylogeny," that is, the development of an individual reflects, imperfectly and incompletely perhaps, the evolutionary development of the species to which the individual belongs. Lamendella (1976) explored the possibility that the development of language in the child, which has received considerable attention since the 1960's, may well parallel in some measure the evolution of language in the human species. Bickerton (1981) pursues the same line of reasoning. Since we now have at least some understanding of the different stages in child language development, we may speculate that these stages of development also reflect to some degree the linguistic history of our species. Lamendella's hypothesis is in my opinion highly plausible, but there is really no solid evidence to support it at the moment.

Despite the enormous advances in our understanding of the human species made during the past century, all this new information sheds very little direct light on the origin and evolution of language. Though we may have more informed speculation than scholars of earlier times, we have no hard answers to the fundamental questions. We do not know when language developed, or even whether the time span involved should be measured in tens of thousands or in millions of years. Nor do we know how it developed, whether gradually and constantly over a long period of time, or episodically with sharp transitions from stage to stage. Finally, *why* it developed when it did (whenever that was) is perhaps the biggest enigma of all. Arguments that it was developed when it was needed for some specific purpose (e.g. big-game hunting, toolmaking, societal organization) strike me as quite implausible. Language is an all-purpose tool; it is not a can opener. It is, as Alfred Russel Wallace suggested in 1869, "an instrument . . . developed in advance of the needs of its possessor" (quoted in Wang 1976: 62). More likely the evolution of language is to be interpreted as an extension of the general cognitive abilities of our ancestors, the adventitious coupling of sound and meaning. The "vocal tract," it should not be forgotten, is an assemblage of organs that evolved with, and still serve, other functions (e.g. breathing, eating). Their use in language is clearly secondary. Similarly, we must assume considerable cognitive preadaptation, for language consists of more than sounds.

At the 1975 conference on language origins, Ralph Holloway (1976: 330) aptly summarized the current state of our knowledge, when, after first lamenting that perhaps the French were right in banning any discussion of the origin of language, he wrote that "for me, at least, the very fact that this Conference has been organized, and that human animals are ready to engage in a great 'garrulity' over the merits and demerits of essentially unprovable hypotheses, is an exciting testimony to the gap between human and other animals."

GENERAL

Benedict, Paul K. 1975. *Austro-Thai: Language and Culture*. New Haven, Conn.
———. 1976. "Sino-Tibetan: Another Look," *Journal of the American Oriental Society* 96: 167–97.
Collinder, Björn. 1977. *Fenno-Ugric Vocabulary*. Hamburg.
Dyen, Isidore. 1959. Review of *Essays in Linguistics*, by Joseph H. Greenberg, *Language* 35: 527–52.
Gamkrelidze, Thomas. 1984. Personal letter.
Greenberg, Joseph H. 1963. *The Languages of Africa*. Bloomington, Ind.
———. 1971. "The Indo-Pacific Hypothesis," in *CTIL* 8.
———. 1976. Public lecture at Stanford University.

———. 1987. *Language in the Americas*. Stanford, Calif.
Grosjean, François. 1982. *Life with Two Languages*. Cambridge, Mass.
Lamb, Sydney M. 1964. "The Classification of the Uto-Aztecan Languages: A Historical Survey," in *UCPL* 34.
Welmers, William E. 1973. *African Linguistic Structures*. Berkeley, Calif.

THE ORIGIN OF LANGUAGE

Bickerton, Derek. 1981. *Roots of Language*. Ann Arbor, Mich.
Clark, W. E. LeGros. 1978. *The Fossil Evidence for Human Evolution*. Chicago.
Du Brul, E. Lloyd. 1976. "Biomechanics of Speech Sounds," in Harnad et al., cited below.
Eldredge, Niles, and Ian Tattersall. 1982. *The Myths of Human Evolution*. New York.
Falk, Dean. 1976. "Comment," in Harnad et al., cited below.
de Grolier, Eric, ed. 1983. *Glossogenetics: The Origin and Evolution of Language*. New York.
Harnad, Stevan R., Horst D. Steklis, and Jane Lancaster, eds. 1976. *Origins and Evolution of Language and Speech*. New York.
Hewes, G. W. 1973. "Primate Communication and the Gestural Origin of Language," *Current Anthropology* 14: 5–32.
Holloway, Ralph L. 1976. "Paleoneurological Evidence for Language Origins," in Harnad et al., cited above.
Itzkoff, Seymour W. 1983. *The Form of Man*. Ashfield, Mass.
Lamendella, John T. 1976. "Relations Between the Ontogeny and Phylogeny of Language: A Neo-Recapitulationist View," in Harnad et al., cited above.
Leakey, Richard E. 1981. *The Making of Mankind*. New York.
Lieberman, Philip. 1975. *On the Origins of Language*. New York.
———. 1984. *The Biology and Evolution of Language*. Cambridge, Mass.
Lyons, John. 1977. "The Origin of Language," in Lyons, *Semantics* 1. Cambridge, Eng.
Marin, Oscar S. M. 1976. "Neurobiology of Language: An Overview," in Harnad et al., cited above.
Marin, Oscar S. M., Eleanor M. Saffran, and Myrna F. Schwartz. 1976. "Dissociations of Language in Aphasia: Implications for Normal Function," in Harnad et al., cited above.
Myers, Ronald E. 1976. "Comparative Neurology of Vocalization and Speech: Proof of a Dichotomy," in Harnad et al., cited above.
Pilbeam, David. 1984. "The Descent of Hominoids and Hominids," *Scientific American* 250,3: 84–96.
Pribram, Karl H. 1976. "Language in a Sociobiological Frame," in Harnad et al., cited above.
Rensberger, Boyce. 1984. "Bones of Our Ancestors," *Science 84* 5,3: 28–39.
Sagan, Carl. 1977. *The Dragons of Eden*. New York.
Wang, William S.-Y. 1976. "Language Change," in Harnad et al., cited above.

GENETIC LINKS BETWEEN FAMILIES

The articles and books in the following bibliography discuss alleged connections between families usually assumed to be unrelated. The families or languages in question follow each source in brackets.

Andronov, M. S. 1961. "New Evidence of Possible Linguistic Ties Between the Deccan and the Urals," in *Dr. R. P. Sethu Pillai Silver Jubilee Commemoration Volume*. Madras. [Dravidian, Uralic]

———. 1968. "Dravidian and Uralian: A Peep into the Pre-History of Language Families," in M. Andronov, *Two Lectures on the Historicity of Language Families*. Annamalainagar. [Dravidian, Uralic]

Bender, M. Lionel. 1981. "Some Nilo-Saharan Isoglosses," in *NS*. [Niger-Kordofanian, Nilo-Saharan]

Bengtson, John D. 1986. "Toward Global Sound Correspondences," unpublished manuscript.

Bergsland, Knut. 1956. "The Uralic 'Half-Eye' in the Light of Eskimo-Aleut," *Ural-Altaische Jahrbücher* 28: 165–72. [Uralic, Eskimo-Aleut]

———. 1959. "The Eskimo-Uralic Hypothesis," *Journal de la Société Finno-Ougrienne* 61: 1–29. [Eskimo-Aleut, Uralic]

Birnbaum, Henrik. 1978. *Linguistic Reconstruction: Its Potentials and Limitations in New Perspective*. Washington, D.C. [Nostratic: Afro-Asiatic, Kartvelian, Indo-European, Uralic, Dravidian, Altaic]

Bomhard, Allan R. 1977. "The Indo-European-Semitic Hypothesis Re-examined," *Journal of Indo-European Studies* 5: 55–99. [Indo-European, Semitic]

———. 1984. *Toward Proto-Nostratic*. Amsterdam. [Indo-European, Afro-Asiatic]

Bonnerjea, Rene. 1971. "Is There Any Relationship Between Eskimo-Aleut and Ural-Altaic?" *Acta Linguistica Acad. Scient. Hungaricae* 21: 401–7. [Eskimo-Aleut, Ural-Altaic]

———. 1975–79. "Some Probable Phonological Connections Between Ural-Altaic and Eskimo-Aleut," *Orbis*, 2 parts, 24 (1975): 251–75, 28 (1979): 27–44. [Ural-Altaic, Eskimo-Aleut]

———. 1978. "A Comparison Between Eskimo-Aleut and Ural-Altaic Demonstrative Elements, Numerals, and Other Related Semantic Problems," *IJAL* 44: 40–55. [Eskimo-Aleut, Ural-Altaic]

Bouda, Karl. 1956. "Dravidisch und Uralaltaisch," *Lingua* 5: 129–44. [Dravidian, Uralic, Altaic]

———. 1960–64. "Tungusisch und Ketschua," *Zeitschrift der Deutschen Morgenländischen Gesellschaft*, 2 parts, 110 (1960): 99-113, 113 (1964): 602–23. [Tungus, Quechua]

———. 1980. "Tschuktschisch und Uralisch II," *Zeitschrift der Deutschen Morgenländischen Gesellschaft* 130: 393–96. [Chukchi, Uralic]

Boyd, Raymond. 1978. "À propos des ressemblances lexicales entre langues niger-congo et nilo-sahariennes," in *Études comparatives*. Paris. [Niger-Congo, Nilo-Saharan]

Burrow, T. 1946. "Dravidian Studies, IV: The Body in Dravidian and Uralian," *Bulletin of the School of Oriental and African Studies* 11: 328–56. [Dravidian, Uralic]

Campbell, John. 1898. "The Denes of America Identified with the Tungus of Asia," *Transactions of the Canadian Institute* 5: 167–223. [Na-Dene, Tungus]

Collinder, Björn. 1934. *Indo-Uralisches Sprachgut*. Uppsala. [Indo-European, Uralic]

———. 1952. "Ural-Altaisch," *Ural-Altaische Jahrbücher* 24: 1–26. [Uralic, Altaic]

———. 1965. *An Introduction to the Uralic Languages*. Berkeley, Calif. [Eurasian: Indo-European, Yukaghir-Uralic, Altaic, Chukchi, Eskimo-Aleut]

Conrady, August. 1916. "Eine merkwurdige Beziehung zwischen den austrischen und indochinesischen Sprachen," in *Kuhn Festschrift*. Munich. [Sino-Tibetan, Austric]

Cop, Bojan. 1974. *Indouralica*. Ljubljana. [Indo-European, Uralic, Altaic]

Cuny, A. 1943. *Recherches sur le vocalisme, le consonantisme et la formation des racines en 'nostratique.'* Paris. [Nostratic]

Décsy, Gyula, ed. 1983. *Global Linguistic Connections*. Bloomington, Ind.

Dolgopol'skij, A. B. 1970. "Gipoteza drevnejshego rodstva jazykov severnoj evrazii," *Proceedings of the Seventh International Congress of Anthropological and Ethnological Sciences (Moscow)* 5: 620–28. [Indo-European, Uralic, Altaic, Kartvelian, Afro-Asiatic]

Elderkin, E. D. 1982. "On the Classification of Hadza," *Sprache und Geschichte in Afrika* 4: 67–82. [Khoisan (Hadza), Afro-Asiatic (Omotic, Chadic), Nilo-Saharan (Kuliak)]

Greenberg, Joseph H. 1987. *Language in the Americas*. Stanford, Calif. [Eurasiatic: Indo-Hittite, Uralic, Yukaghir, Altaic, Korean, Japanese, Ainu, Gilyak, Chukchi-Kamchatkan, Eskimo-Aleut]

Gregersen, Edgar A. 1972. "Kongo-Saharan," *Journal of African Languages* 11: 69–89. [Niger-Kordofanian, Nilo-Saharan]

Haas, Mary R. 1941. "Athabascan, Tlingit, Yuchi and Siouan," *International Congress of Americanists, Proceedings* 25,2: 495–500. [Na-Dene, Yuchi, Siouan]

Hammerich, L. L. 1951. "Can Eskimo Be Related to Indo-European?" *IJAL* 17: 217–23. [Indo-European, Eskimo]

Hamp, Eric P. 1969. "On the Problem of Ainu and Indo-European," in *Eighth Congress of Anthropological and Ethnological Sciences*. Tokyo, 100–102. [Indo-European, Ainu]

Homburger, L. 1941. *Les langues negro-africaines*. Paris. [Niger-Kordofanian, Nilo-Saharan]

———. 1955. "L'Inde et l'Afrique," *Journal de la Société des Africanistes* 25: 13–18. [Dravidian, Semitic]

Hulbert, H. B. 1905. *A Comparative Grammar of the Korean Language and the Dravidian Dialects in India*. Seoul. [Korean, Dravidian]

Illich-Svitych, V. M. 1971–84. *Opyt sravnenija nostraticheskix jazykov*, 3 vols. Moscow. [Indo-European, Kartvelian, Afro-Asiatic, Uralic, Altaic, Dravidian]

Jakobson, Roman. 1942. "The Paleosiberian Languages," *AA* 44: 602–20. [Gilyak, Aleut]

Jenness, Diamond. 1953. "Did the Yahgan Indians of Tierra del Fuego Speak an Eskimo Tongue?" *IJAL* 19: 128–31. [Eskimo, Yamana]

Jensen, H. 1936. "Indogermanisch und Koreanisch," *Germanen und Indogermanen* (Heidelberg) 2. [Indo-European, Korean]

Key, Mary Ritchie. 1984. *Polynesian and American Linguistic Connections*. Lake Bluff, Ill. [Polynesian, Amerind]

Koppelmann, D. H. 1928. *Die Verwandtschaft des Koreanischen und der Ainu-Sprache mit den indogermanischen Sprachen*. Vienna. [Indo-European, Ainu, Korean]

———. 1933. *Die eurasische Sprachfamilie—Indogermanisch, Koreanisch und Verwandtes*. Heidelberg. [Indo-European, Korean, Altaic, Gilyak, Uralic, Ainu, Sumerian]

Lahovary, N. 1957. *La diffusion des langues anciennes du Proche-Orient: leurs relations avec le basque, le dravidien et les parlers indo-européens primitifs*. Berne. Translated in 1963 as *Dravidian Origins and the West*. Bombay. [Basque, Indo-European, Dravidian]

Levin, Saul. 1971. *The Indo-European and Semitic Languages*. Albany, N.Y. [Indo-European, Semitic]

Li, Fang-kuei. 1976. "Sino-Tai," in *GR*. [Sino-Tibetan, Tai]

Lindquist, I. L. 1960. *Indo-European Features in the Ainu Language*. Lund. [Indo-European, Ainu]
Manomaivibool, Prapin. 1976. "Thai and Chinese—Are They Genetically Related?" *CAAL* 6: 11–31. [Tai, Chinese]
Matisoff, James A. 1976. "Austro-Thai and Sino-Tibetan: An Examination of Body-Part Contact Relationships," in *GR*. [Austro-Tai, Sino-Tibetan]
Matsumoto, Nobuhiro. 1928. *Le japonais et les langues austroasiatiques*. Paris. [Japanese, Austroasiatic]
Menges, K. H. 1964. "Altajisch und Dravidisch," *Orbis* 13: 66–103. [Altaic, Dravidian]
———. 1977. "Dravidian and Altaic," *Anthropos* 72: 129–79. [Eastern Nostratic: Dravidian, Altaic, Uralic; Western Nostratic: Indo-European, Kartvelian, Afro-Asiatic]
Menovshchikov, G. A. 1974. "Eskimossko-aleutskie jazyki i ix otnoshenie k drugim jazykovym semjam," *Voprosy Jazykoznanija*, 46–59. [Eskimo-Aleut, Chukchi-Kamchatkan, Uralic, Altaic, Indo-European]
Möller, Hermann. 1911. *Vergleichendes indogermanisch-semitisches Wörterbuch*. Güttingen. [Indo-European, Semitic]
Morice, A. G. 1914. "Northwestern Denes and Northeastern Asiatics," *Transactions of the Canadian Institute* 10: 131–93. [Na-Dene, Chukchi-Kamchatkan, Uralic]
Naert, P. N. 1958. *La situation linguistique de l'ainou, 1: Ainou et indoeuropéen*. Lund. [Indo-European, Ainu]
Nishida, T. 1960. "Common Thai and Archaic Chinese," *Transactions of the Kansai University Institute of Oriental and Occidental Studies* 49: 1–15. [Chinese, Tai]
Pedersen, Holger. 1931. *Linguistic Science in the Nineteenth Century*. Cambridge, Mass. [Nostratic: Semitic, Indo-European, Uralic, Yukaghir, Altaic, Eskimo-Aleut]
Sapir, Edward. 1925. "The Similarity of Chinese and Indian Languages," *Science* 62,*1607*: xii. [Athabascan, Chinese]
Sauvageot, Aurélien. 1930. *Recherches sur le vocabulaire des langues ouralo-altaïques*. Paris. [Uralic, Altaic]
Schuchardt, H. 1912. "Nubisch und Baskisch," *Revue Internationale des Études Basques* 282. [Nubian, Basque]
———. 1913. "Baskisch und Hamitisch," *Revue Internationale des Études Basques* 289. [Basque, Afro-Asiatic]
Schuhmacher, W. W. 1974. "B-C? (A = Indoeuropean, B = Austronesian, C = Eskimo)," *Anthropos* 69: 625–27. [Indo-European, Austronesian, Eskimo]
Shafer, Robert. 1952. "Athabascan and Sino-Tibetan," *IJAL* 18: 12–19. [Athabascan, Sino-Tibetan]
———. 1957. "Note on Athabascan and Sino-Tibetan," *IJAL* 23: 116–17. [Athabascan, Sino-Tibetan]
———. 1963. "Eurasial," *Orbis* 12: 19–44. [Indo-European, Sino-Tibetan]
———. 1965. "The Eurasial Linguistic Superfamily," *Anthropos* 60: 445–68. [Indo-European, Sino-Tibetan]
Shimkin, Dmitri B. 1960. Review of *Aleut Dialects of Atka and Attu*, by Knut Bergsland, *AA* 62: 729–30. [Aleut, Chukchi-Kamchatkan]
Shirokogoroff, S. M. 1931. *Ethnological and Linguistic Aspects of the Ural-Altaic Hypothesis*. Peking. [Uralic, Altaic]
Sinor, D. 1944a. "D'un morphème particulièrement répandu dans les langues ouralo-altaïques," *T'oung Pao* 37: 135–52. [Uralic, Altaic]

———. 1944b. "Indo-européen et ouralo-altaïque," *T'oung Pao* 37: 226–44. [Indo-European, Uralic, Altaic]

Swadesh, Morris. 1952. Review of "Athapaskan and Sino-Tibetan" by Robert Shafer, *IJAL* 18: 178–81. [Athabascan, Sino-Tibetan]

———. 1960. "On Interhemisphere Linguistic Connections," in Stanley Diamond, ed., *Culture in History*. New York. [Amerind, Indo-European, Austronesian, Basque, Afro-Asiatic, Uralic, Eskimo-Aleut, Caucasian, Dravidian, Munda]

———. 1962. "Linguistic Relations Across Bering Strait," *AA* 64: 1262–91. [Eskimo-Aleut, Chukchi-Kamchatkan]

Thalbitzer, William. 1944. "Uhlenbeck's Eskimo-Indoeuropean Hypothesis," *Travaux du Cercle Linguistique de Copenhague* 1: 66–96. [Eskimo-Aleut, Indo-European]

Trombetti, Alfredo. 1902–3. "Della relazioni della lingue caucasische con le lingue camito-semitiche e con altri gruppi linguistici," *Giornale della Società Asiatica Italiana*, 2 parts, 15 (1902), 16 (1903). [Caucasian, Afro-Asiaitic]

———. 1927. "Le lingue dei papua e gl'idiomi dell'Africa," in *Festschrift Meinhof*. Hamburg. [Papuan, African]

Tyler, Stephen A. 1968. "Dravidian and Uralian: The Lexical Evidence," *Language* 44: 798–812. [Dravidian, Uralic]

Uesson, Ants-Michael. 1970. *On Linguistic Affinity: The Indo-Uralic Problem*. Malmö. [Indo-European, Uralic, Yukaghir, Altaic]

Uhlenbeck, C. C. 1942–45. "Ur- und altindogermanische Anklänge im Wortschatz des Eskimo," *Anthropos* 37–40: 133–48. [Indo-European, Eskimo]

Upadhyaya, U. P. 1976. "Dravidian and Negro-African," *International Journal of Dravidian Linguistics* 5: 32–64. [Dravidian, West Atlantic]

Windekens, A. J. Van. 1960. "Contacts linguistiques ainous-tokhariens," *Anthropos* 55: 753–64. [Tocharian, Ainu]

Wulff, Kurt. 1934. *Chinesisch und Tai*. Copenhagen. [Chinese, Tai]

Wurm, Stephen A. 1982. *Papuan Languages of Oceania*. Tübingen. [Indo-Pacific, Australian]

8

Genetic Classification of the World's Languages

This chapter offers a genetic classification of all the world's extant languages (and many of the extinct ones), as best it can be determined from available evidence. The opening section (8.1) discusses problems related to the naming of languages and groups. Section 8.2 presents the principles and conventions I have used in arranging the languages and groups in the classification itself (8.6). Section 8.3 offers an overview of the world's language phyla. Sections 8.4, a general index, and 8.5, a skeleton outline of the major genetic groups (with exemplary languages), provide successive approximations to the complete classification and are intended to help readers orient themselves in the overall classification, where it is easy to become lost. The number following each group in these two indexes indicates the page on which that group begins in the complete classification.

The reader will notice that the taxonomic ambiguities, disputes, and uncertainties emphasized in Chapters 2–6 do not figure in the final classification, which is presented as if all problems had been resolved. Readers who wish to know which portions of the classification are firmly established, and which controversial, should consult the corresponding sections in the text.

The sources used in compiling the classification have been listed at the ends of sections in Chapters 2–6 and in the section Specialists Consulted, but a brief word on how the classification arrived at its present state may be instructive. The original classification was put together in the mid-1970's and was based almost entirely on Voegelin and Voegelin (1977). In late 1979 I became aware that certain parts of the Voegelins' book (which reflected the state of linguistic taxonomy around 1970) had already been superseded by more recent publications, and I began to update the classification to take account of this work.

In 1981 I wrote to some 200 scholars, who I knew from their publications were interested in taxonomy (most linguists are not), and requested their advice on the portions of the classification in which they had expertise. More than 100 of them responded to my request, often with exquisitely long and detailed letters suggesting major revisions, at other times briefly on questions of detail. The vast majority of their suggestions were incorporated into the classification, which has been kept on computer since 1981 to facilitate its revision. At the same time I undertook a more thorough examination of the taxonomic literature and discovered a wealth of information on various groups that was also incorporated into the classification.

Yet the final classification does not always directly reflect the sources and the counsel of the experts, since for many, perhaps most, of the families (at whatever level), I had collected more than one classification. I had had a complete classification to start with (i.e. Voegelin & Voegelin 1977). Grimes (1978) provided another complete classification, though it was based partly on the Voegelins' book. In addition to these two complete classifications I collected many other classifications, of groups large and small, from the linguistic literature and from my own correspondence. So when it came time to decide what the classification of a group should be, I frequently had a half-dozen different classifications of that group. Where all, or most, agreed, there was no problem, but when they differed, as they often did on details and sometimes on major points, reconciliation was required. Although it might seem safest in such instances to choose one of the classifications and follow it faithfully, I quickly realized that this was not the best tactic, because each of the classifications had its own strengths and weaknesses. Limiting myself to one person's classification almost invariably entailed adopting parts of a classification that were clearly inferior to someone else's. I therefore attempted to incorporate into the classification, when there were conflicts between sources, what seemed to me to be the strengths of each classification, always taking into account such factors as who had produced a classification, how it had been produced, on what it was based, and when it was done. The reconciliation of conflicting classifications is a delicate task, at which I have, no doubt, not always been successful. But because classifications continually evolve, particularly when the languages are poorly known and little studied, the classification offered in section 8.6 should be considered provisional in many regards and not the final word. It is intended to stimulate further research, not to put an end to it.

8.1 NAMES

To most people, language names appear straightforward. The English speak English, the French French, and the Chinese Chinese. If Americans,

Canadians, Australians, and New Zealanders also speak English, they still call it English, and it is clearly the same language, with relatively slight dialectal variation. Yet this simple view of language names is really valid only for "famous languages," those languages everyone has at least heard of (e.g. English, Chinese, Japanese, Eskimo), and even here the names often conceal problems the layman is not aware of. For all but a few hundred of the world's roughly 5,000 languages, the names are known only to specialists, the people themselves, and their neighbors, all three of whom frequently have different names for the language in question. In addition, the naming problem is intimately tied up with the language/dialect problem discussed in section 1.2. In much of the world, then, language names do not correspond to neatly defined groups of mutually intelligible dialects. It is common, in fact, for mutually intelligible dialects to be regarded as different languages with distinct names, whether for national (e.g. Swedish, Danish, Norwegian), religious (e.g. Hindi, Urdu), or other political and cultural reasons (e.g. Czech, Slovak). It is equally common for a single language name to subsume a number of very divergent dialects, not all of which are mutually comprehensible (e.g. Romany, Saami [= Lapp], Nahuatl, Quechua). And in between these two extremes there is a multitude of cases where different varieties of speech are considered one language by some, two or more by others (e.g., the two major dialects of Albanian, Gheg and Tosk, which are sometimes accorded the status of distinct languages).

It thus often depends on nonlinguistic factors whether distinct varieties of speech are subsumed under one name or given separate names. In this regard linguistic taxonomy is no different from biological taxonomy, where the species/variety distinction shares many of the same problems as the language/dialect distinction. Dogs and wolves are considered separate species (*Canis familiaris* and *Canis lupus*, respectively) even though they may interbreed and produce viable offspring. On the other hand, some varieties of dogs (e.g. Chihuahuas and Great Danes) do not interbreed and yet are still assigned to the same species. To some extent the naming conventions in both biology and linguistics are a matter of convenience and are affected at the lowest levels of classification by nonbiological and nonlinguistic considerations.

In general, the names adopted in this volume reflect either those of the sources used in compiling the classification or those recommended to me by the scholars with whom I corresponded. In most cases I have not tried to iron out the taxonomic inconsistencies mentioned above; Swedish, Danish, and Norwegian are listed as three distinct languages, whereas Nahuatl is treated as one. The endpoints in the classification thus approximate distinct languages, but both overdifferentiation and underdifferentiation are present in some degree.

Table 8.1. Pejorative Language Names

Pejorative name (language group)	Preferred name	Pejorative name (language group)	Preferred name
Alacaluf (Andean)	Qawasqar	Hottentot (Khoisan)	Nama (or Khoe)
Auca (Andean)	Sabela	Igabo (Edo)	Isoko
Barya (East Sudanic)	Nera	Ingalik (Athabaskan)	None known
Batangan (Meso-Philippine)	Taubuid	Kafir (Indo-Iranian)	Nuristani
Beriberi (Saharan)	Kanuri	Lapp (Finno-Ugric)	Saami
Boni (Cushitic)	Aweer	Matakam (Chadic)	Mafa
Buzi (Mande)	Loma	Mikeyir (East Sudanic)	Shabo
Chama (Tacana)	Ese'ejja	Namshi (Adamawa)	Doyāyo
Dagada (Timor-Alor-Pantar)	Fataluku	Shosho (Plateau)	Birom
Galla (Cushitic)	Oromo	Tagabili (South Mindanao)	Tboli
		Yaghan (Andean)	Yamana
		Zumper (Jukunoid)	Kuteb

Not infrequently a language is known by more than one name (e.g. Irish and Gaelic, Persian and Farsi), and in such common cases I have had to make a choice, though both terms are found in the language index at the end of this volume. In most cases I have tried to adopt the most widely used term or the term preferred by the people who actually speak the language. Unfortunately, these two criteria are often in conflict, and there is a growing movement, which I have followed in many cases, to replace the older, better-established term with the name the people themselves use. In many such cases the older terms are still listed in the language index to this volume to facilitate finding the current equivalent. I have not, however, attempted to provide a complete list of all the language and dialect names and their variant spellings; for these the reader is referred to Voegelin and Voegelin (1977) and Grimes (1984a,b).

In a number of cases the most widely used name is felt by the people who speak the language to be pejorative, and in such cases I have replaced that name with a non-pejorative one. Table 8.1 shows the pejorative language names that have so far come to my attention—with their replacements.

When faced with the problem of selecting a language name for a group of mutually intelligible dialects, each with its own name, different linguists follow different strategies. One strategy is simply to list the separately named dialects as if they were distinct languages (e.g. Swedish, Danish, Norwegian). Another is to "invent" a name that subsumes the dialects in question (e.g. Scandinavian). A third is to use hyphenated names (e.g. Swedish-Danish-Norwegian). Finally, one may choose the name of one dialect (usually the dialect with the most speakers, the highest prestige, or the greatest intelligibility with other dialects) as the language name. I have pointed out that some cases of overdifferentiation (the first strategy) have been allowed to persist in the classification. In other cases it has seemed advisable to list dialects under a single name, and in such cases the last strategy has been preferred. I have avoided hyphenated names (the third strategy) almost entirely, because they are unwieldy and because they are likely to be confused with family names. Invented names (the second strategy) have been used sparingly, and none of the inventions are of my own making. This means that certain dialects, even a few that some people might consider separate languages, will not be found in the classification. Some of these dialect names are listed in the language index, with an indication of the language they are considered to belong to. For those not found in the language index, the reader is advised to consult Voegelin and Voegelin (1977) and Grimes (1984a,b), both of which may be used as indexes to this volume.

Names for language groups have somewhat different problems. In contrast to biology, where a group is named by its discoverer and everyone else is expected to respect that name, in linguistics different scholars often propose different names for the same group. Sometimes a name formerly used for a group becomes unsuitable and is replaced by another (e.g. since around 1950 Hamito-Semitic has been increasingly replaced by Afro-Asiatic; see sections 3.1 and 3.2). In other cases different family names imply different subgrouping hypotheses (e.g. Indo-Hittite vs. Indo-European; see section 2.3). Some presumed families are later found not to be valid genetic nodes, and their names disappear from the classification altogether (e.g. Chari-Nile and Kwa; see sections 3.3 and 3.4). Generally, I have tried to use the family names currently used by specialists; Indo-Hittite thus represents a deviation, for Indo-European is by far the more common term today. I have throughout preferred hyphenated family names to their unhyphenated variants (e.g. Indo-European, Afro-Asiatic vs. Indoeuropean, Afroasiatic; Austroasiatic, rather than Austro-Asiatic, is not an exception to this rule since "Austro-" here means "southern," and thus the meaning of the name is "Southern Asiatic").

8.2 TAXONOMIC CONVENTIONS

The reader who examines the complete classification in section 8.6 will notice that the phyla, families, and languages are sometimes arranged in an order different from that followed in Chapters 2–6. This is because I have adopted a didactic, and largely historical, perspective in the text, but the classification itself follows other principles. This section will explain exactly what those principles and conventions are.

Not only do linguists have different methodological biases in matters of taxonomy (e.g. lexicostatistics vs. traditional comparative approaches), they also have different methods of representing the genetic relationships schematically. Since the present work requires a uniform format for all the world's languages, I have devised one that is intended to maximize readability while expressing the genetic relationships as precisely as possible. All of the classifications collected from the literature, or sent me by colleagues, have been translated into this framework.

In simplest terms, the underlying principle in arranging the groups and languages in the classification is that phyla, stocks, families, and languages (i.e. all genetic units at whatever level) should be ordered so that each is preceded and followed in the classification by the phyla, stocks, families, or languages to which they are most closely related. There are cases where this principle cannot be applied with total consistency because a language or group appears to be equally closely related to more than two languages or groups. But the principle nonetheless has great heuristic value and is useful if its limitations are not overlooked.

Unfortunately, genetic relationships are not always expressed with total precision, and it is often unclear in the literature whether the ordering of the languages is significant or not—and if it is, what that significance is. Since the genetic relationships themselves are so frequently underspecified, I have followed a hierarchy of principles in compiling the classification, which I shall discuss in their order of precedence:

1. Where the information is sufficiently precise I have followed strict *genetic* principles. Languages and groups are listed in an order that puts them closest to the languages or groups to which they are most closely related.

2. In the absence of knowledge of the specific genetic relationships, I have often followed a *geographic* arrangement (e.g. north to south, or east to west). The ordering of the 17 phyla is roughly geographic, starting in Southern Africa (Khoisan) and proceeding around the world to the tip of South America (Amerind). Even at this level genetic considerations are not completely absent: the five constituents of Greenberg's Eurasiatic family (i.e. Indo-Hittite, Uralic-Yukaghir, Altaic, Chukchi-Kamchatkan, and Eskimo-Aleut) are listed consecutively, in anticipation of further consolidation among these groups.

3. In a good many instances I have simply followed the order of presentation in the *source*, without knowing its precise basis.

4. Where it does not violate any known genetic relationships I have tried to let *small groups precede large groups*. This increases readability, since it produces taxonomic structures that branch continuously to the right, making orientation easier within the classification, especially from page to page. In some cases genetic considerations preclude this, and in these rare instances the numbering next to each group (e.g. II, E, 6, d) should allow the reader to identify taxonomic units at the same level, even if they occur on different pages.

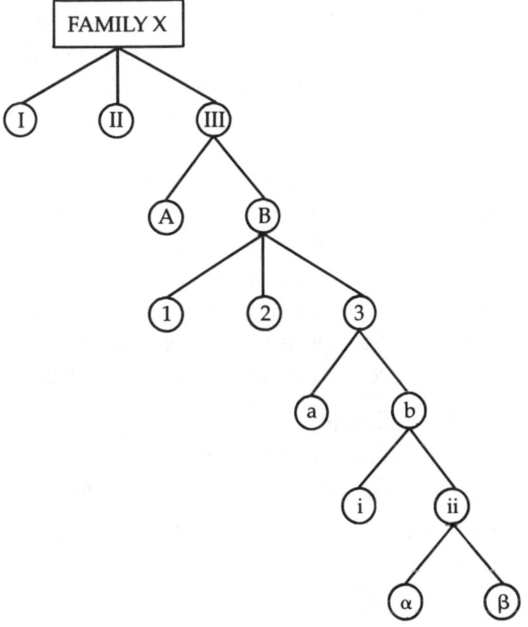

Fig. 8.1. Branching-tree diagram of family X

List 8.1. Representation of the Branching-Tree Diagram of Family X

FAMILY X:
- I PRIMARY BRANCH
- II PRIMARY BRANCH
- III PRIMARY BRANCH:
  - A GROUP
  - B GROUP:
    - 1 SUBGROUP
    - 2 SUBGROUP
    - 3 SUBGROUP:
      - a BRANCH
      - b BRANCH:
        - i SUBBRANCH
        - ii SUBBRANCH:
          - α GROUP
          - β GROUP

The formalism used to represent genetic trees is explained briefly in the introductory "Note on Notation." As stated there, the general principle is that branching trees such as that in Fig. 8.1 are given the representation shown in List 8.1. Each branch is preceded by a letter or number that identifies the taxonomic level of the group. The order in which these identifying tags are used is capital Roman numerals (I,II), capital letters (A,B), Arabic numerals (1,2), lower-case letters (a,b), small Roman numerals (i,ii), and lower-case Greek letters (α,β). If branching continues beyond six levels, the numbers and letters start over, beginning with capital Roman numerals.

The schema illustrated in List 8.1 is sometimes modified by the following abbreviatory convention. Individual languages that are coordinate with groups of languages (i.e. that are at the same hierarchical level) are listed first in the classification, preceded by their quantity. This simply means that

LAMOGAI [6]:
[3]: Longa, Idne, Mok
1 RAUTO [3]: Lamogai, Pulie, Rauto

is a shorter way of expressing:

LAMOGAI [6]:
1 LONGA [1]: Longa
2 IDNE [1]: Idne
3 MOK [1]: Mok
4 RAUTO [3]: Lamogai, Pulie, Rauto

Languages listed in this special initial position fall into three classes: (1) languages that are known to form an independent group within a higher-level family (e.g. Catawba within Siouan), (2) languages that do not seem to belong to any of the groups at a particular level, but whose independent position is perhaps due to a lack of information on the language in question rather than to its proven isolation from the other languages and groups (e.g. the 14 languages listed at the beginning of the Australian phylum), or (3) languages that are the parent of the group that follows (e.g. Latin and Romance). The third category is clearly distinct from the first two, and in fact is used sparingly. It is, however, often impossible to distinguish the first two categories in practice, even though they may be theoretically distinct. If an individual language "fits," taxonomically, between two groups of languages, the abbreviatory convention is not used, for its use would distort the correct genetic structure. This abbreviatory convention is also not used in certain cases where I wish to emphasize the known isolated nature of the language (e.g. Albanian and Armenian within Indo-European). In such cases the failure to use the convention is simply a stylistic variant and should be accorded no special importance.

8.3 OVERVIEW OF LANGUAGE PHYLA

Map 8.1 shows the general geographic distribution of the world's language families. Table 8.2 provides a synopsis of the world's language phyla, offering an indication of the number of languages in each group, the number of speakers in each group, the geographic location of the phyla, and the better-known languages within each group. Estimates of the number of speakers of languages and language groups are notoriously difficult to make with confidence in many cases. I have relied most heavily on Voegelin and Voegelin (1977), Grimes (1984a), and for Oceania, Wurm and Hattori (1981–83).

Grimes, Barbara F., ed. 1978. *Ethnologue,* 9th ed. Dallas.
———. 1984a. *Ethnologue,* 10th ed. Dallas.
———. 1984b. *Index*. Dallas.
Voegelin, C. F., and F. M. Voegelin. 1977. *Classification and Index of the World's Languages*. New York.
Wurm, Stephen A., and Shirô Hattori, eds. 1981–83. *Language Atlas of the Pacific Area,* 2 vols. Stuttgart.

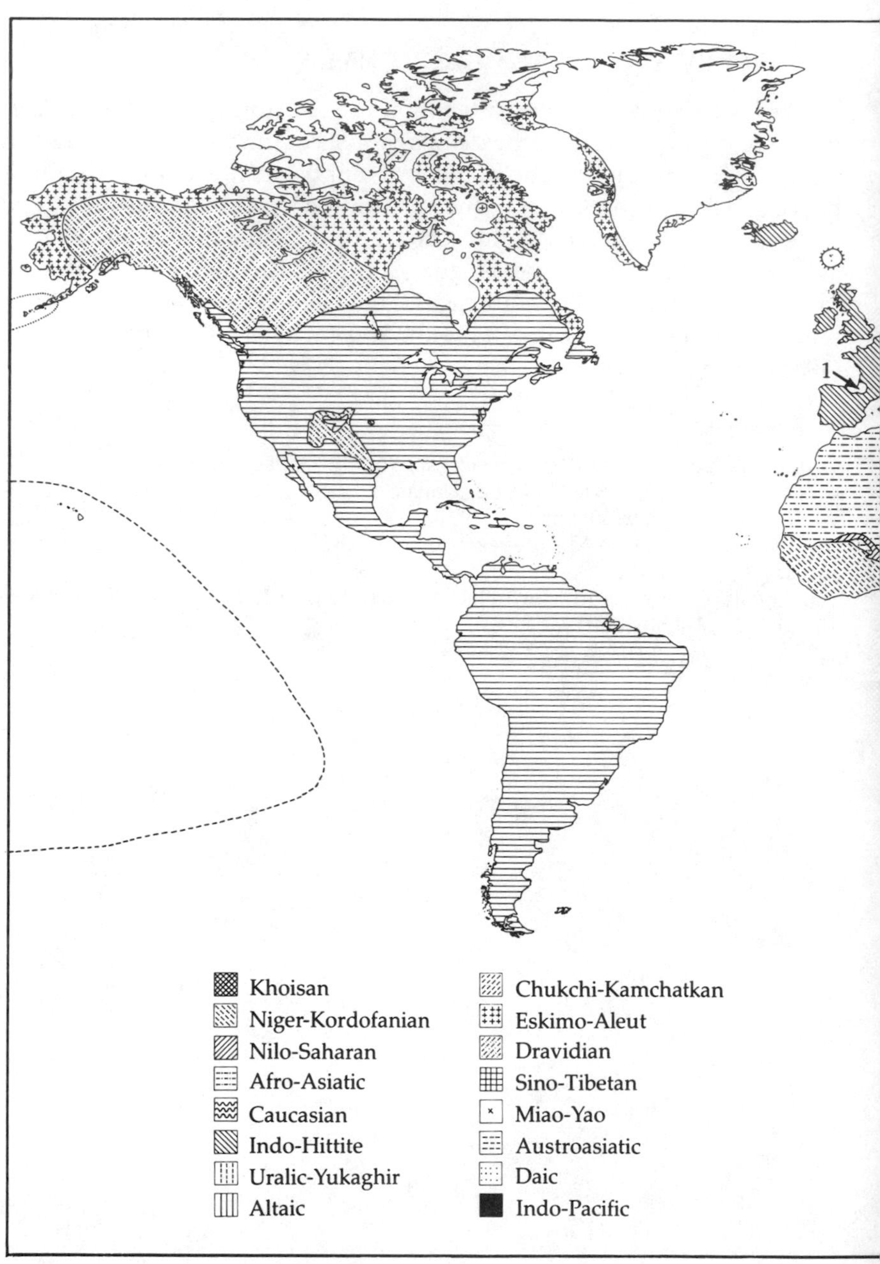

Map 8.1. The world's language families

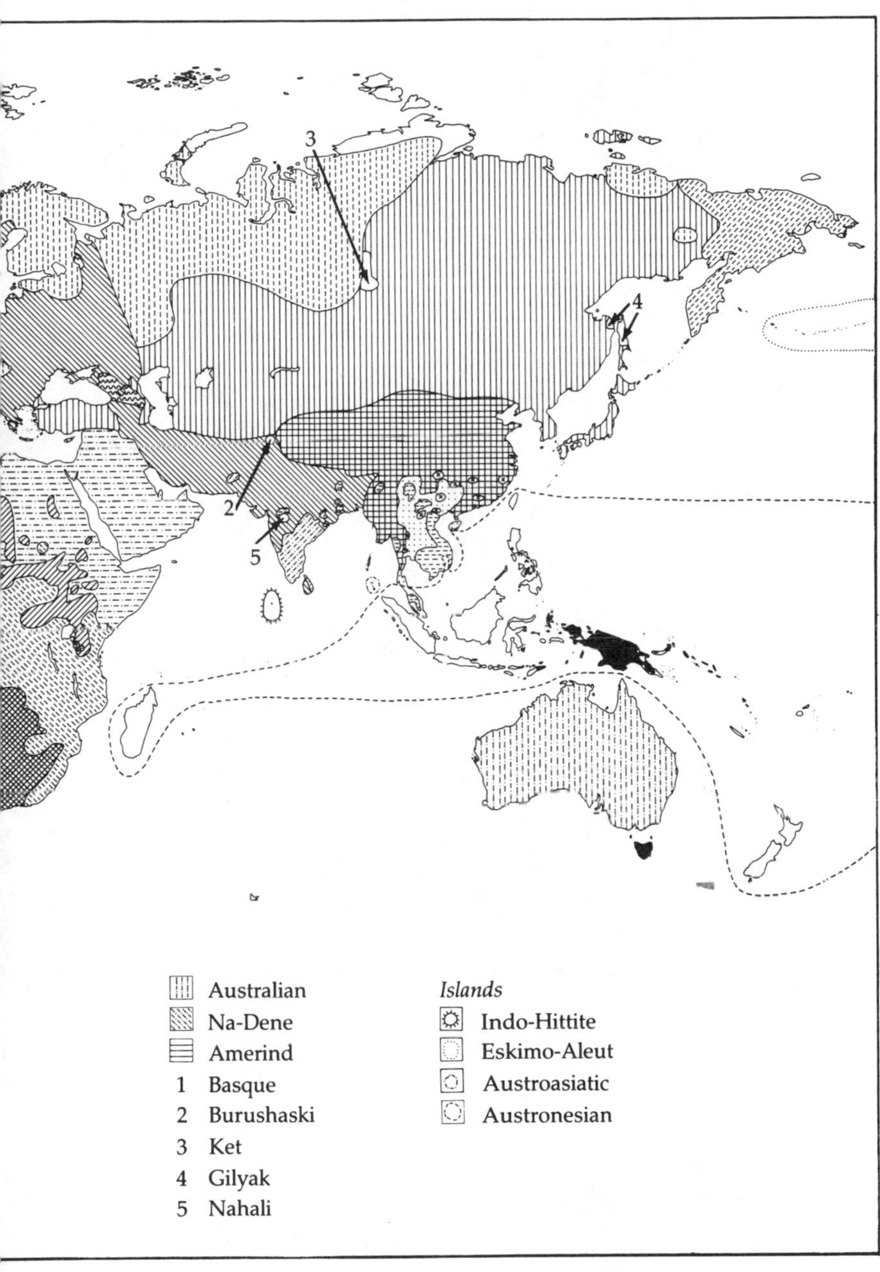
3
4
2
5
Australian
Na-Dene
Amerind
1 Basque
2 Burushaski
3 Ket
4 Gilyak
5 Nahali
Islands
Indo-Hittite
Eskimo-Aleut
Austroasiatic
Austronesian

Table 8.2. *Overview of Language Phyla*

Phylum	Number of extant languages	Number of speakers	Location or country	Better-known languages
KHOISAN	31	120,000	South Africa, Namibia, S Angola, Botswana, N Tanzania	Nama (= Hottentot)
NIGER-KORDOFANIAN	1,064	181,000,000	C and S Africa	Fula (= Fulani), Mandinka, Yoruba, Igbo, Swahili, Kongo, Luganda, Rwanda, Shona, Tswana, Xhosa, Zulu
NILO-SAHARAN	138	11,000,000	C Africa	Kanuri, Luo, Nubian, Maasai, Songhai
AFRO-ASIATIC:	241	175,000,000	N Africa, Near East	
†Ancient Egyptian	—	—	Egypt	†Ancient Egyptian
Berber	30	11,000,000	Algeria, Morocco, Tunisia, Libya, Mauritania, Senegal	Shilha, Kabyle, Riff, Tuareg, Tamazight
Chadic	123	30,000,000	Chad, Niger, Ghana, Nigeria, Cameroon, Central African Republic, Togo, Benin	Hausa
Omotic	34	1,000,000	W Ethiopia, N Kenya	Ometo
Cushitic	35	12,000,000	Somalia, Ethiopia, Sudan, Kenya, Tanzania	Somali, Oromo
Semitic	19	121,000,000	N Africa, Near East	Arabic, Hebrew, Aramaic, Amharic, Tigrinya
CAUCASIAN	38	5,000,000	Caucasus (U.S.S.R.)	Georgian
INDO-HITTITE:	144	2 billion	Europe, SW Asia, India, Americas, Australia, South Africa, New Zealand	
†Anatolian	—	—	Turkey	†Hittite
Armenian	1	5,000,000	U.S.S.R.	Armenian
†Tocharian	—	—	W China	†Tocharian
Indo-Iranian	93	700,000,000	Iran, Afghanistan, Pakistan, India	Romany, Farsi (= Persian), Kurdish, Pashto, Punjabi, Gujarati, Hindi-Urdu, Marathi, Bengali
Albanian	1	4,000,000	Albania	Albanian
Greek	2	10,000,000	Greece	Greek

Italic	16	500,000,000	Rumania, Italy, France, Spain, Portugal, Central and South America	†Latin, Rumanian, Italian, French, Provençal, Catalan, Spanish, Portuguese
Celtic	4	2,500,000	Ireland, Wales, N France	Irish, Welsh, Breton
Germanic	12	450,000,000	Germany, Holland, Scandinavia, Great Britain, North America, Australia, New Zealand, South Africa	German, Yiddish, Dutch, Afrikaans, English, Danish, Swedish, Norwegian, Icelandic
Balto-Slavic	15	290,000,000	U.S.S.R., Poland, Czechoslovakia, Yugoslavia, Bulgaria	Lithuanian, Latvian, Russian, Ukrainian, Byelorussian, Polish, Czech, Slovak, Serbo-Croatian, Bulgarian
URALIC-YUKAGHIR	24	22,000,000	Finland, Estonia, Hungary, U.S.S.R.	Hungarian, Finnish, Saami (= Lapp), Estonian
ALTAIC:	63	250,000,000	Asia	
Turkic	31	80,000,000	Turkey, U.S.S.R., Iran	Turkish, Uzbek, Uighur, Azerbaijani, Turkmen, Tatar, Kazakh, Kirghiz, Chuvash, Bashkir
Mongolian	12	3,000,000	Mongolia, China, U.S.S.R.	Khalkha (= Mongolian)
Tungus	16	80,000	E U.S.S.R., China	Manchu, Evenki
Korean	1	55,000,000	Korea	Korean
Japanese-Ryukyuan	2	115,000,000	Japan	Japanese
Ainu	1	few	N Japan, S Sakhalin Island (U.S.S.R.)	Ainu
CHUKCHI-KAMCHATKAN	5	23,000	NE Siberia (U.S.S.R.)	Chukchi
ESKIMO-ALEUT	9	85,000	Alaska, N Canada, Greenland, NE U.S.S.R.	Eskimo, Aleut
ELAMO-DRAVIDIAN	28	145,000,000	S and E India, S Pakistan	Telugu, Kannada, Tamil, Malayalam
SINO-TIBETAN	258	1 billion	China, Tibet, Nepal, India, Burma, Thailand, Laos	Mandarin, Wu, Yue (= Cantonese), Tibetan, Burmese, Karen
AUSTRIC:	1,175	293,000,000	SE Asia, Oceania	
Miao-Yao	4	7,000,000	S China, N Vietnam, N Laos, N Thailand	Miao, Mien (= Yao)
Austroasiatic:	155	56,000,000	NE India, SE Asia	
Munda	17	6,000,000	NE India	Santali, Mundari
Mon-Khmer	138	50,000,000	NE India, SE Asia, Nicobar Islands	Vietnamese, Mon, Khmer (= Cambodian)
Daic	57	50,000,000	S China, SE Asia	Thai (= Siamese), Lao (= Laotian), Li, Shan, Zhuang, Kam

Continued

Table 8.2. Overview of Language Phyla (continued)

Phylum	Number of extant languages	Number of speakers	Location or country	Better-known languages
Austronesian:	959	180,000,000	Oceania, S Vietnam, Madagascar	
Western	533	179,000,000	Madagascar, Formosa, Indonesia, Philippines, S Vietnam, Kampuchea	Malagasy, Javanese, Sundanese, Malay, Tagalog, Cebuano, Ilokano, Hiligaynon
Eastern (= Oceanic)	426	1,500,000	Melanesia, Micronesia, Polynesia	Fijian, Samoan, Tahitian, Hawaiian
INDO-PACIFIC	731	2,735,000	New Guinea, Timor, Alor, Pantar, Halmahera, New Britain, New Ireland, Bougainville, Solomons, Reef Islands, Santa Cruz, Andaman Islands, Tasmania	†Tasmanian, Enga, Wantoat, Telefol, Iatmul, Asmat
AUSTRALIAN	170	30,000	Australia	Western Desert Language
NA-DENE	34	202,000	Alaska, W Canada, Oregon, California, Arizona, New Mexico	Navajo, Apache
AMERIND:	583	18,000,000	North, Central, and South America	
Kutenai	1	200 (in 1977)	Montana, Idaho	Kutenai
Algic:	16	91,000	Canada, U.S.	
Ritwan	1	10 (in 1980)	N California	Yurok
Algonquian	15	91,000	C and E Canada, C and E U.S.	Ojibwa, Cree, Blackfoot, Cheyenne
Mosan:	27	9,500	NW U.S., SW Canada	
Chimakuan	1	10 (in 1977)	NW Washington	Quileute
Wakashan	6	2,700	SW Canada	Nootka, Kwakwala (= Kwakiutl)
Salish	20	6,800	SW Canada, NW U.S.	Shuswap, Kalispel, Squamish
Keresan	2	7,000	New Mexico	Keres
Siouan-Yuchi	11	21,000	C U.S.	Dakota, Crow
Caddoan	4	1,000	C U.S.	Wichita, Pawnee
Iroquoian	7	15,000	E U.S.	Cherokee, Mohawk
Penutian	68	3,200,000	W Canada, W and SE U.S., S Mexico	Chinook, Zuni, Muskogee (= Creek), Quiche, Cakchiquel, Kekchi, Mam, Yucatec

Hokan	28	55,000	California, Arizona, Texas, Mexico, Colombia	Mohave, Yuma, Tlapanec, Tequistlatec
Tanoan	7	7,400	New Mexico, Oklahoma	Kiowa, Tewa
Uto-Aztecan	25	1,100,000	W U.S., Mexico	Comanche, Hopi, Nahuatl (= Aztec)
Oto-Manguean	17	1,700,000	S Mexico	Otomi, Mixtec, Zapotec
Chibchan-Paezan	43	200,000	Florida, S Mexico, Central America, W South America	Tarascan, Yanomami, Guaymi, Cuna, Paez, Warao, Embera, Cayapa
Andean	18	8,500,000	W South America	Quechua, Aymara, Mapudungu (= Mapuche)
Macro-Tucanoan	47	35,000	NW and E South America	Ticuna, Tucano, Nambikuara, Puinave
Equatorial	145	3,000,000	South America, Caribbean	Guarani, Tupi, Goajiro, Arawak
Macro-Carib	47	50,000	N South America	Galibi (= Carib), Witoto
Macro-Panoan	49	50,000	W South America	Toba, Tacana
Macro-Ge	21	10,000	E South America	Bororo, Chavante

8.4 INDEX TO THE CLASSIFICATION

The following is simply a list of the largest groupings—often called phyla—into which linguists place the world's languages. It serves both as a quick overview of the major language groups presented in the subsequent 10 pages and as a page-number index to the complete classification beginning on p. 301. The first 17 numbered groups span the proposed classification of the world's languages. Although great bodies of research, pursued over centuries, have studied relationships *within* these 17 phyla, few serious attempts have been made to proposed relationships *between* them. Because the assemblage given as 13, Austric, will be unfamiliar and unconventional to many workers, its proposed component groups are given here.

The final four groupings in the list are of languages that for various reasons cannot be placed in the worldwide classification: 18, Language Isolates, lists a handful of languages, such as Basque, that have no obvious relatives anywhere in the world; 19, Unclassified, lists a handful of poorly documented languages that have not yet been assigned by linguists to particular major groups; 20, Pidgins and Creoles, lists a number of languages derived from short- or long-term mixing of one language with one or more others, typically as a result of maritime trade or slaveholding; and 21, Invented, lists the major attempts, like Esperanto, to invent languages from the ground up, for purposes of impartial international communication.

8.5 MAJOR LANGUAGE GROUPS

The following is an outline of section 8.6, Complete Classification. Languages are given in capital-and-lower-case letters, language groups in all capitals. Languages to the right of colons are examples from the language group to the left of the colon. Languages and language groups preceded by a dagger are extinct.

1 **KHOISAN** 301
- I Hadza
- II Sandawe
- III SOUTHERN AFRICA:
  - A NORTHERN: Qxû (= !Kung), Maligo
  - B CENTRAL: Nama (= Hottentot), G//abake
  - C SOUTHERN: ≠Hû, N/huki

2 **NIGER-KORDOFANIAN** 302
- I KORDOFANIAN: Kadugli, Rere
- II NIGER-CONGO:
  - A MANDE: Maninka, Kpelle, Mende
  - B NIGER-CONGO PROPER:
    - 1 WEST ATLANTIC: Fula (= Fulani), Wolof
    - 2 CENTRAL NIGER CONGO:
      - a NORTH CENTRAL NIGER-CONGO:
        - i KRU: Bete
        - ii Dogon
        - iii GUR (= VOLTAIC): Dagbani, More, Senari
        - iv ADAMAWA-UBANGIAN: Mumuye, Gbaya
      - b SOUTH CENTRAL NIGER-CONGO:
        - i IJO-DEFAKA: Kalabiri
        - ii WESTERN:
          - α NYO: Akan, Kposo, Gã
          - β TOGO: Ewe
        - iii EASTERN:
          - α CENTRAL NIGER: Nupe
          - β YORUBA-NORTHERN AKOKO: Yoruba
          - γ EDO: Bini
          - δ LOWER NIGER: Igbo
          - ε JUKUNOID: Jukun
          - ζ DELTA CROSS: Abua
          - η LOWER CROSS: Efik
          - θ UPPER CROSS: Legbo

ι BENUE-ZAMBESI:
- I CARA: Kambari
- II NYIMA:
  - A PLATEAU: Birom
  - B WEL:
    - 1 BENDI-BOKYI: Bendi
    - 2 BANTOID:
      - a NON-BANTU:
        - i MAMBILA-VUTE: Mambila
        - ii TIV-BATU: Tiv
      - b BROAD BANTU:
        - i BANE:
          - α JARAWAN-EKOID: Jarawa
          - β MAMFE: Esimbi
          - γ GRASSFIELDS: Bamun
          - δ MENCHUM: Befang
          - ε BEBOID: Noni
          - ζ TIKAR: Tikar
        - ii NARROW BANTU:
          - α NORTHWEST BANTU: Losengo
          - β CENTRAL BANTU: Swahili, Rwanda, Rundi, Shona, Xhosa, Zulu

3 **NILO-SAHARAN** 317
- I Songhai
- II SAHARAN: Kanuri
- III MABAN: Mesalit
- IV FUR: Fur
- V EAST SUDANIC:
  - A EASTERN:
    - 1 NUBIAN: Mahas
    - 2 SURMA: Me'en
    - 3 Nera
    - 4 EASTERN JEBEL: Gaam
  - B WESTERN:
    - 1 NYIMANG: Nyimang
    - 2 TEMEIN: Ronge
    - 3 TAMA: Merarit
    - 4 DAJU: Sila
  - C NILOTIC:
    - 1 WESTERN: Luo, Nuer
    - 2 EASTERN: Maasai
    - 3 SOUTHERN: Nandi
  - D KULIAK: Ik

VI CENTRAL SUDANIC:
- A WEST CENTRAL:
  - 1 KRESH: Kresh
  - 2 BONGO-BAGIRMI: Gambai
- B EAST CENTRAL:
  - 1 MORU-MADI: Logbara
  - 2 MANGBETU-ASUA: Mangbetu
  - 3 MANGBUTU-EFE: Mamvu
  - 4 Balendru

VII Berta

VIII Kunama

IX KOMUZ:
- A GUMUZ: Bega
- B KOMAN: Komo

4 **AFRO-ASIATIC** 320

I †Ancient Egyptian

II BERBER: Tamasheq, Kabyle, Shilha

III CHADIC: Hausa, Margi

IV OMOTIC: Ometo

V CUSHITIC: Beja, Sidamo, Oromo, Somali

VI SEMITIC: Aramaic, Hebrew, Arabic, Tigrinya, Amharic

5 **CAUCASIAN** 324

I SOUTH: Georgian

II NORTH:
- A NORTHWEST: Kabardian, Abxaz
- B NORTHEAST:
  - 1 NAX: Chechen
  - 2 DAGESTAN: Avar, Dargwa

6 **INDO-HITTITE** 325

I †ANATOLIAN: †Hittite

II INDO-EUROPEAN:
- A Armenian
- B †TOCHARIAN: †Tocharian
- C INDO-IRANIAN:
  - 1 INDIC: Romany, Sinhalese, Hindi, Urdu, Punjabi, Bengali, Gujarati, Marathi, Shina
  - 2 NURISTANI: Kati
  - 3 IRANIAN: Farsi (= Persian), Pashto, Kurdish, Baluchi
- D Albanian
- E GREEK: Greek

- F ITALIC:
  - 1 †OSCO-UMBRIAN: †Oscan
  - 2 LATINO-FALISCAN: Sardinian, Rumanian, Italian, French, Provençal, Catalan, Spanish, Portuguese
- G CELTIC: Irish (= Gaelic), Breton, Welsh
- H GERMANIC: English, German, Yiddish, Dutch, Afrikaans, Danish, Swedish, Norwegian, Icelandic
- I BALTO-SLAVIC:
  - 1 BALTIC: Latvian, Lithuanian
  - 2 SLAVIC: Russian, Polish, Czech, Serbo-Croatian, Bulgarian

7 **URALIC-YUKAGHIR** 328

- I YUKAGHIR: Yukaghir
- II URALIC:
  - A SAMOYED: Nenets
  - B FINNO-UGRIC:
    - 1 UGRIC: Hungarian
    - 2 FINNIC:
      - a PERMIC: Komi, Udmurt
      - b VOLGAIC: Mari, Mordvin
      - c NORTH FINNIC:
        - i SAAMIC: Saami (= Lapp)
        - ii BALTIC FINNIC: Finnish, Estonian

8 **ALTAIC** 328

- I ALTAIC PROPER:
  - A TURKIC: Turkish, Azerbaijani, Uzbek, Kazakh
  - B MONGOLIAN-TUNGUS:
    - 1 MONGOLIAN: Khalkha, Khorchin
    - 2 TUNGUS: Evenki, Manchu
- II KOREAN-JAPANESE: Korean, Ainu, Japanese

9 **CHUKCHI-KAMCHATKAN** 329

- I NORTHERN: Chukchi
- II SOUTHERN: Kamchadal

10 **ESKIMO-ALEUT** 329

- I Aleut
- II ESKIMO:
  - A INUIT: Greenlandic
  - B YUPIK: Central Yupik

11 **ELAMO-DRAVIDIAN** 330
- I †Elamite
- II DRAVIDIAN:
  - A NORTHWEST: Brahui
  - B DRAVIDIAN PROPER:
    - 1 NORTHEAST: Kurux
    - 2 CENTRAL: Telugu
    - 3 SOUTH: Kannada, Tamil, Malayalam

12 **SINO-TIBETAN** 331
- I SINITIC:
  - A BAI: Bai
  - B CHINESE: Mandarin, Wu, Min, Yue (= Cantonese)
- II TIBETO-KAREN:
  - A KAREN: Pa-o, Pho, Sgaw
  - B TIBETO-BURMAN:
    - 1 TIBETIC: Tibetan, Newari
    - 2 BARIC: Garo, Tangsa
    - 3 BURMIC:
      - a KUKI-NAGA: Haka, Mizo, Sho
      - b KACHIN-LUIC: Jinghpaw, Rawang
      - c BURMESE-MOSO:
        - i MOSO: Moso
        - ii BURMESE-LOLO:
          - α BURMIC: Burmese
          - β LOLO: Lisu, Lahu

13 **AUSTRIC** 334
- I MIAO-YAO: Miao, Mien (= Yao)
- II AUSTROASIATIC:
  - A MUNDA: Mundari, Santali
  - B MON-KHMER:
    - 1 NORTH: Khasi, Vietnamese
    - 2 EAST: Khmer (= Cambodian)
    - 3 SOUTH: Mon, Nicobarese
- III AUSTRO-TAI:
  - A DAIC:
    - 1 LATI-GELAO: Lati
    - 2 LI-KAM-TAI:
      - a LI-LAQUA: Li
      - b BE-KAM-TAI:
        - i LAKKIA-KAM-TAI:
          - α Lakkia:

β KAM-TAI:
I KAM-SUI: Kam, Sui
II TAI: Thai (= Siamese), Lao (= Laotian)
B AUSTRONESIAN:
1 ATAYALIC: Atayal
2 TSOUIC: Tsou
3 PAIWANIC: Paiwan
4 MALAYO-POLYNESIAN:
a WESTERN MALAYO-POLYNESIAN:
i NORTHERN PHILIPPINES: Ilokano, Pangasinan, Kapampangan
ii SOUTHERN PHILIPPINES: Maranao, Magindanao
iii MESO-PHILIPPINE: Tagalog, Cebuano, Hiligaynon
iv SOUTH MINDANAO: Bagobo, Tboli
v CELEBES: Bugis, Makassarese
vi BORNEO: Malagasy, Melanau
vii SAMA-BAJAW: Yakan, Sama
viii SUNDIC: Malay, Indonesian, Bali, Sundanese, Achinese, Javanese
b CENTRAL-EASTERN MALAYO-POLYNESIAN:
i CENTRAL MALAYO-POLYNESIAN:
α CENTRAL MALUKU: Taliabo, Geser
β SOUTHEAST MALUKU: Kei, Yamdena
γ TIMOR-FLORES: Sikka, Tetun, Letri Lgona
δ WAIMA'A: Waima'a, Kairui
ε BIMA-SUMBA: Bima, Savu, Manggarai, Ngada
ii EASTERN MALAYO-POLYNESIAN:
α SOUTH HALMAHERA–NORTHWEST NEW GUINEA:
I BOMBERAI: Kaiwai, Onin, Irahutu
II SOUTH HALMAHERA–GEELVINK BAY:
A SOUTH HALMAHERA: Gane, Misool, Waigeo
B GEELVINK BAY: Waropen, Biak, Wandamen
β OCEANIC:
I SARMI-YOTAFA: Sobei, Yotafa
II SIASSI:
A SEPIK-MADANG: Sissano, Gedaged
B RAI COAST–NORTHWEST NEW BRITAIN: Bariai
III MARKHAM: Adzera, Mumeng
IV MILNE BAY–CENTRAL PROVINCE: Bwaidoka, Motu
V KIMBE: Bileki, Vitu
VI NEW BRITAIN: Arawe, Mengen
VII NEW IRELAND–TOLAI: Tolai, Tigak
VIII ADMIRALTY ISLANDS: Seimat, Gele
IX BOUGAINVILLE: Nehan, Halia

- X CHOISEUL: Vaghua, Babatana
- XI NEW GEORGIA: Simbo, Roviana
- XII SANTA ISABEL: Kia, Gao
- XIII SANTA CRUZ: Nembao, Vano
- XIV SOUTHERN NEW HEBRIDES: Aneityum, Lenakel
- XV NEW CALEDONIA: Kumak, Numee
- XVI LOYALTY ISLANDS: Dehu, Nengone
- XVII REMOTE OCEANIC:
    - A MICRONESIAN: Marshallese, Trukese
    - B SOUTHEAST SOLOMONS: Gela, Arosi
    - C CENTRAL & NORTHERN NEW HEBRIDES: Sakao, Motlav
    - D CENTRAL PACIFIC:
        - 1 ROTUMAN-FIJIAN: Rotuman, Fijian
        - 2 POLYNESIAN: Samoan, Tahitian, Maori, Hawaiian

14 **INDO-PACIFIC** 354

- I †TASMANIAN: †Tasmanian
- II ANDAMAN ISLANDS: A-Pucikwar, Onge, Jarawa
- III TRANS–NEW GUINEA:
    - A MAIN SECTION:
        - 1 CENTRAL & WESTERN:
            - a FINISTERRE-HUON: Kate, Wantoat
            - b EAST NEW GUINEA HIGHLANDS: Gadsup, Medlpa
            - c CENTRAL & SOUTH NEW GUINEA–KUTUBUAN: Foe, Asmat, Telefol
            - d ANGAN: Angaataha, Baruya
            - e GOGODALA-SUKI: Suki, Gogodala
            - f MARIND: Boazi, Marind
            - g KAYAGAR: Kaygir, Tamagario
            - h SENTANI: Sentani, Demta
            - i DANI-KWERBA: Dani, Kwerba
            - j WISSEL LAKES–KEMANDOGA: Uhunduni, Ekagi
            - k MAIRASI–TANAH MERAH: Mairasi, Tanah Merah$_1$
            - l WEST BOMBERAI: Karas, Baham
        - 2 EASTERN:
            - a BINANDEREAN: Binandere, Guhu-Semane
            - b GOILALAN: Biangai, Kunimaipa
            - c KOIARIAN: Koiari, Barai
            - d KWALEAN: Kwale
            - e MANUBARAN: Maria
            - f YAREBAN: Yareba
            - g MAILUAN: Magi
            - h DAGAN: Daga

B MADANG–ADELBERT RANGE: Siroi, Waskia
C TEBERAN-PAWAIAN: Dadibi, Pawaian
D TURAMA-KIKORIAN: Kairi, Omati
E INLAND GULF: Minanibai
F ELEMAN: Toaripi, Orokolo
G TRANS-FLY–BULAKA RIVER: Yelmek, Meriam
H MEK: Nalca
I SENAGI: Anggor
J PAUWASI: Dubu
K NORTHERN: Manem, Awyi
L NIMBORAN: Nimboran
M KAURE: Kaure
N SOUTH BIRD'S HEAD: Konda, Barau
O KOLOPOM: Kimaghana
P TIMOR-ALOR-PANTAR: Oirata, Woisika
IV WEST PAPUAN: Amberbaken, Ternate
V EAST BIRD'S HEAD: Meax
VI GEELVINK BAY: Yava
VII SKO: Sko, Warapu
VIII KWOMTARI-BAIBAI: Kwomtari, Baibai
IX ARAI: Rocky Peak
X AMTO-MUSIAN: Amto
XI TORRICELLI: Au, Yahang, Arapesh, Monumbo
XII SEPIK-RAMU: Iatmul, Angoram, Kambot
XIII EAST PAPUAN: Savosavo, Nasioi, Santa Cruz

15 **AUSTRALIAN** 362
I YIWAIDJAN: Iwaidja
II MANGERRIAN: Mangerr
III GUNWINYGUAN: Gunwinygu, Wagiman
IV BURARRAN: Burarra
V MARAN: Alawa
VI WEST BARKLY: Djingili, Wambaya
VII GARAWAN: Garawa
VIII LARAGIYAN: Laragiya
IX DALY: Maranungku, Malakmalak
X DJAMINDJUNGAN: Djamindjung
XI DJERAGAN: Kitja
XII BUNABAN: Bunaba
XIII NYULNYULAN: Nyulnyul
XIV WORORAN: Ungarinjin
XV PAMA-NYUNGAN: Wik-Mungkan, Dyirbal, Western Desert Language

16 **NA-DENE** 365
- I Haida
- II CONTINENTAL NA-DENE:
  - A Tlingit
  - B ATHABASKAN-EYAK:
    - 1 Eyak
    - 2 ATHABASKAN: Tanaina, Chipewyan, Apache, Navajo

17 **AMERIND** 366
- I NORTHERN AMERIND:
  - A ALMOSAN-KERESIOUAN:
    - 1 ALMOSAN:
      - a Kutenai
      - b ALGIC:
        - i RITWAN: †Wiyot, Yurok
        - ii ALGONQUIAN: Blackfoot, Cheyenne, Fox, Micmac
      - c MOSAN:
        - i CHIMAKUAN: Quileute
        - ii WAKASHAN: Kwakwala (= Kwakiutl), Nootka
        - iii SALISH: Bella Coola, Squamish, Kalispel
    - 2 KERESIOUAN:
      - a KERESAN: Keres
      - b SIOUAN-YUCHI: Yuchi, Catawba, Dakota, Winnebago
      - c CADDOAN: Caddo, Wichita, Pawnee
      - d IROQUOIAN: Mohawk, Seneca, Cherokee
  - B PENUTIAN:
    - 1 CANADIAN: Tsimshian
    - 2 WASHINGTON: Chinook
    - 3 OREGON: Santiam, Coos
    - 4 PLATEAU: Klamath, Nez Perce
    - 5 CALIFORNIA:
      - a WINTUN: Wintun
      - b MAIDUAN: Mountain Maidu
      - c YOKUTS: Foothill North Yokuts
      - d MIWOK-COSTANOAN: †Ohlone, Lake Miwok
    - 6 NEW MEXICO: Zuni
    - 7 GULF:
      - a †TUNICA-CHITIMACHA: †Tunica, †Chitimacha
      - b YUKI-WAPPO: Yuki, Wappo
      - c NATCHEZ-MUSKOGEAN: Choctaw, Muskogee (= Creek), Alabama
    - 8 MEXICAN:
      - a Huave
      - b TOTONACAN: Totonac
      - c MIXE-ZOQUE: Mixe, Zoque
      - d MAYAN: Yucatec, Chontal, Tzeltal, Mam, Kekchi, Quiche

C HOKAN:
1 NORTHERN: Shasta, †Yahi, Pomo
2 Washo
3 †SALINAN-CHUMASH: †Salinan
4 SERI-YUMAN: Seri, Yuma, Mohave, Havasupai
5 †WAICURI-QUINIGUA: †Quinigua
6 COAHUILTECAN: Tonkawa
7 TEQUISTLATECAN: *Tequistlatec
8 SOUTHERN: Jicaque, Tlapanec
II CENTRAL AMERIND:
A TANOAN: Kiowa, Taos
B UTO-AZTECAN: Northern Paiute, Comanche, Luiseño, Hopi, Yaqui, Nahuatl (= Aztec)
C OTO-MANGUEAN: Otomi, Mixtec, Mazatec, Chinantec
III CHIBCHAN-PAEZAN:
A CHIBCHAN: Tarascan, Yanomami, Cuna, Tunebo
B PAEZAN: Warao, Itonama, Mura, Embera, Paez, Cayapa
IV ANDEAN: Quechua, Aymara, Zaparo, Mapudungu (= Araucanian), Qawasqar (= Alacaluf)
V EQUATORIAL-TUCANOAN:
A MACRO-TUCANOAN: Puinave, Nambikuara, Ticuna, Tucano
B EQUATORIAL: Shuar, Ayoreo, Guarani, Guahibo, Chipaya, Arawak, Island Carib, †Taino
VI GE-PANO-CARIB:
A MACRO-CARIB: Yagua, Bora, Ocaina, Galibi (= Carib), Hishkaryana
B GE-PANO:
1 MACRO-PANOAN: Lengua, Chimane, Toba, Cashibo, Tacana
2 MACRO-GE: Rikbaktsa, Bororo, Kaingang, Chavante, Cayapo

18 **LANGUAGE ISOLATES:** Basque, Burushaski, Ket, Nahali 377

19 **UNCLASSIFIED:** Warenbori, Taurap, Pauwi, Chiquitano 377

20 **PIDGINS AND CREOLES:** French Creole, Sea Island Creole (= Gulla), Djuka, Tok Pisin, Chinook Jargon 377

21 **INVENTED:** Esperanto, Interlingua 378

8.6 COMPLETE CLASSIFICATION

This section offers a complete genetic classification of the world's languages, arranged in terms of 17 independent phyla. The order in which these phyla are listed is for the most part geographic, beginning in Africa, running through Europe, Asia, and Oceania, and ending in the New World. Languages are given in capital-and-lower-case letters, language groups in all capitals. Languages and language groups preceded by a dagger are extinct. The number of extant languages in each genetic group is given in brackets following the name of the group. Those languages whose phonemic system (i.e., consonants and vowels) may be found in the forthcoming Volume 2 are preceded by an asterisk.

KHOISAN [31]:
I HADZA [1]: Hadza
II SANDAWE [1]: Sandawe
III SOUTHERN AFRICA [29]:
- A NORTHERN [4]: *Qxû (= !Kung), ≠Au.//eî, Maligo, Ekoka
- B CENTRAL [19]:
  - 1 NAMA [3]: *Nama, Dama, !Ora, †Xiri
  - 2 HAI.N//UM [1]: Hai.n//um
  - 3 KWADI [1]: Kwadi
  - 4 TSHU-KHWE [14]:
    - a NORTHEAST [2]: *G//abake, Kwee
    - b NORTH-CENTRAL [3]: Ganade, Shua, Danisin
    - c CENTRAL [1]: Deti
    - d NORTHWEST [4]: Buka, Handa, Xû, *G//ana
    - e SOUTHWEST [4]: Naron, *G/wi, G//ani, N/hain.tse
- C SOUTHERN [6]:
  - 1 TA'A [4]: !Ô, *≠Hû, N/amani, //Ng.!'e
  - 2 !WI [2]: *N/huki, //Xekwi, †/Xam

NIGER-KORDOFANIAN [1,064]:

I KORDOFANIAN [32]:
- A KADUGLI [9]:
  - 1 WESTERN [3]: Tulishi, Keiga, Kanga
  - 2 CENTRAL [4]: Miri, Kadugli, *Katcha, Tumma
  - 3 EASTERN [2]: Krongo, Tumtum
- B KORDOFANIAN PROPER [23]:
  - 1 KATLA [2]: *Katla, Tima
  - 2 HEIBAN [10]:
    - a EASTERN [2]: *Ko, *Warnang
    - b WEST-CENTRAL [8]:
      - i CENTRAL [5]:
        - [1]: *Rere
        - α EBANG-LOGOL [4]:
          - [2]: *Utoro, *Logol
          - I EBANG-LARU [2]: *Ebang, *Laru
      - ii SHIRUMBA [1]: *Shirumba
      - iii WESTERN [2]: *Tiro, *Moro
  - 3 TALODI [6]:
    - [1]: *Tegem
    - a TALODI PROPER [5]:
      - [3]: *Nding, *Jomang, *Tocho
      - i NGILE-DENGEBU [2]: *Ngile, *Dengebu
  - 4 RASHAD [5]: *Tegali, Tagoi, Tingal, Tukum, Turum

II NIGER-CONGO [1,032]:
- A MANDE [29]:
  - [1]: Bobo-Fing
  - 1 NORTHERN-WESTERN [18]:
    - a NORTHERN [13]:
      - i SONINKE-BOZO [2]: *Soninke, Bozo
      - ii SUSU-YALUNKA [2]: *Susu, Yalunka

iii LIGBI-NUMU [2]: Ligbi, Numu
iv VAI-KONO [2]: *Vai, Kono
v MANDEKAN [5]:
α WEST [2]: Mandinka, Xasonke
β EAST [3]: *Maninka, *Bambara, *Dyula
b SOUTHWESTERN [5]:
[3]: *Loko, *Loma, *Kpelle
i MENDE-BANDI [2]: *Mende, Bandi
2 SOUTHERN-EASTERN [10]:
a SOUTHERN [6]:
[2]: Mano, *Dan
i KWENI-TURA [4]: *Kweni, Mwa, Nwa, *Tura
b EASTERN [4]:
[2]: *Bisa, Busa
i SAMO [2]: *Sane, *San
B NIGER-CONGO PROPER [1,003]:
1 WEST ATLANTIC [46]:
[1]: Bijago
a NORTHERN [29]:
i SENEGAL [3]: *Fula (= Fulani), Serer, *Wolof
ii CANGIN [5]: Falor, Lehar, Ndut, Non, Safan
iii BAK [10]:
α BALANT-GANJA [2]: *Balant, *Ganja
β MANJAKU-PAPEL [3]: *Mankan, *Manjaku, Papel
γ DIOLA [5]:
[1]: Bayot
I DIOLA PROPER [4]:
[2]: Karon, Kwatay
A DIOLA-GUSILAY [2]: *Diola, Gusilay
iv EASTERN SENEGAL–GUINEA BISSAU [8]: *Badyara, *Banyun, *Basari, *Bedik, Biafada, Kasanga, Kobiana, Konyagi
v MBULUNGISH-NALU [3]: Baga Mboteni, Mbulungish, Nalu

[1 WEST ATLANTIC]
b SOUTHERN [16]:
[2]: Sua, Limba
i MEL [14]:
[1]: Gola
α TEMNE [8]: Baga Binari, Baga Koga, Baga Maduri, Baga Sitemu, Baga Sobane, Banta, Landuma, *Temne
β BULLOM [5]: Bom, Northern Bullom, *Southern Bullom, Kisi, Krim
2 CENTRAL NIGER-CONGO [957]:
a NORTH CENTRAL NIGER-CONGO [206]:
i KRU [18]:
[3]: Aizi, Kuwaa, *Seme
α EASTERN [3]:
I NORTH [1]: *Bete
II SOUTH [2]: Godie, Dida
β WESTERN [12]:
[4]: Bakwe, *Kru, *Grebo, Tajuason
I KLAU [2]: Klau, Peripheral Klau
II BASSA [2]: Bassa, Dewoin
III WE [4]:
[1]: Krahn
A GUERE [3]: Guere, Wobe, Nyabwa
ii DOGON [1]: *Dogon
iii GUR (= VOLTAIC) [73]:
[1]: *Bariba
α KULANGO-LORHON [2]: Kulango, Lorhon
β SENUFO-TUSYA [15]:
[1]: *Tusya
I SENUFO [14]:
[8]: *Senari, Palaka, Nafana, Tyeliri, Tiefo, Kulele, Karaboro, Viemo
A NATIORO-WARA [2]: Natioro, Wara
B SUPPIRE-MIANKA [2]: *Suppire, *Mianka
C TAGBANA-DYIMINI [2]: Tagbana, Dyimini

γ CENTRAL [55]:
- I KURUMFE-OTI-VOLTA [31]:
  - [1]: Kurumfe
  - A BWAMU-OTI-VOLTA [30]:
    - [1]: Bwamu
    - 1 OTI-VOLTA [29]:
      - a BULI-KOMA [2]: Buli, Koma
      - b OTI-VOLTA PROPER [27]:
        - i EASTERN [5]: Bieri, Wama, Tayari, *Tamari, Nyende
        - ii WESTERN-GURMA [22]:
          - α WESTERN [12]: Notre, *Gurenne, *More, Safalaba, *Dagara, *Kusaal, Kamara, Talne, Nabte, Mampelle, *Dagbani, Hanga
          - β GURMA-YOM [10]:
            - I GURMA [8]: *Kasele, Basari, *Konkomba, Soruba, *Dye, Gangam, *Gurma, *Moba
            - II YOM-NAUDEM [2]: Yom, Naudem
- II DOGHOSE-GURUNSI [24]:
  - A DOGHOSE-GAN [2]: Doghose, Gan
  - B GURUNSI-KIRMA [22]:
    - 1 GURUNSI [18]:
      - a WESTERN [4]: *Kasem, Nuni, *Lyele, Pana
      - b CENTRAL-EASTERN [14]:
        - i CENTRAL [8]: Siti, Winye, Pwo, *Isala, Chakali, *Tampulma, Vagala, Mo
        - ii EASTERN [6]: *Kabre, *Lamba, Tem, Chala, Delo, Bago
    - 2 KIRMA-LOBI [4]:
      - a KIRMA-TYURAMA [2]: *Kirma, *Tyurama
      - b LOBI-DAN [2]: *Lobi, *Dan

iv ADAMAWA-UBANGIAN [114]:
- α ADAMAWA [66]:
  - [5]: Kam, *Longuda, Fali, Nimbari, Kim
  - I WAJA [7]:
    - [5]: Awak, Dadia, Kamu, Tula, Waja
    - A CHAM-MONA [2]: Cham, Mona

[a NORTH CENTRAL NIGER-CONGO]
II CHAMBA [3]: *Chamba, Donga, Wom
III DAKA [4]: Daka, Dirrim, Gandole, Taram
IV DURU [9]: *Doyãyo, Dupa, *Duru, Goom, Kolbila, Kutin, Sari, Sewe, Vere
V MUMUYE-YENDANG [8]:
A MUMUYE [5]: *Mumuye, Gengle, Kumba, Teme, Waka
B YENDANG [3]: Yendang, Kugama, Passam
VI MBUM-MUNDANG [12]:
[4]: *Galke, Mangbai, Pam, Tupuri
A MBUM [4]: *Mbum, Dek, Kali, Lakka
B MUNDANG [2]: Mundang, Gelama
C DAMA-MONO [2]: Dama, Mono
VII YUNGUR [4]:
[2]: Libo, Mboi
A YUNGUR-ROBA [2]: Yungur, Roba
VIII BAMBUKA [4]: Bambuka, Jen, Kanawa, Munga
IX BUA [10]: Bua, Bolgo, Buso, Day, Fanya, *Gula, Kulaal, Koke, Nielim, Tunya
β UBANGIAN [48]:
I GBAYA-GBANZILI [28]:
A GBAYA [4]:
[2]: *Gbaya, Bangando
1 MANZA-NGBAKA [2]: Manza, Ngbaka
B NGBANDI [3]: *Ngbandi, *Sango, *Yakoma
C GBANZILI-SERE [21]:
1 SERE [9]:
a NORTH [2]: *Feroge, Indri
b SOUTH [7]:
i NDOGO-SERE [3]: Ndogo, Sere, Tagbu
ii BAI-VIRI [2]: Bai, *Viri
iii MANGAYA-TOGOYO [2]: Mangaya, Togoyo

2 GBANZILI [12]:
  a EAST [3]:
      [1]: Mundu
    i MAYOGO-BANGBA [2]: Mayogo, Bangba
  b WEST [9]:
      [3]: *Gbanzili, *Bwaka, *Monzombo
    i BAKA-GUNDI [6]: Baka, Bomasa, Bayanga, Ngombe, Gundi, Ganzi

II BANDA [12]:
  A LANGBASI-NGUBU [2]: Langbasi, Ngubu
  B MBANZA-MBANJA [2]: Mbanza, Mbanja
  C NGBUNDU [1]: Ngbundu
  D NGUNDU-GOLO [7]:
    1 NGUNDU-KPAGUA [2]: Ngundu, Kpagua
    2 GUBU-YAKPA [2]: Gubu, Yakpa
    3 LINDA [1]: *Linda
    4 GBI-GOLO [2]: Gbi, Golo

III ZANDE [4]:
  A ZANDE-NZAKARA [2]: *Zande, *Nzakara
  B BARAMBO-PAMBIA [2]: Barambo, Pambia

IV AMADI [2]: Amadi, Dongo

V MONDUNGA [2]: Mondunga, *Mba

b SOUTH CENTRAL NIGER-CONGO [751]:
  i IJO-DEFAKA [5]:
      [1]: Defaka
    α IJO [4]: *Kalabari, *Nembe, Biseni, *Kolokuma
  ii WESTERN [47]:
    α NYO [36]:
      I YI [34]:
        A VOLTA-COMOE [19]:

[b SOUTH CENTRAL NIGER-CONGO]
1 WESTERN [2]: Abure, Eotile
2 CENTRAL [7]:
[2]: *Akan, Abron
a BAULE-AGNI [3]: *Baule, *Anyi, *Chakosi
b NZEMA-AHANTA [2]: *Nzema, Ahanta
3 EASTERN [10]:
[7]: Awutu, Chiripong, *Gonja, *Nkonya, Nawuri, Nchumunu, Nchumburu
a NORTH [3]: Achode, Anyanga, Krachi
B CENTRAL TOGO [15]:
1 NA [8]: Adele, Akpafu, Siwu, *Basila, *Buem, Likpe, Logba, Sele
2 KA [7]: Ahlo, Animere, Avatime, Nyangbo, Bowili, Kebu, Kposo
II GÃ-ADANGME [2]: *Gã, *Adangme
β TOGO [11]:
I EWE-FON [2]: *Ewe, *Fon
II LAGOON [9]:
A POTU [2]: Mbato, *Ebrie
B INTERIOR [5]: Attie, Abe, Abiji, Krobu, *Adyukru
C COASTAL [2]: Aladian, Avikam
iii EASTERN [699]:
α CENTRAL NIGER [11]:
I NIGER-KADUNA [4]:
[1]: *Ebira
A NUPE [3]:
[1]: *Gade
1 NUPE-GWARI [2]: *Nupe, *Gwari
II IDOMA [7]: Alago, *Idoma, *Yala, Akpa, *Igede, *Etulo, *Eloyi
β YORUBA-NORTHERN AKOKO [3]:
[1]: Northern Akoko
I YORUBA [2]: *Yoruba, *Igala
γ EDO [22]:
I DELTA [3]: *Epie, *Engenni, *Degema

II SOUTHWESTERN [5]: Okpe$_1$, *Urhobo, Uvbie, *Isoko, Eruwa
III NORTH-CENTRAL [10]: *Bini, *Esan, Emai, *Iyekhee, Ghotuo, Uneme, North Ibie, Ikpeshi, Sasaru, Ososo
IV NORTHWESTERN [4]: Okpamheri, Uhami, Ukue, Okpe$_2$

δ LOWER NIGER [7]:
[1]: Ekpeye
I IGBO [6]: *Izi, *Igbo, *Ika, *Ukwuani, Ogbah, Ikwere

ϵ JUKUNOID [10]:
I YUKUBEN-KUTEB [2]: Yukuben, *Kuteb
II CENTRAL [8]:
A KPAN-ICEN [2]: *Kpan, Icen
B JUKUN [3]: Ashuku, Nama, *Jukun
C WURBO [3]: Bandawa, Chomo, Jiru

ζ DELTA CROSS [11]:
I CENTRAL DELTA [8]: Ogbogolo, *Ogbia, Kugbo, Mini, *Abua, *Odual, Ogbronuagum, Obulom
II OGONI [3]: *Kana, *Gokana, *Eleme

η LOWER CROSS [8]:
[1]: Obolo
I EFIK [3]: *Efik, *Ibibio, Anaang
II ORON [4]: Okobo, Oron, Ekit, Ibino

θ UPPER CROSS [22]:
[1]: Tita
I EASTERN [9]: *Mbembe, *Legbo, Leyigha, Lenyima, *Loko, Agoi, Lokukoli, Lubilo, Olulumo
II WESTERN [8]: Koring, Kukele, Uzekwe, *Kohumono, Ubaghara, Agwaagwune, Umon, Ukpet
III CALABAR RIVER [4]: Kiong, Korop, Lyoniyorg, Doko

ι BENUE-ZAMBESI [605]:
I CARA [42]:
A EASTERN [24]:
[1]: Amo
1 CHAWAI [2]: Piti, Chawai
2 KURAMA [13]: Kuzamani, Kurama, Rumaya, Ruruma, Binawa, Kono, Surubu, Kaivi, Kiballo, Kitimi, Kinuku, Dungi, Gure
3 JERA [8]: †Kuda, Butu, Gyem, †Taura, *Lemoro, *Janji, Shani, Buji, *Anaguta, *Chokobo

[I CARA]
  B WESTERN [18]:
      [1]: Reshe
    1 LARU-LOPA [2]: Laru, Lopa
    2 KAMBARI-DUKA [15]:
      a KAMBARI [2]: Western Kambari, Eastern Kambari
      b KAMUKU [2]: Ngwoi, Kamuku, †Bassa-Kontagora, †Ashaganna
      c BASSA [7]: Bassa-Kaduna, Bassa-Kuta, Gurmana, Pongu, Bauchi, Ura, Bassa-Kwomu
      d DUKA [4]: Lela, *Duka, Puku, Lyase
II NYIMA [563]:
  A PLATEAU [44]:
      [4]: Ayu, Yashi, Mabo-Barkul, Irigwe
    1 BIROM-MIGILI [4]:
        [2]: Migili, Aten
      a BIROM [2]: *Birom, Fachara
    2 KAJE-KADARA [16]:
        [1]: Katab
      a YESKWA [3]: Yeskwa, Lungu, Koro
      b KAJE [6]: Kamanton, Kagoma, Jaba, Nandu, Izarek, Kaje
      c KADARA [6]: Kadara, Kuturmi, Ikulu, Idong, Doka, Iku
    3 NINZAM-RUKUBA [9]:
        [1]: Rukuba
      a KWANKA [2]: Kwanka, Shall
      b NINZAM [6]: Ninzam, Mada, Gwantu, Nindem, Kaningkon, Kanufi
    4 EGGON [4]: Eggon, Nungu, Ake, Jidda
    5 FYAM [2]: *Fyam, Horom
    6 TAROK [3]: *Tarok, Bashar, Pai
    7 TURKWAM [2]: Turkwam, Arum
  B WEL [519]:
    1 BENDI-BOKYI [9]:
        [1]: Bokyi
      a BENDI [8]: Bekwarra, Bendi, Obanliku, Ukpe, Ubang, Alege, Utugwang, Bumaji

2 BANTOID [510]:
- a NON-BANTU [16]:
  - i MAMBILA-VUTE [8]: *Mambila, Kamkam, Tep, Magu, Kila, Ndoro, Gandua, *Vute
  - ii TIV-BATU [8]: *Tiv, Otank, Emane, Icheve, Evant, Bitare, Abon, Batu
- b BROAD BANTU [494]:
  - i BANE [114]:
    - α JARAWAN-EKOID [20]:
      - I JARAWAN [10]:
        - [2]: Mboa, Nagumi
        - A NIGERIAN [8]: Bile, Mbula, Mama, Lame, Jaku, Gubi, Kulung, *Jarawa
      - II EKOID-MBE [10]:
        - [1]: *Mbe
        - A EKOID [9]: Ndoe, *Ejagham, Efutop, Nde, *Abanyom, Nkem, Nkumm, Nnam, Ekajuk
    - β MAMFE [9]: Esimbi, Amasi, Kenyang, Kitwii, Kinkwa, Menka, Ngwo, Bitieku, Assaka
    - γ GRASSFIELDS [68]:
      - I EASTERN [48]:
        - A NKAMBE [8]: Adere, Limbum, Kofa, Kwaja, Ncha, Ndaktup, Ntem, Yamba
        - B NUN-BAMILEKE [40]:
          - 1 NUN [6]: *Bamun, Mungaka, Bambalang, Baba, Bapi, Bandeng
          - 2 NGEMBA [8]: *Mankon, Mundum, Bafut, Nkwen, Bambui, Pinyin, Awing, Kpati
          - 3 BAMILEKE [26]: Babaju, Fe'fe, *Dschang, Bafussam, Bagam, Balum, Bamaha, Bamendiinda, Bamenkombit, Bamenyam, Banjun, Bangangte, Bangwa, Bapi, Bacham, Bachingu, Bati, Batie, Bamugun, Fomopea, Fongondeng, Foto, Fotuni, *Ngwe, Babuantu, Upper Mundani

[i BANE]
II WESTERN [20]:
A RING [15]:
1 NKOM [8]:
a WEST [4]: *Aghem, Isu, Weh, Bafumen
b CENTRAL [4]: Babanki, Kom, Bum, Oku
2 EAST [7]:
[1]: *Lamnso
a NDOP [6]: Bamessing, Bamessi, Babungo, Bamunka, Bamali, Fanji
B MOMO-NJEN [5]:
1 MOMO [3]: Tadkon, Ngie, Oshie
2 NJEN [2]: Njem, Lower Mundani
δ MENCHUM [6]: Modele, Mukuru, Befang, Bangui, Obang, Okomanjan
ϵ BEBOID [9]:
I WESTERN [4]: Mekaf, Bu, Kinabe, Koshin
II EASTERN [5]: Bebe, Dumbo, Nchanti, Noni, Akweto
ζ TIKAR [2]: *Tikar, Bandobo
ii NARROW BANTU [380]:
α NORTHWEST BANTU [131]:
I ZONE A [43]:
A LUNDU-BALONG [5]: Lundu, Lue, Balong, Bonkeng, *Bafo
B DUALA [7]: Mboko, Kwiri, Su, *Duala, Wori, Pongo, Limba
C BUBI-BENGA [4]: Bubi, Noho, *Yasa, *Benga
D BASAA [6]: Lombi, Bankon, *Basaa, *Tunen, Nyo'o, Mande
E BAFIA [4]: Fa', Mbong, *Kpa, Djanti
F SANAGA [2]: Ki, Yambasa
G EWONDO [5]: Eton, *Ewondo, Bebele, *Bulu, *Fang
H MAKAA-NJEM [7]: *Ngumba, So, Makaa, Njem, Konabem, Mpiemo, Bomwali
I KAKO [3]: Kwakum, Pol, *Yaka

- II ZONE B [41]:
  - A MYENE [1]: *Myene
  - B KELE [7]: Sekyani, Kele, Mbangwe, Wumvu, Kota, Ndasa, Sighu
  - C TSOGO [3]: Tsogo, Kande, Pinji
  - D SIRA [6]: Sira, Sangu, Punu, Lumbu, Mbwisi, Barama
  - E NJEBI [3]: Duma, *Njebi, Tsaangi
  - F MBEDE [6]: Mbede, Mbama, *Ndumu, Ngwii, Ngul, Kaningi
  - G TEKE [9]: Ngu Ngwoni, North Teke, Northeast Teke, West Teke, Central Teke, Bali, East Teke, *South Teke, Wuumu
  - H YANZI [6]: Tiene, Mfinu, Mpuono, Yanzi, Di, Mbuun
- III ZONE C [47]:
  - A NGANDO [2]: *Ngando, Kota
  - B NGUNDI [6]: Ngundi, Pande, *Mbati, Mbomotaba, Bongili, Lobala
  - C MBOSHI [7]: Mboko, *Akwa, Ngare, Koyo, Mboshi, Kwala, Kuba
  - D BANGI-NTOMBA [7]: *Ngiri, *Bobangi, Sengele, Sakata, *Ntomba, *Losengo, Buja
  - E NGOMBE [5]: *Ngombe, Bwela, Bati, Bua, Beo
  - F KELE [6]: Mbesa, So, Gesogo, Lombo, Lokele, Foma
  - G MONGO [6]: *Mongo, Lalia, Ngando, Konda, Mbole, *Ombo
  - H TETELA [5]: *Tetela, Kusu, Nkutu, Yela, *Kela
  - I BUSHONG [3]: Ndengese, Songomeno, *Bushong

β CENTRAL BANTU [249]:

- I ZONE D [17]:
  - A ENYA [3]: Lengola, Mituku, Enya
  - B LEGA-KALANGA [5]: Bali, North Binja, Lega, South Binja, *Holoholo
  - C BIRA-HUKU [6]: Piri, Bira, Nyali, Bodo, Komo, Kare
  - D NYANGA [1]: *Nyanga
  - E BEMBE [2]: Bembe, Buyu

[β CENTRAL BANTU]

II ZONE E [22]:

A LOGOLI-KURIA [7]: Logoli, *Gusii, Kuria, Zanaki, Nata, Sonjo, Ngurimi

B KIKUYU-KAMBA [6]: *Kikuyu, Embu, Meru, *Tharaka, *Kamba, Daiso

C CHAGA [5]: Rwo, Chaga, Rusa, Kahe, Gweno

D NYIKA [4]: Pokomo, Nyika, Digo, *Taita

III ZONE F [13]:

A TONGWE [3]: Tongwe, Bende, Fipa

B SUKUMA-NYAMWEZI [5]: *Sukuma, Nyamwezi, Sumbwa, Kimbu, Bungu

C NYILAMBA-LANGI [5]: Nyilamba, *Rimi, Langi, Mbugwe, Mbugu

IV ZONE G [28]:

A GOGO [2]: Gogo, Kaguru

B SHAMBALA [4]: Tubeta, Casu, Shambala, *Bondei

C ZIGULA-ZARAMO [9]: Zigula, Ngwele, Zaramo, Ngulu, Ruguru, Kami, Kutu, Vidunda, Sagala

D SWAHILI [4]: Tikuu, *Swahili, Pemba, *Komoro

E POGORO [2]: Pogoro, Ndamba

F BENA-KINGA [7]: Sango, Hehe, Bena, Pangwa, Kinga, Wanji, Kisi

V ZONE H [17]:

A KONGO [7]: *Bembe, *Yombe, Kunyi, Ndingi, Mboka, *Kongo, Dondo

B MBUNDU [4]: *North Mbundu, Sama, Bolo, Songo

C YAKA [5]: Yaka, Suku, Hungu, Mbangala, Sinji

D HUNGANA [1]: Hungana

VI ZONE J [30]:

A NYORO-LUGANDA [5]: *Nyoro, *Luganda, Soga, Gwere, Nyala

B HAYA-KWAYA [5]: Karagwe, Haya, Dzindza, Kerebe, Kwaya

C MASABA-LUYIA [6]: *Masaba, *Luyia, *Nyole, Suamia, Nyuli, *Syan

D KONZO [2]: *Konzo, Nande

E SHI-HAVU [7]: Hunde, Havu, Shi, Fuliru, Vira, Kabwari, Tembo

VII ZONE K [26]:

- A HOLU [2]: Yeci, Holu
- B CHOKWE-LUCHAZI [9]: Chokwe, *Luimbi, Luchazi, *Lwena, Mbuunda, Nyengo, Mbwela, Nkangala, Ngangela
- C SALAMPASU-NDEMBO [3]: Salampasu, Ndembo, Ruund
- D KWANGWA [8]: *Luyi, Mbowe, *Kwangali, Masi, Simaa, Sanjo, Kwangwa, Gova
- E SUBIA [2]: Totela, *Subia
- F MBALA [1]: Mbala
- G DIRIKU [1]: Diriku

VIII ZONE L [15]:

- A BWILE [1]: Bwile
- B SONGYE [6]: Kete, Mbagani, Songye, Luna, Budya, *Bangubangu
- C LUBA [5]: *Luba-Kasai, Kanyok, *Luba-Shaba, Hemba, Sanga
- D KAONDE [1]: Kaonde
- E NKOYA [2]: Mbwera, Nkoya

IX ZONE M [24]:

- A RUNGU [4]: Pimbwe, Rungwa, Rungu, *Mambwe
- B NYIKA-SAFWA [7]: *Ndali, Mwanga, Nyiha, Malila, Safwa, Iwa, Tembo
- C NYAKYUSA [1]: *Nyakyusa
- D BEMBA [3]: Taabwa, Bemba, Aushi
- E BISA-LAMBA [5]: *Bisa, Lala, Swaka, Lamba, Seba
- F LENJE-TONGA [4]: Lenje, Soli, *Ila, Tonga

X ZONE N [12]:

- A MANDA [4]: Manda, Matengo, Mpoto, Tonga
- B TUMBUKA [1]: Tumbuka
- C NYANJA [1]: *Nyanja
- D SENGA-SENA [6]: Senga, Kunda, *Nyungwe, *Sena, Rue, Podzo

XI ZONE P [14]:

- A MATUMBI [5]: Ndengereko, Ruihi, Matumbi, Ngindo, Mbunga
- B YAO [5]: *Yao, *Mwera, Makonde, Ndonde, Mabiha
- C MAKUA [4]: *Makua, Lomwe, Ngulu, Chuabo

[β CENTRAL BANTU]

XII ZONE R [9]:

- A SOUTH MBUNDU [4]: *South Mbundu, Ndombe, Nyaneka, *Nkumbi
- B NDONGA [4]: Kwanyama, *Ndonga, Kwambi, Ngandyera
- C HERERO [1]: Herero

XIII ZONE S [22]:

- A SHONA [6]: *Shona, *Zezuru, Manyika, *Karanga, Ndau, Kalanga
- B VENDA [1]: *Venda
- C SOTHO-TSWANA [4]: *Tswana, *Northern Sotho, *Southern Sotho, *Lozi
- D NGUNI [5]: *Xhosa, *Zulu, *Swati, *Ndebele, Ngoni
- E TSWA-RONGA [4]: Tswa, *Tonga, *Tsonga, *Ronga
- F CHOPI [2]: *Chopi, Tonga-Inhambane

NILO-SAHARAN [138]:

- I SONGHAI [1]: *Songhai
- II SAHARAN [5]:
  - A WESTERN [3]:
    - 1 KANURI [2]: *Kanuri, Kanembu
    - 2 TUBU [1]: *Tubu
  - B EASTERN [2]: Zagawa, Berti
- III MABAN [6]:
  - [2]: Mimi$_1$, Mimi$_2$
  - A MABANG [4]:
    - [2]: *Mabang, Mesalit
    - 1 RUNGA-KIBET [2]: Runga, Kibet
- IV FUR [2]: *Fur, Biltine
- V EAST SUDANIC [80]:
  - A EASTERN [18]:
    - 1 NUBIAN [5]:
      - a WESTERN [1]: *Meidob
      - b CENTRAL [3]: *Birgid, *Debri, *Dongolawi
      - c NORTHERN [1]: *Mahas
    - 2 SURMA [8]:
      - [3]: *Murle, Bale, Zilmamu
      - a MAJANG-SHABO [2]: Majang, Shabo
      - b KWEGU [3]: Kwegu, *Suri, Me'en
    - 3 NERA [1]: *Nera
    - 4 EASTERN JEBEL [4]:
      - [1]: *Gaam
      - a AKA-KELO-MOLO [3]: Aka, Kelo, Molo
  - B WESTERN [15]:
    - 1 NYIMANG [2]: *Nyimang, *Dinik
    - 2 TEMEIN [3]: *Ronge, Doni, Dese
    - 3 TAMA [3]:
      - [1]: Merarit
      - a TAMA-SUNGOR [2]: *Tama, *Sungor
    - 4 DAJU [7]:
      - a EASTERN [2]: *Shatt, Liguri
      - b WESTERN [5]: Mongo, Sila, Nyala, Lagawa, Nyalgulgule
  - C NILOTIC [44]:
    - 1 WESTERN [21]:
      - a LUO [14]:
        - i NORTHERN [7]:
          - [5]: *Shilluk, *Anuak, Jur, Thuri, Bor$_1$
          - α MABAN-BURUN [2]: Maban, Burun
        - ii SOUTHERN [7]:
          - [3]: Labwor, Lwo, Adhola
          - α LUO-ACHOLI [4]:
            - [1]: *Luo

                I ALUR-ACHOLI [3]:
                    [1]: *Alur
                    A LANGO-ACHOLI [2]: Lango, *Acholi
        b DINKA-NUER [7]:
            i NUER [2]: *Nuer, Atuot
            ii DINKA [5]: Agar, *Bor$_2$, Padang, *Rek, Kumam
    2 EASTERN [9]:
        a BARI [2]: *Bari, Kakwa
        b LOTUXO-TESO [7]:
            i LOTUXO-MAA [3]:
                α LOTUXO [1]: *Lotuxo
                β ONGAMO-MAA [2]: Ongamo, *Maasai
            ii TESO-TURKANA [4]: Karamojong, Topotha, Turkana, *Teso
    3 SOUTHERN [14]:
        a KALENJIN [12]:
            i NANDI-MARKWETA [5]: Nandi, *Kipsikiis, Keiyo, Tuken, Markweta
            ii ELGON [5]:
                [2]: Sapiny, Kony
                α POK-TERIK [3]: Pok, Ng'oma, Terik
            iii OKIEK [1]: Okiek
            iv PAKOT [1]: *Pakot
        b TATO [2]: Omotik, Datooga
D KULIAK [3]:
    [1]: Ik
    1 NGANGEA-SO [2]: Ngangea, *So
VI CENTRAL SUDANIC [36]:
A WEST CENTRAL [24]:
    1 KRESH [2]: Kresh, Aja
    2 BONGO-BAGIRMI [22]:
        a BONGO [4]: Baka, *Beli, *Bongo, Morokodo
        b SINYAR [1]: Sinyar
        c SARA-BAGIRMI [14]:
            i SARA [6]:
                [1]: Vale
                α SARA PROPER [5]: *Gambai, Kaba, Kaba Dunjo, *Mbai, *Sara
            ii BAGIRMI [8]: Babalia, *Bagirmi, Fongoro, Disa, Gele, Gula, *Kenga, Kuka
        d KARA [3]: Furu, *Kara, *Yulu
B EAST CENTRAL [12]:
    1 MORU-MADI [6]:
        a NORTHERN [1]: *Moru
        b CENTRAL [4]: Avukaya, Kaliko, Logo, *Logbara
        c SOUTHERN [1]: *Madi

2 MANGBETU-ASUA [2]: *Mangbetu, Asua
3 MANGBUTU-EFE [3]: *Mamvu, Mangbutu, Ndo
4 BALENDRU [1]: *Balendru
VII BERTA [1]: *Berta
VIII KUNAMA [1]: *Kunama
IX KOMUZ [6]:
A GUMUZ [1]: Bega
B KOMAN [5]:
1 ANEJ [1]: Anej
2 KWAMA-OPO [4]:
a KWAMA [1]: Kwama
b KOMO-OPO [3]:
i OPO [1]: Opo
ii KOMO-TWAMPA [2]: *Komo, *Twampa

AFRO-ASIATIC [241]:
I †ANCIENT EGYPTIAN [0]: *†Ancient Egyptian, *†Coptic
II BERBER [30]:
A †GUANCHE [0]: †Guanche
B †EAST NUMIDIAN [0]: †East Numidian (= Old Libyan)
C BERBER PROPER [30]:
1 EASTERN [4]:
[1]: Siwa
a AWJILA-SOKNA [3]: Awjila, Sokna, Ghadames
2 TUAREG [3]:
a NORTHERN [1]: Tamahaq
b SOUTHERN [2]: Tamazheq, *Tamasheq
3 WESTERN [1]: *Zenaga
4 NORTHERN [22]:
a ATLAS [2]: *Shilha, *Tamazight
b KABYLE [1]: *Kabyle
c ZENATI [19]:
[7]: Shawiya, Tidikelt, Tuat, *Riff, Ghmara, Tlemcen, Sheliff Basin
i MZAB-WARGLA [5]: Gurara, Mzab, Wargla, Ghardaia, Tugurt
ii EAST ZENATI [7]: Tmagurt, Sened, Jerba, Tamezret, Taujjut, Zwara, Nefusi
III CHADIC [123]:
A MASA [5]: Masa, Zime, Mesme, Marba, *Musey
B EAST [28]:
1 GROUP A [13]:
a SOMRAI [7]:
i GROUP 1 [3]: Somrai, *Tumak, Ndam
ii GROUP 2 [4]: Sarwa, Gadang, Mod, Miltu
b NANCERE [4]:
i GROUP 1 [2]: Nancere, Lele
ii GROUP 2 [2]: Gabri, Kabalai
c KERA [2]: Kera, Kwang
2 GROUP B [15]:
[1]: Mokulu
a DANGLA [11]:
i GROUP 1 [6]: *Dangla, Migama, Mahwa, Jegu, Mogum,Bidiyo
ii GROUP 2 [5]: Mubi, Masmaje, Kajakse, Kujarge, Toram
b SOKORO [3]: Sokoro, Barain, Saba
C BIU-MANDARA [37]:
1 GROUP A [32]:
a TERA [4]:
i GROUP 1 [2]: *Tera, Jara
ii GROUP 2 [2]: *Ga'anda, Hona
b BURA-MANDARA [21]:
i BURA-HIGI [7]:
α BURA [5]:

I GROUP 1 [3]: *Bura, Chibak, Putai
II GROUP 2 [2]: *Margi, *Kilba
β HIGI [2]: *Higi, Bana
ii MANDARA-MATAKAM [14]:
[1]: Sukur
α MANDARA [7]:
[1]: Lamang
I MANDARA PROPER [6]:
[2]: Mandara, Paduko
A GLAVDA [4]: *Glavda, Guduf, Dghwede, Gvoko
β MATAKAM [6]: Mafa, *Mofu, Gisiga, Mada, Hurza, Muktele
c DABA [3]: *Daba, Gawar, Hina
d BATA [4]:
[1]: Gudu
i BATA PROPER [3]: *Bata, *Gude, Nzangi
2 GROUP B [5]:
[2]: *Musgu, Gidar
a KOTOKO [3]:
[1]: *Buduma
i KOTOKO PROPER [2]: Kotoko, Logone
D WEST [53]:
1 GROUP A [32]:
a HAUSA [2]: *Hausa, *Gwandara
b BOLE-ANGAS [24]:
i BOLE-TANGALE [14]:
α BOLE [10]:
[1]: Karekare
I BOLE PROPER [9]: *Bole, Bele, Ngamo, *Maha, Kirfi, Deno, Kubi, Galambu, Gera
β TANGALE [4]:
[1]: *Kanakuru
I TANGALE PROPER [3]: Tangale, Pero, Kupto
ii ANGAS [10]
[1]: Gerka
α ANGAS PROPER [9]:
I GROUP 1 [4]: *Angas, *Sura, *Kofyar, Chip
II GROUP 2 [5]: *Goemai, Montol, Tal, Pyapun, Koenoem
c RON [6]:
[1]: Fyer
i RON PROPER [5]: Ron, Sha, Kulere, Karfa, Shagawu
2 GROUP B [21]:
a BADE-WARJI [12]:
i BADE [3]:
[1]: Duwai
α BADE PROPER [2]: Bade, *Ngizim

ii WARJI [9]: Warji, *Pa'a, Siri, Diri, Jimbin, Miya, Mburku, Kariya, Tsagu
b ZAAR [9]:
i ZAAR PROPER [5]: *Zaar, Barawa, Zeem, Polchi, Geji
ii GURUNTUM [2]: Guruntum, Ju
iii BOGHOM [2]: Boghom, Mangas
IV OMOTIC [34]:
A SOUTH [3]: *Hamar, Ari, Dime
B NORTH [31]:
1 DIZOID [4]: *Dizi, Dorsha, Shako, Nao
2 MAO [4]: Bambeshi, Hozo, Sezo, Ganza
3 GONGA-GIMOJAN [23]:
a GONGA [8]:
i SOUTH [3]: *Kafa, *Mocha, Bosha
ii CENTRAL [1]: Anfillo
iii NORTH [4]: Naga, Guba, Boro, Amuru
b GIMOJAN [15]:
i JANJERO [2]: *Janjero, Fuga
ii OMETO-GIMIRA [13]:
α GIMIRA [2]: Bencho, She
β CHARA [1]: *Chara
γ OMETO [10]:
I WEST [1]: *Basketo
II SOUTH [1]: Male
III CENTRAL [2]: Oyda, *Ometo
IV EAST [6]: *Zayse, Zergulla, Ganjule, Gidiccho, Gatsame, Koyra
V CUSHITIC [35]:
A BEJA [1]: *Beja
B CUSHITIC PROPER [34]:
1 CENTRAL CUSHITIC [5]:
a SOUTH [1]: *Awngi
b NORTH [4]:
[2]: Xamir, *Kemant (= Falasha)
i BILIN-XAMTA [2]: *Bilin, Xamta
2 EASTERN CUSHITIC [22]:
a HIGHLAND [5]:
[1]: *Burji
i SIDAMO [4]:
[2]: *Sidamo, *Gedeo
α KAMBATA-HADIYYA [2]: *Kambata, *Hadiyya
b YAAKUAN-DULLAY [5]:
i YAAKUAN [1]: *Yaaku
ii DULLAY [4]: Harso, *Gawwada, Tsamay, Birale
c LOWLAND [12]:
i AFAR-SAHO [2]: *Afar, Saho

ii OMO-TANA [6]:
  α GALABOID [2]: *Dasenech, †Elmolo, Arbore
  β BAYSO [1]: *Bayso
  γ SAM [3]:
    [1]: *Rendille
    I SOMALI-AWEER [2]: *Somali, *Aweer
iii OROMOID [4]:
  [1]: *Oromo
  α KONSOID [3]: Bussa, *Gidole, *Konso
3 SOUTHERN CUSHITIC [7]:
  a DAHALO [1]: *Dahalo
  b MA'A [1]: *Ma'a
  c RIFT [5]:
    i EAST [2]: Asa, Kw'adza
    ii WEST [3]: *Iraqw, Alagwa, Burunge

VI SEMITIC [19]:
  [0]: †Eblaic
  A †EAST [0]: *†Akkadian
  B WEST [19]:
    1 CENTRAL [6]:
      a ARAMAIC [2]: *†Old Aramaic, †Syriac, *Assyrian, Aramaic
      b ARABO-CANAANITE [4]:
        i CANAANITE [1]: *†Classical Hebrew, *Hebrew, †Phoenician, *†Ugaritic, †Moabite
        ii ARABIC [3]: *†Classical Arabic, *Eastern Arabic, *Western Arabic, *Maltese
    2 SOUTH [13]:
      [1]: †Epigraphic South Arabian, *South Arabian
      a ETHIOPIC [12]:
        i NORTH [2]:
          [0]: *†Geez
          α NORTH PROPER [2]: *Tigre, *Tigrinya
        ii SOUTH [10]:
          α TRANSVERSAL [4]:
            I AMHARIC-ARGOBBA [2]: *Amharic, Argobba
            II EAST GURAGE-HARARI [2]: *Harari, East Gurage
          β OUTER [6]:
            I N-GROUP [2]:
              [0]: *†Gafat
              A N-NORTH GURAGE [2]: Soddo, Goggot
            II TT-GROUP [4]:
              A TT-NORTH GURAGE [1]: *Muher
              B WEST GURAGE [3]:
                [1]: Masqan
                1 CENTRAL & PERIPHERAL [2]: *Central West Gurage, Peripheral West Gurage

CAUCASIAN [38]:
I SOUTH [4]:
[2]: *Georgian, *Svan
A ZAN [2]: *Mingrelian, Laz
II NORTH [34]:
A NORTHWEST [5]:
[1]: *Ubyx
1 ABXAZ-ABAZA [2]: *Abxaz, *Abaza
2 CIRCASSIAN [2]: *Adygh, *Kabardian
B NORTHEAST [29]:
1 NAX [3]:
[1]: *Bats
a CHECHEN-INGUSH [2]: *Chechen, *Ingush
2 DAGESTAN [26]:
a AVARO-ANDI-DIDO [14]:
i AVAR [1]: *Avar
ii ANDI [8]: *Andi, *Botlix, *Godoberi, *Chamalal, *Bagulal, *Tindi, *Karata, *Axvax
iii DIDO [5]:
[1]: *Xvarshi
α DIDO-HINUX [2]: *Dido, *Hinux
β BEZHTA-HUNZIB [2]: *Bezhta, *Hunzib
b LAK-DARGWA [2]: *Lak, *Dargwa
c LEZGIAN [10]:
[2]: *Archi, *Xinalug
i LEZGIAN PROPER [8]: *Lezgi, *Tabasaran, *Agul, *Rutul, *Tsaxur, *Kryts, *Budux, *Udi

INDO-HITTITE [144]:
I †ANATOLIAN [0]:
    [0]: *†Hittite, †Palaic, †Lydian
  A †LUWOID [0]: †Luwian, †Lycian
II INDO-EUROPEAN [144]:
  A ARMENIAN [1]: *†Classical Armenian, *Armenian
  B †TOCHARIAN [0]: *†Tocharian A, *†Tocharian B
  C INDO-IRANIAN [93]:
    1 INDIC [48]:
        [0]: *†Sanskrit
      a ROMANY [1]: *Romany
      b SINHALESE-MALDIVIAN [3]: *Maldivian, *Sinhalese, Vedda
      c NORTHERN INDIA [44]:
        i DARDIC [16]:
          α CENTRAL [5]: *Bashkarik, Maiya, Tirahi, Torwali, *Wotapuri
          β CHITRAL [2]: Kalasha, Khowar
          γ KUNAR [5]: *Dameli, *Gawar-bati, Shumashti, Nangalami, *Pashai
          δ SHINA [4]: *Dumaki, *Phalura, Shina, *Kashmiri
        ii WESTERN [4]:
          α SOUTH [2]: *Marathi, *Konkani
          β NORTHWEST [2]: *Sindhi, *Lahnda
        iii CENTRAL [16]: Parya, Baluj, *Punjabi, *Marwari, *Banjari, *Malvi, *Gade Lohar, *Gujarati, *Bhili, Khandeshi, *Hindi, *Urdu, Dogri, Western Pahari, *Garhwali, *Kumauni
        iv EAST-CENTRAL [5]:
            [2]: *Nepali, *Awadhi
          α BIHARI [3]: *Bhojpuri, *Maithili, Magahi
        v EASTERN [3]:
            [1]: *Oriya
          α BENGALI-ASSAMESE [2]: *Bengali, *Assamese
    2 NURISTANI [5]: *Ashkun, Kalasha-ala, *Kati, Tregami, Wasi-weri
    3 IRANIAN [40]:
      a EASTERN [12]:
        i NORTHEAST [10]:
          α WEST SCYTHIAN [1]: †Scythian, *Ossetic
          β †KHWAREZMIAN [0]: *†Avestan, †Khwarezmian
          γ SOGDIAN [1]: †Sogdian, *Yaghnobi
          δ †BACTRIAN [0]: †Bactrian
          ε EAST SCYTHIAN [8]:
              [1]: †Saka, *Pashto
            I PAMIR [7]:
              A WAKHI [1]: *Wakhi
              B MUNJI-YIDGHA [2]: *Munji, *Yidgha
              C SANGLECHI-ISHKASHMI [2]: *Sanglechi, *Ishkashmi

D SHUGHNI-YAZGULAMI [2]: *Shughni, *Yazgulami
ii SOUTHEAST [2]: *Parachi, *Ormuri
b WESTERN [28]:
i NORTHWEST [21]:
[0]: †Median, †Parthian
α CENTRAL IRAN [8]: *Yazdi, Nayini, Natanzi, Soi, Khunsari, Gazi, Sivandi, Vafsi
β SEMNANI [2]: Semnani, Sangisari
γ CASPIAN [2]: *Gilaki, *Mazanderani
δ TALYSH [2]: *Talysh, Harzani
ϵ ZAZA-GORANI [2]: Zaza, Gorani
ζ BALUCHI [2]: *Baluchi, Bashkardi
η KURDISH [3]: *Kirmanji, *Kurdi, Kermanshahi
ii SOUTHWEST [7]:
α PERSIAN [2]: *†Old Persian, *Farsi (= Persian), *Tajiki
β TATI [1]: *Tati
γ FARS [2]: Fars, Lari
δ LURI [2]: Luri, Kumzari
D ALBANIAN [1]: *Albanian
E GREEK [2]: †Classical Greek, *Greek, Tsakonian
F ITALIC [16]:
1 †OSCO-UMBRIAN [0]: *†Oscan, *†Umbrian, †Sabellian
2 LATINO-FALISCAN [16]:
[0]: *†Faliscan, *†Latin
a ROMANCE [16]:
i SARDINIAN [1]: *Sardinian
ii CONTINENTAL [15]:
α EASTERN [4]:
I NORTH [2]: *Rumanian, *Istro-Rumanian
II SOUTH [2]: *Megleno-Rumanian, *Arumanian
β WESTERN [11]:
I ITALO-ROMANCE [1]:
A †DALMATIAN [0]: †Dalmatian
B ITALIAN [1]: *Italian
II RHAETO-ROMANCE [3]: *Friulian, Ladin, *Romansch
III GALLO-IBERO-ROMANCE [7]:
A GALLO-ROMANCE [3]:
1 NORTH [2]: *Franco-Provençal, *French
2 SOUTH [1]: *Provençal
B IBERO-ROMANCE [4]:
1 NORTH [4]:
a EASTERN [1]: *Catalan
b CENTRAL [1]: *Spanish
c WESTERN [2]: *Galician, *Portuguese
2 †SOUTH [0]: †Mozarabic

G CELTIC [4]:
- 1 †CONTINENTAL [0]: *†Gaulish
- 2 INSULAR [4]:
  - a GOIDELIC [2]: *Irish (= Gaelic), *Scottish Gaelic, †Manx
  - b BRYTHONIC [2]: *Breton, *Welsh, *†Cornish

H GERMANIC [12]:
- 1 †EAST [0]: *†Gothic, †Vandalic, †Burgundian
- 2 NORTH [5]:
  - [0]: *†Runic
  - a EAST [2]: *Danish, *Swedish
  - b WEST [3]: *Norwegian, *Icelandic, *Faroese
- 3 WEST [7]:
  - a CONTINENTAL [5]:
    - i EAST [3]: *German, *Yiddish, Luxembourgeois
    - ii WEST [2]: *Dutch, *Afrikaans
  - b NORTH SEA [2]: *Frisian, *English

I BALTO-SLAVIC [15]:
- 1 BALTIC [2]:
  - a †WEST [0]: *†Old Prussian
  - b EAST [2]: *Latvian, *Lithuanian
- 2 SLAVIC [13]:
  - a EAST [3]:
    - i NORTH [2]: *Russian, *Byelorussian
    - ii SOUTH [1]: *Ukrainian
  - b WEST [6]:
    - i NORTH [2]: *Polish, *Kashubian, *†Polabian
    - ii CENTRAL [2]: *Upper Sorbian, Lower Sorbian
    - iii SOUTH [2]: *Czech, *Slovak
  - c SOUTH [4]:
    - [0]: *†Old Church Slavonic
    - i WEST [2]: *Slovene, *Serbo-Croatian
    - ii EAST [2]: *Macedonian, *Bulgarian

URALIC-YUKAGHIR [24]:
I YUKAGHIR [1]: *Yukaghir, †Chuvantsy, †Omok
II URALIC [23]:
A SAMOYED [4]:
1 NORTH [3]: *Nenets, *Enets, *Nganasan
2 SOUTH [1]: *Selkup, *†Kamas
B FINNO-UGRIC [19]:
1 UGRIC [3]:
[1]: *Hungarian
a OB-UGRIC [2]: *Xanty, *Mansi
2 FINNIC [16]:
a PERMIC [2]: *Udmurt, *Komi
b VOLGAIC [2]: *Mari, *Mordvin
c NORTH FINNIC [12]:
i SAAMIC (= LAPPIC) [3]: *Northern Saami, *Eastern Saami, *Southern Saami
ii BALTIC FINNIC [9]: *Finnish, *Ingrian, *Karelian, Olonets, Ludic, *Vepsian, *Votic, *Estonian, *Livonian

ALTAIC [63]:
I ALTAIC PROPER [59]:
A TURKIC [31]:
[0]: *†Old Turkic
1 BOLGAR [1]: *Chuvash
2 COMMON TURKIC [30]:
a SOUTHERN [7]:
[5]: *Khalaj, *Gagauz, *Turkish, *Crimean Turkish, *Turkmen
i AZERBAIJANI [2]: *Azerbaijani, Qashqay
b EASTERN [3]: *Uighur, *Uzbek, *Salar
c WESTERN [7]:
[1]: *Bashkir
i KUMYK-KARACHAY [3]: *Karachay, *Karaim, *Kumyk
ii TATAR [3]: *Tatar, *Baraba, Crimean Tatar
d CENTRAL [4]: *Nogai, *Karakalpak, *Kazakh, *Kirghiz
e NORTHERN [9]:
i YAKUT [2]: *Yakut, Dolgan
ii TUVA-ALTAI [7]:
[1]: *Khakas
α ALTAI [2]: *Altai, *Northern Altai
β CHULYM-SHOR [2]: *Chulym, *Shor
γ TUVA-KARAGAS [2]: *Tuva, *Karagas
B MONGOLIAN-TUNGUS [28]:
1 MONGOLIAN [12]:
[0]: *†Classical Mongolian
a WESTERN [1]: *Moghol

b EASTERN [11]:
  i DAGUR [1]: Dagur
  ii MONGUOR [4]: *Monguor, Yellow Uighur, *Pao-an, Santa
  iii OIRAT-KHALKHA [6]:
    α OIRAT-KALMYK [2]: Oirat, *Kalmyk
    β KHALKHA-BURIAT [4]:
      I BURIAT [1]: *Buriat
      II MONGOLIAN PROPER [3]: *Khalkha, *Khorchin, *Ordos
2 TUNGUS [16]:
  a NORTHERN [6]:
    [2]: *Even, *Negidal
    i EVENKI [4]: *Evenki, Solon, Manegir, Orochon
  b SOUTHERN [10]:
    i SOUTHWESTERN [1]: †Ju-chen, *Manchu
    ii SOUTHEASTERN [9]:
      α NANAJ [7]: Akani, Birar, *Gold, Kile, *Olcha, *Orok, Samagir
      β UDIHE [2]: *Oroch, *Udihe
II KOREAN-JAPANESE [4]:
  [2]: *Korean, *Ainu
  A JAPANESE-RYUKYUAN [2]: *Japanese, *Ryukyuan

CHUKCHI-KAMCHATKAN [5]:
I NORTHERN [4]:
  A CHUKCHI [1]: *Chukchi
  B KORYAK-ALYUTOR [3]: *Kerek, *Koryak, *Alyutor
II SOUTHERN [1]: *Kamchadal

ESKIMO-ALEUT [9]:
I ALEUT [1]: *Aleut
II ESKIMO [8]:
  A INUIT [3]: Alaskan Inuit, *Canadian Inuit, *Greenlandic
  B YUPIK [5]:
    1 ALASKAN [2]: Alutiiq, *Central Yupik
    2 SIBERIAN [3]:
      [1]: Sirenik
      a CHAPLINO-NAUKAN [2]: *Chaplino, *Naukan

ELAMO-DRAVIDIAN [28]:
I †ELAMITE [0]: *†Elamite
II DRAVIDIAN [28]:
  A NORTHWEST [1]: *Brahui
  B DRAVIDIAN PROPER [27]:
    1 NORTHEAST [2]: *Kurux, *Malto
    2 CENTRAL [13]:
      a KOLAMI-PARJI [4]:
        i KOLAMI-NAIKI [2]: *Kolami, Naiki
        ii PARJI-GADABA [2]: *Parji, *Gadaba
      b TELUGU-KUI [9]:
        i GONDI-KUI [7]:
          α GONDI-KOYA [2]: *Gondi, *Koya
          β KONDA-KUI [5]:
              [1]: *Konda
            I MANDA-KUI [4]:
              A MANDA-PENGO [2]: Manda, *Pengo
              B KUI-KUVI [2]: *Kui, *Kuvi
        ii TELUGU [2]: *Telugu, Savara
    3 SOUTH [12]:
      a TULU [3]: *Tulu, Bellari, *Koraga
      b TAMIL-KANNADA [9]:
        i KANNADA [2]: *Kannada, Badaga
        ii TAMIL-KODAGU [7]:
          α KODAGU [2]: *Kodagu, *Kurumba
          β TODA-KOTA [2]: *Toda, *Kota
          γ TAMIL-IRULA [3]:
              [1]: *Irula
            I TAMIL [2]: *Tamil, *Malayalam

SINO-TIBETAN [258]:
I SINITIC [12]:
  A BAI [4]: Eryuan, Hoking, Bai, Tali
  B CHINESE [8]:
      [0]: *†Archaic Chinese
    1 MIN [2]: *Northern Min, *Southern Min
    2 MANDARIN-YUE [6]:
      a MANDARIN [1]: *Mandarin
      b XIANG [1]: *Xiang
      c WU [1]: *Wu
      d GAN-KEJIA [2]: *Gan, Kejia
      e YUE [1]: *Yue (= Cantonese)
II TIBETO-KAREN [246]:
  A KAREN [14]:
    1 PHO [4]:
        [1]: *Pa-o
      a PHO-PHLON [3]: *Pho, Leke, *Phlon
    2 SGAW-BWE [10]:
        [1]: Brec
      a KAYAH [2]: Kayah, Yinbaw
      b BWE [4]: Bwe, Geba, Gekho, Padaung
      c SGAW [3]: *Sgaw, Pakü, *Mopwa
  B TIBETO-BURMAN [232]:
    1 TIBETIC [75]:
        [2]: Kaman, Hruso
      a NEWARI-PAHRI [2]: *Newari, Pahri
      b DIGARO-MIDU [2]: Digaro, Midu
      c DHIMAL-TOTO [2]: Dhimal, Toto
      d ADI-NISHI [7]: *Lepcha, Adi, Tagen, *Nishi, Apatani, Yano, Lho-pa
      e BODIC [10]:
          [4]: Monpa, Gyarung, Kaike, Ghale
        i TAMANG [4]:
            [2]: *Tamang, Manang
          α GURUNG-THAKALI [2]: *Gurung, *Thakali
        ii TIBETAN [2]: *†Classical Tibetan, *†Zhang-zhung, *Central Tibetan, *Western Tibetan
      f CENTRAL HIMALAYAN [7]:
          [5]: *Magar, Raji, Raute, Kham, *Kusunda
        i VAYU-CHEPANG [2]: Vayu, *Chepang
      g WEST HIMALAYAN [17]:
        i NORTH [4]: Bunan, Thebor, Sumchu, Sungam
        ii NORTHWEST [7]:
          α KANAURI [4]: Kanauri, Chitkhuli, Tukpa, Kanashi
          β MANCHATI [3]: Manchati, Chamba, Rangloi
        iii ALMORA [4]: Rangkas, Darmiya, Chaudangsi, Byangsi
        iv EASTERN [2]: Thami, Bhramu

h EAST HIMALAYAN [21]:
  i WESTERN [8]:
    [2]: *Thulung, Chaurasya
    α BAHING [3]: Bahing, Umbule, *Sunwar
    β DUMI [3]: Dumi, *Khaling, Rai
  ii EASTERN [13]:
    α KHAMBU [3]: Khambu, Nachereng, Kulung
    β BONTAWA [10]:
      [3]: Rodong, Lambichong, Athpare
      I LOHORONG [3]: Lohorong, Yakha, *Limbu
      II WALING [4]: Waling, Rungchenbung, Kiranti, Dungmali
i DZORGAIC [5]: Ch'iang, Dzorgai, Kortse, Pingfang, Thochu
2 BARIC [16]:
  a BODO-GARO [7]:
    [1]: Chutiya
    i BODO [4]: *Bodo, Dimasa, *Tripuri, Lalung, †Moran
    ii GARO [2]: *Garo, *Koch
  b CHANG-TANGSA [9]: Tangsa, Moshang, Shangge, *Nocte, Konyak, Wancho, Phom, Chang, Mon
3 BURMIC [141]:
  a KUKI-NAGA [71]:
    [3]: *Meithei, *Mikir, Mru
    i NORTHERN NAGA [8]:
      [2]: Yimchungru, *Lotha
      α SANGTAM [3]: Lophomi, Thukumi, Pochuri
      β AO [3]: *Ao, Mongsen, Tengsa
    ii EASTERN NAGA [8]:
      α RENGMA [3]: Rengma, Ntenyi, Meluri
      β SIMI [3]: Kezhama, Mao, Zumomi
      γ ANGAMI [2]: *Angami, Chakrima
    iii SOUTHERN NAGA [3]: Maring, *Tangkhul, Kupome
    iv WESTERN KUKI [5]: Maram, Liangmai, Nruanghmei, Khoirao, Zeme
    v NORTHERN KUKI [6]: *Kamhau, Ralte, Siyin, *Thado, Vuite, Zo
    vi OLD KUKI [14]:
      [1]: Kyao
      α LAMGANG [2]: Lamgang, Anal
      β KOLHRENG [3]: Kolhreng, Kom, Tarao
      γ CENTRAL [4]: Chiru, Aimol, Purum, Langrong
      δ WESTERN [4]:
        [1]: Southern Luhupa
        I NORTHERN [2]: Hrangkhol, Biate
        II SOUTHERN [1]: Hallam

vii CENTRAL KUKI [12]:
[1]: Langet
α MIZO [5]: *Mizo, Zahao, Hmar, Pankhu, Paang
β HAKA [2]: Haka, Shonshe
γ LAKHER [4]: *Mara, Tlongsai, Hawthai, Sabeu
viii SOUTHERN KUKI [12]:
α SHO [7]: *Sho, Khyeng, Khyang, Thayetmo, Minbu, Chinbon, Lemyo
β CHINBOK [2]: Chinbok, Ng'men
γ KHAMI [3]: *Khami, Khumi, Ngala
b KACHIN-LUIC [19]:
[1]: Taman, †Chairel
i KACHIN [3]: Jinghpaw, Hkauri, Hka-hku, †Jili
ii LUIC [5]: †Andro, Sengmai, *Kadu, Sak, Chakpa, Phayeng
iii RAWANG [10]: Krangku, Lungmi, Nung, *Rawang, Zithung, Trung, Metu, Melam, Tamalu, Tukiumu
c BURMESE-MOSO [51]:
i MOSO [2]: Moso, Naxi
ii BURMESE-LOLO [49]:
α BURMIC [6]:
I NORTHERN [5]: Phun, Achang, *Maru, Lashi, *Tsaiwa
II SOUTHERN [1]: *Burmese
β LOLO [43]:
[3]: Daignet, Duampu, Nameji, *†Sihia, †Pai-lang, †Tosu
I NORTHERN LOLO [14]:
[11]: Thongho, Pakishan, Kangsiangying, Kiaokio, Nee, Laichau, Tudza, Nuoku, Liangshan, P'ou-la, Sani
A NASÖ [3]: Ulu, Ko-p'u, Weining
II EAST LOLO [2]: Khoany, Mung
III CENTRAL LOLO [6]:
[1]: *Lisu
A LOLO PROPER [5]: Nyi, Chökö, Ahi, Lolopho, Phupha
IV SOUTHERN LOLO [13]:
A PHUNOI [6]: *Phunoi, Pyen, *Bisu, Mpi, Khaskhong, Hwethom
B AKHA [7]: *Akha, Ako, Asong, Phana, Menghwa, Hani, *Lahu
V RESIDUAL LOLO [5]:
[1]: Ugong
A HSIFAN [4]: Manyak, Horpa, Menia, Muli

AUSTRIC [1,175]:
I MIAO-YAO [4]:
A MIAO [1]: *Miao
B YAO [3]: *Laka, *Punu, *Mien (= Yao)
II AUSTROASIATIC [155]:
A MUNDA [17]:
1 NORTH [8]:
a KORKU [1]: *Korku
b KHERWARI [7]:
i SANTALI [2]: *Santali, Turi
ii MUNDARI [5]: *Mundari, *Ho, Korwa, Birhor, Asuri
2 SOUTH [9]:
a CENTRAL [2]: *Kharia, *Juang
b KORAPUT [7]:
i SORA-GORUM [3]:
α GORUM [1]: *Gorum
β SORA-JURAY [2]: *Sora, Juray
ii GUTOB-REMO-GTA' [4]:
α GUTOB-REMO [2]: *Gutob, *Remo
β GTA' [2]: *Plains Gta', Hill Gta'
B MON-KHMER [138]:
1 NORTH [43]:
a KHASI [2]: *Khasi, *Amwi
b PALAUNGIC-KHMUIC [34]:
[1]: Mang
i PALAUNGIC [27]:
α EAST [7]:
[1]: *Danau
I PALAUNG-RIANG [6]:
[1]: *Riang
A PALAUNG [5]: *Shwe, Da'ang, Rumai, Bonglong, Pale

β WEST [20]:
I LAMET-KHAMET [2]: Lamet, Khamet
II WAIC [12]:
A BULANG [5]: Phang, *P'uman$_2$, Plang, Tai-Loi, Kem Degne
B WA-LAWA [7]: *Wa, *Lawa, La, Phalok, Son, En, K'ala
III ANGKUIC [6]: Mok, Angku, Kon Keu, P'uman$_1$, Pou Ma, Kiorr
ii KHMUIC [6]:
α YUMBRI-MRABRI [2]: Yumbri, Mrabri
β MAL-KHMU' [4]:
[1]: *Khmu'
I MAL [3]: *Mal, Phray, Phaï
c VIET-MUONG [7]:
i GROUP I [3]: *Thavung, Pakatan, Arem
ii GROUP II [1]: Poong
iii GROUP III [2]: Mày, *Muòng
iv GROUP IV [1]: *Vietnamese
2 EAST [72]:
a KATUIC [28]:
i WEST [14]:
α SO-BRŨ [10]: So, *Brũ, Mangkong, Tri, Chali, Khua, Leung, Kaleu, Galler, Vân Kìêu
β KUY-SUEI [4]: *Suei, Na Nhyang, *Kuy, Yeu
ii EAST [14]:
[2]: Katang, Tareng
α PACŎH-PHUONG [2]: *Pacŏh, Phuong
β KATU-THAP [3]: *Katu, Kantu, Thap
γ TA-OY-TONG [4]: Ta-Oy, Tong, Ong, Kha In
δ NGEQ-NKRIANG [3]: *Ngeq, Nkriang, Kha Koh
b BAHNARIC [37]:
i SOUTH [8]:
α STIENG-CHRAU [2]: *Stieng, *Chrau

β SRE-MNONG [6]:
[2]: *Sre, Maa'
I MNONG [4]:
[2]: *Eastern Mnong, Biat
A SOUTHERN-CENTRAL [2]: Southern Mnong, *Central Mnong
ii WEST [13]:
[6]: *Loven, Lave, Sok, Sapuan, Cheng, Suq
α NYAHÖÑ-PROUAC [2]: Nyahöñ, Prouac
β OI-THE [2]: Oi, The
γ BRAO-KRAVET [3]: Brao, Kru'ng, Kravet
iii CENTRAL [4]: *Bahnar, Alak, Tampuan, Lmam
iv NORTH [12]:
α EAST [3]:
[1]: Takua
I CUA-KAYONG [2]: Cua, Kayong
β WEST [9]:
[2]: *Rengao, Duan
I JEH-HALĂNG [2]: *Jeh, *Halăng
II SEDANG-TODRAH [5]:
A SEDANG [2]: *Sedang, *Hrê
B TODRAH-MONOM [3]:
[1]: Monom
1 TODRAH [2]: *Modra, *Didra
c KHMER [1]: *Khmer (= Cambodian)
d PEARIC [6]:
i EASTERN [1]: Pear
ii WESTERN [5]:
[1]: Suoy
α SAMRE [2]: Samre, *Somray
β CHONG [2]: Chong, Sa'och
3 SOUTH [23]:
a MONIC [2]: *Mon, Nyah Kur

b ASLIAN [19]:
i SEMANG-JAH HUT [15]:
[1]: *Jah Hut
α SEMANG-SENOIC [14]:
I SEMANG [9]:
[1]: *Che' Wong
A WESTERN [3]: *Kensiu, *Kenta' Bong, Mos
B EASTERN [5]: *Jehai, *Mendriq, *Bateg Deq, *Mintil, *Bateg Nong
II SENOIC [5]:
[1]: *Semai
A NORTH [4]:
[1]: *Temiar
1 LANOH-SEMNAM [3]: *Lanoh, *Sabum, *Semnam
ii SOUTHERN [4]: *Mah Meri, *Semaq Beri, *Semelai, *Temoq
c NICOBAR ISLANDS [2]: Shompen, *Nicobarese
III AUSTRO-TAI [1,016]:
A DAIC [57]:
1 LATI-GELAO [2]: Lati, Gelao
2 LI-KAM-TAI [55]:
a LI-LAQUA [3]:
[1]: Li
i LAQUA-LAHA [2]: Laqua, Laha
b BE-KAM-TAI [52]:
[1]: *Be
i LAKKIA-KAM-TAI [51]:
α LAKKIA [1]: *Lakkia
β KAM-TAI [50]:
I KAM-SUI [6]: Kam, *Mak, Sui, Then, Maonan, Mulao
II TAI [44]:
A NORTHERN [18]: Ch'ien-chiang, Zhuang, Giay, Hsi-lin, Kwei-yang, Ling-yun, Lung-an, Nhang, *Bouyei, Po-se, Qui-chau, *Saek, Tien-chow, T'ien-pa, Zhongjia, Tushan, *Wu-ming, *Yay

[A DAIC]

B CENTRAL [8]: Man Cao-lan, *Nung, Tay, Tho, Tien-pao, Ts'un-lao, Yung-chu'un, *Lung-chow

C SOUTHWESTERN [18]: *Khamti, *Khün, *Lao (= Laotian), Lü, Maw, Phu Thai, Phuan, *Shan, *Thai (= Siamese), Northern Thai, Southern Thai, *White Tai, *Black Tai, Red Tai, Tay Nua, Ya, Yuan, Yunnan Shant'ou

B AUSTRONESIAN [959]:
- 1 ATAYALIC [2]: *Atayal, *Sedeq
- 2 TSOUIC [4]:
  - [1]: *Rukai
  - a TSOUIC PROPER [3]:
    - i NORTHERN [1]: *Tsou
    - ii SOUTHERN [2]: *Kanakanabu, *Saaroa
- 3 PAIWANIC [8]:
  - [5]: *Bunun, *Paiwan, *Puyuma, *Saisiyat, *Ami
  - a SINICIZED [3]: Kavalan, *Pazeh, *Thao, †Ketangalan, †Basay, †Taokas, †Papora, †Babuza, †Hoanya, †Siraya
- 4 MALAYO-POLYNESIAN [945]:
  - a WESTERN MALAYO-POLYNESIAN [374]:
    - [3]: *Chamorro, *Palauan, *Yapese
    - i NORTHERN PHILIPPINES [53]:
      - α NORTHERN LUZON [41]:
        - I NORTHERN CORDILLERAN [15]:
          - [6]: *Isnag, *Yogad, Adasen, Malaweg, *Agta, Itawis
          - A GADDANG [2]: *Gaddang, *Ga-dang
          - B IBANAG-ATTA [2]: *Ibanag, *Atta
          - C DUMAGAT [5]:
            - [1]: *Umiray Dumaget
            - 1 NORTHERN [4]: Southeast Cagayan Agta, Kasiguranin, *Casiguran Dumagat, Paranan
        - II ILOKANO [1]: *Ilokano
        - III SOUTH-CENTRAL CORDILLERAN [25]:
          - A CENTRAL CORDILLERAN [18]:
            - [1]: Isinai

1 KALINGA-ITNEG [5]:
[1]: *Itneg
a KALINGA [4]: Kalinga-Itneg, *North Kalinga, *Central Kalinga, *South Kalinga
2 NUCLEAR CORDILLERAN [12]:
[1]: *Balangaw
a IFUGAO [3]: Kiangan, *Central Ifugao, *East Ifugao
b BONTOK-KANKANAY [8]:
i BONTOK [4]: Sadanga, East Bontok, South Bontok, *Central Bontok
ii KANKANAY [4]: Kankanay-Itneg, *North Kankanay, Central Kankanay, South Kankanay
B SOUTHERN CORDILLERAN [7]:
[1]: *Ilongot
1 PANGASINIC [6]:
[1]: *Pangasinan
a BENGUET [5]:
[1]: I'wak
i IBALOI-KARAW [2]: *Inibaloi, Karaw
ii KALLAHAN [2]: *North Kallahan, South Kallahan
β BASHIIC-CENTRAL LUZON-NORTHERN MINDORO [12]:
I BASHIIC [4]:
[1]: Yami
A IVATAN [3]: *Itbayaten, *Ivatanen, Babuyan
II CENTRAL LUZON [5]:
[2]: Sinauna, *Kapampangan
A SAMBALIC [3]: *Tina, Botolan, *Bolinao
III NORTHERN MINDORO [3]: *Iraya, Alangan, Tadyawan
ii SOUTHERN PHILIPPINES [23]:
α SUBANUN [5]:
[2]: *Siocon Subanon, Kalibugan
I EASTERN [3]: *Sindangan, Salug, Lapuyan

[a WESTERN MALAYO-POLYNESIAN]
    β MANOBO [15]:
        I NORTH [3]: Kagayanen, *Binukid, Kinamigin
        II CENTRAL [8]:
            A SOUTH [3]:
                    [1]: Obo
                1 ATA-TIGWA [2]: *Ata, *Tigwa
            B EAST [3]: *Agusan, *Dibabawon, Rajah Kabungsuan
            C WEST [2]: *Ilianen, *Western Bukidnon
        III SOUTH [4]:
                [2]: Tagabawa, *Sarangani Manobo
            A COTABATO [2]: *Kalamansig, Tasaday
    γ DANAO [3]:
            [1]: *Magindanao
        I MARANAO-IRANON [2]: *Maranao, Iranon
  iii MESO-PHILIPPINE [54]:
    α SOUTH MANGYAN [3]:
            [1]: *Hanunoo
        I BUHID-TAUBUID [2]: *Buhid, Taubuid
    β KALAMIAN [2]: *Kalamianen, Agutaynon
    γ PALAWAN [5]: *Batak, *Tagbanwa, Palaweño, *Molbog, Banggi
    δ CENTRAL PHILIPPINES [44]:
        I TAGALOG [3]: *Tagalog, Lubang, Marinduque
        II BIKOL [8]:
                [1]: $Pandan_1$
            A INLAND [5]:
                    [1]: Iriga
                1 BUHI-DARAGA [4]:
                        [1]: Buhi
                    a LIBON-DARAGA [3]:
                            [1]: Libon
                        i OAS-DARAGA [2]: Oas, Daraga

B COASTAL [2]: Virac, *Naga

III MANSAKAN [8]:

[1]: Davaweño

A NORTH [1]: Kamayo

B EASTERN [4]:

[2]: Isamal, Caraga

1 MANDAYAN [2]: Mandayan, *Mansakan

C WESTERN [2]: *Kalagan, *Tagakaolo

IV MAMANWA [1]: *Mamanwa

V BISAYAN [24]:

A SOUTH [5]:

1 SURIGAO [3]: Surigaonon, Jaun-Jaun, Kantilan

2 BUTUAN-TAUSUG [2]: *Tausug, Butuanon

B CEBUAN [2]: *Cebuano, Boholano

C CENTRAL [8]:

1 WARAYAN [3]:

[1]: Gubat

a SAMAR-WARAY [2]: North Samar, *Waray

2 PERIPHERAL [4]: Camotes, Bantayan, Masbate, *Hiligaynon

3 ROMBLON [1]: Romblonanon

D BANTON [2]: Banton, Odionganon

E WEST [7]:

1 KUYAN [2]: *Kuyunon, Datagnon

2 KINARAYAN [2]: Kinaray-a, $Pandan_2$

3 NORTH-CENTRAL [2]: Looknon, Bulalakawnon

4 AKLAN [1]: Aklanon

iv SOUTH MINDANAO [5]:

[2]: Bagobo, *Tiruray

α BILIC [3]:

[1]: *Tboli

I BLAAN [2]: *Cotabato Bilaan, *Sarangani Bilaan

[a WESTERN MALAYO-POLYNESIAN]

v CELEBES [61]:

α SANGIR-MINAHASAN [10]:

I SANGIRIC [5]: Talaud, Sangir, *Sangil, Bantik, Ratahan

II MINIHASAN [5]: *Tonsea, *Tondano, *Tombulu, *Tontemboan, *Tonsawang

β MONGONDOW-GORONTALO [9]:

I MONGONDOW [2]: Ponosakan, Mongondow

II GORONTALO [7]: Bintauna, Kaidipang, Bolango, Atinggola, Suwawa, Gorontalo, Buol

γ CENTRAL SULAWESI [25]:

[1]: Banggai

I EASTERN [3]: Saluan, Andio, Balantak

II WEST-CENTRAL [21]:

[1]: Balaesan

A TOMINI [8]: Tolitoli, Tomini, Bolano, Dondo, Dampelasa, Kasimbar, Petapa, Ndau

B KAILI-PAMONA [8]: Kaili, Pipikoro, Lindu, Sedoa, Napu, Bada, Rampi, Pamona

C BUNGKU-MORI [4]: Bungku, Mori, Lalaki, Mekongka

δ SOUTH SULAWESI [9]: Makassarese, *Bugis, Mandar, *Sa'dan, Massenrempulu, Pitu Ulunna Salo, Mamuju, Seko, Wotu

ϵ MUNA-BUTON [8]: Muna, *Wolio, South Buton, Buton, Tukang-Besi, Bonerate, Kalaotoa, Layolo

vi BORNEO [109]:

[1]: Ida'an

α NORTHEAST [33]:

I MURUT-TIDONG [12]:

A MURUT [7]: Selungai Murut, *Kolod, *Sumambu, Paluan, *Timugon, Beaufort Murut, Keningau Murut

B TIDONG [5]: Tidong, Sembakung, Baukan, Kalabakan, Serudung

II DUSUN-BISAYA [15]:

A DUSUN [11]: Gana, Kuijau, *Kadazan-Dusun, Lotud, Papar, Rungus, *Eastern Kadazan, Klias River Kadazan, Kimaragang, Garo, Tebilung

B BISAYAN [4]: Tatana, Northern Bisaya, Southern Bisaya, Tutong$_1$

III PAITANIC [6]: Dumpas, Lingkabau, Abai Sungai, Tambanua, Upper Kinabatangan, Lobu

β APO DUAT [5]: Lundayeh, Kelabit, *Sa'ban, Lengilu, Putoh

γ REJANG-BARAM [17]:

I LOWER REJANG [3]: *Melanau, Kanowit, Tanjong

II REJANG-BINTULU [4]: *Bintulu, Lahanan, Kajaman, Bukitan

III BARAM-TINJAR [5]: Lelak, Narom, Kiput, Tutong$_2$, Berawan

IV REJANG-SAJAU [5]: Punan Bah, Punan Merap, Sajau Basap, Burusu, Basap

δ LAND DAYAK [12]: Silakau, Lara', Jagoi, Singgie, Biatah, *Bukar Sadong, Bekati', Benyadu', Kembayan, Ribun, Djongkang, Sanggau

ε KAYAN-KENYAH [29]:

[1]: Punan-Nibong

I KAYAN [17]:

[1]: Murik Kayan

A WESTERN [8]: *Rejang Kayan, Baram Kayan, Mendalam Kayan, Kayan Mahakam, Busang, Bahau, Kayan River Kayan, Wahau Kayan

B MODANG [2]: Modang, Segai

C MULLER-SCHWANER "PUNAN" [6]: Aoheng, Havongan, Kereho-Uheng, Bukat, Punan Aput, Punan Merah

II KENYAH [11]:

[5]: Bakung Kenyah, Sebob Kenyah, Tutoh Kenyah, Punan Tubu, Wahau Kenyah

A MAIN KENYAH [6]: Western Kenyah, Upper Baram Kenyah, Bahau River Kenyah, Kayan River Kenyah, Mahakam Kenyah, Kelinyao Kenyah

ζ BARITO [12]:

I EAST [4]: *Lawangan, Dusun Deyah, *Ma'anyan, *Malagasy

II WEST [6]:

A NORTHWEST [2]: *Dohoi, *Siang

B SOUTHWEST [4]: *Kapuas, *Katingan, Kahayan, Bakumpai

III MAHAKAM [2]: Tunjung, Ampanang

vii SAMA-BAJAW [20]:

[4]: *Abaknon, Batuan, *Yakan, *Sibutuq

α SULU-BORNEO [16]:

I INNER SULU SAMA [3]: *North Sama, Central Sama, South Sama

II WESTERN SULU SAMA [1]: *Pangutaran

[a WESTERN MALAYO-POLYNESIAN]

III BORNEO COAST BAJAW [12]:

[1]: Jama Mapun

A NORTH BORNEO [3]: Kota Belud, Kawang, Putatan

B INDONESIAN [8]: Sulamu, Kajoa, Roti, Jaya Bakti, Poso, $Tongian_1$, $Tongian_2$, Wallace

viii SUNDIC [46]:

[4]: *Javanese, *Sundanese, Mbaloh, Gayo

α LAMPUNG [2]: *Lampung, Komering

β BALI-SASAK [3]: *Bali, Sasak, Sumbawa

γ SUMATRA [10]:

[3]: Lom, Mentawai, Enggano

I NORTHERN [2]: Simeulue, Nias

II BATAK [5]:

[1]: Simalungan

A NORTHERN [2]: Alas, Karo Batak

B SOUTHERN [2]: *Toba Batak, Mandailing

δ MALAYIC [27]:

[1]: *Madurese

I MALAYIC DAYAK [2]: Iban, Malayic Dayak

II MALAY-MOKLEN [13]:

A MOKLEN [2]: Moklen, Moken

B MALAYAN [11]:

1 PARA-MALAY [4]: *Minangkabau, *Urak Lawoi', Duano', Rejang

2 ABORIGINAL MALAY [4]: Temuan, Orang Hulu, Orang Kanaq, Orang Seletar

3 LOCAL MALAY [3]: *Malay, *Indonesian, Orang Laut

III ACHINESE-CHAMIC [11]:

[1]: Achinese

A CHAMIC [10]:

1 NORTH [1]: Huihui

2 SOUTH [9]:

a PLATEAU [3]: Jarai, Rhade, *Haroi

b COASTAL [6]:

i CHAM-CHRU [3]: *East Cham, *West Cham, *Chru

ii RAGLAI [3]: South Raglai, *North Raglai, Cacgia Raglai

- b CENTRAL-EASTERN MALAYO-POLYNESIAN [371]:
  - i CENTRAL MALAYO-POLYNESIAN [89]:
    - α CENTRAL MALUKU [37]:
      - [1]: Teor
      - I WEST [5]:
        - [1]: Ambelau
        - A BURU-TALIABO [4]:
          - [1]: Buru
          - 1 SULA-TALIABO [3]:
            - [1]: Taliabo
            - a SULA [2]: Sula, Mangoli
      - II EAST [31]:
        - A BANDA [3]:
          - [1]: Banda
          - 1 SERAN LAUT [2]: Geser, Watubela
        - B SERAM [28]:
          - 1 EAST SERAM [3]: Bobot, Masiwang, Seti
          - 2 NUNUSAKU [25]:
            - [1]: Kayeli
            - a CENTRAL SERAM [2]: Nuaulu, Manusela
            - b THREE RIVERS [8]:
              - [1]: Wemale
              - i AMALUMUTE [7]:
                - [1]: Atamanu
                - α NORTHWEST SERAM [6]:
                  - [4]: Saleman, Hulung, Loun, Lisabata
                  - I ULAT INAI [2]: Naka'ela, Alune
            - c PIRU BAY [14]:
              - i WEST [5]:
                - [1]: Asilulu
                - α HOAMOAL [4]:
                  - I EAST [2]: Boano, Wakasihu
                  - II WEST [2]: Manipa, Luhu, †Batumerah

[b CENTRAL-EASTERN MALAYO-POLYNESIAN]

ii EAST [9]:

[1]: Teluti

α SERAM STRAITS [8]:

[3]: Kaibobo, Hitu, Paulohi

I ULIASE [5]:

[1]: Kamarian

A HATUHAHA [4]: Saparua, Haruku, Nusalaut, Amahai

β SOUTHEAST MALUKU [9]:

[1]: Selaru

I KEI-ARU [8]:

[3]: Kei, Yamdena, Selwasa

A ARU [5]:

[2]: Ujir, Kola

1 SOUTH [3]: Dobel, Barakai, Tarangan

γ TIMOR-FLORES [24]:

[2]: Helong, Naueti

I FLORES-LEMBATA [3]: *Sikka, Lamaholot, Kedang

II TIMOR [19]: Roti, Timorese, *Tetun, *Kemak, Tukudede, Mambai, Galoli, Idate, Lakalei, Wetar, Roma, Kisar, *Letri Lgona, Dai, Dawera, Masela, Damar, Teun, Serua

δ WAIMA'A [3]: Waima'a, Habu, Kairui

ϵ BIMA-SUMBA [16]: Bima, Kodi, Weyewa, Lamboya, Wanukaka, Anakalangu, Mamboru, East Sumbanese, *Savu, Ndao, *Manggarai, Riung, *Ngada, Ende, Lio, Palu'e

ii EASTERN MALAYO-POLYNESIAN [482]:

α SOUTH HALMAHERA–NORTHWEST NEW GUINEA [56]:

I BOMBERAI [9]:

[1]: Kaiwai

A ONIN [6]: Uruangnirin, Onin, Sekar, Arguni, Bedoanas, Erokwanas

B KUIWAI [2]: Irahutu, Nabi

II SOUTH HALMAHERA–GEELVINK BAY [47]:

A SOUTH HALMAHERA [23]:

1 SOUTH [2]: Gane, East Makian

2 CENTRAL-EAST [21]:
  [14]: Buli, Maba, Patani, Sawai, Weda, Misool, Amber, Wajamli, Bichole, Giman, Salawati, Waigeo, Batanta, As
  a RAJA EMPAT [7]: Maya, Maden, Palamul, Matbat, Laganyan, Kawe, Gebe
B GEELVINK BAY [24]:
  [6]: Waropen, *Mor$_2$, Iresim, Yaur, Yeretuar, Tandia
  1 BIAKIC [4]: Biak, Ron, Dusner, Meoswar
  2 YAPEN [14]:
    a EAST [2]: Wabo, Kurudu
    b CENTRAL-WESTERN [12]: Wandamen, Ansus, Woi, Pom, Aibondeni, Marau, Munggui, Papuma, Busami, Serui-Laut, Wadapi-Laut, Ambai

β OCEANIC [426]:
  [1]: Maisin
  I SARMI-YOTAFA [6]:
    A SARMI [3]: Sobei, Bongo, Tarpia
    B YOTAFA [3]: Yotafa, Ormu, Kayupulau
  II SIASSI [44]:
    A SEPIK-MADANG [22]:
      1 SEPIK [13]:
        a WESTERN [5]: Sera, *Sissano, Tumleo, Ali, Ulau
        b EASTERN [8]:
            [1]: Kis
          i KAIRIRU [2]: Kairiru, Kaiep
          ii MANAM [5]: Wogeo, Bam, Sepa, *Manam, Medebur
      2 MADANG [9]:
        a BEL [6]:
          i NORTHERN [5]: *Takia, *Megiar, *Matukar, *Gedaged, Bilbil
          ii SOUTHERN [1]: *Ham
        b ASTROLABAN [3]: Wab, *Biliau, Mindiri

[β OCEANIC]

- B RAI COAST–NORTHWEST NEW BRITAIN [22]:
  - 1 RAI COAST [7]:
    - [2]: *Sio, Mangap
    - a KORAP [3]: Lukep, Malasanga, Barim
    - b ROINJI-NENGAYA [2]: Nengaya, Roinji
  - 2 BARIAI-NGERO [8]:
    - a NGERO [4]: Tami, Mutu, Gitua, Malamalai
    - b BARIAI [4]:
      - i CAPE GLOUCESTER [2]: Maleu, Kilenge
      - ii KOVE-BARIAI [2]: Bariai, *Kove
  - 3 HUON GULF [7]:
    - a YABIM-BUKAWAC [5]: *Yabim, *Bukawac, Lae, Labu, *Kela
    - b KAIWA-SIBOMA [2]: Kaiwa, Siboma

- III MARKHAM [23]:
  - A ADZERA [14]:
    - 1 LOWER WATUT [3]: Silisili, Dangal, Maralango
    - 2 MARKHAM PROPER [7]: *Adzera, Wampur, Unank, Sukurum, Ngariawan, Sirasira, Wampar
    - 3 BUSU [4]: Sirak, Guwot, Musom, Yalu
  - B BUANG [6]: *Mumeng, Piu, Kapin, *Mapos, *Manga, Vehes
  - C HOTE [3]: Hote, Yamap, Misim
- IV MILNE BAY–CENTRAL PROVINCE [54]:
  - A MILNE BAY [41]:
    - 1 EASTERN [3]: *Misima, Nimowa, *Tagula
    - 2 WESTERN [38]:
      - a MINIAFIA-UBIR [2]: *Miniafia, Ubir
      - b MUKAWA [6]: Doga, Anuki, Mukawa, Gapapaiwa, Boianaki, Wataluma
      - c KAKABAI [2]: Dawawa, Igora
      - d TAUPOTA-WEDAU [5]: Wedau, Taupota, Garuwahi, *Kehelala, Kukuya
      - e SUAU [3]: *Suau, Bohutu, Wagawaga
      - f DUAU [5]: Tubetube, Duau, Bunama, Kurada, Mwatebu

g DOBU [5]: Sewa Bay, *Dobu, Molima, Galeya, Bosilewa
h GUMASI [1]: Gumasi
i BWAIDOKA [6]: Yamalele, Fagululu, Kalokalo, *Bwaidoka, Diodio, *Iduna
j KILIVILA [3]: Budibud, *Muyuw, Kilivila
B CENTRAL PROVINCE [13]:
1 WESTERN [6]: Mekeo, *Roro, Kuni, *Nara, *Gabadi, Doura
2 EASTERN [7]:
a MOTU-SINAGORO [3]: *Motu, *Sinagoro, *Keapara
b MAGORI [4]: Ouma, Magori, Yoba, Bina
V KIMBE [6]:
A NAKANAI [2]: Melamela, *Bileki
B WILLAUMEZ [3]: Xarua, Bola, Bulu
C BALI-VITU [1]: Vitu
VI NEW BRITAIN [16]:
[1]: Tumuip
A ARAWE [3]: Arawe, Moewehafen, Gasmata
B LAMOGAI [6]:
[3]: Longa, Idne, Mok
1 RAUTO [3]: Lamogai, Pulie, Rauto
C WHITEMAN [3]: Pasismanua, Kapore, Mangseng
D MENGEN [3]: Uvol, Mamusi, *Mengen
VII NEW IRELAND–TOLAI [21]:
A PATPATAR-TOLAI [10]: Barok, Patpatar, *Sursurunga, *Tangga, Lihir, Konomala, Kandas, Siar, *Tolai, *Duke of York
B NORTHERN NEW IRELAND [7]: Lavongai, *Tigak, *Kara, Tiang, Nalik, Notsi, Tabar
C ST. MATTHIAS [2]: Mussau, Tenis
D MADAK [2]: Lamusong, *Madak
VIII ADMIRALTY ISLANDS [23]:
A WESTERN [2]:
1 WUVULU [1]: Wuvulu
2 NINIGO [1]: *Seimat, †Kaniet

[β OCEANIC]

B EASTERN [21]:

1 MANUS [16]:

a NORTHWEST ISLANDS [7]: Hermit, Sisi, Sori, Ponam, Andra, Leipon, Loniu

b WEST [4]: Lindrou, Levei, Mondropolon, Likum

c EAST [5]: *Gele, Nali, Mokerang, Papitalai, Titan

2 SOUTHEAST ISLANDS [5]: Baluan, Lenkau, Penchal, Nauna, Pak

IX BOUGAINVILLE [14]:

A NORTH & EAST [12]:

1 NORTH-NEHAN [9]:

a NEHAN [1]: *Nehan

b NORTH [7]:

i BUKA [3]: *Halia, Solos, *Petats

ii SAPOSA-TINPUTS [4]: *Saposa, Hahon, *Tinputs, *Teop

c PAPAPANA [1]: Papapana

2 EAST [3]: *Mono, *Uruava, *Torau

B WEST [2]: Banoni, Piva

X CHOISEUL [4]:

A NORTHWEST [3]: Vaghua, Varisi, Ririo

B CENTRAL-EASTERN [1]: *Babatana

XI NEW GEORGIA [10]:

A EAST [2]: Marovo, Vangunu

B WEST [8]: Ghanongga, Lungga, *Simbo, Nduke, *Roviana, Ughele, Kusaghe, Hoava

XII SANTA ISABEL [7]:

A WEST [2]: *Kia, Laghu

B CENTRAL [3]: Kokota, Zazao, Blablanga

C EAST [2]: Maringe, *Gao

XIII SANTA CRUZ [6]:

A UTUPUA [3]: *Nembao, Asumboa, Tanimbili

B VANIKORO [3]: Buma, *Vano, Tanima

XIV SOUTHERN NEW HEBRIDES [8]:

[1]: *Aneityum

A ERROMANGA [2]: *Sie, Ura

B TANNA [5]: *Kwamera, *Whitesands, North Tanna, *Lenakel, Southwest Tanna

A NORTHERN [13]:
    1 FAR NORTH [4]: Yalayu, *Kumak, *Caac, *Yuaga
    2 NORTH [7]:
        [3]: Pwapwa, Pwaamei, *Hmwaveke
        a NEMI [4]: Jawe, Nemi, *Fwai, Pije
    3 CENTRAL [2]: *Cemuhi, *Paici
B SOUTHERN [11]:
    1 SOUTH [9]:
        a GROUP I [5]: Arho, Arha, *Ajie, Orowe, Neku
        b GROUP II [2]: Nere, *Tiri
        c GROUP III [2]: *Xaracuu, *Xaragure
    2 FAR SOUTH [2]: Dubea, *Numee
XVI LOYALTY ISLANDS [3]: *Iaai, *Dehu, *Nengone
XVII REMOTE OCEANIC [156]:
    A MICRONESIAN [9]:
        [1]: *Nauruan
        1 MICRONESIAN PROPER [8]:
            [3]: *Gilbertese, *Marshallese, *Kusaiean
            a PONAPEIC-TRUKIC [5]:
                i PONAPEIC [2]: *Mokilese, *Ponapean
                ii TRUKIC [3]: *Trukese, *Carolinian, *Ulithian, †Mapia
    B SOUTHEAST SOLOMONS [22]:
        1 GELA-GUADALCANAL [7]:
            [1]: *Bughotu
            a GELA [2]: *Gela, *Lengo
            b GUADALCANAL [4]: *Ghari, *Talise, Malango, Birao
        2 MALAITA–SAN CRISTOBAL [15]:
            a MALAITA [11]:
                [1]: *Longgu
                i NORTHERN [5]: *Lau, *To'abaita, *Kwara'ae, Langalanga, *Kwaio
                ii SOUTHERN [5]: Dori'o, *'Are'are, *Marau, *Oroha, *Sa'a
            b SAN CRISTOBAL [4]: *Arosi, *Fagani, Bauro, Kahua

[XVII REMOTE OCEANIC]

C CENTRAL & NORTHERN NEW HEBRIDES [94]:
1 EAST SANTO [5]:
a NORTH [1]: *Sakao
b SOUTH [4]: Lorediakarkar, *Shark Bay, Butmas, Polonombauk
2 MALEKULA INTERIOR [12]:
[1]: *Labo
a SMALL NAMBAS [4]: Letemboi, Repanbitip, Dixon Reef, Nasarian
b MALEKULA CENTRAL [7]: Katbol, Lingarak, Vinmavis, Litzlitz, Larevat, Maragus, *Big Nambas
3 NORTHEAST NEW HEBRIDES–BANKS ISLANDS [77]:
a EAST NEW HEBRIDES [29]: Hiw, *Toga, *Lehali, Lehalurup, *Motlav, *Mota, *Vatrata, *†Alo-Teqel, *Mosina, *Nume, Koro, Wetamut, *Lakona, *Merlav, *Marino, Central Maewo, Baetora, *Northeast Aoban, Nduindui, *Raga, Apma, Sowa, Seke, Sa, *North Ambrym, *Lonwolwol, Dakaka, Port Vato, *Southeast Ambrym, *Paama
b WEST SANTO [24]: Valpei, *Nokuku, Vunapu, Piamatsina, *Tolomako, Tasmate, Wusi, Akei, Malmariv, Navut, Lametin, Morouas, Roria, Fortsenal, Amblong, Wailapa, *Tangoa, Araki, Narango, Tambotalo, Aore, *Malo, Tutuba, Mafea
c MALEKULA COASTAL [16]: Malua Bay, Vovo, Mpotovoro, Mae, Vao, *Atchin, *Uripiv, Unua, *Rerep, *Aulua, Burmbar, Port Sandwich, *Maskelynes, Axamb, Malfaxal, *Southwest Bay
d EPI [5]: *Lewo, Bierebo, *Baki, Maii, Bieria
e CENTRAL NEW HEBRIDES [3]: *Namakura, *North Efate, *South Efate

D CENTRAL PACIFIC [31]:
1 ROTUMAN-FIJIAN [3]:
[1]: *Rotuman
a FIJIAN [2]:
i WEST [1]: Nadroga
ii EAST [1]: *Fijian
2 POLYNESIAN [28]:
a TONGIC [2]: *Niuean, *Tongan

b NUCLEAR POLYNESIAN [26]:
  i SAMOIC OUTLIER [17]:
      [7]: *Samoan, Niuafo'ou, *Tuvalu, *East Uvea, Pukapuka, Rennellese, *Pileni
    α SOUTHERN [5]: *Tikopia, *West Uvea, *Emae, *Mele, *West Futuna
    β NORTHERN [3]: Sikaiana, *Luangiua, Takuu
    γ MICRONESIAN [2]: *Kapingamarangi, *Nukuoro
  ii EASTERN POLYNESIAN [9]:
      [1]: *Rapanui (= Easter Island)
    α CENTRAL [8]:
      I TAHITIC [5]: *Tahitian, Tongareva, *Rarotongan, *Pa'umotu, *Maori, †Moriori
      II MARQUESIC [3]: *Mangareva, *Marquesan, *Hawaiian

INDO-PACIFIC [731]:
I †TASMANIAN [0]: *†Tasmanian
II ANDAMAN ISLANDS [4]:
A GREAT ANDAMANESE [1]:
1 †NORTHERN [0]: †Aka-Cari, †Aka-Kora, †Aka-Bo, †Aka-Jeru
2 CENTRAL [1]: †Aka-Kede, †Aka-Kol, †Oko-Juwoi, *A-Pucikwar, †Akar-Bale, †Aka-Bea
B SOUTH ANDAMANESE [3]: Onge, Jarawa, Sentinel
III TRANS–NEW GUINEA [505]:
[5]: *Oksapmin, *Morwap, Molof, Usku, Tofamna
A MAIN SECTION [267]:
1 CENTRAL & WESTERN [216]:
[2]: Dem, Mor_1
a FINISTERRE-HUON [67]:
i HUON [22]:
[1]: *Kovai
α EASTERN [8]: *Kate, *Mape, *Dedua, Sene, Momare, Migabac, *Kube, *Kosorong
β WESTERN [13]: *Ono, Sialum, Nomu, Kinalakna, Kumokio, *Selepet, *Timbe, *Komba, *Tobo, *Yaknge, *Burum, Mesem, *Nabak
ii FINISTERRE [45]:
[1]: Abaga
α ERAP [11]: Nuk, Nek, Nakama, Munkip, Numanggang, Sauk, Gusan, Finungwa, Nimi, *Urii, Mamaa
β WANTOAT [4]: Irumu, Yagawak, Bam, *Wantoat
γ GUSAP-MOT [7]: Ufim, Nahu, *Rawa, Nekgini, Neko, Ngaing, Gira
δ WARUP [8]: Dahating, Bulgebi, Guiarak, Morafa, Forak, Degenan, Yagomi, Asat
ε YUPNA [9]: Mebu, Nankina, Gabutamon, Domung, *Bonkiman, Wandabong, Nokopo, *Kewieng, Isan
ζ URUWA [5]: Som, Sakam, Yau, Komutu, Weleki
b EAST NEW GUINEA HIGHLANDS [38]:
[2]: *Wiru, Kenati
i KALAM [3]:
[1]: Gants
α KALAM-KOBON [2]: *Kalam, Kobon
ii EASTERN [7]:
[1]: Owena
α GADSUP-AUYANA-AWA [3]: *Gadsup, *Auyana, *Awa
β TAIRORA [3]: *Tairora, *Binumarien, *Waffa
iii EAST-CENTRAL [8]:
[2]: *Gende, *Kamano
α SIANE [2]: *Siane, Yabiyufa
β GAHUKU [2]: *Gahuku, *Benabena
γ FORE [2]: *Fore, *Gimi

iv CENTRAL [9]:
[1]: *Medlpa
α CHIMBU [3]: *Chimbu, *Chuave, Nomane
β WAHGI [2]: *Wahgi, *Nii
γ JIMI [3]: *Narak, *Maring, Ganja
v WEST-CENTRAL [9]:
[1]: *Huli
α ENGA [5]: *Enga, Katinja, Nete, Lembena, Ipili
β ANGAL-KEWA [3]: *Angal, *Kewa, *Sau
c CENTRAL & SOUTH NEW GUINEA–KUTUBUAN [59]:
i KUTUBUAN [5]:
α EAST [2]: *Foe, Fiwaga
β WEST [3]: *Fasu, *Some, *Namumi
ii CENTRAL & SOUTH NEW GUINEA [54]:
[2]: Somahai, *Kamula
α ASMAT-KAMORO [8]: *Iria, *Asienara, *Kamoro, *Sempan, *Central Asmat, Casuarina Coast Asmat, Citak Asmat, North Asmat
β AWYU-DUMUT [14]:
[7]: *Sawuy, Kotogut, Mapi, Ederah, Kia, Upper Digul, Upper Kaeme
I AWYU [4]: *Siagha, *Pisa, *Aghu, Airo
II DUMUT [3]: *Kaeti, *Wambon, Wanggom
γ OK [13]:
I LOWLAND [5]: *Southern Kati, *Northern Kati, *Yonggom, *Ninggirum, Iwur
II MOUNTAIN [8]: *Telefol, *Tifal, *Kauwol, *Faiwol, Setaman, *Bimin, *Mianmin, *Ngalum
δ AWIN-PA [2]: *Awin, *Pa
ε EAST STRICKLAND [3]: *Nomad, Agala, Konai
ζ BOSAVI [8]: *Beami, Onabasulu, *Kaluli, Kasua, Kware, Tomu, *Bainapi, Sonia
η DUNA-POGAYA [2]: *Duna, Pogaya
θ MOMBUM [2]: *Mombum, Koneraw
d ANGAN [12]:
[1]: *Angaataha
i ANGAN PROPER [11]: *Simbari, *Baruya, *Safeyoka, *Kawatsa, *Kamasa, *Yagwoia, *Ankave, *Ivori, *Lohiki, *Menya, *Hamtai
e GOGODALA-SUKI [3]:
[1]: *Suki
i GOGODALA [2]: *Gogodala, *Waruna
f MARIND [6]:
i BOAZI [2]: *Boazi, *Zimakani
ii MARIND PROPER [2]: *Marind, *Bian Marind
iii YAQAY [2]: *Yaqay, *Warkay

g KAYAGAR [3]: *Kaugat, *Kaygir, *Tamagario
h SENTANI [4]:
[1]: Demta
i SENTANI PROPER [3]: *Sentani, Nafri, Tanah Merah$_2$
i DANI-KWERBA [11]:
i SOUTHERN [6]:
[1]: Wano
α DANI [2]: *Western Dani, *Grand Valley Dani
β NGALIK-NDUGA [3]: North Ngalik, South Ngalik, Nduga
ii NORTHERN [5]:
[2]: Saberi, Samarokena
α KWERBA [3]: *Kwerba, Airoran, Sasawa
j WISSEL LAKES–KEMANDOGA [4]:
[1]: *Uhunduni
i EKAGI-WODANI-MONI [3]: *Ekagi, *Wodani, *Moni
k MAIRASI–TANAH MERAH [4]:
[1]: Tanah Merah$_1$
i MAIRASI [3]: Mairasi, Northeastern Mairasi, Semimi
l WEST BOMBERAI [3]:
[1]: *Karas
i WEST BOMBERAI PROPER [2]: *Iha, *Baham
2 EASTERN [51]:
a BINANDEREAN [16]:
[1]: *Guhu-Semane
i BINANDEREAN PROPER [15]: *Suena, *Yekora, *Zia, *Binandere, Ambasi, *Aeka, *Orokaiva, Hunjara, *Notu, Yega, Gaina, Baruga, Mawae, Dogoro, *Korafe
b GOILALAN [5]: *Biangai, *Weri, *Kunimaipa, Tauade, Fuyuge
c KOIARIAN [6]:
i KOIARIC [3]: *Koita, *Koiari, *Mountain Koiari
ii BARAIC [3]: *Managalasi, *Barai, *Ömie
d KWALEAN [2]: *Humene, *Kwale, †Mulaha
e MANUBARAN [2]: Doromu, *Maria
f YAREBAN [5]: Bariji, *Yareba, Doriri, Sirio, Abia
g MAILUAN [6]: *Magi, Domu, Morawa, Binahari, Bauwaki, Laua
h DAGAN [9]: Onjob, Maiwa, Jimajima, *Daga, Mapena, Turaka, Gwedena, Ginuman, Sona
B MADANG–ADELBERT RANGE [102]:
1 MADANG [58]:
a RAI COAST [29]:
i EVAPIA [5]: Sinsauru, Asas, Sausi, Kesawai, Dumpu
ii KABENAU [5]: Arawum, Kolom, *Siroi, Lemio, Pulabu
iii YAGANON [4]: Yabong, Ganglau, Dumun, Saep
iv PEKA [4]: Usino, Sumau, Urigina, Danaru

v NURU [7]: Usu, *Erima, Duduela, Kwato, Rerau, Jilim, Yangulam
vi MINDJIM [4]: Bom, Male, Bongu, Songum
b MABUSO [29]:
[1]: Kare
i KOKON [3]: *Girawa, Munit, Bemal
ii GUM [6]: Sihan, Gumalu, Isebe, *Amele, *Bau, Panim
iii HANSEMAN [19]: Rapting, Wamas, Samosa, Murupi, Saruga, Nake, Mosimo, Garus, Yoidik, Rempi, Bagupi, Silopi, Utu, Mawan, Baimak, Matepi, Gal, Garuh, Kamba
2 ADELBERT RANGE [44]:
a PIHOM-ISUMRUD-MUGIL [28]:
[1]: Mugil
i PIHOM [22]:
[2]: Amaimon, Wasembo
α KAUKOMBARAN [4]: Pay, Pila, Saki, Tani
β KUMILAN [3]: *Ulingan, Bepour, Moere
γ TIBORAN [5]: Kowaki, Mawak, Hinihon, Musar, Wanambre
δ OMOSAN [2]: Koguman, Abasakur
ϵ NUMAGENAN [6]: Wanuma, Yaben, Yarawata, Bilakura, Parawen, Ukuriguma
ii ISUMRUD [5]:
[1]: Dimir
α KOWAN [2]: Korak, *Waskia
β MABUAN [2]: Malas, Bunabun
b JOSEPHSTAAL-WANANG [12]:
i JOSEPHSTAAL [7]:
[2]: Osum, Wadaginam
α SIKAN [2]: Sileibi, Katiati
β POMOIKAN [3]: Pondoma, Ikundun, Moresada
ii WANANG [5]:
[1]: Paynamar
α ATAN [2]: Atemple, Angaua
β EMUAN [2]: Emerum, Musak
c BRAHMAN [4]: Isabi, Biyom, Tauya, Faita
C TEBERAN-PAWAIAN [3]:
[1]: *Pawaian
1 TEBERAN [2]: *Dadibi, *Podopa
D TURAMA-KIKORIAN [4]:
[1]: *Kairi
1 TURAMA-OMATIAN [3]: Omati, Ikobi, Mena
E INLAND GULF [3]:
[1]: Ipiko
1 MINANIBAI [2]: *Minanibai, *Tao, †Karami, †Mahigi

F ELEMAN [7]:
- [2]: Purari, Tate
- 1 EASTERN [2]: *Toaripi, Uaripi
- 2 WESTERN [3]: Opao, Keuro, *Orokolo

G TRANS-FLY–BULAKA RIVER [28]:
- 1 BULAKA RIVER [2]: *Yelmek, *Maklew
- 2 TRANS-FLY [26]:
  - a KIWAIAN [7]: *Southern Kiwai, Wabuda, Bamu Kiwai, Morigi, Kerewo, *Northeastern Kiwai, *Arigibi
  - b TIRIO [4]: Tirio, Aturu, Lewada, Mutum
  - c EASTERN TRANS-FLY [4]: *Bine, Gidra, Gizra, *Meriam
  - d PAHOTURI [3]: *Agöb, Idi, *Waia
  - e MOREHEAD & UPPER MARO RIVERS [8]:
    - [2]: Yey, Moraori
    - i NAMBU [2]: *Nambu, Dorro
    - ii TONDA [4]: Upper Morehead, Lower Morehead, *Tonda, Kanum

H MEK [9]:
- 1 WESTERN [6]: Kosarek, Nipsan, *Nalca, Korapun, Goliath, Eipo
- 2 EASTERN [3]: Ketengban, Sirkai, Kinome

I SENAGI [2]: *Anggor, *Dera

J PAUWASI [4]:
- 1 EASTERN [2]: Yafi, Emumu
- 2 WESTERN [2]: Dubu, Towei

K NORTHERN [32]:
- 1 BORDER [12]:
  - a WARIS [7]: *Waris, *Manem, Senggi, Waina, Daonda, Simog, *Amanab
  - b TAIKAT [2]: *Awyi, *Taikat
  - c BEWANI [3]: Pagi, Kilmeri, Ninggera
- 2 TOR–LAKE PLAIN [20]:
  - [3]: Turu, Mawes, Uria
  - a CENTRAL LAKE PLAIN [7]: Baburiwa, Taogwe, Taori-Kei, Tori Aikwakai, Papasena, Weretai, Taori-So
  - b EAST LAKE PLAIN [3]: Taworta, Dabra, Foau
  - c TOR [7]: Berik, Bonerif, Mander, Itik, Kwesten, Maremgi, Wares

L NIMBORAN [3]: Mekwei, Kemtuk, *Nimboran

M KAURE [5]:
- [2]: Sause, Kapori
- 1 KAURE PROPER [3]: Kaure, Narau, Kosare

N SOUTH BIRD'S HEAD [10]:
- 1 SOUTH BIRD'S HEAD PROPER [6]: Barau, Arandai, Tarof, Kasuweri, Puragi, Kampong Baru
- 2 INANWATAN [2]: Inanwatan, Duriankere
- 3 KONDA-YAHADIAN [2]: Konda, Yahadian

O KOLOPOM [3]: *Kimaghana, *Riantana, *Ndom

- P TIMOR-ALOR-PANTAR [18]:
  - [7]: Oirata, Lovaea, Fataluku, Kairui, Bunak, Kolana, Tanglapui
  - 1 ALOR-PANTAR [11]:
    - [1]: Makasai
    - a ALOR [6]: Kui, *Woisika, Abui, Kelon, Kafoa, Kabola
    - b PANTAR [4]: *Blagar, Tewa, Nedebang, Lamma

IV WEST PAPUAN [24]:
- [1]: Amberbaken
- A BIRD'S HEAD [10]:
  - 1 NORTH-CENTRAL [4]:
    - a NORTH [2]: Karon Pantai, Madik
    - b CENTRAL [2]: Karon Dori, Brat
  - 2 WEST [6]: Kuwani, Tehit, Kalabra, Seget, Moi, Moraid
- B BORAI-HATTAM [2]: Borai, Hattam
- C NORTHERN HALMAHERA [11]:
  - 1 SOUTH [2]: Ternate, Tidore
  - 2 NORTH [9]: Galela, Tobelo, Loda, Ibu, Sahu, Modole, Tabaru, Pagu, *West Makian

V EAST BIRD'S HEAD [3]:
- [1]: Mantion
- A MEAX [2]: Meax, Meningo

VI GEELVINK BAY [5]:
- [1]: Yava
- A EAST GEELVINK BAY [4]: Turunggare, Baropasi, Bauzi, Bapu

VII SKO [8]:
- A VANIMO [4]: *Sko, Sangke, Wutung, *Vanimo
- B KRISA [4]: Krisa, Rawo, Puari, *Warapu

VIII KWOMTARI-BAIBAI [5]:
- [1]: Pyu
- A KWOMTARI [2]: Kwomtari, *Fas
- B BAIBAI [2]: Baibai, Biaka

IX ARAI [6]: *Rocky Peak, Iteri, Bo, *Ama, Nimo, Owiniga

X AMTO-MUSIAN [2]: Amto, Musian

XI TORRICELLI [48]:
- [1]: *Urim
- A WEST WAPEI [3]: *One, Seta, Seti
- B WAPEI-PALEI [20]:
  - [1]: *Urat
  - 1 WAPEI [12]: Yis, Yau, *Olo, *Elkei, *Au, *Yil, Alu, *Ningil, Gnau, Galu, Yapunda, Valman
  - 2 PALEI [7]: Nambi, Agi, Aruop, *Kayik, Aiku, Bragat, Aru
- C MAIMAI [6]:
  - [3]: Laeko, Beli, Wiaki
  - 1 MAIMAI PROPER [3]: Siliput, *Yahang, Heyo
- D KOMBIO-ARAPESH [9]:
  - 1 KOMBIO [6]: Eitiep, Lou, Kombio, Yambes, Aruek, Wom
  - 2 ARAPESH [3]: *Mountain Arapesh, *Southern Arapesh, Bumbita

E MARIENBERG [7]: Bungain, Mandi, Muniwara, Urimo, Kamasau, Elepi, Buna
F MONUMBO [2]: *Monumbo, Lilau
XII SEPIK-RAMU [98]:
[1]: Gapun
A SEPIK [43]:
[1]: *Biksi
1 UPPER SEPIK [5]:
[1]: *Abau
a IWAM [2]: *Iwam, Amal
b WOGAMUSIN [2]: *Wogamusin, *Chenapian
2 RAM [3]: Karawa, Bouye, Autu
3 TAMA [5]: Kalou, Pasi, Pahi, *Mehek, *Mayo
4 YELLOW RIVER [3]: *Namie, Ak, Awun
5 MIDDLE SEPIK [11]:
[1]: Yerakai
a NUKUMA [2]: *Kwoma, *Kwanga
b NDU [8]: *Ngala, *Manambu, *Kaunga, *Abelam, *Boiken, Sawos, *Iatmul, Kwasengen
6 SEPIK HILL [15]:
a SANIO [6]: *Sanio, Paka, Gabiano, Piame, Bikaru, *Hewa
b BAHINEMO [7]: Bitara, Bahinemo, Mari, Bisis, Watakataui, Kapriman, Sumariup
c ALAMBLAK [2]: Kaningara, *Alamblak
B LEONARD SCHULTZE [6]:
1 WALIO [4]: Walio, Pai, Yabio, Tuwari
2 PAPI [2]: Papi, Duranmin
C NOR-PONDO [6]:
1 NOR [2]: *Murik, Kopar
2 PONDO [4]: *Chambri, Yimas, Karawari, *Angoram
D RAMU [42]:
1 YUAT-WAIBUK [13]:
a MONGOL-LANGAM [3]: Langam, Mongol, Yaul
b YUAT-MARAMBA [6]:
[1]: Maramba
i YUAT [5]: Changriwa, Mekmek, Miyak, Biwat, Bun
c WAIBUK [4]: Waibuk, Aramo, Pinai, Wapi
2 RAMU PROPER [29]:
a GRASS [5]:
[1]: *Banaro
i GRASS PROPER [4]: *Kambot, Aion, Adjora, Gorovu
b ARAFUNDI [2]: Alfendio, Meakambut
c ANNABERG [3]:
[1]: Rao
i AIAN [2]: Anor, Aiome

d RUBONI [8]:
i OTTILIEN [5]: Watam, Gamei, Kaian, Bosman, Awar
ii MISEGIAN [3]: *Giri, Sepen, Mikarew
e GOAM [11]:
i ATAITAN [4]: Andarum, Igom, Tangu, Tanguat
ii TAMOLAN [7]: Romkun, Breri, Kominimung, Igana, Akrukay, Itutang, Midsivindi

XIII EAST PAPUAN [23]:
A YELE-SOLOMONS–NEW BRITAIN [12]:
1 YELE-SOLOMONS [5]:
[1]: *Yele
a †KAZUKURU [0]: †Kazukuru, †Guliguli, †Dororo
b CENTRAL SOLOMONS [4]: Bilua, Baniata, Lavukaleve, *Savosavo
2 NEW BRITAIN [7]:
[5]: Sulka, Kol, Wasi, Anem, Panaras
a BAINING-TAULIL [2]: *Baining, *Taulil, †Butam
B BOUGAINVILLE [8]:
1 EAST [4]:
a NASIOI [2]: *Nasioi, Nagovisi
b BUIN [2]: *Buin, Siwai
2 WEST [4]:
[2]: Konua, Keriaka
a ROTOKAS [2]: *Rotokas, Eivo
C REEF ISLANDS–SANTA CRUZ [3]:
[1]: *Aiwo
1 SANTA CRUZ [2]: *Santa Cruz, *Nanggu

AUSTRALIAN [170]:
[14]: *Enindhilyagwa, Ndjébbana, *Yanyuwa, Gagudju, Kungarakany, Mangarayi, †Mingin, Nakkara, *Nunggubuyu, *Tiwi, Waray, Limilngan, Umbugarla, Gunbudj, Murrinh-Patha
I YIWAIDJAN [4]:
[2]: Margu, Amurag
A YIWAIDJIC [2]: *Iwaidja, *Maung
II MANGERRIAN [1]: Mangerr
III GUNWINYGUAN [9]:
[3]: Jawony, Rembarrnga, *†Ngandi, Ngalakan
A GUNWINYGIC [3]: Warlang, *Gunwinygu, *Ngalkbon
B YANGMANIC [3]:
[2]: *Wagiman, Wardaman
1 NOLGIN [1]: †Dagoman, Yangman
IV BURARRAN [2]: Guragone, *Burarra
V MARAN [2]:
[1]: *Alawa
A MARIC [1]: †Warndarang, Mara
VI WEST BARKLY [3]:
[1]: *Djingili
A WAMBAYAN [2]: *Ngarndji, *Wambaya
VII GARAWAN [2]: *Garawa, Waanyi
VIII LARAGIYAN [2]: Laragiya, Wulna
IX DALY [9]:
A MOIL [1]: *Ngenkikurrunggur
B BRINKEN-WAGAYDY [5]:
1 BRINKEN [3]: *Marithiyel, *Marimanindji, *Maringarr
2 WAGAYDY [2]: *Wadjiginy, *Maranungku
C MALAKMALAK [3]:
1 DALY [1]: *Madngele
2 MALAKMALAK PROPER [2]: *Dyeraidy, *Malakmalak
X DJAMINDJUNGAN [3]: Djamindjung, Nungali, Ngaliwuru
XI DJERAGAN [3]:
A MIRIWUNGIC [2]: Gadjerawang, Miriwung
B KITJIC [1]: *Kitja
XII BUNABAN [2]: Bunaba, Guniyan
XIII NYULNYULAN [2]: *Nyulnyul, †Yawuru, †Warwa, Nyigina
XIV WORORAN [3]: Wunambal, *Ungarinjin, Worora
XV PAMA-NYUNGAN [109]:
[5]: †Muk Thang, †Dhuduroa, *Kala Lagaw Ya (= Mabuiag), †Muruwari, Warumungu, Flinders Island, Barrow Point, *Bandjalang, †Pallangahmiddang
A YUULNGU [7]: *Djinang, *Dhangu, *Dhuwal, Djinba, *Ritharngu, Dhay'yi, Yan-nhangu
B TANGIC [2]: *Lardil, Gayardilt

C PAMAN [25]:
- 1 NORTHERN [3]: †Gudang, *Atampaya, †Wudhadhi, Tjungundji, *†Mpalityanh, †Yupngayth, *†Linngithigh, *†Ngkoth, *†Yinwum, *†Aritinngithigh, *Awngthim, *†Mbiywom
- 2 MIDDLE [7]: *Wik-Me'anha, Wik-Ngathana, *Wik-Mungkan, Wik-Iiyanh, *Kugu-Muminh, Pakanha, Ayabadhu
- 3 WESTERN [2]: Thaayorre, *Yir Yoront
- 4 NORTH-EASTERN [2]: Kaantyu, *Umpila
- 5 LAMALAMIC [4]: Umbindhamu, *Umbuygamu, Mbariman-Gudhinma, *Lama-Lama, †Gugu Warra
- 6 COASTAL [1]: Koko Pera, *†Gog Nar
- 7 CENTRAL [4]: *Thaypan, Aghu-Tharnggala, †Gogo Mini, †Dagalag, Kawarrangg, *Oykangand
- 8 NORMAN [1]: *Kurtjar, †Kuthant, †Walangama
- 9 FLINDERS [1]: *Gugadj
- 10 †SOUTHERN [0]: *†Agwamin, *†Mbabaram, *†Mbara
- 11 †MAYABIC [0]: †Mayi-Kutuna, †Mayi-Kulan

D YALANJIC [2]: *Guugu Yimidhirr, *Gugu Yalandyi

E YIDINYIC [2]: *Dyaabugay, *Yidiny

F DYIRBALIC [2]: *Dyirbal, *Warrgamay

G NYAWAYGIC [1]: *Nyawaygi, †Wulguru

H MARIC [5]:
- [0]: †Guwa, †Yanda, †Yirandhali
- 1 KAPU [2]: Gunggari, Birria
- 2 MARI [3]: Gugu Badhun, †Gudjala, †Yilba, †Biri, †Giya, †Yiningay, †Wadjalang, †Gayiri, †Gangulu, †Bidyara, †Yiman, Margany, Guwamu

I WAKA-KABIC [1]:
- 1 †KINGKEL [0]: †Darambal, †Bayali
- 2 †THAN [0]: †Gureng Gureng, †Gabi
- 3 MIYAN [1]: †Wuliwuli, *Waga, †Barunggam, †Muringam

J †DURUBALIC [0]: †Turrubal, †Gowar

K GUMBAYNGGIRIC [1]: *Gumbaynggir, *†Yaygir

L YUIN-KURIC [1]:
- 1 KURI [1]: †Yugambal, †Nganyaywana, *Dyangadi, *†Gadang, †Awabakal
- 2 †YUIN [0]: †Gudungura, *†Ngarigu, *†Thawa, †Dyirringany, †Dhurga, *†Dharawal
- 3 †IYORA [0]: †Darkinyung, †Dharuk

M WIRADHURIC [2]: *†Gamilaraay, Ngiyambaa, Wiradhuri

N BAAGANDJI [1]: Baagandji

O †YOTAYOTIC [0]: †Yotayota, †Yabula-Yabula

P †KULINIC [0]:
- 1 †KULIN [0]: *†Wemba Wemba, †Nari Nari, †Wathawurung, †Kolakngat, *†Wuywurrung
- 2 †BUNGANDIDJ [0]: †Bungandidj, †Kuurn Kopan Noot

Q †NGARINYERIC-YITHAYITHIC [0]: *†Ngarinyeri, †Ngayawung, †Yuyu, †Keramin, †Yitha-Yitha
R KARNIC [14]:
  1 PALKU [2]: *Lhanima, *Pitta-Pitta
  2 ARABANA [1]: *Arabana
  3 KARNA [6]: Midhaga, Garuwali, Yarluyandi, Ngamini, Yandruwandha, *Diyari
  4 NGURA [3]: *Wangkumara, Badjiri, Bidjara
  5 YARLI [2]: *Malyangaba, Yardliwarra
S WAGAYA-WARLUWARIC [3]:
  1 WAGAYA [1]: Wagaya
  2 WARLUWARIC [2]: Yindjilandji, Warluwara
T KALKATUNGIC [1]: *Kalkatungu, *†Yalarnnga
U ARANDIC [3]:
  1 ARTUYA [1]: *Kaititj
  2 URTWA [2]: *Alyawarra, *Aranda, †Lower Aranda
V SOUTH-WEST [31]:
  1 NGUMBIN [5]: *Walmajarri, Djaru, Gurindji, Mudburra, Ngarinman
  2 MARNGU [3]: *Garadyari, Mangarla, *Nyangumarta
  3 NGAYARDA [8]: *Ngarla, *Nyamal, *Nyiyabali, †Tjurruru, *Kariyarra, Martuyhunira, Nhuwala, *Yindjibarndi, Binigura
  4 MANTHARDA [3]: *Wariyangga, Djwarli, *Thargari
  5 KANYARA [2]: *Dhalandji, *Bayungu
  6 †KARDU [0]: *†Yinggarda, †Maya, †Malgana, *†Nhanda
  7 WADJARI [3]: *Wadjari, Wirdimay, *Karlamay
  8 WATI [2]: †Wirangu, *Warnman, *Western Desert Language
  9 NGARGA [3]: Warlmanpa, *Warlpiri, *Ngardi
  10 †NYUNGAR [0]: *†Nyungar
  11 NGADJUNMAYA [1]: *Ngadjunmaya
  12 YURA [1]: *Adynyamathanha, †Banggarla, †Kaurna

NA-DENE [34]:
I HAIDA [1]: *Haida
II CONTINENTAL NA-DENE [33]:
A TLINGIT [1]: *Tlingit
B ATHABASKAN-EYAK [32]:
1 EYAK [1]: *Eyak
2 ATHABASKAN [31]:
a TANAINA-AHTNA [2]: *Tanaina, Ahtna
b INGALIK-KOYUKON [3]:
[1]: Ingalik
i KOYUKON-HOLIKACHUK [2]: Holikachuk, Koyukon
c TANANA-UPPER KUSKOKWIM [4]:
i TANANA [3]: Upper Tanana, Tanacross, Tanana
ii UPPER KUSKOKWIM [1]: Upper Kuskokwim
d TUTCHONE [2]: Northern Tutchone, Southern Tutchone
e TAHLTAN-KASKA [2]: Tahltan, Kaska
f †TSETSAUT [0]: †Tsetsaut
g PACIFIC COAST [2]:
i OREGON [1]:
α †UMPQUA [0]: †Umpqua
β TOLOWA-GALICE [1]: *Tolowa, *†Galice
ii CALIFORNIA [1]:
α HUPA [1]: *Hupa
β †MATTOLE-WAILAKI [0]: †Mattole, *†Wailaki
h CANADIAN [12]:
i HAN-KUTCHIN [2]: Han, Kutchin
ii HARE-CHIPEWYAN [4]:
α HARE-SLAVE [3]: *Hare, Dogrib, *Slave
β CHIPEWYAN [1]: *Chipewyan
iii BEAVER-SEKANI [2]: Beaver, Sekani
iv CARRIER-CHILCOTIN [3]:
α CHILCOTIN [1]: Chilcotin, †Nicola
β BABINE-CARRIER [2]: Babine, *Carrier
v †KWALHIOQUA [0]: †Kwalhioqua
vi SARCEE [1]: *Sarcee
i APACHEAN [4]:
[1]: *Kiowa Apache
i NAVAJO-APACHE [3]:
[1]: Eastern Apache
α WESTERN APACHE–NAVAJO [2]: *Western Apache, *Navajo

AMERIND [583]:
I NORTHERN AMERIND [164]:
A ALMOSAN-KERESIOUAN [68]:
1 ALMOSAN [44]:
a KUTENAI [1]: *Kutenai
b ALGIC [16]:
i RITWAN [1]: *†Wiyot, *Yurok
ii ALGONQUIAN [15]:
[0]: *†Beothuk
α BLACKFOOT [1]: *Blackfoot
β ALGONQUIAN PROPER [14]:
[8]: *Cheyenne, *Arapaho, *Cree, *Ojibwa, *Potawatomi, *Menominee, *Fox, †Illinois, *Shawnee
I EASTERN [6]: *Micmac, *Passamaquoddy, *Eastern Abenaki, Western Abenaki, †Loup A, †Loup B, *†Massachusett, †Narragansett, †Mohegan, †Quiripi, †Unquachog, †Mahican, *Munsee, Unami, †Nanticoke, *†Powhatan, †Carolina
c MOSAN [27]:
i CHIMAKUAN [1]: *†Chemakum, *Quileute
ii WAKASHAN [6]:
α NORTHERN [3]: *Heiltsuk, *Haisla, *Kwakwala (= Kwakiutl)
β SOUTHERN [3]: Makah, *Nitinat, *Nootka
iii SALISH [20]:
α BELLA COOLA [1]: *Bella Coola
β SALISH PROPER [19]:
I COAST [8]:
A CENTRAL [8]:
1 NORTHERN [2]: *Comox, †Pentlatch, Seshelt
2 SQUAMISH [1]: *Squamish
3 †NOOKSACK [0]: †Nooksack
4 HALKOMELEM [1]: *Halkomelem
5 STRAITS [2]: *Clallam, *Northern Straits
6 LUSHOOTSEED-TWANA [2]: *Lushootseed, *Twana
B †TILLAMOOK [0]: *†Tillamook
II TSAMOSAN [4]:
A INLAND [2]: *Upper Chehalis, *Cowlitz
B MARITIME [2]: Quinault, Lower Chehalis
III INTERIOR [7]:
A NORTHERN [3]: Lillooet, Thompson, *Shuswap
B SOUTHERN [4]: *Columbian, *Okanagan, *Kalispel, *Coeur d'Alene

2 KERESIOUAN [24]:
  a KERESAN [2]: *Eastern Keres, *Western Keres
  b SIOUAN-YUCHI [11]:
    i YUCHI [1]: *Yuchi
    ii SIOUAN [10]:
      α CATAWBA [1]: *Catawba, †Woccon
      β SIOUAN PROPER [9]:
        I MANDAN [1]: *Mandan
        II NORTHERN PLAINS [2]: *Crow, *Hidatsa
        III MISSISSIPPI VALLEY [6]:
          A DAKOTA [1]: *Dakota
          B DHEGIHA [3]: *Omaha, *Osage, †Quapaw, Kansa
          C CHIWERE-WINNEBAGO [2]: *Chiwere, *Winnebago
        IV †SOUTHEAST [0]:
          A †EAST [0]: *†Tutelo
          B †SOUTH [0]: *†Biloxi, *†Ofo
  c CADDOAN [4]:
    [0]: †Adai
    i SOUTHERN [1]: *Caddo
    ii NORTHERN [3]:
      α WICHITA [1]: *Wichita
      β PAWNEE-KITSAI [2]:
        I KITSAI [0]: *†Kitsai
        II PAWNEE [2]: *Pawnee, *Arikara
  d IROQUOIAN [7]:
    i NORTHERN [6]:
      [0]: †Laurentian, †Huron
      α FIVE NATIONS [5]:
        [0]: †Susquehannock
        I MOHAWK-ONEIDA [2]: *Mohawk, *Oneida
        II SENECA-ONONDAGA [3]:
          A ONONDAGA [1]: *Onondaga
          B SENECA-CAYUGA [2]: *Seneca, Cayuga
      β TUSCARORA [1]: *Tuscarora, *†Nottoway
    ii SOUTHERN [1]: *Cherokee
B PENUTIAN [68]:
  1 CANADIAN [1]: *Tsimshian
  2 WASHINGTON [1]: †Lower Chinook, *Upper Chinook
  3 OREGON [3]:
    a TAKELMAN [1]:
      i TAKELMA [0]: *†Takelma
      ii KALAPUYA [1]: *Santiam, †Tfalati, †Yonkalla
    b COAST [2]:
      i COOS [1]: *Coos
      ii YAKONAN [1]: *†Alsea, *Siuslaw

- 4 PLATEAU [3]:
  - a KLAMATH [1]: *Klamath
  - b SAHAPTIN–NEZ PERCE [2]: *Sahaptin, *Nez Perce
  - c †MOLALE-CAYUSE [0]: *†Molale, †Cayuse
- 5 CALIFORNIA [13]:
  - a WINTUN [3]: Nomlaki, *Patwin, *Wintun
  - b MAIDUAN [3]: *Mountain Maidu, Northwest Maidu, *Southern Maidu
  - c YOKUTS [1]: *Foothill North Yokuts, †Foothill South Yokuts, *†Valley Yokuts
  - d MIWOK-COSTANOAN [6]:
    - i †COSTANOAN [0]:
      - α †NORTHERN [0]: †Ohlone, †San Jose, †San Francisco, †Santa Cruz
      - β †SOUTHERN [0]: *†Rumsen, *†Mutsun, †Soledad, †Monterey
    - ii MIWOK [6]:
      - α WESTERN [2]: *Coast Miwok, *Lake Miwok
      - β EASTERN [4]: *Central Sierra Miwok, *Southern Sierra Miwok, *Northern Sierra Miwok, *Plains Miwok
- 6 NEW MEXICO [1]: *Zuni
- 7 GULF [7]:
  - a †TUNICA-CHITIMACHA [0]:
    - i †CHITIMACHA [0]: *†Chitimacha
    - ii †TUNICA-ATAKAPA [0]: *†Tunica, *†Atakapa
  - b YUKI-WAPPO [2]: Yuki, *Wappo
  - c NATCHEZ-MUSKOGEAN [5]:
    - i †NATCHEZ [0]: *†Natchez
    - ii MUSKOGEAN [5]:
      - α WESTERN [1]: *Choctaw
      - β EASTERN [4]:
        - [2]: *Mikasuki, *Muskogee (= Creek), †Apalachee
        - I ALABAMA-KOASATI [2]: *Alabama, *Koasati
- 8 MEXICAN [39]:
  - a HUAVE [1]: *Huave
  - b TOTONACAN [2]: *Totonac, *Tepehua
  - c MIXE-ZOQUE [6]: *Mixe, Oluta, *Sayula, *Sierra Popoluca, Texixtepec, *Zoque
  - d MAYAN [30]:
    - i HUASTECAN [1]: *Huastec, †Chicomuceltec
    - ii YUCATECAN [4]: *Yucatec, Itza, Lacandon, *Mopan
    - iii GREATER TZELTALAN [5]:
      - α CHOLAN [3]: *Chol, *Chontal, †Cholti, *Chorti
      - β TZELTALAN [2]: *Tzeltal, *Tzotzil
    - iv GREATER KANJOBALAN [6]:
      - α CHUJEAN [2]: *Tojolabal, *Chuj

β KANJOBALAN [4]:
[1]: Mocho
I KANJOBAL-JACALTEC [3]: Kanjobal, *Acatec, *Jacaltec
v EASTERN [14]:
α GREATER MAMEAN [4]:
I MAMEAN [2]: *Teco, *Mam
II IXILAN [2]: *Aguacatec, *Ixil
β GREATER QUICHEAN [10]:
[2]: Uspantec, *Kekchi
I QUICHEAN [6]: *Quiche, *Achi, Sacapultec, Sipacapa, *Tzutujil, *Cakchiquel
II POCOM [2]: Pocomam, *Pocomchi
C HOKAN [28]:
1 NORTHERN [11]:
[2]: *Karok, *Shasta, *†Chimariko
a PALAIHNIHAN [2]: *Achumawi, *Atsugewi
b †YANAN [0]: *†Yana, †Yahi
c POMO [7]:
[1]: *Southeastern Pomo
i RUSSIAN RIVER & EASTERN [6]:
[1]: *Eastern Pomo
α RUSSIAN RIVER [5]:
[2]: *Northeastern Pomo, *Northern Pomo
I SOUTHERN [3]: *Southern Pomo, *Central Pomo, *Kashaya
2 WASHO [1]: *Washo
3 †SALINAN-CHUMASH [0]: †Salinan, *†Chumash, †Esselen
4 SERI-YUMAN [11]:
a SERI [1]: *Seri
b YUMAN [10]:
i KILIWA [1]: *Kiliwa
ii DELTA-CALIFORNIAN [2]: *Cocopa, *Diegueño
iii RIVER [3]: *Mohave, *Yuma, *Maricopa
iv PAI [4]:
α PAIPAI [1]: *Paipai
β UPLAND YUMAN [3]: *Walapai, *Havasupai, *Yavapai
5 †WAICURI-QUINIGUA [0]: †Waicuri, †Maratino, †Quinigua
6 COAHUILTECAN [1]:
[1]: *Tonkawa, †Karankawa
a †COAHUILTECAN PROPER [0]: *†Coahuiltec, †Cotoname, *†Comecrudo
7 TEQUISTLATECAN [2]: *Tlamelula, *Tequistlatec
8 SOUTHERN [2]:
[1]: *Jicaque, †Yurimangui
a TLAPANECAN [1]: *Tlapanec, *†Subtiaba

II CENTRAL AMERIND [49]:
- A TANOAN [7]:
  - 1 KIOWA-TOWA [2]: *Kiowa, Towa
  - 2 TEWA-TIWA [5]:
    - a TEWA [1]: *Tewa
    - b TIWA-PIRO [4]:
      - i PIRO [0]: *†Piro
      - ii TIWA [4]:
        - α NORTHERN [2]: *Taos, *Picuris
        - β SOUTHERN [2]: *Isleta, *Sandia
- B UTO-AZTECAN [25]:
  - 1 NUMIC [8]:
    - a WESTERN [2]: *Northern Paiute, *Mono
    - b CENTRAL [3]: Koso, *Shoshone, *Comanche
    - c SOUTHERN [3]: *Kawaiisu, *Southern Paiute, *Chemehuevi
  - 2 TÜBATULABAL [1]: *Tübatulabal
  - 3 TAKIC [4]:
    - [0]: †Gabrielino
    - a SERRAN [1]: †Kitanemuk, *Serrano
    - b CUPAN [3]:
      - [1]: *Luiseño
      - i CAHUILLA-CUPEÑO [2]: *Cahuilla, *Cupeño
  - 4 HOPI [1]: *Hopi
  - 5 PIMIC [4]:
    - a PIMAN [2]: *Pima, *Pima Bajo, *†Tepecano
    - b TEPEHUAN [2]: *Northern Tepehuan, *Southern Tepehuan
  - 6 TARACAHITIC [3]:
    - [0]: †Tubar
    - a TARAHUMARA-GUARIJÍO [2]: *Tarahumara, Guarijío
    - b CAHITA [1]: *Yaqui, †Opata, *†Cahita
  - 7 CORACHOL [2]: *Cora, *Huichol
  - 8 AZTECAN [2]:
    - a †POCHUTLA [0]: *†Pochutla
    - b AZTEC PROPER [2]: *Pipil, *†Classical Nahuatl, *Nahuatl (= Aztec)
- C OTO-MANGUEAN [17]:
  - 1 AMUZGO [1]: *Amuzgo
  - 2 OTOMIAN [6]:
    - a NORTHERN [2]: *Chichimeca, *Pame
    - b CENTRAL [2]: *Mazahua, *Otomi
    - c SOUTHERN [2]: Matlatzinca, Ocuiltec
  - 3 MIXTECAN [3]:
    - a TRIQUE [1]: *Trique
    - b MIXTEC-CUICATEC [2]: *Mixtec, *Cuicatec
  - 4 POPOLOCAN [4]:
    - a MAZATEC [1]: *Mazatec

b IXCATEC-CHOCHO [3]:
i IXCATEC [1]: *Ixcatec
ii CHOCHO-POPOLOC [2]: Chocho, Popoloc
5 CHINANTECAN [1]: *Chinantec
6 ZAPOTECAN [2]: *Chatino, *Zapotec
7 †MANGUEAN [0]: †Mangue, *†Chiapanec
III CHIBCHAN-PAEZAN [43]:
A CHIBCHAN [27]:
[4]: *Tarascan, *†Cuitlatec, *Xinca, *Lenca, Paya
1 YANOMAM [4]: *Sanuma, *Yanomami, Yanomamö, Ninam
2 NUCLEAR CHIBCHAN [19]:
[2]: *Motilon, *Cuna
a MISUMALPAN [2]: †Matagalpa, *Miskito, Sumo
b RAMA [2]: Rama, Guatuso, †Guetar
c TALAMANCA [4]: *Cabecar, *Bribri, *Teribe, *Borunca
d GUAYMI [2]: *Guaymi, Buglere
e †ANTIOQUIA [0]: †Katio, †Nutabe, †Anserma, †Arma
f ARUAK [4]: †Atanque, †Guamaca, *Ica, Cagaba, Chimila, Malayo
g CHIBCHAN PROPER [3]:
[0]: *†Chibcha, †Sinsiga, †Duit
i TUNEBO [3]: Eastern Tunebo, *Central Tunebo, Western Tunebo
B PAEZAN [16]:
[2]: *†Timucua, *Warao, †Kunza, †Betoi, *†Chimu, *Itonama
1 †HUARPE [0]: †Allentiac, †Millcayac
2 †JIRAJARAN [0]: †Ayoman, †Gayon, †Jirajara
3 MURA [1]: *Mura, †Matanawi
4 NUCLEAR PAEZAN [13]:
[0]: †Andaqui
a CHOCO [8]: *Embera, *Saija, Catio, Caramanta, Chami, Tado, Baudo, *Waunana, †Runa
b INTER-ANDINE [2]:
i COCONUCAN [1]: *Guambiano, †Coconuco, †Totoro
ii PAEZ [1]: *Paez
iii †POPAYAN [0]: †Popayan
c BARBACOAN [3]:
i PASTO [1]: *Cuaiquer, †Barbacoas
ii CAYAPA-COLORADO [2]: *Cayapa, *Colorado
IV ANDEAN [18]:
A †NORTHERN [0]:
[0]: †Culli, †Sec, †Leco
1 †CATACAO [0]: †Catacao, †Colan
2 †CHOLONA [0]: †Cholona, †Hibito
B URARINA-WAORANI [2]: Urarina, *Waorani, †Omurano
C CAHUAPANAN-ZAPAROAN [7]:
1 CAHUAPANAN [2]: Chayahuita, Jebero
2 ZAPAROAN [5]: *Zaparo, *Andoa, *Arabela, Cahuarano, *Iquito

D QUECHUAN [2]: *Quechua A, *Quechua B
E AYMARAN [2]: *Aymara, *Jaqaru
F SOUTHERN [5]:
1 PUELCHE [0]: *†Puelche
2 MAPUDUNGU [2]: *Mapudungu (= Araucanian), Huilliche
3 QAWASQAR-YAMANA [2]: *Qawasqar (= Alacaluf), *Yamana
4 PATAGONIAN [1]: *Tehuelche, †Teushen, *†Selknam, †Haush
V EQUATORIAL-TUCANOAN [192]:
A MACRO-TUCANOAN [47]:
[9]: †Auishiri, Canichana, Capishana, †Gamella, *Iranshe, Koaia, *Movima, Muniche, Natu, †Pankararu, Shukuru, Uman
1 CATUQUINAN [2]:
a NORTHERN [0]: †Catawishi
b SOUTHERN [2]: †Bendiapa, †Burua, *Canamari, Catuquina, †Parawa, †Taware, †Tucundiapa
2 HUARI [2]: Huari, Masaca
3 ARUTANI-SAPE [3]: Arutani, Sape, Macu
4 NAMBIKUARAN [4]: Northern Nambikuara, *Southern Nambikuara, Sabanes, Sarare
5 PUINAVE-MAKU [6]:
[1]: *Puinave
a MAKU [5]: *Hupda, Guariba, Nadëb, Yahup, *Cacua
6 TICUNA-YURI [1]: *Ticuna, †Yuri
7 TUCANOAN [20]:
[1]: Miriti
a EASTERN [12]:
i NORTHERN [3]: *Tucano, *Guanano, Piratapuyo
ii CENTRAL [6]:
α BARA [1]: Tuyuca
β DESANO [2]: Desano, Siriano
γ TATUYO [3]: *Tatuyo, Carapana, Yuruti
iii SOUTHERN [3]:
α MACUNA [1]: Macuna
β BARASANO [2]: *Northern Barasano, *Southern Barasano
b CENTRAL [1]: *Cubeo
c WESTERN [6]:
[1]: Tanimuca
i NORTHERN [4]:
[2]: Coreguaje, Tetete, †Tama
α SIONA-SECOYA [2]: *Siona, *Secoya, †Macaguaje
ii SOUTHERN [1]: Orejon
B EQUATORIAL [145]:
[4]: *Cayuvava, *Camsa, †Taruma, *Trumai, †Tusha, *Yuracare
1 PIAROA-SALIBA [2]: Piaroa, Saliba
2 †TIMOTE [0]: †Cuica, †Timote

3 JIVAROAN [8]:
[2]: *Cofan, †Esmeralda, *Yaruro
a CANDOSHI [2]: *Candoshi, Taushiro
b JIVARO PROPER [4]: Achuar, Shuar, *Huambisa, *Aguaruna
4 ZAMUCOAN [2]: *Ayoreo, Chamacoco
5 KARIRI-TUPI [46]:
a †KARIRI [0]: †Dzubucua, †Kamaru, †Kiriri, †Sapuya
b TUPI [46]:
[2]: Purubora, Yuqui
i ARIKEM [1]: †Arikem, †Kabishiana, Karitiana
ii MONDE [4]: Arua, Gavião, Surui, Monde, †Digüt
iii RAMARAMA [1]: Arara, †Ramarama, †Uruku, †Urumi
iv YURUNA [1]: Yuruna, †Manitsawa, †Shipaya
v TUPARI [5]: *Guarategaya, Kepkiriwat, Makurapi, Tupari, Wayoro
vi TUPI-GUARANI [32]:
[2]: Guayaki, Juma
α GROUP I [25]:
[9]: Apiaca, Aweti, Ava, Kamayura, Kayabi, Emerillon, †Karipuna, Oyampi, Pauserna, †Sheta, †Takunape, Tapirape
I KAWAHIB [3]: †Paranawat, *Tenharim, Tukumanfed, Wirafed
II TENETEHARA [8]: Amanaye, †Anambe, Tembe, *Guajajara, Guaja, *Asurini, Arawete, Parakanã, Urubu
III TUPI [5]: *Guarani, *Kaiwa, Tapiete, Guarayu, *Nhengatu, †Potiguara
β GROUP II [2]: *Cocama, Omagua
γ GROUP III [3]: Mawe, *Munduruku, *Siriono, †Kuruaya
6 MACRO-ARAWAKAN [83]:
[1]: Katembri, †Otomaco
a TINIGUAN [1]: Tinigua, †Pamigua
b GUAHIBAN [5]: †Churuya, *Guahibo, *Cuiba, Guayabero, Macaguan, Playero
c ARAWAKAN [76]:
[1]: †Guamo, †Taino, Chamicuro
i ARAWAN [7]: †Arawa, Culina, †Pama, Paumari, Sewacu, †Sipo, Deni, Yamamadi, Yuberi, Banawa
ii CHIPAYAN [3]: *Chipaya, Uru, Callahuaya, †Caranga
iii CHAPACURAN [11]:
α GUAPORE [8]:
I CHAPACURA [2]: Chapacura, Itene, †Quitemoca
II WANYAM [6]: Cabishi, Cujuna, Cumana, Mataua, Wanyam, Urunamacan
β MADEIRA [3]: Pakaasnovos, Tora, Urupa
γ †OCORONO [0]: †Herisobocono, †Ocorono, †San Ignacio

iv MAIPURAN [54]:
[0]: †Shebayo
α BANIVA-YAVITERO [1]: †Baniva, Yavitero
β PARESSI-SARAVECA [1]: *Paressi, †Saraveca
γ PRE-ANDINE [15]:
[1]: *Amuesha
I †AMAZONIAN [0]: †Marawa, †Waraicu
II CUTINANA [1]: Cushichineri, †Cuniba, †Cutinana
III JURUA-PURUS [2]: Casharari, †Catiana, †Inapari, Apurina, †Maniteneri, †Wainamari
IV MONTANA [11]:
[3]: *Piro, †Pucapacuri, Puncuri, Sirimeri
A CAMPA [6]: *Ashaninca, Asheninca, Pajonal, Caquinte, *Machiguenga, *Nomatsiguenga
B HARAKMBET [2]: *Amarakaeri, Huachipaeri
δ WAPISHANAN [1]: *Wapishana
ε SOUTHERN [9]:
I PARANA [3]: Chane, Guana, *Terena
II BOLIVIAN [6]: *Baure, Cashiniti, Chiquito, Cozarini, *Ignaciano, Trinitario
ζ EASTERN [5]:
[1]: Palicur
I XINGU [4]: Custenau, Yawalapiti, Mehinaku, Waura
η NORTHERN [22]:
[2]: *Island Carib, †Arua, †Jaoi, *Resigaro
I CAQUETION [1]: Achagua, †Caquetio
II GUAYUPEAN [0]: †Sae
III ORINOCO [3]: Guarequena, Bare, Guinao, †Mawacua, †Maipure
IV PIAPOCAN [1]: Piapoco
V TA-ARAWAKAN [3]: *Goajiro, †Guanebucan, *Arawak, Paraujano
VI RIO NEGRO [12]:
A IZANENI [7]: Baniwa, Curripaco, Pacu, Cuati, Mapanai, Moriwene, Izaneni
B MARITIPARANA [2]: Cabiyari, †Matapi, *Yucuna
C WIRINA [1]: †Wirina, Yabaana
D †TARIANAN [0]: †Itayaine, †Tariano
E †YAPURA A [0]: †Mariate, †Wainuma
F YAPURA B [2]: Cawishana, Yumana, †Passe, †Manao

VI GE-PANO-CARIB [117]:
A MACRO-CARIB [47]:
[1]: *Andoke, †Cucura
1 PEBA-YAGUAN [1]: †Peba, †Yameo, *Yagua

2 BORA-WITOTO [9]:
- a BORAN [4]: *Bora, Faai, Imihita, *Muinane
- b WITOTOAN [5]:
  - [3]: Fitita, *Ocaina, Nonuya, †Orejone, †Miranya, †Coeruna
  - i WITOTO PROPER [2]: *Meneca, *Murui

3 CARIB [36]:
- a NORTHERN [28]:
  - i COASTAL [2]:
    - α †VENEZUELAN [0]: †Chayma, †Cumanagoto, †Yao, †Tamanaco
    - β SIERRA DE PERIJA [2]: Japreria, *Yukpa
    - γ †OPONE-CARARE [0]: †Opone, †Carare
  - ii WESTERN GUIANA [3]: Mapoyo, Yabarana, Panare, †Quaca, †Pareca
  - iii GALIBI [1]: *Galibi (= Carib)
  - iv EAST-WEST GUIANA [21]:
    - α GROUP 1 [3]: *Wayana, *Apalai, †Roucouyene, †Aracaju, *Trio
    - β GROUP 2 [4]: Wama, Urukuyana, Triometesen, Kumayena
    - γ GROUP 3 [5]: Pianakoto, Saluma, †Paushi, Cashuena, Chikena, *Waiwai
    - δ GROUP 4 [5]: †Paravilhana, Wabui, Sapara, Yauapery, Waimiri, †Crichana, Paushiana, †Bonari
    - ε GROUP 5 [4]: *Makushi, *Pemon, Patamona, Akawaio, †Arinagoto
  - v NORTHERN BRAZIL [1]:
    - α †GROUP 1 [0]: †Palmella, †Pimenteira
    - β GROUP 2 [1]: †Yaruma, Chicão
    - γ †GROUP 3 [0]: †Pariri, †Apiaka, †Arara, †Yuma
- b SOUTHERN [8]:
  - i SOUTHEASTERN COLOMBIA [1]: †Hianacoto, †Guaque, Carijona
  - ii XINGU BASIN [2]: *Bakairi, Nahukwa
  - iii SOUTHERN GUIANA [5]: Ye'cuana, Wayumara, Parukoto, *Hishkaryana, *Kashuyana

B GE-PANO [70]:

1 MACRO-PANOAN [49]:
- a †CHARRUAN [0]: †Charrua, †Chana, †Güenoa
- b †LULE-VILELA [0]: †Lule, *†Vilela
- c MASCOIAN [5]: Guana, Northern Lengua, Southern Lengua, Sanapana, Emok
- d MOSETEN [1]: *Chimane
- e MATACO-GUAICURU [9]:
  - i GUAICURUAN [4]: †Abipon, Kadiweu, †Guaicuru, †Guachi, Mocovi, *Toba, Pilaga
  - ii MATACO [5]: *Chulupi, *Chorote, Nocten, *Vejoz, Maca

f PANO-TACANA [34]:
i PANOAN [25]:
α SOUTHERN [3]: *Chacobo, Pacahuara, Caripuna, †Sinabo, †Zurina
β SOUTH-CENTRAL [5]:
[2]: *Amahuaca, Parquenahua
I YAMINAHUA-SHARANAHUA [3]: Yaminahua, Poyanawa, †Shipinawa, †Tushinawa, *Sharanahua
γ SOUTH-EASTERN [5]: *Cashinahua, Morunahua, Catuquina, Shahuanahua, Camanahua
δ WESTERN [1]: *Cashibo
ε NORTH-CENTRAL [6]: *Capanahua, *Shipibo, Isconahua, †Remo, Marubo, †Capuibo, Sensi, Niarawa, †Pichobo, †Araua, †Atsahuaca
ζ NORTHERN [4]: *Matses, Mayubo, Rëmoxbo, Pisabo
η EASTERN [1]: Kasharari
ii TACANAN [9]:
[1]: Yamaluba, †Arasa, †Guariza
α †CHIRIGUA [0]: †Maropa, †Chumana, †Sapiboca
β TIATINAGUA-TACANA [8]:
I TIATINAGUA [2]: *Ese'ejja, *Huarayo
II ARAONA-TACANA [6]:
A ARAONA [3]: Capachene, Mabenaro, Araona
B CAVINEÑA-TACANA [3]:
1 CAVINEÑA [1]: *Cavineña
2 TACANA PROPER [2]: *Tacana, Reyesano, †Toromono
2 MACRO-GE [21]:
[5]: Rikbaktsa, Fulnio, Guato, Opaye, †Oti, Caraja
a BORORO [3]:
i BORORO PROPER [2]: *Bororo, Umotina, †Aravira
ii OTUKE [1]: Otuke, †Covare, †Coraveca, †Curucane, †Tapii
b BOTOCUDO [1]: Botocudo
c †CHIQUITO [0]: †Chiquito
d †KAMAKAN [0]: †Kutasho, †Masacara, †Menien, †Mongoyo, †Kamakan
e †PURI [0]: †Puri, †Coroado, †Coropo
f YABUTI [2]: Aricapu, Yabuti
g MASHAKALI [1]: *Mashakali
h GE-KAINGANG [9]:
i KAINGANG [2]:
[0]: †Dorin
α NORTHERN [2]: *Kaingang, Xokleng, †Chiqui
β SOUTHERN [0]: †Amho, †Ingain, †Gualachi

ii GE [7]:
- α CENTRAL [2]:
  - I †ACROA [0]: †Acroa, †Aricobe, †Guegue
  - II ACUA [2]: *Chavante, Cherente
- β NORTHWEST [5]: *Apinaye, Suya, Kreen-Akarore, *Cayapo, *Canela

LANGUAGE ISOLATES[a] [5]: *Basque, *Burushaski, *Ket, *Gilyak, *Nahali, *†Sumerian, *†Etruscan, *†Hurrian, †Meroitic

UNCLASSIFIED[a] [16]: Warenbori (New Guinea), Taurap (New Guinea), Yuri (New Guinea), Busa (New Guinea), Nagatman (New Guinea), Porome (New Guinea), Pauwi (New Guinea), Massep (New Guinea), Carabayo (Colombia), Guaviare (Colombia), Yari (Colombia), Mutus (Venezuela), Yuwana (Venezuela), Kohoroxitari (Brazil), Arara (Brazil), Chiquitano (Bolivia)

PIDGINS AND CREOLES [37]:

I SWAHILI-BASED [1]: Asian Swahili

II ZULU-BASED [1]: *Fanagalo

III ENGLISH-BASED [17]:
- A ATLANTIC [10]: *Sea Island Creole (= Gulla), Guyanese, *Western Caribbean Creole, Lesser Antillean Creole, *Krio, Wescos, *Djuka, *Saramaccan, *Sranan, Pitcairnese
- B PACIFIC [7]: Hawaiian Creole, Roper River Creole, Torres Strait Pidgin, *Tok Pisin, *Bislama, Solomon Pijin, Micronesian Pidgin

IV DUTCH-BASED [1]: Dutch Creole

V GERMAN-BASED [1]: Unserdeutsch

VI FRENCH-BASED [1]: *French Creole

VII SPANISH-BASED [3]: Bamboo Spanish, *Chavacano, Palenquero

VIII PORTUGUESE-BASED [8]: *Indo-Portuguese, Macanese, *Malacca Creole, Timor Pidgin, *Crioulo, *Fa d'Ambu, Papiamento, Cafundo Creole

[a]The difference between a *language isolate* and an *unclassified* language is the following. A language isolate is a language with a reasonable amount of documentation that has been evaluated by scholars for a sufficient period of time to know that the language is not closely related to any other known language or group. An unclassified language is typically that of a recently discovered ethnic group. In such cases little or nothing is known of the language of these people, or what is known has not yet come to the attention of someone who could classify it on this basis. It is likely that the unclassified New Guinea languages are members of Indo-Pacific; almost certainly the unclassified South American Indian languages are members of one of the South American branches of Amerind. This list of unclassified languages merely represents those that have come to my attention. There are still uncontacted tribes in South America, and peoples whose distinct languages have escaped notice elsewhere in the world, especially in Southeast Asia, New Guinea, and Africa.

IX RUSSIAN-BASED [0]: †Russo-Norsk
X NAGA-BASED [1]: *Naga Pidgin
XI MALAY-BASED [1]: Bazaar Malay
XII MOTU-BASED [1]: *Hiri Motu
XIII CHINOOK-BASED [1]: *Chinook Jargon

INVENTED [2]: *Esperanto, *Interlingua

Postscript 1991

During the decade that I compiled and refined the classification given in this book, no one was more aware of its constant state of flux than I. Nor did I imagine that the classification frozen in type in 1987 (and in fact finalized in 1985) would be immune to further change—at every level of the classification. This is *not* to say that I thought everything was still up for grabs, but rather that some reshuffling and further consolidation were by no means ruled out. I did not, however, anticipate the significant and unexpected developments that have in fact taken place during the past five years. This Postscript will then bring things up to date, but the rest of the book is unchanged.

In assembling the classification given in this book, my primary intention was to define linguistically valid taxa (i.e., families of languages more closely related to each other than to any language outside the family) in a hierarchical structure usually expressed in the form of a tree. Above all else I wished to avoid putting together languages (and language families) that did not really constitute valid taxa and thus do not lead to valid historical inferences. At the highest level I would now make two changes. The family called Caucasian in section 2.5 should be broken up into two distinct families, North Caucasian and South Caucasian, each of which is more closely related to other families than to the other, as discussed below. Following a suggestion by Sergei Starostin I now use Caucasian in place of North Caucasian, and Kartvelian in place of South Caucasian. Furthermore, I would now remove Korean-Japanese-Ainu from Altaic, leaving Altaic with its traditional constituents: Turkic, Mongolian, and Tungus. These taxonomic revisions raise the number of supposedly independent stocks to 20, shown in List 9.1, as well as a few language isolates like Basque, Burushaski, Gilyak, †Etruscan, and †Sumerian.

List 9.1. The World's Language Families (1987)

KHOISAN	SINO-TIBETAN
NIGER-KORDOFANIAN:	YENISEIAN
I KORDOFANIAN	NA-DENE
II NIGER-CONGO	AFRO-ASIATIC
NILO-SAHARAN	KARTVELIAN
AUSTRALIAN	ELAMO-DRAVIDIAN
INDO-PACIFIC	INDO-HITTITE
AUSTRIC:	URALIC-YUKAGHIR
I AUSTROASIATIC	ALTAIC
II MIAO-YAO	KOREAN-JAPANESE-AINU
III DAIC	CHUKCHI-KAMCHATKAN
IV AUSTRONESIAN	ESKIMO-ALEUT
(NORTH) CAUCASIAN	AMERIND

In section 7.3 I briefly discussed several proposals for more comprehensive classifications that would reduce the number of independent families in List 9.1, and I also raised the possibility that all human languages may ultimately share a common origin, though I emphasized that such questions have long been considered unapproachable by traditional historical linguists. Over the past five years a radically different view—but one with clear precursors in the late nineteenth and early twentieth centuries—has come to be advocated by a small but growing number of scholars who believe not only that all presently extant languages are related, but that this can be shown by traditional comparative linguistics. A summary of recent work from this perspective may be found in Ruhlen (1991a).

LONG-RANGE COMPARISON

It is not possible to understand why some linguists see genetic diversity where others see uniformity without approaching the problem historically. Today the vast majority of linguists, in this country at least, subscribe to the view that Indo-Hittite has never been shown to be related to any other language or language family. The explanation usually offered for this total lack of relatives is that the comparative method in linguistics is limited to the last 5,000–10,000 years, beyond which time phonetic and semantic changes will have obliterated all trace of genetic affinity—if such ever existed.

There are, however, a number of things wrong with this traditional and widely accepted view of the limitations of comparative linguistics. First of all, it would indeed be a remarkable coincidence if the Indo-Hittite family turned out not only to be the family in terms of which comparative linguistics was first discovered some 200 years ago, but also the measure of the temporal limits of the method itself. The blind acceptance of this belief in the twentieth century has led to a view of classification wherein the world is conceived of as if it were made up of numerous Indo-Hittite-sized families, among which there are simply no apparent connections. This possibility cannot be ruled out *a priori*, for it is theoretically possible that, while Indo-Hittite is only 6,000–8,000 years old, the temporal gap between Indo-Hittite and its closest relative might be one or two million years. This is precisely the traditional belief—except that the date of necessary divergence is set at ten thousand years or more, not at two million.

What is really wrong with the traditional view is that it is simply false. Consider, for example, Proto-Indo-European **nepōt-* 'nephew,' which hardly differs from modern Rumanian *nepot* 'nephew.' This and many other similar examples that could be adduced show clearly that the idea that everything has changed beyond recognition after 6,000 years cannot be taken seriously. Furthermore, it was already known to be false in the nineteenth century, when many genetic connections were discovered among Eurasian families by linguists of no less repute than Rasmus Rask. At the beginning of the twentieth century, scholars such as Henry Sweet, Holger Pedersen, and Alfredo Trombetti pointed out the inconsistency of Indo-Europeanists treating the Indo-European pronoun system, *m-* 'I' vs. *t-* 'you' (sg.), as a pattern inherited from Proto-Indo-European, while conveniently ignoring the presence of a similar pattern in Uralic, Altaic, Chukchi-Kamchatkan, and Eskimo-Aleut. The interpretation of the same pattern in different ways according to one's preconceived expectations and assumptions can hardly be called scientific. Toward the close of the twentieth century, scholars such as Vladislav Illich-Svitych, Aron Dolgopolsky, and Joseph Greenberg have similarly stressed the distribution of this pronominal pattern and its genetic import. Despite the constant dissent of a few linguists throughout the twentieth century, Indo-Europeanists have in general maintained vehemently, down to the present day, the fiction that Indo-Hittite has no known relative. They have done this, I believe, for a number of reasons (Ruhlen 1988a, Bengtson 1988), some of which Sweet (1901: vi) pointed out almost a century ago:

> In philology, as in all branches of knowledge, it is the specialist who most strenuously opposes any attempt to widen the field of his methods. Hence the advocate of affinity between the Aryan [Indo-European] and the Finnish [= Finno-Ugric] languages need not be alarmed when he hears that the majority of Aryan philologists reject the hypothesis. In many cases this rejection merely means that our specialist

has his hands full already, and shrinks from learning a new set of languages. . . . Even when this passively agnostic attitude develops into aggressive antagonism, it is generally little more than the expression of mere prejudice against dethroning Aryan from its proud isolation and affiliating it to the languages of yellow races; or want of imagination and power of realizing an earlier morphological stage of Aryan; or, lastly, that conservatism and caution which would rather miss a brilliant discovery than run the risk of having mistakes exposed.

Furthermore, many of the early proposals—but by no means all—were quite bad and were justifiably rejected by Indo-Europeanists, in particular certain comparisons with Semitic that were based mostly on typological factors and on the earnest hope that the languages of Christian Europe were related to the languages of the Bible. An additional factor has been the ever-increasing specialization in academia throughout the twentieth century, which has encouraged scholars to occupy a narrow and cozy niche—usually a single language family or even a single language for linguists—to which all their attention is devoted. Under these circumstances, widely distributed traits are not likely even to be noticed, much less understood. An entirely analogous situation befuddled the classification of American Indian languages throughout this century, as discussed in section 6.3.1.

Another factor that has prevented more comprehensive taxonomies from developing has been a confusion between *classification* and *reconstruction*, the latter usually requiring regular phonological correspondences. Thus, Sarah Thomason (1990) claims that "the traditional proof of genetic relationship . . . is the discovery of recurring sound/meaning correspondences that permit phonological reconstruction, together with the establishment of systematic correspondences in other grammatical subsystems that permit grammatical reconstruction." In a similar vein Theodora Bynon (1977: 271) claims that Greenberg's "use of basic vocabulary comparison not simply as a *preliminary* to reconstruction but as a *substitute* for it is . . . controversial." This is a surprising statement, since Greenberg has never claimed—and never would claim—that classification is a "substitute" for reconstruction. The two are distinct enterprises, and classification does not require reconstruction. In fact, just the opposite is true, in that reconstruction *does* require a prior classification; otherwise there would be nothing to reconstruct.

There is a final element in the question of "long-range comparison" that needs to be dispelled. Many linguists believe that Greenberg uses unconventional, even intuitive, methods that are quite different from the methodology of traditional historical linguistics, which is usually equated with reconstruction and regular sound changes. This view is clearly evident in the remarks of Thomason and Bynon above and has recently appeared widely in the media in this country. Yet nothing could be further from the truth. The reasons for this widespread misconception are, I believe, the following. Historical linguistics has always been dominated by specialists in Indo-Hittite, for obvious historical reasons. But for Indo-Hittite the problem of classification was essentially resolved by Sir William Jones in 1786 when he outlined five branches of this family. Thus for Indo-Hittite, classification has never been a central problem, though a few new branches were later discovered.

When, however, one is faced not with an already defined family like Indo-Hittite, but with a thousand African languages whose relationships are unknown, the problems are quite different. At this stage one must begin with the comparison of the languages involved in order to detect closely related families, and then, by the comparison of these, higher-level taxa. Greenberg has called this process "multilateral comparison," but it is really no different from the initial step of the comparative method. As we saw in Chapter 6, Greenberg's method of classification "by inspection" has been derided by American Indianists who reject the idea that such a simple method could produce reliable results (Goddard 1987: 656). This, however, is not the view of the eminent evolutionary biologist Ernst Mayr (1988: 268): "From the earliest preliterary days, organisms were grouped into classes by their outward appearance, into grasses, birds, butterflies, snails, and others. Such grouping 'by inspection' is the expressly stated or unspoken starting point of virtually all systems of classification." The problem with historical linguistics is that this initial step in the comparative method has always been "unspoken," and Greenberg's attachment of a new name to this process has led some to believe he is employing a new and unreliable method. In fact, he is simply starting the only way one can.

In the final analysis, of course, whether or not Indo-Hittite can be shown to be related to other families depends not on *a priori* methodological considerations, but on the empirical evidence that can be adduced in favor of such relationships. Let us turn then to a review of the evidence that has been put forward by the advocates of a Eurasiatic, or Nostratic, family in which Indo-Hittite is but one component.

Nostratic/Eurasiatic

The Nostratic family, as defined by Illich-Svitych, connects Indo-Hittite with five other families, whereas Greenberg's Eurasiatic family overlaps this definition, as seen in Fig. 9.1. The Nostratic family is supported by over 700 etymologies (Illich-Svitych 1967, 1971–84; Dolgopolsky 1984, to appear), and Greenberg (to appear) offers about 500 etymologies in support of Eurasiatic. Finally, Bomhard (1990) proposed 483 Nostratic etymologies, though he argues for a different set of sound correspondences from those used by the Soviets.

Fig. 9.1. Comparison of Illich-Svitych's Nostratic and Greenberg's Eurasiatic

The differences between Nostratic and Eurasiatic derive from the different methodologies used by the Nostraticists and by Greenberg. Since its first adumbration by Holger Pedersen at the start of this century, Nostratic has been defined—somewhat amorphously—as those language families that can be shown to be related to Indo-Hittite. Furthermore, Nostraticists insist on comparing reconstructed proto-languages for each family and thus exclude, for the time being anyway, those families that have not yet been reconstructed in sufficient detail for broader comparison. Two points should be made. First, this definition of Nostratic is unabashedly Eurocentric and really is not a proper taxonomic definition at all. Second, a taxonomic definition that depends on the quality of the linguistic literature stands little chance of constituting a valid taxon.

Greenberg, on the other hand, approaches the problem of Indo-Hittite relatives from a totally different perspective, that of a taxonomist who merely classifies the entities under consideration, but without requiring reconstruction and without attributing any special importance to Indo-Hittite. Furthermore, Greenberg does not deny that Afro-Asiatic, Kartvelian, and Dravidian are related to the families he includes in Eurasiatic, but he considers these relationships more remote. With the growing awareness of the importance of classification—prior to reconstruction—by at least some Nostraticists, the differences between Eurasiatic and Nostratic show signs of reconciliation. With regard to Afro-Asiatic there seems to be a growing consensus that this family is related to Nostratic as a sister language rather than as a daughter language, as Greenberg and Harold Fleming had already proposed. Recently Starostin (1989a) has expressed the same view: "I prefer presently to exclude Afro-Asiatic material from the Nostratic comparisons. This does not mean, of course, that Afro-Asiatic parallels for Nostratic roots . . . are all accidental 'look-alikes.' They may purely reflect a relationship on some deeper level between Afro-Asiatic and Nostratic." Furthermore, in the same paper Starostin presents substantial and convincing evidence connecting Nostratic and Dene-Caucasian (see below), but he does not claim that the Dene-Caucasian families are Nostratic (as the traditional definition would require). He sees rather that they are two higher-level families that are related to each other and to Afro-Asiatic. Finally, Starostin (1990) suggests that Dravidian is the most divergent branch of Nostratic (minus Afro-Asiatic), thus bringing his views further in line with those of Greenberg. Starostin's perspective is similar to that of Greenberg in that it concentrates on defining the hierarchical relationships of the world's language families rather than simply trying to prove that X is related to Y.

With regard to the Asian families that Greenberg includes in Eurasiatic—but which have been generally excluded from Nostratic—there is really little conflict. These families have all been included in Nostratic by one or another scholar, and Dolgopolsky has included Eskimo-Aleut in Nostratic from his earliest work. Thus, these families have generally been excluded from Nostratic because they had not been reconstructed, not because they did not belong. This leaves Kartvelian as the sole remaining difference between Eurasiatic and Nostratic, and it seems certain that this difference too can eventually be resolved.

Amerind

The publication of Greenberg's (1987) revolutionary classification of American Indian languages into just three families provoked a storm of controversy that parallels in many ways that which greeted his African classification some forty years ago. Even before the appearance of Greenberg's book—and without even seeing its contents—Lyle Campbell (1986) called for Greenberg's classification to be "shouted down." Under such circumstances it is not surprising that Campbell later delivered a thoroughly negative review of Greenberg's book to the journal *Language* (Campbell 1988). Terrence Kaufman (1990: 63) claims that "many of Greenberg's (1987) and Ruhlen's (1987) [this book] avowed values are subversive and should be explicitly argued against." Ives Goddard (1987: 657) gave an equally negative review of Greenberg's book, claiming that "the equations it generates do not require any historical explanation." A minority of scholars, however, recognized the importance of Greenberg's work from the outset, and Dell Hymes's (1987: 659) review stands in stark contrast to the assessments of Campbell, Kaufman, and Goddard: "Greenberg has demonstrated what has been suspected, namely, that almost all the indigenous languages of the New World are genetically related as what he appropriately calls 'Amerind.' So much, I think, is certain."

My own study of Greenberg's book, and of the 23 volumes of notebooks upon which it is based (Greenberg 1981), has led me to conclude that the case for Amerind is even stronger than Greenberg's book implied, which is hardly surprising for a pioneering work of this nature. First, there are about 150 additional Amerind etymologies that Greenberg split among various Amerind subgroups instead of uniting them as Amerind etymologies (Ruhlen 1989a). Second, the unpublished Amerind notebooks contain additional Amerind etymologies, as well as substantial additional evidence for those already listed in the book. Finally, I have found that claims (Thomason 1990) that the Amerind pronominal pattern *n-/m-* 'I/you' is an archaic residue of stable nasal sounds is demonstrably false. As shown in Ruhlen (1989b), this pattern is virtually absent outside of the Amerind family, though within Amerind it is the most frequent pronominal pattern, and its wide distribution in the Americas has been noted for almost a century.

In light of what has been said in section 6.3.1 concerning the taxonomic nonsense advocated by many American Indian specialists, it is hardly surprising that the practitioners of the failed Phase III paradigm should react hostilely to its demise. What is surprising is the extent to which these critics have indulged in outright distortions of Greenberg's book, charges that are answered in detail in Ruhlen (1988b) and Greenberg (1989, 1990a, 1990b). Since many scholars read reviews of books they would never actually look at, no doubt some such scholars have accepted what Greenberg's critics have said in their reviews at face value, without ever checking Greenberg's book. It is for that reason that a few examples of this criticism are in order.

In his review in *Language,* Campbell (1988: 594–95) discusses the "Xinca-Lenca problem" (i.e. are these two languages related?): "An example of one of these often-repeated long-shot proposals is instructive. The Xinca-Lenca hypothesis was first proposed by Lehmann in 1920 . . . and accepted by Sapir; it became entrenched in the literature and is reflected in *Language in the Americas* as part of Greenberg's Chibchan. Nevertheless, *Lehmann's evidence is the only data ever published in support of the hypothesis* [emphasis mine]. I assess his evidence in its entirety. . . . In sum, not one single cognate set proposed by Lehmann is without serious problems; the Xinca-Lenca hypothesis thus has no support." Campbell apparently is trying to create the impression that Greenberg's book is little more than a stringing together of previously ill-supported groupings like Xinca-Lenca. Anyone who takes the time to read Greenberg's book will find that Xinca and Lenca figure in no less than 78 of Greenberg's lexical etymologies for Chibchan-Paezan and Amerind. Thus Campbell's claim that the only evidence connecting these two languages is Lehmann's is simply false.

Goddard (1987: 657) criticizes Greenberg for loose semantics, meaning that the semantic connections are implausible. As an example he cites

Greenberg's grouping of words meaning "excrement," "night," and "grass" in a single etymology. Most linguists would agree that these three meanings have little in common. However, an examination of the etymology itself reveals Goddard's trick, for what he has done is to cite the furthest semantic connections in the etymology while completely excluding the basic core meanings. What we find in the etymology in question are words denoting "dark in color." In Almosan the meaning is "black" and the overall distribution of the meanings in North and South America suggests that this was the original meaning. In Keresiouan we find "dark in color" in Iroquoian and "green" in Keresan. In Penutian the meaning has completely shifted to "green" and its close semantic connections "grass" and "blue." In South America Macro-Ge preserves the original meaning of "black" in Proto-Ge, while other languages in this group have shifted the meaning to "dirty." Finally, in the Equatorial group the meaning is "excrement." As in the previous example, a comparison of Greenberg's book with the allegations of his critics reveals what can only be called a willful distortion of the evidence. It should be noted that Campbell (1988: 600) also criticizes Greenberg's lax semantic standards: "G[reenberg]'s forms are quite permissive in semantic latitude. Semantic equations such as the following are not convincing: 'excrement/night/grass.'"

While critics have spent most of their time trying to discredit Greenberg's classification, others have begun to compare Greenberg's three families with the world's other language families in order to identify the origin of each. Already in 1986 Greenberg, Turner, and Zegura suggested, in an article comparing dental, serological, and linguistic data, that there were three migrations from Asia to the New World, the first resulting in the Amerind family, the second in the Na-Dene family, and the third, the Eskimo-Aleut family. Powers (1990) provides archaeological evidence for three distinct migrations to the New World, at roughly 14,000 B.P., 11,000 B.P., and 4,000 B.P. Linguistic evidence for three distinct migrations, which would require a comparison of these three families with Old World families, was not given in the Greenberg, Turner, and Zegura article, but has subsequently been developed for all three migrations. Eskimo-Aleut, as the easternmost member of Eurasiatic, probably represents the most recent migration. The next most recent incursion into the Americas was carried out by the ancestors of the Na-Dene, which was shown during the 1980s to be related to a different set of Old World families in a phylum now called Dene-Caucasian (see below). Finally, the Amerind phylum itself, which constituted the first migration sometime before 12,000 B.P., is most closely related to Eurasiatic as a whole. That is, though it is not a member of Eurasiatic, it is closer to Eurasiatic than to any other family. Linguistic evidence for this connection may be found in Ruhlen (1989e) and is summarized in Ruhlen (1990a). An investigation of the internal structure of the Amerind family is given in Ruhlen (1991b).

Dene-Caucasian

During the early part of this century Edward Sapir, after making a string of brilliant taxonomic discoveries (discussed in Chapter 6), came to the conclusion that the Na-Dene Family, which he himself had identified, was more closely related to the Sino-Tibetan family than to other native American languages. In a letter to Alfred Kroeber in 1920 he wrote: "I am just now interested in another big linguistic possibility. I tremble to speak of it, though I've carried the germinal idea with me for years. I do *not* feel that Na-dene belongs to the other American languages. . . . Do not think me an ass if I am seriously entertaining the notion of an old Indo-Chinese [=Sino-Tibetan] offshoot into N.W. America. . . . At least I know that Déné's a long shot nearer to Tibetan than to Siouan" (Golla 1984: 350). Exactly one year later he wrote to Kroeber again regarding the same subject, this time even more emphatic than before:

> I have long wanted to write you about Nadene and Indo-Chinese, but my evidence accumulates so fast it is hard to sit down and give an idea. Let me say this for the present. If the morphological and lexical accord which I find on every hand between Nadene and Indo-Chinese is "accidental," then every analogy on God's earth is an accident. It is all so powerfully cumulative and integrated that when you tumble to one point a lot of others fall into line. I am now so thoroughly accustomed to the idea that it no longer startles me. For a while I resisted the notion. Now I can no longer do so. (Golla 1984: 374)

For reasons that are not entirely clear, Sapir never published any evidence for this connection. It seems likely that in the wake of Michelson's hostile critique of Algonquian-Ritwan (see section 6.3.1) and Pliny Goddard's equally negative review of Na-Dene (see section 6.2.1), Sapir decided that even more remote genetic connections than these would simply not be considered seriously by other linguists and he effectively ceased taxonomic work after around 1925. Sapir's unpublished Na-Dene–Sino-Tibetan comparative notebooks are now stored in the American Philosophical Society library in Philadelphia, and Americanists view the whole idea of a genetic connection between Na-Dene and Sino-Tibetan as yet another of Sapir's failed long-shots. According to Campbell (1988: 593), "Needless to say, no specialist today embraces this claim."

Ironically, one of the major discoveries in linguistic taxonomy during the 1980s has been the elaboration of a *Dene-Caucasian* family, in which Na-Dene and Sino-Tibetan are two components. This line of research began in the Soviet Union and for a while escaped the attention of American scholars. The initial step was Sergei Starostin's (1984) comparison of (North)

Caucasian, Sino-Tibetan, and Yeniseian (whose sole surviving language is Ket), in which he showed that these three families formed a higher-level family that he called Sino-Caucasian. The following year V. A. Chirikba presented evidence connecting Basque with (North) Caucasian, an idea that had already been suggested by Alfredo Trombetti in 1926. A year later Sergei Nikolaev (1986), in a comparison of (North) Caucasian and Na-Dene, showed that these two families too were unmistakably related to each other, and the overall family was renamed Dene-Caucasian to indicate this fact. Sapir's idea of a Sino-Tibetan–Na-Dene connection was thus resurrected by Soviet scholars, though without ever comparing the two families that had led Sapir to his conclusions.

The Soviet work on Dene-Caucasian became better known in this country at the Rice University symposium on the genetic classification of languages in March, 1986 (Shevoroshkin and Manaster-Ramer 1991). Since that time John Bengtson (1991a) has provided substantial additional support for Dene-Caucasian by making the first multilateral comparison of the family, which for Bengtson includes Burushaski and Sumerian, as well as the families compared by the Soviets. Furthermore, Bengtson (1991b) proposes that Basque, (North) Caucasian, and Burushaski form a subfamily, which he calls Macro-Caucasian, within the Dene-Caucasian phylum. (It should be noted that Claude Boisson [1989] has made an exhaustive comparison of Sumerian with both Nostratic and Dene-Caucasian, and he leans toward a stronger connection with the former than with the latter.) I have compared Starostin's (1982) Proto-Yeniseian reconstructions with Na-Dene etymologies (Ruhlen 1989c) and with Nahali, providing additional connecting links for Dene-Caucasian (Ruhlen 1989d). (Heinz-Jürgen Pinnow, however, considers Nahali a member of Austroasiatic.) In light of the various proposals mentioned above I would now incline toward including the following families in Dene-Caucasian: Basque, (North) Caucasian, Burushaski, Sumerian, Nahali, Sino-Tibetan, Yeniseian, and Na-Dene. The inclusion of Nahali and Sumerian seems to me the least secure.

MONOGENESIS

If we accept both Greenberg's Eurasiatic proposal and the Soviets' Dene-Caucasian phylum, then the number of distinct families is reduced to about a dozen, as shown in List 9.2, and a logical next step would be to compare these families with each other to see whether further consolidation is possible. Such research has been practically forbidden in this century by the myth that Indo-Hittite has no known relatives and the related myth that the comparative method in linguistics is limited to a time depth of 5,000–10,000 years (Ruhlen 1988a, 1990b), conveniently the assumed age of Indo-Hittite.

List 9.2. The World's Language Families (1991)

I KHOISAN
II NIGER-KORDOFANIAN:
A KORDOFANIAN
B NIGER-CONGO
III NILO-SAHARAN
IV AUSTRALIAN
V INDO-PACIFIC
VI AUSTRIC:
A AUSTROASIATIC
B MIAO-YAO
C DAIC
D AUSTRONESIAN
VII DENE-CAUCASIAN:
A Basque
B (NORTH) CAUCASIAN
C Burushaski
D Nahali
E SINO-TIBETAN
F YENISEIAN
G NA-DENE
VIII AFRO-ASIATIC
IX ELAMO-DRAVIDIAN
X KARTVELIAN
XI EURASIATIC:
A INDO-HITTITE
B URALIC-YUKAGHIR
C ALTAIC
D KOREAN-JAPANESE-AINU
E Gilyak
F CHUKCHI-KAMCHATKAN
G ESKIMO-ALEUT
XII AMERIND

With these myths now demolished by the work of the Soviet Nostraticists and the impending volumes by Greenberg (to appear) on Eurasiatic and Dolgopolsky (to appear) on Nostratic, a number of linguists have once again turned to the perennial problem of the interrelationships of all the world's language families. John Bengtson and I (1988), employing Greenberg's multilateral approach, have proposed some two dozen etymologies connecting all of the world's language families, and many more are known. A careful comparison of all the world's language families—until recently almost an illicit enterprise (Matisoff 1990)—will uncover many additional connections, and within a few years, I believe, the fact that all extant human languages share a common origin will be as casually accepted as is the opposite opinion today. Now that the dike of Indo-Hittite isolation has finally burst, it is only a matter of time before the resulting wave spreads to all of the world's language families. Independent of the work of Bengtson and Ruhlen (1988), Soviet linguists have been approaching this same problem from their own Nostratic perspective of comparing reconstructed families, but their conclusions are not substantially different from ours. Starostin (1989a) has shown many convincing connections between Nostratic and Dene-Caucasian, and Ilja Peyros (1989) has adduced evidence connecting these two families with Austric. Shevoroshkin (1989a) presented evidence connecting Nostratic, Dene-Caucasian, Amerind, Australian, and Indo-Pacific, and Kaiser and Shevoroshkin (1988) noted similarities between Nostratic and the two African phyla, Nilo-Saharan and Niger-Kordofanian. The Czech linguist Vaclav Blažek (1989) has also made important contributions to global comparisons. Both approaches thus arrive at essentially the same conclusion, namely, that all of the world's language families—and hence all of the world's extant languages—share a common origin. This opinion is admittedly at variance with the prevailing views of the great majority of linguists, just as the Amerind family is discounted by the majority of American Indian specialists, but I believe both hypotheses are correct. Furthermore, they are not in my opinion particularly difficult taxonomic questions, and the failure to recognize both taxa is due more to a lack of understanding of basic taxonomic principles than to the alleged paucity of evidence. The really difficult—and to my mind most interesting—taxonomic problems involve determining the degrees of relationship among the world's language families, not the fact of relationship itself.

It is important here to emphasize once again, as I did in section 7.3, that the fact that all *extant* languages appear to form a single family does not alone imply the correctness of monogenesis. We only have information on the languages spoken by modern humans, *Homo sapiens sapiens*. We have no direct evidence on the communicative systems used by earlier hominids, whether contemporaneous with modern humans, such as the Neanderthals, or much earlier, such as *Homo erectus* or *Australopithecus afarensis*. How then did language develop? There are basically two poles to this question, though one can conceive of numerous intermediate possibilities. At one pole is the possibility that all hominids prior to *Homo sapiens sapiens* were speechless, so to speak, and that language developed solely—and probably rapidly, like a child learning a language—in modern humans, leading perhaps to the extinction of all other hominids. At the other pole is the idea that linguistic abilities in hominids developed gradually over a very long time period so that earlier hominids would have had some kind of language which over several million years developed in modern humans into what we call human language. I personally find the idea that language could have evolved *ex nihilo* to its present complexity in 100,000 years or so implausible, but it is hard to back up this belief with any kind of hard evidence. My view is that all extant languages have developed from a single language that was spoken perhaps 100,000 years ago, but that this language was in no sense primitive. It was in all probability a language not qualitatively different from the 5,000 languages spoken today. The mind of modern humans has not changed since our appearance on the earth, and I doubt that our languages have either. Stephen Jay Gould (1988: 18–20) expresses this same point of view, though not in the context of language, when he writes that

> At some point, modern *Homo sapiens* split off from an ancestral group and founded our own species. They were us from the beginning, are us now, and shall be us until we blow ourselves up or genetically engineer ourselves out of current existence. *Homo sapiens* . . . is an entity, not a tendency. Once we arose as a species—and 100,000 to 250,000 years ago in Africa is our best current assessment of time and place—we were probably pretty much ourselves in terms of mental organization. . . . I would reverse our usual perspective. . . . We are stunned by what our Ice Age ancestors could do. I think that we should look the other way, onward from the origin of our species. Is it not remarkable that all of what we call civilization, all of agriculture, of the arts and sciences, of technology, of life in complex cities, could be built by the unchanged power resident in the mind of a creature who evolved a large brain for reasons obviously unrelated to this future potential?

And it is not, in my view, likely that this creature accomplished these remarkable achievements without a fully developed capacity for language from the inception.

HUMAN GENETICS

Ironically, the event perhaps destined to have the greatest impact on historical linguistics was the discovery by human geneticists during the 1980s that the structure of the human population based on genes—its basic clusters and their hierarchical arrangement in a family tree—bears a striking resemblance to proposals made by linguists on the basis of human language. This discovery was unexpected, at least among linguists, for two reasons. First, it had become virtually an article of faith during the twentieth century that "there is no deterministic connection between language and gene pools or culture" (Campbell 1986: 488). And second, even if there *was* some correlation between the evolution of genes and languages, linguistic evolution is so much swifter than genetic evolution that the two processes could hardly be expected to result in the same groupings (Bateman et al. 1990a: 9–10). Yet this is exactly what L. L. Cavalli-Sforza and his colleagues reported in 1988 in a paper that has already sent shock waves through the field of historical linguistics.

It is of course true that any person, with any genes, can learn any human language with native proficiency, provided only that he is raised as a child in an environment where the language is spoken. Black Americans speak English, an Indo-Hittite language, but genetically they are very similar to black Africans, who speak non-Indo-Hittite languages. Thus in this case black Americans are genetically like black Africans, but linguistically like white Europeans. The reason for this discrepancy between genes and languages is hardly a mystery. As is well known, it was the European slave trade which kidnapped blacks from Africa and brought them to the Americas to sell. Over time the original African languages were replaced by English in the U.S.A., and by French, Spanish, or Portuguese elsewhere in the Americas. What Cavalli-Sforza and colleagues found, however, is that when one eliminates such anomalies, which have known historical explanations or prehistorical explanations that can reasonably be inferred, a generally consistent genetic tree emerges that resembles remarkably the linguistic classification given in this book. As to why there should be such a correlation, Cavalli-Sforza and colleagues (1990: 18) offer the following answer.

> The central question is *why there should be any congruence between genetic and linguistic evolution.* The main reason is that the two evolutions follow in principle the same history, namely, sequence of fissions. Two populations that have separated begin a process of differentiation of both genes and languages. These processes need not have exactly constant evolutionary rates, but rough proportionality with time is a reasonable expectation for both. They should therefore be qualitatively congruent, except for later events such as gene flow or language replacement. These may blur the genetic and the linguistic picture, but our conclusion is that they do not obscure it entirely.

Cavalli-Sforza's comparison of the genetic tree and the linguistic phyla is shown in Fig. 9.2.

Two groups of linguists in particular have expressed outrage at the proposed genetic findings. First of all, Indo-Europeanists were dismayed to find Indo-Hittite connected to other Eurasian families in a fashion reminiscent of the Nostratic/Eurasiatic proposal. The noted Indo-Europeanist Paul Hopper (1989) lashed out against the alleged linguistic-genetic correlations by claiming that "linguistic hustlers" (Nostraticists and Greenbergians) had "induced . . . responsible human biologists" (Cavalli-Sforza and colleagues) into believing that there is some correlation between the distribution of genes and the distribution of languages. Hopper refers derisively to families such as Niger-Kordofanian, Afro-Asiatic, Nilo-Saharan, and Austroasiatic as "broad-based guesses," which are not to be confused with "factually established genetic categories" like Indo-Hittite.

The other group of scholars who were more than dismayed by the genetic findings were the American Indian specialists, who were in the midst of their orgy of anti-Greenberg invective (Ruhlen 1988b). At a time when Greenberg's book was being condemned by one American Indian expert after another, Cavalli-Sforza found that, on the basis of their genes, the native populations of the Americas fell into the *same* three groups that Greenberg had identified on the basis of language one year before. For scholars like Goddard and Campbell, such findings were devastating to their posi-

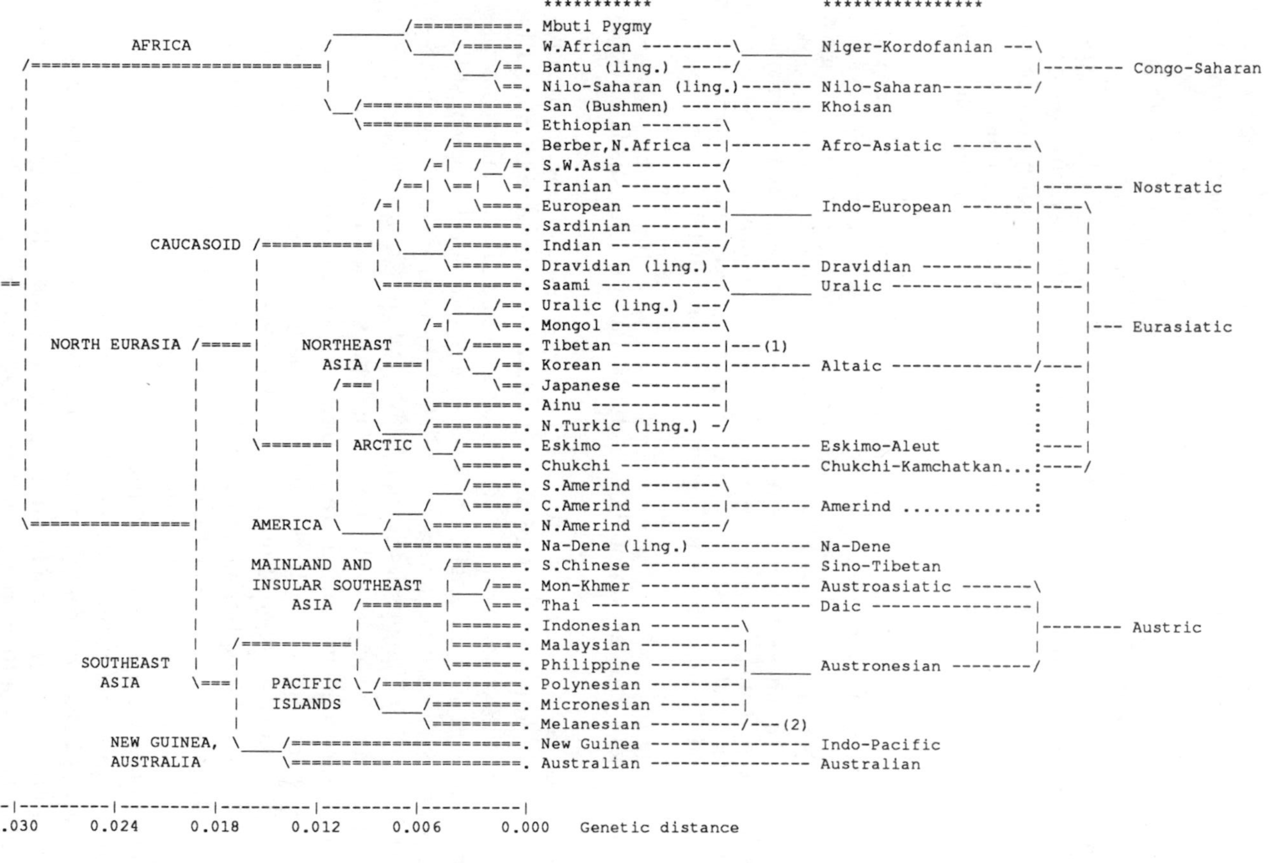

Fig. 9.2. Comparison of the genetic tree and linguistic phyla (Cavalli-Sforza et al. 1988)

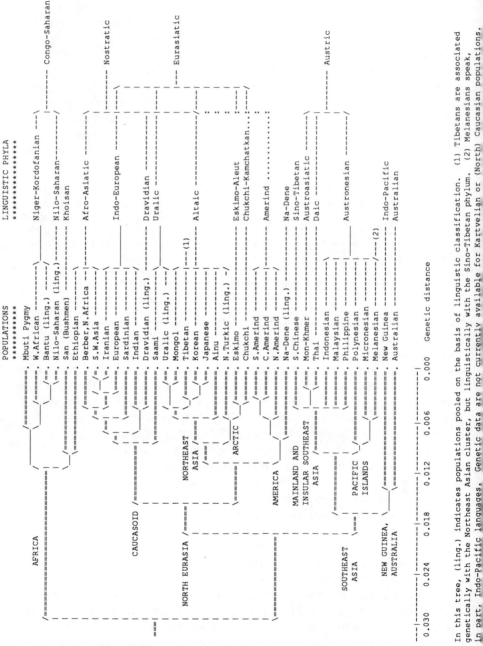

tion and could not go unchallenged, for if another scientific discipline—with its own methods and its own data—should arrive at the same classification as Greenberg, such independent corroboration can hardly be easily dismissed. The American Indianists' strategy had been to unanimously condemn Greenberg's book, distorting and misrepresenting it in the process, so that other scholars would simply accept their verdict without checking the facts themselves. This strategy had worked remarkably well for Truman Michelson and Pliny Goddard against Edward Sapir's proposals around 1920, and it continued to be widely used throughout the twentieth century. The danger that the genetic findings posed was that *outsiders*, who were not likely simply to accept the verdict of self-appointed experts, were being brought into the debate. Furthermore, these outsiders had found exactly what Goddard did not want, Greenberg's three families.

Goddard's response to these unwelcome developments was a joint article with six biologists from the Smithsonian Institution (Bateman et al. 1990a), who began by noting with alarm the "instant fame" of Cavalli-Sforza's paper "which received the rare accolade of rapid review in *Science*, . . . *Nature*, . . . and *Natural History*." Bateman et al. claim that Cavalli-Sforza's "main conclusion, that there is 'considerable parallelism between genetic and linguistic evolution' . . . is undermined by analysis of an inadequate database by inappropriate methods" (2). But they are later forced to admit (Bateman et al. 1990b: 177) that they are "unfamiliar with the data, methods, and models of human population genetics." This raises the interesting question of how they knew a database with which they were unfamiliar was inadequate. Later they make it clear that the existing literature on human genetics is not even worth investigating. We should rather start from scratch at the level of the individual human: "Extant hominids are sufficiently abundant and widespread to allow large-scale demographic sampling" (1990a: 13). Just round up a batch of these critters and test them. In sum, the article by Bateman et al. is replete with pretentious terminology (such as the use of "extant hominids" in place of "people"), an amusing figure showing that "languages evolved after the ability to speak" (10), a plethora of demonstrably false claims ("Languages lack the widespread but nonuniversal attributes that characterize major groups of organisms" [5] conveniently ignores the Eurasiatic pronominal pattern *m-/t-* 'I/you' and the Amerind pattern *n-/m-* 'I/you.'), and a virtual absence of any evidence that Native American populations do not fall into the three groups as claimed by Cavalli-Sforza and Greenberg. Bateman et al.'s final argument, that they cannot judge the work because they do not have access to either the database or the methodological considerations upon which the article was based, seems disingenuous, considering that such information could hardly be given in a paper with a strict five-page limitation. However, the work from which this article was extracted, which runs to almost 1,000 pages, is now approaching publication (Cavalli-Sforza et al. 1991), and the chapter devoted to the Americas, which I have read in manuscript, leaves little doubt that if Greenberg's Amerind had not already existed, Cavalli-Sforza and colleagues would have had to invent such a term themselves. Such is the story that human genes tell for the Americas.

It should be noted that Cavalli-Sforza's finding of a high degree of correlation between linguistic and genetic classifications is but one of many such discoveries made for different regions of the world during the 1980s, work that is briefly reviewed in Ruhlen (1991a). For Africa, Laurent Excoffier and his colleagues (1987: 151) found that "genetic differentiation clearly parallels the clustering of major linguistic families." For the island of Sardinia, Alberto Piazza and colleagues (1988) found that "languages and genes have a similar geographical distribution even at a microareal level." With regard to Europe, Guido Barbujani and Robert Sokal (1990: 1816) report that "of the 33 gene-frequency boundaries discovered . . . , 31 are coincident with linguistic boundaries marking contiguous regions of different language families, languages, or dialects." In an investigation of the Yanomami Indians of South America, Barbujani, Oden, and Sokal (1989: 386) concluded that "both at the level of variation among dialect groups as well as within such groups the regions of rapid genetic change agree with observable linguistic differences. These findings support conclusions from other studies on the relation of genetics and language."

Although the idea that there is a general congruence between languages and different ethnic groups fell out of favor in the twentieth century, for a variety of reasons, the general correlation was in fact noticed long ago. According to Trombetti (1905: 55), "Language, it is true, is not a trait that is directly inherited like physical structure, but in reality agreement between languages and races is the rule, disagreement, the exception." Nor did this correlation escape the notice of Charles Darwin (1859: 405): "If we possessed a perfect pedigree of mankind, a genealogical arrangement of the races of man would afford the best classification of the various languages now spoken throughout the world; and if all extinct languages, and all intermediate and slowly changing dialects, had to be included, such an arrangement would, I think, be the only possible one."

I believe that we now stand on the threshold of a multi-disciplinary investigation into human prehistory that will lead, and is already leading, to a more precise understanding of the history of our species than has hitherto seemed possible. The independent evidence of historical linguistics, human genetics, and archaeology is beginning to be integrated into a coherent and consistent framework for understanding human evolution over the past 100,000 years. This is not to say that all three of these disciplines yet agree on all particular points, much less that any of these fields is correct in all of its claims. But what is now known seems very promising. As Stephen Jay Gould (1989: 22) puts it, "The reconstruction of the human family tree—its branching order, its timing, and its geography—may be within our grasp. Since this tree is the basic datum of history, hardly anything in intellectual life could be more important." In a similar vein the British archaeologist Colin Renfrew (1991a) has recently written that "in a couple of decades, I predict, we shall see emerging a new synthesis between historical linguistics, prehistoric archaeology, and molecular genetics." I would go even further. I believe we can see it emerging even today.

BIBLIOGRAPHIC UPDATE

Since this book went to press some five years ago I have become aware of some sources that were inadvertently omitted, while other works have either come to my attention or were published during this time.

General

There are a number of good introductions to historical and comparative linguistics, the most recent being Bynon (1977), Hock (1986), and Anttila (1989). All of these works, however, emphasize historical rather than comparative aspects and devote most of their attention to the Indo-Hittite family; for these reasons they are largely complementary to this book. Fleming (1987b) offers a world-wide survey of linguistic classification. For the importance of statistics in historical linguistics, see Embleton (1986). On the emerging synthesis between genetics, archaeology, and linguistics, see Greenberg, Turner, and Zegura (1986), Cavalli-Sforza et al. (1988, 1991), Shevoroshkin (1989b, 1990, 1991), Turner (1989), and Renfrew (1991a, b). Within the linguistic community there has developed in recent years a reaction against the widespread belief that the period of linguistic taxonomy is basically over, owing to the alleged limitations of the comparative method. A newsletter, *Mother Tongue*, was founded by Harold Fleming in 1986 specifically to confront these erroneous and unjustified beliefs. An especially good introduction to the problems of fossil evidence for hominid prehistory is given in Lewin (1987).

Khoisan

Additional etymologies connecting Sandawe and Hadza to Khoisan are given in Fleming (1987a). General works on the family may be found in Vossen and Keuthmann (1986). Also of interest is Traill (1986).

Niger-Kordofanian

For an overview of the family, see Bendor-Samuel (1988). Meeussen (1980a, b) provides Bantu reconstructions.

Nilo-Saharan

Recent contributions to this perennially neglected family include Bender (1989, 1991).

Australian

Blake (1988) argues, on the basis of pronouns, that the traditional classification of Australian languages is incorrect, and that the family consists of two basic branches, Pama-Nyungan and non-Pama-Nyungan. Dixon and Blake (1979–) present general surveys of various Australian languages.

Indo-Pacific

Foley (1986) presents an overview of Papuan languages.

Austric

Edmondson and Solnit (1988) contains a series of studies on comparative Daic (Kadai), including an extensive set of Proto-Kam-Sui reconstructions by Graham Thurgood. Benedict (1990) argues that Japanese is a member of Austro-Tai, closest in fact to Austronesian. Such a classification disagrees, however, with those of Greenberg (to appear), who places it in Eurasiatic, and Starostin (1991), who considers it a member of Altaic within Nostratic.

Additional Austronesian etymologies have been proposed in Blust (1980, 1983–84, 1985), and Blust's definitive Austronesian etymological dictionary is eagerly awaited.

Dene-Caucasian

The basic works defining Dene-Caucasian are Starostin (1984), Nikolaev (1986), and Bengtson (1991a, b), all of which are contained in Shevoroshkin (1991). Ruhlen (1989d) supplies some connecting links between Yeniseian and other families, particularly Na-Dene.

Klimov (1986) provides an overview of the (North) Caucasian languages, as does Catford (1991). Until Nikolaev and Starostin's etymological dictionary of (North) Caucasian is published, the list of Caucasian roots given in Nikolaev and Starostin (1986) will have to suffice. The extinct Hurrian, and the closely related Urartian, languages have recently been shown by Diakonov and Starostin (1986) to belong to the Eastern branch of the Caucasian family. Ivanov (1985) argues that the extinct language Hatti belongs to the Western branch of (North) Caucasian.

Proto-Yeniseian reconstructions, and the etymologies upon which these are based, are given in Starostin (1982). An English translation of the reconstructions is given in Ruhlen (1989d).

For Sino-Tibetan, Starostin (1989b) presents a new reconstruction of Old Chinese phonology. Ramsey (1987) offers an overview of the languages of China, including the many non-Chinese languages of the south. Sagart (1990) suggests that Chinese is more closely related to Austronesian than to Tibeto-Burman.

A number of recent works by Pinnow (1984, 1985a, b, 1986a, b, 1988, 1990) continue his many contributions to the Na-Dene family. Pinnow, it should be stressed, has been one of the staunchest supporters of the Na-Dene affiliation of Haida, a "pseudo-controversy" that now appears over. Ruhlen (1989c) proposes additional Na-Dene etymologies based on Greenberg's unpublished Na-Dene notebook.

Afro-Asiatic

Diakonov (1988) and Perrot (1988) offer overviews of the family, while Ehret (1989) gives some 800 reconstructed roots. Stolbova (1987) presents an extensive list of West Chadic reconstructions.

Kartvelian

General surveys of the family are given in Klimov (1986) and in Catford (1991).

Eurasiatic

The Eurasiatic family is defined, with supporting evidence, in Greenberg (to appear). Dolgopolsky (to appear) presents his version of Nostratic, whereas Bomhard (1990) offers a somewhat different version of Nostratic based on the glottalic theory of Indo-Hittite consonantism. An English translation of Illich-Svitych's (1967) Nostratic reconstructions is given in Kaiser (1989).

In addition to the standard Indo-Hittite etymological dictionary by Pokorny (1959), we now have Mann (1984–87) and Décsy (1991). During the past several years the homeland and spread of the Indo-Hittite languages has once again become a focus of research in both archaeology and linguistics. Gamkrelidze and Ivanov (1984, 1990), Renfrew (1987, 1989), and

Dolgopolsky (1988) all agree in locating the Indo-Hittite homeland in Anatolia (modern Turkey), an idea that fits well with Sturtevant's Indo-Hittite hypothesis. Renfrew attempts to connect the spread of Indo-Hittite with the spread of agriculture from the Near East around 8,000 years ago, a date some two millennia older than the commonly accepted one. Mallory (1989) presents a view of the origin of the Indo-Hittite family more in line with the traditional views of Marija Gimbutas.

For Uralic, Rédei (1986–88) has replaced earlier works as the definitive etymological dictionary of the family; Décsy (1990) also presents a list of Uralic roots, but not those restricted to Finno-Ugric, for which the work by Rédei must be consulted. The standard etymological dictionary for the Samoyed family is Janhunen (1977).

For Altaic, Starostin (1991) presents a reconsideration of this family, which for Starostin includes Korean and Japanese, in addition to Turkic, Mongolian, and Tungus. Shibatani (1990) surveys both Ainu and Japanese.

Mudrak (1986) offers a list of Chukchi-Kamchatkan reconstructions, and Mudrak (1989) gives a list of Eskimo-Aleut reconstructions.

Amerind

Regna Darnell's (1990) biography of Sapir provides interesting insights into Sapir's taxonomic work, as does Victor Golla's (1984) edition of the Sapir-Kroeber correspondence. A compendium of Algonquian reconstructions is given in Aubin (1975), and Lincoln and Rath (1980) provide a list of North Wakashan roots. Berman (1990) offers additional Algic etymologies. Kinkade (1988) presents a thorough examination of Proto-Salish color terminology, and Galloway (1988) offers some Proto-Central Salish reconstructions. DeLancey, Genetti, and Rood (1988) suggest additional Penutian etymologies, and Callaghan (1988) presents a list of Proto-Miwok-Costanoan cognate sets. Rensch (1989) offers an etymological dictionary of the Chinantec languages, considered a single (highly diversified) language in this book. Kaufman (1992) argues that Oto-Manguean is closest to Hokan, the two considered by Greenberg (1987) to be members of Central Amerind and Northern Amerind, respectively.

For South America, several general surveys have recently appeared, including Klein and Stark (1985), Payne (1990), and Derbyshire and Pullum (1986, 1990, 1991).

Anttila, Raimo. 1989. *Historical and Comparative Linguistics*. Amsterdam.

Aubin, George F. 1975. *A Proto-Algonquian Dictionary*. Ottawa.

Barbujani, Guido, Neal L. Oden, and Robert R. Sokal. 1989. "Detecting Regions of Abrupt Change in Maps of Biological Variables," *Systematic Zoology* 38: 376–89.

Barbujani, Guido, and Robert R. Sokal. 1990. "Zones of Sharp Genetic Change in Europe Are Also Linguistic Boundaries," *Proceedings of the National Academy of Sciences* 87: 1816–19.

Bateman, Richard, Ives Goddard, Richard O'Grady, V. A. Funk, Rich Mooi, W. John Kress, and Peter Cannell. 1990a. "Speaking of Forked Tongues: The Feasibility of Reconciling Human Phylogeny and the History of Language," *Current Anthropology* 31: 1–24.

———. 1990b. "On Human Phylogeny and Linguistic History: Reply to Comments," *Current Anthropology* 31: 177–83.

Bender, M. Lionel. 1989. *Topics in Nilo-Saharan Linguistics.* Hamburg.

———. 1991. "Subclassification of Nilo-Saharan," in M. Lionel Bender, ed., *Proceedings of the 4th Nilo-Saharan Linguistics Colloquium*, 1–34. Hamburg.

Bendor-Samuel, John, ed. 1988. *The Niger-Kordofanian-Congo Language Family.* Berlin.

Benedict, Paul. 1990. *Japanese–Austro-Tai.* Ann Arbor.

Bengtson, John D. 1988. "Beyond Whitney's 'Tenth Lecture': New Horizons in Comparative Linguistics," in Sheila Embleton, ed., *The Fourteenth Lacus Forum 1987.* Lake Bluff, Ill.

———. 1991a. "Notes on Sino-Caucasian," in Shevoroshkin, ed., 1991.

———. 1991b. "Some Macro-Caucasian Etymologies," in Shevoroshkin, ed., 1991.

Bengtson, John D., and Merritt Ruhlen. 1988. "Global Etymologies," ms.

Berman, Howard. 1990. "New Algonquian-Ritwan Cognate Sets," *IJAL* 56: 431–34.

Blake, Barry J. 1988. "Redefining Pama-Nyungan," in *Yearbook of Australian Linguistics* 1.

Blažek, Vaclav. 1989. "Materials for Global Etymologies," in Shevoroshkin 1989b.

Blust, Robert. 1980. "Austronesian Etymologies," *Oceanic Linguistics* 19: 1–181.

———. 1983–84. "Austronesian Etymologies II," *Oceanic Linguistics* 22–23: 29–149.

———. 1985. "Austronesian Etymologies III," *Oceanic Linguistics* 25: 1–123.

Boisson, Claude. 1989. "Sumerian/Nostratic/Sino-Caucasian Isoglosses," ms.

Bomhard, Allan R. 1990. *A Sample of the Comparative Vocabulary of the Nostratic Languages*, ms.

Bynon, Theodora. 1977. *Historical Linguistics.* Cambridge, Eng.

Callaghan, Catherine A. 1988. "Proto Utian Stems," in William Shipley, ed., *In Honor of Mary Haas.* Berlin.

Campbell, Lyle. 1986. "Comment," *Current Anthropology* 27: 488.
——. 1988. Review article of *Language in the Americas*, by Joseph H. Greenberg, *Language* 64: 591–615.
Catford, J. C. 1991. "The Classification of Caucasian Languages," to appear in Sydney Lamb and E. Douglas Mitchell, eds., *Sprung from Some Common Source: Investigations into the Prehistory of Languages*. Stanford, Calif.
Cavalli-Sforza, L. L., Alberto Piazza, Paolo Menozzi. 1991. *History and Geography of Human Genes*. Princeton.
Cavalli-Sforza, L. L., Alberto Piazza, Paolo Menozzi, and Joanna Mountain. 1988. "Reconstruction of Human Evolution: Bringing Together Genetic, Archaeological and Linguistic Data," *Proceedings of the National Academy of Sciences* 85: 6002–06.
——. 1990. "Comment," *Current Anthropology* 31: 16–18.
Chirikba, V. A. 1985. "Baskskij i severokavkazskie jazyki," in *Drevnjaja Anatolija*. Moscow.
Darnell, Regna. 1990. *Edward Sapir: Linguist, Anthropologist, Humanist*. Berkeley.
Darwin, Charles. 1859. *On the Origin of Species*. London.
Décsy, Gyula. 1990. *The Uralic Protolanguage: A Comprehensive Reconstruction*. Bloomington, Ind.
——. 1991. *The Indo-European Protolanguage: A Computational Reconstruction*. Bloomington, Ind.
DeLancey, Scott, Carol Genetti, and Noel Rude. 1988. "Some Sahaptian-Klamath-Tsimshianic Lexical Sets," in William Shipley, ed., *In Honor of Mary Haas*. Berlin.
Derbyshire, Desmond C., and Geoffrey K. Pullum, eds. 1986–91. *Handbook of Amazonian Languages*, 3 vols. Berlin.
Diakonov, Igor M. 1988. *Afrasian Languages*. Moscow.
Diakonov, Igor M., and Sergei A. Starostin. 1986. *Hurro-Urartian as an Eastern Caucasian Language*. Munich.
Dixon, R. M. W., and Barry J. Blake, eds. 1979–. *Handbook of Australian Languages*, 3 vols. Amsterdam.
Dolgopolsky, Aron. 1984. "On Personal Pronouns in the Nostratic Languages," in Otto Gschwantler, Károly Rédei, and Hermann Reichert, eds., *Linguistica et Philologica*. Vienna.
——. 1988. "The Indo-European Homeland and Lexical Contacts of Proto-Indo-European with Other Languages," *Mediterranean Language Review* 3: 7–31.
——. To appear. *Nostratic Comparative Vocabulary*. ms.
Edmondson, Jerold A., and David B. Solnit, eds. 1988. *Comparative Kadai: Linguistic Studies Beyond Tai*. Arlington, Tex.
Ehret, Christopher. 1989. *A Reconstruction of Proto-Afroasiatic*, ms.
Embleton, Sheila M. 1986. *Statistics in Historical Linguistics*. Bochum.

Excoffier, Laurent, Béatrice Pellegrini, Alicia Sanchez-Mazas, Christian Simon, and André Langaney. 1987. "Genetics and History of Sub-Saharan Africa," *Yearbook of Physical Anthropology* 30: 151–94.

Fleming, Harold. 1986– . *Mother Tongue*. Boston.

———. 1987a. "Hadza and Sandawe Genetic Relations," *Sprache und Geschichte in Afrika* 7: 157–88.

———. 1987b. "Toward a Definitive Classification of the World's Languages," *Diachronica* 4: 159–223.

Foley, William A. 1986. *The Papuan Languages of New Guinea*. Cambridge, Eng.

Galloway, Brent D. 1988. "Some Proto-Central Salish Sound Correspondences," in William Shipley, ed., *In Honor of Mary Haas*. Berlin.

Gamkrelidze,T. V., and V. V. Ivanov. 1984. *Indoevropejskij jazyk i indoevropejtsy*, 2 vols. Tbilisi.

———. 1990. "The Early History of Indo-European Languages," *Scientific American* (March): 110–16.

Goddard, Ives. 1987. Review of *Language in the Americas*, by Joseph H. Greenberg, *Current Anthropology* 28: 656–57.

Golla, Victor, ed. 1984. *The Sapir-Kroeber Correspondence*. Berkeley.

Gould, Stephen Jay. 1988. "Honorable Men and Women," *Natural History* (March), 16–20.

———. 1989. "Grimm's Greatest Tale," *Natural History* (February), 20–26.

Greenberg, Joseph H. 1981. *Amerindian Notebooks*, 23 vols., ms.

———. 1987. *Language in the Americas*. Stanford, Calif.

———. 1989. "Classification of American Indian Languages: A Reply to Campbell," *Language* 65: 107–14.

———. 1990a. "Indo-European Practice and American Indianist Theory in Language Classification," to appear in Allan Taylor, ed., *Language and Prehistory in the Americas*. Stanford, Calif.

———. 1990b. "The American Indian Language Controversy," *Review of Archaeology* 11, 2: 5–14.

———. To appear. *Indo-European and Its Closest Relatives: The Eurasiatic Language Family*. Stanford, Calif.

Greenberg, Joseph H., Christy G. Turner II, and Stephen L. Zegura. 1986. "The Settlement of the Americas: A Comparison of Linguistic, Dental, and Genetic Evidence," *Current Anthropology* 27: 477–97.

Hock, Hans Henrich. 1986. *Principles of Historical Linguistics*. Berlin.

Hopper, Paul J. 1989. Review of *Language Contact, Creolization, and Genetic Linguistics*, by Sarah Grey Thomason and Terrence Kaufman, *American Anthropologist* 91: 817–18.

Hymes, Dell. 1987. Review of *Language in the Americas*, by Joseph H. Greenberg, *Current Anthropology* 28: 659–62.

Illich-Svitych, Vladislav M. 1967. "Materialy k sravnitel'nomu slovarju nostraticheskix jazykov," *Etimologija* (Moscow) 1965: 321–96.

——. 1971–84. *Opyt sravnenija nostraticheskix jazykov*, 3 vols. Moscow.

Ivanov, Vjacheslav V. 1985. "Ob otnoshenii xattskogo jazyka k severnozapadnokavkazskim," in *Drevnjaja Anatolija*. Moscow.

Janhunen, Juha. 1977. *Samojedischer Wortschatz. Gemeinsamojedische Etymologien*. Helsinki.

Kaiser, Mark, 1989. "V. M. Illič-Svityč's Early Reconstructions of Nostratic," in Shevoroshkin (1989b).

Kaiser, Mark, and Vitaly Shevoroshkin. 1988. "Nostratic," *Annual Review of Anthropology* 17: 309–29.

Kaufman, Terrence. 1990. "Language History in South America: What We Know and How to Know More," in Payne, ed., 1990.

——. 1992. "Tlapaneco-Subtiaba, Otomangue, and Hokan," to appear in Allan Taylor, ed., *Language and Prehistory in the Americas*. Stanford, Calif.

Kinkade, M. Dale. 1988. "Proto-Salishan Colors," in William Shipley, ed., *In Honor of Mary Haas*. Berlin.

Klein, Harriet E. Manelis, and Louisa R. Stark, eds. 1985. *South American Indian Languages: Retrospect and Prospect*. Austin, Tex.

Klimov, G. A. 1986. *Vvedenije v kavkazskoe jazykoznanije*. Moscow.

Lewin, Roger. 1987. *Bones of Contention*. New York.

Lincoln, Neville J., and John C. Rath. 1980. *North Wakashan Comparative Root List*. Ottawa.

Mallory, J. P. 1989. *In Search of the Indo-Europeans*. London.

Mann, Stuart E. 1984–87. *An Indo-European Comparative Vocabulary*. Hamburg.

Matisoff, James A. 1990. "On Megalocomparison," *Language* 66: 106–20.

Mayr, Ernst. 1988. "Toward a Synthesis in Biological Classification," in Ernst Mayr, *Toward a New Philosophy of Biology*. Cambridge, Mass.

Meeussen, A. E. 1980a. *Bantu Grammatical Reconstructions*. Tervuren, Belgium.

——. 1980b. *Bantu Lexical Reconstructions*. Tervuren, Belgium.

Mudrak, Oleg A. 1986. "Proto-Chukchi-Kamchatkan Roots," ms.

——. 1989. "Eskaleutian Roots," in Shevoroshkin 1989b.

Nikolaev, Sergei L. 1986. "Sino-kavkazkie jazyki v Amerike," ms. [English translation in Shevoroshkin 1991.]

Nikolaev, Sergei L., and Sergei Starostin. 1986. "North Caucasian Roots," ms. [Revised version in Shevoroshkin 1991.]

——. To appear. *(North) Caucasian Etymological Dictionary*. Stanford, Calif.

Payne, Doris L., ed. 1990. *Amazonian Linguistics: Studies in Lowland South American Languages*. Austin, Tex.

Pejros, Ilja I. 1989. "Dopolnenie k gipoteze S. A. Starostina o rodstve nostraticheskix i sinokavkazskix jazykov," in *Lingvisticheskaja rekonstruktsija i drevnejshaja istorija vostoka*. Moscow.

Perrot, Jean, ed. 1988. *Les langues dans le monde ancien et moderne, vol. 3: Les langues chamito-sémitiques*. Paris.

Piazza, A., R. Griffo, N. Cappello, M. Grassini, E. Olivetti, S. Rendine, and G. Zei. 1988. "Genetic Structure and Lexical Differentiation in Sardinia," to appear in Alberto Piazza and L. L. Cavalli-Sforza, eds., *Language Change and Biological Evolution*. Stanford, Calif.

Pinnow, Heinz-Jürgen. 1984. "Sprachhistorische Untersuchung zur Stellung des Haida," in *Gedenkschrift Gerdt Kutscher.*

——. 1985a. "Sprachhistorische Untersuchung einiger Tiernamen im Haida," *Abhandlungen der Völkerkundlichen Arbeitsgemeinschaft* (Nortorf) 39.

——. 1985b. "Das Haida als Na-Dene-Sprache: Materialien zu den Wortfeldern und zur Komparation des Verbs," *Abhandlungen der Völkerkundlichen Arbeitsgemeinschaft* (Nortorf) 43–46.

——. 1986a. "Die Zahlwörter des Haida in sprachvergleichender Sicht," *Abhandlungen der Völkerkundlichen Arbeitsgemeinschaft* (Nortorf) 47.

——. 1986b. "Säugetiernamen des Haida und Tlingit: Materialien zu ihrer historischen Erforschung," *Abhandlungen der Völkerkundlichen Arbeitsgemeinschaft* (Nortorf) 50.

——. 1988. "Verwandtschafts- und andere Personenbezeichnungen im Tlingit und Haida," *Abhandlungen der Völkerkundlichen Arbeitsgemeinschaft* (Nortorf) 62.

——. 1990. "Die Na-Dene-Sprachen im Lichte der Greenberg-Klassifikation," *Abhandlungen der Völkerkundlichen Arbeitsgemeinschaft* (Nortorf) 64.

Pokorny, Julius. 1959. *Indogermanisches Etymologisches Wörterbuch*. Bern.

Powers, W. R. 1990. "The Peoples of Eastern Beringia," in *Prehistoric Mongoloid Dispersals* 7: 53–74. Tokyo.

Ramsey, S. Robert. 1987. *The Languages of China*. Princeton.

Rédei, Károly, ed. 1986–88. *Uralisches Etymologisches Wörterbuch*. Budapest.

Renfrew, Colin. 1987. *Archaeology and Language: The Puzzle of Indo-European Origins*. London.

——. 1989. "The Origins of Indo-European Languages," *Scientific American* (October): 106–14.

——. 1991a. "Before Babel: Speculations on the Origins of Linguistic Diversity," *Cambridge Archaeological Journal* 1.

——. 1991b. "World Languages and Human Dispersals: A Minimalist View," to appear in J. A. Hall and I. C. Garvey, eds., *Power, Wealth and Belief: Essays in Honour of Ernest Gellner*. Cambridge, Eng.

Rensch, Calvin R. 1989. *An Etymological Dictionary of the Chinantec Languages*. Arlington, Tex.

Ruhlen, Merritt. 1988a. "The Origin of Language: Retrospective and Prospective," to appear in Alberto Piazza and L. L. Cavalli-Sforza, eds., *Language Change and Biological Evolution*. Stanford, Calif. [Russian version in *Voprosy Jazykoznanija* (1991)]

——. 1988b. "Is Algonquian Amerind?," to appear in Ruhlen 1991c.

——. 1989a. "Additional Amerind Etymologies," to appear in Ruhlen 1991c.

——. 1989b. "First- and Second-Person Pronouns in the World's Languages," to appear in Ruhlen 1991c.

——. 1989c. "Na-Dene Etymologies," to appear in Ruhlen 1991c.

——. 1989d. "Proto-Yeniseian Reconstructions (after Starostin 1982), with Extra-Yeniseian Comparisons," to appear in Ruhlen 1991c.

——. 1989e. "Linguistic Origins of Native Americans," ms.

——. 1990a. "Phylogenetic Relations of Native American Languages," in *Prehistoric Mongoloid Dispersals* 7: 75–96. Tokyo.

——. 1990b. "The Amerind Root MALIQ'A 'Swallow, Throat' and Its Origin in the Old World," to appear in Ruhlen 1991c.

——. 1991a. "An Overview of Genetic Classification," in John A. Hawkins and Murray Gell-Mann, eds., *Evolution of Human Languages*. Redwood City, Calif.

——. 1991b. "The Amerind Phylum and the Prehistory of the New World," in Sydney Lamb and E. Douglas Mitchell, eds., *Sprung from Some Common Source: Investigations into the Prehistory of Languages*. Stanford, Calif.

——. 1991c. *Studies in Linguistic Taxonomy*.

Sagart, Laurent. 1990. "Chinese and Austronesian are Genetically Related," ms.

Shevoroshkin, Vitaly. 1989a. "Methods in Interphyletic Comparisons," *Ural-Altaische Jahrbücher* 61: 1–26.

——, ed. 1989b. *Reconstructing Languages and Cultures*. Bochum.

——, ed. 1990. *Proto-Languages and Proto-Cultures*. Bochum.

——, ed. 1991. *Sino-Caucasian Languages*. Bochum.

Shevoroshkin, Vitaly, and Alexis Manaster-Ramer. 1991. "Some Recent Work on the Remote Relations of Languages," in Sydney Lamb and E. Douglas Mitchell, eds., *Sprung from Some Common Source: Investigations into the Prehistory of Languages*. Stanford, Calif.

Shibatani, Masayoshi. 1990. *The Languages of Japan*. Cambridge, Eng.

Starostin, Sergei A. 1982. "Prajenisejskaja rekonstruktsija i vneshnie svjazi enisejskix jazykov," *Ketskij sbornik*, Leningrad, 144–237.

——. 1984. "Gipoteza o geneticheskix svjazjax sinotibetskix jazykov s enisejskimi i severnokavkazskimi jazykami," *Lingvisticheskaja rekonstruktsija i drevnejshaja istorija vostoka* 4, Moscow, 19–38. [English translation in Shevoroshkin 1991.]

———. 1989a. "Nostratic and Sino-Caucasian," in Vitaly Shevoroshkin, ed., *Explorations in Language Macrofamilies*. Bochum.

———. 1989b. *Rekonstruktsija drevnekitaiskoi fonologicheskoi sistemy*. Moscow.

———. 1990. "A Statistic Evaluation of the Time-Depth and Subgrouping of the Nostratic Macrofamily," paper presented at the Cold Spring Harbor symposium on evolution.

———. 1991. *Altajskaja problema i proisxozhdenije zhaponskogo jazyka*. Moscow.

Stolbova, O. V. 1987. "Sravniteljno-istoricheskaja fonetika i slovarj zapadnochadskix jazykov," in V. J. Porxomovskij, ed., *Afrikanskoe istoricheskoe jazykoznanije*. Moscow.

Sweet, Henry. 1901. *The History of Language*. London.

Thomason, Sarah Grey. 1990. "Hypothesis Generation vs. Hypothesis Testing: A Comparison Between Greenberg's Classifications in Africa and in the Americas," to appear in Allan Taylor, ed., *Language and Prehistory in the Americas*. Stanford, Calif.

Traill, Anthony. 1986. "Do the Khoi Have a Place in the San? New Data on Khoisan Linguistic Relationships," *Sprache und Geschichte in Afrika* 7: 407–40.

Trombetti, Alfredo. 1905. *L'unità d'origine del linguaggio*. Bologna.

———. 1926. *Le origini della lingua basca*. Bologna.

Turner, Christy G. II. 1989. "Teeth and Prehistory in Asia," *Scientific American* 260 (February): 88–96.

Vossen, Rainer, and Klaus Keuthmann. 1986. *Contemporary Studies on Khoisan* 2. Hamburg.

A Guide to the World's Languages

VOLUME 1: CLASSIFICATION

Index of Personal Names

In these indexes an "f" after a number indicates a separate reference on the next page, and an "ff" indicates separate references on the next two pages. Clusters of references grouped with a "passim" fall within three pages of each other (e.g., 13, 16, 17, 20 would be entered as 13–20 passim, whereas 13, 14, 18, 20 would not).

Language Group Index

This is an index to the *more important* language families that appear in the complete classification (section 8.6). It does not list every genetic group in the classification. In particular, several kinds of groups have been systematically eliminated, as follows. (1) Most groups consisting of a single language, such as KABYLE and BERTA (but a few exceptions to this general rule remain, e.g. ALBANIAN and ALEUT). (2) Many geographical (or other generic) subdivisions of a more general group, such as EAST CHADIC, MIDDLE PAMAN, and ANGAN PROPER, which should be sought under CHADIC, PAMAN, and ANGAN, respectively. In cases where what appears to be a subdivision (e.g. WEST ATLANTIC) is in fact an independent entity (there is no EAST ATLANTIC or NORTH ATLANTIC), the group is of course retained and is listed twice (in this case under WEST ATLANTIC and ATLANTIC, WEST). (3) All groups with names such as "GROUP A" or "GROUP 1" have been omitted.

The rules of alphabetization of group names follows the same principles outlined in the introduction to the Language Index. As in the Language Index homonymous names are distinguished by specifying a higher-level grouping after each:

SEPIK (SEPIK-MADANG)
SEPIK (SEPIK-RAMU)

Language Index

This index contains all of the roughly 5,000 languages classified in Chapter 8. The number following each language indicates the page on which that language appears in the classification (section 8.6). When more than one number follows a language the final number indicates the page number in the classification, the others are references in the text of the book.

Compound language names are alphabetized according to the following principles. (1) If the first word is a common adjective, then the language is alphabetized according to the second word (e.g. "Eastern Pomo" is to be found under "Pomo, Eastern" and "Alaskan Inuit" under "Inuit, Alaskan"). (2) If both words appear meaningless to the average reader, the language name is alphabetized according to the first word (e.g. "Abai Sungai" and "Jaya Bakti" are listed as such in the index). (3) In a limited number of cases a language name is listed under both its first and second words (e.g. both "Kelinyao Kenyah" and "Kenyah, Kelinyao" appear in the index). This dual approach is followed because there are in fact other "Kenyah" languages, even though to most people both terms seem equally opaque.

It is not uncommon for two (or more) entirely different languages to have the same name. When they are genetically and/or geographically close to each other scholars sometimes distinguish them by subscripts (e.g. $Mimi_1$ and $Mimi_2$, Mor_1 and Mor_2). Usually, however, homonymous names are not even noticed, much less distinguished. For example, in addition to the fairly well-known Yao (= Mien) language of Southeast Asia, there are two other languages called Yao in the classification, one a member of the Bantu family in Africa, the other belonging to the Carib family of South America. Homonymous names are distinguished in the index by following each with its family affiliation, in this case:

Yao (BANTU)
Yao (CARIB)
Yao (MIAO-YAO)

More perplexing than the problem of identical names is the fact that in some instances the name most often associated with a language is, for reasons discussed in section 8.1, replaced by a different name in the classification. I have tried to anticipate where such replacements are likely to confuse the average reader and have provided cross references in such cases. Thus, "Gypsy→ Romany, 286, 325" means that the language of the Gypsies is called Romany and is listed as such on those pages. I have, however, used this system of cross-references sparingly and only for the most common variants. This is an index to the world's languages as listed in section 8.6. Both Voegelin and Voegelin (1977) and Grimes (1984) provide indexes to the more than 25,000 names associated with the world's languages and their dialects and either book may be used as a more general index to this volume to identify other language and dialect names.

Grimes, Barbara F., ed. 1984. *Index to the Tenth Edition of Ethnologue: Languages of the World*. Dallas.

Voegelin, C. F., and F. M. Voegelin. 1977. *Classification and Index of the World's Languages*. New York.